IARIA

SECURWARE 2016

The Tenth International Conference on Emerging Security Information, Systems and Technologies

July 24 - 28, 2016

Nice, France

SECURWARE 2016 Editors

Carla Merkle Westphall, University of Santa Catarina, Brazil

Hans-Joachim Hof, Munich University of Applied Sciences, Germany

Geir Køien, University of Agder, Norway

Lukáš Králík, Tomas Bata University in Zlin, Czech Republic

Martin Hromada, Tomas Bata University in Zlin, Czech Republic

Dora Lapkova, Tomas Bata Univerzity in Zlin, Czech Republic

Printed from e-media with permission by:

Curran Associates, Inc.
57 Morehouse Lane
Red Hook, NY 12571

Some format issues inherent in the e-media version may also appear in this print version.

Printed by Curran Associates, Inc. (2016)

International Academy, Research, and Industry Association (IARIA)
412 Derby Way
Wilmington, DE 19810

Phone: (408) 893-6407
Fax: (408) 527-6351

petre@iaria.org

Additional copies of this publication are available from:

Curran Associates, Inc.
57 Morehouse Lane
Red Hook, NY 12571 USA
Phone: 845-758-0400
Fax: 845-758-2633
Email: curran@proceedings.com
Web: www.proceedings.com

Table of Contents

SECURWARE 2016

Forward

The Tenth International Conference on Emerging Security Information, Systems and Technologies (SECURWARE 2016), held between July 24-28, 2016 in Nice, France, continued a series of events focusing related topics on theory and practice on security, cryptography, secure protocols, trust, privacy, confidentiality, vulnerability, intrusion detection and other areas related to low enforcement, security data mining, malware models, etc.

Security, defined for ensuring protected communication among terminals and user applications across public and private networks, is the core for guaranteeing confidentiality, privacy, and data protection. Security affects business and individuals, raises the business risk, and requires a corporate and individual culture. In the open business space offered by Internet, it is a need to improve defenses against hackers, disgruntled employees, and commercial rivals. There is a required balance between the effort and resources spent on security versus security achievements. Some vulnerability can be addressed using the rule of 80:20, meaning 80% of the vulnerabilities can be addressed for 20% of the costs. Other technical aspects are related to the communication speed versus complex and time consuming cryptography/security mechanisms and protocols.

Digital Ecosystem is defined as an open decentralized information infrastructure where different networked agents, such as enterprises (especially SMEs), intermediate actors, public bodies and end users, cooperate and compete enabling the creation of new complex structures. In digital ecosystems, the actors, their products and services can be seen as different organisms and species that are able to evolve and adapt dynamically to changing market conditions.

Digital Ecosystems lie at the intersection between different disciplines and fields: industry, business, social sciences, biology, and cutting edge ICT and its application driven research. They are supported by several underlying technologies such as semantic web and ontology-based knowledge sharing, self-organizing intelligent agents, peer-to-peer overlay networks, web services-based information platforms, and recommender systems.

To enable safe digital ecosystem functioning, security and trust mechanisms become essential components across all the technological layers. The aim was to bring together multidisciplinary research that ranges from technical aspects to socio-economic models.

The conference had the following tracks:

- Security challenges with new technologies
- Security technologies
- Applied security technologies and systems
- Cryptography
- Security management
- Risk and security
- Security frameworks, architectures and protocols

In addition, SECURWARE 2016 included the mini-symposium:

- **ASTaS 2016, Applied Security Technologies and Systems**

We take here the opportunity to warmly thank all the members of the SECURWARE 2016 technical program committee, as well as all the reviewers. The creation of such a high quality conference program would not have been possible without their involvement. We also kindly thank all the authors that dedicated much of their time and effort to contribute to SECURWARE 2016. We truly believe that, thanks to all these efforts, the final conference program consisted of top quality contributions.

Also, this event could not have been a reality without the support of many individuals, organizations and sponsors. We also gratefully thank the members of the SECURWARE 2016 organizing committee for their help in handling the logistics and for their work that made this professional meeting a success.

We hope SECURWARE 2016 was a successful international forum for the exchange of ideas and results between academia and industry and to promote further progress related to security in all its aspects. We also hope that Nice, France provided a pleasant environment during the conference and everyone saved some time enjoy the beautiful French Riviera.

SECURWARE 2016 Advisory Committee

Juha Rőning, University of Oulu, Finland
Catherine Meadows, Naval Research Laboratory - Washington DC, USA
Mariusz Jakubowski, Microsoft Research, USA
William Dougherty, Secern Consulting - Charlotte, USA
Hans-Joachim Hof, Munich University of Applied Sciences, Germany
Peter Müller, IBM Zurich Research Laboratory, Switzerland
Vladimir Stantchev, Institute of Information Systems, SRH University Berlin, Germany
Syed Naqvi, Birmingham City University, UK

SECURWARE 2016 Industry Liaison Chair

Rainer Falk, Siemens AG - München, Germany

SECURWARE 2016 Research/Industry Chair

Mariusz Jakubowski, Microsoft Research, USA

ASTaS 2016 Mini-Symposium organizers

Lukáš Králík, Tomas Bata University in Zlin, Czech Republic
Martin Hromada, Tomas Bata University in Zlin, Czech Republic
Dora Lapkova, Tomas Bata Univerzity in Zlin, Czech Republic

SECURWARE 2016

Committee

SECURWARE Advisory Committee

Juha Rőning, University of Oulu, Finland
Catherine Meadows, Naval Research Laboratory - Washington DC, USA
Mariusz Jakubowski, Microsoft Research, USA
William Dougherty, Secern Consulting - Charlotte, USA
Hans-Joachim Hof, Munich University of Applied Sciences, Germany
Peter Müller, IBM Zurich Research Laboratory, Switzerland
Vladimir Stantchev, Institute of Information Systems, SRH University Berlin, Germany
Syed Naqvi, Birmingham City University, UK

SECURWARE 2016 Industry Liaison Chair

Rainer Falk, Siemens AG - München, Germany

SECURWARE 2016 Research/Industry Chair

Mariusz Jakubowski, Microsoft Research, USA

SECURWARE 2016 Technical Program Committee

Habtamu Abie, Norwegian Computing Center - Oslo, Norway
Afrand Agah, West Chester University of Pennsylvania, USA
Maurizio Aiello, National Research Council of Italy - IEIIT, Italy
Jose M. Alcaraz Calero, University of the West of Scotland, United Kingdom
Alessandro Aldini, University of Urbino, Italy
Firkhan Ali Bin Hamid Ali, Universiti Tun Hussein Onn Malaysia, Malaysia
David Argles, Haven Consulting, UK
George Athanasiou, KTH Royal Institute of Technology, Sweden
Benjamin Aziz, University of Portsmouth, UK
Fabrizio Baiardi, University of Pisa, Italy
Ilija Basicevic, University of Novi Sad, Serbia
Lejla Batina, Radboud University Nijmegen, The Netherlands
Carlos Becker Westphall, Federal University of Santa Catarina, Brazil
Francisco Jose Bellido Outeiriño, University of Cordoba, Spain
Malek Ben Salem, Accenture Technology Labs, USA
Jorge Bernal Bernabé, University of Murcia, Spain
David Bissessar, Canada Border Services Agency, Canada
Catalin V. Birjoveanu, "Al.I.Cuza" University of Iasi, Romania
Lorenzo Blasi, Hewlett-Packard, Italy

Albert Levi, Sabanci University, Istanbul, Turkey
Zhuowei Li, Microsoft, USA
Giovanni Livraga, Università degli Studi di Milano - Crema, Italy
Jaime Lloret Mauri, Polytechnic University of Valencia, Spain
Jiqiang Lu, Institute for Infocomm Research, Singapore
Rongxing Lu, Nanyang Technological University, Singapore
Flaminia L. Luccio, University Ca' Foscari Venezia, Italy
Wissam Mallouli, Montimage, France
Feng Mao, EMC, USA
Milan Marković, Banca Intesa ad Beograd, Serbia
Juan Manuel Marín Pérez, University of Murcia, Spain
Claudia Marinica, ENSEA/University of Cergy-Pontoise/CNRS - Cergy-Pontoise, France
Olivier Markowitch, Université Libre de Bruxelles, Belgium
Stefan Marksteiner, JOANNEUM RESEARCH, Austria
Gregorio Martinez, University of Murcia, Spain
Wojciech Mazurczyk, Warsaw University of Technology, Poland
Catherine Meadows, Naval Research Laboratory, USA
Alexandre Melo Braga, Fundação CPqD, Brazil
Weizhi Meng, City University of Hong Kong, Hong Kong
Carla Merkle Westphall, Federal University of Santa Catarina, Brazil
Aleksandra Mileva, University "Goce Delcev", Republic of Macedonia
Jelena Milosevic, Università della Svizzera italiana, Lugano, Switzerland
Leslie Milton, University of Maryland, College Park, USA
Ajaz Hussain Mir, National Institute of Technology Srinagar - Kashmir, India
Hasan Mirjalili, EPFL - Lausanne, Switzerland
Rabeb Mizouni, Khalifa University of Science, Technology & Research (KUSTAR) - Abu Dhabi, UAE
Fadi Mohsen, University of North Carolina at Charlotte, USA
Theodosis Mourouzis, University College London, U.K.
Jose M. Moya, Universidad Politécnica de Madrid, Spain
Peter Mueller, IBM Zurich Research Laboratory , Switzerland
Yuko Murayama, Iwate Prefectural University, Japan
Alexios Mylonas, Staffordshire University, UK
Daniel A. Nagy, Eotvos Lorand University of Sciences, Budapest, Hungary
Antonio Nappa, IMDEA Software Institute, Spain
Syed Naqvi, Birmingham City University, UK
David Navarro, Ecole Centrale de Lyon, France
Nuno Neves, University of Lisbon, Portugal
Mehrdad Nojoumian, Florida Atlantic University, USA
Jason R.C. Nurse, Cyber Security Centre - University of Oxford, UK
Andres Ortiz, Universidad de Málaga, Spain
Federica Paganelli, National Interuniversity Consortium for Telecommunications (CNIT), Italy
Alwyn Roshan Pais, National Institute of Technology Karnataka, India
Carlos Enrique Palau Salvador, Universidad Politecnica de Valencia, Spain
András Pataricza, Budapest University of Technology and Economics, Hungary
Ella Pereira, Edge Hill University, UK
Pedro Peris López, Universidad Carlos III de Madrid, Spain
Zeeshan Pervez, University of the West of Scotland, UK
Christoph Pohl, Munich University of Applied Sciences, Germany

Ion Tutanescu, University of Pitesti, Romania
Shambhu Upadhyaya , State University of New York at Buffalo, USA
Yevgeniy Vahlis, Bionym Inc., Canada
Miroslav Velev, Aries Design Automation, USA
José Francisco Vicent Francés, University of Alicante, Spain
Andrea Visconti, Università degli Studi di Milano, Italy
Calin Vladeanu, "Politehnica" University of Bucharest, Romania
Tomasz Walkowiak, Wrocław University of Technology, Poland
Wendy Hui Wang, Stevens Institute of Technology - Hoboken, USA
Rafael Weingartner, Federal University of Santa Catarina (UFSC), Brazil
Edgar Weippl, SBA Research, Austria
Wenhua Wang, Marin Software Company, USA
Ronald Watro, BBN Technologies, USA
Steffen Wendzel, Fraunhofer FKIE, Bonn, Germany
Matthias Wieland, Universitaet Stuttgart, Germany
Wojciech Wodo, Wroclaw University of Technology, Poland
Yongdong Wu, Institute for Infocomm Research, Singapore
Yang Xiang, Deakin University - Melbourne Burwood Campus, Australia
Mengjun Xie, University of Arkansas at Little Rock, USA
Wun-She Yap, Universiti Tunku Abdul Rahman, Malaysia
Sung-Ming Yen, National Central University, Taiwan
Xie Yi, Sun Yat-Sen University - Guangzhou, P. R. China
Heung Youl Youm, KIISC, Korea
Amr Youssef, Concordia University - Montreal, Canada
Petr Žáček, Tomas Bata University in Zlin, Czech Republic
Shengzhi Zhang, Florida Institute of Technology, USA
Jun Zhang, Deakin University, Geelong Waurn Ponds Campus, Australia
Wenbing Zhao, Cleveland State University, USA
Yao Zhao, Beijing Jiaotong University, P. R. China
Xinliang Zheng, Frostburg State University, USA
Albert Zomaya, The University of Sydney, Australia

Copyright Information

A Generic Feature-based Detection for Facebook Spamming Groups

Meng-Jia Yen
Taiwan Semiconductor
Manufacturing Co. Ltd.
Hsinchu, Taiwan
e-mail: inscy3@hotmail.com

Yang-Ling Hwang
Chung Shan Medical University
Taichung, Taiwan
e-mail: yanling_h@yahoo.com

Cheng-Yu Tsai
Institute for
Information Industry
Taipei, Taiwan
e-mail: josephtsai@iii.org.tw

Fu-Hau Hsu
National Central University
Taoyuan, Taiwan
e-mail: hsufh@csie.ncu.edu.tw

Chih-Wen Ou
National Central University
Chunghwa Telecom Co. Ltd.
Taoyuan, Taiwan
e-mail: frankou@cht.com.tw

***Abstract*—Facebook spammers often use Facebook groups to propagate spam because every member will automatically receive a notification of the post when a new message is posted on the group's wall. Hence, a Facebook group which is created to scatter spam is called a *spamming group*. Even though detection of e-mail spam or Web-based spam has been developed for a long period of time, current Facebook mechanisms still cannot efficiently remove spamming groups. In this study, we propose a new spamming group detection approach for Facebook.**

Keywords–Facebook; spamming group; online social network

I. INTRODUCTION

Online social networks (OSNs) provide new platforms for Internet users around the world to communicate with each other. In March 2015, Facebook had 1.44 billion monthly active users [1]. Different from email spamming which can be directly conducted by sending spam to any email addresses, a Facebook user can not directly contact another Facebook user if they are not friends. Even if they are friends, directly sending unwelcome messages to friends can result in message blocking. Hence, Facebook spammers often use Facebook groups instead to propagate spam.

A Facebook group, which is similar to a real world group created for various reasons, is a collection of Facebook users who create a space on Facebook for organizing, sharing information, and exchanging resources for themselves. A Facebook group's *wall* is a Web page of a Facebook group which allows the group members to post text, images, links, or media. Group members can comment and respond directly on these items on the group's wall. By default configuration, when a group member posts on a group's wall, all members belonging to this group will receive a notification automatically.

To be a member of a certain group, a Facebook user can join a group by the following two methods: (1)Go to the desired group and send a request to the administrator(s) of the group. (2)Ask a friend, who has been a member of the desired group, to add him to the group. A user is defined as a *volunteer*, if he is added to a Facebook group through the first method. And a user is defined as an *invitee*, if he is added to a Facebook group through the second method.

A Facebook group member can invite his friends to join his group directly without the invitees' confirmation. Such a convenient invitation mechanism allows a spammer to add compromised user accounts and their friends to a Facebook spamming groups created by the spammer. Then, whenever a new spammer-crafted message is posted on a spamming group, every member receives a notification of the spamming post automatically. Spamming on Facebook significantly differs from the traditional email spam and Web-based spam malware [2]. Significant effort was spent on email spam detection [3] [4] in recent years, but few studies have focused on understanding the spamming activities in Facebook groups. Most previous spam-related studies identify email spam based on pattern/signature filtering strategies or manual user report mechanism [5]. However, according to Rahman et al. [2], there is only a low overlap (10%) between the keywords associated with email spam and those they found on Facebook. Besides, photos are more frequently used in Facebook spam. Because Facebook spam has different properties than e-mail spam, existing email spam detection solutions are not suitable for Facebook spamming group detection. There are few studies discussing about how to prevent spamming on Facebook. Gao et al. [6] detect and characterize spam campaigns by using wall messages on the Facebook. You [7] implemented a text filtering mechanism to classify groups by using specific keywords. Facebook currently provides a report mechanism for users to report spamming groups when they think that some groups have obviously spam contents or any other unwelcome contents. Spamming activities violate Facebook's Community Standards. But a report [8] shows that the current report mechanism of Facebook, which heavily relies on the cooperation of users, is not effective in removing spamming groups. Our experiments also show that many active spamming groups survive at least for five months (between December 2013 and April 2014). As a result, it is an important issue to develop a new approach to detect Facebook spam.

In this study, we propose a new approach to detect spamming groups according to their features. To this end, four of these features are targeted by spamming group detection including relationships among members, and members' social activities in a Facebook group. The rest of this paper is organized as follows: Section II describes related work in this field. Section III describes what the system design principles are and what kinds of feature are selected by us for the spamming group detection. Section IV shows the effectiveness of the prototype implementation. Section V addresses that more features could be adopted to improve the detection accuracy. Such adoption will be included in the future work. Section VI concludes this paper.

II. Related Work

This section compares our approach with a text message classifier [7], which filters the text feature (e.g., group's name, description and posts) to find the spamming groups. This text message classifier is easy to be bypassed because the groups' name and description can be modified at any time. Moreover, the keywords used in email spam significantly differ from those used on Facebook [2]. This classifier needs a large database, which must be maintained continuously. Our mechanism does not rely on keywords and databases. We only use the training data (about 200 samples) to keep our approach working without extra storage and resources. Therefore, we demonstrated that our mechanism can effectively detect spamming groups.

III. System Design

After observing diverse Facebook spamming groups and surveying various reports, we found that spamming groups have the following special features. These features consider not only the relationships among members of a group (e.g., information provided in the invitation record of a group) but also characteristics of social activities made by members in a group (e.g., number of clicks on the post "like" buttons made by normal users). These features play important roles in identifying a spamming group in our system.

Spamming group owners may use compromised accounts or use social techniques to entice normal users to add their friends [9] to a spamming group. If a spamming group has relatively few members, the impact of its spam will be reduced. The more members a spamming group has, the more impact its spam can produce. Hence, the member number of a group can be an factor indicating the influence of a post of the group. Most spamming groups either do not allow members to post any kind of messages on the groups' walls or require that posts from members must be approved by group administrators before appearing on the walls. Some spamming groups may allow members to post messages. However, the posts may be deleted quickly to keep spam on the top of walls. Compared to literal posts, image posts are easier to catch readers' eyes. In order to achieve a better effect of propaganda, a spammer would like to post an image post rather than a plain text post. The proportion of volunteers to invitees in a spamming group is significantly less than the proportion of volunteers to invitees in a normal group. This finding is intuitive because normal users seldom like to voluntarily join an unwelcome spamming group. Users always prefer to spend time on something that actually attracting them. For example, if someone is not interested in a post, it is unlikely that he will click the like button of the post. Annoying messages posted by spammers usually get very few number of "like" button clicks made by normal users.

Our approach detects a spamming group based on the group features described in Table I. These features include propagation ability, attractiveness, posting permission, and social impression. A *liker* of a group is a member of the group who has clicked the like button of a post on the group wall. Instead of calculating the number of clicks on the like buttons of all posts on a group wall, we calculate the distinct likers of all posts in the group so that even if a user has clicked the like button of every post on a group wall, this user is still counted as one liker.

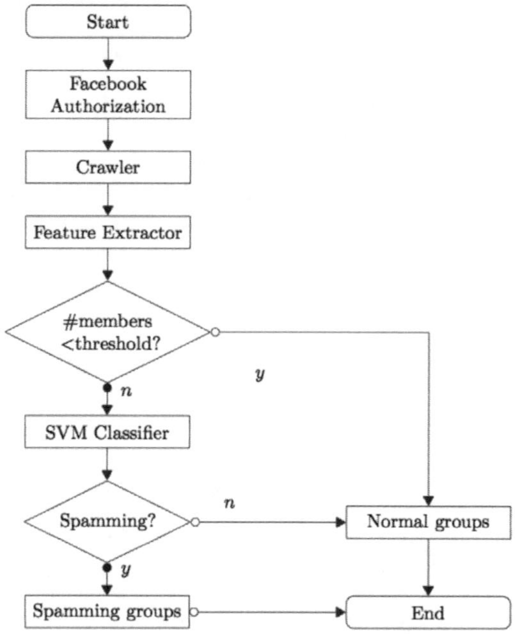

Figure 1. Prototype System Flow chart

The purpose of this study is to develop a prototype system which can identify spamming groups. Figure 1 illustrates the flow chart of our prototype system. Firstly, our prototype system extracts features from a Facebook group specified by a user. After extracting features, our prototype system assesses the number of members of this group. As we have discussed, a typical spamming group is unlikely to have a small number of members. If the number of members is less than a given small threshold, it can be directly classified as a normal group. Even though we might misjudge a spamming group with few members as a normal group in the classification with a small threshold, the number of victims suffering from this false negative is relative small. Secondly, if a group is not classified as a normal group, it is delivered to classifier, which performs classification based on the features listed in Table I. In this prototype system, we use a support vector machine (SVM) as our classifier because it is appropriate for a case which only has a small number of features and the number of output classes is only two. In our case, the outputs are classified-as-normal and classified-as-spamming.

IV. Experiment

Our approach requires a crawler and a classifier. The crawler collects information from Facebook. A machine-learning based classifier is trained by the information collected

TABLE I. FEATURES USED IN OUR APPROACH

Index	Feature	Description
1	Propagation ability	the number of members in a group
2	Attractiveness	the proportion of image posts to the total posts in a group
3	Posting permission	the proportion of distinct posters to all posts in a group
4	Social impression	the proportion of distinct likers to all members in a group

TABLE II. SUMMARY OF DATASET

Group type	training	testing	Total
Normal	100	104	204
Spamming	100	232	332

TABLE III. EXPERIMENT RESULTS

Group type	testing	classified as normal	classified as spamming
Normal	104	98	6
Spamming	232	20	212

from Facebook. It will be able to identify new arriving unclassified Facebook group samples in the testing stage. We implemented a prototype in a host installing Microsoft Windows 7 x64 with Intel(R) core(TM) dual core i5-4430@3.00GHz and 8G RAM. The Average Facebook API response time in normal status is under 200 ms [10]. Our prototype was executed five hundred times to train its classifiers and extract group features. Our prototype checks 100 groups within 20 seconds. Compared with other methods, we provided a real-time and more accurate solution to detect spamming groups.

We qualified 536 Facebook groups shown in Table II, collected during a three-month period from December, 2013 to February, 2014. Each collected Facebook group was manually inspected. Those 100 benign groups and 100 spamming groups were used for training the classifier. The rest of collected groups were used for testing its performance. The experiment result shows the false positive rates, false negative rates, and total error rates in Table III. There are six normal groups misclassified as spamming groups, and 20 spamming groups were erroneously identified as normal groups. Therefore, the false positive rate, false negative rate, and the total error rate of our current approach are 5.77%, 8.62%, and 7.73% respectively.

V. DISCUSSION

We only use four features in this current approach. More features can be adopted in the future work. The invitation record is considered a potential useful feature, since the spamming is a typical abuse of the invitation mechanism of a Facebook group. Attackers invite friends of those compromised accounts, and these benign invitees usually do not actively add their friends to these unwelcome spamming groups. Thus, there is no recursive invitation, which means the number of invitees is restricted naturally. This observation leads to one heuristic: the invitation records can indicate whether a group is abusing the invitation mechanisms. Based on this heuristic, the first feature may be the abuse of invitation, defined as the proportion of invitees to all members in a group. This feature is used to measure whether the invitation mechanism of Facebook is abused in a group. After considering the extent of abuse of invitation, we may also assess the structure of invitation relationships of a group. To this end, some scores may be required for such assessment. We believe that the inclusion of more features will improve the accuracy of the detection. This part of enhancement will be included in the future work.

Our approach makes the following contributions. First, our approach provides an accurate mechanism to identify a spamming group which is better than current Facebook report mechanism. Second, our approach greatly increases spammers' cost to build a spamming group. Third, our approach is flexible to adopt new features to classify spamming groups.

VI. CONCLUSIONS

Facebook groups are abused frequently by spammers. In this study we design and implement a prototype to automatically detect spamming groups. We compare the differences of accuracy between two feature sets. One set contains the four accessed features and the other contains all seven features. Experimental result shows that when only the four accessed features are used, the total error rate of this prototype system is 7.74%.

REFERENCES

[1] Facebook, "Facebook company info," 2016, http://newsroom.fb.com/company-info/.

[2] M. S. Rahman, T.-K. Huang, H. V. Madhyastha, and M. Faloutsos, "Efficient and scalable socware detection in online social networks," in Presented as part of the 21st USENIX Security Symposium (USENIX Security 12). Bellevue, WA: USENIX, 2012, pp. 663–678. [Online]. Available: https://www.usenix.org/conference/usenixsecurity12/technical-sessions/presentation/rahman

[3] C. Kreibich, C. Kanich, K. Levchenko, B. Enright, G. M. Voelker, V. Paxson, and S. Savage, "Spamcraft: An inside look at spam campaign orchestration," in Proceedings of the 2Nd USENIX Conference on Large-scale Exploits and Emergent Threats: Botnets, Spyware, Worms, and More, ser. LEET'09. Berkeley, CA, USA: USENIX Association, 2009, pp. 4–4. [Online]. Available: http://dl.acm.org/citation.cfm?id=1855676.1855680

[4] Y. Xie, F. Yu, K. Achan, R. Panigrahy, G. Hulten, and I. Osipkov, "Spamming botnets: Signatures and characteristics," in Proceedings of the ACM SIGCOMM 2008 Conference on Data Communication, ser. SIGCOMM '08. New York, NY, USA: ACM, 2008, pp. 171–182. [Online]. Available: http://doi.acm.org/10.1145/1402958.1402979

[5] Facebook, "How do i deal with spam?" 2016, https://www.facebook.com/help/217854714899185.

[6] H. Gao, J. Hu, C. Wilson, Z. Li, Y. Chen, and B. Y. Zhao, "Detecting and characterizing social spam campaigns," in Proceedings of the 10th ACM SIGCOMM Conference on Internet Measurement, ser. IMC '10. New York, NY, USA: ACM, 2010, pp. 35–47. [Online]. Available: http://doi.acm.org/10.1145/1879141.1879147

[7] Y.-S. You, "A study on facebook for spamming group detection," Master's thesis, National Tsing Hua University, August 2013.

[8] Facebook, "What is facebook doing to protect me from spam?" 2016, https://www.facebook.com/help/637109102992723.

[9] N. O'Neill, "The rise of scam facebook groups," 2010, http://www.adweek.com/socialtimes/the-rise-of-scam-facebook-groups/312867.

[10] Facebook, "Platform status," 2016, https://developers.facebook.com/status/.

Beyond the Dolev-Yao Model: Realistic Application-Specific Attacker Models for Applications Using Vehicular Communication

Christoph Ponikwar, Hans-Joachim Hof
MuSe - Munich IT Security Research Group
Department of Computer Science and Mathematics
Munich University of Applied Sciences (MUAS), Germany
Email: christoph.ponikwar@hm.edu, hof@hm.edu

Smriti Gopinath, Lars Wischhof
Department of Computer Science and Mathematics
Munich University of Applied Sciences (MUAS), Germany
Email: smriti.gopinath@hm.edu, wischhof@hm.edu

***Abstract*—In recent time, the standards for Vehicular Ad-hoc Networks (VANETs) and Intelligent Transportation Systems (ITSs) matured and scientific and industry interest is high especially as autonomous driving gets a lot of media attention. Autonomous driving and other assistance systems for cars make heavy use of VANETs to exchange information.They may provide more comfort, security and safety for drivers. However, it is of crucial importance for the user's trust in these assistance systems that they could not be influenced by malicious users. VANETs are likely attack vectors for such malicious users, hence application-specific security requirements must be considered during the design of applications using VANETs. In literature, many attacks on vehicular communication have been described but attacks on specific vehicular networking applications are often missing. This paper fills in this gap by describing standardized vehicular networking applications, defining and extending previous attacker models, and using the resulting new models to characterize the possible attackers interested in the specific vehicular networking application. The attacker models presented in this paper hopefully provide great benefit for the scientific community and industry as they allow to compare security evaluations of different works, characterize attackers, their intentions and help to plan application-specific security controls for vehicular networking applications.**

Keywords–security; attacker model; VANET; V2X; ITS.

I. INTRODUCTION

Vehicular networking applications are a subset of applications used in Intelligent Transportation Systems (ITSs). They typically need security controls, especially, when safety is at stake. For a constructive planning of security controls, it is of benefit to have a model of a typical attacker, a so-called attacker model. Typical attack classes are impersonation, data tampering, sybil attacks, or Denial of Service (DOS) attacks, please refer to [1] for a survey on these attacks. However, these attack classes are very general and their severity differs from application to application. Hence, it is beneficial to have application-specific attacker models for vehicular networking applications. This paper presents vehicular networking applications specific attacker models. These attacker models could be used for security control planning as well as evaluation of security controls. Also, standardized attacker models as in this paper are hopefully a great benefit for the scientific community to compare evaluations of different papers and modeling real world attackers.

This paper is structured as follows: Section II presents related work and shows the gap this paper is closing. Section III gives an overview on vehicular networking applications. Section IV presents a classification of attackers that is used for the application-specific attacker models introduced in Section V. Section VI concludes the paper.

II. RELATED WORK

The field of attack modeling has a long history with some of it rooting in reliability engineering and the vault tree analysis which got adopted and adapted as attack trees [2]–[4] in the realm of secure systems engineering. Because of its detailed and explicit nature the attack tree modeling approach is best suited when goals of an attacker have been elicited and actual mitigation should be developed. The approach taken here categorizes attackers based on different aspects that are derived from their goal, which in return tries to take advantage of a specific vehicular networking application. Others use a game theory based approach to infer intentions, objectives and strategies of attackers [5], we derive these from the vehicular networking application that the attacker tries to exploit.

The often cited Dolev-Yao attacker model [6] models the attacker as an active saboteur. He is omnipotent and can therefore intercept, eavesdrop, or modify all communication of the network. Furthermore, the attacker can pose as a legitimate communication partner and can therefore initiate a communication with every participant in the network. Compromising or breaking cryptographic primitives is not possible for a Dolev-Yao attacker. Networks in an Intelligent Transportation System (ITS) aren't limited to the Internet, instead they consist of Vehicular Ad-hoc Networks (VANET), enabling ad-hoc communication. Cellular technologies, like Long Term Evolution (LTE), can provide connectivity to the Internet. Roadside Units (RSU) or other stationary participants could be connected via traditional electrical or optical wired technologies to other separated networks or the Internet. The Dolev-Yao model is far too imprecise for such a complex networking structure and it only depicts a special type of attacker. This attacker is also unrealistically strong by being omnipotent, which gets increasingly unlikely the more complex and diverse a network becomes. This was previously pointed out in regards to sensor networks [7][8]. Especially, it is pointed out that physical security should not be expected because an attacker can easily get access to those nodes and perform a take over or compromise cryptographic secrets [7]. In such a way, an outside attacker becomes an inside participating one. To sum it up, the Dolev-Yao model is far too imprecise and unrealistically strong to be of use for security controls planning in realistic vehicular networking scenarios.

A realistic attack scenario is the exploitation of low level software or hardware vulnerabilities in the network stacks of wireless transceivers. The existence and importance of these vulnerabilities has been discussed in various publications, [9]–[12]. This scenario marks the lower bound of attack scenarios that are discussed in this paper. While still being relevant specifically to wireless communication, cellular or ad-hoc, it is also not specific to only one vehicular networking application and the root cause of vulnerable soft- and hardware proliferates through all the layers of current systems and is not specific to wireless communications. Therefore, this is not in focus for this publication. Instead, the main contribution is the combination and extension of previous attacker models by [6][7][13] and the detailed description of realistic attacker models via the extended model. Most of the previous works [14]–[18], are missing realistic attacker models. Some like [15]–[17] use categories of attacks, like impersonation, data tampering, sybil, or DOS attacks and describe each attacker based on its category. [18] is really close to defining realistic attacker models by defining categories of attackers, like driver, road side or infrastructure.

Realistic attacker models are needed to better understand who might be the attacker of a system, for better comparison and ultimately needed to make risk based decisions about whether to implement security controls and how to guard against a specific realistic attacker.

III. Vehicular Networking Applications

A general classification of vehicular networking applications uses two classes: *safety applications* and *non-safety applications*. For realistic attacker models, a more fine-grain categorization is needed. The classes used in this paper are described in the following. Please refer to [1] for a detailed description of the vehicular networking applications.

A. Cooperative Sensing (Safety)

Cooperative Sensing applications use V2X communication for situation awareness, e.g., to reduce risks of accidents while driving.

Road Hazard Signalling (RHS): When a vehicle picks up a standardized condition [19], an application broadcasts these conditions to other recipients using a Decentralized Environmental Notification Messages (DENM) [20]. Conditions include emergency vehicle approaching, slow vehicle, stationary vehicle, emergency electronic brake lights, wrong way driving, adverse weather condition, hazardous location, traffic condition, roadwork, and human presence on the road.

Cooperative Collision Avoidance (CCA): When a vehicle senses a possible collision with an approaching vehicle based on Cooperative Awareness Messages (CAM) [21] received from nearby vehicles, the driver gets a warning. Two distinct collision warning applications has been specified: Intersection Collision Risk Warning (ICRW) (a warning is triggered if a collision is likely to happen at an intersection) and Longitudinal Collision Risk Warning (LCRW) (a warning is displayed to the driver if a front or rear end collision is likely)[22].

B. Cooperative Maneuvering

Applications apply V2X communication for driving automation functions in the levels 3 to 5 as defined in SAE J3016 [23].

Cooperative Adaptive Cruise Control (CACC): To optimize resource usage by forming a convoy or platooning and reducing speed alteration via an extended horizon where minor changes can be leveled out.

Cooperative Merging Assistance (CMA): To avoid collisions vehicles and roadside units (RSU) cooperate and negotiate merging maneuvers.

Cooperative Automated Overtake (CAO): For takeover maneuvers either in a fully autonomous self-driving or a driver assistance scenario, cooperation among vehicles to improve safety is needed.

C. In-Vehicle Internet Access

Internet-based applications are offered to passengers and in distraction reduced versions even to the driver.

D. Mobility Monitoring and Configuration

The status of a vehicle can be remotely queried and modified. This application includes control of auxiliary heating systems as well as software and firmware updates. Usually, the accessed vehicle is in a parked position during the interactions of this application.

IV. Attacker Model

There are already different characteristics for attackers known in literature, some described in the following paragraphs and extended if needed.

Insider Attacker vs. Outsider Attacker [7][13]: An outsider attacker is restricted because he does not participate in regular communication. An insider attacker on the other hand is a regular participant in the communication. A participant could become an insider attacker e.g., when hacked or infected with malware.

Active Attacker vs. Passive Attacker [7][13]: A passive attacker only eavesdrops on communication. An active attacker on the other hand acts in the network, e.g., by creating and inserting messages, by replaying messages, or by modifying existing messages.

Static Attacker vs. Dynamic Attacker [7]: An attacker adapting his behavior based on the behavior of network environment or attack target is called a dynamic attacker. Static attackers on the other hand do not adapt to changes whatsoever. An example of a static attack is the most basic form of malware which doesn't utilize a command and control infrastructure and is build only for a specific purpose, like sending spam. An example of a dynamic attack is an attacker of an Advanced Persistent Threat campaign, which adapts to security measures or changes his goal based on the detected environment around it.

Cooperative Attacker [7] **vs. Individual Attacker**: Attackers colluding to reach a common goal (e.g., destabilization of the network) are called cooperative attackers. An attacker limited to its own abilities is called an individual attacker.

Local Attacker vs. Extended Attacker [13] **extension: Global Attacker** [7]: How much influence an attacker has is an important criteria for the scope and impact a given attack can develop. Limited by his physical abilities, a local attacker can only influence participants in his ad-hoc communication vicinity. An attacker controlling multiple network segments has the ability to execute more sophisticated attacks that need a greater area of influence. This so-called global attacker has the ability to access every message of the network. But based on the diversity and complexity of ITS network architecture, this type of attacker is limited to the infrastructure providers or to attackers that can influence or execute control over this communication infrastructure.

Malicious Attacker vs. Rational Attacker [7][13] **extension: Opportunistic Attacker**: An indiscriminate attacker who does not care about losses, resource usage, or consequences and targets functionality of participants or the network is called malicious attacker. A rational attacker tries to reach a certain goal by the cheapest means possible and is focused on his benefit or profit. An attacker who only executes an attack when an opportune circumstance occurs is called an opportunistic attacker.

Table I shows the profile matrix based on the attacker characteristics described above that is used in the rest of this paper to describe application-specific attackers.

TABLE I. GENERAL ATTACKER PROFILE MATRIX

Attacker Properties			
Membership:	insider		outsider
Method:	active		passive
Adaptability:	dynamic		static
Organization:	cooperative		individual
Scope:	global	extended	local
Motivation:	malicious	rational	opportunistic

Based on this profile matrix, specific attackers can be modeled. The worst possible attacker is shown in Table II. The worst possible attacker is the most powerful attacker one can think of. As described in Section II for the Dolev-Yao model, such a powerful attacker is quite unlikely to appear in most realistic scenarios (however, there is one valid scenario listed below).

TABLE II. WORST ATTACKER PROFILE MATRIX

Attacker Properties			
Membership:	insider		~~outsider~~
Method:	active		~~passive~~
Adaptability:	dynamic		~~static~~
Organization:	cooperative		~~individual~~
Scope:	global	~~extended~~	~~local~~
Motivation:	malicious	~~rational~~	~~opportunistic~~

Table III shows the weakest possible attacker of the application specific attacker model.

TABLE III. WEAKEST ATTACKER PROFILE MATRIX

Attacker Properties			
Membership:	~~insider~~		outsider
Method:	~~active~~		passive
Adaptability:	~~dynamic~~		static
Organization:	~~cooperative~~		individual
Scope:	~~global~~	~~extended~~	local
Motivation:	~~malicious~~	~~rational~~	opportunistic

The worst attacker and weakest attacker are both ends of the application specific attacker model presented in this paper. However, in most vehicular networking applications a realistic attacker model lies between the worst attacker and the weakest attacker. The following section presents the realistic attacker models applicable for each vehicular networking application presented in Section III.

V. APPLICATION SPECIFIC ATTACKER MODELS

For each vehicular networking application (see Section III.), different specific attacker profiles are described in this section.

A. *Cooperative Sensing (Safety)*

Attackers interfering with safety functions are always inadvertently or intentionally risking to cause damage to themselves or other humans besides causing financial damage. It is important to keep this in mind especially when judging about the motivation of a certain attacker.

A perpetrator is stuck in traffic, he then decides to push a button that forces his vehicle to send out false road hazard warnings to influence other vehicles. In an ideal situation for the attacker, the victim vehicles fall for his false claims. He might pose as an emergency vehicle, send out false wrong way driving warnings, roadwork, or human presence on the road to clear a lane, to speed past other vehicles. He is an active dynamic insider acting as an individual, with local reach, see table IV. As stated previously, fiddling with safety functions is borderline malicious activity. The speeding attacker might still try to be rational about the reliance of the successful deceiving of other traffic participants as they might simply ignore his false claims or he might overlook real hazards.

TABLE IV. SPEEDSTER PROFILE MATRIX

Attacker Properties			
Membership:	insider		~~outsider~~
Method:	active		~~passive~~
Adaptability:	dynamic		~~static~~
Organization:	~~cooperative~~		individual
Scope:	~~global~~	~~extended~~	local
Motivation:	~~malicious~~	rational	~~opportunistic~~

Another group taking advantage of this safety application may be a single or group of environmentalists or annoyed residents. Their goal might be to reduce the speed of vehicles, no matter what the rest of the community decided on to be acceptable. There are two basic technical approaches these attacker can pursue either they try to jam valid RSUs (Denial of Service), see Table V, or they try to compromise or mimic a valid RSU, see TableVI.

TABLE V. OUTSIDER TRAFFIC CALMING PROFILE MATRIX

Attacker Properties			
Membership:	~~insider~~		outsider
Method:	active		~~passive~~
Adaptability:	~~dynamic~~		static
Organization:	~~cooperative~~		individual
Scope:	~~global~~	~~extended~~	local
Motivation:	~~malicious~~	~~rational~~	opportunistic

When being able to communicate to other vehicles other attacks are possible, like trying to get the vehicles to alter their route, because of hazard warnings like weather conditions or

TABLE VI. INSIDER TRAFFIC CALMING PROFILE MATRIX

Attacker Properties			
Membership:	insider		~~outsider~~
Method:	active		~~passive~~
Adaptability:	~~dynamic~~		static
Organization:	~~cooperative~~		individual
Scope:	~~global~~	~~extended~~	local
Motivation:	~~malicious~~	~~rational~~	opportunistic

fake traffic conditions. But a single RSU or a fake one has only a limited area of influence.

A small step up for the attacker who is compromising RSUs, see Table VI, to slow vehicles down, would be if he does not stop after controlling one RSU. He would try to get control over a larger area to have a bigger influence on victim vehicles, see Table VII. By doing so he poses a greater risk to safety in that area by exercising his power over an area and colluding RSUs, to make the false or modified warnings look authentic.

TABLE VII. SOPHISTICATED TRAFFIC MANIPULATION PROFILE MATRIX

Attacker Properties			
Membership:	insider		~~outsider~~
Method:	active		~~passive~~
Adaptability:	dynamic		~~static~~
Organization:	cooperative		~~individual~~
Scope:	~~global~~	extended	~~local~~
Motivation:	~~malicious~~	rational	~~opportunistic~~

To prevent duplicate information, the following attack model omits the table, because the attacker resembles the worst case attacker as pictured in Table II. The attacker could be a foreign power either state sponsored or independent but the goal of this group would be to put on a stranglehold on safety related functions to unleash massive chaos by using infrastructure to flood victims with false hazard, collision warning and creating non existent vulnerable road users in front of vehicle, to get the safety systems to collapse and shutdown. During such an attack the goal of the attacker would be to create human casualties or at least create huge financial losses and impediment. The whole purpose of such a malicious attack is to weaken the position of an opponent and to strengthen their own, this could be also achieved by holding the infrastructure ransom and threatening to vandalize the infrastructure. To have such a large scale effect the attacker needs to compromise the infrastructure by ether common vulnerabilities or by compromising the provider of it.

The last three attacker types in this section dedicated are derived from the weakest attacker, see Table III. The goal of these attackers is to acquire knowledge about nearby vehicles. This goal is similar to the snooping individual who uses the manufacturer build in monitoring as described in Table XIII. The difference between these three type of attackers is their scope, whether they have only local, extended or global reception. A local influence might be easy to establish, only one receiver is needed. For extended visibility, more receivers are required, but for global reach the RSU to attacker receiver ratio must be one-to-one. This would be easy to achieve for an worst case attacker as he does not only want to have control over some infrastructure but wants to have control over all available ones.

B. Cooperative Sensing (Information/Non-Safety)

In comparison to the safety relevant applications mentioned before, informational cooperative sensing application do not have an immediate life threatening aspect. The application for exchanging dynamic mapping information is particularly interesting as it might be used to improve the driver's experience, but could be misused to annoy the driver or even to literally navigate him into dangerous situations. One attacker who is trying to annoy drivers or shop owners sets up a fake RSU to send out false information about points of interest. This might reach from false opening hours to false location information. This can be considered as trolling, wasting someone's time and resources and annoying people to no end, as presented in Table VIII. He is rather static, a individual opportunistic attacker with only a local scope.

TABLE VIII. TROLLING VIA FALSE INFORMATION PROFILE MATRIX

Attacker Properties			
Membership:	insider		~~outsider~~
Method:	active		~~passive~~
Adaptability:	~~dynamic~~		static
Organization:	~~cooperative~~		individual
Scope:	~~global~~	~~extended~~	local
Motivation:	~~malicious~~	~~rational~~	opportunistic

The second type of attacker are criminals, see Table IX, that use technology to make their activities easier. In case of mapping information, they could try to trick the driver via the navigation system to take another route, to send the driver to an abundant place to either rob or kidnap him. It may be enough to setup some fake RSUs or compromise a few, software wise or physically, to mislead or manipulate the victims systems. A single criminal or a group of them may feed dynamic false information into the systems near their victim and may even deploy multiple RSUs to have a higher chance of misleading the driver. When considering criminals as attackers, the differentiation whether their motivation is malicious or rational depends on where the perpetrators want to reuse their scheme, like a business, or if they are outright hitmen. But whether the latter one would invest in the technology and know-how to ease his job of executing a paid for assassination is questionable. Nonetheless intentional criminal activity would be considered malicious.

TABLE IX. FALSE INFORMATION AS CRIMINAL ACTIVITY SUPPORT

Attacker Properties			
Membership:	insider		~~outsider~~
Method:	active		~~passive~~
Adaptability:	dynamic		~~static~~
Organization:	cooperative		~~individual~~
Scope:	~~global~~	extended	~~local~~
Motivation:	malicious	~~rational~~	~~opportunistic~~

C. Cooperative Maneuvering

When considering cooperative maneuvering, one distinguishes if a non-cooperative fallback is available or not. If a non-cooperative fallback is available, the attacker might be just like the trolling one mentioned in Table VIII as no real harm is possible because a safe downgrade to non cooperative assistance is available. If no fallback is available, there is a safety issue. CACC should have a non cooperative companion ACC. For the cooperative automated overtake application especially in an autonomous driving environment, the safety implications are obvious. An attacker sending false awareness information is only different from the worst case attacker (see Table II) in regards to his reach as he is locally limited and to the organizational aspect as he is an individual, see Table X.

TABLE X. INTENTIONALLY FALSE CAM ATTACKER PROFILE MATRIX

Attacker Properties			
Membership:	insider		~~outsider~~
Method:	active		~~passive~~
Adaptability:	dynamic		~~static~~
Organization:	~~cooperative~~		individual
Scope:	~~global~~	~~extended~~	local
Motivation:	malicious	~~rational~~	~~opportunistic~~

D. In-Vehicle Internet Access

A malware author who uses the Internet connectivity as an initial attack vector to infect software components in a vehicle is summarized in Table XI. This type of an active attack depends heavily on the design of the vehicular internet access capabilities. If the vehicle itself does not have Internet enabled or capable components and merely provides an access point for other smart devices to get access, than the attack surface is reduced. Still, an outside attacker could try to attack the access point software or more generally common software components among vehicles of the same manufacturer or across the industry, that is reachable via the Internet. The ability of an attacker to adapt his malware or the ability of it getting new orders via an command and control infrastructure makes him an dynamic opponent. As an individual attacker who uses the Internet as the initial access vector to his victims, his capabilities are also limited by the ability to directly connect to a victim or whether the victim has to make the initial connection. In this case, he would resort to common scenarios like water hole, or phishing attacks, where the victim connects to an Internet resource who serves an exploit kit targeted at software vulnerabilities. Nevertheless the attackers scope is limited in the sense of the initial attack vector to a local one, further more he is going to act in a rational way, as he wants to make a profit of off his work.

TABLE XI. VEHICULAR MALWARE INITIAL ATTACK VECTOR

Attacker Properties			
Membership:	~~insider~~		outsider
Method:	active		~~passive~~
Adaptability:	dynamic		~~static~~
Organization:	~~cooperative~~		individual
Scope:	~~global~~	~~extended~~	local
Motivation:	~~malicious~~	rational	~~opportunistic~~

E. Mobility Monitoring and Configuration

There are cases where an owner or an agent of the owner (modder, tuner) could be seen as an attacker from the perspective of a vehicle manufacturer. In this case, the owner or his agent tries to manipulate the vehicle, e.g., to decrease the mileage count of a car. It is obvious that the owner or his agent can access all available communication, hence he is an insider attacker. He also has the ability to modify the hardware of software and react to security controls in place. For example, extraction of cryptographic keys from firmware images is a well-known approach in the car hacking and chip tuning community. Hence, the attacker is an adaptive attacker. Attacks usually affect only one vehicle. A special case is an attack on an online service portal of the manufacturer. If all vehicles of this manufacturer can be modified remotely, the attack could have an extended scope, but the initial vulnerability is still local to the service portal. The owner of a vehicle is a rational attacker as he is resource sensitive. If the use of a vehicle hack has less value than the money needed to execute the hack, the owner likely will not execute the attack. See Table XII for a summary.

TABLE XII. MODDER/TUNER PROFILE MATRIX

Attacker Properties			
Membership:	insider		~~outsider~~
Method:	active		~~passive~~
Adaptability:	dynamic		~~static~~
Organization:	~~cooperative~~		individual
Scope:	~~global~~	~~extended~~	local
Motivation:	~~malicious~~	rational	~~opportunistic~~

Another attacker is a control freak attacker. His goal is snooping on his or her spouse, child, or anybody else using the vehicle. As the owner of the vehicle, the active insider individual attacker can use the location tracking or monitoring ability for the legitimate purpose (e.g., finding his vehicle or creating an automatic driver's logbook) but also use it to spy on persons he lends the vehicle to. He does not need to change his behavior as tracking devices are already build into most vehicles. He is very opportunistic as he uses the abilities of the existing monitoring system. Only his own vehicle is affected. The properties of the control freak attacker are summarized in Table XIII.

TABLE XIII. CONTROL FREAK PROFILE MATRIX

Attacker Properties			
Membership:	insider		~~outsider~~
Method:	active		~~passive~~
Adaptability:	~~dynamic~~		static
Organization:	~~cooperative~~		individual
Scope:	~~global~~	~~extended~~	local
Motivation:	~~malicious~~	~~rational~~	opportunistic

An extension of the control freak attacker is an attacker attacking a centralized location information system of a manufacturer. If such a centralized system (e.g., a service portal) exists and the user can query it for the position of his vehicle (e.g., to find a parked car), it could be an attractive target. The attacker is an outside attacker but he must be highly motivated, persistent, and dynamic. When attacking the system, the possession or control of multiple vehicles might be advantageous but the attacker is still considered to be individual and locally limited to the attacked system, that stores the location information. The attacker is not interested to create outages or service interruption as he is interested in the functioning system and especially in the data it gathers, therefor he can be considered being rational. See Table XIV for a summary of this attacker.

TABLE XIV. MASS SURVEILLANCE PROFILE MATRIX

Attacker Properties			
Membership:	~~insider~~		outsider
Method:	active		~~passive~~
Adaptability:	dynamic		~~static~~
Organization:	~~cooperative~~		individual
Scope:	~~global~~	~~extended~~	local
Motivation:	~~malicious~~	rational	~~opportunistic~~

The last two attacker models are still fit into the V2X communication and application paradigm, although they are centered around the existence of systems run by the manufacturer and misusing or exploiting weaknesses in them, which are reachable via the Internet.

VI. CONCLUSION AND FUTURE WORK

This paper presented a survey on current vehicular networking applications, including Cooperative Sensing (Safety), Cooperative Sensing (Information/Non-Safety), Cooperative Maneuvering, In-Vehicle Internet Access, and Mobility Monitoring and Configuration. Novel attacker models are presented that focus on realistic application-specific attacks instead of general attacks on vehicular networks.

TABLE XV. ATTACKER MODEL OVERVIEW

Attacker Properties		
1	Speedster	IV
2	Outsider Traffic Calming	V
3	Insider Traffic Calming	VI
4	Sophisticated Traffic Manipulation	VII
5	Massive Financial Damages and Human Casualties	II
6-8	Information Gathering with three different scopes	III
9	Trolling via false information	VIII
10	False information as criminal activity support	IX
11	Intentionally false CAM attacker	X
12	Vehicular malware initial attack vector	XI
13	Modder/Tuner	XII
14	Control Freak	XIII
15	Mass Surveillance	XIV

Our contribution describes 15 realistic attacker profiles in its main Section V, an summary is given in table XV. These attacker models allow for a more focused planning of security controls for vehicular networks, as well as a better comparability of security evaluations using these attacker models.

Using this attacker modeling approach for evaluation and providing in-depth examples on how to benefit from it in particular vehicular communication applications is reserved for future work.

REFERENCES

[1] C. Ponikwar and H.-J. Hof, "Overview on security approaches in intelligent transportation systems," SECURWARE 2015 : The Ninth International Conference on Emerging Security Information, Systems and Technologies, 2015, pp. 160–165.

[2] C. Salter, O. S. Saydjari, B. Schneier, and J. Wallner, "Toward a secure system engineering methodolgy," in Proceedings of the 1998 workshop on New security paradigms. ACM, 1998, pp. 2–10.

[3] B. Schneier, "Attack trees," Dr. Dobbs journal, vol. 24, no. 12, 1999, pp. 21–29.

[4] A. P. Moore, R. J. Ellison, and R. C. Linger, "Attack modeling for information security and survivability," DTIC Document, Tech. Rep., 2001.

[5] P. Liu, W. Zang, and M. Yu, "Incentive-based modeling and inference of attacker intent, objectives, and strategies," ACM Transactions on Information and System Security (TISSEC), vol. 8, no. 1, 2005, pp. 78–118.

[6] D. Dolev and A. C. Yao, "On the security of public key protocols," Information Theory, IEEE Transactions on, vol. 29, no. 2, 1983, pp. 198–208.

[7] H.-J. Hof, "Sichere dienste-suche in sensornetzen," Ph.D. dissertation, Institut fr Telematik an der Universität Karlsruhe (TH), 2007.

[8] H.-J. Hof and M. Zitterbart, "Scan: A secure service directory for service-centric wireless sensor networks," Computer Communications, 2005, pp. 1517–1522.

[9] C. Mulliner, N. Golde, and J.-P. Seifert, "Sms of death: From analyzing to attacking mobile phones on a large scale." in USENIX Security Symposium, 2011.

[10] C. Mulliner, "On the impact of the cellular modem on the security of mobile phones," Ph.D. dissertation, Technische Universitt Berlin, Fakultt IV - Elektrotechnik und Informatik, 2012.

[11] R.-P. Weinmann, "Baseband attacks: Remote exploitation of memory corruptions in cellular protocol stacks." in WOOT, 2012, pp. 12–21.

[12] ——, "Baseband exploitation in 2013: Hexagon challenges," in Pacsec 2013, 2013.

[13] M. Raya and J.-P. Hubaux, "Securing vehicular ad hoc networks," Journal of Computer Security, vol. 15, no. 1, 2007, pp. 39–68.

[14] M. Amoozadeh, A. Raghuramu, C.-N. Chuah, D. Ghosal, H. M. Zhang, J. Rowe, and K. Levitt, "Security vulnerabilities of connected vehicle streams and their impact on cooperative driving," Communications Magazine, IEEE, vol. 53, no. 6, 2015, pp. 126–132.

[15] V. Hoa La and A. Cavalli, "Security Attacks and Solutions in Vehicular Ad Hoc Networks: A Survey," International Journal on AdHoc Networking Systems, vol. 4, no. 2, Apr. 2014, pp. 1–20.

[16] N. Nikaein, S. K. Datta, I. Marecar, and C. Bonnet, "Application distribution model and related security attacks in vanet," in 2012 International Conference on Graphic and Image Processing, 2012, pp. 876 808–876 808.

[17] I. A. Sumra, I. Ahmad, H. Hasbullah, and J.-l. B. A. Manan, "Classes of attacks in vanet," in Electronics, Communications and Photonics Conference (SIECPC), 2011 Saudi International. IEEE, 2011, pp. 1–5.

[18] T. Leinmüller, R. K. Schmidt, E. Schoch, A. Held, and G. Schäfer, "Modeling roadside attacker behavior in vanets," in GLOBECOM Workshops, 2008 IEEE. IEEE, 2008, pp. 1–10.

[19] European Telecommunications Standards Institute, "ETSI TS 101 539-1 V1.1.1 (2013-08): Intelligent Transport Systems (ITS); V2x Applications;Part 1: Road Hazard Signalling (RHS) application requirements specification," Aug. 2013.

[20] ——, "ETSI TS 102 637-3 V1.1.1 (2010-09): Intelligent Transport Systems (ITS); Vehicular Communications; Basic Set of Applications; Part 3: Specifications of Decentralized Environmental Notification Basic Service," Sep. 2010.

[21] ——, "ETSI TS 102 637-2 V1.2.1 (2011-03): Intelligent Transport Systems (ITS); Vehicular Communications; Basic Set of Applications; Part 2: Specification of Cooperative Awareness Basic Service," Mar. 2011.

[22] ——, "ETSI TS 101 539-3 V1.1.1 (2013-11): Intelligent Transport Systems (ITS); V2X Applications; Part 3: Longitudinal Collision Risk Warning (LCRW) application requirements specification," Nov. 2013.

[23] SAE International - On-Road Automated Vehicle Standards Committee, "Taxonomy and Definitions for Terms Related to On-Road Motor Vehicle Automated Driving Systems," Jan. 2014.

Cost-Effective Biometric Authentication using Leap Motion and IoT Devices

Louis-Philip Shahim, Dirk Snyman, Tiny du Toit, Hennie Kruger
School of Computer-, Statistical- and Mathematical Sciences
North West University,
Potchefstroom, South Africa.
e-mail:lp.shahim6@gmail.com; {dirk.snyman, hennie.kruger, tiny.dutoit}@nwu.ac.za

Abstract — **Biometric authentication is a popular method for information security defense and access control. With the availability of small computing Internet of Things (IoT) devices in conjunction with a hardware peripheral that is able to track hand geometry, multifactor authentication becomes cost-effective and mobile. The proposed system would attempt to authenticate system users by combining both a user's hand geometry scan, along with a series of gestures while simultaneously using machine learning classification techniques for user classification. Cancelability will be insured with a novel steganography implementation for user biometric information.**

Keywords – biometrics; information security; internet of things (IoT); leap motion; multifactor authentication.

I. INTRODUCTION

Biometrics have long been used as an accepted user authentication method and have been implemented as a security measure in many real world systems including personal computers, mobile devices (cell phones and tablets), and also physical access control systems [1][2][3]. Biometrics are the digitalization and analysis of a person's innate physical or biological characteristics and the use thereof to distinguish between persons that are to be afforded access to specific systems, information or physical areas [1][3]. By encoding a person's physical attributes the disadvantages of traditional password based security, like passwords being lost or stolen, can be overcome [1][3]. One of the factors that hampers the acceptance of biometric authentication systems is that the cost of the development and implementation has traditionally been high due to factors such as biometric hardware, computational processing power, infrastructure integration, user training, and research and testing [1][3]. Cost still remains an ever present consideration for organizations when deciding to implement novel approaches over existing traditional methods. This factor raises the question whether traditional biometrics can be accomplished at a lower cost by using non-traditional methods and/or hardware.

With the current influx of new augmented computer interaction possibilities (i.e., new and non-traditional ways to control computers), a wide range of technological facets such as voice-, image- and movement control are receiving a lot of attention [3][4]. This leads to advancements in hardware capability and a definitive decrease in the cost of related hardware. Hardware peripherals (like the Leap Motion Controller (LMC)) that extend the basic functionality of computers to include support for the aforementioned facets are becoming more commonplace [2]. In order to facilitate these interactions, the hardware is implicitly working with information that can be harnessed for biometric identification. Chan *et al.* [2] mentions the possibility of partial sign language gesture recognition using the LMC. The recognition of simple gesture interactions could be implemented as a form of biometric identification due to the latent biometric information it conveys.

The advent of the IoT movement [5][6] presents a myriad of small computing systems that display reasonable processing power and connectivity capabilities at a cost point far lower than traditional computer systems. The IoT is the interaction of everyday objects over the internet or similar networks by embedding computer systems that add smart functionality or an implied "intelligence" to these objects [5][6].

By combining the two above mentioned paradigms, this paper proposes a system that would implement the required hardware and software in an environment that uses augmented user interaction techniques in order to authenticate system users. Using a LMC for advanced hand scanning, a user would be able to gain access to a system or physical area (interfacing with electronic components of traditional security systems to be controlled by the RPi) by having their hand geometry scanned, combined with a series of gestures to incorporate a technique called multifactor authentication [2] in an inexpensive way. Because the LMC requires no direct touch (compared to traditional fingerprint scanners), an applicable scenario for such a system could be to allow medical surgeons access to an operating theatre once they have disinfected their hands and would not like to touch any surfaces before entering. By simply gesturing towards the authentication system, access will be granted if the surgeon is duly authorized thereto.

The rest of this paper is structured as follows: Section II presents system design in terms of security, hardware, interpretation of biometric information, and advantages and disadvantages. The conclusion and future direction for this research is presented in Section III.

II. SYSTEM DESIGN

A. Security considerations

Literature [1][3] mentions a series of considerations (other than cost) that should be central to decision making relating to biometric systems and the biometric traits on which the system functions. Among others, these include:

1) Reliability – The system needs to be always operational and available and therefore hardware should be able to handle many interactions without fail.

2) Error incidence and accuracy – Errors may be introduced to the system by external factors like user aging or environmental changes. The accuracy of the system (false-acceptance vs. false-rejection rates) should be balanced to ensure security while promoting usability.

3) User acceptance – Users need to embrace the technology in order for the biometric authentication method to be successful. Unobtrusive technologies get accepted more easily.

4) Ease of use – The biometric technology should be easy to use, preferably without extensive training.

5) Security application – The choice of biometric authentication method should fit the level of security expected for the specific application.

6) Cancelability – Cancelable biometrics (CB) refer to the obfuscation of stored personal biometric information in such a manner that prohibits the reconstruction of said information by third parties using computational techniques [9]. This ensures the anonymity of users who submit their data to biometric authentication systems by ensuring that their specific information is difficult to decipher by any party other than the intended system. One the main categories of CB is that of biometric salting [9]. This entails the transform of biometric information using transform parameters native to the user in question. E.g., using hand information retrieved from the LMC as transform parameters.

7) Maturity of technology – Traditionally the maturity of the technology, i.e., the technology is often implemented and how well it is supported, determines its longevity. This is also based on prevailing standards that are expected of a proven technology. The LMC, when implemented as a biometrics device, should conform well to these factors mentioned above except for the maturity of the technology. Due to the novel nature of the application it is to be expected that the maturity level is to be quite low.

B. *Hardware*

With the LMC's advanced hand and finger tracking capabilities, the position, velocity and orientation, supplemented by hand geometry information, are reported upon with accuracy and reduced latency [8]. Chan *et al.* [2] present the implementation of an LMC to assume the role of a biometric authentication device by harnessing the abovementioned information. The low cost factor of this device makes this implementation even more favorable in situations where cost is of substantial concern. One drawback of this approach is that the LMC is a peripheral device that still requires a computer system to connect it to as the device cannot function in a standalone way. This disadvantage will add to the associated cost of implementation. However, because the IoT is such a phenomenon presently, many low cost alternatives to traditional computer systems have become commonplace. One of the most widely known computer systems for IoT development is the Raspberry Pi (RPi) platform [6][7]. The RPi presents a balance between size, connectivity, processing power and cost making it an ideal IoT device to serve as an electronic interface (e.g., for interaction with existing physical security systems) alongside traditional computers that drive peripheral devices like the LMC. The information from the LMC can be analyzed locally using methods such as those described by Chan *et al.* [2] but augmenting the result of the analysis by transmitting instructions to the RPi to effect remote digital electronics based tasks, for instance the arming or disarming of alarm systems across interconnected networks (like the Internet) where the RPi serves as an intelligent node for electronic systems interaction. The RPi can further be used for the communication with remote sensors such as movement- or sound sensors.

C. *Interpreting biometric information*

In order to interpret the implicit biometric information that is conveyed by the LMC and harness it in order to do biometric authentication, [2] proposes the use of machine learning techniques (see [8] for more examples on machine learning in biometrics). The readings obtained from the LMC (or other biometric devices) can be presented to a machine learning algorithm as features. The machine learning algorithms (each to their own internal structure) represent data that was gathered from users as a model against which to assess biometric access attempts at runtime. These models for biometric classification are usually biased to have a high precision, but low recall rate (i.e., to favor low false-acceptance rate at the expense of high false-rejection rates). The following algorithms are often implemented for biometric classification [2][8][11][12]: Naïve Bayes classifiers, Random Forrest classifiers, Support Vector Machines, Gaussian Mixture Models, and Artificial Neural Networks.

D. *Advantages/Disadvantages*

Advantages of the proposed approach to biometric authentication include: *a)* Ease of use and convenience. *b)* The low cost factor. *c)* Security aspects should be good when compared to passwords because authentication is based on gestures and hand information that cannot be stolen or guessed. *d)* Auditability in terms of being able to connect users to a specific event or activity. *e)* Well suited for environments where typing is difficult or unwanted (e.g., surgeon in theatre).

Disadvantages include: *a)* The technology is still in its infancy and is not mature. *b)* While accuracy of authentication is expected to be high for small organizations, it may pose a problem with many users. *c)* Error incidence due to changes in a person's hands due to injury, old age, or illness.

E. *Comparison with literature*

Table 1 presents a cursory summary of a selection of systems from literature in comparison to the idea proposed in this paper. The proposed novelty of this idea is the combination of the resulting LMC biometric authentication system with an environment where IoT devices interact with existing security infrastructure. The idea further proposes the inclusion of novel cancelability by employing a new steganography approach for the storage and retrieval of biometric user information. The steganography algorithm will include biometric information of each user as transform parameters. To further illustrate the approach, Fig. 1 presents a graphical representation of the proposed algorithmic framework.

TABLE 1: COMPARISON OF SYSTEMS FROM LITERATURE.

Biometric device	Biometric task	Cancelability	Algorithm	IoT	
LMC	3D signature recognition	None specified	Naïve Bayes/Support vector machine	No	[11]
LMC	Gesture based biometrics	None specified	*k*-nearest neighbor classifier	No	[12]
LMC	Hand geometry and gestures	None specified	Random forest classifier	No	[2]
LMC	Hand geometry and gestures	Stenographical encryption based on biometric information	Machine learning classification and novel steganography	Yes	[this paper]

III. CONCLUSION AND FUTURE WORK

This paper presented the proposed idea of a LMC as a low cost biometric authentication device by its combination with an RPi as an IoT device. The next stage in this research will be to investigate different implementation possibilities. Further investigation into the underlying hardware and software topics is warranted to gauge the feasibility of these technological aspects before experimental implementation can commence. Issues in terms of information security that need to be investigated are: Classification methods need to be researched to ensure the highest possible accuracy of implemented classifiers. The implementation of secure cancelable biometrics to ensure user anonymity. Dlamini *et al.* [10] present the encryption of user credentials in transit and rest by using steganography to "hide" user information in images rather than commonly used user databases. If a common user database is breached, all of the users' information contained therein may be exposed. Future work may include the incorporation of biometrics (read from the LMC) as parameters for use in such a steganography engine as implemented by Dlamini *et al.* [10]. This results in a steganography algorithm that encodes the user information in a picture based on their own unique traits rather than arbitrary encryption keys which may be computationally deduced. The premise is that even when one user's information is identified from the image, the fidelity of other users' information remains intact because the encryption parameters are unique to each user. Finally, extensive real world experimentation is planned with the resulting system to identify any inherent security flaws.

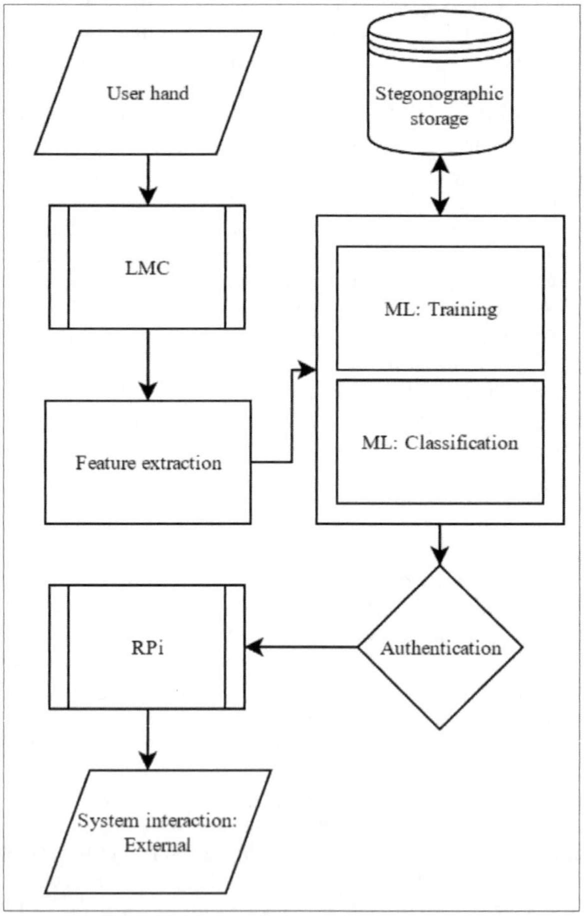

Figure 1. Graphic representation of the algorithm.

REFERENCES

[1] S. Liu and S. Silverman, "A practical guide to biometric security technology," IT Professional, vol. 3, no. 1, 2002, pp. 27-32.

[2] A. Chan, T. Halevi, and N. Memon, "Leap Motion Controller for Authentication via Hand Geometry and Gestures," In Human Aspects of Information Security, Privacy, and Trust, 2015, pp. 13-22.

[3] A. K. Jain, K. Nandakumar, and A. Ross, "50 Years of Biometric Research: Accomplishments, Challenges, and Opportunities," Pattern Recognition Letters, 2016. [Online]. Available from: http://www.sciencedirect.com/science/article/pii/S0167865515004365.2016.06.10.

[4] X. Wang, S. K. Ong, and A. Y. C. Nee, "A comprehensive survey of augmented reality assembly research," Advances in Manufacturing, vol. 4, no. 1, 2016, pp. 1-22.

[5] F. Xia, L. T. Yang, L. Wang, and A. Vinel, "Internet of things," International Journal of Communication Systems, vol. 25, no. 9, 2012, p. 1101.

[6] M. Maksimović, V. Vujović, N. Davidović, V. Milošević, and B. Perišić, "Raspberry Pi as Internet of things hardware: performances and constraints," Design issues, vol. 3, 2014, p. 8.

[7] MagPi, "Raspberry Pi 3 is out now! Specs, Benchmarks & More," 1 March 2016. [Online]. Available from: https://www.raspberrypi.org/magpi/raspberry-pi-3-specs-benchmarks/. 2016.03.01.

[8] G. Damousis and S. Argyropoulos, "Four Machine Learning Algorithms for Biometrics Fusion: A Comparative Study," Applied Computational Intelligence and Soft Computing, vol. 2012, 2012, p. 6.

[9] C. Rathgeb and A. Uhl. "A survey on biometric cryptosystems and cancelable biometrics." EURASIP Journal on Information Security 2011.1, 2011, pp. 1-25.

[10] M.T. Dlamini, J. Eloff, H.S. Venter, M. Eloff, K. Chetty, and J. Blackledge. "Securing cloud computing's blind-spots using strong and risk-based MFA," In International Conference on Information Resource Management, 2016, pp. 58:1-28.

[11] I. Nigam, M. Vatsa, and R. Singh. "Leap signature recognition using hoof and hot features," In 2014 IEEE International Conference on Image Processing (ICIP), 2014, pp. 5012-5016.

[12] M. Piekarczyk and M.R. Ogiela, "On using palm and finger movements as a gesture-based biometrics," In 2015 International Conference on Intelligent Networking and Collaborative Systems (INCOS), 2015, pp. 211-216.

Node Compromise Detection Based on Parameter Grouping in Wireless Sensor Networks

Manyam Thaile, O. B. V. Ramanaiah
Dept. of CSE, JNTUH College of Engineering
Hyderabad, Telangana State, India
e-mails: {manyamthaile, obvramanaiah}@gmail.com

***Abstract*—Node Compromise Detection (NCD) is an essential requirement for dealing with potential attacks in randomly deployed, unattended and not tamper resistant wireless sensor networks applications. Behaviour based concepts, such as false information communication by a compromised node (ZoneTrust), are reported in literature. In our work, more effective parameters, namely, packet sending rate, depletion of node energy, node location, and node non-availability are identified for NCD. All these parameters are used to detect a compromised node either conjunctively (AND model) or disjunctively (OR model). The OR model is suitable for military surveillance; and the AND model is suitable for weather monitoring applications. The OR model incurs a lot of overhead whereas the AND model suffers from high risk of attack. To alleviate these demerits Parameter Grouping (PG) concept is proposed to retain the merits of both AND and OR models. An extensive NS-2 based simulation work was carried out and found that the proposed NodeTrust-based PG improves the system performance substantially.**

***Keywords*—node compromise detection; software attestation; parameter grouping; wireless sensor network security**

I. Introduction

A Wireless Sensor Network (WSN) consists of a large number of sensor nodes, which perform sensing, processing and communication. There are different types of WSN applications, i.e., smart home security, battlefield surveillance, civil structure condition monitoring, crop pest control, etc. The sensor nodes have constrained resources such as limited battery energy, low computing power and low memory.

An attacker can easily capture the sensor nodes and compromise them due to the vulnerabilities of the sensor networks, i.e., unattended nature, low computing power (incapability to run software-based security concepts), lack of tamper-resistant hardware and unreliable communication, etc.

The node compromisation is a serious security threat to all WSN applications, because when a node is compromised, an attacker can launch a variety of attacks and inject malicious code. A compromised node is a trusted node (benign node) that has been taken control over by an attacker [8]. An attacker can compromise a sensor node in two ways:

- An attacker can physically capture a sensor node, connect it to a high-end computing system, steal the security keys, inject the malicious code, and thereby making the node compromised.
- An attacker can logically (remotely) connect a sensor node to high-end computing system, steal the secret keys, and inject the malicious code to make the node compromised.

To mitigate the damage incurred by compromised nodes, the system should detect and revoke the nodes at the earliest [12]. For addressing these issues, researchers have recently proposed various node compromise detection schemes, as well as revokation techniques. There are two approaches for handling Node Compromising [9], namely, prevention schemes, and detection schemes, as shown in Figure 1.

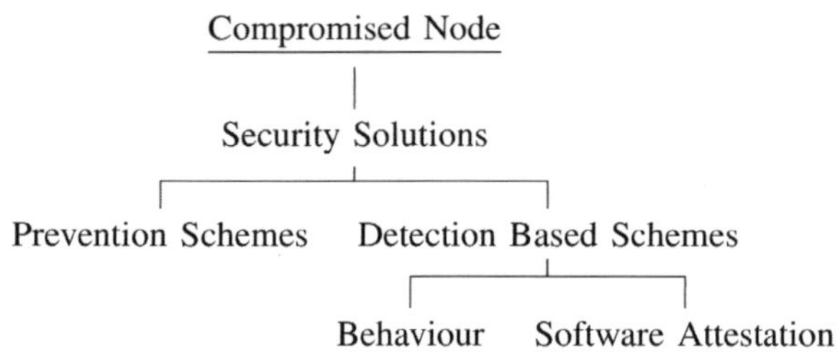

Figure 1. Security Solutions for Compromised Nodes.

Jun-Won Ho et al. [1] proposed a scheme named *ZoneTrust (ZT)* based on the concept of trust of a zone. If a zone is untrusted, then the base station applies the software attestation for each and every node in the zone. The drawbacks of this approach are:

- It is necessary for the base station to communicate with each and every sensor node of the untrusted zone which results in high communication overhead.
- Software attestation is applied on every node in the untrusted zones, in which some of the nodes are not compromised. This leads to computation overhead.
- Due to communication and computation overheads, ZoneTrust scheme consumes a lot of energy of the nodes.
- ZoneTrust considered only one parameter to determine untrusted zone, that is, false information communication.

In our previous work, packet arrival time (odd time of arrival) is used to detect a compromised node [14].

This paper proposes a better scheme with minimal overhead called *Parameter Grouping (PG)*. It identifies the untrusted nodes based on the five identified parameters of the behavior based approach, namely, packet sending rate, node energy depletion, node location, false information and non-availability of sensor nodes. Then, base station applies software attestation on those identified nodes to decide the compromised nodes. Afterwards it revokes them immediately.

The rest of paper is organized as follows: Existing literature on NCD is reviewed in Section II. Network model, as well as attacker model are discussed in Section III. Section IV elaborates our proposed scheme (Parameter Grouping). Section V presents the simulation results. Finally, the paper concludes with Section VI.

II. RELATED WORK

The prevention-based techniques are the first approach of defense for protecting sensor nodes using cryptography. The encryption and authentication are the primary measures in a prevention-based technique, based on key management, as that introduced in the security framework SPINS [7]. However, in case the first approach of defense is broken the compromised nodes could extract security-sensitive information (e.g., secret key), leading to breaches of security.

Thus, developing detection-based techniques as the second approach of defense has become of paramount importance. Detection based techniques aim at identifying misbehaviour and to check integrity of software. Detection based techniques are divided into two major categories as shown in Figure 1: Behaviour based and Software attestation based schemes.

The Behaviour based schemes detect misbehaviour of sensor nodes based on different parameters. For example, packet arrival time, packet arrival rate, packet sending rate, node location, node energy, etc. [5][6][11]. These techniques detect only misbehaviour, but fail to check integrity of malicious code.

The software-attestation based techniques have been proposed to detect the malicious code of sensor nodes. Specifically, the base station checks whether the flash image codes have been maliciously altered by performing attestation in randomly chosen portions of image codes or the entire codes [2][3][4]. These techniques detect only malicious code, but fail to detect misbehaviour of sensor nodes. The security architecture of wireless sensor networks [13] is shown Figure 2. The vertical comparison given in Figure 2 indicates that the various WSN security issues are addressed in every layer of the protocol stack from physical to application layers.

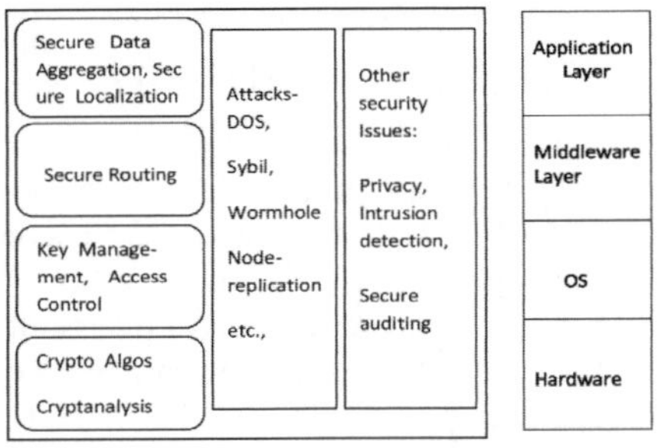

Figure 2. Security Architecture for WSN.

III. SYSTEM MODEL

A. Network Model

The sensor network considered for our study is a static network in which a sensor node does not change its location once deployed. Besides, it is assumed that the base station is a trustworthy node. The communication between a sensor (leaf) node and base station takes place in two levels: from sensor node to Zone Head (ZH), and from ZH to base station. It is assumed that in every zone a sensor node nearest to base station is named as ZH. The proposed architectural model is depicted in Figure 3.

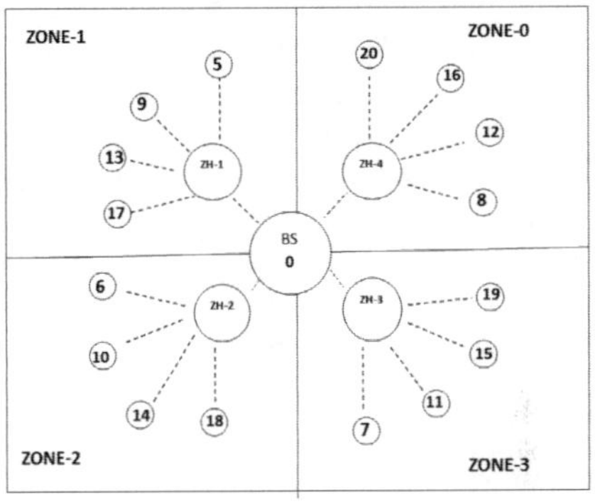

Figure 3. Architecture of Wireless Sensor Network.

B. Attacker Model

We assume that an attacker attempts to compromise as many nodes as possible in each zone. An attacker physically captures sensor nodes or remotely accesses them, compromises them, and re-deployes them back at different locations.

The attacker injects malicious code in all the captured nodes. This results in high packet sending rate, as well as faster depletion of compromised node's energy. The compromised nodes will be unavailable for the duration of the attack injection. Hence, it is to be noted that certain parameter values change unexpectedly.

C. AND-OR Model

The AND-OR Model estimates the trust of sensor nodes based on the behavioural parameters such as packet sending rate, depletion of node energy, node location, false information and non-availability of a node.

The evaluation of five parameters is follows:

- PSR (Packet Sending Rate): It can take different values, namely, HIGH, LOW, and NORMAL. If this parameter has value HIGH, then it is considered as satisfied (i.e., true).
- DNE (Depletion of Node Energy): It takes three values, namely, LOW, NORMAL, and HIGH. If DNE is equivalent to HIGH, then it is considered as true.
- NL (Node Location): Two values are possible, namely, Changed, and Unchanged. If NL is equivalent to Changed, then it is considered as true.

- FI (False Information): Two values are possible, namely, TRUE, and FALSE. If a node reports/communicates False Information, then the value of FI parameter is set to TRUE; else FALSE.
- NAN (Non Availability of Node): It takes two values, namely, YES and NO. If a node sends information periodically to ZH, it indicates its availability in the WSN; then NAN is set to NO; otherwise, YES.

The AND model identifies a node as untrustworthy, if it satisfies all the above five parameters simultaneously. In other words, the node is declared as untrustworthy when the conjunction of the five parameters is true. If at least one parameter is not true, then that node is not declared as untrust.

A node where all the identified parameters are valid/satisfied is declared as untrusted. Some (not all) parameters may be satisfying at each and every node of the network; and it might be the case that some nodes are already compromised. But the AND model does not detect these compromised nodes because all the parameters are not satisfying at those compromised nodes. Obviously, this model increases the vulnerability of the network for attacks (i.e., High risk).

The condition of AND model to be verified at i^{th}node is C_i=$(PSR_i \wedge DNE_i \wedge NL_i \wedge FI_i \wedge NAN_i)$. Node Status, NS is defined as follows:

$$NS(Node_i, TimeInterval_k) = \begin{cases} Untrust, if(C_i == True) \\ Trust, else \end{cases} \quad (1)$$

where PSR: **P**acket **S**ending **R**ate, DNE: **D**epletion of **N**ode **E**nergy, NL: **N**ode Location, FI: **F**alse **I**nformation and NAN: **N**on-**A**vailability of **N**ode.

The OR model categorizes a node as untrusted, which satisfies at least one of the above mentioned five parameters. In other words, the node is declared as untrusted when the disjunction of the five parameters is true. If all the parameters are not satisfied simultaneously, then only a node is declared as trust.

When more and more parameters are identified for NCD, only some (not all) parameters may be satisfied in case of a large number of nodes. As per OR Model, these nodes, where at least one parameter is valid, are identified as untrustworthy. This increases the number of nodes to be applied the software attestation to decide whether they are really compromised or not (Even if one parameter is satisfied by a node, it calls for software attestation for compromised node detection). This increases the software attestation overhead for OR model.

The condition of OR model to be verified at i^{th}node is C_i=$(PSR_i \vee DNE_i \vee NL_i \vee FI_i \vee NAN_i)$. Node Status, NS is defined as follows:

$$NS(Node_i, TimeInterval_k) = \begin{cases} Untrust, if(C_i == True), \\ Trust, else \end{cases} \quad (2)$$

The main motivation of Parameter Grouping is to strike the balance between risk of attack and attestation overhead. The OR model has a main advantage of low risk, whereas the AND model has the chief advantage of low overhead. To retain the merits of both, it is required to combine the two approaches. One way to achieve this is to group the parameters based on some criteria. Then, apply OR model among the groups, and the AND model within each group. In other words, a group is declared as satisfying when all the group parameters are true (AND model). All the groups are evaluated on the same lines. Then the node under observation is declared as untrusted only when the disjunction of all the groups' outcomes is true (OR model). Table I shows the comparison of AND and OR Models.

TABLE I. AND-OR MODEL COMPARISON.

Model	Risk	Attestation Overhead	False +ve	False -ve
AND	High	Low	No	Yes
OR	Low	High	Yes	No

Let the probability of a node declared as untrustworthy when all the parameters are considered individually be p_1, and the probability of the same node declared as untrustworthy when some (potentially distinct subset or group) of the parameters are considered conjunctively is p_2. It can be intuitively derived that $p_2 < p_1$. Based on this, the following conclusion is drawn:

Less number of nodes will be identified as untrustworthy in Parameter Grouping Model than the OR Model. It means that PG model results in less overhead in software attestation.

Let q_1 be the probability of a node declared as untrustworthy when all the parameters are considered as conjunctively, and q_2 be the probability of the same node declared as untrustworthy when disjunctions of groups of parameters are considered. It can be intuitively derived that $q_2 > q_1$. Based on this, the following conclusion is drawn:

Relative to AND Model, more number of nodes will be identified as untrustworthy in Parameter Grouping Model. It implies that more number of nodes are declared as untrustworthy when any one group of parameters is valid. It means that false negative rate (attack risk) is reduced compared to AND Model. It is to be observed that AND and OR models helps each other to mitigate the disadvantage of the other.

We can deploy AND-OR model and Parameter Grouping in different types of applications of WSNs, namely, military surveillance, weather monitoring etc.,

We discuss parameter grouping in detail in the next section.

IV. PARAMETER GROUPING

The motivation for parameter grouping is to overcome the demerits of AND, as well as OR Models. Parameter grouping is done based on their inter-relationship, for example, packet sending rate and depletion of node energy are inter-related as high packet sending rate results in high Depletion of Node Energy (DNE). The parameters mentioned earlier are categorized into three groups, namely, G1, G2, and G3, where G1={Packet Sending Rate, Depletion of Node Energy }, G2={Node Location, False Information}, G3={Non-Availability}. Mathematically, the concept of parameter grouping is explained below:

$$Node_iSusp = \begin{cases} (PSR_i \wedge DNE_i) \vee (NL_i \wedge FI_i) \vee (NAN_i) \\ or \\ (G1_i \vee G2_i \vee G3_i) \end{cases} \quad (3)$$

where G1=$(PSR_i \wedge DNE_i)$, G2=$(NL_i \wedge FI_i)$, G3=(NAN_i), and i^{th} node is suspected.

A. Group1 (G1)

The parameters, namely, PSR and DNE are made as one group, say G1. It means that the conjunction of the two parameters becomes true only when both the parameters are satisfied. If at least one parameter is not satisfied, the group outcome becomes negative irrespective of the other parameter's validity. Here G1= (PSR $\wedge$ DNE).

Packet Sending Rate: It is assumed that each sensor node sends a packet to ZH in every interval. The packets sent by all the members of the zone are maintained in a table. If any one node sends more number of packets abnormally, that is noticed by ZH. Then it determines that node's PSR value is True. Mathematically, PSR value of a ith node at time interval k is

$$PSR(Node_i, TimeInterval_k) = \begin{cases} True, p_i > Th \\ False, else \end{cases} \quad (4)$$

where p_i is a number of packets received by i^{th}.

Depletion of Node Energy: As every node sends only one packet regularly to ZH, its battery energy depletes (consumes) uniformly. If some node's energy depletes quite fast (might be due to high packet sending rate), it becomes abnormal. The ZH notices this abnormality and suspects that node is compromised. Our assumption is that if any node's energy is decreasing more than threshold value in each interval, then that node's DNE value is considered as True.

$$DNE(Node_i, TI_k) = \begin{cases} True, Pre_{en} - Cur_{en} > Th \\ False, else \end{cases} \quad (5)$$

where i is $node_{id}$, k is time interval, TI is $TimeInterval_k$, Pre_{en} is the node's energy in the previous interval and Cur_{en} is the node's energy in the current interval.

After finding out the values of PSR and DNE, the G1's validity and then equation 3 are to be evaluated.

B. Group2 (G2)

The parameters, node location and false information are considered as one group. The reason for combining the two parameters is when an attacker physically captures a node, makes it compromised, and replaces it back at different location usually. As it is compromised, the node is likely to send false information to ZH. In other words, a node is suspected only when its location is changed and the information communicated by it to ZH is incorrect/unusual. G2= (NL $\wedge$ FI). If at least one parameter is false, then G2 is false.

Node Location: As we are dealling with static sensor network, nodes' location remains unchanged usually. The ZH maintains the locations of all the nodes, and suspects those nodes which change their locations unusually.

$$NL(Node_i, TI_k) = \begin{cases} False, if(Org_{loc} == Cur_{loc}) \\ True, else \end{cases} \quad (6)$$

where i is $Node_{id}$, k is time interval, Org_{loc} is the node's orginal location, and Cur_{loc} is the node's current location. **False Information**: A sensor node is expected to communicate to ZH in a predefined format with an expected size, which is coherent with all other nodes reports. Contrary to this, if ZH notices incorrect and/or unusual information (in terms of size and format), that node is suspected.

After finding out the values of NL and FI, the G2's validity and then equation 3 is to be evaluated.

C. Group3 (G3)

This group has the only one parameter, NAN. Any new parameter which is coherent with this will be added to the group. If a particular node is unavailabe for communication because of physical capturing and compromisation activity, it is observed by ZH as unusual or abnormal. Then that node is declared as suspicous.

Algorithm 1 NAN algorithm

```
Gather all NodeID's & timestamp
Search all the nodes exist or not
if missing time > th then
    G3 or NAN=True
else
    G3 or NAN=False
end if
```

By substituting the values of G1, G2, and G3 the equation 3 is evaluated. If at least one of the Group $(G1, G2, G3)$ is true, then the corresponding is node considered as untrusted. The ZH informs to base station, when the untrusted nodes are identified.

V. SIMULATION

An extensive simulation study was carried out using NS2 simulator (NS2.35) on Ubuntu platform. As mentioned in Section III the network model consists of four zones with a total of 25 nodes including four zone heads and one base station, as shown in Figure 3. The routing and transport protocols used in our simulation are DSDV (Destination Sequenced Distance Vector) and UDP (User Datagram Protocol), respectively. The energy model is also included to know the residual battery energy of a node whenever required. Simulation was carried out based on the proposed concept of Parameter Grouping, and results are analyzed.

A. Experimental Analysis

All the parameters considered in simulation and their values/ranges are specified in Table II. The simulation was carried out by changing the number of nodes as 25, 30, 40, and 50. The atomic unit of time for our simulation is 1 sec. Behaviour of sensor nodes is analyzed based on the statistics gathered during the simulation.

TABLE II. SIMULATION PARAMETERS.

Parameter	Value
Simulation Time	20 Seconds
Area	100 × 100
Time Intervals	1 Second
Traffic Type	UDP
Routing protocol	DSDV
Energy Model	Yes
No.of Nodes	25,30,40,50

Node Trust, The first experiment was carried out by setting the number of nodes as 25 and statistics, namely, event time, nodeID, energy, location (both x and y), the number of packets transmitted are collected and tabulated in Table III. It is to be observed that all the parameters are taking values as expected. No parameter is found with abnormal value. Hence, it is concluded that all the nodes in four zones are trustworthy. In other words, no node is found that is untrustworthy. This is also supported by the report of our NCD reporting system (based on NS2 simulation).

TABLE III. NODE TRUST.

Sender					
Time	NodeID	Energy	X-value	Y-value	#packets
.	.	.	.	.	.
11.7036	13	10.00	12.0000	20.0000	1
11.1895	5	9.99	8.0000	24.0000	1
11.0475	7	10.00	95.0000	72.0000	1
11.7449	10	10.00	60.0000	14.0000	1
11.0791	9	10.00	16.0000	25.0000	1
11.1886	8	10.00	28.0000	94.0000	1
11.7540	14	10.00	65.0000	18.0000	1
11.1138	15	10.00	85.0000	90.0000	1
11.8824	11	10.00	80.0000	82.0000	1
11.3390	6	10.00	71.0000	12.0000	1
11.1443	16	10.00	33.0000	90.0000	1
11.3334	12	10.00	35.0000	90.0000	1

The second simulation was carried out assuming that the attack took place. It means that some nodes are physically captured, compromised and re-located back at different locations. By observing the values of the identified parameters in Table IV, abnormality can be noted.

With respect to node 8 entry in Table IV, G1 parameters: PSR and DNE are true; and hence, the G1 also becomes true. Similarly G2's truth value (based on location and false information , as well as, G3's truth value becomes true. Hence 5, 8, and 10 are untrusted.

If we assume that a WSN is deployed for military surveillance application, an attacker can make the captured node to always report false (or misleading) information. For example, a particular compromised node reporting vehicle motion all the time.

Node Compromise Detection and Revocation: where Ntype is Node type, SN is suspicious node, CD is compromised node, ED is energy depletion and NAN is Non-Availability of Node.

TABLE IV. NODE UNTRUSTED.

Sender					
Time	NodeID	Energy	X-value	Y-value	#packets
.	.	.	.	.	.
11.1383	16	10.00	33.0000	90.0000	1
11.2395	13	10.00	12.0000	20.0000	1
11.9203	14	9.99	65.0000	18.0000	1
11.7560	5	9.99	12.7100	31.4100	1
11.3239	8	9.97	28.0000	94.0000	201
11.7636	9	9.99	16.0000	25.0000	1
11.2148	15	10.00	85.0000	90.0000	1
11.8340	12	9.99	35.0000	90.0000	1
11.3681	7	10.00	95.0000	72.0000	1
11.4029	10	9.97	60.0000	14.0000	201

TABLE V. COMPROMISED NODES.

NodeID	Energy	X	Y	packets	Ntype	CD	Comments
8	-	28.00	94.00	201	SN	yes	packets>Th
8	0.03	28.00	94.00	-	SN	yes	ED>Th
10	-	60.00	14.00	201	SN	yes	packets>Th
10	0.03	60.00	14.00	-	SN	yes	ED>Th
5	-	13.26	32.26	1	SN	yes	false location
6	-	-	-	-	SN	yes	NAN
11	-	-	-	-	SN	yes	NAN

As mentioned in Section I, the node is declared as compromised (NCD) if a node is untrustworthy and if the code is altered. It is to be noted that whether the code is altered or not is known through software attestation process; see Table V for the NCD report of the proposed and developed system. The compromised nodes are 5, 6, 8, 10, and 11 as per the report of the developed system. The MD5 (Message Digest) algorithm [16][17] is used for attestation. Compromised nodes can be revoked in two ways, first; one re-configure code of the compromised nodes, and secondly remove from the sensor network and replace with new nodes.

B. Performance Analysis

Let 'k' be the number of zones, each having 'm' number of nodes as its members on an average. If we assume that at least one zone is untrustworthy, then it is necessary for the BS to communicate the code for software attestation to each and every node of that zone (as per ZoneTrust concept). Hence, the communication cost is of the order n=$k \times m$ (total number of the nodes). Hence, the communication cost of ZoneTrust is O(n).

If we use the Parameter Grouping concept, the complexity decreases to O(k), where $k << n$. It is due to the need of BS to communicate only with identified untrusted nodes.

As explained above, the computation complexity (to run MD5 algorithm) of ZoneTrust is O(n), whereas that of the proposed PG concept is O(k) where $k << n$.

We apply the standard metrics of performance for detection systems [15].

- **False Positives**: It means that some benign nodes are reported as compromised. The PG model eliminates false positive reports. Systems with a low percentage of false positives are accurate.

- **False Negatives:** It implies that compromised nodes are reported as benign nodes. The PG model avoids false neagtive also.

Figures 4, 5, 6, and 7 show the performance between Parameter Grouping and ZoneTrust concepts in terms of Detection time, Number of Nodes to be Software Attested, communication overhead and computation overhead, respectively.

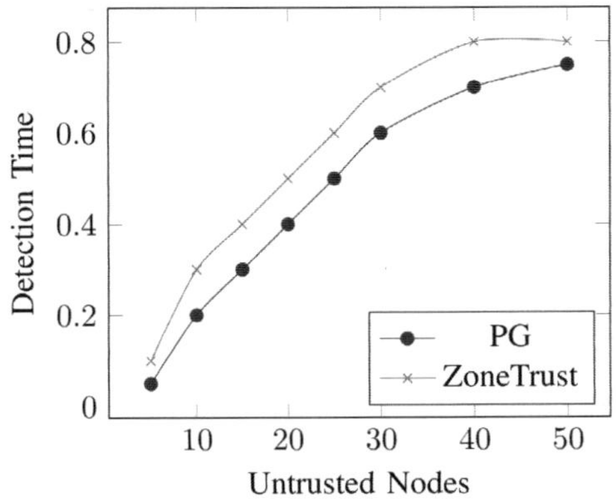

Figure 4. #Untrusted Nodes Vs Detection Time.

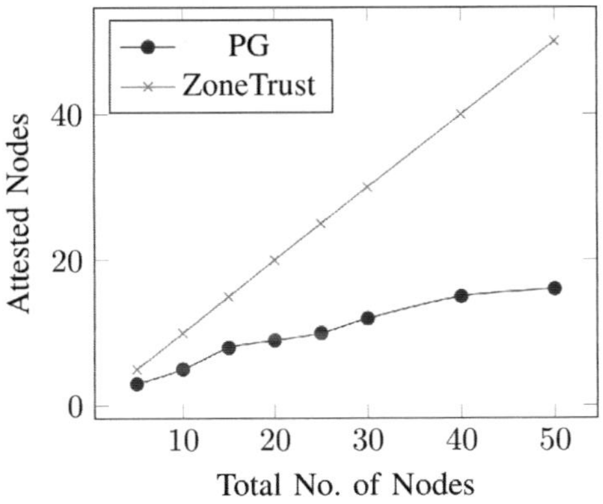

Figure 5. #Untrusted Nodes Vs #Nodes to be Attested.

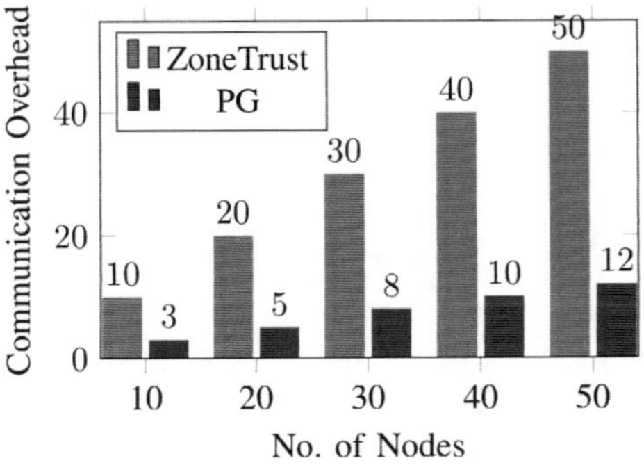

Figure 6. Communication Overhead between ZT and PG.

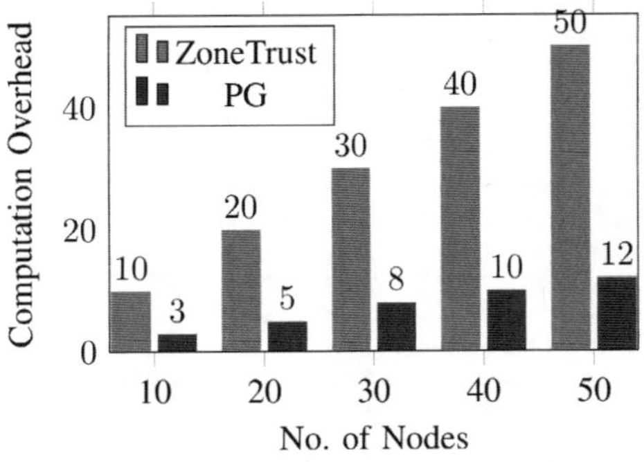

Figure 7. Computation Overhead between ZT and PG.

VI. Conclusion and Future Work

In this paper, Parameter Grouping concept for NCD in WSN was proposed, simulated and analyzed. The analysis, as well as simulation results prove that the computation and communication cost of the proposed method is O(k), whereas that of ZoneTrust method is O(n) where K is the number of zones and n is the total number of sensor nodes in WSN and $k << n$.

The proposed solution is to carry out further experimentation of Parameter Grouping concept by considering various node compromise models based on probability theory. The models are basic uniform, basic gradient, intelligent uniform, and intelligent gradient. This is to increase security and decrease the overhead of the system.

References

[1] Jun-Won Ho, Matthew Wright, and Sajal K. Das, "ZoneTrust: Fast Zone-Based Node Compromise Detection and Revocation in Wireless Sensor Networks Using Sequential Hypothesis Testing," IEEE Transactions on Dependable and Secure Computing, July/August 2012, vol. 9, no. 4, pp. 494-511.

[2] T. Abuhmed, N. Nyamaa, and D. Nyang, "Software-Based Remote Code Attestation in Wireless Sensor Network," Proc. of IEEE GLOBECOM, December. 2009.

[3] T. Park and K. G. Shin, "Soft Tamper-Proofing via Program Integrity Verification in Wireless Sensor Networks," IEEE Trans.Mobile Computing, May/June 2005, vol. 4, no. 3, pp. 297-309.

[4] A. Seshadri, A. Perrig, L. van Doorn, and P. Khosla, "SWATT:SoftWare-Based Attestation for Embedded Devices," Proc. IEEE Symp. Security and Privacy (S & P), May 2004.

[5] Mary Mathews, Min Song, Sachin Shetty, and Rick McKenzie, "Detecting Compromised Nodes in Wireless Sensor Networks," Software Engineering, Artificial Intelligence, Networking, and Parallel/Distributed Computing, August 2007, vol .1, pp. 273-278.

[6] F. Li and J. Wu, "Mobility Reduces Uncertainty in MANET," Proc. IEEE INFOCOM, May 2007.

[7] Perrig A, et al., "SPINS: security protocols for sensor networks," Presented at the 17th ACM international Conference on Mobile Computing and Networks (MobiCOM), 2001.

[8] Daniele Raffo, "Security Schemes for the OLSR Protocol for Ad Hoc Networks," 2005

[9] Miao Xie, Song Han, Biming Tian, and Sazia Parvin, "Anomaly detection in wireless sensor networks: A survey," Journal of Network and Computer Applications, July 2011, vol. 34, no. 4, pp. 1302–1325.

[10] Tao Li, Min Song, and Mansoor Alam, "Compromised Sensor Nodes Detection: A Quantitative Approach," The 28th An IEEE International Conference on Distributed Computing Systems Workshops, 2008.

[11] Vinayaka S.N, and M Dakshayini, "COMPRO-MOTO: An efficient approach for identifying compromised nodes in wireless sensor networks," International Journal of Computers and Technology, May 22, 2014, vol. 13, no. 7.

[12] B. Li, and R. Doss, "Fast Recovery from Node Compromise in Wireless Sensor Networks," An IEEE Third International Conference on New Technologies, Mobility and Security (NTMS), 2009

[13] Available online: http://www.wsn-security.info/Security_Map.htm (accessed on 1.05.2016).

[14] Manyam Thaile, and O.B.V Ramanaiah, "Node Compromise Detection Based on NodeTrust in Wireless Sensor Networks," An IEEE International Conference on Computer Communication and Informatics (ICCCI), Jan. 07 – 09, 2016, pp. 193-197, Coimbatore, INDIA

[15] Yi-Tao Wang, and Rajive Bagrodia, "ComeSen: A Detection for Identifying Compromised Nodes in Wireless Sensor Networks," SECURWARE 2012: The Sixth International Conference on Emerging Information, Systems and Technologies, pp. 148-156, 2012.

[16] S. Bruce, "Applied cryptography: protocols, algorithms and source code in C," John Wiley and Sons, Canada, 1996.

[17] S. Goldwasser, S. Micali, and R. Rivest, "A digital signature scheme secure against adaptive chosen-message attacks," J. Comput., vol. 17, no. 2, pp. 281-308, 1988.

Embedded Security Testing with Peripheral Device Caching and Runtime Program State Approximation

Markus Kammerstetter and Daniel Burian

Secure Systems Lab Vienna, Automation Systems Group
Institute of Computer Aided Automation
Vienna University of Technology
Vienna, Austria
Email: {mk,dburian} @ seclab.tuwien.ac.at

Wolfgang Kastner

Automation Systems Group
Institute of Computer Aided Automation
Vienna University of Technology
Vienna, Austria
Email: k @ auto.tuwien.ac.at

Abstract—**Today, interconnected embedded devices are widely used in the Internet of Things, in sensor networks or in security critical areas such as the automotive industry or smart grids. Security on these devices is often considered to be bad which is in part due to the challenging security testing approaches that are necessary to conduct security audits. Security researchers often turn to firmware extraction with the intention to execute the device firmware inside a virtual analysis environment. The drawback of this approach is that required peripheral devices are typically no longer accessible from within the Virtual Machine and the firmware does no longer work as intended. To improve the situation, several ways to make the actual peripheral devices accessible to software running inside an emulator have been demonstrated. Yet, a persistent problem of peripheral device forwarding approaches is the typically significant slowdown inside the analysis environment, rendering resource intense software security analysis techniques infeasible. In addition, security tests are hard to parallelize as each instance would also require its own embedded system hardware. In this work, we demonstrate an approach that could address both of these issues by utilizing a cache for peripheral device communication in combination with runtime program state approximation. We evaluated our approach utilizing well known programs from the GNU core utilities package. Our feasibility study indicates that caching of peripheral device communication in combination with runtime program state approximation might be an approach for some of the major drawbacks in embedded firmware security analysis but, similar to symbolic execution, it suffers from state explosion.**

Keywords–Embedded Systems; Security Analysis; State Explosion; Program Slicing; Virtual Machine Introspection.

I. INTRODUCTION

The widespread use of embedded systems in security critical environments calls for better security testing techniques. However, testing embedded system firmware in its native environment imposes severe restrictions. Embedded systems can often be interfaced over debugging interfaces such as JTAG (Joint Test Action Group) or serial communication, but they typically only provide very basic debugging functionalities insufficient for more powerful security analysis techniques based on dynamic instrumentation. A possible solution to these problems is to create a VM (Virtual Machine) that emulates the entire embedded system. Since only the most common hardware is emulated by existing emulators, such as QEMU, real world embedded devices may require implementing additional peripheral device emulators. Yet, extending a VM with peripheral devices can not only be too time consuming for a resource constrained embedded security audit, but the information on the internals of these peripherals might not be available in the first place. Ultimately, this renders the emulation based approach infeasible in many cases. Previous work [3, 10] showed how peripheral devices can be transparently connected to a VM. This allows the embedded system firmware to run inside an emulator as if it were running on the original hardware with the peripheral devices directly attached. The extracted system firmware can thus be inspected outside its original system environment. The drawback of the peripheral device forwarding approach is the typically significant slowdown of device communication and the lack of possibilities to parallelize slow analysis runs or to leverage snapshots in presence of external peripheral device states. Since typical security testing techniques such as fuzz testing are highly repetitive in nature, in this work, we evaluate an approach utilizing caching of peripheral device communication in combination with runtime program state approximation. Our approach could ultimately render existing dynamic firmware security analysis techniques more powerful by enabling functions such as snapshotting, test parallelization or testing without physical access to the embedded system. We show that the challenge is not the caching itself but the sufficiently accurate approximation of the embedded program state to decide which peripheral device response in the cache needs to be returned to the firmware under test. We address this problem with runtime program state approximation and show that, similar to symbolic execution, the approach suffers from state explosion. Specifically, the contributions presented in this paper are as follows:

- We present a peripheral device caching approach for embedded security testing.
- We present a state variable detection heuristic allowing runtime program state approximation as key to peripheral device communication caching.
- We evaluate the feasibility of our approach with programs from the GNU core utilities and show that it might be usable to address persistent drawbacks in embedded firmware security analysis in the future.

The remainder of this paper is organized as follows. Section II provides an overview of related work. In Section III, we explain how peripheral devices are typically accessed from within an embedded operating system and describe why these devices are a challenge for current embedded system security testing methods. In Section IV, we present our peripheral caching approach leveraging runtime program state approximation which is described in Section V. The results of our feasibility study are presented in Section VI. The conclusions and suggestions on further work can be found in Section VII.

II. Related Work

In previous work, at least two different peripheral device forwarding approaches have been implemented. In [10], Zaddach et al. presented the Avatar framework allowing existing tools such as the QEMU emulator or symbolic execution tools to be connected to embedded target systems. Based on memory mappings, their system can forward peripheral device access from the emulator to the corresponding memory region of the peripheral device on the target embedded system. Similarly, Kammerstetter et al. presented the PROSPECT framework [3], an operating system centric approach that forwards peripheral device accesses from within the kernel in the VM to a stub on the embedded target device via a network connection. In addition to peripheral device communication forwarding, Koscher et al. presented SURROGATES [6], a system that uses Field Programmable Gate Arrays (FPGAs) to speed up the connection between the forwarding system (i.e., Avatar or PROSPECT) and the embedded hardware itself. In contrast, our work does not focus on the peripheral device forwarding techniques themselves, but instead adds a peripheral device communication caching layer in between the VM and the target device. We thus aim to simplify embedded security testing by enabling powerful mechanisms such as snapshotting, parallelization or testing without the analysis environment being connected to the real embedded system. The concept underlying our caching heuristic is related to the problem of program slicing where our peripheral caching system identifies states of the program slice that deal with peripheral hardware access. In general, program slicing typically focuses on source code and has been broadly covered by Weiser et al. [9], Korel et al. [5], Frank Tip [8] and Binkley et al. [1]. More recently, Kiss et al. [4] and Cifuentes et al. [2] also covered the problem of slicing binary executables. Considering the work on binary slicing, our cache heuristic is loosely related as the cache needs to identify states in a program slice based on the runtime environment of the process. We thus aim at identifying individual states in a program slice of the running process without extracting the whole program slice.

III. Peripheral Device Access

By leveraging peripheral device forwarding, medium to large scale embedded systems can be analyzed for security vulnerabilities. Within this work, we exemplary focus on embedded systems that utilize Linux on a MIPS architecture such as routers or Cyber Physical System (CPS) components. These systems are typically composed of a System-on-Chip (SoC) containing a processor, ROM, SRAM and I/O Controllers. The I/O Controllers are used to connect the SoC to external components such as DRAM, flash memory or peripheral devices (see Figure 1). Depending on the embedded system use cases, connected external peripheral devices are often customly designed by system manufacturers and can range from simple sensors and actuators to complex modules such as communication interfaces or security modules.

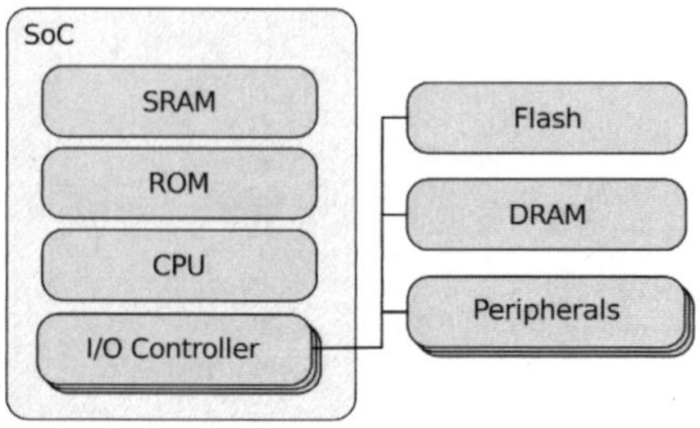

Figure 1. Typical Embedded System Hardware.

A. Challenges in Embedded System Security Testing

The security of embedded systems can be tested in several ways. The manufacturer of an embedded system typically has very detailed information about all components within the system and can thus resort to techniques such as whitebox security auditing and source code security analysis. Embedded systems often provide JTAG or serial console access allowing developers to access the running system. Depending on the specific implementation, these interfaces can provide a varying range of device access ranging from simple status readout to full dynamic system analysis. If the embedded system does not already provide tools for dynamic system analysis, the tester may be able to install necessary tools via an exposed debugging interface. However, embedded systems are typically resource constrained and tailored to a specific task. Without the resources to run additional software like debuggers on the system, dynamic analysis on the device itself is often infeasible. In addition, the operating system kernel may be tailored to the specific use case of the system with debugging or system analysis features stripped to reduce hardware requirements and thus production costs. Whenever dynamic security analysis on the embedded system is not feasible, analysts typically aim at extracting the firmware from the device for further investigation. This can either involve static analysis techniques on the firmware with its well known limitations [7], as well as dynamic analysis approaches utilizing debugging interfaces such as JTAG or VM emulation. At this point, the challenge arises that embedded systems typically make extensive use of peripheral devices that are typically not available from within the VM. The analyst thus needs to resort to peripheral device forwarding frameworks such as Avatar or PROSPECT that have limitations on their own. Specifically, forwarding peripheral device communication is typically impeded by a significant slowdown and a lack of possibilities to parallelize slow analysis runs as each testing instance would require its own connected embedded target system.

B. Communication with Peripheral Devices

On UNIX systems such as Linux, peripheral devices are accessible via system calls that are handled by the kernel which in turn uses device specific hardware drivers for the actual device communication (Figure 2). In our test environment, the peripheral devices are represented as character devices. Depending on which commands the device driver supports, a user space program with the right permissions can thus access these devices with system calls such as `open`, `read`, `write` or `close`. To enable dynamic analysis on an otherwise resource constrained system, we utilize the PROSPECT framework [3]. The Linux kernel and all encompassing software running on the system are extracted from the embedded system and moved into an emulator such as QEMU.

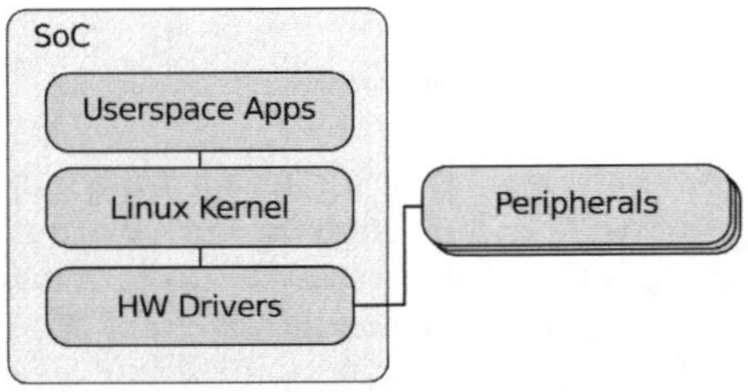

Figure 2. Typical Embedded System Software Stack.

To allow programs in the VM to communicate with the peripheral devices in a way similar to the original embedded system, PROSPECT replaces the embedded system software on the original hardware with a server stub that forwards all device communication over a network connection to the peripheral devices. We thus tunnel all device communication from the VM to the peripheral devices via a network connection such as TCP/IP over Ethernet. This allows us to run the embedded system software inside the analysis environment and thus enables the use of resource intense analysis techniques. Although the analysis environment typically provides significantly more system resources such as file system space, CPU speed or RAM, previous research showed that due to the peripheral device forwarding [3] most device communication will be significantly slowed down. Besides, another drawback is that each VM will require a dedicated set of embedded system hardware.

IV. Caching Peripheral Device Communication

Considering security testing techniques such as fuzz testing, tests are typically highly repetitive and focused on very specific (i.e., security critical) code regions in the firmware. Triggered by each of those very similar test cases, the firmware of the embedded system performs the very same communication actions with its peripheral devices over and over again. For instance, consider a Real Time Clock (RTC) peripheral device that would be queried by the embedded firmware each time a network packet is received. Although the security analyst might only target the network packet handling code in the firmware with the fuzz tester, the peripheral device communication to the RTC would still need to be carried out as otherwise the firmware would stop to function and could not be tested. As long as the values returned from the RTC allow the firmware to continue its normal execution, it is not necessary that the returned values are actually correct. Although two subsequently read timestamps should represent an amount of time that has passed between the successive reads, the functionality of the firmware during the focused fuzz tests will in most cases not be impeded by the fact that the time itself is not correct. By adding a peripheral device communication cache between the analysis environment and the embedded system, the repetitive device communication actions could be stored so that during the highly similar test cases valid device responses can be served from the cache. Ultimately, this would enable very powerful supporting technologies such as snapshotting, parallel testing or even testing without the embedded system attached.

A. Caching Strategies

In the first step, we implemented a cache between the PROSPECT driver and its stub on the target device (Figure 3). For each peripheral device interaction, the cache receives the following information:

- Process Id (PID) and Thread Group Id (TGID)
- Name of the peripheral device
- Command type and command data

When the cache receives a command, it has to decide between two options:

1) Cache hit - An appropriate device response is already in the cache. The cached response is returned to the program without querying the actual device.

2) Cache miss - The cache has not stored a suitable device response. In this case, the cache first needs to bring the hardware into the state it would normally be before this request. This is done by resetting the hardware and replaying all communication that the requesting program performed until this point. The approach can thus forward the new command to the peripheral device, store the new reply and forward it to the VM. This means that the cache needs to retain information not just about the commands and their replies, but also about the previous command history for each VM.

The main challenge is to find a strategy that can be applied to decide whether for a specific firmware program state a valid peripheral device response is already in the cache. We explored several strategies and describe them in the following:

1) Choosing Responses by Command: Very simple devices may be cached by command. To do so, the device must either be stateless, or the device's state must be deducible from the command. For example, if the device is a simple switch that is only controlled by an open and close command, the cache does not need any information other than the command itself to react accordingly. For instance, whenever the cache receives a control request to turn on the switch it could just return the cached response confirming that the switch has been turned on. However, as soon as a single control command can return different responses this approach is no longer applicable. An example where this approach would not work is the above mentioned RTC module which would return a different timestamp value for every read command.

2) Choosing Responses by Command and Command History: An improved strategy is to store information about the previously issued commands to a peripheral device. Based on the command history, the cache can decide if a suitable device response is already in the cache or not. A simplified deterministic example could be a program that reads from a peripheral device representing an incrementing counter with an initial reset. After reset, the program would read continuously increasing counter values (i.e., 1, 2, 3, etc.) on each execution. The read command itself may look the same, but depending on which and how many commands were issued to the peripheral device before, the replies to each command need to be different for every call. If the cache can learn a sufficient amount

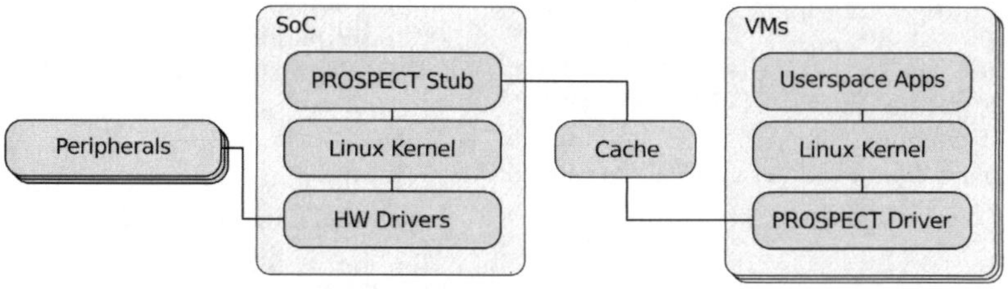

Figure 3. Embedded System Testing Utilizing PROSPECT with an Intermediate Cache.

of requests and replies from the first *training* execution, it can replay the answers every subsequent time the program is executed. The problem with this strategy is that even if the behavior of the peripheral device is deterministic, it becomes insufficient as soon as multiple threads access the same device. In this case, the thread scheduler will cause a different execution order of threads for the same input and the behavior from the perspective of the cache will no longer be deterministic. Since the cache would need to consider all possible thread execution orders to respond to future requests, the strategy quickly becomes ineffective with an increasing amount of program indeterminism. Listing 1 shows an example where two threads cause the mentioned problem by accessing a temperature sensor and a communication interface at the same time.

```
def Thread1():
  while(True):
    temp = readTemperature()
    if (temp > max):
      sendMessage("High temperature")
    sleep(0.1)

def Thread2():
  while(True):
    statusMsg = getStatusMessage()
    statusMsg += readTemperature()
    sendMessage(status)
    sleep(2)
```

Listing 1. Threading Example with Read-Loop.

3) Choosing Responses by Program State Approximation: A more advanced strategy is to find a heuristic to identify abstract program states reflecting the current position within the program flow. When program execution is started, the program typically makes use of resources such as the CPU or stack memory. We could thus derive a set of relevant CPU registers (i.e., the instruction register, the stack pointer, the general purpose registers) and use this information to determine in which state the program currently resides in. Whenever a peripheral device is accessed (e.g., with a `read` system call), we use the program state to determine whether there is already a known peripheral device response in the cache. If this is not the case, we forward the peripheral device communication from the analysis environment to the real system and cache the response for later use. However, considering typical program constructs such as a loop reading a temperature value (Listing 1), it is very likely that the CPU registers will be identical within the `readTemperature()` function at the call site of the `read` system call for different loop iterations. It is thus necessary to include the program stack into the state computation so that the state of the outer function will be considered as well. However taking the stack memory into account, determining the program states gets much more challenging as it is no longer clear which memory regions are relevant with regard to the peripheral device communication. If the state approximation granularity is too low, many irrelevant memory regions will influence the program state approximation and different program states will be derived for the same peripheral device communication action (*state duplication*). As a result, most of the device accesses would be cache misses. In contrast, if the granularity is too high, we would get wrong cache hits and the program would receive invalid peripheral device responses. In the following, we present the runtime program state approximation approach we took and the results we were able to obtain with it.

V. Runtime Program State Approximation

On an Operating System (OS), the program state can be determined through its allocated memory (i.e., stack and heap), the CPU registers and handles received from the OS kernel (e.g., file handles). However, especially considering binary executables where the source code is not available, determining which variables need to be considered during the determination of the program state is considered to be a hard problem related to program slicing [2, 4]. Since it would not be feasible to deterministically detect exact program states, we implemented a heuristic (Figure 4) that attempts to approximate sufficiently exact program states to use them for our caching approach.

A. System Call Interception and Kernel/VM Hooking

In the first two steps of the heuristic (Figure 4), we need to intercept the systems calls used for peripheral device communication. For each intercepted system call, we need to decide whether the system call is utilized for communication with a device that is forwarded through PROSPECT. Furthermore, for runtime program state approximation we need to have access to the internals of the OS kernel and the program accessing the device as well. This includes the state of the virtual memory at the time of a call, the CPU registers and open file handles. We implemented and practically tested the following methods to obtain the required low-level information.

1) Virtual Machine Introspection (VMI): The first method was implemented by extending QEMU with a Virtual Machine Introspection (VMI) module. VMI has the advantage that any low-level state information from the machine including physical memory or otherwise hard to access kernel internals can not only be accessed and read, but can be modified just the same. An additional advantage is that any introspection logic runs directly on the host machine and not inside the VM, leading to significantly higher performance. Although the VMI approach is very powerful, our VMI module implementation uncovered two major drawbacks. First, due to the low level VMI operates on, important functions inside the kernel such as those providing paging information and memory mapping need

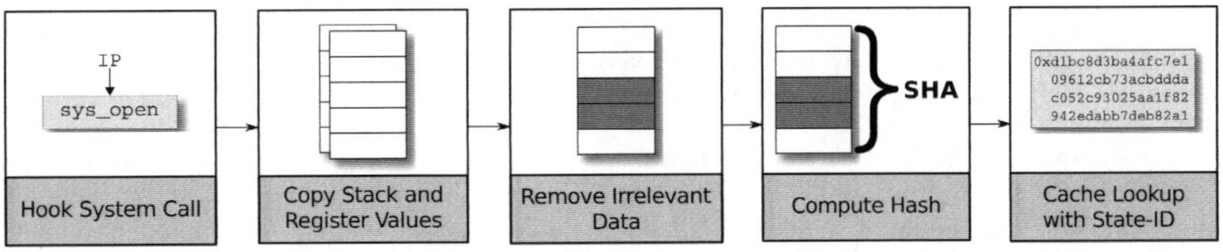

Figure 4. State Approximation Heuristic.

to be reimplemented. Even worse, important offsets to internal kernel structures can be configuration dependent requiring frequent adaptations of the VMI analysis code. Second, to reliably hook system calls, Translation Block Chaining (TBC) needs to be disabled. TBC is an optimization technique the QEMU emulator uses to drastically speed up emulation. Translation blocks are basic blocks of code from the guest system that are translated to the host system architecture. With TBC, these blocks are chained together and cached so that they do not have to be translated again each time the process counter arrives at that specific address. However, due to the caching, the program addresses within these cached blocks are no longer processed by QEMU's TBC lookup logic which ultimately causes our hooks on those addresses to no longer get executed. Disabling the TBC optimization allows reliable VMI hooking but at the same time significantly slows down the emulator.

2) Kernel Module: The second state approximation method was implemented as a loadable Linux kernel module running within the QEMU guest system. Since PROSPECT already performs system call hooking from within the kernel, we extended it with functions to read registers and mapped virtual memory regions of the calling process. Compared to the VMI approach, using a kernel module simplifies access to swapped out pages and kernel structures.

3) File Handles: Each time an `open` system call is used to return a new file handle, the value of the file handle is determined by the operating system kernel. Since the returned file handles frequently differ between executions, we use a file descriptor tracking mechanism. The mechanism places a hook on the `open` and `close` system calls. It can thus track the currently active file descriptors and remove them from the stack region of interest by overwriting the descriptors with zero bytes.

4) Registers: The register content has a central role in our program state variable detection heuristic. While the most important register to be utilized in this case is the instruction pointer, we found that the subset of registers leading to the best results also included the return address, the stack pointer and several general purpose registers.

B. *Hash Computation and State-ID Matching*

In the last two steps of the heuristic (Figure 4), we compute the SHA-256 digest and use it for cache lookup. The digest is computed on the concatenated stack region of interest and the register set. Using the previously described state variable detection heuristic, we ensure that hash digest results in a granularity that is suitable for cache lookups. The cache lookup is implemented as a large dictionary where the SHA-256 hash value is used as index to a device response data field of arbitrary size.

VI. RESULTS

Our feasibility study shows that our approach works for less complex programs but suffers from the well known state explosion problem for more complex programs. The low complexity programs we tested required less information from stack and registers to correctly determine the program state. However, with growing program complexity, it becomes more challenging to accurately determine a unique state suitable for cache lookups resulting in state duplication and cache misses. Since the number of these duplicates rises exponentially with increasing program complexity, similar to symbolic execution, the approach leads to the state explosion problem. In that regard, the MIPS architecture turned out to be especially challenging due to its standard calling convention and the resulting difficulty of stack frame unwinding. To test our approach, we used programs from the GNU core utilities and treated their file system accesses as peripheral device accesses with our caching approach in between. We tested 3 program classes:

1) Low Complexity Programs:
For very simple programs such as `cat`, `head`, `sum` and `wc`, our caching approach hardly depends on stack frame information, no heap information is required and only a small subset of the registers is sufficient to correctly determine the program states for peripheral caching. Within a single execution the cache could thus already learn all necessary responses and use them correctly. At that point we were able to completely remove the program's input files and still obtain the identical program flow with our caching approach.
2) Medium Complexity Programs:
Medium complexity programs such as `expand` rely on dynamic heap memory management. As a result, some of the relevant program states for device access may depend on the information stored at those memory regions. Using peripheral caching for programs like `expand`, the lack of information on heap content led to duplicate states. These could be compensated for by utilizing several training executions until the cache had learned all possible states including duplicates. It also required minor manual adaptations of the considered stack parameters within the heuristic. We believe that this problem can be addressed in future work and the heuristic could be greatly improved by adding proper stack unwinding. Monitoring the heap state would be an advantage, but is not mandatory. Without proper stack unwinding and manual adaptations, medium complexity programs currently present the limit of our approach.
3) Higher Complexity Programs
Higher complexity programs such as `sort` not only heavily rely on dynamic heap memory management, but

they also store a large amount of relevant state information on the heap. The problem and its possible solution are thus similar to medium complexity programs, but in comparison the number of duplicate states is much higher and can no longer be handled through manual adaptations. We believe that with stack unwinding and dynamic memory allocation monitoring the problem can be improved, but higher complexity programs will remain challenging.

VII. Conclusion and Future Work

Our feasibility study showed that the presented peripheral caching concept could be an approach for some of the major drawbacks in embedded firmware security analysis. When applying typical embedded security testing techniques such as fuzz testing, sufficiently precise caching of peripheral device communication could thus enable powerful features such as snapshotting or test parallelization. After sufficient cache training the firmware can even be tested without requiring physical access to the embedded system. We showed that the problem is related to program slicing and may lead, similar to symbolic execution, to the well known state explosion problem. We created a VMI-based as well as a kernel-module based implementation and tested the feasibility of our approach with programs from the well known GNU core utilities package. Our results show that the peripheral caching approach works for low and medium complexity programs. However, depending on the architecture and the difficulty of stack frame unwinding, the program state approximation can become increasingly difficult. In future work, we're looking forward to port our approach to embedded architectures such as ARM allowing more precise stack unwinding. We believe that this will further increase the precision of the program state approximation so that more complex programs can be addressed with our approach as well. Furthermore, we aim to implement a kernel module/VMI hybrid implementation to benefit from the speed improvements of running the program state approximation heuristic outside the VM while still utilizing the OS kernel insight provided through a kernel module.

Acknowledgements

The research was funded by the Austrian Research Funding Agency's (FFG) KIRAS security research program through the $(SG)^2$ project under national FFG grant number 836276, the AnyPLACE project under EU H2020 grant number 646580, and IT security consulting company Trustworks KG.

References

[1] David W Binkley and Keith Brian Gallagher. Program Slicing. *Advances in Computers*, 43:1–50, 1996.

[2] Cristina Cifuentes and Mike Van Emmerik. Recovery of jump table case statements from binary code. In *Program Comprehension, 1999. Proceedings. Seventh International Workshop on*, pages 192–199. IEEE, 1999.

[3] Markus Kammerstetter, Christian Platzer, and Wolfgang Kastner. Prospect: Peripheral proxying supported embedded code testing. In *Proceedings of the 9th ACM Symposium on Information, Computer and Communications Security*, ASIA CCS '14, pages 329–340, New York, NY, USA, 2014. ACM.

[4] Akos Kiss, Judit Jász, Gábor Lehotai, and Tibor Gyimóthy. Interprocedural static slicing of binary executables. In *Source Code Analysis and Manipulation, 2003. Proceedings. Third IEEE International Workshop on*, pages 118–127. IEEE, 2003.

[5] Bogdan Korel and Janusz Laski. Dynamic program slicing. *Information Processing Letters*, 29(3):155–163, 1988.

[6] Karl Koscher, Tadayoshi Kohno, and David Molnar. Surrogates: Enabling near-real-time dynamic analyses of embedded systems. In *Proceedings of the 9th USENIX Conference on Offensive Technologies*, WOOT'15, pages 7–7, Berkeley, CA, USA, 2015. USENIX Association.

[7] Bingchang Liu, Liang Shi, Zhuhua Cai, and Min Li. Software vulnerability discovery techniques: A survey. In *Multimedia Information Networking and Security (MINES), 2012 Fourth International Conference on*, pages 152–156. IEEE, 2012.

[8] Frank Tip. A survey of program slicing techniques. *Journal of programming languages*, 3(3):121–189, 1995.

[9] Mark Weiser. Program slicing. In *Proceedings of the 5th International Conference on Software Engineering*, ICSE '81, pages 439–449, Piscataway, NJ, USA, 1981. IEEE Press.

[10] Jonas Zaddach, Luca Bruno, Aurelien Francillon, and Davide Balzarotti. Avatar: A Framework to Support Dynamic Security Analysis of Embedded Systems' Firmwares. In *Network and Distributed System Security (NDSS) Symposium*, NDSS 14, February 2014.

The Principle of 3D Sensors

Miroslav Marcaník, Michal Šustek, Pavel Tomášek
Tomas Bata University in Zlín
Faculty of Applied Informatics
Nad Stráněmi 4511, 760 05, Zlín
{marcanik, sustek, tomasek}@fai.utb.cz

Jiří Dvořák
Brno University of Technology,
Faculty of Mechanical Engineering
Antonínská 548/1, 601 90, Brno
dvorak@fme.vutbr.cz

***Abstract* - Gradual development of modern trends with more emphasis on visualization and measurement accuracy have resulted in the continuous improvement of measuring instruments, which are very closely linked to Personal Computers and/or Programmable Logic Controllers to the displaying unit and leads to greater utilization of 3D technology. 3D technology is used in security, biometrics, and in many other fields. This contribution is focused on understanding the issues of scanning and its advantages and disadvantages. It serves as a complete overview of the structure of the 3D sensors.**

Keywords – 3D sensors; sensors; CCD; CMOS.

I. INTRODUCTION

The greater emphasis on accuracy, versatility, speed, and price is the result of the continual development of production, automation, and research of 3-dimensional measurements of objects. These 3D technologies became more important with the development of integrated computer technologies.

The binary system is a numbering system which is used to express a value using only characters 0 and 1. The binary system belongs to a group of positional number systems with base 2, which is a specific number as expressed by the power of 2. The numbers registered in the binary system are called binary numbers. Record of numbers in the binary system is complemented by a 'B' or 'b', which is used as a subscript on the last digit or acronym BIN. [1]

Thus, the control input/output information becomes only the values "YES" or "NO" because that specifies whether the previous cycle is performed correctly, satisfies the specified tolerances, but it does not describe the influences, facts and events that preceded the input. Since the control input/output is mainly done visually, it is necessary to adapt the technique using geometry [2]. This path is very appealing, but it may happen that our elected sensing principle is imperfect and must subsequently find a new algorithm for image processing. The main representative of 3D shooting is CCD (Charge-Coupled Device) [3] and/or CMOS (Complementary Metal–Oxide–Semiconductor) [3] camera. The separation of signals may be difficult in practice, because there are plenty of influencing factors. Quality can be affected by the most essential settings, such as the arrangement of cameras, illuminators and environment. This setting is applied in film and art photography as well. A big part is affected by lighting or suitable arrangement of illuminators - object - cameras. If we have neglected these factors, we put programmers in a position where they spend most of their time creating and optimizing algorithms for finding the proper results in the image. Some problems and disruptive factors can be eliminated by polarization and absorption filters, semi-permeable mirrors, light reflectors and diffusers [4].

Photometric systems can be difficult to connect with the PCs and their operation systems but, generally, they use simple methods of image processing. Scanning is performed using surface or line CCD camera with a greater emphasis on minimization of measurement errors [2].

The rest of the paper is structured as follows. Section II serves as an introduction to optical radiation and the principle of its operation. Section III describes two construction types for scanning device and their advantages and disadvantages. The last section describes the types of methods used for 3D scanning.

II. OPTICAL RADIATION

A 3D sensor utilizes electromagnetic waves radiated by the scanned object to obtain information on shape, position and object properties. The object may be an active source of optical radiation, or passive, which only reflects or modifies the incident radiation from another source. The most significant properties are light rays, straight lines, independence of each other and no interaction with each other. The law of reflection and refraction is applied. Optical radiation has the same properties as the electromagnetic wave [2].

For the velocity (in $m \cdot s^{-1}$) we have the relation:

$$v = \frac{1}{\sqrt{\varepsilon\mu}} \quad (1)$$

Permittivity (ε) is a physical quantity describing the relationship between the vectors of the electric field intensity and electric induction in a material or vacuum. Permeability (μ) expresses the influence of the material or environment on a magnetic field [5].

Since it is a very small probability that the scanning takes place in vacuum, we extend this pattern for the environment where the scanning is performed. The relation to calculate the diverse environment is given below:

$$v = \frac{c}{\sqrt{\varepsilon_r}} \qquad (2)$$

where c = $2{,}998 \cdot 10^8$ $m \cdot s^{-1}$ is the speed of light in vacuum and ε_r the relative permittivity environment.
The speed of light is also affected by refractive index. Maxwell explains the relation between the absolute refractive index n_0 and the dielectric constant ε_r:

$$\varepsilon_r = n_0^2 \qquad (3)$$

Radiation can also be characterized by wavelength (λ), which is always smaller than in vacuum. The relation between λ and n is expressed by:

$$\lambda_n = \frac{\lambda_0}{n_0} \qquad (4)$$

III. Principle of Video Camera

The principle of the video camera is the same as the digital camera. Reflected electromagnetic waves (visible light) from the object pass through the objective and fall onto the photosensitive sensor. Consequently, the input image is converted to an electronical signal by the sensor and then it is saved using the internal electronics.

A. Objective

The camera uses the lens optical system for imaging. Lenses are divided into two basic groups: lens (refractors) and mirrors (reflectors). Reflectors create an image of direct, apparent and the same as the subject. Two types of mirrors are used - concave and convex. Concave mirrors create a mirror image that is direct, apparent and reduced. Convex are dependent on the distance from the focus and the mirror. If we show the object positioned between the focal point and highlight of mirrors, it creates a picture of the direct and virtual object located further from the focus. On the other hand, it appears as an image inverted and real. The size of the result image can be dependent on the position of the lenses as well as reduction or enlargement. The main advantages include the absence of reflectors chromatic aberration and it is easier to manufacture large mirrors. Figure 1 shows the main representatives of mirror telescopes which are Cassegrain [6] and Newtonian [6] telescopes.

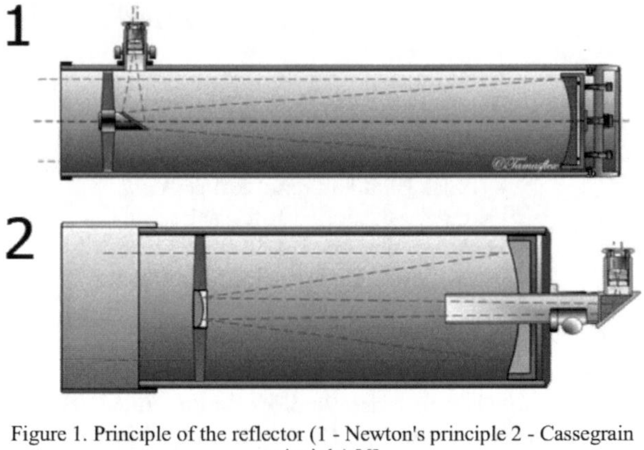

Figure 1. Principle of the reflector (1 - Newton's principle 2 - Cassegrain principle) [6]

Refractors use an optically isotropic medium which is bounded by two spheres (or one spherical and one plane). It is called the lens (spherical lens). Lenses limited by non-spherical surfaces (e.g. part of the cylinder, ellipsoid, etc.) are called aspherical lenses. The lens has a different refractive index than its surroundings. The emerging picture when viewing the lens depends on the type of lens (converging, diverging) and the position of the object against the lens. A diffusing lens creates an image directly. The size of the resulting image may be larger or smaller against to original image [6].

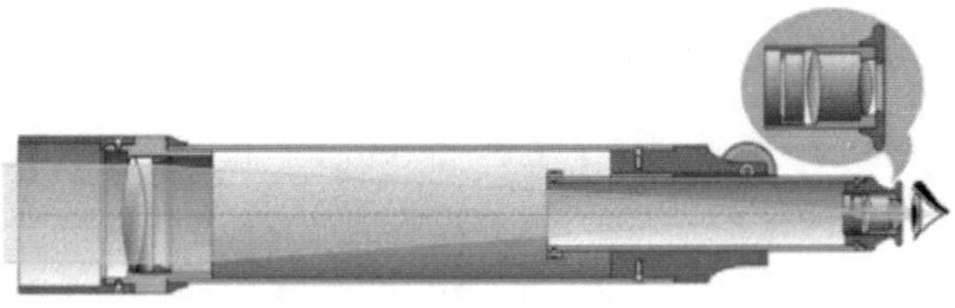

Figure 2. Principle refractor [6]

B. CCD vs CMOS

Nowadays, technologies are dominated by two data recorders.

CCD is the most frequently used imaging chip in compact cameras. Its manufacture is relatively simple, but costly. The output information from the CCD chip is not a digital, but an analog, and must be digitized. The utilization of the Analog / Digital converter (A/D) means higher power consumption and slowing down the flow of data. Light-sensitive cells on CCD have a square shape and the output from the CCD is via bus. The individual rows or columns of photosensitive cells are connected to the bus. Data is sent to the bus row by row. Simpler embodiments but slower data read. That arrangement of the CCD chip is called progressive CCD chip. In contrast, the chip known as an interlaced CCD chip is easier to manufacture.
The principle is very simple. First to third column is on its own register (subtraction for mini sort memory), fourth to sixth also have their own pair. They are deducted gradually in these values of individual registers, which leads to higher

speed retrieval of data from the chip (in this case, it would be 2-3 times).

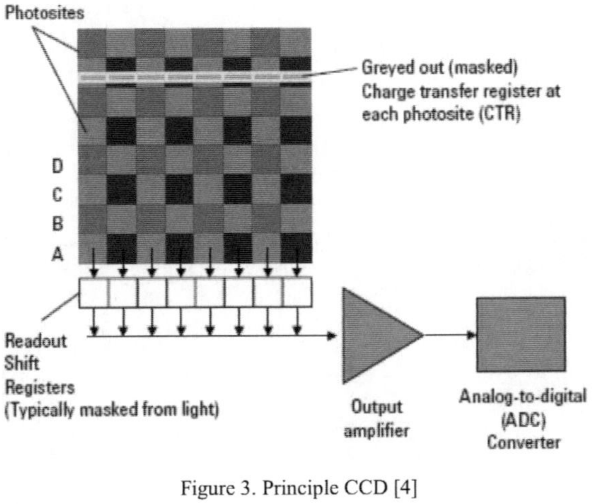

Figure 3. Principle CCD [4]

CMOS chip is predominantly used in digital cameras and gradually expands into digital compacts. CMOS chip is structurally a very complex matter, but it is cheaper to produce because it is produced in the same way as computer processors. Circuits that digitize an image at the CCD for all pixels gradually are directly part of the CMOS chip - each photoreceptor cell has these circuits directly at each other. Digitalization of the image is thus, performed in each photosensitive cell at the same time. This reduces the time required for reading the image of the CMOS chip and reduces power consumption. On the other hand, the area sensitive to light is only a tiny part of the overall chip because the other areas are digitizing circuitry. This is solved by color filters. These filters use Red – Green – Blue – additive color model (RGB) or Cyan – Magenta – Yellow – Key (CMYK). Filter miniature lens which focuses the rays illuminating the surface of photoreceptor cell only to place, which is the light-sensitive. The number of cells per micrometer rises up to tens of million. Another advantage is the data output from the CMOS chip goes suddenly as matrix. This increases the speed of a collection of data from the CMOS chip. In particular, this property is desirable for high speed filming. Older and cheaper CMOS chips cause undesired spreading to nearby hubs light-sensitive cells. Overall, this phenomenon manifested itself as lighter or darker bands on the scene known as the effect of striped shirt - a man in a one color shirt looks like he is wearing striped one. This undesirable phenomenon of "leakage" of electrons can sometimes be observed on the CCD chip as well. A new generation of CMOS does not suffer from this defect anymore [4].

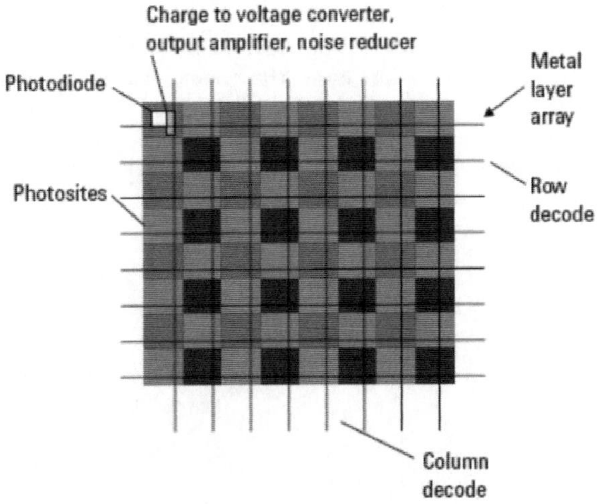

Figure 4. Principle CMOS [4]

IV. PRINCIPLES 3D SCANNING

3D sensors are coming to the forefront and are more and more commonly used in all possible sectors because of the development of technology and the increasing demand and popularity of virtual reality. Some examples include construction, architecture, industrial machinery, navigation, etc. Perhaps in all applications, it is necessary to have coordinates in a 3D space. The scanning is dependent on the position of the object, its speed, color, shape, and angle of rotation. The advent of modern technology and optics, which is still used for 2D scanning, expanded to methods for measuring the third dimension. Today, there are mainly two methods of measuring. The first one is a triangulation and the second is a light interference. The gradual development of technologies brings about the third method. This method is called Time of Light (TOF) and uses the knowledge of the speed of light.

A. Triangulation

Triangulation is very often used as a method which requires a very complicated structure of the measuring sensor. It is divided into two categories: active triangulation and passive triangulation.

The principle of the active triangulation involves photogrammetric reconstruction of the scanned object. The surface of scanned object is illuminated by the light source and simultaneously scanned by the CCD sensor [7].

The principle of passive triangulation involves photogrammetric reconstruction of the scanned object on the basis of its projection on the sensor surface device. One dimension is lost during projection and it is needed to renew on the basis of a common information from multiple sources [7].

The principle can be seen in Figure 5. The light signal is transmitted from the laser source to the object. The object reflects the light ray to the camera. The angle of the transmitted ray from the source is constant, but the CCD sensor depending on the spend ray of the dimmed sensor. The connector between the light source and the CCD sensor is called triangulation base (baseline). Thanks to the knowledge of two angles and the length of the triangular base, we can calculate the distance of a point, and then save the coordinates for later calculations and rendering [8].

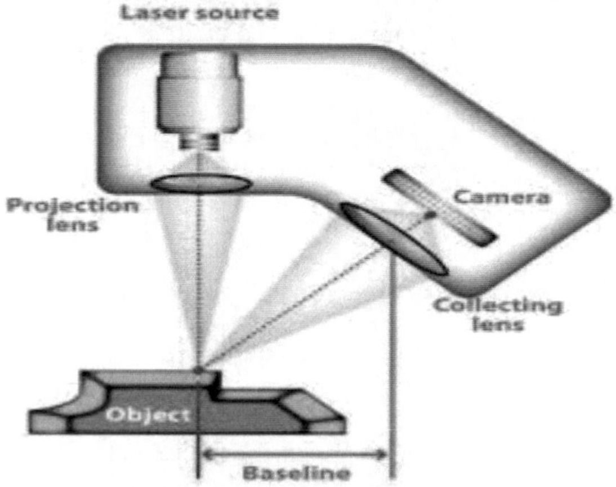

Figure 5. Principle triangulation [5]

To mark the surface, the following are used:

- the light beam (1D triangulation),
- light (2D triangulation),
- Structured light beam (3D triangulation).

Disadvantages:

- higher purchase price and better facilities,
- time demands when evaluating the Record,
- the limiting factor may be the memory size and especially the quality of the recording,
- more necessary knowledge of issues,
- treatment of subjects.

B. Interferometry

Interferometry is a method suitable for very precise measurements over a short distance. The principle is based on light interference. The principle can be seen in Figure 6. The light source - the laser - is transmitted through the polarization splitter - a part on the measured object. The reflected signal is combined with polarization ray splitter reference called carrier wave and they may interfere together. The resulting wave interference is given by equation (5) [8]:

$$I(x,y) = |I_1(x,y)|^2 + |I_2(x,y)|^2 + 2|I_1(x,y)||I_2(x,y)|\cos(j_1(x,y) - j_2(x,y)) \quad (5)$$

Disadvantages:

- Technologically intensive production;
- Demanding quantitative interpretation of results;
- Susceptibility to interference.

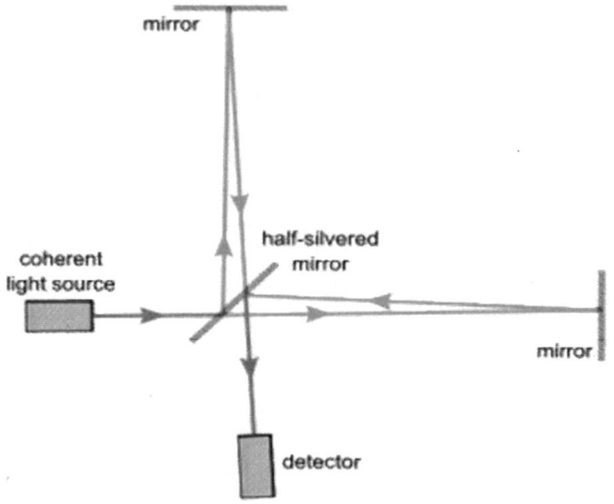

Figure 6. Principle Interferometry [8]

C. TOF

This is a method that uses the knowledge of the speed of modulated light signal that is emitted from the transmitter and subsequently reflected towards the receiver. The use of this method requires very precise time value. The principle can be seen in Figure 7. The distance of sensing object can be computed from formula 6, where "t" is the total time from sending a signal to the one more acceptation and "c" is the speed of light (c = 2.998 * 108 m / s) [8].

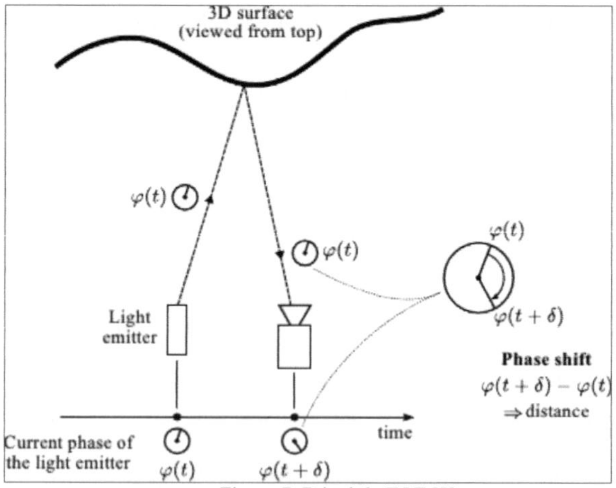

Figure 7. Principle TOF [8]

$$s = \frac{c * t}{2} \quad (6)$$

Disadvantages:

- High-accuracy time measurement required
- Measurement of light pulse return is inexact, due to light scattering
- Difficulty to generate short light pulses with fast rise and fall times

- Usable light sources (e.g. lasers) suffer low repetition rates for pulses

V. CONCLUSION

We can find a lot of potential in utilization of 3D sensors in all sectors from an overall perspective. A big boom was registered mainly in the improvement of cartography, digitization, security etc. The main objective of this article was to suggest the basic concepts, definitions, types and principles of various kinds of sensors. The summary of the information in this article suggests that the expansion of 3D scanners and 3D technologies and their general application over time will be more necessary than previously thought. The main advantage of 3D sensors is the utilization of three-dimensional space, which has been in seclusion so far and was not the main goal. The authors believe that 2D sensor will be partially or completely replaced by 3D sensors in a few years. Although we area ware that 3D sensors are more expensive because it is necessary to place greater emphasis on accuracy and designing of 3D scanners, they do provide an improved visualization.

ACKNOWLEDGMENT

This work was supported by Internal Grant Agency of Tomas Bata University under the project No. IGA/FAI/2016/25.

REFERENCES

[1] Binary System. PLC Automatization [online]. [cit. 2016-07-18]. Available from: http://plc-automatizace.cz/knihovna/data/soustava/dvojkova-binarni-soustava.htm

[2] Kreidl M. and R. Šmíd. Technical diagnosis: sensors, methods, signal analysis. 1st ed. Praha: BEN - technical literature, 2006. Sensors non-electrical quantities. ISBN 80-7300-158-6.

[3] Šnajdárek, Ladislav. Methods 3d Laser Scanning Workpieces In Process Plan. Brno, 2008. Bachelor's Thesis. Brno University Of Technology. Supervision: Ing. Miroslav Opl.

[4] Digimanie. Mobile phones with cameras: CMOS sensor chips vs CCD [online]. Web, 2009 [cit. 03/31/2016]. Available from: http://www.digimanie.cz/fotomobily-snimaci-cipy-cmos-vs-ccd/2885

[5] Zheng, D., Liu, T., Zhou, L., Xu, Y., Electromagnetic absorbing property of the flaky carbonyl iron particles by chemical corrosion process (2016), Journal of Magnetism and Magnetic Materials, 419, pp. 119-124. DOI: 10.1016/j.jmmm.2016.06.008

[6] The section for children and young Czech Astronomical Society. Section for children and young Czech Astronomical Society [online]. Web: Web, 2006 [cit. 03/31/2016]. Available from: www.mladez.astro.cz

[7] Islam, S.C., Herrmann, M., Beigang, R., A THz triangulation and imaging system and its applications, (2007) IRMMW-THz2007 - Conference Digest of the Joint 32nd International Conference on Infrared and Millimetre Waves, and 15th International Conference on Terahertz Electronics, art. no. 4516600, pp. 498-499. Cited 2 times.

[8] Marcaník M. and J. Dvorak. Use of 3D sensors for the protection of critical infrastructure elements and soft targets. Zlín: Tomas Bata University in Zlín, 2015. ISBN 978-80-7454-559-7.

[9] A. Zatočilová. Straightness measurement and evaluation of rotary axes forged using photogrammetry and image analysis [online]. Brno, 2014 [cit. 03/31/2016]. Available from: http://dl.uk.fme.vutbr.cz/zobraz_soubor.php?id=2310. PhD. Technical University Brno. Supervisor Doc. Ing. Jan Brandeis, PhD.

[10] Hubálek, J. microsensors and microelectromechanical systems. Institute of Microelectronics, Faculty of Electrical Engineering and Communication [online]. Brno © 2004-2015, 10. 11. 2015 [cit. 11/11/2015]. Available from: http://www.umel.feec.vutbr.cz/bmms/prednasky/BMMS-01.pdf.

[11] Mechatronics | Introduction: Sensors [online]. 2010 [cit. 11/10/2015]. Available from: http://mechmes.websnadno.cz/dokumenty/pri-mn-s-10_senzory_uvod.pdf

[12] Skoupý, P. 3D optical measurement and scanning systems for engineering. Brno: Brno University of Technology, Faculty of Mechanical Engineering, 2007. [cit. 11/11/2015]

[13] Brunet, F. Contributions to Parametric Image Registration and 3D Surface Reconstruction. Clermont-Ferrand, 2010. [cit. 2015-11-11]. Available from: http://www.brnt.eu/publications/brunet2010phd.pdf. Universite d'Auvergne.

[14] Schroeder, K. Martin, and B. Lorensen, Visualization Toolkit: An Object-Oriented Approach to 3D Graphics, 4th Edition. Kitware, December 2006 [cit. 2015-11-11]

[15] Janková, M.; Dvořák, J. The ICT possibilities in the virtual universities cyberspace. In Mathematics, Information Technologies and Applied Sciences 2014 (post-conference proceedings of selected papers extended versions). Brno: MITAV 2014, 2014. s. 59-65. ISBN: 978-80-7231-978- 7.

A Secure Frequency Hiding Index for Encrypted Databases

Somayeh Sobati Moghadam

Université Lumière Lyon 2
Email: Somayeh.Sobati-moghadam@univ-lyon2.fr

***Abstract*—Cloud computing offers the opportunity of data outsourcing as well as the data management tasks. However, for the sake of various privacy issues, confidential data must be encrypted before outsourcing to the cloud. But query processing over encrypted data without decrypting the data is a very challenging task. Deterministic (DET) encryption scheme allows encrypting data while still enabling efficient querying over encrypted data. The inherit merits of DET make it very suitable and efficient scheme for cloud data outsourcing. But the security of DET scheme is still a challenge while DET is vulnerable to frequency attacks. We present a new scheme for indexing encrypted data, which hides data frequency to achieve a strictly stronger notion of security. The proposed indexing method is secure against frequency attacks, hence, data cannot be recovered from indexes. Moreover, our scheme is still efficient for query processing.**

Keywords–Data outsourcing; data privacy; querying encrypted data.

I. INTRODUCTION

A naive solution to preserve privacy is encrypting data before outsourcing to the cloud. In the context of relational databases, the state-of-the-art solutions use property preserving encryption schemes. Property preserving encryption schemes enable processing query over encrypted data without decryption. For instance, order preserving encryption scheme (OPE), preserves the order of ciphertexts as original plaintexts, means OPE preserves the order property. Deterministic (DET) scheme encrypts the same plaintext into the identical ciphertexts, thus, the equality property is preserved [1]. Property preserving encryption schemes are undoubtedly efficient schemes while enabling queries to be directly processed over encrypted data. But such schemes leak some information about the plaintext.

DET scheme allows the server to perform a large number of queries which means it can perform `SELECT` with equality predicates, equality `JOIN`, `GROUP BY`, `COUNT`, `DISTINCT`, etc. [2]. DET scheme is vulnerable to frequency attacks, while DET leaks the frequency distribution of underlying data. In frequency attacks, an adversary not only has access to the encrypted data but also has some prior knowledge about the plaintext domain and its frequency distribution. Frequency attack does not impose any threat when the underlying data has uniform frequency distribution [3]. If the frequency distribution of plaintext not uniform, DET scheme must be replaced with a probabilistic encryption scheme, but it makes query processing impossible over encrypted data.

CryptDB is a first practical system uses property preserving schemes to support a wide range of queries processing over encrypted data. As the best of our knowledge, other systems like BigQuery demo [4], Always Encrypted [5], Cipherbase [6] and Relational Cloud [7] use a DET scheme too. As a result, they are vulnerable to frequency attacks. Naveed et al. in [8] demonstrate that a large fraction of the records from DET encrypted columns, can be decrypted by frequency attacks.

We present a new scheme to improve the security of DET by hiding the frequency of plaintexts. The proposed scheme hides the frequency of plaintexts by means of a new indexing scheme. In our scheme, the indexes have a uniform distribution,and hence the proposed scheme is robust against frequency attacks. While increasing security, our scheme preserves the functionality of DET scheme. This scheme can be applied as an alternative to a DET scheme.

II. FREQUENCY HIDING SCHEME

The basic idea is to create an index such that no frequency information from repeated plaintexts leaks. Note that this index should still enable querying while hiding the frequency of data. Therefore, any plaintext value of frequency f is mapped into multiple index values. Thus, the target distribution remains close to flat, i.e., uniform Intuitively, if t distinct plaintext values are mapped into $m > t$ unique values that are of the same frequency, none of these target values can be explicitly mapped to the corresponding plaintext values by the frequency attacks.

To enable efficient query processing, we propose to add some auxiliary metadata for an attribute A at the server side. In our solution, we add an auxiliary column named $EqIdx$ (**Eq**$uality$ $checking$ **Idx**) along an attribute `A`. This column allows equality checking over `A`. To create $EqIdx$ column, first the values of A are sorted in ascending order. Then, an incremental ID is assigned to the sorted values, which are stored in $EqIdx$ column. As a result, for each plaintext value v_i, we have f_i distinct values in the column $EqIdx$, from s_i to l_i. We call s_i and l_i as boundaries of v_i.

In order to query processing, the user should keep the boundaries of each plaintext value; otherwise, when the user has a query, he cannot know how to transform the values in a query. Storing the corresponding boundaries at the user side induces storage overhead which is in contrary with the benefits of data outsourcing. Thus, we store an auxiliary table that maintains the information about the boundaries for each plaintext value. We call this table as *frequency table*, fT. Frequency table's values are encrypted, thus, leak no information about the plaintext values. In order to query processing, the user first sends a query to retrieve the corresponding boundaries from frequency table. Then, using the result of the first query, the user sends another query to retrieve the desired values.

A. Building Index

To simplify our discussion, let us assume a relational table T consists of one column A (additional columns, if any, can be processed similarly) and we wish to encrypt and store it at a service provider. The encrypted version of T is T' at the server side. Considering A has t distinct values $\{v_1, v_2, ..., v_t\}$ with the frequencies $\{f_1, f_2, ..., f_t\}$. First, we sort the plaintext values in ascending order. Then, we assign incremental values in to the sorted data. We store the incremental values in an auxiliary column called $EqIdx$ along the encrypted values of A, $E(A)$. Note that the encryption scheme for encrypting A's values could be a scheme with high security guarantees (e.g., a randomize encryption scheme that encrypts the same plaintexts into the different ciphertexts). Each plaintext value v_i is mapped into f_i distinct values I_i in $EqIdx$ such that $I_i \in [s_i, l_i]$ $\forall i = 1, ..., f_i$. In other words, all values in an interval like $[s_i, l_i]$ are corresponded to the same plaintext v_i.

B. Building Frequency Table

Frequency table fT consists of two attributes, the first one maintains the encryption of distinct plaintext values and the second attribute stores the encrypted boundaries corresponding to the plaintext values.

As we explained before, for any distinct plaintext values v_i in attribute A, we have two corresponding boundaries s_i and l_i, $i = 1, ..., t$. s_i and l_i are concatenated $< s_i \parallel l_i >$, and encrypted with a key k, $E_k(< s_i \parallel l_i >)$. v_i is encrypted with the same key, $E_k(v_i)$. Then, $E_k(< s_i \parallel l_i >)$ and $E_k(v_i)$ $i = 1, ..., t$ are stored in the attributes $E(Boundaries)$ and $E(A')$ in fT, respectively. Figure 1 shows an example of frequency table and $EqIdx$ for attribute A.

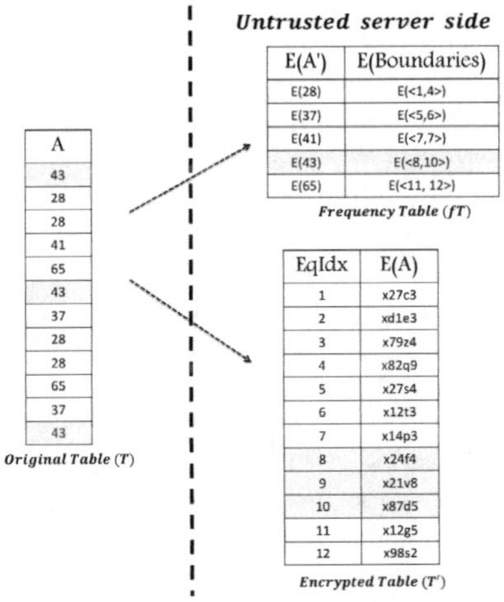

Figure 1. Metadata at the server side. Ciphertexts shown are not full-length.

C. Query Processing

Considering a simple query example like "`SELECT * FROM T WHERE A=`v_i". First, the user sends a query to retrieve the boundaries of v_i from fT. Therefore, the user encrypts v_i with k and sends the following query:
`SELECT` E_k`(Boundaries) FROM` fT `WHERE` $E(A')$`=E(`v_i`)`. When the user receives the result, he decrypts and recovers the corresponding boundaries s_i and l_i. Subsequently, the user sends a query using the extracted boundaries to retrieve all values that have $EqIdx$ between s_i and l_i:
`SELECT E(A) From T`$'$ `WHERE` $s_i \leq$ `EqIdx` $\leq l_i$.
Finally, the user decrypts the final results returned back by the server.

Confidentiality in our approach relies on the secure cryptographic scheme using for encryption of data and corresponding metadata. Uniform distribution in $EqIdx$ hides the frequency of data. Thus, our solution is robust against frequency attacks. Note that the drawback of this scheme is its inefficiently for data updating. Typically, our indexing method uses the distribution of plaintext, while update operations may change it, rendering re-calculation unavoidable.

III. CONCLUSION

In this paper, we propose a new scheme that can effectively resist against frequency attacks in cloud data outsourcing. The adversary in our scenario has knowledge of the frequency of original data in a database. In the proposed scheme, all sensitive data are encrypted at the server side and some metadata is used to query encrypted data. A new indexing scheme is introduced to hide the frequency of data. The proposed solution, not only provides robust security guarantees against frequency attacks, also allows efficient and correct query processing over encrypted data. We plan to introduce security proof for the proposed scheme and extend it in order to support any query over encrypted data.

REFERENCES

[1] M. Bellare, A. Boldyreva, and A. O'Neill, "Deterministic and efficiently searchable encryption," in CRYPTO, 2007, pp. 535–552. [Online]. Available: http://dx.doi.org/10.1007/978-3-540-74143-5_30

[2] R. A. Popa, "Building practical systems that compute on encrypted data," Ph.D. dissertation, Massachusetts Institute of Technology, 2014.

[3] T. Sanamrad, L. Braun, D. Kossmann, and R. Venkatesan, "Randomly partitioned encryption for cloud databases," in DBSec, 2014. [Online]. Available: http://dx.doi.org/10.1007/978-3-662-43936-4_20

[4] Google Encrytped Big Query. [Online]. Available: https://github.com/google/encrypted-bigquery-client (retrieved: May, 2016)

[5] Always Encrypted. [Online]. Available: https://msdn.microsoft.com/enus/library/mt163865(v=sql.130).aspx (retrieved: May, 2016)

[6] A. Arasu, S. Blanas, K. Eguro, R. Kaushik, D. Kossmann, R. Ramamurthy, and R. Venkatesan, "Orthogonal security with cipherbase," in CIDR 2013, 2013. [Online]. Available: http://www.cidrdb.org/cidr2013/Papers/CIDR13_Paper33.pdf

[7] Relational cloud. [Online]. Available: http://relationalcloud.com/ (retrieved: June, 2016)

[8] M. Naveed, S. Kamara, and C. V. Wright, "Inference attacks on property-preserving encrypted databases," in SIGSAC, 2015, pp. 644–655. [Online]. Available: http://doi.acm.org/10.1145/2810103.2813651

Analysis of Direct Punch in Professional Defence Using Multiple Methods

Dora Lapkova, Milan Adamek
Department of Security Engineering
Tomas Bata University in Zlin
Zlin, Czech Republic
e-mail: {dlapkova, adamek}@fai.utb.cz

Lukas Kralik
Department of Informatics and Artificial Intelligence
Tomas Bata University in Zlin
Zlin, Czech Republic
kralik@fai.utb.cz

***Abstract*— This article is focused on a complex analysis of a direct punch. The direct punch is only one technique in a complex system – a professional defence. The professional defence is a necessary part of a physical protection, which is a basis in every security system. During this research, several methods were used for the measurement of velocity, force, body movement, etc., during a punch. The main goal was to find out the most significant characteristics of a direct punch. The second goal was to find some dependencies among groups of people with different training level in professional defence. Some parts of these experiments were published in the past, but this article contains the results of all the methods used.**

Keywords- direct punch; professional defence; complex analysis; velocity; force

I. INTRODUCTION

The direct punch is one of the basic elements of the majority of martial arts, sports and systems [1][2]. In professional defence, the direct punch is used to stop an attacker and to increase the distance between the defender and the attacker.

The direct punch (Figure 1) is delivered by the arm following a direct line. The hitting area is a closed fist [4]. In the following experiment, the punch was delivered by the back hand.

Figure 1. Direct punch [3]

The professional defence [5] is a field which is primarily focused on the legal protection of personal interests against an attack. It covers various areas - the theory and the practice of defence, attack and prevention, scientific disciplines such as the tactics (e.g., skill in the counter attack), the strategy (the precautionary action) and the operation (the behaviour after a conflict situation). Moreover, it includes the knowledge of somatology and the chosen parts of crisis management, especially the phases of the conflict and solutions to conflict situations [5]. The professional defence is a necessary part of a physical protection, which is a basis in every security system. Without good quality physical protection, we cannot have effective security technologies and whole security system. The professional defence is the protection of client's interests against the attack. The motivation is a salary, because it is a full-time job. On the other hand, a self-defense is the protection of our own interests against the attack. We can help other person too but our motivation is not the salary but a justice and a willingness of the help.

The aim of this article is to describe the complex analysis of the direct punch. This study took five years and, during this time, five methods of measurement were used – the measurement of the velocity (camera Olympus i-Speed 2) [6-8], the measurement of the force (strain gauge type SRK-3/V and strain gauge L6E-C3-300kg) [3][9][10][11], the measurement of the body movement (system VICON) and the measurement of the local muscle load (EMG = Electromyography). The second aim is to find some dependencies among groups of people with different training level. All results from each experiment are published together in this article in separate sections.

During our study, the strain gauge type SRK-3/V suffered from many errors [12]. That was the reason why it was replaced by strain gauge L6E-C3-300kg. The results for the first strain gauge are not presented in this article because the data was corrupted, therefore irrelevant.

In Section 2, the measurement of the velocity is described. Section 3 presents the measurement of the force. Next, in Section 4, we describe the measurement of the movement during the direct punch. In Section 5, we divided people into four groups according to their training level. In Section 6, the results and the most important graphs and tables are presented. We conclude in Section 7.

Our motivation is a lack of research in this area. In Czech Republic, prof. Straus [13] did the similar research with less people and with help only one method of the measurement. In the world, this area has less quality research and articles.

II. MEASUREMENT OF VELOCITY

A high-speed camera Olympus i-Speed 2 [14] was used for measuring of velocity. This camera had a CMOS 800x600 sensor, full resolution recordings to 1000 fps (fps = frames per second) and 33000 fps maximum recording speed [15]. We used a recording speed of 1000 fps [8].

The measuring station (Figure 2) consists of a punching bag and a construction of its suspension. A paper with two perpendicular lines was stuck on the right of the punching bag. The horizontal line was for leading the hand during movement. The aim of the vertical line was to determine the beginning of data analysis. The result was that all direct punches were measured in the same distance from punching bag. This distance was 60mm. The end of the measuring was at the moment when the movement of the hand stopped on axis "x" – the deformation of punching bag was at the maximum [6][7][8].

Figure 2. Measuring station with camera [8]

A total of 61 participants took part in the experiment; 48 men and 13 women.

During the experiment, each person made one, two or three strikes. During the measurement, the target was positioned in such manner that the center of the punching bag was in line with the striking person´s shoulder. That way the punches have the maximum velocity and force (as there is no decomposition of force or velocity into the other axes). The person was made to stay in the same place for the whole experiment. Any unnecessary movement (e. g. lunge etc.) would lead to data distortion [8].

III. MEASUREMENT OF FORCE

The strain gauge sensor L6E-C3-300kg (Figure 3) works as unilaterally cantilever bending beam [10]. During force delivery, the biggest deformation of sensor is in places with the thinnest walls – there are metal film strain gauges which change their electrical resistance depending on deformation. Strain gauges are plugged in Wheatstone bridge and this way it is possible to convert the difference of resistance to an electrical signal which we can processed [10].

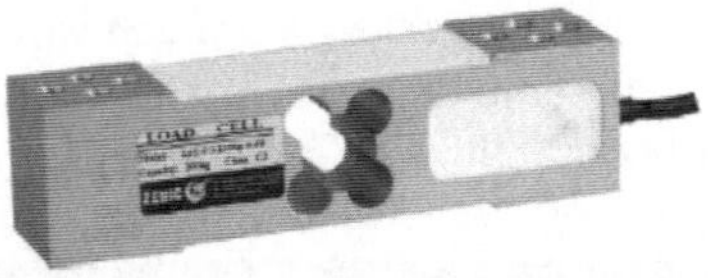

Figure 3. Strain gauge sensor L6E-C3-300kg [10]

The sensor is connected to the computer, which is used for data storage, through the strain gauge. The strain gauge type TENZ2334 is an electronic appliance that converts the signals to data that is stored in memory. The core of the appliance is a single-chip microcomputer that controls all of the activities. The strain gauge sensor is connected to this appliance via four-pole connector XLR by four conductors. The number of values measured by the sensor averages around 600 measurements per second while the data is immediately stored in the memory of a device with a capacity of 512 kB [5].

The strain gauge sensor mentioned above was placed on the measuring station according to the following schematic (Figure 4):

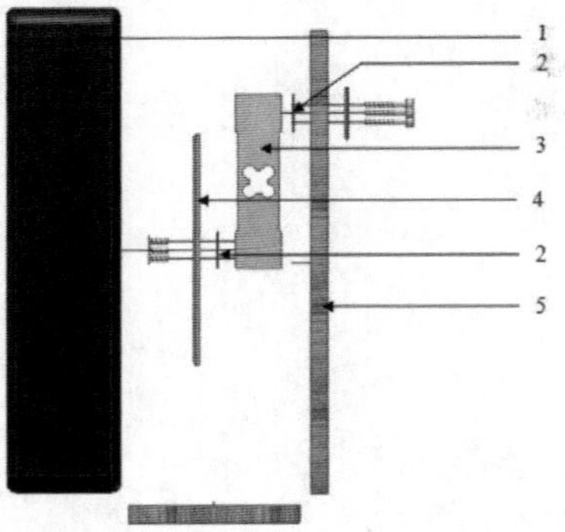

Figure 4. Measuring station schematic [10]

1 – punching bag (made from hardened vinyl filled with foam)
2 –template
3 – strain gauge sensor L6E-C3-300kg
4 – board (200 x 200 x 5 mm)
5 – punching bag base

A total of 220 participants took part in the experiment; 192 men and 28 women. All participants were between 19 and 25 years of age. During the experiment, each person made ten strikes.

IV. MEASUREMENT OF MOVEMENT DURING MAKING OF DIRECT PUNCH

The aim of this experiment was to visualize body movement during making of the direct punch. The system VICON, which is located in University Hospital in Brno (Figure 5), was used for this experiment. The laboratory is equipped with 8 video cameras (in height 1,4 m – 2,5 m) and illuminated by rings radiating infrared light with wavelength of 780nm. Retro-reflexive markers and infrared light allow scanning of the whole trajectory of motion with accuracy of few hundredths of a millimeter. The type of cameras used was MX20+ with the resolution of 1600 x 1280 pixels and the frequency of 120 fps (frames per second).

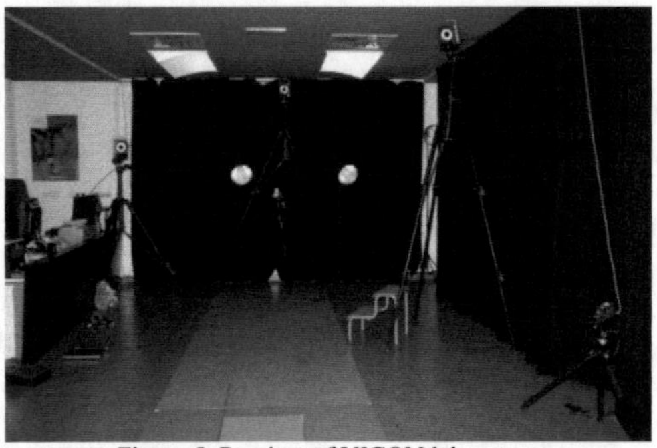

Figure 5. Preview of VICON laboratory

Special markers (retro-reflexive markers) were placed on selected body parts (Figure 6).

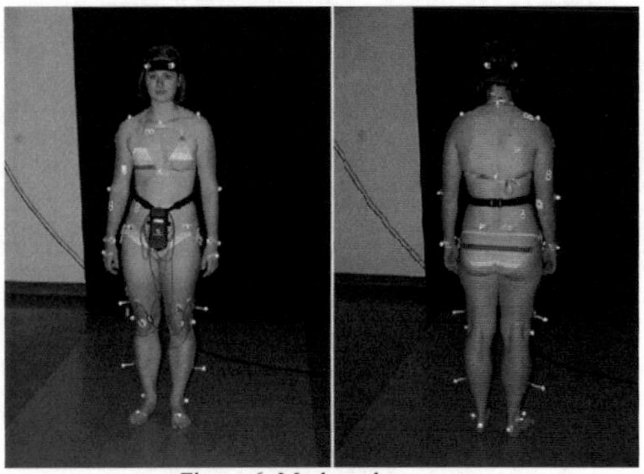

Figure 6. Marker placement

During this experiment, a local muscle load was also measured with the help of EMG. The main hypothesis is that the level of training affects the utilization of individual muscles. The better trained person uses more muscles and makes the technique more effective. EMG is used in medicine, but it can also be used for measuring a local muscle load. An eight-channel EMG (3000 Hz) was used and it was connected to great muscles via electrodes. The monitored muscles were (Figure 7):

- *M. palmaris brevis* (1)
- *M. biceps brachii* (2)
- *M. triceps brachii* (3)
- *M. deltoideus, spinal part* (4)
- *M. trapezius* (5)
- *M. pectoralis major* (6)
- *M. latissimus dorsi* (7)
- *M. obliquus externus abdominis* (8)

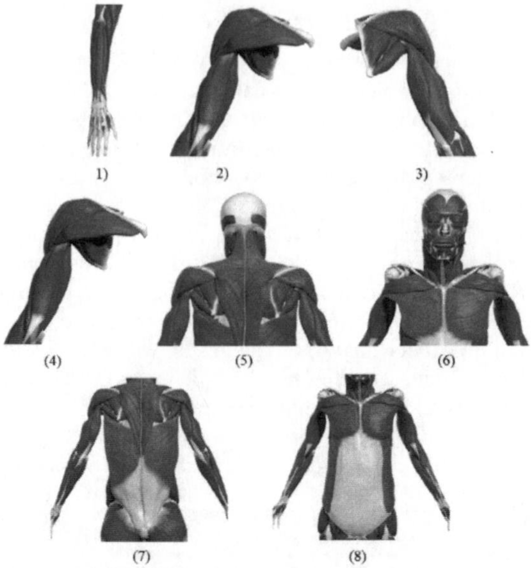

Figure 7. Monitored muscles

The experiment was performed with 21 participants: 15 men and 6 women in age of 19 – 30 years. Each direct punch was performed 10 times in a row.

V. GROUPS OF PEOPLE

These experiments were done at Tomas Bata University in Zlin and in University Hospital in Brno. Most people who participated in the experiment were students from 19 to 30 years of age.

Based on previous training and experience, the participants were divided into the following categories [3][6][7][8][9][10][11][12]:

- Untrained – These people have never done any combat sport, martial art or combat system. They had no theoretical knowledge of the striking technique. The technique was presented to these people before the experiment for safety reasons. Noted further as UTM (for men) and UTW (for women).
- Mid-trained - These people had the theoretical knowledge of striking techniques and did attend the Special physical training course for at least six months. The course was focused on self-defence and professional defence. Noted further as MTM (for men) and MTW (for women).
- Trained – These people have attended the Special physical training course for two or more years or practiced a combat sport or martial art for the same time period. Noted further as TM (for men) and TW (for women).
- Self-trained - These people did practice or still do practice (for less than 2 years) some combat sport, martial art or combat system. As there is no

guarantee of the quality of the training they are separated into their own category. Noted further as STM (for men) and STW (for women).

TABLE I. NUMBER OF PARTICIPANTS

Methods of measurement	Total number of participants	Men	Women
Measurement of velocity	61	48	13
Measurement of force	220	192	28
VICON + EMG	21	15	6

A different number of people participated in each experiment (see Table 1).

VI. RESULTS

In this section, the results will be presented with the help of graphs and tables. The aim was to show the most important and interesting results.

During the data analysis, two pieces of software were used – MINITAB and Microsoft Office Excel.

A. Results from the measurement of the velocity

Figures 8 to 10 depict the dependencies of mean velocity as a function of time. It is expected that trained men have the highest velocity and untrained women the lowest velocity. But these big differences are very interesting, together with differences among each group according to training level.

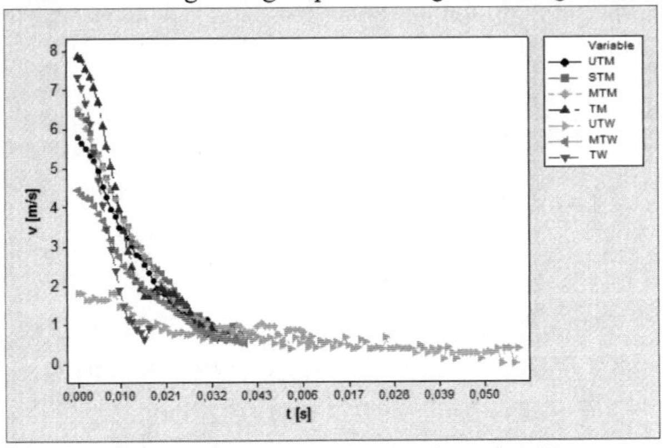

Figure 8. Dependence of mean velocity on time [8]

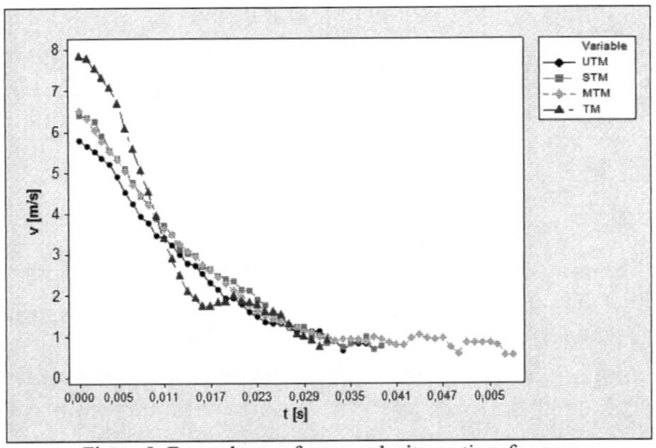

Figure 9. Dependence of mean velocity on time for men

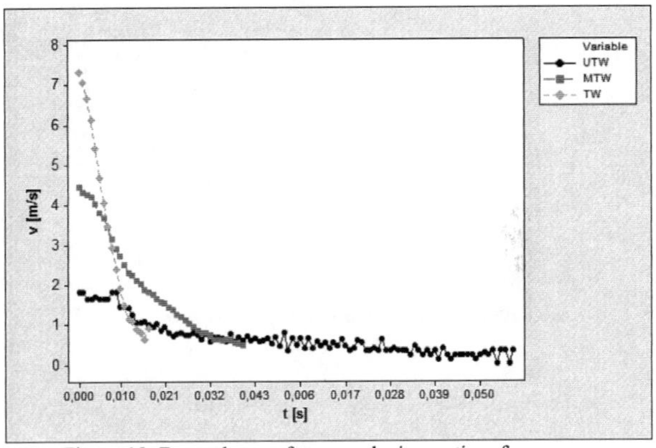

Figure 10. Dependence of mean velocity on time for women

Clear differences among groups according to training level are evident from Figure 8 to 10. There are not only differences in maximum velocity, but also in time of direct punch. Very interesting is the fall of velocity. There is a very sharp fall in groups of trained men and women. Other groups have a less sharp fall.

Table 2 presents the statistical data from the measurement of the velocity.

TABLE II. VELOCITY [8]

	Mean	Standard deviation of mean	Coefficient of variation	Minimum
UTM	3.06	1.6	52.61	0.77
STM	3.16	1.76	55.83	0.7
MTM	3.05	1.82	60.35	0.57
TM	4.55	2.43	54.25	1.15
UTW	0.67	0.44	66.66	0
MTW	2.14	1.25	58.25	0.47
TW	3.65	2.37	64.29	0.69
	Median	**Maximum**	**Number of samples**	
UTM	2.81	5.86	10	

STM	2.76	6.44	7
MTM	2.76	6.52	32
TM	4.46	7.87	39
UTW	0.58	1.82	1
MTW	1.82	4.46	16
TW	3.35	7.34	6

B. Results from the measurement of the force

Figure 11 and 12 show the dependence of the mean force as a function of time. In Figure 12, we display only a part of the whole graph of force for increased readability.

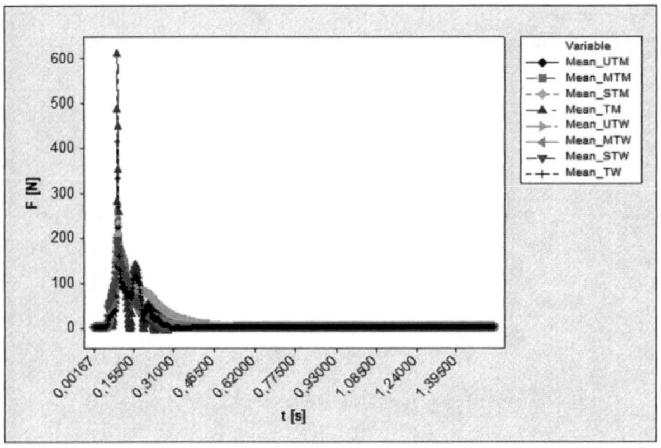

Figure 11. Dependence of mean force on time – whole [3]

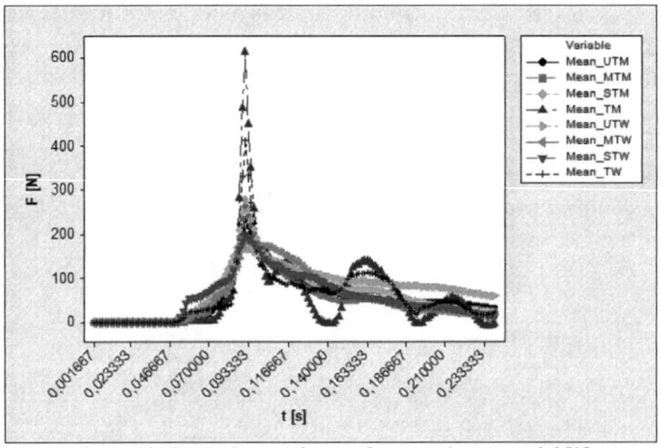

Figure 12. Dependence of mean force on time – partial [3]

Figure 13 and 14 show dependencies of mean force as a function of time for men and for women separately.

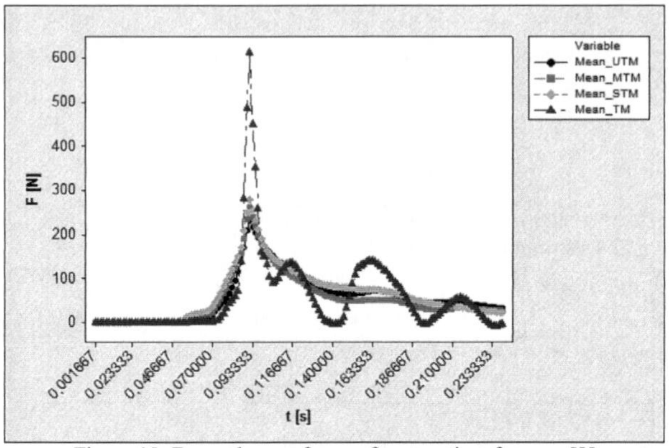

Figure 13. Dependence of mean force on time for men [3]

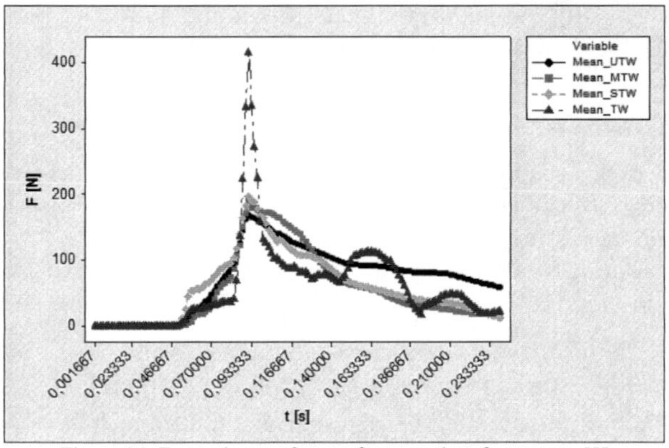

Figure 14. Dependence of mean force on time for women [3]

Table 3 shows the results for each category – especially the mean value for the force, the maximum force and the standard deviation.

TABLE III. RESULTS OVERVIEW FOR EACH CATEGORY

	Mean	Standard deviation of mean	Coefficient of variation	Maximum
UTM	23.148	48.08	240.59	233.76
MTM	17.522	44.512	313.25	260.37
STM	28.42	55.91	228.37	279.12
TM	27.75	88.92	499	612.7
UTW	15.17	36.157	265.72	169.9
MTW	20.76	45.779	254.28	192.09
STW	81.66	66.21	88.7	220.2
TW	40.78	78.56	256.9	415

C. Results from VICON system and EMG

For this experiment, the participants were a trained and an untrained woman, with the scanned marker placed on the back of the hand and in one case on the elbow. The process of direct punch was compared. As it is depicted in Figure 15, there is a difference in arm trajectory. It is clear that trajectories for direct punch of the untrained woman are absolutely different. Also, the marker on the elbow shows a visible round motion. The trained woman has both trajectories almost the same and direct.

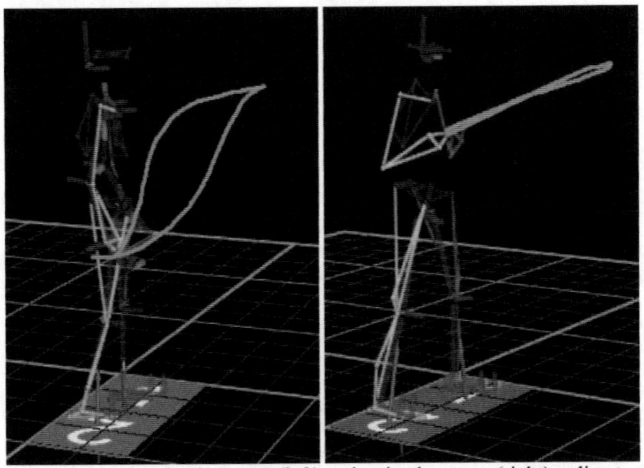

Figure 15. Untrained woman (left) and trained woman (right) – direct punch

Figure 16 and 17 show that the EMG diagram for both women are very similar. The most visible difference is in utilization of abdominal muscles and triceps.

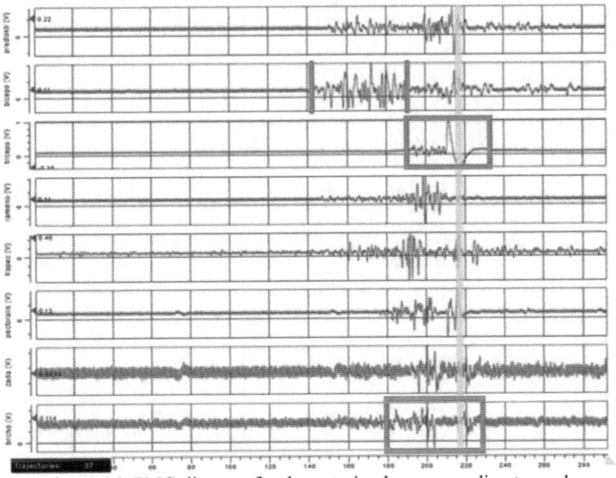

Figure 16. EMG diagram for the untrained woman – direct punch

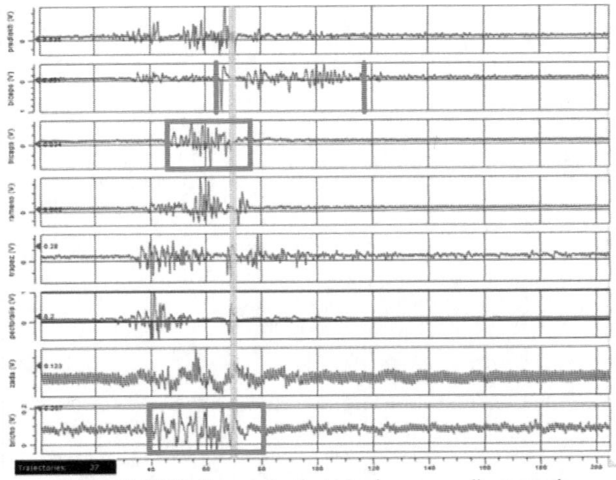

Figure 17. EMG diagram for the trained woman – direct punch

The trained woman (Figure 17) used these muscles more intensely than the untrained woman. A smaller difference is in the time of utilization of biceps that is shorter for the untrained woman (Figure 16).

VII. Conclusion

During a long term study, five methods were used for the analysis of the direct punch.

The first method was to measure the velocity of the direct punch. Very interesting results are in the column Maximum, because we can see that differences between trained men and trained women are not too big. The difference is only 0.53 m/s (6.73%). In the case of force, the difference is bigger, 197.7 N (32.27%).

The fall of velocity and force is also very interesting. There is a very sharp fall in the group of trained men and women. Other groups have a less sharp fall.

The body movement was visualized very precisely with the help of the system VICON. We can see significant differences between the two groups of people divided according to their training level.

This complex analysis showed that is possible to measure significant differences among people with different training level. In the future, the data analysis will be continued and the aim will be to find other dependencies.

Acknowledgment

This work was supported by the Ministry of Education, Youth and Sports of the Czech Republic within the National Sustainability Programme project No. LO1303 (MSMT-7778/2014) and also by the European Regional Development Fund under the project CEBIA-Tech No. CZ.1.05/2.1.00/03.0089 and also by the Internal Grant Agency of Tomas Bata University under the project No. IGA/CebiaTech/2016/006.

REFERENCES

[1] G. Blower, "Boxing: Training, Skills and Techniques," Crowood, 2007.

[2] D. Levine and J. Whitman, "Complete Krav Maga". 2007.

[3] D. Lapkova, M. Adamek, and Z. Kominkova Oplatkova, "Analysis of direct punch force in professional defence." In: Proceedings 29th European Conference on Modelling and Simulation ECMS 2015. Germany: Digitaldruck Pirrot GmbH, 2015, s. 564-569. ISBN 978-0-9932440-0-1.

[4] Z. Reguli, "Inovation SEBS a ASEBS." Biomechanics of combat sports and martial arts. [online]. [cit. 2016-05-30]. 2011, Available: http://www.fsps.muni.cz/inovace-SEBS-ASEBS/elearning/biomechanika/biomechanika-upolovych-sportu

[5] D. Lapkova, M. Pospisilik, M. Adamek, and Z. Malanik, "The utilisation of an impulse of force in self-defence". In: XX IMEKO World Congress: Metrology for Green Growth.Busan, Republic of Korea, 2012, s. 0-6. ISBN: 978-89-950000-5-2.

[6] D. Lapkova, Z. Malanik, and M. Adamek, "Use of the high-speed camera in self-defence". In: Annals of DAAAM for 2011 & Proceedings of the 22nd International DAAAM Symposium "Intelligent Manufacturing & Automation: Power of Knowledge and Creativity". Vienna: DAAAM International Vienna, 2011, s. 1531-1532. ISBN 978-3-901509-83-4.

[7] D. Lapkova and M. Adamek, "Analysis of Direct Punch with a View to Velocity." In Proceedings of the 2014 International conference on Applied Mathematics, Computational Science and Engineering. Craiova : Europment, 2014, s. 0-9. ISSN 2227-4588. ISBN 978-1-61804-246-0.

[8] D. Lapkova and M. Adamek, "Statistical and Mathematical Classification of Direct Punch." In: Proceedings of the 38th International Conference on Telecommunication and Signal Processing (TSP 2015). Prague: Asszisztencia Szervezo Kft., 2015, s. 486-489. ISBN 978-1-4799-8497-8. ISSN 1805-5435.

[9] D. Lapkova, M. Pluhacek, and M. Adamek, "Computer Aided Analysis of Direct Punch Force Using the Tensometric Sensor". In: Modern Trends and Techniques in Computer Science: 3rd Computer Science On-line Conference 2014 (CSOC 2014). Springer, 2014, s. 507-514. ISBN 978-3-319-06739-1. ISSN 2194-5357.

[10] D. Lapkova, M. Pluhacek. Z. Kominkova Oplatkova, and M. Adamek, "Using Artificial Neural Network for the Kick Techniques Classification – an Inticial Study". In: Proceedings 28th European Conference on Modelling and Simulation ECMS 2014. Germany: Digitaldruck Pirrot GmbH, 2014, s. 382-387. ISBN 978-0-9564944-8-1.

[11] D. Lapkova, L. Kralik, and M. Adamek, "Possibilities of force measuring in professional defence." In: IMEKO XXI World Congress. Prague: Czech Technical University in Prague, 2015, s. 280-285. ISBN 978-80-01-05793-3.

[12] D. Lapkova and M. Adamek, „Using strain gauge for measuring of direct pucnh force." In: IMEKO XXI World Congress. Prague: Czech Technical University in Prague, 2015, s. 285-288. ISBN 978-80-01-05793-3.

[13] J. Straus and V. Porada, "Concise biomechanics of extreme dynamic loading on organism". Jurisprudencija [online]. 2005, s. 18-23 [cit. 2012-06-27]. Available: http://www3.mruni.eu/padaliniai/leidyba/jurisprudencija/juris58.pdf#page=18.

[14] J. Pesek, "High speed digital imaging system I-Speed 2 and its application." Brno, 2008. Bachelor's thesis. Brno University of Technology. Advisor doc. Dr. Ing. Vladimír Pata.

[15] M. Baron, "Measurement and evaluation of high-speed processes using high-speed camera system Olympus i-SPEED 2". Zlín, 2010. Thesis. Tomas Bata University in Zlin. Advisor doc. Dr. Ing. Vladimír Pata.

Methodology of Determination of Uncertainties by Using Biometric Device iCAM 7000

Hana Talandova, Lukas Kralik, Milan Adamek
Faculty of Applied Informatics
Tomas Bata University in Zlin
Zlin, Czech Republic
Email :{talandova, kralik, adamek}@fai.utb.cz

***Abstract* - The iris recognition is known for a long time. Identification by iris is positively perceived by the public, like fingerprinting. Devices for acquiring images are cheaper and smaller, compared with other technologies. This article aims to verify the reliability of the scanner of the iris in different conditions. The measurement is performing on the scanner iCAM7000. The measurement is performing in different lighting conditions, in the artificial lighting, reduction in the lighting conditions and in daylight. Thereafter the percentage of success of authorization is measured during physical activity.**

Keywords - Iris recognition; Identification; iCAM 7000; Percentage of success

I. INTRODUCTION

Biometric analysis of an iris is relatively new and rapidly evolving field, which is primarily used to uniquely identify individuals. Identification by an iris is relatively well known for a long time [2]. A full implementation of this technology in practice was not possible because of low-quality digital sensors. Currently, iris recognition is considered to be one of the most reliable technologies and one of the most secure methods of identification [11] [13] [14] [15].

There are several research publications which deal biometric devices [3] [4] [5]. However, little attention is paid to the effectiveness of these devices. For this reason, in this paper, we address the state of the art in terms of efficiency of biometric equipment.

This paper describes and analyses iris scanner reliability under various lighting conditions and the probability of correct recognition.

The rest of the paper is structured as follows. The Section II contains the Introduction to the iris recognition. The Section III describes the iris scanner iCAM7000. The Section IV contains details of the scanning procedure. While, The Section V explains the methods of measurement and followed by the results. And finally in Section VI, the contribution of our work is described in the conclusion.

II. IRIS

The iris is formed together with the eye in the prenatal development in the third month. Within the structure of the iris (Figure 1) a pattern is formed until the eighth month of gestation, although the pigment will be established in the postnatal period. The iris is composed of collagen fibers which form certain patterns. The color of the iris is different form person to person, and this color is created by the pigment melanin. The size of the iris is about 11 mm. The structure is stable during a person's live and remains similar after mechanical damage too. In our picture, it is possible to detect 266 features [1] [2] [6].

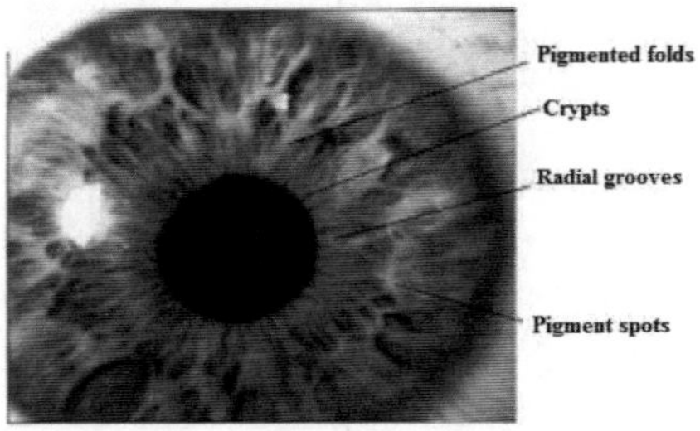

Figure 1. The external features of the iris (adapted from [8])

A. *The external features of the iris*

- Pigment spots - Random clump of pigment cells on the surface of the cornea, ciliary occurrence in the area.
- Crypts – A dark place where the iris is thin, the incidence at the interface between the ciliary and papillary zones.
- Pigmented folds - The bottom layer of the iris around the pupil.
- Radial grooves - Occurrence near the pupil and extending radially towards the edge of the iris.

III. THE IRIS SCANNER ICAM7000

The scanning of an iris was performed by the scanner iCAM7000 (Iris identification Systems; series Iris Access® 7000) [10]. This scanner scans the iris in a fully automatic way and also captures the image of the face around eyes. iCAM 7000 has a voice and a visual interface, which makes it faster and more accurate to scan the iris and subsequently identify/verify a person. 60 – 70% of iris visibility is sufficient for successful identification of a person [10].

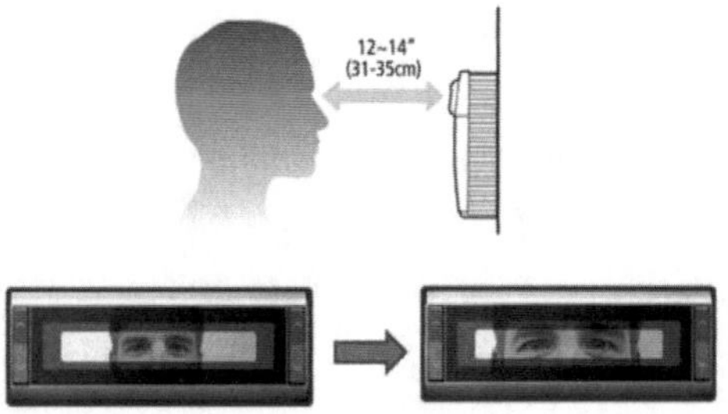

Figure 2. The necessary distance for capturing an image (adapted from [10])

The iCAM is activated when the user approaches or provides the identification card. The scanner is able to take a picture from the distance of 31 – 35 cm (Figure 2). The scanner uses the dot indicated in Figure 2, which is projected on the root of the nose; this helps the user adjust and correct the eye position. When the user is in the correct position, the orange dot is changed to green. The whole process is completed with a voice command to easier capture the image [10].

IV. Iris scanning

The processing procedure is divided into four parts: segmentation, normalization, extraction and comparison (Figure 3).

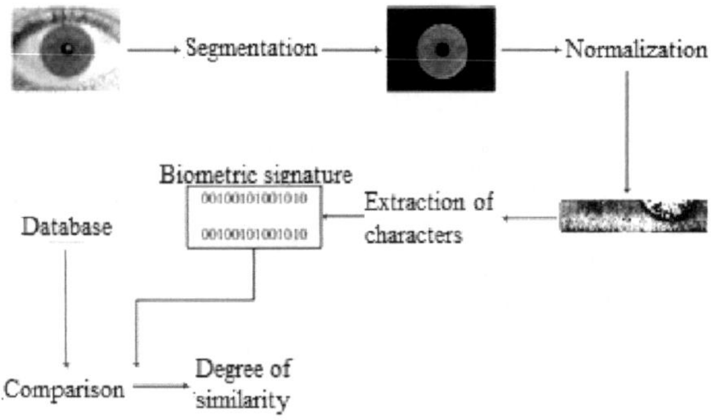

Figure 3. The processing procedure of iris (adapted from [9])

1) Capturing an image

Various negative factors may occur during the image capturing from the sensor. They can result in deterioration of image processing. There are many negative influences (for examples: noise, blur, etc.) After the elimination of these effects, the accuracy of the biometric system is increased. The sensor transforms all colour images into grey spectrum and it eliminates tone colour aberration.

Color aberrations can arise as a result of charge-coupled device sensors (CCD sensors) used. After this process, it is necessary to normalize the colour spectrum of the captured image for better edge enhancement [3] [4].

2) Segmentation

The second step is segmentation, which determines the position of the iris and the pupil (Figure 4). This part of analysis is among the slowest processes in the whole system. This is caused by the necessity to determine the position of the iris and the pupil, and to correct all the edges of the captured image.

Various algorithms exist to detect edges of the image, such as Cannes's edge detector algorithm. This algorithm is based on identification of gradient among nearby pixels [8] [9].

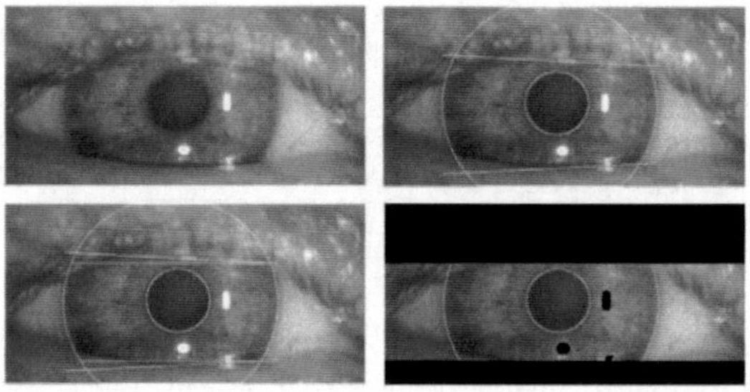

Figure 4. Segmentation with eye image (adapted from [7])

3) Normalization

The coordinates of points from the scanned iris and its centre are the basis of normalization. The method works by converting the annulus shaped iris into a rectangular shape. The resulting image is a rectangle with coordinates of radiuses and angles. On the short side of the rectangle i.e. vertical axis, there are radiuses of a circle and on the long side i.e. horizontal axis, angular coordinates. This is a transfer of Cartesian coordinates into polar coordinates [7] [9].

4) Extraction of characters

The following step is an extraction of characters, when the input data are extracted and encoded in major characters. The result is a two-bit piece of information that contains the coordinates of the iris [7] [9].

5) Comparison

This is the last step where the comparison of characters with the template stored in the database takes place and the result is called the degree of similarity. The degree of similarity shows the similarity between the code templates and the code of the iris. If the characters match the template stored in the database, the system allows the access and in the opposite case the access is denied. The comparison was carried out using the Hamming distance between two points [9].

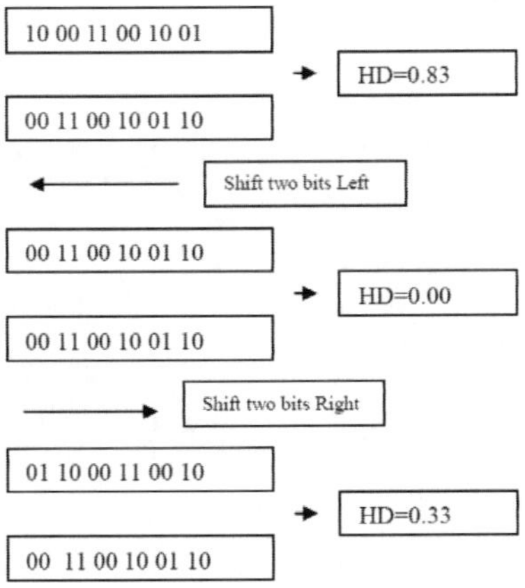

Figure 5. Shifting process (adapted from [7])

The Hamming distance of two templates is calculated, one template is shifted left and right bit-wise and a number of Hamming distance values are calculated from successive shifts (Figure 7). One shift is defined as one shift left, and one shift right of a reference template. In this example, one filter is used to encode the templates, so only two bits are moved during a shift. The lowest Hamming distance, in this case zero, is used since this corresponds to the best match between the two templates [7].

V. METHODS OF MEASUREMENT AND RESULTS

Several measurements were carried out in various conditions to verify the reliability of the iris scanner:

- Visibility in poor lighting - The measurement was performed in daylight, in poor light conditions and under artificial lighting.
- During physical exertion - The measurement was performed after physical exertion.

Six subjects were used for the measurements. Each time there were 10 measurements. The success percentages of these measurements were recorded in result tables.

The first measurement was performed in various light conditions in order to investigate the success percentage of authorization under these circumstances. Furthermore, the influence of glasses and contact lenses was investigated. Thereafter, the measurement of success percentage of authorization was performed during physical activity.

TABLE I. THE MEASUREMENTS IN VARIOUS LIGHT CONDITIONS

	Daylight	Low light conditions	Artificial light
Subject 1 - Without glasses	100%	100%	100%
Subject 2 - Without glasses	100%	100%	100%
Subject 3 - Without glasses	100%	100%	100%
Subject 4 - With glasses	60%	90%	90%
Subject 5 - With glasses	80%	90%	90%
Subject 6 - Contact lens	100%	100%	100%

Table 1 shows a comparison of measurements in different light conditions. There are measurements in daylight, in poor light conditions and in artificial lighting. In the case of subjects without glasses, the success rate is 100%. In the case of subjects wearing glasses, the success rate was between 60% - 90%. This may be due to the number of diopters of the subject. As can be seen in the case of subject 6, contact lenses have no effect on identification.

TABLE II. MEASUREMENT DURING PHYSICAL EXERTION

	Physical exertion
Subject 1	100%
Subject 2	100%
Subject 3	100%
Subject 4	100%
Subject 5	100%

In Table 2, we can see the success percentage of authorization after physical activity. The measurement was performed on 3 subjects who put a physical strain on their bodies, and subsequently used the scanner for identification. In all subjects, the physical exertion had no effect on authorization. However, in the case of subject 5, who had run for 5 minutes up the stairs, the identification took much longer in order for the person to be recognized.

VI. CONCLUSION

Iris recognition methodology is known for a long time, but its full implementation in practice was possible only with the extension of high-quality digital sensors.

Identification by iris is positively perceived by the public, like fingerprinting. Compared to other technologies, devices for taking pictures are smaller and cheaper.

The main objective of this paper was to create comparative measurements for future work. The measurements were performed on the scanner iCAM7000. The measurements were carried out in different light conditions, in artificial lighting, poor light conditions and in daylight. In the daylight, it was found that the measured data showed a lower percentage of success in measuring with a lot of diopters. The use of contact lenses was found to have no effect on the device function. Another measurement was focused on the effect of physical activity on authorization. Based on the measurements, we conclude that physical activity has almost no effect on user authorization to access.

The future work will be related to artificial intelligence and utilization of neural networks for recognizing and identifying persons by iris. The results from artificial intelligence measurements and from the measurements performed in this work (iCAM7000) will be compared. The goal of this work is to increase efficiency of biometric identification by iris in various light conditions.

ACKNOWLEDGMENT

With support by grant No. IGA/FAI/2016/027 and IGA/CebiaTech/2016/006 from IGA (Internal Grant Agency) of Thomas Bata University in Zlin. This work was supported by the Ministry of Education, Youth and Sports of the Czech Republic within the National Sustainability Programme project No. LO1303 (MSMT-7778/2014).

REFERENCES

[1] R. Rak, V. Matyas, and Z. Řiha, Biometrics and identity of a person in forensic science and commercial applications. 1. Praha: Grada Publishing, a.s., 2008. ISBN 978-80-247-2365-5.

[2] H. Li, L. Li and K. Tok, "Advanced topics in biometric," New Jersey: World Scientific, 2012, xv, pp. 500, ISBN 978-981-4287-84-5.

[3] L. Ma, T. Tan, Y. Wang, and D. Zhagn. "Efficient iris recognition by characterizing key local variations," IEEE Transactions on image processing: a publication of the IEEE Signal processing Society, 2004, vol. 13, pp. 739–50. ISSN 1057-7149.

[4] M. Elgamal and N. Al-biqami, "An efficient feature extraction method for iris recognition based on wavelet transformation," International Journal of Computer and Information Technology, 2013, vol. 2, iss.3, s. 521-527. ISSN 2279-0764.

[5] C. L. Tiesse, L. Martin, L. Torres, and M. Robert, "Person identification technique using human iris recognition," In Proc. Vision Interface. May 2002, pp. 294-299.

[6] A. K. Jain, A. A. Ross, and K. Nandakumar, "Introduction to biometrics," 1., New York: Springer, 2011, pp. 311. ISBN 9780387773261.

[7] S. Gupsa, V. Doshi, A. Jain, and S. Iyer, "Iris Recognition System using Biometric Template Matching Technology," International Journal of Computer Applications 2010, vol. 1, pp.4 . ISSN 0952-8091.

[8] H. Talandova, Study about application of biometric systems in the industry of commercial security. Zlin, 2010. Bachelor thesis. UTB in Zlin.

[9] M. Luzny, The Reliability of iris scanners for the biometric indetification if individuals. Zlin, 2015. Bachelor thesis. UTB in Zlin.

[10] Iris ID, Inc. iCAM 7000: User Manual.USA [2012].

[11] M. Faundez-Zanuy, "Biometric security technology," IEEE A&E Syst.Mag., Jun. 2006 vol. 21, no. 6, pp. 15–26.

[12] J. Mansfield and J. L. Wayman, "Best practices in testing and reporting performance of biometric devices," U.K. Government Biometrics Working Group, 2002. [Online]. Available:http://www.npl.co.uk/upload/pdf/biometrics_bestprac_v2_1.pdf [retrieved June 2016]

[13] P. Phillips, W. T. Scruggs, A. J. O'Toole, P. J. Flynn, K. W. Bowyer, C. L. Schott, and M. Sharpe, "FRVT 2006 and ICE 2006 large-scale results," Nat. Inst. Standards Technol., 2007. [Online]. Available: http://www.frvt.org/FRVT2006/docs/FRVT2006andICE2006LargeScaleReport.pdf [retrieved June 2016]

[14] Independent Biometric Group, "Comparative biometric testing round 6 public report," 2006 [Online]. Available: http://www.biometricgroup.com/reports/public/comparative_biometric_testing.html[retrieved June 2016]

[15] K. Bowyer, K. Hollingsworth, and P. Flynn, "Image understanding for iris biometrics: A survey," Comput. Vision Image Understand, 2008, vol. 110, no. 2, pp. 281–307.

Scanning Probe Microscopy Used for 3D Topography Image Acquisition of Marks on Cartidge Cases in Forensic Ballistics

Milan Navrátil, Vojtěch Křesálek, Adam Koutecký
Department of electronics and measurements
Faculty of applied informatics
Tomas Bata University in Zlín
Zlín, Czech Republic
e-mails: {navratil, kresalek, a_koutecky}@fai.utb.cz

Zdeněk Maláník
Department of Security Engineering
Faculty of applied informatics
Tomas Bata University in Zlín
Zlín, Czech Republic
e-mail: malanik@fai.utb.cz

Abstract— **In spite of the significance of tool mark analysis in forensic ballistics, the image acquisition and comparison of tool marks remains a difficult and time consuming effort. This work deals with modified scanning probe microscopy applied to examination of marks on the surface of fired cartridge cases. Marks after firing pin are represented by 3-D topography image from measured data and compared according to images taken from confocal microscope and scanning electron microscope.**

Keywords - forensic balistic; scanning probe microscopy; firing pin; cartridge case; marks; 3D; topography.

I. INTRODUCTION

The identifying of the weapon which perpetrator used for shooting includes the basic questions of forensic ballistics. This individual identification is based on the axiom that the components of the weapon which are in the contact with the shot and cartridge case, leave on their surface characteristic marks. They are a unique reflection of micro roughness of contacted surface.

From a historical point of view, one of the earliest references related to the rifling of firearms is in a book by Harold Peterson [1]. In the early part of the 20th century, the science of firearm and tool mark identification was recognized by numerous judicial systems in several countries around the world. Legal recognition was due, in part, to the efforts of several individuals that had conducted research and experiments into the identification of fired projectiles and cartridges cases to the specific firearms.

In the middle part of the 20th century, the science of firearm and tool mark identification continued to evolve. For example, in the United States, the Scientific Crime Detection Laboratory (SCDL) began operations at Northwestern University in 1929, followed by formation of the Federal Bureau of Identification (FBI) Laboratory in 1932. Moreover, many other countries also recognized the requirement to provide this type of forensic analysis and established firearm and tool mark sections either in existing laboratories or as new laboratories. Over the next few years, several laboratories were established and commenced operations, especially in many of the larger cities in Canada, the United Kingdom, and the United States and in Europe.

In 1969, as a result of individual's effort in scientific research in the field of firearm and toolmark identification, Association of Firearm and Toolmark Examiners (AFTE) was founded.

In the last part of the last century, the science of firearms and toolmark identification has continued to evolve with a greater number of forensic scientists being employed as firearm and tool-mark examiners around the world. The science has greatly benefited from the numerous technological advances that have occurred during this period. These advances include innovations in one of the primary tools of the firearm and toolmark examiner — the binocular comparison microscopes. The immense majority of the current comparison microscopes have been equipped with digital cameras and closed circuit television (CCTV) units, which allow for direct viewing on a monitor or instant documentation using digital photomicrography. The most significant advances during this period include the tremendous growth, popularity, and relatively inexpensive cost of computers. The ability to fully utilize the immense potential of computers has allowed science overall, and forensic science more specifically, to take full advantage in development of several useful 'tools' for use within the firearms laboratory. The ongoing development of computers has provided the firearms and toolmark examiner with such useful equipment as the current Integrated Ballistics Identification System (IBIS) from Forensic Technology (Quebec, Canada) which combines a traditional 2D light microscopy image with software for image comparison and database search [2].

In recent years, researchers have started to explore a next generation of techniques for tool mark imaging. These methods produce 3D images of tool marks. Several technologies have been considered, for example, focus-variation microscopy, confocal microscopy, point laser profilometry, atomic force microscopy or scanning interferometry. Mentioned techniques require expensive equipment and often the sample preparation is not trivial. For example, we can mention very fast method called TopMatch GS-3 [3]. It is 3D scan acquisition based on GelSight imaging technology that uses an elastomeric sensor and enhanced photometric stereo [4][5][6][7]. The another novel application of sensing technology, based on chromatic white light, acquires highly detailed topography and luminance data of cartridge cases simultaneously [8]. Atomic Force Microscopy (AFM) technique in forensic science was used with combination of Fourier Transform Infrared Attenuated Total Reflectance (FTIR/ATR) spectroscopy in analysis of Gun-Shot Residue (GSR) to test their ability to determine shooting distance and discrimination of the powder manufacturers [9]. Using this method for tool mark analysis is not suitable because regular Scanning Probe Microscopes (SPM) and among them especially atomic force microscope are the best techniques to measure very smooth surfaces. For larger samples, such as cartridge cases, an analogy of scanning probe microscopy was required. This work shows the possibility of the assembled system and also indicates possible trends for the future.

In Section 2, the principle of general scanning probe microscopy and our custom scanning system are described. Section contains series of acquired images from scanning electron, scanning probe and optical microscopy of measured cartridge cases together with their mutual comparison. Section 4 presents a conclusion and an indication of the future work.

II. Scanning Probe Microscopy

In general, scanning probe microscopy (SPM) is a technique to examine materials with a solid probe scanning the surfaces. The SPM is relatively new for materials characterization compared with light and electron microscopy. It can examine surface features whose dimensions range from tenth of a millimetre to atomic spacing. The main characteristic of the SPM is a sharp probe tip that scans a sample surface. The tip must remain in very close proximity to the surface because the SPM uses near-field interactions between the tip and a sample surface for examination. This near-field characteristic eliminates the resolution limit associated with optical and electron microscopy because their resolution is limited by the far-field interactions between light or electro waves and specimens. The lateral and vertical resolution of an SPM can be better than 0.1 nm, particularly the vertical resolution. The lateral range of an SPM measurement is up to about 100 μm, and its vertical range is up to about 10 μm. The SPM must operate in vibration-free environment due to atomic proximity between the tip and the sample.

For surface morphology measurement, the mode of SPM using atomic forces is very often utilized. Operation is based on surface scanning using an elastic cantilever with a sharp tip. The tip is moved closer to the surface with a small constant force. The tip height ranges from hundreds of nanometers up to 2 μm and tip curvature radius ranges from 2 to 60 nm. Interaction of the tip and the surface is detected by the reflection of the laser beam from the top of a cantilever on the four-segment photodiode detector.

Every SPM system consists of several basic components: a probe and its motion sensor, scanner, electric controller, computer and vibration isolation system. The scanner controls the probe that moves over the sample in three dimensions in a precise way (1 pm if atomic resolution is required). To achieve this level of precision, a scanner is made of piezoelectric materials. Moreover, the scanner must be well calibrated to eliminate piezoelectric effects (nonlinearity, hysteresis, creep of material). There are four operational modes in the STM: constant current, constant height, spectroscopic and manipulation modes. The most commonly used mode is the constant current mode, where the feedback loop controls the scanner moving up and down to maintain a constant tunnelling current [10].

In case of forensic ballistics, the size of marks (shots, cartridge cases, parts of gun, etc.) is often many times greater than limits of SPM method. It is not possible to use commercial instruments without any physical adjustment of the sample because there is a danger that the sample can be reversibly modified or damaged. For SPM systems, the maximal size of scanned area rarely exceeds 100 μm. Another limitation is the maximal height of the sample, which is often about 1 cm together with surface roughness of the examined sample. From reasons mentioned above, there was a need to modify or design custom scanning systems allowing measuring larger samples with larger roughness of the surfaces.

A. Custom SPM system

Our custom scanning system differs in several important aspects from the above described general SPM system. The present configuration of the system can examine only metallic samples. It consists of stationary conductive probe with sharp tip, stage connected to system of servomotors (Mercury M110 1DG) controlled by stepper controllers (Mercury C-862) through the computer and own user software (programmed in MATLAB), it is illustrated in Figure 1. As a feedback, a change in resistivity of the used electronic circuit is employed. This change is caused by the physical contact of the tip and sample; it is measured with multimeter (Hewlett Packard 34401A). Switch SW1 represents contact between the tip and sample. Resistors R_1 = 1 MΩ and R_2 = 100 Ω participate in overall measured circuit resistance. Schema of the electronic circuit can be seen in Figure 2.

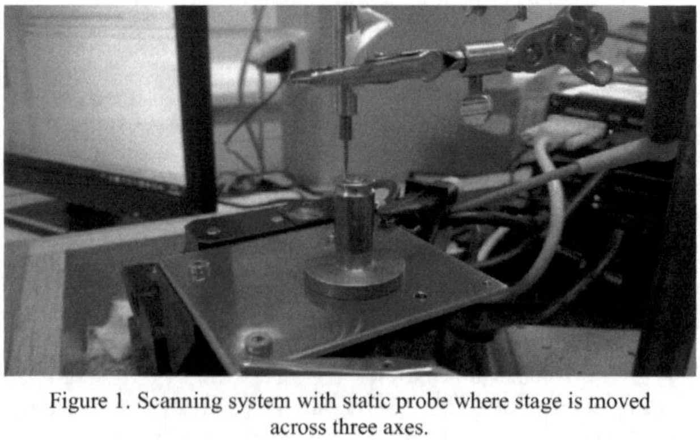

Figure 1. Scanning system with static probe where stage is moved across three axes.

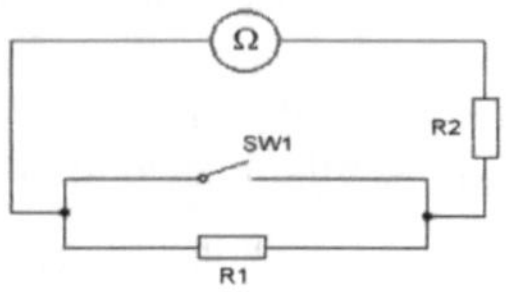

Figure 2. Simple electronic circuit for feedback system.

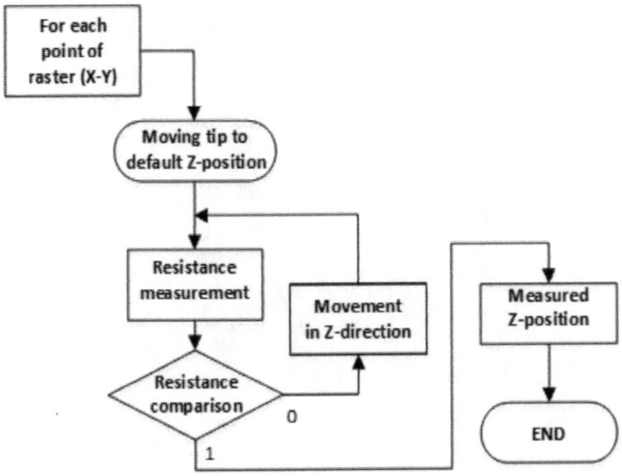

Figure 3. Flowchart of approaching cycle.

This system allows the measurement of larger objects (from few millimetres up to about 5 cm), maximal scanned area is 5 x 5 mm. On the other hand, examined object must be conductive, lateral and vertical resolution are given by chosen scanning raster and limited by curvature radius of the probe and also by used stepper motors. It can be said that the scanning system works in spectroscopy mode. For each point in chosen regular rectangular raster, the approach cycle is successively accomplished to get Z-coordinate which corresponds to topography of the sample, which is illustrated in Figure 3. All three coordinates are stored in common SPM data format for further visualisation and analysis.

The accuracy of the system and the level of details during scanning are dependent on chosen raster size, approaching distance in Z-axis and its velocity. They are inversely related to the total time of scanning process. On the basis of repeated spectroscopy measurement at one single point of the sample it was found out that relative slow approaching velocity of the stage in Z-axis (in range up to 5 μm per second) leads to uncertainty below 0.2 micrometers. On the other hand, velocities over 15 μm per second exceed uncertainty of 1 micrometer. The correct and adequate settings of system parameters is a question of compromise between quality and measurement duration. Lots of important information is shown in main window of the user application during running measurement. It also includes the current 3D graph together with measured topography profile, estimated time of end measurement, information about stage movement and many others.

B. Scanning probe with a sharp conductive tip.

The indispensable part of the scanning system is the tip. Maximal resolution we can reach with this system is given by curvature radius of the tip. The curvature radius of used tip was reached by mechanical sharpening and was measured with optical microscopy and also with scanning electron microscopy. Comparison of these two methods can be seen in Figure 4 and Figure 5, where different determination of curvature radius is obtained. The images from SEM method

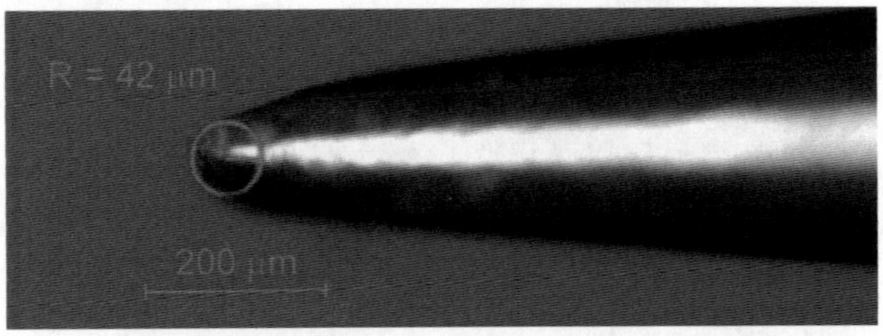

Figure 4. Image of the used sharp conductive tip measured with optical microscope.

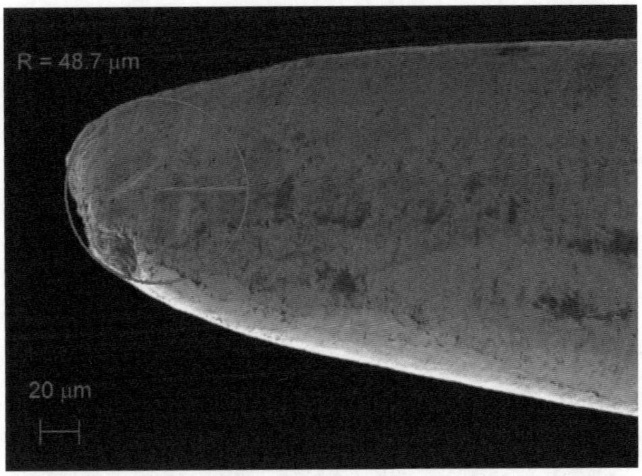

Figure 5. Image of the used sharp conductive tip measured with SEM.

have much better resolution so that measured values are more accurate.

According with this value, the scanning raster is chosen, in our case it was 50 μm. Additionally, the method is based on resistivity change at contact during approach. Regarding to possible physical damage of the tip or sample in case of non-conductive contact (dust, impurity) because stage is approaching the tip until resistivity change of the electronic circuit occurs, tip attachment is also very important. From this reason, the tip has possibility of free movement in Z-axis inside guide conductive casing which is fixed and the tip always get back to the same position.

III. RESULTS AND DISCUSSION

For test measurement, two available firearms with different specific marks of firing pin were chosen (Glock 17 and Walther PPQ). For every single gun, several fired cartridge cases were collected and then the marks after firing pin measured and analysed. Two of typical cartridge cases from individual firearms were subjected to measurement with our SPM method. For comparison of obtained topography images to images taken using contemporary method, scanning electron microscopy (SEM) as well as confocal microscopy were used, see Figure 6 – Figure 12.

All cartridge cases were scanned using SPM in the same way, with the same system parameters, raster in both lateral axes was 50 μm, total scanned area from 4000 μm to 3000 μm, depending on size of individual mark. Initial

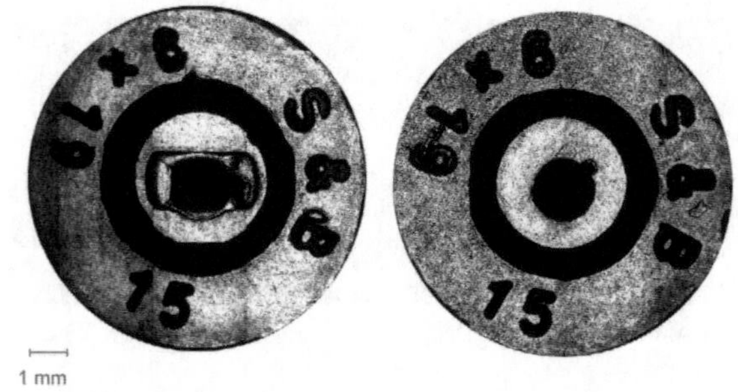

Figure 6. Visualised cartridge cases on primer side using confocal microscope.

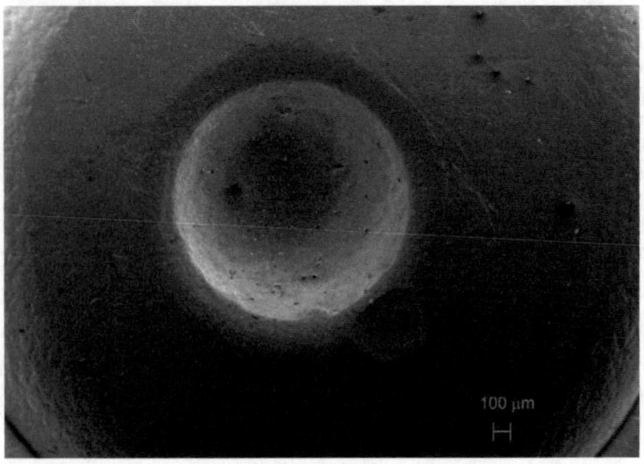

Figure 7. Image of mark after firing pin on cartridge case fired from Walther PPQ measured with SEM.

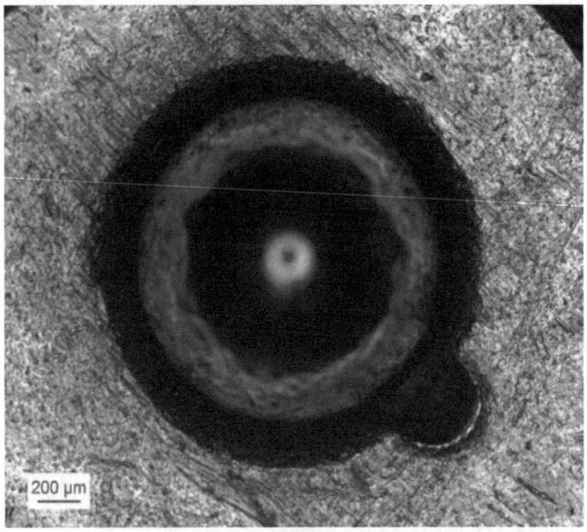

Figure 8. Image of mark after firing pin on cartridge case fired from Walther PPQ measured with optical microscope.

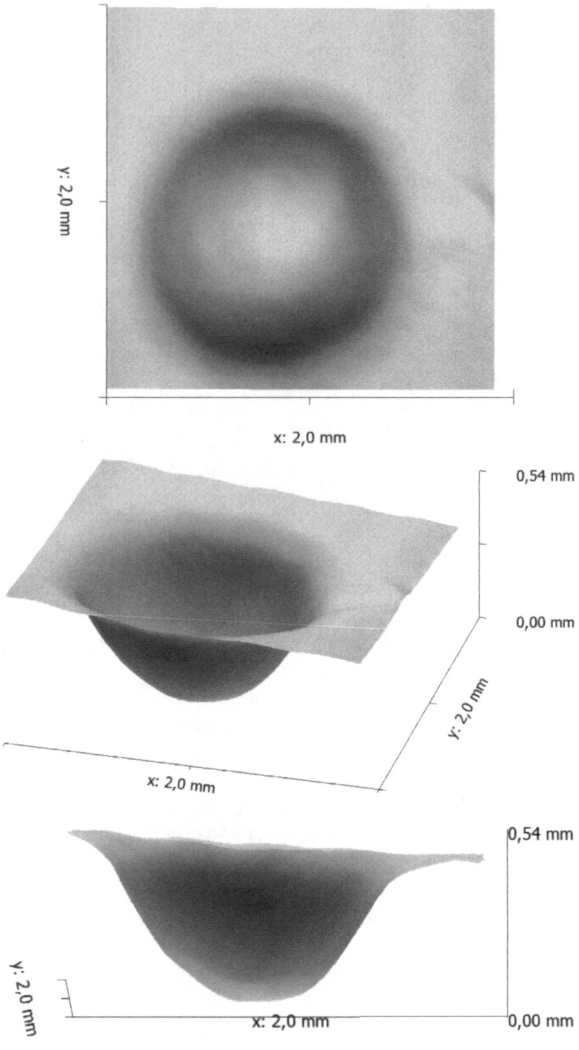

Figure 9. Views on 3D scan of mark after firing pin (Walther PPQ) using our SPM method.

sample positioning on the stage and the tip distance were manually performed. Approaching speed was set 5 µm/s. The scanning process of one mark took approximately 8 hours. All measured data was processed in Gwyddion software [11] which is a modular program for SPM data visualization and analysis [12]. Plane leveling was applied to raw SPM data. The plane was computed from all the image points and was subtracted from the data. The last modification lay in data trimming according to region of interest.

As it can be seen from Figure 9 and Figure 12, the level of detail is very poor, but we have information about spatial penetration of the firing pin, which is another useful information. According to this, we can compare shape of firing pin, its abrasion level so that its possible malfunction can be predictable.

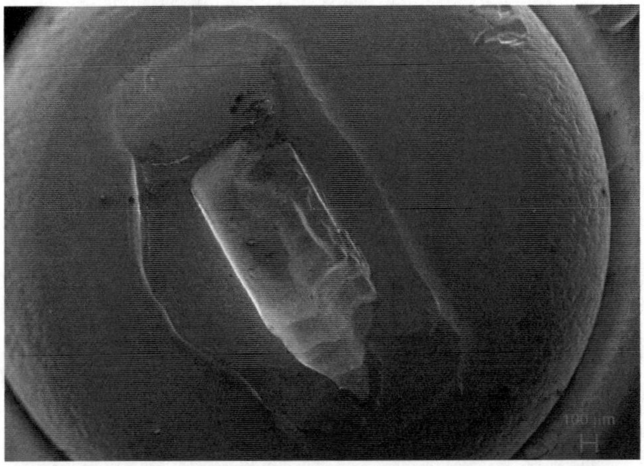

Figure 10. Image of mark after firing pin on cartridge case fired from Glock 17 measured with SEM.

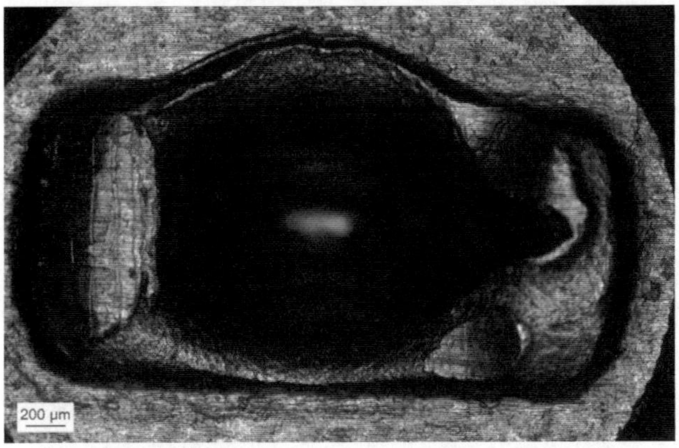

Figure 11. Image of mark after firing pin on cartridge case fired from Glock 17 measured with optical microscope.

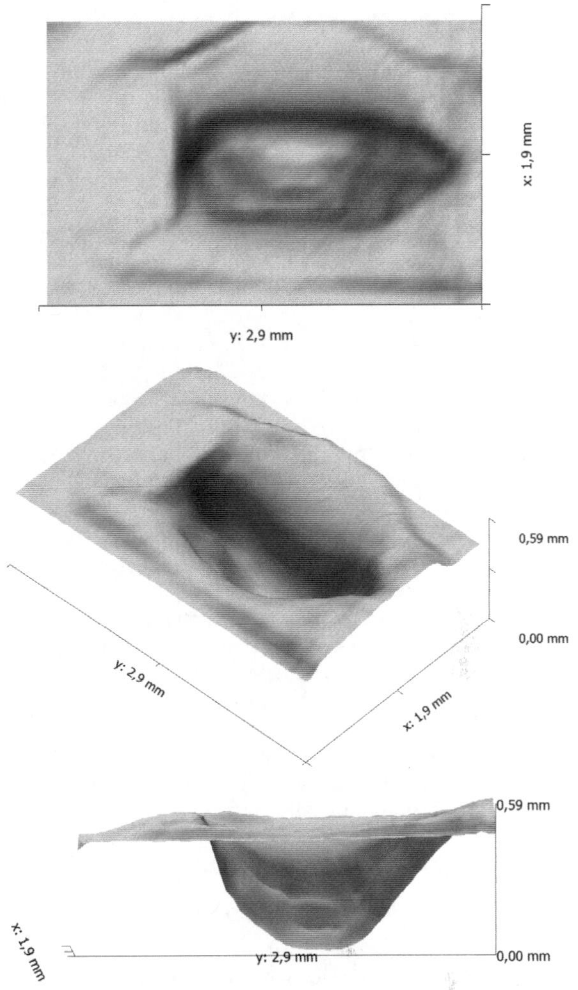

Figure 12. 3D scan using our SPM method of mark after firing pin (Glock 17)

Figure 7 and Figure 10 show SEM images that have, from principal, unique resolution (can reach values of 0.02 nm) and large depth of field (the order of micrometers at 10^4 magnification). We can observe very fine details, images look plastic, but they are still only 2-D images. Moreover, this type of instrument does not belong to common laboratory equipment and its cost is very high.

Figure 6 shows reduced images from confocal microscopy, which provides, except others, non-contact surface profilometry with resolution of 0.15 µm. It can slice clean thin optical sections so that it is able to compose a 3-D topography image. The problem is for surfaces where there is a steep decrease of the material. This represents edge and deep inner part of mark after firing pin on the primer which would be evident from Figure 6 and real comparison of the cartridge case.

For marks after firing pin, STM method can be considered as efficient, especially if the resolution improves. Furthermore, not only topographic images can be the result of this measurement. Another little modification of this method it will lead to simultaneous acquisition of contact potential, which gives us information about homogeneity of metal crystal lattice and its imperfections.

IV. CONLCUSION AND FUTURE WORK

In spite of the significance of tool mark analysis in forensic sciences, the image acquisition and comparison of tool marks remains a difficult and time consuming effort. The comparison, in our case, is based on the fact that microscopic firearm imperfections are transferred to a fired cartridge case.

In this study, we were concerned with marks after firing pin on fired cartridge casings that were measured with custom SPM method. As a result of these measurements, 3-D topography images were acquired. For the verification and comparison of obtained results, images of the same samples were measured with available optical methods (scanning electron microscopy and confocal microscopy).

Using our SMP method, one single cartridge case was scanned in order of hours which is impractical at this moment; but, there are also possibilities and reserves which allows us increasing the scanning time. In future work, construction of near field microwave microscope can be the promising improvement from the point of time consumptions. It is based on impedance change between the tip and the sample in microwave spectra. Additionally, it is non-contact method so that the possibility of tip or sample damage falls behind. The tip is only moved in constant height above the conductive sample within the raster and the resonant curves of coaxial resonator are measured. Image brightness component is arranged according to changes of resonant curves.

The lateral resolution is limited by curvature radius of the tip. By mechanical sharpening we were able to decrease the radius below 50 micrometres which is still not enough to observe details necessary to comparison of tool marks. Using methods like chemical milling of the tip [12] or stretching of the thin wire when heated the curvature radius of the conductive tip can be dramatically reduced. As a consequence of mentioned improvements, 3D scan of measured surface can be taken in much shorter time with better resolution then it is presented here. It is evident, that any SPM method for surface topography measurement is much time-consuming then optical methods. Every method has pros and cons, always it depends what information the user wants to get and what is the worth.

Moreover, every single scanned surface can be mathematically described as a unique vector of numbers; for example, moment characteristics or Fourier descriptors [14] can be utilized in combination of suitable segmentation methods. These complementary aspects can be helpful in tool mark comparison and firearms identification.

ACKNOWLEDGMENT

This work was supported by the Ministry of Education, Youth and Sports of the Czech Republic within the National Sustainability Programme Project No. LO1303 (MSMT-7778/2014) and also by the European Regional Development Fund under the project CEBIA-Tech No. CZ.1.05/2.1.00/03.0089.

REFERENCES

[1] H. L. Peterson, "The Fuller Collection of American Firearms: America's Military Long Arms. Eastern National Park & Monument Association, 1967.

[2] J. Hamby and J. Thorpe, "The History of Firearm, and Toolmark Identification. AFTE Journal", vol. 31, no. 3, 1999, pp. 266-284.

[3] R. Lilien, "Applied Research and Development of a ThreeDimensional Topography System for Firearm Identification using GelSight", USA, Patent No. 248639, 2015.

[4] R. Li, "Touching is believing: sensing and analyzing touch information with GelSight", 2015, PhD. Thesis, Massachusetts Institute of Technology.

[5] R. Li and E. Adeslon, "Sensing and recognizing surface textures using a gelsight sensor", In: Proceedings of the IEEE Conference on Computer Vision and Pattern Recognition, 2013, pp. 1241-1247.

[6] R. Lilien, "Applied Research, and Development of a Three-Dimensional Topography System for Imaging and Analysis of Striated and Impressed Tool Marks for Firearm Identification using GelSight", Department of Justice Award 2013-R2-CX-K005, Document 248962, 2015

[7] R. Tomcik, Cadre Forensics, "A Successful Case of End-User Involvement". National Criminal Justice Reference Service [online], 2014, [retrieved: 06, 2016], Available at: https://www.ncjrs.gov/pdffiles1/nij/247272.pdf

[8] A. Makrushin et al., "3D imaging for ballistics analysis using chromatic white light sensor" [online], In: Proc. SPIE 8290, Three-Dimensional Image Processing (3DIP) and Applications II, [retrieved: 06, 2016], DOI: 10.1117/12.908105, Available at: http://proceedings.spiedigitallibrary.org/proceeding.aspx?doi=10.1117/12.908105#

[9] Y. Mou, J. Lakadwar, J. Rabalais, and J. Wayne, "Evaluation of shooting distance by AFM and FTIR/ATR analysis of GSR", Journal of forensic sciences, vol. 53, no. 6, 2008, pp. 1381-1386.

[10] Y. Leng, „Materials characterization: introduction to microscopic and spectroscopic methods", 2nd ed. Weinheim: J. Wiley, c2013, ISBN 978-3-527-33463-6.

[11] D. Nečas and P. Klapetek, "Gwyddion: an open-source software for SPM data analysis", Cent. Eur. J. Phys., vol. 10, no.1, 2012, pp. 181-188

[12] P. Klapetek, "Quantitative data processing in scanning probe microscopy: SPM applications for nanometrology", First edition, New York: William Andrew/Elsevier, 2013. Micro & nano technologies, ISBN 1455730580.

[13] M. Fotino, "Tip sharpening by normal and reverse electrochemical etching", Review of Scientific Instruments, 1993, 64(1), 159, [retrieved: 06, 2016], DOI: 10.1063/1.1144419. ISSN 00346748. Available at: http://scitation.aip.org/content/aip/journal/rsi/64/1/10.1063/1.1144419

[14] K. Arbter, W. E. Snyder, H. Burkhardt and G. Hirzinger, "Application of affine-invariant Fourier descriptors to recognition of 3-D objects", in IEEE Transactions on Pattern Analysis and Machine Intelligence, vol. 12, no. 7, pp. 640-647, Jul 1990.

Security of Seniors – The Detection and Prevention of Falls

Lubomír Macků
Faculty of Applied Informatics
Tomas Bata University in Zlín
Zlín, Czech Republic
e-mail: macku@fai.utb.cz

Markéta Matějíčková
EUROALARM Ltd.
Praha, Czech Republic
e-mail: matejickova@euroalarm.cz

***Abstract*— The paper deals with the issue of seniors security, namely the security problems related to falls of independently living elderly citizens. Various possibilities of their fall detection are studied. We analyze the historical development, current capabilities and efficiency of different approaches and methods. We address the willingness and ability of seniors to actively use technology, detection limits, privacy, personal data security and other important factors. In addition, we discuss the challenges, current shortcomings, issues and trends in fall detection or operation reliability in real-life conditions. The main future goal would be to maintain the personal privacy and security of irrelevant information in modern fall detection systems.**

Keywords-security; seniors; emergency response; fall detection; smart phones; assistive technology; senior inspect; witrack.

I. Introduction

Worldwide, the number of persons over 60 years is growing faster than any other age group. According to the World Health Organization (WHO) study [1] approximately 28-35% of people aged 65 and over fall each year. This number is even increasing to 32-42% for those over 70 years of age. In fact, the number of falls increases exponentially with age-related biological changes. Falls are defined here as "inadvertently coming to rest on the ground, floor or other lower level, excluding intentional change in position to rest on furniture, leaning on the walls or other objects". Falls and consequent injuries are major public health problems that often require medical attention. They lead to 20-30% of mild to severe injuries, and are underlying cause of 10-15% of all emergency department visits and account for 40% of all injury deaths. If preventive measures are not taken in immediate future, the numbers of injuries caused by falls is projected to double in the year 2030.

In addition, falls may also result in post-fall syndrome that includes dependence, loss of autonomy, confusion, immobilization and depression, which will lead to a further restriction in daily activities. Such dependence is shown, for example, in a study by S. M. Friedman et al. [2], where authors state that each syndrome may lead to the other. Namely, an individual who falls may subsequently develop fear of further falls. This distinction underlies the concept of primary prevention, in which the onset of fear of falling is prevented, versus secondary prevention, in which fear of falling is prevented from progressing. Falls consequences can significantly mitigate their early detection combined with an effective emergency system.

The effect of automatic fall detection units on the fear of falling was studied by S. Brownsell et al. [3] on the group of participants, who had experienced a fall in the previous six months. Most users who wore their fall detectors at least occasionally felt more confident and independent and considered that the detector improved their safety.

One of determining factors influencing the severity of fall consequences in older people is the amount of time spent lying on the floor or ground [4]. This is particularly critical when a person cannot call for help, for instance when she/he has lost consciousness or is alone when the fall occurs. Even when uninjured, 47 % of people who have experienced a fall were unable to get back up without help. Lying on the floor due to a fall event for one hour or more is defined as a "long-lie". Experiencing a "long-lie" event is associated with serious injuries, higher mortality rates and hospital admissions, as well as consequent care home admissions.

Therefore, calling for help systems and other technological equipment for detecting, preventing, and mitigating falls consequences have become a social necessity and it is very important to use reliable and sufficiently sensitive systems..

A fall detection system could be defined as a system which detects falls and alerts a designated person or emergency services in order to facilitate rapid assistance. A system causing too many false alarms is inconvenient for the system supervisor while the not responding system can result in injuries or even in death.

For these and other reasons, some fall detection studies originated a few years ago, for example Noury and collective [5] in 2008 or a similar analysis [6] published in 2012 by Mubashir and other co-authors. In recent years, there has been rapid development in the field of fall detection and so some systems are missing in the above studies, such as those based on the use of smart phones and the like. These missing trends are described in this work.

In section II., individual systems are described. Starting with *"The first call for help system"*, continuing with the *"Automatic fall detection"* and, at the end, the *"Mobile personal airbag"* system. In section III., more recent and some complex projects are mentioned. Also the possibility of using smartphones in the area of fall detection can be found here. Section IV. concludes the article and suggests future possible developments in the area.

II. INDIVIDUAL SYSTEMS

A. *The first call for help system*

The first call for help system, in English often called Medical Alarm or Personal Emergency Response System (PERS) was developed in Germany in the early 70s of the 20th century by Wilhem Hormann [7]. The system was programmed to send messages after pressing a button. The button (transmitter) was designed to be worn by a senior living alone. The cost was 795 USD and was offered through Popular Science magazine in October 1975.

B. *Automatic fall detection*

Research on automatic fall detection progressed through the nineties of the twentieth century. Lord and Colvin [8] studied the causes and consequences of falls in the elderly, they tried to prevent falls and suggested the use of an accelerometer to detect a fall. The first detector prototype was developed in the fall of 1998. It used a piezoelectric shock sensor for detecting abnormal peaks caused by the fall and a mercury tilt switch for detecting the orientation of the falling user.

One of the first attempts to detect the fall based on video cameras was described by Wu [9] in 2000. Results showed that the horizontal and vertical speed can be utilized to distinguish a fall from normal activities.

In 2002, Prado et al. [10] developed a prototype system for detecting fall based on two dual-axis accelerometers placed in a patch worn on the user back at his cross level. The same year, Norbert Noury [11] developed a smart sensor with evaluation algorithm. The prototype contained a piezoelectric accelerometer, vibration sensor and a switch responsive to the position. Unfortunately, it turned out that the vibration sensor is too sensitive.

T. Degen et al. [12] introduced a fall detector for elderly people in the form of a wristband in 2003. The device was comfortable to wear, but its reliability was only 65%.

Some of the acceleration based fall detectors can be seen in Table 1.

In 2004, Sixsmith et al. [20] used a variety of cheap infrared cameras mounted on the wall. The alarm started when there was no observed activity over long period of time or during the detection of a fall. Attempts (20 falls + 10 attempts without falling) unfortunately showed that only 30% of falls were properly detected.

Several groups around the world were engaged in the new devices development in 2006. Kang et al. [21] have developed a bracelet, in which the fall monitoring and modules for measurement of the single-channel electrocardiogram (ECG), blood pressure, pulse oximetry, breathing, and temperature were merged. Nyan et al. [22] have conducted fall detection experiments based on a high-speed camera and three gyroscopes installed in the undershirt. The gyroscopes were concretely placed on the chest, arm and at the waist. The camera was used to study the position of the body during the fall, while the angular velocity was the guideline for the fall detection. Miaou et al. [23] reported fall detection based on the panoramic camera and information about the user (the height to width ratio and Body Mass Index (BMI)). This system brought a 70% accuracy without user information and 81% accuracy with this information. Alwan et al. [24] suggested a fall detection system based on floor shocks sensing by a piezoelectric sensor. It showed 100% detection rate, but falls simulations were carried out with dummies.

Srinivasan et al. [25] studied the automatic detection of the fall based on triaxial accelerometer and passive infrared detectors (PIR) in 2007. The triaxial accelerometer worn by the user was placed at the waist for fall detection while the PIR detectors were mounted on the wall to provide information about the horizontal movement. The same year Almeida et al. [26] presented the stick with a gyroscope, which helped detect the downfall and measured the number of steps. The fall detection was based on the angular velocity evaluation.

In 2008, Doukas and Maglogiannis suggested a combination of accelerometer and a microphone placed on a leg [27]. Based on the short-time Fourier transformation

TABLE I. COMPARISON OF ACCELERATION BASED FALL DETECTORS

Study	Year	Objective	Detection technique	Tested	SP/SE	Detector location
Kangas et al.[13]	2009	prototype verification	exceeding the threshold value; min.2 phase	20 persons	100% / 97%	wrists, head, waist
Shan et al.[14]	2010	investigation of a pre-impact fall detector	support vector machines (SVM)	5 persons	100% / 97,5%	waist
Bourke et al. [15]	2010	comparision of novel fall detection algorithms	considering the fall impact, the velocity and the person posture	20 persons	SP: 100%	waist
Lai et al. [16]	2011	several acceleration sensors for joint sensing fall events	exceeding the threshold value; compared acceleration in 3 axes	9 persons	Accuracy 92.92%	neck, hand, waist, foot
Yuwono et al. [17]	2012	verification of a sophisticated fall detection method	machine learning, perceptron network structure adaptation	8 persons	99% / 98,6%	waist
Kerdagari et al. [18]	2012	investigation of the performance of different classification algorithms	machine learning; combination of several methods	50 persons	SE: 90.15%	waist
Cheng et al. [19]	2013	daily activity monitoring and fall detection	exceeding the threshold value; using a decision tree	14 persons	95%/97,6%	chest, thigh

it was described that during the impact the low-frequency sound signals with high amplitude are formed and can be used to detect falls. The same year, Bourke et al. [28] introduced a fall detection system and algorithm that were incorporated into a custom designed garment.

Tzeng et al. [29] used in 2010 a pressure sensor in the floor to identify fall strength combined with infrared camera to detect the movement of a person. Bianchi et al. [30] developed a fall detection system based on barometric pressure sensor and a triaxial accelerometer located at the waist. On the basis of the barometric pressure difference between the waistline and the earth, the experimental results showed that the obtained sensor information was useful for the fall detection.

C. *Mobile personal airbag*

It is a 2009 pilot project for the protection against injuries from falls [31]. Behind this project stands a Japanese scientist Toshiyjo Tamura and his team. The researchers designed a wearable device containing a fall detector directly connected to the airbag. The signal containing information about the acceleration and angular velocity was used for the airbag activation. Sixteen people were monitored during a fall simulation. Based on the data an algorithm was designed so that the downfall was evaluated 300 ms before the actual impact of people on the ground. This signal was then used to start the 2.4 liter airbag. Although this system can help to prevent injuries due to falling, other research/development is required to miniaturize the inflation system.

III. MORE RECENT PROJECTS

A. *Fallwatch project*

The French company Vigilio S.A. launched a project FallWatch [32] funded by the FP7-SME program with the timeframe 2009 - 2012. The challenge was to develop a new generation of fall detection devices, including call for help system, which would be effective in minimizing the consequences of falls. FallWatch is a miniature radio communicating wearable device in the form of an adhesive patch. The project deals with the fall from the moment it occurs, i.e., from its detection through the cause investigation to desired action. Fall-Watch may be regarded as a context-aware system. The user wears a "patch" and FallWatch constantly monitors the kinematic variables and classifies the situation according to three degrees of state activity: low, medium and high. Another component is the home central unit that monitors activity using signals from PIR detectors and classifies the situation according to three-level scale (no activity, normal activity, exceptional activity).

B. *Smartphones as a fall detection system*

Developers are trying to detect the fall using smart phones since 2010. Dai et al. [33] introduced the fall detection based on mobile phones in 2010 and recently the detection based on triaxial accelerometers becomes more and more popular.

In 2012, Fang et al. [34] compared the accuracy of fall detection for smart phones placed on the waist, chest and thigh, and found that its chest location is the most appropriate. The advantage of using a smartphone to detect the fall is the possibility of simultaneous use for sending warning messages and / or tracking the person who needs help.

Koshmak et al. [35] experimented with detection of a fall with 7 skiers. They had with them a smart phone when skying downhill and the pulse and blood oxygen saturation were measured. The measured values were unexpectedly variable in critical situations.

Also, Kau and Chan [36] conducted a study with smartphones. Fall was detected using a triaxial accelerometer and electronic compass.

C. *The Senior Inspect project*

A purely Czech product in the fall detection area is the Senior Inspect project. The project was developed by The CleverTech spin-off company.

The spin-off company allows the important process called technology transfer in

academic environment to take place and is usually founded by university

staff with contribution from external specialists or companies. The CleverTech is a spin-off company consisting of Faculty of Biomedical Engineering at Czech Technical University (CTU) in Prague, First faculty of medicine at Charles University in Prague and some external entities. The first testing of the product began in 2010, the commercial use in 2013 [37].

The user wears a small communications unit and in a critical situation presses the SOS button. The system also enables a range of advanced automatic features in case the user is unable to press the button by himself/herself. When setting off an alarm in the surveillance center the position is determined and the voice call is established directly with the user through the communication unit. On the base of the individual assistance profile and the user agreement the next procedure is selected (the family, professional associations, integrated rescue system etc. are contacted). Key benefits include:

- simplicity of use
- possibility of the communication, localization
- panic button
- the support for proper use
- automatic detection of emergency situations (including the fall)

D. *FATE Solution*

The Polytechnic University of Catalonia project Fall Detector for the Elderly (FATE), which was launched in 2012 with EU funding, should soon bring results. The FATE system is being developed to be an affordable and reliable system capable of detecting falls both inside and outside home [38]. The system consists of two main elements plus a series of secondary elements. The main elements are:

- highly sensitive fall detector incorporating accelerometers, capable of running a complex, specific fall detection algorithm in order to provide accurate fall detection.

- telecommunications layer based on wireless technologies. It consists of an indoors telecommunications network based on Zigbee, a central computer (with or without Internet connection) and a mobile phone communication with the central computer and the fall sensor via Bluetooth. All incidences and measures are stored in the server, so that they can be used as a monitoring data for the carers/doctors thus improving subject fall prevention and treatment. Once detected and confirmed, fall events are communicated by the mobile phone (or Internet, if this service is available) to relatives or health service providers.

Secondary elements are:

- bed presence sensor to dismiss false falls (if the person lies on the bad in a sudden way while wearing the fall detector) to control the time the person spends in bed (to detect potential health problems or behavior anomalies) and to detect falls from the bed (as the user may decide not to wear the fall sensor during sleeping hours).
- i-Walker to detect fall risk for elders with significant gait difficulties, i.e., walker with integrated automatic brake, tilt sensors and with pressure sensors placed in the handle.

E. Personal motion sensor with the fall detection IMSAFE.

Individual Mobility Sensor for Automatic Fall Evaluation (IMSAFE) [39] is based on a combination of the power converter placed in shoe soles with accelerometer located in the belt measuring stroke, orientation and deviation from the pattern posture (Fig. 1). The device was developed in the form of 2 different prototypes in 2012 at the University of San Diego. The declared detection accuracy of this project is high, 97.14%.

F. Czech project ARTEMIS

Another Czech project monitoring the health condition comes from student Marek Novak. This student was awarded a prize in 2013 for his project Artemis [40], whose aim was to develop the concept of wireless modules for monitoring and processing of physiological parameters.

Here, the sensors wirelessly transmit data to a central unit in the form of a wristwatch (hereinafter referred to as watch), which performs filtering, processing and data displaying. The watch enables communication with similar devices, and network access. Miniature sensors are wearable on clothing or can be worn as bracelets. Such sensors are sensor for measuring an electrocardiogram (ECG), a motion sensor for detecting a fall, global positioning system (GPS) location sensor, temperature, transmissive pulse oximetry and several others. The watch is equipped with a 1.8-inch color display.

Figure 1. IMSAFE - fall detection in the soles [39]

From a technological perspective, the application runs on inexpensive low-power communication modules Nordic nRF24L01+ and MRF49XA with low power consumption. For controlling STM32L microcontrollers are used. The whole implementation uses as a power supply ordinary Li-Ion battery. Communication with the public networks is provided via Bluetooth and Global System for Mobile Communication (GSM).

From the application point of view, ARTEMIS provides an inexpensive and convenient all age groups monitoring, from newborns to seniors. The next version should be based on the platform Intel Quark, which allows with integrated Wi-Fi even better wireless options.

G. Kinect, game console

Putting Microsoft Kinect game console on the market aroused an interest for many researchers dealing with the camera fall detection. This console detects the motion using sensors and the response action is based on the player motion without the need of any control device touching. Stone et al. [41] introduced in 2013 two state detection techniques and verified the system using a relatively large set of data from thirteen households. The detection algorithm was based on the following measured variables: minimum and average vertical speed, the maximal vertical acceleration and the shading rate (which is evaluated for each of the pixels). This data set included 3339 days (i.e. 9 years) of continuous data, holding 454 falls, of which 445 were performed by actors and nine cases involved real falls in a normal situation.

Further study using the game console Kinect was elaborated at Lawrence Technological University [42]. The authors utilized three types of Kinect sensors: a standard camera, an infrared (IR) camera, and a microphone array. The IR camera detects points projected by a laser and automatically converts them into a depth map. The cameras are calibrated so that the depth map pixels correspond to the pixels in the standard camera images. They also use a Kinect software development kit (SDK) which is a free software package providing a variety of useful tools. The software automatically detects the 3D location. Additionally, the floor plane is automatically detected. Two algorithms to detect falls using the Kinect SDK were developed. The first algorithm uses only joint position data. This algorithm calculates the distance from the floor to each joint. If the maximum distance is less than some threshold value, a fall is detected. The second algorithm calculates the velocity of each joint in the direction normal to the floor plane. The velocities are averaged over all joints and many frames. If this average velocity is lower (downward velocities are defined as negative) than some threshold value, a fall is detected.

Voice recognition is used to reduce false positive reports. After a fall is detected, the event is validated using the Kinect microphone array and a voice recognition system.

Once a fall is detected, a new thread is created to ask the user if he requires assistance. The thread waits for a response of yes or no. In the case of a yes, a fall is reported. In the case of a no, the report is canceled. A timer is also set. If the timer ends without receiving a yes or no response, a fall is reported.

Falls are reported through email or Multimedia Messaging Service (MMS) with attached pictures of the event.

The system has been tested quite extensively even with people using canes, crutches, and walkers and works reliably. It offers an affordable way of fall detection. One major concern is that a simulated fall may be significantly different from an actual fall.

H. *WiTrack project*

Since 2013, the WiTrack project is in its prototype stage. It is a 3D monitoring which works even if the person is occluded from the WiTrack device or in a different room. This project originated at Massachusetts Institute of Technology (MIT). The system tracks the 3D motion of a user using the radio signals reflected from his body. WiTrack does not require the user to carry any wireless device, yet its accuracy exceeds current radio frequency (RF) localization systems, which require the user to hold a transceiver [43]. It operates at a fairly low-power, transmitting only 0.75 milliwatts. This signals strength is 100 times lower than the Wi-Fi and even 1000 times lower than the broadcast signal from a GSM phone. WiTrack can determine not only the center of the human body, but also monitors the movement of the limbs and head. The detection accuracy is 96.9%. WiTrack may be part of the user electronics and has wide possibilities of usage, not just a fall detection, but also appliance control or playing games.

IV. CONCLUSION

Although it may seem that, with all technological development nowadays, fall detection must be a simple matter, it is actually not. Currently, this complex problem does not have a standardized solution. Reliable, inexpensive and senior friendly devices for the fall detection are still not available on the market despite the fact that they become essential in order to provide a rapid assistance and to prevent fear of falling among seniors.

Most often, detection methods are based on signals from accelerometers and gyroscopes placed in the various types of equipment and on the video detection. Lately, efforts are being made towards the smart phones use and more free of charge applications are becoming available.

One of the shortcomings of current solutions is loss of privacy, mainly when using video detection but not only. The smart phone fall detection needs to solve the problems associated with limited battery capacity and the need for recharging. Also, the smart phones cannot compete with the complex solutions that sophisticate systems provide.

Helpful would be a public database of accelerometer signals and video signals of fall situations. Since it is not acceptable to subject older people to simulated falls, the data are severely limited. Most reported studies used young volunteers to simulate falls. Unfortunately, even if there was a public database the simulated data might not match those of the real seniors´ daily life situations.

Sharing source codes of the algorithms would also be helpful.

The future fall detection development will probably includes using more sophisticated smart mobile phones because of their decreasing price and increasing hardware potential. In the commerce sphere, the extension of systems like the Senior Inspect with other health functions has huge potential. The combination of systems which are able to monitor the user without using wearable devices inside his home with some suitable device used outside will definitely succeed. The main goal will be to maintain the privacy and security of irrelevant information (the data obtained in the time during which falls do not occur), but simultaneously to monitor and capture sufficient data when it is crucial.

REFERENCES

[1] World Health Organization, “WHO global report on falls prevention in older age”, Geneva, Switzerland, iv, 47 p. ISBN 92-415-6353-2, 2008

[2] S. M. Friedman, B. Munoz, S. K. West, G. S. Rubin, L. P. Fried, "Falls and fear of falling: which comes first? A longitudinal prediction model suggests strategies for primary and secondary prevention," Journal of the American Geriatrics Society, 50(8), pp. 1329-1335, 2002.

[3] S. Brownsell and M. S. Hawley, "Automatic fall detectors and the fear of falling," Journal of telemedicine and telecare 10(5), pp. 262-266, 2004.

[4] F. J. T. Thilo, S. Hahn, S. Bilger, J. M. Schols, R. J. Halfens, "Involvement of older people in the development of fall detection systems: a scoping review," BMC geriatrics 16.1, 2016.

[5] N. Noury, P. Rumeau, A. K. Bourke, G. ÓLaighin, J. E. Lundy, "A proposal for the classification and evaluation of fall detectors," Irbm 29.6, 2008, pp. 340-349.

[6] M. Mubashir, L. Shao, L. Seed, "A survey on fall detection: Principles and approaches," Neurocomputing 100, 2013, pp. 144-152.

[7] "Emergency Dialer," Popular Science, p. 104, October 1975.

[8] C. J. Lord and D. P. Colvin, "Falls in the elderly: Detection and assessment," Engineering in Medicine and Biology Society, 1991. Vol. 13: 1991., Proceedings of the Annual International Conference of the IEEE. IEEE, 1991, pp. 1938-1939.

[9] G. Wu, "Distinguishing fall activities from normal activities by velocity characteristics," Journal of biomechanics 33.11, pp. 1497-1500, 2000.

[10] M. Prado, J. Reina-Tosina, L. Roa. "Distributed intelligent architecture for falling detection and physical activity analysis in the elderly," Engineering in Medicine and Biology, 2002. 24th Annual Conference and the Annual Fall Meeting of the Biomedical Engineering Society EMBS/BMES Conference, 2002, Proceedings of the Second Joint. Vol. 3. IEEE, 2002, pp. 1910-1911.

[11] N. Noury, "A smart sensor for the remote follow up of activity and fall detection of the elderly," Microtechnologies in Medicine & Biology 2nd Annual International IEEE-EMB Special Topic Conference on. IEEE, 2002, pp. 314-317.

[12] T. Degen, H. Jaeckel, M. Rufer, and S. Wyss, "SPEEDY: a fall detector in a wrist watch," Proc. Seventh IEEE International Symposium on Wearable Computing, 2003, pp. 184-187.

[13] M. Kangas, I. Vikman, J. Wiklander, P. Lindgren, L. Nyberg, T. Jämsä, Sensitivity and specificity of fall detection in people aged 40 years and over. Gait & posture, 29(4), pp. 571-574, 2009.

[14] S. Shan and T. Yuan, "A wearable pre-impact fall detector using feature selection and support vector machine," In Signal Processing (ICSP), 2010 IEEE 10th International Conference on, IEEE, October 2010, pp. 1686-1689.

[15] A. K. Bourke et al. "Assessment of waist-worn tri-axial accelerometer based fall-detection algorithms using continuous unsupervised activities," Engineering in Medicine and Biology Society (EMBC), 2010 Annual International Conference of the IEEE. IEEE, 2010, pp. 2782-2785.

[16] C. F. Lai, S. Y. Chang, H. C. Chao, Y. M. Huang, "Detection of cognitive injured body region using multiple triaxial accelerometers for elderly falling," Sensors Journal, IEEE, 11(3), pp. 763-770, 2011.

[17] M. Yuwono, B. D. Moulton, S. W. Su, B. G. Celler, H. T. Nguyen, "Unsupervised machine-learning method for improving the performance of ambulatory fall-detection systems," Biomed Eng Online, 11(9), 2012.

[18] H. Kerdegari, K. Samsudin, A. R. Ramli, S. Mokaram, "Evaluation of fall detection classification approaches," In Intelligent and Advanced Systems (ICIAS), 2012 4th International Conference on (Vol. 1, pp. 131-136). IEEE, June 2012, pp. 131-136.

[19] J. Cheng, X. Chen, M. Shen, "A framework for daily activity monitoring and fall detection based on surface electromyography and accelerometer signals," Biomedical and Health Informatics, IEEE Journal of, 17(1), 2013, pp. 38-45.

[20] A. Sixsmith and N. Johnson. "A smart sensor to detect the falls of the elderly," Pervasive Computing, IEEE 3.2, pp. 42-47, 2004.

[21] J. M. Kang, T. Yoo, H. C. Kim, "A wrist-worn integrated health monitoring instrument with a tele-reporting device for telemedicine and telecare," Instrumentation and Measurement, IEEE Transactions on 55.5, 2006, pp. 1655-1661.

[22] M. N. Nyan, F. E. Tay, A. W. Y. Tan, K. H. W. Seah, "Distinguishing fall activities from normal activities by angular rate characteristics and high-speed camera characterization," Medical engineering & physics 28.8, pp. 842-849, 2006.

[23] S. G. Miaou, P. H. Sung, C. Y. Huang, "A customized human fall detection system using omni-camera images and personal information," Distributed Diagnosis and Home Healthcare, 2006, D2H2, 1st Transdisciplinary Conference on. IEEE, 2006, pp. 39-42.

[24] M. Alwan, P. J. Rajendran, S. Kell, D. Mack, S. Dalal, M. Wolfe, R. Felder, "A smart and passive floor-vibration based fall detector for elderly," Information and Communication Technologies, 2006. ICTTA'06. 2nd. Vol. 1. IEEE, 2006, pp. 1003-1007.

[25] S. Srinivasan, J. Han, D. Lal, A. Gacic, "Towards automatic detection of falls using wireless sensors," Engineering in Medicine and Biology Society, 2007. EMBS 2007. 29th Annual International Conference of the IEEE. IEEE, 2007, pp. 1379-1382.

[26] O. Almeida, M. Zhang, J. C. Liu, "Dynamic fall detection and pace measurement in walking sticks," High Confidence Medical Devices, Software, and Systems and Medical Device Plug-and-Play Interoperability, 2007. HCMDSS-MDPnP. Joint Workshop on. IEEE, 2007, pp. 204-206.

[27] C. Doukas and I. Maglogiannis, "Advanced patient or elder fall detection based on movement and sound data," Pervasive Computing Technologies for Healthcare, 2008. PervasiveHealth 2008. Second International Conference on. IEEE, 2008, pp. 103-107.

[28] [1] A. K. Bourke, P. W. van de Ven, A. E. Chaya, G. M. OLaighin, J. Nelson, "The design and development of a long-term fall detection system incorporated into a custom vest for the elderly," In Conference proceedings:... Annual International Conference of the IEEE Engineering in Medicine and Biology Society. IEEE Engineering in Medicine and Biology Society. Annual Conference, 2007, pp. 2836-2839.

[29] H. W. Tzeng, M. Y. Chen, M. Y. Chen, "Design of fall detection system with floor pressure and infrared image," System Science and Engineering (ICSSE), 2010 International Conference on. IEEE, 2010, pp. 131-135.

[30] F. Bianchi, S. J. Redmond, M. R. Narayanan, S. Cerutti, N. H. Lovell, "Barometric pressure and triaxial accelerometry-based falls event detection," Neural Systems and Rehabilitation Engineering, IEEE Transactions on 18.6, 2010, pp. 619-627.

[31] T. Tamura, T. Yoshimura, M. Sekine, M. Uchida, O. Tanaka, "A wearable airbag to prevent fall injuries, " Information Technology in Biomedicine, IEEE Transactions on 13.6, 2009, pp. 910-914.

[32] Y. Depeursinge, J. Krauss, M. El-Khoury, "Device for monitoring the activity of a person and/or detecting a fall, in particular with a view to providing help in the event of an incident hazardous to life or limb," U.S. Patent No. 6,201,476. 13 Mar. 2001.

[33] J. Dai, X. Bai, Z. Yang, Z. Shen, D. Xuan, "Mobile phone-based pervasive fall detection," Personal and ubiquitous computing 14.7, pp. 633-643, 2010.

[34] S. H. Fang, Y. C. Liang, K. M. Chiu, "Developing a mobile phone-based fall detection system on android platform," Computing, Communications and Applications Conference (ComComAp), 2012. IEEE, 2012, pp. 143-146.

[35] G. A. Koshmak, M. Linden, A. Loutfi, "Evaluation of the android-based fall detection system with physiological data monitoring," Engineering in Medicine and Biology Society (EMBC), 2013 35th Annual International Conference of the IEEE. IEEE, 2013, pp. 1164-1168.

[36] L. J. Kau, C. S. Chen, "A smart phone-based pocket fall accident detection, positioning, and rescue system." Biomedical and Health Informatics, IEEE Journal of 19.1, pp. 44-56, 2015.

[37] Senior Inspect - detail information [Online], Available from: http://www.seniorinspect.cz/cs/podrobne-informace.html, 2015.03.16

[38] FATE PROJECT - Fall Detector for the Elderly [Online], Available from: http://fate.upc.edu/index.php, 2015.03.11

[39] IMSAFE: Individual Mobility Sensor for Automatic Fall Evaluation, Functional Cardiovascular Engineering Laboratory [Online], Available from: http://web.eng.ucsd.edu/~pcabrales/imsafe.html, 2015.03.06

[40] Czech School: Six students on the Intel ISEF [Online], Available from: http://www.ceskaskola.cz/2014/04/sestice-studentu-jede-na-intelisef.html, 2015.03.05

[41] E. E. Stone, M. Skubic, "Fall detection in homes of older adults using the Microsoft Kinect," Biomedical and Health Informatics, IEEE Journal of 19.1, pp. 290-301, 2015.

[42] C. Kawatsu, J. Li, C. J. Chung, "Development of a fall detection system with Microsoft Kinect," Robot Intelligence Technology and Applications 2012. Springer Berlin Heidelberg, pp. 623-630, 2013.

[43] F. Adib, Z. Kabelac, D. Katabi, R. C. Miller, "3d tracking via body radio reflections," 11th USENIX Symposium on Networked Systems Design and Implementation (NSDI 14), 2014, pp. 317-329.

Improvement of CPRNG of the PM-DC-LM Mode and Comparison with its Previous Version

Petr Zacek, Roman Jasek, David Malanik
Faculty of Applied Informatics
Tomas Bata University
Zlin, Czech Republic
e-mail: {zacek, jasek, dmalanik}@fai.utb.cz

***Abstract*—This paper presents the last results from our research focused on proposing the polymorphous mode of operation of block ciphers. The first attempt was based on Chaotic Pseudo-Random Number Generator (CPRNG) using logistic maps and it is called Polymorphous Mode – Deterministic Chaos – Logistic Maps mode (PM-DC-LM). CPRNG controls the polymorphous behavior of this mode. The CPRNG returns two values, *g* and d. Value g represents the last three digits of the number generated by CPRNG and the value *d* represents the last digit. Based on these two values, function F is controlled. In the initially proposed actual version, the CPRNG was limited in generating values ending by digits from one to nine. Thus, this leads to a non-optimal probabilistic distribution of values *g* and *d*. Therefore, an improvement is necessary. This paper shows the principle for improving the CPRNG in the PM-DC-LM mode and how to ensure the whole interval of values for g and d is generated, including numbers ending with zero. The principle is applied on the CPRNG and then it is tested. The differences between the actual and the upgraded version of the PM-DC-LM are described using the probabilistic distribution of generated values *g* and *d*. The entropies for values *g* and *d* of actual and upgraded versions are also calculated. These calculations are based on one million samples of values *g* and *d*.**

Keywords - Deterministic Chaos; Logistic Map; CPRNG; Symmetric Cryptography; Block Cipher; Block Cipher Mode of Operation; PM-DC-LM.

I. Introduction

Our designed Polymorphous Mode (PM) with its subversion PM-DC-LM was described by P. Zacek et al. [6] even though it was not named this way in that publication. This paper concentrates on testing one part of PM-DC-LM, namely CPRNG.

The motivation of our paper is to test the behavior of the used CPRNG built on a deterministic chaos – logistic maps and discuss the possibilities of the CPRNG used.

We discuss the possibilities of how to derive the initialization values for CPRNG from the initialization vector (*IV*). The last part shows the testing of CPRNG on real data. Real data were two random generated *IV* of 256-bit length. The values x_n were calculated for the first one million values x_n. The comparison of the appropriateness of CPRNG is based on entropies calculated from the probabilistic distributions of values *d* and *g*, which are generated by CPRNG.

Section 2 provides a brief description of the PM-DC-LM mode. Section 3 describes the internal logic of the used CPRNG. Section 4 is about the properties and possibilities of the CPRNG. In Section 5, the testing of the CPRNG is provided. The paper ends with a conclusion, in Section 7.

II. Description of PM-DC-LM mode

The acronyms "PM", "DC", and "LM" mean it is "Polymorphous Mode" with using the "Deterministic Chaos", and "Logistic Maps" as the type of deterministic chaos. This name depends on the type of the deterministic chaos and PM is used as the basis. The mode is mostly described in [6], where it was designed for the first time. Because of the polymorphous behavior of this mode, we changed the equation of the calculation for the next key. In contrast to the original, we used one more value named *g*. Value *g* is derived as the last three digits of value x_n from CPRGN.

III. Description of the used CPRNG

The used CPRNG is described in this section. The CPRNG is fully described, and it is the same as in the material. It is based on the deterministic chaos logistic map, which operates in the following equation

$$x_n = rx_{n-1}(1 - x_{n-1}) \qquad (1)$$

where *r* is the control parameter, x_n is the actual value and x_{n-1} is the previously generated value. If value *r* is a real number above 3.57, the system behaves chaotically for most of the values. Based on this fact, we choose real numbers in the interval <3.9, 4.0) to avoid numbers near the values of 3.82842712... In this generator, value *r* is generated from *IV*. Value x_i should be a real number from the interval (0, 1). The first value $x \rightarrow x_0$ is calculated using the following equations, where the first one is for values of $r > 3.9$ and the second is for $r = 3.9$ [2][6].

$$x_0 = 10(r - 3.9) \qquad (2)$$

$$x_0 = 10^{-15} \qquad (3)$$

The value r is calculated from the initialization vector before the encryption. The algorithm how to calculate the value from the initialization vector is also described in [6][7].

IV. Properties of Proposed CPRNG and Possibilities

Because of the polymorphous structure of the proposed mode, the parts could be changed. According to CPRNG, the following features can be changed:

- We can change the type of deterministic chaos.
- We can change the principle how to calculate the values of r and x_0 as their precision.

A. Type of deterministic chaos

As the other parts could be changed, the type of the deterministic chaos could also be changed. Consequently, the way how to derive the initial values for CPRNG must be changed, too.

B. Derivation of values r and x_0

The actual derivation of value r is as follows:, (also described in the material [6])

1. Express *IV* as a binary number.
2. Split the *IV* into the same blocks of the length as precision p.
3. Represent it as numbers 0 and 1.
4. Calculate the sum of numbers 0 and 1 at their corresponding position modulo 10.
5. Concatenate sums as digits after to 3.9.

Ideally, we want to have different CPRNG for all IVs. The above principle is not the best. It leads to collisions. For example, if we have two *IV*s IV_1 = 0110 and IV_2 =1001, the value r is the same -> r = 3.91111. There are two ways to avoid the mentioned collisions.

1. Using a non-collision hash function before converting the *IV* into value r.
2. Representing the *IV* as a decimal number with fixed length (including leading zeros) and then concatenating all digits after value r.

These two possibilities have advantages and disadvantages as well. The first possibility should be secure if the non-collision function is used. It should also be quicker, and problems with the representation of long float numbers will happen less frequently. The second possibility does not lead to collisions at all, but we need to operate with long float numbers. For example, the value r computed from *IV* 256-bit length has 79 digits after the decimal point, so the representation of these numbers could be a problem [6][7].

The derivation of value x_0 could be changed as well.

- We can independently derivate it to value r.
  - Using another different algorithm for derivation of the value r from the same *IV*
  - Using the second *IV* for value x_0

V. Testing of CPRNG

A. Values d and g

We tested the first ten values from two different generators of deterministic chaos based on two randomly generated different *IV*s with length 256 bits, which were different in the last bit.. The precision p (number of digits in the value r after 3.9) of the r was chosen as 14 (maximal in the Python 3.x, which was used for testing). The results are shown below.

IV_1 = 111111…1000
IV_2 = 111111…1001

r_1 from IV_1 = 3.911132271809247
r_2 from IV_2 = 3.911132271809248

x_1 = 0.11132271809247
x_2 = 0.11132271809248

The first ten values generated by generator number one based on values r_1 and x_1:
[0.3869282003850097, 0.9277783349901382, 0.26206814046285243, 0.7563677304170022, 0.720726194443333, 0.787232496718318, 0.6551048496504891, 0.8836909470612287, 0.40199109175011855, 0.9402137244001353]

The first ten values generated by generator number one based on values r_2 and x_2:
[0.38692820038504017, 0.9277783349901654, 0.2620681404627615, 0.756367730416833, 0.7207261944436724, 0.7872324967177322, 0.6551048496518054, 0.8836909470596319, 0.40199109175491127, 0.94021372440381]

The first ten values g returned by generator number one and the corresponding first ten values d (digits highlighted in red color).
[097, 382, 243, 022, 333, 318, 891, 287, 855, 353]
The first ten values g returned by generator number two and the corresponding first ten values d (digits highlighted in red color).
[017, 654, 615, 833, 724, 322, 054, 319, 127, 381]

As can be seen from the results above, the first ten values g from generator number two are 100% different from the first ten values g from generator number one. The value d is different in 90% of the cases. So, although the *IV*s are different by only one bit, the generators behave quite differently.

The ideal probabilistic distribution of values d and g should be indistinguishable from the probabilistic distribution of the random values. For the value of d, the probability should be 1/10 for any number from 0 to 9 which is unreachable, because using the deterministic chaos is always distinguishable from the random distribution. For demonstration, the CPRNG was tested on the first million values of x. The results are represented by the graphs below.

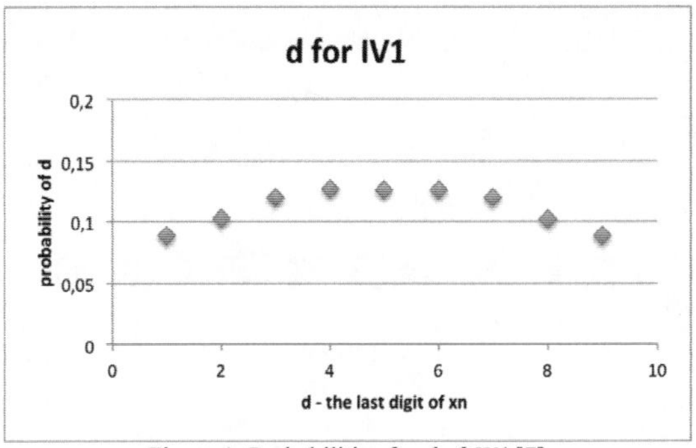

Figure 1. Probabilities for d of *IV1* [7]

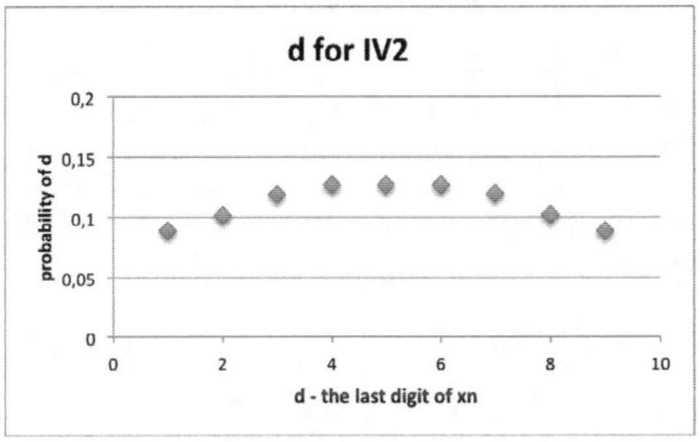

Figure 2. Probabilities for d of *IV2* [7]

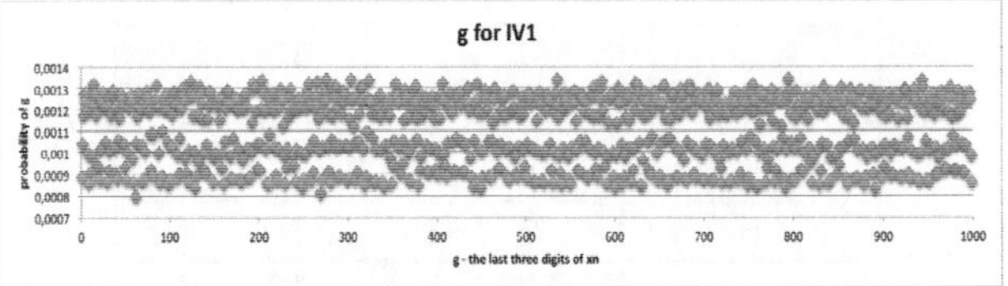

Figure 3. Probabilities for g of *IV1*

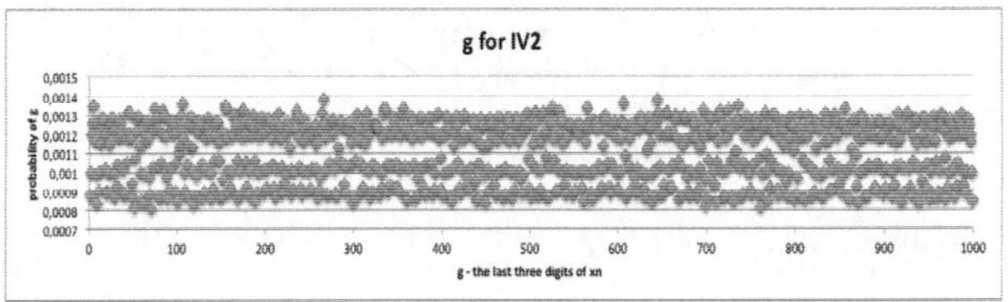

Figure 4. Probabilities for g of *IV2*

Figures 1 and 2 show the deterministic appearance of the probabilistic distribution for the values d generated by CPRNGs while the probabilities look more or less similar for both *IVs*. Figures 3 and 4 show the probabilistic distribution for the values g generated by CPRNGs. Probabilities oscillate around the most suitable value 0.001, concretely from 0.0008 to 0.0014. For more random-looking distribution, another type of pseudo-random number generator should be used or the CPRNG should be improved.

The probabilistic distribution shown in Figures 3 and 4 could be rewritten in more detail in the following Table 1 using values c.

TABLE I. PART OF PROBABILISTIC DISTRIBUTION OF *G* AS OCCURRENCE *C* OF *G* IN *IV1* AND *IV2* (*G* FROM 951 TO 970)

g	c for *IV1*	c for *IV2*	*g*	c for *IV1*	c for *IV2*
951	864	857	961	898	894
952	1008	1002	962	977	1006
953	1199	1177	963	1222	1248
954	1257	1250	964	1230	1307
955	1238	1239	965	1285	1293
956	1274	1294	966	1265	1287
957	1176	1162	967	1190	1216
958	1023	1054	968	1010	1072
959	900	861	969	923	855
960	0	0	970	0	0

Non-randomness of probabilistic distribution can be seen in detail in Table 1, where probabilities for values g from 951 to 970 are represented by numbers c according to the occurrences of g per one million generated values by CPRNG. The number c should be approximately 1000 in the perfect distribution. As can be seen, g values ending by digits different from zero are the only possible outcomes of CPRNG. Thus, the value of g; the last three digits from generated number x = 0.26206814046285240 will be 524 instead of 240. Based on this fact, potential occurrences for values g ending by zero are distributed among the others. Consequently, based on this fact and deterministic behavior of CPRNG it leads to maximums in the distribution. For proper and stable distribution, the CPRNG should be changed accordingly to generate the entire range of g values including numbers ending in zero.

B. Entropy for values g and d

The degree of randomness of CPRNG could be measured by evaluating the entropy for values g and d based on their probabilistic distribution. The entropy for values g was calculated fro (4) and for values d using (5).

$$H(g) = -\sum_{g=000}^{999} p_g . \log(p_g) \qquad (4)$$

$$H(d) = -\sum_{d=0}^{9} p_d . \log(p_d) \qquad (5)$$

The entropy should be maximal. The maximum for the entropy for values g could be calculated from (6) and for values d from (7).

$$H(g)_{max} = -\left(0.001 \cdot \log(0.001) \cdot 1000\right) \cong 6.9077 \qquad (6)$$

$$H(d)_{max} = -\left(0.1 \cdot \log(0.1) \cdot 10\right) \cong 2.3026 \qquad (7)$$

On the other hand, the minimal entropy is 0. When (4) is applied to the probabilistic distribution for values g, obtained from the first one million values x from CPRNG based on the *IV1*, the entropy H is around 6.793. The entropy for values g based on the *IV2* is similar, 6.792.

Similarly, the entropy H for the probabilistic distribution for values d, obtained from CPRNG based on the *IV1*, is 2.1878 and for the *IV2* the entropy is 2.1877.

Based on these results, using the CPRNG may be assigned as sufficient and useful for generating pseudo-random numbers.

VI. POSSIBILITIES AND IMPROVEMENTS

There are many possibilities how to improve CPRNG for the PM-DC-LM or generally for the PM. The first possibility is the counting with values g and d ending in zero. This could be achieved by representing values g as the second, the third, and the fourth digit from the end of values x and similarly the second digit from the end as values d. According to it, the function F in the PM-DC-LM should be changed to count with the different values d. This means, the function F should be able to operate with 10 states instead of 9.

A. *Evaluation of improvement – probabilistic distribution*

In this section, the utilization of the proposed possible improvement is evaluated and shown. The testing of updated CPRNG was done on the same two randomly generated values *IV1* and *IV2* as before. The probabilistic distributions for values d obtained from the improved CPRNG are shown in Figures 5 and 6.

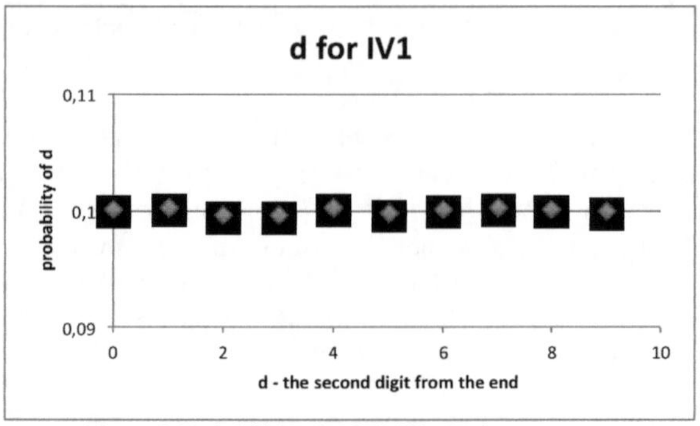

Figure 5. Probabilities for d of *IV1* after improvement

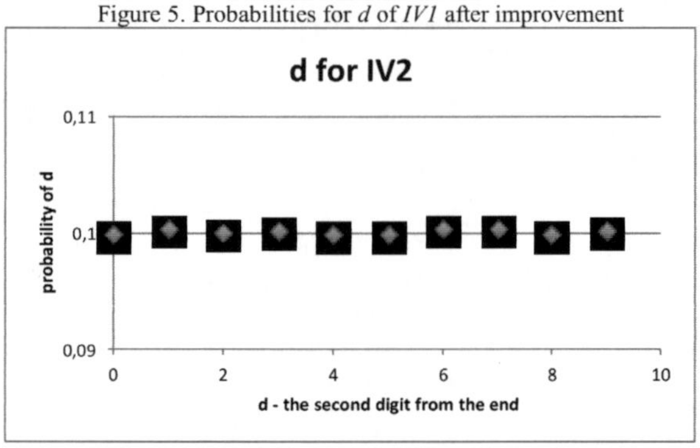

Figure 6. Probabilities for d of IV1 after improvement

As can be seen from Figures 5 and 6, the probabilistic distributions after improvement are closer to the random distribution. The detailed view is shown in Table 2 below as values c, where value c stands for a number of the occurrence of digit d in the first one million generated values x.

TABLE II. OCCURRENCE OF *D* IN *X*

d	*c* for *IV1*	*c* for *IV2*
0	100055	99801
1	100215	100243
2	99688	99908
3	99582	100087
4	100308	99769
5	99731	99842
6	100168	100239
7	100255	100290
8	100049	99738
9	99949	100083

As we can see from Table 2, the occurrence for values c is closer to the ideal. The probabilistic distributions of values g are shown in Figures 7 and 8.

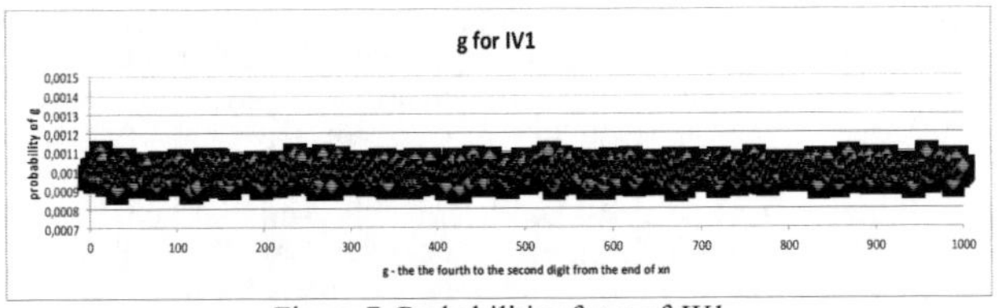

Figure 7. Probabilities for g of *IV1*

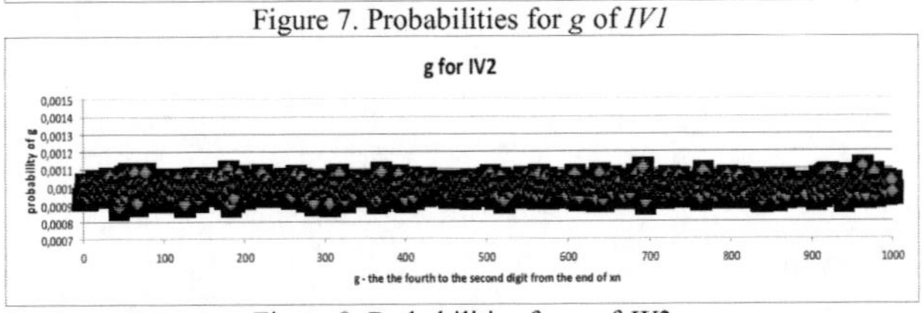

Figure 8. Probabilities for g of *IV2*

As we can see from Figures 5 and 6, the probabilistic distributions are getting closer to the optimal probability 0.001. The oscillation around the ideal value is compressed and optimized.

The probabilistic distribution shown in Figures 3 and 4 could be rewritten more detailed using the values c.

TABLE III. PART OF PROBABILISTIC DISTRIBUTION OF G AS OCCURRENCE C OF G IN *IV1* AND *IV2* (G FROM 951 TO 970)

g	c for IV1	c for IV2	g	c for IV1	c for IV2
951	1026	1027	961	952	1006
952	1029	1034	962	988	1113
953	967	995	963	1025	1024
954	980	1025	964	996	1050
955	1040	1018	965	1014	980
956	988	989	966	1004	1038
957	979	985	967	977	945
958	1091	1017	968	991	992
959	988	950	969	993	993
960	955	1002	970	1023	1017

As we can see in Table 3, after improvement, all values g could be obtained from CPRNG. Thus, the limitation in values ending by zero was removed. In the next section, the calculation of the entropies will be done as the confirmation of the improvement.

B. *Evaluation of improvement – entropy*

The maximal entropies are the same as (6) and (7) show. When (4) is applied to the new values of the probabilistic distribution for values g of the improved CPRNG, the entropies are $H = 6.9072$ for *IV1* and $H = 6.9073$ for *IV2*. Similarly, with using (5), the entropies for values d are $H = 2.3026$ for *IV1* and $H = 2.3026$ for *IV2*.

C. *Comparison after and before improvement*

The CPRNG is compared based on the entropies for values d and g after and before the improvement. The random (pseudo-random) generators should have the entropy close to its maximal value. The entropies for designed CPRNG used in the PM-DC-LM are summarized in Table 4.

TABLE 4. COMPARISON OF ENTROPIES OF CPRNG AFTER AND BEFORE IMPROVEMENT

	H(d)max	H(d)	H(d)improved	H(g)max	H(g)	H(g)improved
for IV1	2.30258509	2.18778925	2.30258215	6.90775527	6.79255874	6.90724147
for IV2	2.30258509	2.18774009	2.30258304	6.90775527	6.79248131	6.90725673

As we can see from Table 4, the entropies of improved CPRNG are closer to their maximal value for both probabilistic distributions for values g and d.

VII. CONCLUSION

In this paper, the CPRNG based on logistic maps used in our mode PM-DC-LM was tested. Some possibilities and ways for upgrading and changing the CPRNG were discussed. One of the possible mentioned ways, namely how to set CPRNG on two random generated *IV*s, was tested. The CPRNG was run one million times, and the probabilistic distribution of values g and d were shown in graphs. Consequently, the entropies for probabilistic distribution were calculated and compared with the maximal value of their corresponding entropies.

The CPRNG is distinguishable from the random distribution, as long as it is deterministic, whereas whole distribution looks sufficient and balanced even so before the improvement. After improvement, the entropies were calculated, and all were compared in Table 4. When the CPRNG was improved, a more random distribution was achieved than before.

For future research, it would be sensible to try to change the type of deterministic chaos or try to change the CPRNG to another general used PRNG. It would also be interesting to change the algorithm determining how the values r and x_n are derived from *IV*. We are planning to do further security analysis of the used CPRNG algorithm using the NIST statistical test suite and NIST randomness tests.

ACKNOWLEDGMENT

This work was supported by the Tomas Bata University Internal Grant Agency, Project No.: IGA/FAI/2015/47; further, it was supported by financial support from the Ministry of Education of the Czech Republic research project NPU I No.: MSMT-7778/2014; as well as by the European Regional Development Fund, CEBIA-Tech Project No.: CZ.1.05/2.1.00/03.0089

REFERENCES

[1] M. S. Bellovin. Columbia University. Modes of Operation Columbia, USA, 2009 [cit. 30.1.2015]. Online at: https://www.cs.columbia.edu/~smb/classes/s09/l05.pdf [accessed June 2016]

[2] E. W. Weisstein. "Logistic Map." From MathWorld--A Wolfram Web Resource. http://mathworld.wolfram.com/LogisticMap.html [accessed June 2016]

[3] Modes Development. In: National Institute of Standards and Technology: Computer Security Resource Center [online]. 2001, http://csrc.nist.gov/groups/ST/toolkit/BCM/modes_development.html [accessed June 2016]

[4] J. C. Sprott, Chaos and Time-Series Analysis, Oxford University Press, 2003

[5] R. Senkerik, M. Pluhacek, I. Zelinka, D. Davendra, and Z. Oplatkova, "A brief survey on the chaotic systems as the pseudo random number generators",, in Interdisciplinary Symposium on Complex Systems, vol 14. Emergence, Complexity and Computation (ISCS 2014),, Springer International Publishing, 2015, pp. 205-214, doi:10.1007/978-3-319-10759-2_22

[6] P. Zacek, R. Jasek, and D. Malanik, "Using the Deterministic Chaos in Variable Mode of Operation of Block Ciphers", in Artificial Intelligence Perspectives and Applications, R. Silhavy, et al., Editors. 2015, Springer International Publishing. p. 347-354, DOI: 10.1007/978-3-319-18476-0_34

[7] P. Zacek, R. Jasek, and D. Malanik, "Possibilities and Testing of CPRNG in Block Cipher Mode of Operation PM-DC-LM", ICNAAM 2015 - 13th International Conference of Numerical Analysis and Applied Mathematics, in press.

Severity Assessment of Security Incidents

Lukas Kralik, Petr Stipek, Roman Senkerik, Roman Jasek
Department of Artificial Intelligence and Informatics
Faculty of Applied Informatics, Tomas Bata University in Zlin
Zlin, Czech Republic
{kralik, stipek, senkerik, jasek}@fai.utb.cz

Abstract—**This paper demonstrates the possible utilization of multi-criteria decision making methods as a different approach to a severity assessment of security incidents. This may support incident management and help with faster decisions. The demonstrated example is based on the Fuller's method. This method helps with determination of criteria weights that are utilized for an overall evaluation and prioritization of security incidents. The main objective was to propose a very simple and fast method that will be suitable for small and medium companies.**

Keywords-severity assessment; security; incident; incident management; security management, multi-criterial decision making; MCDM.

I. INTRODUCTION

An issue of security incidents and their resolving is inseparably connected with the field of Information and Communication Technologies (ICT). It is necessary to look for more and more effective ways to prevent security incidents due to the increasing heterogeneity, complexity and pressure of confidentiality, integrity, availability or non-repudiation. Each security incident is bound with time pressure, which requires automated and clearly defined steps. One of these steps is a severity assessment of a security incident. It is absolutely necessary since it strongly affects the whole investigation process of the occurred incident.

This paper demonstrates the possibilities of utilization of Multi-Criteria Decision Making methods (MCDM) to assess the severity of the security incidents. This may serve as a basis for the new approach to severity assessment of security incidents.

The main objective of current research is to use the simplest MCDM methods to assess the severity. The process described in Section IV of this paper only demonstrates possible utilizations of MCDM. Values for criteria weights may vary for each company. Also, it is important to mention that this method is intended as a support for already implemented incident management tools and for small and medium companies.

The paper is divided into three parts. The first part is focused on basic terms and necessary theory which introduce readers into issues of security incidents. The following part describes solutions for security incidents and used methods with multi-criteria evaluation. And the final part is about the severity assessment of security incidents. This may help security managers in companies with prioritization of security incidents and their solution.

A. *Security incident – basic terms*

A security incident is an event in the information system, which causes disruption of confidentiality, integrity, availability or non-repudiation of information due to the failure of security measures or violation of security policy [1]-[5].

A suspected violation of a security policy or an attempt to overcome security measures is very often regarded as a security incident. A security incident usually has the following course: Incident Detection - Analysis of the Incident - Response to the Incident. Detection may be either automatic, based on the information from some monitoring system, or manual, i.e., the incident is reported by someone. The company, which wants to deal with the security incidents and effectively solve them, should have an appropriate security standard and also it must properly present such standard to employees. The next step is the formation of a team, which will be responsible for receiving reports, evidence and solving of incidents, etc. In many cases, this team is called Information Security Incident Response Team (ISIRT). The number of ISIRT members depends on the total number and frequency of security incidents and, of course, on the size of the company. For a proper function, ISIRT must have an adequate equipment, means and mainly authority [5]-[13].

The question is than as to how to determine the severity of the incident. There are many possible ways and approaches. The severity of the incident can be determined based on the value of an impact. In other words, the incident has a financial or a non-financial impact to the company. Another solution is to determine the severity of the incident according to the number and expertise of people who have to deal with the incident (more details are given in Section III). It can be assumed that a different number of people or teams with diverse levels of knowledge will participate in finding solution of various incidents [7]-[9][11]-[13].

1) *Security standard*

Each security standard must contain three basic elements. The first one is a definition of the security incident. The security incident must be clearly and understandably described with appropriate examples. These examples should be placed in the attachment.

The next part of the security standard is information about security incident report. Contact should involve address on the intranet, e-mail, phone and the office or workplace address. It is necessary to take into the account that the network infrastructure may not work.

And the last one is a structure of a security incident report - form for reporting incidents [5][9][12][13].

2) Security incident log

Creation of the security incident log is necessary for successful resolving of the particular incident. Information listed in this log includes:

- When the incident has occurred - due to the fact that the incident may be related to other events; it is always advisable to ascertain the exact time.
- Where the incident has occurred - the exact place and its description will enable the investigative team to respond quickly.
- Who committed the incident - the identity of the intruder can sometimes be difficult to identify, but we should try to get about him as much relevant information as possible.
- How the incident has occurred - sometimes we do not have enough information, but we should try to build a probable scenario describing the incident.
- What was the target of an attack - we should also distinguish whether the system was directly attacked or used to preparation for another attack.
- Which security attribute was compromised - integrity, confidentiality, availability and/or non-repudiation.
- What was the nature of the incident – if the incident was intentional or unintentional and if unintentional, thus if there was negligence or lack of knowledge of security policy.
- What measures have been overcome - whether the measures at the physical, logical, organizational, personnel or technical security.
- What asset has impaired - hardware, software (operating system, applications, and databases), network, data, etc.
- What is the probability that the incident will be repeated again - rather low, medium, high or certain [5][9][12][13].

3) Equipment of ISIRT

The team should have developed procedures for dealing with specific types of incidents, and these procedures should be still updated with new types of incidents occurring. Also, they should have prepared a communication plan to make it clear who has to inform whom, or who decides on further action etc.

A basic equipment of this team is a common room (war room), where it will be possible to meet and agree on the next steps in the event of an incident [12][13].

Last but not least, they need access to adequate software and hardware resources - for example, the team will need to make a copy of configuration, logs or possibly an entire partition of the infected system [12][13].

B. Simplified procedure for investigation of an incident

The whole procedure has 7 steps. The biggest problem in practice is in step 3. A top management usually requires immediate recovery of operations, thus there may be no time for ensuring clues and finding causes. However, ignoring this step makes environment/conditions for another step, namely step 6, more difficult. Appropriate measures should be proposed to prevent the recurrence of the incident. Choosing a suitable measure is so difficult, thus the company has no other option than hope that the incident will not occur again [3]. The 7 steps of the procedure are:

1. Identify where a security incident has occurred;
2. As quickly as possible, prevent further damage;
3. Analyze the cause of the security incident and collect clues for further analysis;
4. Remove the cause and restore functionality;
5. Assess damage;
6. Design and implement appropriate measures to prevent a recurrence of this incident;
7. Inform others (employees, top management...) on the results of the investigation [2][6][7].

II. LIFE CYCLE OF SOLUTION OF INCIDENT

To propose a solution of security incidents, we used modified Deming's Plan – Do – Check – Act (PDCA) cycle, which is demonstrated on Figure 1. The life cycle of solution of incidents (security) is composed of 4 parts:

1. Formulation and planning of security incident management;
2. Deployment and operation of security incident management;
3. Evaluation of the incident,
4. Development of security incident management and its improvement [12].

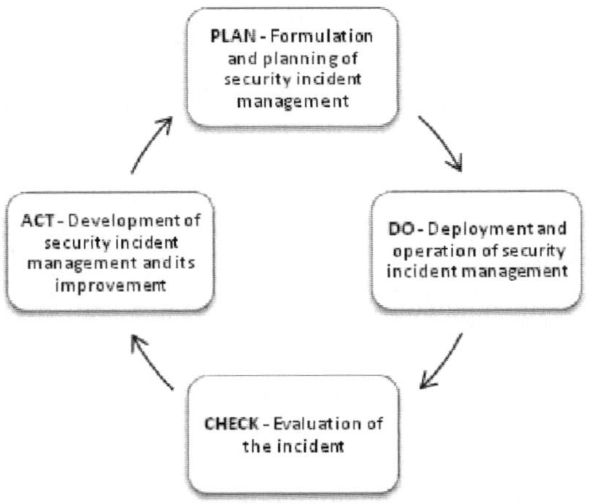

Figure 1. Modified PDCA cycle (adapted from [12])

A. *Formulation and Planning of Security Incident Management*

Incident Management System, which is based on the organization's security policy, is designed in this phase of the cycle. The main activities in this phase of the life cycle are:

- Preparation and publication policy management of security incidents, including the allocation of the relevant competences and responsibilities.
- Description of the process for reporting security incidents.
- The definition of documents and documentation requirements for employees who are involved in a security incident.
- Verification of the validity of current security documents and documentation management process due to security incidents.
- Building of a team to deal with security incidents, including the determination of competences and obligations within the team and specifying of contact connection.
- Design of crisis scenarios and processes in the event of a crisis state of the organization due to a security incident.
- Plan of staff training in the issue of security incidents and their solving.
- Plans, procedures and methods for testing the process of solving security incidents [8].

B. *Deployment and Operation of Security Incident Management*

It represents the actual deployment of the entire process into practical use in the company. The following groups of activities are carried out in this phase of the life cycle:

- Event detection;
- Identification, determination, preparation of solutions;
- Solving of security incident.

1) Event detection

This is a key moment for the successful solving of the security incident. The reason is very simple. In this phase, the user of information system encounters the security event. But it is very important that the user is able to recognize and classify the event. Is this event a security incident or not? This is a question which the user must answer. So, it is crucial to spread awareness about the security between users of information system and other employees. The security system will be effective only if employees are able to detect and recognize the incident in time.

Sufficient primary information is another important point for the future solving of the security incident. That is the reason why the essential part of solution is an administrative nature – filling forms, building reports, etc. The basic document is the form for the security event report.

2) Identification, determination and preparation of solutions

The decision is the following step for solving a security incident –is it a security incident which has to be solved by the incident team? This decision is in competence of the security team. The main objectives of the employees to support the security team are:

- Find out as much information as possible about the security event.
- Make primary identification and classification of the incident.
- Make documentation about the information found.
- Inform the security team and, eventually, the incident team [12].

Primary identification of the incident is a significant activity. Important actions during this activity are related to determination and ensuring of:

- Cause of security incident
- Place where security incident occurred
- Way how security incident occurred
- Scope of affected assets [12].

3) Solving of security incident

The incident team should verify and analyze all obtained information very fast and decide if they can solve the incident by internal resources or if they will need help from an external expert. It is essential to make detailed documentation of the whole process of solving of the security incident. This documentation might be used for future solution of identical or similar security incidents [12].

C. *Evaluation of the incident*

Evaluating the security incident switches security management from the passive role to the active role, respectively, proactive. The solving of the incident dispels the current complications of the company. Subsequent analysis of the incident should bring benefits to the company to overcome complications. This means lessons from the causes of the incident and subsequently updates of a security risk analysis. On the basis of this fact, risks are revised. The content of the evaluation phase is:

- A more detailed analysis of the incident and its conclusions;
- Updating data about solutions of security incidents;
- Lessons from the incident for the needs to increase security awareness within the company;
- Impact of the incident on the process and content management of security incidents [12].

At the periodical evaluation of security in the company, conclusions resulting from security incidents are used for development and improvement of the security management system [11][12].

D. Development of security incident management and its improvement

In this phase, the experiences gained in dealing with security incidents are included into the security management system of the entire organization. The main aim of this phase is to generalize obtained knowledge from the security incident. The prime activities are:

- Generalize conclusions from the security incident towards risk analysis, its implementation and management.
- Generalize impacts of the incident on Security Management - update the security documentation, etc.
- Identify and implement any changes to the Security Management System [12].

This last phase represents the final feedback, when the experience, skills and knowledge gained during the solving of the security incident reflects into the strategic level of Security Management and Security Policy of the company.

III. Assessment of Severity of Incident

It is very often a problem to correctly determine the severity of the incident. In addition, the severity may vary throughout the life cycle of the incident. For example, at the beginning of the investigation of the incident, it may seem that this is a security incident with a negligible impact on the company and later, during the investigation, it may prove that the original assumption was wrong [11]-[13].

If companies already have established the process that could be used with some exaggeration as an incident management and the severity of each incident is determined in this process, then their approach is very different [12] [13]. It is understandable that different companies use various number of degrees to reflect the severity of the incident and also individual levels have other names [7][11]. However, it is striking that for determining the degree of severity, the companies do not have defined clear rules [13].

If a company conducted a risk analysis, then it can be relatively easy to determine the severity of the incident based on the value of the asset which confidentiality, integrity or availability has been or may be compromised [11][12]. The proposal of criteria for determining the severity of the incident follows:

The severity should be defined by 4 levels:

- low (1 point)
- middle (2 points)
- high (3 points)
- critical (4 points)

Depending on the amount of affected users:

- one or few users (1)
- whole department (2)
- whole branch (3)
- whole company (4)

According to the level that will deal with the incident:

- technical (IT) support (1)
- lower management (2)
- middle management (3)
- top management (4)

Who should be familiar with the incident:

- one or a few employees of the company (1)
- all employees (2)
- own employees and persons outside the company (3)
- own employees and the public(4)

By level of expertise:

- first level of support (1)
- system administrator (2)
- security expert (3)
- security company (4)[13]

There are a lot of security standards and guidelines which define more criteria (e.g. Computer Security Incident Handling Guide from National Institute of Standards and Technology) [1]. With respect to the size and scope of company, these four levels for assessment of the severity of the incident should be enough for most small companies. As it is shown in the following table (Table I.), it is the most selected criteria (selected by more than half of participants) in a survey with around 50 participants.

TABLE I. CRITERIA FOR SEVERITY ASSESMENT

Criterion	Respondents
Depending on the amount of affected users	*41*
According to a level that will deal with the incident	*36*
Who should be familiar with the incident	*30*
By level of expertise	*34*
By value of affected asset	22
Probability of occurrence	8
Affecting of system functionality	11
Time from occurrence to response	15
Incident priority	11
Availability of known solution	5
Probability of recurrence	7

There are many appropriate methods based on MCDM. These methods should be divided into basic (the most simple), advanced and comprehensive (the most difficult). In this case, Fuller's method is recommended because it is very simple and also each company may customize assessment of severity of security incident according to their needs.

A. *Fuller's method*

This is also known as a method of the Fuller's triangle or mainly the pairwise comparison. This method exists in many modifications and it is determined for finding of preferential relations between a pair of criteria. In the simplest modification of this method, the number of preferences is found out with the respect to all other criteria [14][15][17]. This should be done according to Table III. If criterion in a row is more important than a criterion in a column, then number 1 is typed into the cell, otherwise use 0. In agreement with the number of preferences, normalized weights are determined by the following equation [16]

$$v_i = \frac{f_i}{m(m-1)/2} \tag{1}$$

f_i .... number of preferences of i-th criterion
m .... number of criteria
$m(m-1)/2$ .... number of comparisons

The disadvantage is the fact that, when some criterion has 0 preferences, than its weight will be 0. That is a problem because this criterion is not insignificant [15][16].

Also, there is a modification that respects indifference (same significant criteria). In this case, the cell is filled by the number 0.5 [14][17].

B. *Determining of criteria weights*

As mentioned, this assessment is based on the simply pairwise comparison. Also there are 4 criteria which are compared (Table I.):

1. Depending on the amount of affected users;
2. According to a level that will deal with the incident;
3. Who should be familiar with the incident;
4. By level of expertise.

TABLE II. PAIRWISE COMPARISON

Pair of criteria	Preference		
	first	same	second
1 – 2	4	10	5
1 – 3	1	3	15
1 – 4	5	9	5
2 – 3	4	4	11
2 – 4	6	7	6
3 – 4	2	12	5

Comparison was made on the base of interviews with security managers from security agencies and industry companies (Table II.). Following comparison (Table III.) is a median of selected preferences by participants. Nevertheless, it is important to realize that these values may vary. Every company may have a different opinion on the importance of an individual criterion and simultaneously, they should prefer totally different criteria.

TABLE III. PAIRWISE COMPARISON

	1	2	3	4
1	X	0,5	0	0,5
2	0,5	X	0	0,5
3	1	1	X	0,5
4	0,5	0,5	0,5	X

With the utilization of equation 1, final criteria weights are listed in Table IV. These weights will be used for an overall evaluation and severity assessment according to equation 2.

TABLE IV. CRITERIA WEIGHTS

Criterion	Weight [-]
Depending on the amount of affected users	0.167
According to a level that will deal with the incident	0.167
Who should be familiar with the incident	0.417
By level of expertise	0.250

C. *Severity assessment*

Every criterion has a scale with 4 values corresponding to the severity level for each criterion. The overall severity is normalized and expressed as a dimensionless number:

$$S = \sum_{i=1}^{n} C_i \cdot W_i \tag{2}$$

S .... Severity
C_i .... Value of the i-th criterion
W_i .... Weight of the i-th criterion

In practice, most incidents are not so important or dangerous for system stability [6][8][10]. This may cause difficult prioritization of individual incidents. Simple and small modifications in proposed process should make this prioritization better. The mentioned modification is in scale for each criterion and also companies may propose their own criteria with utilization of this proposed assessment.

The main benefit of the proposed procedure is in speed and simplicity. These two factors are the most important for small companies. Also, this procedure may extend existing incident management in medium companies and provide faster decision making.

IV. Conclusion and Future Work

Security incidents and their solutions are an essential part of life of IS/ICT managers, as well as of ordinary users. Absolute security of an information system is not guaranteed by implementation of any security policy. Although the implementation of various security functions and measures are part of ensuring security, vulnerabilities remain in the information system and these vulnerabilities represent risks. The existence of these vulnerabilities is the possibility of the security incident with direct or indirect impact on everyday operations of companies. Therefore, it is essential that each company pay attention to the definition and the implementation of security management system, its control and audit. At the same time, companies should also deal with efficient and professional management of security incidents. Incidents can be controlled intuitively or in a structured way - professionally. Only a professional approach allows gaining benefits from security incidents - experience, skills and knowledge from solutions of previous security incidents.

The next step in this research is extending the set of criteria which will focus on different aspects (financial and technical/technological impact). The method for the determining of criteria weights will be change for more comprehensive and sophisticated based on intelligent systems (probably fuzzy approach). The main goal for future work and research is a development of continual severity assessment procedure. The final work will be compared with existing assessment methods and also it will be tested in practice.

Acknowledgment

This work was supported by the Ministry of Education, Youth and Sports of the Czech Republic within the National Sustainability Programme project No. LO1303 (MSMT-7778/2014) and also by the European Regional Development Fund under the project CEBIA-Tech No. CZ.1.05/2.1.00/03.0089 and also by the Internal Grant Agency of Tomas Bata University under the project No. IGA/CebiaTech/2016/006.

References

[1] NIST, "Special Publication 800-61 – Computer Security Incident Handling Guide, Revision 2: 800-861", 2012.

[2] International Organization for Standardization ISO/IEC 27000-Information technology-Security techniques-Information security management systems-Overview and vocabulary.

[3] International Organization for Standardization ISO/IEC TR 18044:2004- Information technology - Security techniques - Information security incident management.

[4] International Organization for Standardization ISO/IEC 27001 - Technology-Security Techniques - Information Security Management Systems-Requirements.

[5] Czech. Act nr. 181/2014 sb. Cyber Security Act. 2014.

[6] P. Doucek "IS/ICT Security Incidents and theire Solutions," System Integration vol. 3, Prague 2005, pp. 77-85.

[7] L. Wan-Soo and J. Sang-Soo, "A Study on Information Management Model for Small and Medium Enterprises," Recent Advances in E-Activities, Information Security and Privacy, Spain, WSEAS Press, 2009, pp. 84-87 ISSN: 1790-5117. ISBN: 978-960-474-143-4.

[8] K. Prislan and I. Bernik, "Risk Management with ISO 27000 Standards in Information Security," In Advances in E-Activities, Information Security and Privacy, Venezuela WSEAS Press 2010, pp. 58-63 ISBN: 978-960-474-258-5.

[9] L. Kralik and R. Senkerik, "Proposal for Security Management System," Recent Advances in Electrical Engineering and Educational Technologies. Proceedings of the 2nd International Conference on Systems, Control and Informatics (SCI 2014), Athens, 2014. p. 77-80. ISBN 978-1-61804-254-5.

[10] S. Fenz and A. Ekelhart, "Formalizing Information Security Knowledge," 4th International Symposium on Information, Computer, and Communications Security, ACM, 2009, pp. 183-194, 10.1145/1533057.1533084.

[11] L. Kralik, R. Senkerik, and R. Jasek, "Different Aproaches to Security Incidents and Proposal of Severity Assessment of Security Incident," The Ninth International Conference on Emerging Security Information, Systems and Technologies (SECURWARE 2015), IARIA, Aug. 2015, pp. 185-189, ISBN: 978-1-61208-427-5.

[12] L. Kralik, R. Senkerik, and R. Jasek, "Model for comprehensive approach to security management," International Journal of System Assurance Engineering and Management, vol. 7, pp. 129-137, Jun. 2016, doi: 10.1007/s13198-016-0420-8.

[13] L. Kralik, R. Senkerik and R. Jasek, "Integrated security system management and incident management from the perspective of organizational structure," International Conference on Logistics, Informatics and Service Sciences (LISS 2015), IEEE, Jul. 2015, pp. 1-6, doi: 10.1109/LISS.2015.7369766.

[14] M. Cerny and D. Gluckaufova. "Multicriterial evaluation in practice", Statni nakladatelstvi technicke literatury, 1982.

[15] J. Fotr and L. Svecova, "Managerial decisions: processes, methods and tools," Ekopress, 2010. ISBN 978-80-86929-59-0.

[16] J. Krupka, M. Kasparova, and R. Machova, "Decision Processes," University of Pardubice, 2012, ISBN 978-80-7395-478-9.

[17] W. Ho, X. Xu, and P. K. Dey, "Multi-criteria decision making approaches for supplier evaluation and selection: A literature review," European Journal of Operational Research, Elsevier, 2010, pp. 16-24, ISSN: 0377-2217.

Methodology of Future Security Studies

The Proposal of New Prognostic Method for the Creation of Security Forecasts

Jan Valouch, Hana Urbančoková
The Faculty of Applied Informatics
Tomas Bata University in Zlin
Zlin, Czech Republic
e-mail: valouch@fai.utb.cz, e-mail: urbancokova@fai.utb.cz

Abstract – **The security futurology is the science of the future, which deals with the theory, study and creation of variants of possible developments in the security situation. When creating reliable forecasts, it is necessary to use the scientific methods. Futurologists use a wide range of qualitative and quantitative forecasting methods. This article describes the basic assumptions of the proposal of a new universal prognostic method. An important aspect of the proposal is the efficiency, reliability, speed and the verifiability of method of forecasting of the security situation. An universal prognostic method for the creation of security forecasts does not currently exist.**

Keywords-security futurology; forecasting methodology; security forecast; security situation; futurologists.

I. INTRODUCTION

Futurology (also called futures studies) is an interdisciplinary science which aims to create forecasts in the form of visions and scenarios of possible developments. These forecasts are based on the application of rational and scientific findings and methods. Security is a subject of theoretical research, as a specialized part of social sciences. A part of future studies is a security futurology, which deals with the future and development of the security situation in social groups, objects, sectors, companies, regions, states, the universe, etc. Security futurology field includes:

- Military security,
- Economic security,
- Political security,
- Societal security
- Cultural security,
- Environmental security [1].

Besides the above mentioned sectors of security, many specific types of security exist, e.g., cyber security, data security, network security, energy security, food security, public security, human security, communications security, etc. [1].

Future studies are also classified according to the approach to the creation of a forecast into the following two groups:

- Explorative futurology (the aim is to search for answers to the question "What happens if....?"),
- Normative futurology ("What must be done for something to happen ....?").

Many predictions (technology, military, information technology (IT) security, etc.) were mistaken. For example: "I think there is a world market for maybe five computers," (T. Watson, CEO of IBM, 1943), "Cellular phones will absolutely not replace local wire systems," (M. Cooper, inventor, 1981), "I predict the Internet in 1996 [will] catastrophically collapse," (R. Metcalfe, 3Com, 1995), etc.

In the case of forecasting security situations, reliable and verifiable forecasts must be processed that help especially in the decision-making. Forecasts can be verified in several ways (application of multiple methods, expert correction, etc.). Other benefits of futurology studies include:

- Warning of the impacts of adverse developments,
- Support in seeking optimal solutions to the problems of society,
- Forecasting of future states,
- Support the preparation for the negative impacts
- Search for new ideas and of long term targets,
- Learning, extension of knowledge of stakeholders,
- Adaptation, increasing the ability to adapt.

Prognostic methods should permit the processing of forecasts in accordance with the fundamental principles of prognostication (complexity, systematicness, verifiability, determination, continuity, coordination, fortuitousness, efficiency, focus on practice, dynamism, quantification, method, etc.) [2].

Futurologists use a lot of scientific methods for predicting the future, but there is no universal method that can be used in forecasting of the security situation [5]. The procedure for designing new methods should include:

- Analysis of the subject of security futurology,
- Comparison of forecasting methods,
- Reliability analysis of forecasts of security development,
- The relationship between attacks (threats) and the technology and tools,
- A proposal of the optimal process of security forecasts formation
- A proposal methods and tools,
- Availability of techniques and tools, processing large volumes of data.

Section 2 describes the basics of forecasting methodology. A summary of forecasting methods is presented in Section 3. All specific methods will be explained in greater detail in future works.

There is no universal method that can be used in forecasting of the security situation. The main objective of this proposal is fast and reliable forecasting method. This method should be based on the specifications of the individual sectors of security.

II. METHODOLOGY OF FORECASTING

Future studies in their current form mainly include forecasting, planning, programming, future studies, future research, technological and social forecasting (foresighting), creation of alternative scenarios, the construction of indicators of future development etc.[5]

The prognosis is a key outcome of the process of forecasting. The prognosis is a statement about the future of the object or condition that is based on scientific facts. The prognosis does not indicate what will happen, but what could happen [6].

The forecasts should be based on the analysis of regularities of social and economic development, identification and evaluation of social needs and interests, identification and evaluation of economic and security goals and development priorities.

Basic phases of forecasting include:

- Identifying and defining the problem of prognosis,
- Preparation of process of developing forecasts
- Obtaining information,
- Sorting of information,
- Analysis of information
- Select suitable methods for creating forecasts,
- Implementation of selected methods,
- Elaboration forecasts,
- Stylization of forecasts,
- Verification of forecasts [5].

III. FORECASTING METHODS

Futurologists use a lot of scientific methods for forecasting the future. Application of an appropriate method is dependent on many factors, such as fields, type, range and target of forecast, time horizon, available data, knowledge and experience, etc. During the processing of a forecast, a combination of several forecasting methods is usually used. A basic classification of forecasting methods includes:

- qualitative methods
- quantitative methods [3].

Qualitative methods are based on knowledge, experience and opinion of experts. These methods are also referred to as subjective, reflection or intuitive. These methods are used in situations where there is not enough data from the past. The advantage of quantitative methods is the use of a relatively large amount of expert information. Conversely, the disadvantages are unsystematic evaluation of acquired information and also bias of experts. These methods are more suitable for long-term prognosis [4].

Quantitative methods (also referred to as objective methods, statistical methods) are based on application of statistical analysis of historical data [10]. These methods use mathematical models and equations for determining of time horizons in the future. These methods assume that the identified trends and their measurable indicators will continue well into the future [7]. The main advantage of the application of quantitative methods is an objective and accurate verification of predictions. These methods are suitable for the formation of short- and medium-term forecasts [2].

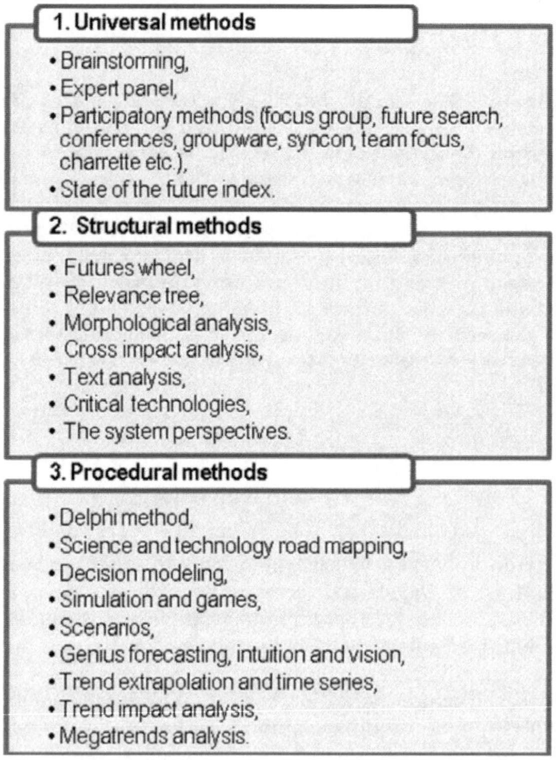

Figure 1. Classification of forecasting methods

In contrast to the aforementioned classification of forecasting methods in accordance with the degree of subjectivity, the same group of methods can be classified also according to the application within the prognostic activities:

- Universal method
- Structured methods,
- Procedural methods [3][4].

Universal methods are widely used and are suitable for processing of most types of forecasts within different time periods and different sectors. Structural methods are applicable in identifying and exploring the object of interest and its structure. Procedural methods are used primarily for processing of chronological sequence analysis of monitored indicators in different periods of time. Procedural methods are particularly suitable for creating of development trends of monitored objects to the future [7][11].

Figure 1 shows the list and classification of forecasting methods. A more detailed explanation of the methods can be found in [4].

IV. APPLICATION OF METHODOLOGY

The new method (universal quantitative and qualitative method, which is based on the specifications of individual sectors of security) can be applied for example in military security. Military security includes, for example, the following predictions:

- Military conflicts,
- Arms spending,
- Development of missile technology,
- Development in military structures, organizations,
- Development of the number of persons in the armed forces, and determining the roles of the armed forces,
- The cooperation of the armed forces and their participation in the Alliance,
- Methods of warfare,
- Content of military doctrinal documents,
- Military art, strategy, operational art, tactics,
- Military education,
- Development of science and research in the military,
- Method of preparing troops,
- Military capabilities,
- The possibility of the defense industry, etc.

The new approach is especially well suited for predicting military security [8][9].

V. CONCLUSION AND FUTURE WORK

Futurologists use a lot of scientific methods for forecasting the future. The field of security futurology uses universal, structural and procedural methods. There is no universal method that can be used in forecasting of the security situation. The new method should be based on the specifications of the individual sectors of security (military, political, societal, economic and environmental security). The method should combine and optimize the qualitative and quantitative methods. Scenario methods are very useful for predicting the security situation. An important requirement is the rapid collection of expert and statistical data and processing them using computer technology.

REFERENCES

[1] J. Eichler, International security in the early 21st century. Prague: DoD CR, AVIS, 2006, 304 p. ISBN 80-7278-362-2. In Czech.

[2] J. Valouch, "Forecasting methodology", in Security Technologies, Systems and Management , vol 5, Czech Republic Zlín: VeRBuM, 2015, pp. 34-50. ISBN 978-80-87500-67-5. In Czech.

[3] M. Potůček (ed.), Manual of forecasting methods. Prague: Sociological publishing company (SLON). 2006, 196 p. ISBN 80-86429-55-5. In Czech.

[4] N. Slocun, Participatory Methods Toolkit. A Practitioners Manual. Brusels: King Baudouin Foundation, 2003, 167 p. ISBN 90-5130-447-1.

[5] F. Petrášek, Futurology study. Prague: Oeconomica. 2009, 274 p. ISBN 978-80-245-1517-5. In Czcech.

[6] M. Zeman, Cautionary forecasting. Prague: Horizont. 1998, 200 p. ISBN 80-7012-095-9. In Czcech.

[7] L. Buřita, "Prognostic methods and their applications in the defense sector", in: Defence and Strategy. vol 1, Czech Republic, Brno, 2015, pp. 47-60.

[8] J. Valouch, "Basics of security futurology", in Security Technologies, Systems and Management , vol 5, Czech Republic Zlín: VeRBuM, 2015, pp. 17-33. ISBN 978-80-87500-67-5. In Czech.

[9] O. Vejmelka, Military explanatory dictionary of selected operational concepts. Prague: DoD Czech Republic, 2004. 359 p.

[10] World futures studies federation. [online]. c. 2016. Available from: http://www.wfsf.org/. [retrieved: May, 2016]

[11] S. Hendrych, The Treatise on futurology. [online]. c. 2015. Available from: www.hendrychst.cz /. [retrieved: June, 2016]

Measurement of Electromagnetic Interference of Electronic Devices

Hana Urbancokova, Jan Valouch, Stanislav Kovar, Milan Adamek
Tomas Bata University in Zlin
Faculty of Applied Informatics
Zlin, Czech Republic
e-mail: {urbancokova, valouch, skovar, adamek}@fai.utb.cz

Abstract — **Measuring levels of electromagnetic interference, which are emitted by electronic devices, must be carried out in specialized laboratories that are equipped with an anechoic or semi-anechoic chamber. Electromagnetic interference of electronic devices is measured in these chambers at a distance of several meters; therefore, this interference is included in the far-field of electronic devices. Another possibility of measuring of electromagnetic interference is the measurement in a Gigahertz Transversal Electromagnetic (GTEM) cell. Unlike the chambers, the GTEM cells measure electromagnetic interference in the near-field of devices. Since the chambers are often fully booked, manufacturers of electronic devices can not test products in every phase of their development. The measurement of electromagnetic interference of electronic devices in the GTEM cell might be a possible alternative measure for manufacturers.**

Keywords- Electromagnetic compatibility; Electromagnetic interference; Intrusion and hold-up alarm systems; Electronic device; Level of interference signals.

I. INTRODUCTION

Nowadays, the level of electromagnetic interference (EMI), which is normally found in our surroundings, can be a serious problem for the operation of electronic devices. The level of EMI is sometimes so high that it can cause malfunction or damage, and even the destruction of electronic devices. Because every electronic equipment, system or device is not only a receiver of electromagnetic interference, but it is also the source of interference, the problem with EMI is growing [1].

We face the question of problems of electromagnetic interference from the very development of electronic devices. One of the aims of the manufacturers is to bring to the market a product, which has a high resistance to electromagnetic interference. Also, this product should not produce electromagnetic radiation that could disrupt the functionality of other electronic equipment in its surroundings during its current operations. For this reason, manufacturers must test their products in laboratories of electromagnetic compatibility (EMC) [2] [3].

Specialized generators that can produce various types of electromagnetic interference are used for most of the tests for electromagnetic susceptibility of electronic devices. These generators are quite expensive but their cost is negligible in contrast to the construction of the anechoic or semi-anechoic chamber. For example, the Haefely AXOS5 Compact Immunity Tester costs € 19,000 and constructing and equipping the semi-anechoic chamber may require the investment of € 450,000 and more. Therefore, some manufacturers have invested money in the purchase of such generators and they carry out themselves the most basic tests of electromagnetic susceptibility of devices at the time of development. Subsequently, when the finished product is tested in an accredited EMC laboratory, the manufacturer can be sure that the product meets the criteria in international technical standards for electromagnetic susceptibility for selected types of electromagnetic interference. For manufacturers, the problem is testing of electromagnetic radiation of their products when they want to find out the level of electromagnetic interference emitted by a new product during its development. The anechoic or semi-anechoic chambers are used for this type of tests in the EMC laboratories, however, these chambers are often fully occupied due to their small number and the repeated tests for testing of electromagnetic interference of device is expensive for manufacturers.

All electrical and electronic devices must be designed in accordance with the standards for EMC. In the field of electromagnetic interference, the components of intrusion and hold-up alarm systems (I&HAS) are tested in accordance with the international standard CSN EN 55022 ed.3. This technical standard determines uniform requirements for the high-frequency interference level of the information technology equipment, defines limits on the levels of the EMI and the methods of measurement [4] [5].

The aim of this paper is to publish the measured levels of electromagnetic interference radiated by the basic set of intrusion and hold-up alarm system in the semi-anechoic chamber and GTEM cell. The basic difference in the measured levels of EMI is based on the type of the measured electromagnetic interference. Electromagnetic interference, which is located in the far-field of an electronic device, is recorded in the semi-anechoic chamber while the interference in a near-field is recorded in the GTEM cell. In a further research, these data will be used for analysis, which answers the question whether the GTEM cell can be an adequate substitute for a semi-anechoic chamber for the measurements of EMI of electronic devices.

In Section II, the (semi)anechoic chamber is described and Section III focuses on the basic characteristics of the GTEM cell. In Section IV, we describe the set of I&HAS on which the level of electromagnetic interference was measured in the semi-anechoic chamber and the GTEM cell; in addition, this section discussed the measuring instruments used. In Section V, the results of the measurements are shown.

II. (SEMI) ANECHOIC CHAMBER

An ideal space for testing and measuring of EMC parameters of electronic equipment is an absorption chamber. This chamber is electromagnetically impermeable (electromagnetic shielding) through the outer structure of a well-conductive metal material. In our case, the semi-anechoic chamber was built from the panels that were of galvanized sheet steel with a thickness of 2.0 mm.

The interior of the chamber is covered with an electromagnetically absorbent material which significantly reduces the internal reflections in a broad frequency. This absorbent material can be made of a ferrite or a carbon with a styrofoam. The absorption chamber exists in two versions both as the anechoic chamber or semi-anechoic chamber.

The anechoic chamber has covered with an absorbent material, not only interior walls and ceiling but also the entire floor. As such, the anechoic chamber simulates unlimited open area. In practice, we often encounter a semi-anechoic chamber (shown in Figure 1), which has covered with an absorbent material only the ceiling and walls and simulates the open area with reflections from the ground plane.

The absorbent material can be placed on the floor in the semi-anechoic chamber if it is required under the technical standards or requirements of the manufacturer of the equipment under test (EUT).

Figure 1. Semi-anechoic chamber

The absorbent material converts the energy of the incident wave into heat using the magnetic or dielectric losses. Due to the price, dielectric materials are preferred, such as the different toughened foam materials of polystyrene, polypropylene or polyurethane that contain electro-conductive or graphite fillers. Most frequently, these materials have the shape of a pyramid or cone, but we can also encounter the absorber surface area. The main disadvantage is that a quality anechoic chamber is technologically and financially very demanding [5] [6] [7].

III. GTEM CELL

The GTEM cell (shown in Figure 2) is a specially constructed shielded space which allows the measurement of EMC parameters of small electronic devices. The GTEM cell enclosure is made of conductive material and has the shape of a pyramid. The rear internal space is covered with the absorbent material, the side walls are left bare to act as a waveguide. The antenna or field probe is placed in front of the cell and the EUT is placed in the space between the absorber and the antenna or field probe (transducer) [8].

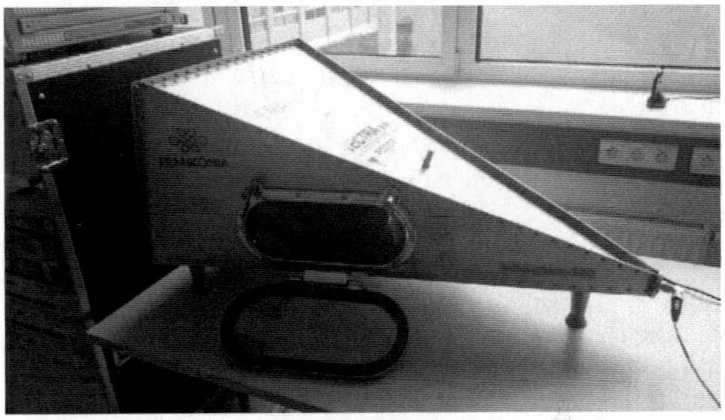

Figure 2. GTEM cell

The GTEM cells can be of different sizes depending on the septum height from 0.25 m to 2.0 m. The GTEM cell is considerably smaller and its price is much lower in contrast to the anechoic or semi-anechoic chamber [9].

IV. SET OF I&HAS AND MEASURING INSTRUMENTS

This basic set of intrusion and hold-up alarm system belongs to the product lines of Oasis and includes the following components:

- Control panel JA 82-K
- Accumulator 12V, 2.4Ah
- Mains power module
- Keypad JA-81E
- Passive infrared detector JS-20
- Siren SA-913TM

The control panel was powered from the mains supply 240V/50Hz and the control panel with accumulator and mains power module were closed in the plastic box. The electromagnetic radiation of this set was tested in the semi-anechoic chamber and GTEM cell in the EMC laboratory at the Tomas Bata University in Zlin in the Czech Republic.

The used semi-anechoic chamber was from the manufacturer Frankonia and was equipped with a BiLog antenna CBL 6112, which is the broadband biologarithmic-periodic antenna which operates with a range from 30 MHz to 2 GHz. The polarization of this antenna can be varied (horizontal or vertical polarization) and the height of the antenna is adjustable from 0.8 m to 4.0 m above the ground plane.

The BiLog antenna was connected to the EMI test receiver ESU8 with a range of 20 Hz to 8 GHz by using the switching and control units OSP130 and OSP150. The whole set was controlled by a computer with EMC Software EMC32 for simplifying control of the antenna, the setting of limits and higher quality display of measured data.

The used GTEM cell 250 from the manufacturer Frankonia had a maximum septum height of 250 mm and was suitable for the measurement of electromagnetic radiation of small electronic devices. The measuring probe EFS-10 was located inside the cell and it was connected to the test receiver ESPI (Rohde & Schwarz), which had an operating frequency from 9 kHz to 7 GHz.

V. THE RESULTS OF SELECTED MEASUREMENTS

The equipment under test was the basic set of I&HAS. We measured the levels of electromagnetic interference of this set in the semi-anechoic chamber and GTEM cell. The set of I&HAS was measured in the mode where the whole set was in the ON state (state of guarding) or when the alarm was induced.

The selected measurements from the semi-anechoic chamber and GTEM cell are shown in Figures 3, 4, 5 and 6. In the figures, the x-axis shows the frequency from 30 MHz to 1 GHz and the y-axis shows the measured level of electromagnetic interference. The levels of electromagnetic interference are stated in the specific unit dBμV/m. The red line, which is in the figures from the semi-anechoic chamber, shows the maximum level of electromagnetic interference, which the EUT can generate at the respective frequencies. This maximum level is defined by the standard CSN EN 55022 ed. 3. If the measured interference of the EUT exceeds this red line, it means that the device generates the interference which endangers functionality of electronic devices in its surrounding area and this EUT can not have the Certificate of the EMC tests.

Two coloured lines are shown in the figures from the semi-anechoic chamber. This is because each measurement was carried out in both polarities of the antenna. The antenna height was 250 cm above the ground plane. From our previous series of measurements, we determined that this was the ideal antenna height for the measurement of this EUT. The highest levels of electromagnetic interference emitted by the EUT were recorded at this height.

Figure 3 shows the electromagnetic interference generated by the EUT in the ON state. This EMI was recorded in both polarities of the receiving antenna. As apparent from the figure, the biggest differences in the levels of the electromagnetic interference of the EUT, when the polarity of the antenna was changed, have been recorded in the frequency range from 40 MHz to 80 MHz and then from 120 MHz to 220 MHz.

Figure 4 shows the set of intrusion and hold-up alarm system in the state of alarm. We also carried out two measurements for both polarities of the receiving antenna. With the antenna in the horizontal position (green line), a clearly recorded electromagnetic interference generated by the siren can be observed, which announced the alarm by the sound signal in the frequency range from 180 MHz to 280 MHz.

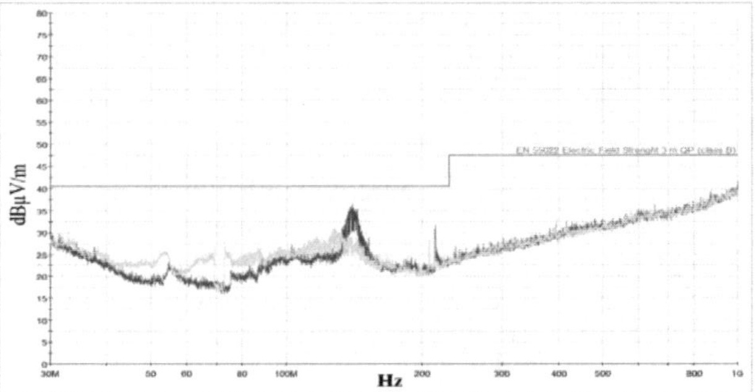

Figure 3. Semi-anechoic chamber - the EMI of the EUT in the ON state – the antenna in the horizontal (blue line) and vertical (green line) polarization

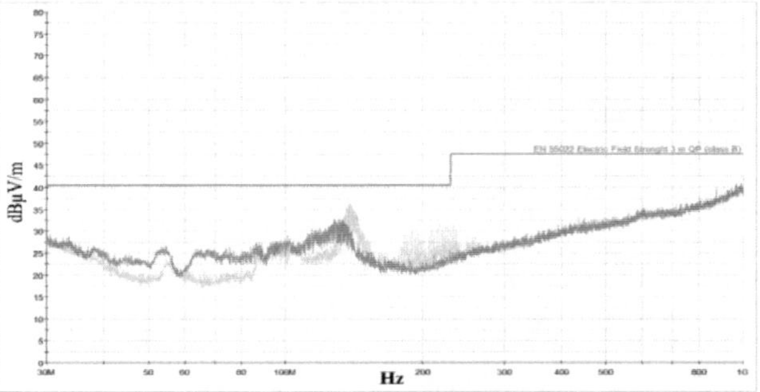

Figure 4. Semi-anechoic chamber - the EMI of the EUT in the state of alarm – the antenna in the horizontal (green line) and vertical (violet line) polarization

In the GTEM cell, we carried out same measurements as in the semi-anechoic chamber. In Figure 5 and Figure 6, the limit of 40 dBμV/m has been highlighted in red for better orientation and comparability of measurement data. The x-axis shows the frequency from 30 MHz to 1 GHz and the y-axis shows the measured level of electromagnetic interference in the unit dBμV/m.

Figure 5 shows the set of I&HAS in the ON state. As in the semi-anechoic chamber, the significant electromagnetic interference of EUT has been measured in the GTEM cell in the frequency range from 100 MHz to 200 MHz.

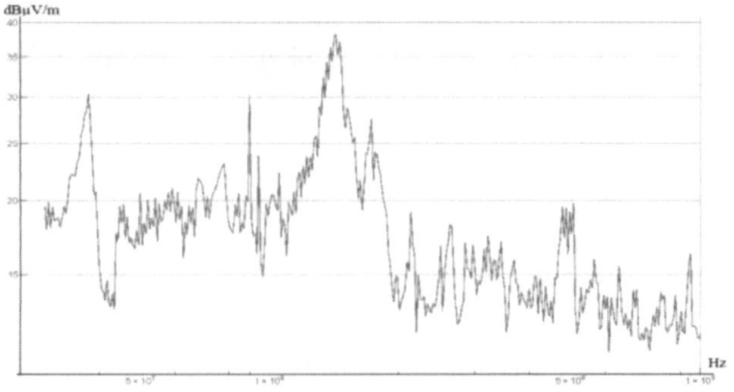

Figure 5. GTEM cell - the EMI of the EUT in the ON state

The difference between the measured data can be observed especially in the frequency range from 30 MHz to 50 MHz and from 200 MHz to 1GHz. These differences can be attributed to the fact that a certain low electromagnetic interference stably occurs in the semi-anechoic chamber and it overlapped interference which was emitted by the EUT. It is also necessary to take into consideration that electromagnetic interference measured in the near-field should have a higher level than electromagnetic interference measured in the far-field of the EUT.

Figure 6 shows set of I&HAS in the state of alarm.

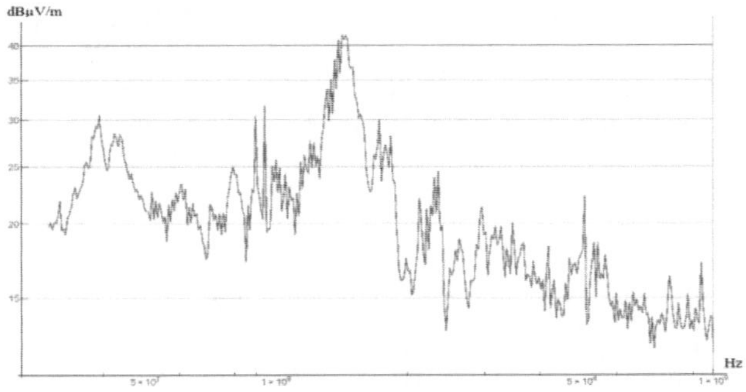

Figure 6. GTEM cell - the EMI of the EUT in the state of alarm

The level of interference of the EUT in a state of alarm recorded in the GTEM cell at a frequency of 150 MHz exceeded the limit of 40 dBμV/m, which is determined by the standard CSN EN 55022 ed. 3. Due to the fact that interference in the near-field is higher than in the far-field and this limit is proposed for measurements in the far field, this result was to be expected.

VI. CONCLUSION AND FUTURE RESEARCH

The measured levels of electromagnetic interference radiated by the set of components of intrusion and hold-up alarm system in the ON state or state of alarm indicate that the measurements from the semi-anechoic chamber and GTEM cell are partially similar. The similarity in measured levels EMI of far-field and near-field the EUT indicates that there is the possibility of using GTEM cells as an adequate substitute for a semi-anechoic chamber in design time of electronic devices and it could be of great significance for manufacturers of these devices.

In all cases, electromagnetic interference of the EUT reached the highest level at a frequency of approximately 150 MHz. However, since the GTEM cell records electromagnetic interference in the near-field of the device and semi-anechoic chamber records the interference in the far-field of the device, the levels of EMI in the GTEM cell are noticeably higher. When the EUT was in the ON state, the level of EMI is closer to the border of 40 dBμV/m in the GTEM cell than in the semi-anechoic chamber. In the case of measurements when the set of I&HAS was in the state of alarm, the border of 40 dBμV/m was even exceeded in GTEM cell. However, exceeding of this limit was not very pronounced.

In future research, we will examine and analyze the measured data and we will carry out other measurements on other types of electronic devices. If it is established that the measured levels of EMI in the GTEM cell are stably higher than in the semi-anechoic chamber, the GTEM cell can be an adequate substitute for a semi-anechoic chamber intended to the pre-certification measurements of EMI of small electronic devices, however, with the necessary modifications of the maximum level of electromagnetic interference which is defined in the standard CSN EN 55022 ed. 3.

ACKNOWLEDGMENT

This work was supported by the Ministry of Education, Youth and Sports of the Czech Republic within the National Sustainability Programme project No. LO1303 (MSMT-7778/2014) and also by the European Regional Development Fund under the project CEBIA-Tech No. CZ.1.05/2.1.00/03.0089 and also by the Internal Grant Agency of Tomas Bata University under the project No. IGA/CebiaTech/2016/005

REFERENCES

[1] H. Urbancokova, J. Valouch, and M. Adamek, "Testing of an Intrusion and Hold-up Systems for Electromagnetic Susceptibility - EFT/B, " International Journal of Circuits, Systems and Signal Processing, volume 9, USA, Oregon: North Atlantic University Union, 2015, pp. 40-46, ISSN: 1998-4464.

[2] E. Vaculik and P. Vaculikova, Electromagnetic compatibility of electrotechnical systems: A practical guide to technology limitations HF electromagnetic interference, 1st ed, Grada Publishing, Prague, 1998, p. 487, ISBN 80-716-9568-8. (in Czech)

[3] J. Valouch, "Electromagnetic Compatibility of Alarm Systems - Legislative and Technical Requirements," Security Magazin, Issue No 106, 2/2012, Prague: Security Media, 2012, pp. 32-36, ISSN 1210- 8273.

[4] CSN EN 55022 ed. 3. Information technology equipment - Characteristics of high-frequency disturbance - Limits and methods of measurement, Prague: Czech office for standards, metrology and testing, 2011. (in Czech)

[5] J. Valouch, "Technical requirements for Electromagnetic Compatibility of Alarm Systems," International Journal of Circuits, Systems and Signal Processing, volume 9. USA, Oregon: North Atlantic University Union, 2015, pp. 186 – 191, ISSN: 1998-4464.

[6] J. Svacina, Electromagnetic compatibility: principles and notes, Issue No. 1, Brno: University of Technology, 2001, p. 156, ISBN 8021418737. (in Czech)

[7] T. Rybak and M. Steffka, Automotive electromagnetic compatibility (EMC), Boston: Kluwer Academic Publishers, 2004, ISBN: 1-4020-7713-0.

[8] F. A. Po'ad, M. Zarar, M. Jenu, C. Christopoulos, and D.W.P. Thomas, "Estimation of Electric and Magnetic Shielding Effectiveness of a Metallic Enclosure with Apertures," International RF and Microwave Conference, IEEE, 2006, pp. 291-295, DOI: 10.1109/RFM.2006.331088, ISBN 0-7803-9744-4.

[9] D. Li, Y. Yuan, and M. Xie, "Generating field strength measurement standard in GTEM cell by using transfer standard," International Conference on Microwave and Millimeter Wave Technology, IEEE, 2010, pp. 2033-2036, DOI: 10.1109/ICMMT.2010.5525186, ISBN 978-1-4244-5705-2

Object Oriented Role-Based Access Control

Petr Stipek, Lukas Kralik, Roman Senkerik
Faculty of Applied Informatics
Tomas Bata University in Zlin
Zlin, Czech Republic
Email: stipek@fai.utb.cz, kralik@fai.utb.cz, senkerik@fai.utb.cz

***Abstract* — This paper focuses on issues related to Security Design and Access Control in Object-Oriented Software projects by pointing out some common implementation problem sources, and their solutions. Further, the study presents an innovative way of extending the Role-Based Access Control (RBAC) Model for large and dynamically-growing projects. Specifically, the emphasis is placed on Scalability Allocation Rights to users, based on their roles. The proposed approach seeks to minimize the bindings of Application Logic from the Functional Logic Allocation and the Verification of Individual Rights.**

Keywords - software security; object-oriented programming; weakly-typed languages; ACL;RBAC; CRUD; ORM/ODM

I. Introduction

Ensuring security against unauthorized access is an integral part of nearly all systems. This is evident not only in security demands on simple claims relating to displaying selected parts of applications to user groups, but also in the very sophisticated - and interdependent relationship between the rights of users. Typically, the gradual expansion of systems allows modifications, which are consistent with the software evolution processes. Each phase of the evolution presents advantages - as well as difficulties that might potentially force developers to violate or abandon proven concepts regarding the fulfillment of the requirements of a final product. A common challenge that devlopers face is dealing with an inconsistent design that leads to a complex development and maintainance of the system. For example, while the maximum utilization of Integrated Development Environment (IDE) tools can perform code-refactoring, this is only effective in cases when careful documentation, via annotations, is adopted. This way, one avoids writing control symbols via primitive data types - which inherently may cause needless financial expenses.

There are many ways to design an Access Control List (ACL) [3]. Different combinations also exist for approaches - including RBAC [1][8]; Attribute Based Access Control (ABAC)[9]; or approaches based on the Create, Read, Update and Delete (CRUD) Operations [2][5][6]. Basically, it is either a user - or a group of users with allocated roles who can be assigned, or have permission to, or be withdrawn access to a part of a system.

In Section 1, the basic principles regarding what should be followed or held in the design of ACL are described. This is followed by a comparison between generally-used design patterns and mechanisms. Section 3, presents the main disadvantages of ACLs. In Section 4, an Object-Oriented Approach, suitable for appliactions using Object Relational Mapper/Object-Document Mapping, (ORM/ODM), is also presented. Finally - in Section 5, the Performance Impact of our proposal is discussed.

II. Basic principles

This section presents some basic principles underlying the preparation of applications′ security structures. This approach helps to consider a few choices and takes into consideration our own requirements to select the best approach.

A basic presumption in effective design approaches is that all dependencies of the Application Logic from the users, user-accounts, and their roles, are removed. For instance, in an Invoice Price Calculation Model, the user or their role, is generally considered irrelevant. Rather, what is more important, is the knowledge of what operations can or cannot run. This means that whether or not the current user fulfills the conditions necessary for authorization, an authorization service that provides and manages the current user account, according to law and regulations has to be provided. At the moment, when a project reaches a state where it is necessary to set a security policy, quite a number of developers tend to advance the implementation of security policy in the code on the basis of customer specifications using an authentication service.

While there is nothing wrong with this process in principle, a common problem often surfaces in the later stages of development. This challenge, in particular, is related to creating information about user accounts - or their roles, in the code and in places where it would be needed to access user-roles instead of asking the authentication services; whether the specified permissions are assigned or not (See comparison in Figure 1).

Running both approaches will lead to the same results with negligible performance impact. Fixing roles in the model however, results in a scattered security policy throughout the system instead of being managed centrally [9][10]. In case of any change to the security policy, the entire code must be revised and all the potential occurrences must have to be checked. Such a system is more inclined to errors due to improper authentication – and, it is far more difficult to maintain the consistency of the overall security policy documentation of system roles.

```
class EntityModelOne
{
    /** @var IAuthorizator */
    private $authorizator;

    public function __construct(IAuthorizator $authorizator)
    {
        $this->authorizator = $authorizator;
    }

    /**
     * Creates new record only if user has a permission.
     * @param array $data
     * @throws AuthenticationException
     */
    public function createNew(array $data)
    {
        if (!$this->authorizator->isAllowed("createNewEntity"))
            throw new AuthenticationException();

        // Method content
    }
```

```
class EntityModelTwo
{
    /** @var IAuthorizator */
    private $authorizator;

    public function __construct(IAuthorizator $authorizator)
    {
        $this->authorizator = $authorizator;
    }

    /**
     * Creates new record only if user has Admin role.
     * @param array $data
     * @throws AuthenticationException
     */
    public function createNewRecord(array $data)
    {
        if (!$this->authorizator->isInRole("AdminRole"))
            throw new AuthenticationException();

        // Method content
    }
```

Figure 1. Authentication during the Creating of a new Record in the Modeling, Verification of Rights (viz left); and Verification by Role (viz right)

A. *Permission collision avoidance*

A modern trend in applications development has to do with the design of modular applications with completely separate and independent components. This is particularly evident in Open Source projects, where hundreds of different developers create modules for a specific framework. This trend increases the potential risk of permission collision when composing the application. Since prefix titles are often used in prevention, there is always a real risk of missing these out in the assignment of prefixes. It is prudent therefore, to anticipate permission collisions during compiling or testing - when the application can fail, rather than in the production version - when full operation with client data is used.

This is consistent with the reasons advanced above for the introduction of the term "permissions resources", which essentially divides privileges into smaller units – thus minimizing the risk of collisions. For weakly-typed languages, these resources are defined as a text-string. However, a much better way is to use objects like structures in strongly-typed languages, so that the textual expression resource name can be replaced for the entire class name; serving as a source of authority (See comparison in Figure 2). In case of building a program that would include two classes of the same name, an exception occurs when one compiles it - and the program will not even start.

```
/**
 * Shows record if user has a permission.
 * @param int $id
 * @throws AuthenticationException
 */
public function showRecord($id)
{
    if (!$this->authorizator->isAllowed("entityResource"
        , "read")) {
        throw new AuthenticationException();
    }

    // Method content
}
```

```
/**
 * Shows record if user has a permission.
 * @param MyEntity $entity
 * @throws AuthenticationException
 */
public function createEntity(MyEntity $entity)
{
    if (!$this->authorizator->isAllowed($entity
        , MyEntityResource::CREATE)) {
        throw new AuthenticationException();
    }

    // Method content
}
```

Figure 2. Avoiding Resource Permission Collisions; Text Form (viz left); Object Form (viz right)

B. *Application of CRUD operations*

With the entry of ORM [4] tools for mapping database data on the object-structure in applications, another layer nestled between the model and the database containing the repositories and services is formed. This is essentially designed to work with the entities. At the same time, there are attempts to unify the implementation of the authorization process with the interlayer - consistent with basic database operations, e.g creating, reading, editing and deleting records. For each entity, four permissions were created using for which the developers implemented the security function. This allowed the creation of generic class managing entities (Figure 3), thereby significantly reducing the spread of homogeneous source codes, and speeding up its development in a system with a large number of entities.

In most cases, these operations are quite enough. For example - in the Web-content management system context, in this way we manage the application development lifecycle. But which of the permissions does one require, for example, to publish a page by a Senior Editor?

Is it an operation to create or edit? In this case, we need help by creating additional permissions.

```
abstract class GenericService
{
    /**
     * Returns class of generic entity
     * @return string
     */
    abstract protected function getEntityClass();

    /**
     * Creates new record from entity
     * @param $entity
     * @throws AuthenticationException
     */
    public function createEntity($entity)
    {
        // Check if entity is equal to generic entity class
        $this->assertEntitityType($entity);

        if (!$this->authorizator->isAllowed($this->getEntityClass(), "create"))
            throw new AuthenticationException();

        // Method content of creation
    }
    // Other methods
```

Figure 3. Demonstration of a Generic Service for Managing Weakly-typed Language Entities

C. Misprint minimisation

Man is a fallible creature, and it is very easy to make a misprint in writing code. If a programmer makes a mistake in the source code, the compiler reports an error. In most cases, the IDE in which the application is being developed, posts the error directly. However, if we connect the information controlling the program logic to text strings, then there is no better tool for performing such compilations. When this occurs, not even a robust IDE is able to estimate whether it is just text for later "bubbling" to the user; or to control characters. Object design is a popular approach in many systems - but not all developers can fully understand this approach and utilize all of the benefits that it brings. Occurrences of control character sequences are more advantageous to bind in constants tied to objects which have to be applied to them or semantically related. The added value is used for accuracy verification by the compiler so as to detect a misprint; while simultaneously, the IDE will offer its lists by enabling one to interactively cooperate with constants. Some developers however, reject this approach because it creates redundant writing – i.e. the extra burden to rethink how and where to place constants, or have no experience with good working practices (especially developers working with weakly-typed languages).

III. THE DISADVANTAGES AND LIMITATIONS OF ACL

The above-mentioned procedures are suitable for most applications in practice. However, owing to their functional principles, there are restrictive limits that are particularly felt in large and modular systems.

A. Violation of the Single Responsibility Principle

Too often, the open concept allows developers to design a system carelessly - instead of using best-practice principles, which would ensure the better sustainability of the system throughout its life-cycle. Most developers make errors to a varying degree when writing code and begin to merge the application´s object-structure, thereby limiting readability, scalability and testability. This increases the risk of error. An example can be data entities, to which constants are added and used for access control, instead of defining objects exclusively for this purpose and thus minimizing binding in the system.

B. Gross Allocating Rights

Access control does not necessarily influence the accessibility of specific records. If one needs to grant user access just to certain articles in the Content Management System, one can either set the rights for all - or for none. This can be done with definitions depending on the user (for example, a property right, the position of the head against the author, etc.). But if one wants to add access to an item that does not exist in the system´s logical connection to the user or their role, then this cannot be achieved. Further, the introduction of auxiliary information for approach management violates the Single Responsibility Principle (SRP).

C. Keeping the documentation and permissions management

It may seem that, in the documentation process, nothing is inherently damaged. A separate document is created that describes the rights of individual roles in the system, and appropriate comments are created in the source code. Unfortunately, experiences from practice demonstrate that these mechanisms do not always work. Often - under pressure, there are sudden changes, communication noises, and all these changes are either completely undocumented or not commented on in the system. Overall, the principle of keeping two documents is difficult to maintain. Rather, it is more suitable to structure an application so that both could be managed uniformly and centrally; though it will rely on information from source-codes. When designing a unified standard that contains all the key information; the creation of automatically-generated documentation that is updated after every intervention in the system is not considered to be a big problem. This may simultaneously build more milestones for the development of safety measures.

The whole situation of the doubling of the documentation may still be complicated by the need for the creation of administration rights for management authority, where there is also a need to rewrite information about the function and impact of individual rights.

IV. The Object-Oriented Design of Access Control

In the previous section, it was shown how to use an object-oriented approach to improve the development of an ACL. So it is valuable considering how to compose a concept that would create some sort of framework to manage permissions. Additionally, framework features also include definitions of the scope of the proceedings - separated from the application logic, thus allowing scalability and self-documentation.

First, it is necessary to clarify several major changes and their impact on the structure of the safety logic.

A. Resource Permission Abstraction

The classical ACL model is restrictive due to the subtleties of how to assign permissions and owing to the fact that we have verified them against the object classes [3]. If we used a system where each entity uses a unique identifier (see Figure 4) within its own class, thereby defining their common interface to be able to obtain this key, and the transfer of specific instances of objects, one is able to obtain the name of the source that is its unique identifier. This then serves for the assignment of authorization services to obtain information on this source and to return a message saying if permission is set or not.

It must be noted that even standard entities either have a single identifier, or obtain one to perform a set of operations with relational-data or data-dependent objects. Solutions can be found in resolvers registrations for a particular object-type specified class or common interface. When creating a resource name, a resolver is necessary; and can be obtained from the specified object.

It is also necessary to convert the source-object into text or numbers so that the authentication service will be able to manage these objects in the database and to search for them. We could also store entire objects - but this approach is only suitable for document-oriented databases like MongoDB.

```
public function createEntity($entity)
{
    // Check if entity is equal to generic entity class
    $this->assertEntitityType($entity);

    if (!$this->authorizator->isAllowed($this->getEntityClass(), "create"))
        throw new AuthenticationException();

    // Method content of creation
}
```

Figure 4. Replacement of a Permission Resource by an Entity

B. Rights specification

The term 'resource permissions' represents a set of rules, settings and related information on how to handle data (see Figure 5) was introduced above. Principally, via this step, an attempt has been made to separate the security information objects outside the application logic and to form the basis for the documentation of the individual permissions. This source tells us - by entity or class of data shields, how to obtain information about a particular record (instance), under which the resource and its formal description fall hierarchically. It also allows one to create a collection of permissions that can be allocated over the object and verify whether they are associated with roles in the system. Another important benefit of this proposal is its ability to structurally rank these in hierarchies – not only as individual resources, but also permissions. Also, the entire system can be divided into logical units and an overall map of all privileges can be created. Ultimately, the outcome may generate documentation or create a tool that allows for the allocation and revocation of privileges because all of the information is managed in one place.

```
class MyEntityResource implements IResource {
    const READ = "read", CREATE = "create", UPDATE = "update", REMOVE = "remove";
    /** Name of parent resource for a hierarchical arrangement
     * @return string */
    function getParentResourceClass(){
        return MyModuleResource::class;
    }
    /** Returns target class type
     * @return string */
    function getTargetCLass(){
        return MyEntity::class;
    }
    /** Closure accessing entity primary key
     * @return Closure */
    function getPrimaryKeyGetter(){
        return function (IEntity $entity) {
            return $entity->getId();
        };
    }
    /** General name for documentation
     * @return string */
    function getName(){
        return "My entity";
    }
    /** General description for documentation
     * @return string */
    function getDescription(){
        return "CRUD operations over the My entity";
    }
    /** Setup all entity privileges definition
     * @param PrivilegeCollection $privileges */
    function setupPrivileges(PrivilegeCollection $privileges){
        $privileges->addGlobal(self::READ, "Show record", "Description");
        $privileges->addGlobal(self::CREATE, "Create op.", "Detailed description");
        $privileges->addGlobal(self::UPDATE, "Update op.", "Detailed description");
        $privileges->addGlobal(self::REMOVE, "Remove op.", "Detailed description");
    }
```

Figure 5. Sample Resource Permissions for One Entity

C. Expansion Permission Problems

Extending control permissions to a specific instance and data brings with it a big problem. This is termed the "default permissions" before first starting the system. The more options one has - the more "permissions" one needs to initialize. To simplify this process one has to rely on the advantage of the inheritance of both user roles and individual permissions. With a suitable algorithm, one can set the authorization service so that it is cumulatively associated with the higher-level roles and the permission subordinate roles [7].

This procedure is sufficient to define permissions on the lowest layers of the tree structure (Figure 6) and roles in the upper layers. This only defines additional permissions, which arise just for that role, and 'bubble up' to the other parent layer.

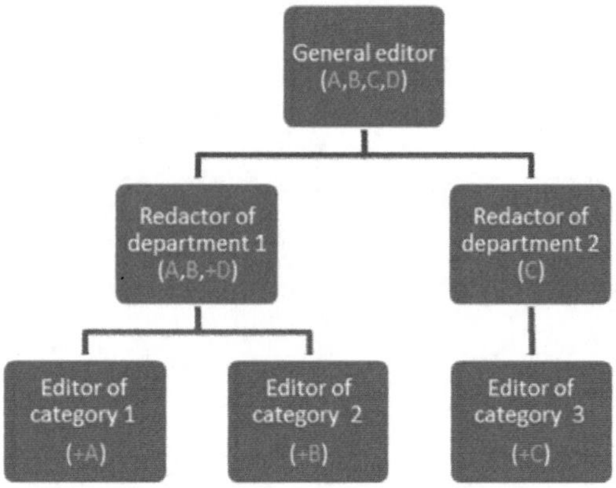

Figure 6. Cumulative Assignment of Permissions to Parent-roles (Green: Defined manually; Orange: inherited)

D. The Multiple Assignment of Rights to Overall Resources of the Same Type

By restricting the permissions to the distinction between instances, one loses the ability to mass configure the rights of target group resources. This limitation can be compensated for by the "inheritance" of individual permissions within one source - or privileges superior to the source. Logically, there is a possibility to divide these into Local Law (i.e. applied individually over instances); and Global Law (i.e. applicable to all instances) groups. Altering the setting of inheritance rights from local to global eliminates this restriction. For authentication services, it is necessary to know how to work with these additions. Inheritance can also be used to restrict the necessary definition permissions over their resources. For example, by assigning rights on the creation of article categories, one wants to enable someone to create individual articles within this category.

In contrast to roles, rights calculation must be performed in the opposite direction from the highest layer to the lowest. At the same time, it is not enough to work on only the grantgranting and refusing access - but a third, neutral state, must be introduced with the right to take over from the parent permissions.

E. Creating Resources on the Run

In order to fulfill the functionality of the above points, the implementation mechanism to manage these resources is still missing.

This requires a solution which offers a manual implementation approach to all services that manage entities and to data for which access needs to be managed. It would be necessary to implement at least a 'create a resource' entity after creating and deleting a source before deleting entities. One can include call changes and record any events; but it is not necessary to ensure that this concept will work.

Manual implementation can be dispensed with by using the abilities of some ORM/ODM implementations – i.e. so-called "listener" or "subscriber" services that invoke special application extensions on selected groups of objects that are triggered when changes in state entities occur. Their purpose is simple and built on objects′ additional events, without affecting the integrity of their content and functionality.

F. Ownership of Resources and Events

In some cases, we need to decide the access to a resource based on information regarding its ownership. It is very questionable whether the owner information should be part of the functional logic - or a component of the management approach, since this data is often only used as functional logic to filter the records or to access relational records. Their movement outside the influence entity would complicate querying databases. On the other hand, it would turn into a violation of the Single Responsibility Principle, so that the information about the owner should be stated at the source, not the entity. Both cases, however, can be resolved relatively quickly so that the resulting behavior will be similar. If we want to note the information about a property with entities, then we have to note the method by which the owner is obtained. In higher programming languages, we use the Lambda expressions or Closures for this purpose to advantage. Setting the property will be part of the functional logic.

For property management inside these resources purposes, we can automate it by just slipping the logged user object to the authorization service through which it obtains this identity and assigns it a new source. To simplify folding database queries, one needs to create an object that returns a partial database command connecting the required tables, which will simply be included into the desired filter command.

In the same way as a property, we can also keep information about the latest update, or delete the record.

V. OBJECT ACCESS PERFORMANCE IMPACTS

The crucial question however, is how this approach will have an impact on the application performance.

One can notice the significant impact when the call first acts on database queries. The percentage impact is very difficult to calculate and depends on the complexity and size of the entire model.

Negative impacts can partially cancel out the pre-calculations and there is a need for a suitable caching intermediate results application and for the results for each role in the system. After application caching, let us move on to the complexity of the search at list-level.

Another negative effect is due to the fact that there are doubled insert and delete commands to the database in the case of the creation and deletion of records. This concept is unsuitable for example, for monitoring systems - but rather, will assist in the development of Customer Relationship Management (CRM) systems.

The concrete results and ensuing comparison of the performance impact model applications - at least, are not yet known, because this model is currently in the testing phase.

VI. CONCLUSION

The main advantage of the above-mentioned approach is the centralization of security logic and related documentation in an ideal case as separated models from application logic. It allows one to have a greater detailed and more sensitive control of access to resources, (applications), without the side-effect of the expansion of privileges because of their structuring options due to heredity and to relations that are defined only in security logic. Additionally, the approach also helps in the production of more effective code by means of developer tools.

Future work will focus on three key areas, herein below:

Firstly, the work will focus on how to make preprocessed combinations of privileges, roles and all of the relations between them. This would be ideal for boosting the performance of authorization services and the minimization of latency.

Secondly, the focus will be on designing a security policy documentation generator, based on structure and definitions of all permissions - throughout all resources. This approach would generate feedback about the range and complexity of the (given) security policy.

Thirdly, we will focus on the creation of a Security Coverage measuring tool that will be able to analyze source codes and generate feedback about the degree of security (insecurity). It will also focus on the concrete role of access - or permission, requirements for accessing any part of a code. This would serve as a foundation of extant knowledge for developers.

ACKNOWLEDGMENT

This work was supported by:

Grant No.: IGA / Cebia Tech / 2015/036, Tomas Bata University in Zlin Internal Grant Agency.

REFERENCES

[1] D. Ferraiolo and R. Kuhn,"Role-Based Access Controls," Baltimore, 15th National Computer Security Conference, 1992,pp. 554–563

[2] O. M. Pereira, M. Rui, R. L. Aguiar, and Y. M. Santos,"CRUD-DOM: A Model for Bridging the Gap between the Object-Oriented and the Relational Paradigms," Fifth International Conference on Software Engineering Advances. IEEE, 2010,pp. 114-122, DOI: 10.1109/ICSEA.2010.25, ISBN 978-1-4244-7788-3

[3] R. S. Sandhu and P. Samarati, "Access control: principle and practice," IEEE Communications Magazine (Volume 32, Issue:9),1994, pp. 40-48, DOI: 10.1109/35.312842, ISSN 0163-6804.

[4] H. Song and L. Gao,"Use ORM Middleware Realize Heterogeneous Database Connectivity," Spring Congress on Engineering and Technology IEEE," 2012, pp. 1-4, DOI: 10.1109/SCET.2012.6341925. ISBN 978-1-4577-1964-6.

[5] C. O. Truica, F. Radulescu, A. Boicea, and I. Bucur, "Performance Evaluation for CRUD Operations in Asynchronously Replicated Document Oriented Database," 20th International Conference on Control Systems and Computer Science. IEEE, 2015, pp. 191-196, DOI: 10.1109/CSCS.2015.32, ISBN 978-1-4799-1780-8.

[6] O. M. Pereira, D. D. Regateiro, and R. L. Aguiar, "Distributed and Typed Role-based Access Control Mechanisms driven by CRUD Expression," International Journal of Computer Science: Theory and Application, ORB Academic Publisher 2014, pp. 1-11, [Online] Available from: http://www.orb-academic.org/index.php/journal-of-computer-science

[7] A. A. Elliott and G. S. Knight, "Role Explosion: Acknowledging the Problem," In Proceedings of the 2010 International Conference on Software Engineering Research & Practice, 2010

[8] C. Feltus, M. Petit, and M. Sloman, "Enhancement of Business IT Alignment by Including Responsibility Components in RBAC,"Proceedings of the CAiSE 2010 Workshop Business/IT Alignment and Interoperability (BUSITAL2010), 2010, pp. 61-75

[9] M. Munz, L Fuchs, M. Hummer, and G. Pernul, "Introducing Dynamic Identity and Access Managemen in Organisations," 11th International Conference on Information Systems Security, 2015, pp. 139-158, DOI: 10.1007/978-3-319-26961-9_0

[10] R Sandhu, D Ferraiolo,and R Kuhn, "The NIST model for role-based access control: towards a unified standard,", ACM workshop on Role-based access control, 2000

Introduction to Web Security and Evaluation Methods of Web Application Vulnerabilities

Petra Holbíková, Roman Jasek
Department of Artificial Intelligence and Informatics
Faculty of Applied Informatics, Tomas Bata University in Zlin
Zlin, Czech Republic
e-mail: holbikova@fai.utb.cz, jasek@fai.utb.cz

Abstract—**In this paper, we focus on basic security rules of Web applications or Websites, as well as recommendations for developers in terms of what should be avoided while creating Web applications. The paper is divided into two parts. In the first part we describe the basic security rules and common Web risks. In the second part, a system for risk assessment of vulnerability - Common Vulnerabilities Score System is introduced and described.**

Keywords - Web Security; Secure Socket Layer; Threat Risk Modelling; Common Vulnerabilities Score System; Basic Web Security; Security Risks.

I. INTRODUCTION

There are basic principles to secure Web sites and Web applications that are recommended to always be used. The effort to minimize the vulnerability of Web applications is already evident in the initial design. Integrating several programming languages into one project potentially increases the risk of a security error. Some of the possible impacts include theft and misuse of users personal data, financial repercussions on the company operating the Web applications, reputation harm or technical consequences - destruction of the entire application, or its theft [11]. A list of common potential hazards and errors is generally considered as the minimum of what developers have to test while developing their applications [7].

The essential set of recommendations will be presented in the following sections. In Section 2 we describe the basic security rules, like types and usage of Secure Socket Layer certificate [7], why it is advisable to regularly update the system, common mistakes at form validation and passwords creation. The last part of Section 2 is dedicated to top 10 risks in Web applications. In Section 3 we describe Common Vulnerability Scoring System and its Base metrics scoring system [10].

II. BASIC SECURITY RULES

Secure Socket Layer (SSL) certificate is one of the most common and basic ways to secure Websites. It is used for secure communication and data transfer between Web browsers and Web servers. SSL is mostly used in situations where, for example, sensitive data is entered by the user in a login form and includes username and password. Other examples of SSL use include cases of stored sensitive information in user accounts such as credit card numbers, emails, address and passwords, or communications and trusted information exchanges. To provide secure connection, an SSL certificate is installed on the Web server. The SSL certificate has two functions. The first function is to authenticate the identity of the website and the second is to encrypt transmitted data.

A. SSL Certificates

Choosing a trusted certification authority is an important part of an SSL certificate selection. The most used certification authority is probably Symantec, due to its cooperation with Verisign, GeoTrust, Thawte and low-cost Rapid SSL authorities. SSL certificates can be divided into two groups. The certificates in the first group are based on the number of owned domains or subdomains [9].

- Single Certificate protects communications between the server and a Web browser only for one domain or subdomain
- Wildcard certificate can be used for one domain and unlimited number of its subdomains
- Multi-Domain certificate is used for secure multiple domain names

The second type of certificates is based on the level of validation.

- Domain Validation certificate covers basic encryption and verification of the ownership of the domain name registration.
- Organization Validation certificate also authenticates additional details of the owner.
- Extended Validation (EV) certificate provides the highest degree of security. The user is informed within the Web browser by the icon of padlock on the left side of uniform resource locator (URL) and a green address bar. The most frequent usage of this type of certification is in the financial and banking sector.

The last type of SSL certificate, which is also often used, is a Code Signing Certificate. This certificate allows developers and software companies to sign their applications that are intended for distribution over the Internet [8].

B. Regular system updates

Although some safety information is visible to the user, other safety information is better to be hidden from the user or potential attackers, especially if well-known and widely available open source Content Management System (CMS) or system is used.

It is a good idea to hide information, such as what kind of system type, what version, or information on bug reports is used. If a potential attacker finds out what system is used and its version, it is much easier to lead a targeted attack on a website. Knowledge of the system version can be used to detect information about weaknesses in various databases or existing exploit program. A common defense method against the exploit attacks is to perform regular updates.

Detailed error information should not be provided to the users themselves. A typical situation is when users log into their account. It is not advisable to show the user what part (username or password) was wrongly filled out. If the potential attacker sees what information in a login form is correctly filled, the attacker can then focus on the part that is filled wrong.

C. Form validation, file upload and passwords

Other weak points of Web applications are any input fields for users to type in information, weak user passwords or file uploads on the frontend.

Form validation is recommended on both sides of the Web application. The Web browser can validate filled-out data by JavaScript, as well as on the server side filled-out data are validated in the programing language in which the application is programmed. The Web browser can seize small errors and limit user in using some types of characters. These initial validations, however, can be overcome. After that, the server captures and filters these surpassed validations. On the server side, the inserted code is also removed. Otherwise, the inserted code can damage databases.

File Upload Form is a simple way for an attacker to upload harmful files on the server. The basic rules are limit file size and multipurpose internet mail extensions (MIME) types. Thereafter, it is appropriate to store files outside the document root and rename files during-their uploading to a Web server. At the same time, users who are not logged in should not be allowed to upload files.

In the password case, the user should be informed how a strong password looks like. The password length is generally recommended to be at least 8 characters. Another rule for a password creation is to combine characters. It is not recommended to use any common words. These passwords can be broken by brute force attack where attackers use dictionaries - Dictionary attack.

The longer and more complicated the password, the safer it is.

It is appropriate to choose a combination of uppercase and lowercase letters, numbers and characters. It is advised to use those characters that can be found any language keyboard. All these rules are possible to be set up and filtered in the Web browser and then passed to the user.

Another recommendation, which cannot be part of the user limitation, is not to use any personal information in a password. Also, it is not recommended to use your name or the names of your loved ones, nicknames or date of birth, ID card numbers or any words that can be easily connected with a user. The user should use a different password for each service, or at least modify it. Passwords should be changed regularly [7].

D. OWASP Top 10

OWASP is an official name for Open Web Application Security [6]. Project OWASP Top 10 analyses Web risks at three-year intervals and monitors the changing trends in Web applications vulnerability. These risks are frequently only a fraction of developer testing [6]. The summary of common security risks is shown in Table 1 and Table 2. Table 1 shows the most common security risks of years 2004 and 2007.

TABLE I. OWASP TOP 10 2004, 2007 COMPARISON [6]

	2004	2007
1	Unvalidated Input	Cross Site Scripting
2	Broken Access Control	Injection Flaws
3	Broken Authentication and Session Management	Malicious File Execution
4	Cross Site Scripting	Insecure Direct Object References
5	Buffer Overflow	Cross Site Request Forgery
6	Security Misconfiguration	Information Leakage and Improper Error Handling
7	Improper Error Handling	Broken Authentication and Session Management
8	Insecure Storage	Insecure Cryptographic Storage
9	Application Denial of Service	Insecure Communications
10	Insecure Configuration Management	Failure to Restrict URL Access

Table 2 shows the continuation of OWASP Top 10 research of security risks for years 2010 and 2013.

TABLE II. OWASP TOP 10 2010, 2013 COMPARISON [6]

	2010	2013
1	Injection	Injection
2	Cross Site Scripting	Broken Authentication and Session Management
3	Broken Authentication and Session Management	Cross-Site Scripting
4	Insecure Direct Object References	Insecure Direct Object References
5	Cross Site Request Forgery	Security Misconfiguration
6	Injection Flaws	Sensitive Data Exposure
7	Insecure Cryptographic Storage	Missing Function Level Access Control

8	Failure to Restrict URL Access	Cross-Site Request Forgery
9	Insufficient Transport Layer Protection	Using Components with Known Vulnerabilities
10	Unvalid Redirects and Forwards	Unvalidated Redirects and Forwards

In general terms, it can be said that the security risks trends have not particularly changed.

III. THREAT RISK MODELING

There are several methods for vulnerability and security assessment of the site. The best known methods are STRIDE and DREAD used by Microsoft [11]. Their names are derived from the initial letters of the evaluated categories.

Another extended evaluation methodology is AS / NZS 4360: 2004 Risk Management that became the first formal standard for documenting and managing risks [5].

The US Department of Homeland Security (DHS) has introduced a group of National Infrastructure Advisory Council Vulnerability Disclosure Working Group which works with the outputs from Cisco Systems, Symantec, ISS, Qualys, Microsoft, CERT / CC, and eBay. One of the outcomes of this group is the system used for assessing the vulnerability of Web applications, Common Vulnerability Scoring System (CVSS) [2][3].

The first version of this system was established in February 2005 with the aim of creating an open and standardized evaluation of the degree of severity of software vulnerabilities. Subsequent development standards continued until the current version (April 10, 2016) CVSSv3.0 introduced in 2015.

The basic score is computed using six metrics that can be divided into two subgroups. The first subset is Exploitability.

- **Attack vector (AV)** is a metric system that asks from which source might be the attack led. Four options are evaluated - network, adjacent network, local or physical.
- **Access Complexity (AC),** metric system is figuring out how easy or difficult it is to use the detected error. The options are high or low.
- **Privileges Required (PR),** metric system describes the level of privileges that an attacker must have to be able to successfully exploit errors. The values are none, low or high. The highest rating has the value none.
- **User Interaction (UI)** metric system determines whether the vulnerability can be exploited only by an attacker or if a user different from the attacker, is involved. The best score are obtained by Web sites where there is no user interaction.

The second subgroup, called Impact metrics, includes an assessment of Confidentiality (C), Integrity (I) and Availability (A) impacts. We ask whether there is a data destruction, irreparably damaged data or unavailability of data or service. For the evaluation, three evaluation levels of severity are used.

The last component of the basic evaluation is a metric Scope. It indicates if the error affects only the funds managed by the same authority or not [1].

The Base Score is a function of the Impact and Exploitability sub score equations, where the Base Score is defined as,

If (Impact sub score =< 0) 0 else,
Scope Unchanged Round up (Minimum [(Impact + Exploitability),10])
Scope Changed Round up (Minimum [1.08 × (Impact + Exploitability),10])

and the Impact sub score (ISC) is defined as,

$$\text{Scope Unchanged } 6.42 \times ISC_{Base}$$
$$\text{Scope Changed } 7.52 \times [ISC_{Base}-0.029] - 3.25 \times [ISC_{Base}-0.02]^{15}$$

where,

$$ISC_{Base} = 1 - [(1-C) \times (1-I) \times (1-A)] \quad (1)$$

And the Exploitability sub score is,

$$\text{Exploitability} = 8.22 \times AV \times AC \times PR \times UI \quad (2)$$

AV .... Attack Vector
AV.................. Attack Complexity
PR .... Privileges Required
UI .... User Interaction
C...................... Confidentiality Impact
I...................... Integrity Impact
A .... Availability Impact

The calculated final Base Score is evaluated form 0 to 10. The lower the score, the smaller the vulnerability rate. Scoring can be converted into a verbal evaluation, as shown in Table 3.

TABLE III. QUALITATIVE SEVERITY RATING SCALE [5]

Rating	CVSS Score
None	0.0
Low	0.1 – 3.9
Medium	4.0 – 6.9
High	7.0 – 8.9
Critical	9.0-10.0

Other metrics can be used for more comprehensive evaluation of the vulnerability of Web applications. They are classified into two groups. Temporal Metrics measure the current state of the use of techniques, availability of the code, the existence of patches or workaround that may vary over time. This metrics system has three parts – Exploit Code Maturity (E), Remediation Level (RL) and Report Confidence (RC). Environmental Metrics group describes the impact of vulnerability. This metrics system customizes the CVSS score depending on the importance of the affected information technology asset to organization, measured in terms of Confidentiality (CR), Integrity (IR) and Availability (AR).These two systems are shown in Fig. 1.

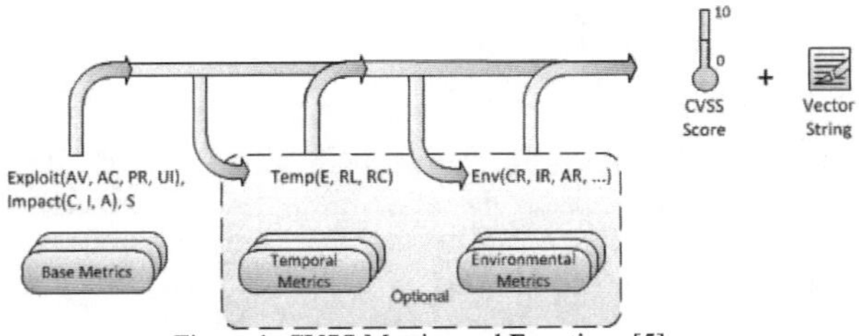

Figure 1. CVSS Metrics and Equations [5]

These two additional metrics are used for clarification of the score system and are optional. The basic metrics is sufficient for security risks assessment of most Web sites [4].

IV. CONCLUSION

Web security is one of the basic issues while creating Web applications. This article outlines the basic rules of Web application security and constitutes one of the methods of assessing Web applications security. The first section summarizes the applicable rules for Web applications creation, like SSL certificates, creating passwords and input forms. The second part describes the method Common Vulnerability Scoring System, Base Metric Group, due to which we can obtain basic CVSS score of Web application. This work is the basis for further development of this method and its application on fuzzy logic.

REFERENCES

[1] H. Li, R. Xi and L. Zhao "Study on the distribution of CVSS environmental score" ICEIEC 2015 - Proceedings of 2015 IEEE 5th International Conference on Electronics Information and Emergency Communication, art. no. 7284502, 2015, pp. 122-125.

[2] H. Holm and K. K. Afridi "An expert-based investigation of the Common Vulnerability Scoring Systém", Computers and Security, 53, 2015, pp. 18-30.

[3] G. Spanos and L. Angelis "Impact Metrics of Security Vulnerabilities: Analysis and Weighing", Information Security Journal, 24 (1-3), 2015, pp. 57-71.

[4] I. V. Anikin "Information security risk assessment and management method in computer networks", 2015 International Siberian Conference on Control and Communications, SIBCON 2015 - Proceedings, art. no. 7146975, 2015.

[5] Common Vulnerability Scoring System v3.0: Specification Document. FIRST [Online]. Available from: https://www.first.org/cvss/specification-document [retrieved June 2016]

[6] OWASP [online]. Avaiable from: https://www.owasp.org [retrieved June 2016]

[7] Why File Upload Forms are a Major Security Threat. Acunetix [Online].Available from: http://www.acunetix.com/websitesecurity/upload-forms-threat [retrieved June 2016]

[8] What is an SSL certificate? Verisign [Online]. Available from: https://www.verisign.com/en_US/domain-names/web-presence/website-optimization/ssl-certificates/index.xhtml

[9] Symantec [online]. Available from: https://www.symantec.com/ [retrieved June 2016]

[10] Scafrone, K., Mell, P. "An analysis od CVSS version 2 vulnerability scoring", Proceeding of the 3rd International Symposium on Empirical Software Engineering and Measurement, IEEE, 2009, pp.516-525

[11] Microsoft [online]. 2016, Available form: https://msdn.microsoft.com [retrieved June 2016]

Electromagnetic Weapons as Means of Stopping Vehicles

A Proposal of a Stationary Electromagnetic Device for Stopping Vehicles

Jan Valouch, Hana Urbančoková
The Faculty of Applied Informatics
Tomas Bata University in Zlin
Zlin, Czech Republic
e-mail: valouch@fai.utb.cz, e-mail: urbancokova@fai.utb.cz

Abstract – **The development of automobile technology is associated with the increase of application of electronic elements. One possible method to stop the vehicle is to disrupt the operation of electronic systems using a high power electromagnetic pulse. This article describes the design idea of a stationary generator of electromagnetic pulses that would be useful for stopping vehicles at checkpoints, at the entrances to the object and in front of sensitive infrastructure. An important aspect of the proposal is the effectiveness of the generator with respect to the electromagnetic immunity of vehicles.**

Keywords-direct energy weapons; car; vehicle; electromagnetic susceptibility; high power microwave; non-lethal weapons.

I. INTRODUCTION

Electromagnetic weapons are referred to as Directed Energy Weapons (DEW). These weapons use highly focused energy to damage targets. The energy could be delivered via electromagnetic radiation, sound, or subatomic particles. The DEW, which operate in the frequency range of 100 KHz - 1 GHz (Directed Energy Weapons - Radio Frequency DEWRF) and in the range from 1 to 300 GHz (microwave, DEWM) are devices designed to disrupt, degrade, or destroy electronic and electrical systems [1]. Automobiles contain a large number of electronic systems. Electromagnetic pulse (EMP) coupled into the electronic circuits of the vehicles can interfere with the operation of the electronic control unit [2]. Disruption of the function of the control unit may result in the engine stalling. This effect allows:

- Stopping the engine stationary or slow moving vehicles (e.g., vehicles used for bank robberies, drug-handovers, within the needs of detention persons or identification of criminals, or when the driver breached the traffic rules),
- Stopping speeding vehicles,
- Protection of convoys (reduce the risk of attack from other vehicles - collision, shooting) [3].

Only a few companies produce electromagnetic devices for stopping vehicles. These devices are used for the needs of police, army, special operations units or protecting of important events [4]. These electromagnetic weapons are very expensive. This article describes the design idea of a stationary generator of electromagnetic pulses that would be useful for stopping vehicles at checkpoints, at the entrances to the object and in front of sensitive infrastructure. Initial ideas and design conditions of stationary electromagnetic system for stopping vehicles:

- The system will be used for stopping vehicles at the entrances to objects [5],
- Security personnel will use the system to stop suspicious vehicles [4],
- The system will be integrated with the access control system for use in security applications (this solution is missing),
- The system can be integrated with an alarm security system and video surveillance system (this solution is missing),
- The system can be activated automatically in response to a negative event (e.g., an attempt to break into the object, a vehicle in the vicinity of object, etc.),
- The power level of system will be set efficiently with a view of electromagnetic immunity vehicles,
- Possible inclusion of the system into a series of technical standards to complement alarm systems.

Project schedule should include:

- Analysis of design of contemporary DEW (USA, Germany, China, Australia, etc.),
- Comparison of contemporary devices and systems used for stopping vehicles,
- Analysis of the requirements of technical standards for electromagnetic immunity of vehicles,
- Selection of the type of generator of electromagnetic pulses (several solutions exist),
- The proposal the automatic generator control (main advantage of suggested approach),
- Simulation of the effects-similarly [4],
- Main goal-Creating a product prototype.

DEW basic description is given in Section 2. Contemporary electromagnetic systems for stopping vehicles are described in Section 3. Detailed information about the proposed system (use of alarm outputs of the access control system or cameras, detectors, wiring, etc.) will be addressed in our future work.

II. Directet Energy Weapons

Electromagnetic weapons that operate in radio wave and microwave (DEWRF and DEWM) ranges use electromagnetic impulses. These weapons use two types of the generators: narrowband (HPM- High Power Microwave) and wideband (UWB- Ultra Wide Band). UWB weapons emit radiation in a wide frequency range, but with a low energy density. These devices are suitable where it is not possible to accurately identify the characteristics of the target- especially its working frequencies. HPM weapons emit pulses at the individual frequencies with very high power. The impact on the target is very effective, because the impulse resonates with the known frequency of the attacked device [1].

High-Power Microwave (HPM) electromagnetic energy can be produced as a near-instantaneous pulse created through special electrical equipment that transforms battery power, or powerful chemical reaction or explosion, into intense microwaves that are very damaging to electronics [2].

For the HPM systems some types of generators can be used like: MILO- Magnetically Line Isolated Oscillator, RKA-Relativistic Klystron Amplifier, TWT-Traveling Wave Tube, BWO-Back Wave Oscillator [3], MWCG-Cherenenkov generator, Vircator-Virtual Cathode Oscillator, reltron, magnetron, gyrotron [4], etc. UWB Generator use as power component: special spark gaps, laser-activated semiconductor switches, quick switches for disconnecting circuits with inductance [4].

III. Contemporary Electromagnetic Systems for Stopping Vehicles

Figure 1 shows the system HPEMcarStop, which is produced by a company Diehl BGT Defence GmbH & Co., Roethenbach/Pegnitz, Germany [5]. The company produces HPEM (High Power Electro Magnetics) effectors in the form of systems with product names: HPEMcarStop and HPEMcheckPoint. System HPEMcarStop can be used, e.g., for activities by the police, army, special operations units or protection of important events (e.g., the Olympic Games).

Figure 1. The system HPEMcarStop (adapted from [5])

The system is designed so that EMP operates on the target vehicle from its front side; it means that the EMP generator is installed on a platform in the rear part of the vehicle. HPEMcarStop was successfully tested with more than 60 different types of vehicles and allows stopping the target vehicle at a distance of 3 to 15 m with more than 75% success rate. HPEMcheckPoint is designed to the stopping of vehicles at checkpoints and in front of important objects (e.g., the critical infrastructure). It combines a system HPEMcarStop with another source HPEM, which is located on trailer.

Figure 2 shows the next system for stopping a car with the designation HPEMcase. This mobile system is used to influence command and data centers, computers, alarm systems control devices, surveillance installations, as well as all other kinds of electronics. Maximum peak radiated power is 365 MW and operating frequency 350 MHz [5].

Figure 2. The System for protecting buildings and persons HPEMcase (adapted from [5])

Other manufacturers, which produce similar devices are: the company Eureka Aerospace (Pasadena, California, USA, system RF Safe Stop) or British company e2v (Chelmsford, England, system HPEMS) [6] [7].

IV. Electromagnetic Immunity of Automotive Technology

During the research, it is necessary to analyze the requirements of the standards for electromagnetic immunity of automotive technology. Verification of Electromagnetic Compatibility (EMC) requirements is performed for automobiles, e.g., in compliance with European Directive 2006/28/ EC and with standards ISO 11451, 11452, 7637, CISPR 12, CISPR 25, SAE J1133, etc.

Vehicle manufacturers also use their own standards (e.g., BMW- GS 95002, Jaguar, Land Rover- CS2010JLR, Renault- 36.00.808, etc.). These standards are stricter than international standards. These standards contain information about the requirements of testing electromagnetic immunity (type tests, signal levels, etc.) for automotive components.

V. Conclusion and Future Work

An effective way to stop a vehicle is to disrupt the operation of electronic systems using high power electromagnetic pulses, which can be generated using electromagnetic weapons. We presented the idea to use a stationary generator of electromagnetic pulses for stopping vehicles at checkpoints and at the entrances to the object. An important aspect of the proposal is the comparison of contemporary devices and systems used for stopping vehicles and analysis of the requirements of technical standards for electromagnetic immunity of vehicles. A novelty is the possibility of automatic generator control through integration with the alarm system. The output signal of the alarm system can trigger a HPM generator. The engine of vehicles within the radiation zone will stop and will not work as long as the HPM source is switched on. Another possibility is to use a camera system to identify the type of vehicle and its speed. This is one of the possible ways to adjust power of generator. It is not advisable to calibrate HPM generator for one type car. Suitable orientation of the antenna HPM generator is important, regardless of the car construction (cars with metalized windows and a full steel body or cars based on carbon fiber and aluminum). To achieve the best possible result (vehicle stop), target cars must be radiated from the front. Exposure time of HPM signals required to stop the vehicle is dependent on the vehicle type, construction, speed, etc.

REFERENCES

[1] H. Urbancokova, J. Valouch and S. Kovar, "Stopping of transport vehicles using the power electromagnetic pulses," in: Przegląd Elektrotechniczny. vol 91, no 8. Poland, Warszawa, 2015, pp. 101-104.

[2] C. Wilson, High Altitude Electromagnetic Pulse and High Power Microwave Devices: Threat Assesment. Washington, D.C.: Congressional Research Service, p. 25, 2008.

[3] L. Drazan, "Electromagnetic Weapons Threat to Industrial Society" Conference Proceedings BTSM. Zlín, Tomas Bata Univerzity in Zlín 2013, pp. 10-15.

[4] K. Hong and S. Braidwood, "Stopping Car Engines Using High Power Electromagnetic Pulses" Electromagnetics in Advanced Applications (ICEAA), International Conference on Electromegnetics in Advance Applications, September 20-24, 2010, pp. 378-381. ISBN 978-1-4244-7366-3.

[5] Diehl Bgt Defence. White Paper on HPEM Technology Roethenbach/Pegnitz, Germany, 2013. [online]. Available from: http://www.vdi.de/. [retrieved: June, 2016]

[6] Eureka Aerospace. High-Power Electromagnetic System for Stopping Vehicles. [online]. Available from: http://www.eurekaaerospace.com. [retrieved: June, 2016]

[7] E2v Bringing life to technology. Directed Energy Weapons Systems DEWs. [online]. Available from: http://www.e2v.com/. [retrieved: June, 2016]

An Empirical Survey on how Much Security and Privacy Customers Want in Instant Messengers

Thomas Paul

Munich University of Applied Sciences
Lothstrasse 64, Munich, Germany
e-mail: thomas.paul91@gmail.com

Hans-Joachim Hof
MuSe – Munich IT Security Research Group
Munich University of Applied Sciences
Lothstraße 64, Munich, Germany
e-mail: hof@hm.edu

Abstract— **Instant messengers are popular communication tools used by many people for everyday communication, as well as for work related communication. Following the disclosure of a massive surveillance system by Edward Snowden, many users became aware of the risks of unsecure communication. Users increasingly ask for secure communication. However, unsecure instant messengers are still popular nowadays. This could be due to the fact, that, besides the large number of available instant messengers, no instant messenger fully satisfies the users preferences. To research the acceptance of security mechanisms in instant messengers, this paper presents an evaluation of user preferences for secure instant messengers. A user survey was conducted to rate the acceptance of security mechanisms typically used by instant messengers. The survey clearly shows that users ask for security functionality. The paper presents the features of an ideal instant messenger that fulfills all the user preferences identified by the survey. A market simulation shows that the ideal instant messenger has a high potential for commercial success.**

Keywords-Instant Messaging; instant messenger; security; usability.

I. INTRODUCTION

Today, instant messengers like WhatsApp are important for communication between people, even outrunning the once popular SMS (Short Message Service) [8]. Instant messengers are communication clients for instant messaging networks. Instant messaging networks provide a service called instant messaging that allows transmitting real-time text messages to other users or groups of users. Most instant messaging networks allow users to also transmit pictures or arbitrary files. Following the disclosure of Edward Snowden, secure communication became popular in the press, as well as in user preferences. However, current instant messenger usage does not show a signification shift from unsecure instant messengers to secure instant messengers. This could be due to the fact that none of the existing secure instant messenger fulfills the preferences of the now security-aware users. To fill this gap, the work presented in this paper analyzes user preferences for secure instant messengers. A user survey was conducted to rate the acceptance of security mechanisms typically used by instant messengers. The results of the survey should help developers of future instant messengers to decide on security features to implement.

This paper is structured as follows: Section II discusses related work. Section III presents the design of the user survey. Section IV discusses in detail the findings of the user survey. Section V presents the features of an ideal instant messenger fulfilling all the user preferences identified by the survey. A market simulation is used to show the potential of this ideal instant messenger. Section VI summarizes the findings of the paper.

II. RELATED WORK

There are several studies on instant messenger usage, e.g., [8][11][12][13]. In [8], the popularity of SMS and instant messengers is analyzed. The authors of [11] research how the usage of WhatsApp differs from the usage of SMS. The authors of [12] present a study on how users use instant messaging in building and maintaining social relationships. In [13], the motivation of users for switching instant messengers is discussed. However, most studies focus on one distinct instant messenger and the usage of instant messaging. They do not focus on security preferences of users. Analyzing not only one but several instant messengers helps to identify the features most asked for by users in each messenger. When planning future instant messengers, this knowledge could help to increase the focus on the intended users.

Other publications, e.g., [9][10], have a focus on security, but they analyze only existing security features of instant messengers and attacks on these instant messengers. In [9], security features of instant messengers and attacks on instant messaging are presented. The authors of [10] focus only on attacks on instant messaging. User preferences for secure instant messaging are out of scope of these papers.

In contrast, the user survey presented in this paper focuses on preferences of users regarding security- and privacy-related features of instant messengers. The results of this paper are intended to give a hint on the ideal combination of features that should be included when implementing future instant messengers. The focus of this paper is on stand-alone instant messengers, instant messaging in social messaging platforms is not considered.

III. Survey Design

The survey consists of four parts:

1. Socio-demographic questions.
2. General questions about instant messaging.
3. Security-related questions.
4. Choice Based Conjoint Analysis.

Each part of the survey is discussed in detail in the following subsections.

A. Demographic Questions

The demographic questions include the typical questions about age and sex. Age groups where: <18, 18-24, 25-29, 30-39,40-49,50-59, 60+.

B. General Questions About Instant Messaging

This part of the survey analyzes the degree of brand awareness and usage of popular instant messenger networks. The instant messengers considered in the user survey presented in this paper can be divided into two major groups:

- Instant messengers without focus on security: Facebook Messenger, Hangouts, Hike, Kakao Talk.Kik, Line, Skype, Snapchat, Tango, Viber, and WhatsApp.
- Security-conscious instant messengers with end-to-end encryption: ChatSecure, iMessage, myEnigma, SIMSme, surespot, Telegram, TextSecure, Threema, and Wire.

The list with security-conscious instant messengers shows that there are already several secure alternatives for instant messaging. It is an interesting question if people are using these messengers and if not, why not?

C. Security-related Questions

In this section of the survey, participants are asked about their preferences for security features. The list of security features consists of the security features present in the security-conscious instant messengers (ChatSecure, iMessage, myEnigma, SIMSme, surespot, Telegram, TextSecure, Threema, and wire). Users can express their preferences on a scale ranging from 1 (unimportant) to 5 (very important).

Topics of the questions in this section of the survey:

- *Importance of transparency of security features*: does the user want to know what is going on concerning security or does he want security to "just happen behind the scenes"? Does users trust software developers and instant messaging network providers or do they want to have the possibility for external audits?
- *Importance of provider and server location*: Is it important for users that instant messaging network providers are based in Europe and use only servers at European locations or do the users not care about server location, even if the servers are located in the USA with its low data privacy protection level?
- *Convenience versus Security*: If security comes at the cost of a more complicated handling of the instant messenger, is this acceptable for users?
- *Trust in chat partners*: Do users prefer to have control over the content they send to their chat partners?

D. Choice Based Conjoint Analysis

The Choice Based Conjoint Analysis (CBC) [3] is a popular analysis methodology in marketing. CBC is used to survey product preferences of users. CBC can be used to find out, which features or which combination of features users prefer. This section gives a very short introduction into CBC, necessary for understanding of the results of the survey. Please refer to [2] for a thorough discussion of CBC. The core of CBC is to offer customers several concepts of a product and the customer selects the one product concept it likes most (or none). This approach is quite similar to how customers decide on real markets. Hence, the methodology is quite natural for the participants of the survey. The disadvantage of CBC is its inefficiency, resulting in surveys that need a lot of reading of different product concept descriptions by the participants. Figure 1 shows an example of concept choice from the user survey. The question (in German) is: "If you have to chose one of these instant messengers, which would you take?". Concepts are described by attributes. Attributes have two or more levels. For example, if a concept includes an attribute "price",

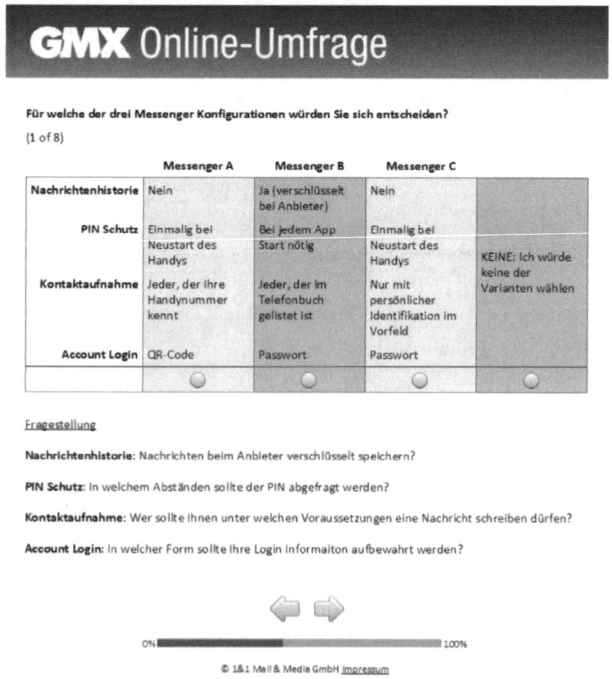

Figure 1. Example concept selection from the survey

levels may be "1.99 €", "2.50€", and "2.98 €". For the survey presented in this paper, concepts are instant messengers with different features (= attribute levels). CBC is only suitable for concepts that need a small number of attributes for description, [4] suggests having a maximum of six attributes. Hence, the selection of security- or privacy-relevant features of an Instant Messenger was restricted to those features that are visible to a user. Security features with little or no user interaction are not considered. Existing Instant Messengers are analyzed to come up with realistic security- or privacy-relevant attributes.

The following attributes were chosen for the survey:

- Message history.
- PIN (Personal identification number) protection of instant messenger.
- Type of contact establishment.
- Type of account login.

These attributes and their levels are described in the following and can be seen in Figure 1.

An instant messenger with a *message history* stores sent and received instant messages on a server. In general, a message history can be stored either on a device or on the servers of the instant messaging network. Storing a message history on servers of the instant messenger network poses a risk for user privacy as the servers may be infiltrated and the message history may be stolen or the instant messaging network provider accesses the message history, e.g., to customize advertisement for users. As users today often use multiple devices and change devices often, it is assumed that only a message history stored on the server of the Instant Messenger network provider is realistic.

Hence, the only levels for attribute message history are

- message history and
- no message history.

A *PIN* can be used to restrict access on an instant messenger. A PIN prevents attackers from getting access to the messenger if an attacker has physical access to the device. Also, a PIN can be used to derive a key for encryption of sensitive information of the instant messenger on the device. However, entering a PIN is a hassle for users, see [6][7] for a discussion of the usability problems of PINs and passwords. Hence, the survey distinguishes PIN usage based on the frequency of the usage (once after restart of device, every time the instant messenger is opened).

The levels for attribute PIN protection are:

- PIN must be entered when opening the instant messenger,
- PIN must be entered once after restart of the instant messenger (typically when device is restarted), and
- No PIN.

Another security relevant feature is how users *establish contact* for the first time. The most secure way of contact establishment is meeting in person and exchanging fingerprints of keys used for communication. For example, the instant messenger Threema uses this approach. However, this approach is time-consuming and may be impossible in some cases. Another approach for contact establishment is to only allow contact establishment to parties that have mutual phone book entries (user A has stored the telephone number of user B in his phone book and user B stored the telephone number of user A in his phone book). This approach assumes that the instant messenger is used on a mobile phone. The disadvantage of this approach is that it requires transferring the phone book of the mobile phone an instant messenger is running on to the instant messaging network. This is a serious privacy issue, as phone books hold much information on the social environment of users. Also, if a phone book is transferred to an instant messaging network, much of the data transferred belongs to users that did not explicitly agree to this transfer. Another approach for contact establishment is to allow everybody that knows the phone number of a user to contact this user. The problem with this approach is that a possibly publically known value (phone number) is considered to be secret.

The levels for attribute contact establishment are:

- Meeting in person.
- Mutual phone book entries.
- Phone number known.

Several instant messengers require an *account login* to protect access to the instant messaging network. Account login can be password based or it can use a QR-code that is scanned by the instant messenger on the device. Entering passwords is considered to be a hassle for users, see [6][7] for a discussion on the user-friendliness of passwords.

Possible levels for attribute account login are:

- Password-based account login
- QR-Code based account login

TABLE I. summarizes attributes and levels used for the survey presented in this paper.

TABLE I. FEATURES AND THEIR CHARACTERISTICS FOR CHOICE-BASED CONJOINT ANALYSIS

Attribute	***Message history***	***PIN protection***	***Contact establishment***	***Account login***
Level	Yes	When opening App	Meeting in person	Password
	No	Once after restart	Mutual phone book entries	QR-Code
		No PIN	Phone number known	

Figure 2 shows an overview of the data analysis of the survey. A utility function is used to calculate the part-worth utility of the different levels of an attribute. A concatenation function is used to calculate the conjoint utility.

Hence,

$$U_p = \psi[f_1(x_{1p}), f_2(x_{2p}), \dots, f_i(x_{ip})] \quad (1)$$

, where U_p is the conjoint utility of product p, Ψ the concatenation function, f_i the utility function of attribute i, and x_{ip} the level of attribute i for product p.

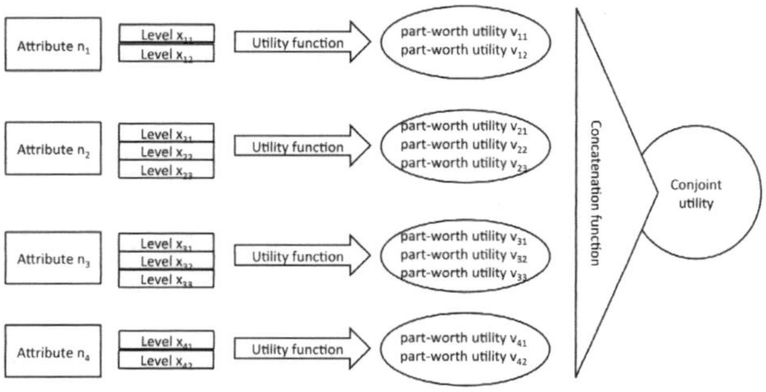

Figure 2. Data analysis

The following utility function is used for this survey:

$$v_{ip} = \sum_{k=1}^{K_i} \beta_{ik} * x_{ikp} \qquad (2)$$

, where v_{ip} is the part-worth utility of attribute i for product p, K_i is the total number of levels for attribute i, β_{ik} is the part-worth utility of level k for attribute i, and x_{ikp} is a variable that is 1 if level k of attribute i is present in product p and 0 otherwise.

Concatenation function (3) is used for this survey:

$$U_p = \sum_{i=1}^{I} v_{ip} \qquad (3)$$

where U_p is the conjoint utility of product p, v_{ip} is the part-worth net value of attribute i of product p, and I is the total number of attributes.

Inserting (2) in (3) leads to

$$U_p = \sum_{i=1}^{I} \sum_{k=1}^{K_i} \beta_{ik} * x_{ikp} \qquad (4)$$

IV. EVALUATION OF THE USER SURVEY

The survey in German language was sent to 200,000 customers of the two participating German freemail providers GMX und Web.de. Hence, it is very likely that most participants of the survey are located in Germany. 1720 users participated in the survey, 640 of them completed the survey. In the following, only the completed survey questionnaires are considered. Participants did not get any incentives for the participation in the survey.

60% of the participants are male, 40% female. 85% of the participants are older then 30 years. The participation in the survey grew with the age of the users. 58% of all participants use instant message clients.

Instant messenger usage varies with age: while nearly all young participants use instant message clients, 64% of the people of age 60 or above do not use instant message clients. This is compliant to the results of [8] that state that older people prefer SMS to instant messengers.

The survey found that the market of instant messengers is dominated by three big players: WhatsApp (81%), Skype (36%), and Facebook Messenger (29%). The figures show that users use more than one instant messenger. This is due to the fact that different instant messengers are used in different social groups a user belongs to. Threema, an instant messenger with focus on security, is only used by 7% of all users. The figures for WhatsApp and Threema are in the same order of magnitude as in a similar study in 2015 about instant messenger distribution in Germany [1].

80% of all participants stated that it is very important or important to have information about the security features of an instant messenger client. This indicates that security is important for users. However, this contrasts to the heavy usage of WhatsApp, an instant messenger with little security features.

52% of participants thought that it is important or very important that the source code of the instant messenger is open source. 24 % thought that it is unimportant or very unimportant to have open source software. These results show that participants distrust the providers of instant messenger software.

70% of participants prefer servers of the instant messenger network to be located only in Europe. Only 8% thought that the location of a server is unimportant. This shows that users are clearly aware of the Internet scale spying activities of several governments. Also, this number shows that users become more and more sensitive to security and privacy issues in communication.

One important security feature is hiding messages from unauthorized access. However, this security requirement clashes with a convenience feature: message preview on the lock screen. Users clearly vote for convenience when asked for a choice between convenience and security: 45% of participants want messages to show on the lock screen in contrast to 29% of participants that considered this feature to be unimportant or very unimportant.

Another security feature popular, e.g., in Snapchat, is to make screen shots impossible such that received messages cannot be recorded. 45% of participants regarded it important that communication partners cannot take screenshots of the instant message conversation. 29% thought that this feature is unimportant or very unimportant. It is interesting that a similar question of the survey gets the opposite result: when asked, if received images should only be visible in the messenger not outside, 42% disagreed, only 34% agreed.

The CBC analysis using the attributes message history, PIN protection, contact establishment, and account login was used to compare different instant messenger concepts, see Section III.D for details on attributes used and their respective levels. The analysis of the importance of the attributes showed, that for the participants, PIN protection and contact establishment are the most important attributes.

The participants prefer to have a PIN protection of the instant messenger, but they want to enter the PIN only once after restart. Again, users decide for a lower level of security if the choice is security or convenience. However, the survey also shows that users consider PIN protection important, hence they decided for a more convenient but less secure instant messenger concept but they did not choose the most unsecure instant messenger concept (no PIN).

The participants prefer to allow only those persons to contact them that are in their phone book. Again, the users ignore privacy issues (transfer of phone book to instant messaging network) if the choice is privacy or convenience.

The participants voted to have a message history in an instant messenger.

The participants prefer to use traditional passwords for account logon. They do not want to use the more convenient login using a QR code. It is assumed that this is the case because users are not used to QR codes.

V. MARKET SIMULATION

A market simulation is used to show the potential market shares that an instant messenger that is based on the results of the survey can get. Part-worth utilities from the CBC are used for a market simulation using the Sawtooth Simulator (http://www.sawtoothsoftware.com/). The following concepts of instant messengers are used for the market simulation:

- WhatsApp Configuration: A configuration similar to the popular WhatsApp instant messenger.
- Threema Configuration A: A configuration similar to the secure instant messenger Threema. As Threema offers multiple features, two Threema configurations were used.
- Threema Configuration B: See Threema Configuration A.
- Best Configuration: A configuration using only those features with best part-worth utility.
- Worst Configuration: A configuration using only those features with worst part-worth utility.

See TABLE II. for details of the levels selected for the configurations above.

Figure 3 shows the results of the market simulation: 68% of the customers would choose the best configuration instant messenger. Only 18% respective 16% would vote for Threema B/A, 8,26% for WhatsApp. However, it should be noted, that instant messenger usage follows the network effect [5]. The network effect states that a network is more valuable for a user if it has many participants. Hence, well established Instant Messenger networks like WhatsApp will always be very popular for new users and new messengers have problems getting a critical mass of users. However, the market simulations shows great potential for a new instant messenger designed based on the results of the survey presented in this paper.

TABLE II. WHATSAPP CONFIGURATION FOR MARKET SIMULATION

Attribute	***Message history***	***PIN protection***	***Contact establishment***	***Account login***
WhatsApp	No	No PIN	Phone number known	Password
Threema A	No	Once after restart	Mutual phone book entries	Password
Threema B	No	When opening App	Meeting in person	QR-Code
Best	Yes	Once after restart	Mutual phone book entries	Password
Worst	No	No PIN	Meeting in person	QR-Code

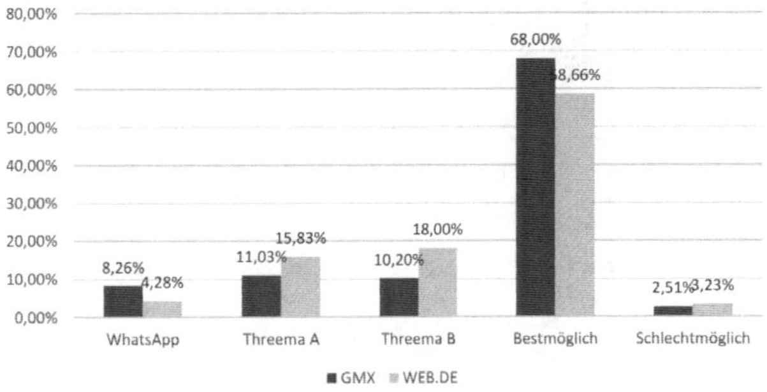

Figure 3. Results of the market simulation

VI. CONCLUSION

This paper presents the results of a survey on user preferences for instant messengers with a special focus on security and privacy features. The survey holds some interesting insights into user preferences in secure instant messengers, e.g., that instant messenger users have a desire for security and privacy protecting instant messengers. However, they are not willing to accept inconveniences to have a higher level of security. Security features are accepted if they require only little or no user effort. If users have the choice between convenience and security, they decide for convenience. The insights of this paper are suitable for improving the development of secure instant messengers in the future. The most popular unsecure messenger used is WhatsApp, the most popular secure messenger is Threema. However, the survey showed that both messengers do not fit well to the preferences of users. The results of the survey were used to design a new instant messenger with the most promising features. A market simulation shows that this instant messenger has a great potential. If network effects were neglected, this instant messenger would gain 68% of market share in contrast to 8% for a WhatsApp-like instant messenger and 15%-18% for a Threema-like messenger.

ACKNOWLEDGEMENT

The authors want to thank Adrian Klie and the 1&1 Internet SE (part of the United Internet Group) for their support of this work. The survey would not have been possible without their help.

REFERENCES

[1] Deutsches Institut für Vetrauen und Sicherheit im Internet (DIVSI), "Allgemeine Geschäftsbedingungen (AGB) of communication providers" [Online], Available from: https://www.divsi.de/wp-content/uploads/2015/10/2015-10-22_DIVSI_AGB-Umfrage_Charts.pdf, [retrieved: June, 2016].

[2] Swatooth Software Inc., "The CBC System for Choice-Based Conjoint Analysis – Version 8" [Online], Sawtooth Software Technical Paper Series, Available from:
https://sawtoothsoftware.com/download/techpap/cbctech.pdf, [retrieved: June, 2016], February 2013.

[3] J. Louviere and G. G. Woodworth, "Design and Analysis of Simulated Consumer Choice or Allocation Experiments: An Approach Based on Aggregate Data", Journal of Marketing Research , vol. 20, no 4, American Marketing Association, DOI:10.2307/3151440, November 1983, pp. 350-367.

[4] P. E. Green and V. Srinivasan, "Conjoint Analysis in Marketing Research: New Developments and Directions", Journal of Marketing, vol. 54, no 4, American Marketing Association, DOI: 10.2307/1251756 , October 1990, pp. 3-19.

[5] M. L. Katz and C. Shapiro, "Systems Competition and Network Effects", The Journal of Economic Perspectives, vol. 8, no. 2, American Economic Association, ISSN 08953309, Spring 1994, pp. 93-115.

[6] H.-J. Hof, "Towards Enhanced Usability of IT Security Mechanisms – How to Design Usable IT Security Mechanisms Using the Example of Email Encryption", International Journal On Advances in Security, vol. 6, no. 1&2, ISSN 1942-2636, 2013, pp. 78-87.

[7] H.-J. Hof, "User-Centric IT Security – How to Design Usable Security Mechanisms", The Fifth International Conference on Advances in Human-oriented and Personalized Mechanisms, Technologies, and Services (CENTRIC 2012, 2012), pp. 7-12.

[8] Institut für Demoskopie Allensbach, "WhatsApp on the Rise", Allensbacher Kurzbericht – 17.01.2014, [Online], Available from: http://www.ifd-allensbach.de/uploads/tx_reportsndocs/PD_2014_01.pdf [retrieved: June, 2016].

[9] M. Mannan and P.C. van Oorschot, "Secure Public Instant Messaging: A Survey", Proceedings of the 2nd Annual Conference on Privacy, Security and Trust(PST'04), Fredericton, NB, Canada, 2004, pp. 69-77.

[10] N. Leavitt, "Instant messaging: a new target for hackers", Computer, vol. 38, no. 7, ISSN 0018-9162, 2005, pp. 20-23.

[11] K. Church and R. de Oliveira, "What's up with whatsapp?: comparing mobile instant messaging behaviors with traditional SMS", Proceedings of the 15th international conference on Human-computer interaction with mobile devices and services", ACM New York, ISBN 978-1-4503-2273-7, 2013, pp. 352-361.

[12] W. Wang, J.J. P.-A. Hsieh, and B. Song, "Understanding User Satisfaction With Instant Messaging: An Empirical Survey Study", International Journal of Human-Computer Interaction, vol. 28, no. 3, 2012, pp. 153-162,

[13] A. C. Y. Hou, "Switching Motivations on Instant Messaging: A Study Based on Two Factor Theory", Multidisciplinary Social Networks Research, Series Communications in Computer and Information Science, vol. 540, 2015, pp. 3-15.

The Mathematical Modeling of Road Transport in Context of Critical Infrastructure Protection

Jan Mrazek, Lucia Duricova, Martin Hromada
Faculty of applied informatics
Tomas Bata University in Zlin
Zlin, Czech Republic
e-mail: {mrazek, duricova, hromada}@fai.utb.cz

***Abstract*—The failure of critical infrastructure is becoming a more and more debated topic in the society. There is a need to plan and implement a functional and secure critical infrastructure. Road transportation has significant influence over the correct functioning of critical infrastructure. A case of disruption of security and functionality leads to distortion between other elements. This process causes a disturbance or paralysis of critical infrastructure. The first part of the article focuses on transport critical infrastructure and its importance for maintaining vital societal function. Road transportation has also significant influence over the correct functioning of critical infrastructure. Next, we present different approaches to dynamic modeling of the impacts of road transportation. The presented approaches provide some basic knowledge to implement dynamic modeling into practice. The conclusion of the article focuses on the design of dynamic modeling in road transportation, based on a deterministic approach. Conclusion outputs are seen as a fundamental baseline for selected processes of security project Resilience 2015.**

Keywords-critical infrastructure; crisis situation; extraordinary event; mathematical models of road transport; road critical infrastructure.

I. INTRODUCTION

The paper describes the use of mathematical models for modeling impacts on critical road infrastructure [2]. Critical road infrastructure has an effect on our lives. Even a simple accident can significantly disturb or even paralyze the continuity of road transportation [3]. For this reason, it is necessary to pay attention to the critical infrastructure. This article is primarily focused on the identification and designation of critical infrastructure [1]. Another aspect addressed in the paper is the mathematical modeling in road transport. When applying mathematical models to road transportation, one needs to timely minimize the negative impacts on society and on other critical infrastructure sectors [5].

II. CRITICAL INFRASTRUCTURE

Critical infrastructure is mostly known as an element or a system whose functional degradation leads to a significant impact on national security. National security considers the basic needs of the population of a country, its health and economy.

Individual elements of critical infrastructure have linkages to each other which guarantee the correct functioning of individual elements. These linkages ensure the interdependence of its various sectors and elements.

The elements we call critical infrastructure in particular. These elements are determined by the cross-cutting and sector specific criteria if the element of critical infrastructure is part of the European Critical Infrastructure. In this case, it is considered as an element of European critical infrastructure [14].

A. The Cross-cutting Criteria

In order to assess the severity of the impact of disruption to a critical infrastructure element, we consider the elements from the following perspectives:

(a) casualties criterion (assessed in terms of the potential number of fatalities or injuries);
(b) economic effects criterion (assessed in terms of the significance of economic loss and/or degradation of products or services; including potential environmental effects);
(c) public effects criterion (assessed in terms of the impact on public confidence, physical suffering and disruption of daily life; including the loss of essential services).

B. The Sectoral Criteria

The sectoral criteria to identify critical infrastructure elements are set by Government Decree no. 432/2010 Coll.[14], on criteria for determining the elements of critical infrastructure.

The basic classification of sector specific criteria to identify critical infrastructure elements are: [14]

- Energy.
- Water management.
- Food and agriculture.
- Health.
- Transport.
- Communication and information systems.
- Financial market and currency.
- Emergency services.
- Public administration.

III. Critical Road Infrastructure

The individual elements of the critical road infrastructure are important for the state not only for passengers, but also for materials. These elements include rail, water, air or road transport. The individual elements are also at risks that can affect them through any linkage to crisis or emergency situations. These situations can impair or limit the functionality of this state. In case of limited functionality, there is a disruption of its security. In our case, we focus on the road critical infrastructure which could be described as the most important element in the transport [6].

The current state of road infrastructure can be analyzed from two perspectives. The first view is regarding road safety. The second view shows us linkages with other elements of critical infrastructure.

Traffic safety is influenced by two inputs. The first entry is homeland security, which is aimed at reducing accidents and creating traffic rules. External security includes anti-terrorism, vandalism, the elements etc.

We can conclude that road transport is the most vulnerable and the most significant element of the critical infrastructure.

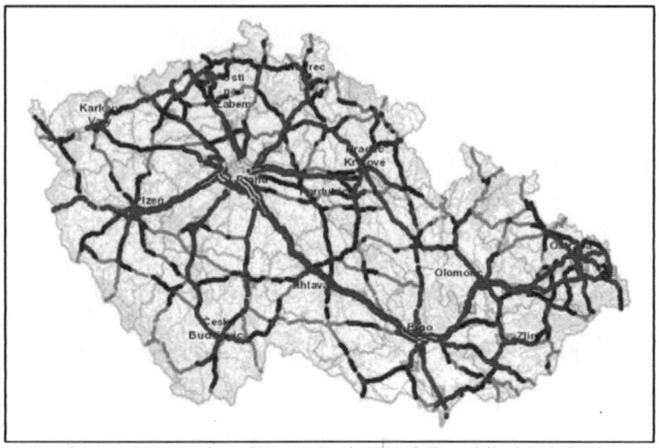

Figure 2. Intensity of Transport in Czech Republic 2015. [13]

When looking at Figure 2, we can see that the riskiest places in the Czech Republic are the main arteries of motorways and Class I roads. The biggest risk for the Czech Republic is without any doubt the D1 motorway. Looking at Figure 2, it is possible to draw attention to the utilization of major roads. They are overloaded by a large number of vehicles.

IV. Mathematical Models of Road Transport

The goal of mathematical modeling in road transport is what the most trusted model vehicle movements and their interaction in traffic. One of the criteria is the failure of random factors and variables. These models can then be divided into stochastic and deterministic. The difference between these two models is substantial. Stochastic models operate with the probability of certain events and take into account the random effects, while deterministic models with random effects are not counted. Deterministic model is act upon strict mathematical, statistical and logical relationships. These relations predetermine the behavior [9] [10].

A very important role in modeling road transport is the request for range of investigated network. This fact is closely related to the requirement for input data. When modeling large transport networks, we can generalize some detail or possibly neglected. For small transport networks, it cannot be afforded such a procedure, it is necessary to give weight to each transport movement. In this model we divide the macroscopic and microscopic or their combination. When you merge macroscopic and microscopic models, there is a new model that we call mesoscopic. With this model it is possible to meet only rarely. [9], [10]

A. Makroscopic Model

The most commonly are used to simulate large-scale communication networks. These models are mainly used for prognostic purposes.

$$q = v * k \tag{1}$$

Where q = intensity of transmission services [ks·h-1];v = the current speed of vehicle [km·h-1];k = density of vehicles in the stream [ks·km-1].

Greenshields model is among the simplest and oldest linear model. It is based on measuring the speed and intensity when the help of these data we can calculate the density. Fundamental assumption is the linear dependency of velocity on the density. The following formula expresses this dependency: [5]

$$v(k) = v_{max} * \left(1 - \frac{k}{k_{max}}\right) \tag{2}$$

where v_{max} = maximum speed [km·h^{-1}]; k_{max} = density congestion [ks·km^{-1}].

In areas with a low density, this model acts as unrealistic. This behavior is caused by insufficient speed and density is then symmetric parabolic dependence on the density of intensity. At lower densities it leads to maximum intensity.

B. Microscopic model

They are based on modeling of individual vehicles driving along the road when there is a consideration as the communication parameters and the vehicle and the driver behavior. During a traffic simulation we meet mostly these models.

Input parameters are achieved vehicles vehicle speed, engine power, size, acceleration and deceleration. Other essential parameters for input features are network users and their interaction. The input data are never accurate, mainly due to the uniqueness of each participant and the vehicle. The determination of acceleration depending on the environmental conditions is essential. Generally, we can express the acceleration in microscopic models as follows:

$$a = f(v, \Delta v, \Delta x) \tag{3}$$

where a = acceleration [m·s^{-2}]; v = speed [m·s^{-1}]; Δv = relative speed relative to the preceding vehicle [m·s^{-1}]; Δx = distance from the preceding vehicle [m].

Consequently, the examination of the traffic flow, we filter out two basic ways of influencing the vehicle between them. The first approach is developed based on observance of a safe distance between vehicles, and when changing the speed of the vehicle prior. The second approach is based on the distance between vehicles. [12], [4]

Weidman's model – The model is a reaction of the driver, which is carried out at a certain distance and the difference in speed between the vehicles. This difference estimated driver only relatively. Using the model, we are looking threshold level drivers that are running in its decisions. These limits are divided into four categories:

- Free movement.
- Approximation.
- Monitor.
- Emergency braking.

These four categories are shown in Figure 3, which you can see below:

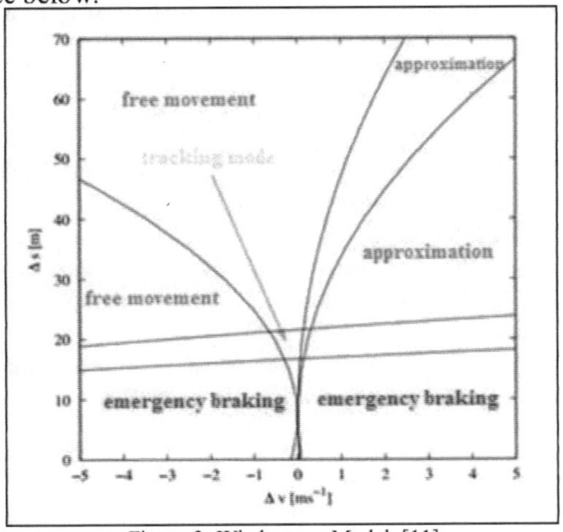

Figure 3. Wiedemann Model. [11]

In the free movement the drivers try to or do reach maximum speed. In cases where an increase of density on the road is, there occurs a state where the vehicle is traveling at a higher speed than the preceding vehicle for this vehicle approaching. Once there is the approaching to the vehicle prior to the vehicle driver tries to adjust not only the speed of the preceding vehicle but also its driving style. This leads to copying of previous vehicle, not only in terms of speed but also in view of maintaining a constant distance between vehicles. At this point, the most important element is the reaction time of the driver, which can lead to two different states. The first condition can be described as the best possible, and that is the driver can react quickly and reduce the existing distance between vehicles. The second condition leads to a bad reaction that could cause a collision.

Gipps model – This model can be also known as non-crash. It is based on the speed limit, when as the result of this action is no crash. This model was the first realistic model. The positive aspect is its ability to reproduce the characteristics of real traffic flow without necessity introducing parameters. These properties are not related to the driver. The driver is limited to maximum accelerations and decelerations that are in full speed distance between vehicles and the relative speed. Therefore, the vehicle will never exceed the maximum speed and acceleration should in the free flow of traffic drop to zero. On the basis of the vehicle speed in the traffic flow calibration has been experimental data expressed by the following formula:

$$v_n(t+\tau) \le v_n(t) + 2{,}5 a_n \tau * \left(1 - \frac{v_n(t)}{V_n}\right) * \sqrt{\left(0{,}025 + \frac{v_n(t)}{V_n}\right)} \quad (4)$$

Where a_n = maximum vehicle acceleration [m·s^{-2}]; τ = the reaction time of the driver [s]; V_n = target vehicle speed corresponding free traffic without restrictions [m·s^{-1}]; $v_n(t)$= vehicle speed at time t[m·s^{-1}] [11]

IDM model – The biggest advantage of the above mentioned model is the number of input parameters. These source parameters are intuitive character. From this perspective, it saves a great deal of time because they do not have to work on long analysis to obtain the input data. The basic equation of this model is expressed dependence acceleration:

$$a_i(s_i, v_i, \Delta v_i) = a_{i0}\left[1 - \left(\frac{v}{v_{i0}}\right)^{\delta} - \left(\frac{s_{opt}(v_i, \Delta v_i)}{s_i}\right)^2\right] \quad (5)$$

Where a_i = acceleration of the vehicle [m·s^{-2}]; a_{iO} = comfortable acceleration [m·s^{-2}]; v_{iO}= target vehicle speed [m·s^{-1}]; v= vehicle speed [m·s^{-1}]; s_{opt} = optimum distance vehicles [m]; s_i = immediate distance from the preceding vehicle [m]; δ = acceleration factor of realism of the reference vehicle.[11]

Usefulness of the models has in every sector its pros and cons. In the community of mathematicians and physicists dealing with this issue it has become the most recognized IDM model also termed as "Intelligent Driver Model". Gipps and Wiedemann models and are most prevalent in simulation software. [7], [8]

V. The Use of Dynamic Modeling of the Impacts of Road Transport

Macroscopic and microscopic models have their uses for modeling in road transport. The output element of these models is the evaluation of vehicle movement and their interaction in the road. We can say that it is modern approaches. On this basis, we developed a group of authors on the subject of dynamic system modeling in road transport. This system is based on a deterministic approach. The basis of this system is the analysis section where it disposes critical element and detour routes on the basis of the macroscopic model. The brain of the system is the algorithm that evaluates the performance parameters of the sections, the degree of intensity transmittance pass routes in the transport and effects of operating parameters on alternate roads.

In Figure 4. below we can see the progress of the algorithm for dynamic system modeling the impact of road transport:

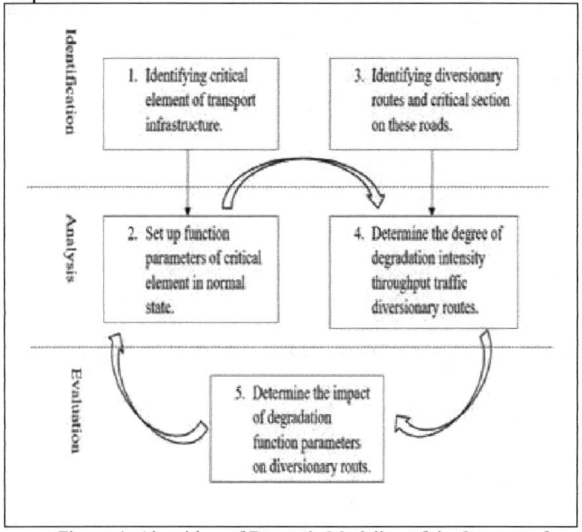

Figure 4. Algorithm of Dynamic Modeling of the Impacts of Road Transport. [1]

Step 1. Identifying critical element in road infrastructure - In case of rejection of a critical element of road transport is the first step no doubt his identification. The identification is based on a directive of the European Union, which leads to their identification and subsequent designation by sectoral and cross-cutting criteria. To be able to fulfill the cross- cutting criteria, you need to model the results of the impact that these values be able to compare the values of crosscutting. This hypothesis is the initial step due to confirm or refute criticism.

Step 2. Determination of critical element functional parameters in a normal state - After identifying follows assessment of functional parameters critical element in a normal state. This means that a certain intensity and traffic throughput as the latest phase in this step set these parameters along the entire route, where this is a critical element.

Step 3. Finding detour routes and critical sections of these routes - At a time when there is lose of a critical element we need to be prepared for alternative roundabout routes. Certainly we should not forget the possible risk sections also on alternative routes so that we are ready for the emergence of other events.

Step 4. Determine the degree of intensity throughput traffic on the detour routs. Determination of functional parameters should be done not only on the main road but also on alternative routes. Functional parameters means to determine the intensity of transmission traffic across alternative route.

Step 5. Determination of the impact on functional parameters on alternate roads. Finally, to represent a number of casualties and economic loss. The final statement gives us lost gross domestic product (GDP) and additional operating costs.

VI. CONCLUSION

Road transport is for every state a significant element of the critical infrastructure. In the case of disruption or failure of this element can lead to other serious threats to some typical elements of critical infrastructure. This fact can achieve a negative impact not only on society. From this perspective, we must not neglect prevention and quality response to this potential threat. Above presented tool is built on the foundations of existing instruments. This tool is not only suitable for real-time analysis but also a far better overview in the art. The aim of dynamic modeling is effective to minimize the expected impact. Road transport is important for any company in many ways and therefore it is necessary to pursue this issue more intensive than before. Increasing the security of critical infrastructure element significantly will affect the security and other elements that are connected with a linkage.

ACKNOWLEDGMENT

This work was supported by Internal Grant Agency of Tomas Bata University under the project No. IGA/FAI/2016/015.

This work was supported by the research project VI20152019049 "RESILIENCE 2015: Dynamic Resilience Evaluation of Interrelated Critical Infrastructure Subsystems", supported by the Ministry of the Interior of the Czech Republic in the years 2015-2019.

REFERENCES

[1] M., Hromada and L., Lukas: Methodology for selected critical infrastructure elements and elements system resilience evaluation. In: The 2015 IEEE Symposium on Technologies for Homeland Security, Waltham, USA (2015), ISBN 978-1-4799-1737-2

[2] L., Lukáš and M., Hromada: Simulation and Modelling in Critical Infrastructure Protection, In: International journal of mathematics and computers in simulation, pp. 386-394 (2011), ISSN: 1998-0159

[3] S., Attal (2008) Markov chains and dynamical systems: The open system point of view, 2008. Available from: http://math.univ-lyon1.fr/~attal/Mesarticles/cosa_attal.pdf

[4] Ni, D. Equilibrium traffic flow models [online]. 2012[cit. 2015-03-24]. Available: http://people.umass.edu/ndh/TFT/Ch05%20Equilibrium.pdf

[5] R., Bogo, L., Gramani and E., Kaviski. (2015) Modelling the flow of vehicles by the macroscopic theory. Revista Brasileira de Ensino de Física, volume 37, Issue 1, 2015, pp. 1-8.

[6] G., Oliva, S., Panzieri and R., Setola. (2010) Agent-based input– output interdependency model, International Journal of Critical Infrastructure Protection, 3(2010), 79-82.

[7] G., Upreti, P.V., Rao, R.S., Sawhney and I., Atuahene and R., Dhingra. (2014) Increasing transport efficiency using simulation modeling in a dynamic modeling approach, Journal of Cleaner Production (Special Volume: Making Progress Towards More Sustainable Societies through Lean and Green Initiatives), 85(2014),433-441. doi:10.1016/j.jclepro.2014.09.002

[8] W., Young, A., Sobhani, M.G., Lenné and M., Sarvi. (2014) Simulation of safety: A review of the state of the art in road safety simulation modelling, Accident Analysis & Prevention,
66(2014), 89-103. doi:10.1016/j.aap.2014.01.00

[9] T., Apeltauer. (2013) Microscopic traffic models in work zones. [Habilitační práce]. Brno: University of Technology, 2013. (in Czech)

[10] T., Apeltauer, P., Holcner and J., Macur. (2009) Verification of some models of traffic flow, článek v Silnice a železnice, ISSN 1801-822X, KONSTRUKCE Media, Ostrava, 2009. (in Czech)

[11] Apeltauer, T., Holcner, P., Macur, J. (2013) Validation of microscopic traffic models based on GPS precise measurement of the vehicle dynamics. Promet - Traffic&Transportation, 2013, Vol. 25, pp. 157-167.

[12] Apeltauer, T. (2011) Romodis – rozvoj moderních dopravních inteligentních systémů (modul 8 – Využití simulačních modelů v dopravě) [online]. 2011 [cit. 2015-03-24]. Dostupné z: http://www.romodis.cz/files/169118867.pdf (in Czech)

[13] Nationt traffic census. *RMD* [online].
Praha: Ředitelství silnic a dálnic, 2010 [cit. 2016-03-31]. Available from:
http://scitani2010.rsd.cz/pages/map/default.aspx

[14] Act n. 432/2010 Coll. Government Regulation on criteria for determining critical infrastructure element, 2010 [cit. 2016-03-30]. Dostupné z: https://www.zakonyprolidi.cz/cs/2010-432

Linkages Types with an Emphasis on Important Critical Infrastructure Sectors

Martin Hromada
Department of Security Engineering
Faculty of Applied Informatics, Tomas Bata University in Zlin
Zlin, Czech Republic
email: hromada@fai.utb.cz

Frantisek Paulus
Population Protection Institute in Lazne Bohdanec
Lazne Bohdanec, Czech Republic
email: frantisek.paulus@ioolb.izscr.cz

***Abstract*— This paper presents and evaluates theoretical approaches applied to the interdependencies description of important critical infrastructure areas. It describes the theoretical basis, and, in some cases, their practical application, with an emphasis on the important critical infrastructure sectors (e.g. Energy, Transport, Information and Communication Technologies). Other important critical infrastructure sectors (e.g. Water Management, Health Care, and Emergency Services) are not emphasized in this publication because they are addressed in the security research project RESILIENCE 2015. The aim of the article is to define the linkage types as a framework and baseline for resilience functional parameters definition, which is crucial for objective and relevant critical infrastructure resilience establishment. The article outcomes can also be seen as an analytical input to the above mentioned project activities.**

Keywords- critical infrastructure; important critical infrastructure sector; linkage; dependence; interdependence.

I. Introduction

One of the basic attributes of the critical infrastructure is its network nature. Therefore, the interdependence of the various sectors and elements contained in it creates logical patterns.

In the Czech Republic, considerable attention has been given to important sectors of critical infrastructure (CI) in recent years. In the process of identifying a designation of CI elements, and addressing their protection, however, only individual sectors were taken into account and impacts of inter-linkages at inter-sectoral level were not considered. In addition, research into this issue has not been adequately developed. Reflection necessity of basic CI attribute, which is the interaction between the different sectors and their elements, was not been taken into account when assessing the criticality of the process or in providing protection. Recent prevailing approach, when the important CI sectors protection of major is dealt separately [1], [2], with regards to the basic characteristics of the system, need to be perceived as a weak and unsustainable.

The following text summarizes selected theoretical approaches to the classification of types of linkages between important CI infrastructure sectors/elements, published in domestic and foreign scientific literature, and, therefore offers the possibility of their further use for the needs of the research project. The rest of the paper is divided in three sections The first section discusses and presents the theoretical and philosophical framework in context of critical infrastructure dependencies and interdependencies in the wider context. The second and main section presents the outcomes of our state of the art analysis in connection with types of linkages classification approaches. The analysis structure represents the needs of security project RESILIENCE 2015 which was mentioned above. The last section presents the synthesis of the analysed solutions and analysis in selected areas.

II. Types of Linkages Classification Approaches Analysis

Critical infrastructure is seen as a System of systems, and, therefore a fundamental condition that must be met is the linkages between the system's elements.

Generally, for linkages of any type within any system, it is necessary to distinguish with regard to the designed level. Figure 1 [3] illustrates this approach and distinguishes linkages between the CI systems and linkages inside the system between the individual elements.

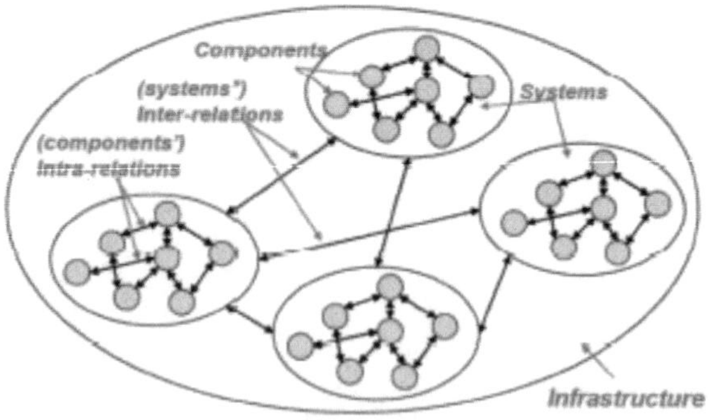

Figure 1. Linkages inside the CI [11]

Research on dependency linkages between the important CI and their elements in the Czech Republic is still a subject of scientific interest. Therefore, in the literature, this topic is addressed only marginally. The fundamental works published [4][5][6] are generally analysing the existing foreign sources. Foreign research studies that could significantly contribute to addressing the typology of linkages were also published in the Czech Republic.

In the foreign literature, the topic of linkages in CI sectors is widely addressed. One of the most important sources can be considered an article by Rinaldi et al. [7]

which bring together experts from the Czech Republic well as foreign experts. The approaches in that publication are also reflected partly or completely in published practical applications [8][9][10], as well as in conceptual documents [11].

Rinaldi et al. [7] offer several possible approaches to categorizing linkages. In terms of the direction of functional failure, linkages can be of type dependency or interdependency.

A linkage dependency is an expression that applies when infrastructure B is affected by infrastructure A, but infrastructure A is not within the same infrastructure linkages affected by B. Dependence is a one-sided type of linkage. An example of such a link is shown in Figure 2.

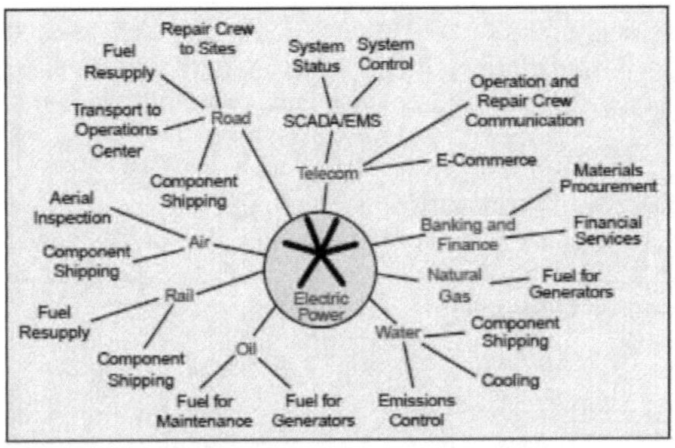

Figure 2. Example of dependency - dependency on electricity [7]

Linkage interdependency is an expression that applies when CI A is dependent on CI B through a certain linkage, and CI B is dependent on CI A through other linkage. Linkage of interdependence is a two-sided type of linkage. An example of such a linkage is shown in Figure 3.

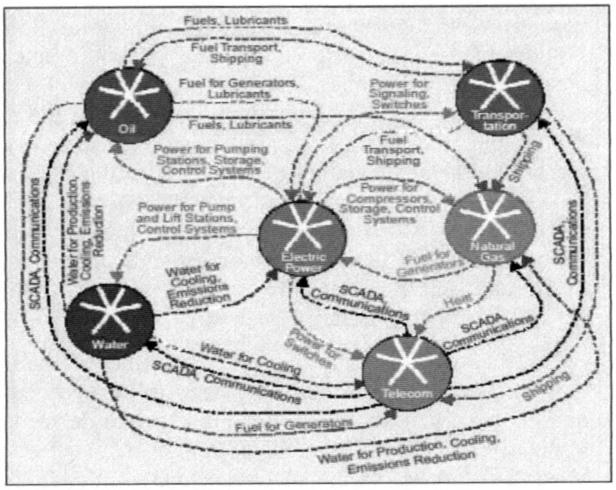

Figure 3. Example interdependency - the interdependence between selected CI sectors [11]

Regarding categorization of linkages in terms of their action direction, Rostek, Markuci & Adamec [6] report that, if CI A positively / negatively affects CI B through a linkage, it is not a requirement that CI B was dependent on CI A. It is, therefore, a sign that expresses a kind of precursor patterns of dependency and its ability of stimulatory or inhibitory effect.

Rinaldi et al. [7] exclusively emphasize the use of the term interdependency whose content concept corresponds to the most real systems and their holistic perspective.

In the same publication from Rinaldi et al. [7], another possible approach is further hinted at, which is based on the ability of CI sectors and their components interactions. Despite the fact that this case only dealt with the individual sectors, respectively their elements characteristics, and did not deal with direct linkages typology, this approach can be considered inspirational to the general perception of linkages between the CI sectors. From this perspective, it provides the following types of sectors:

- Supported,

The industry is dependent on the function of other sectors and their role is predominantly passive.

- Supportive,

The industry is able to influence the function of other sectors and their role is predominantly active.

Categorization of linkages within the systems is not addressed exclusively as part of research activities targeted at CI analysis. For example, it is possible to include the publication of Bühne et al. [12], which gives basic linkages typology used in the process of phenomena modelling. Bühne et al. [12] indicate linkages:

- Requirements,

Requires the existence / need another object (required).

- Exclusivity,

Linkage to selected object precludes the selection of another object.

- Help / advice,

It describes the positive relationship - object has a positive influence on another object.

- Obstacles,

It describes the relationship when the object has a negative impact on another object.

Another approach to linkages classification was presented by Rinaldi et. al [7] . In relation to the general classification, according to the direction of dependency linkage and interdependence linkage, in this context there is more evolved the interdependency linkage types and further categorized into the following classes of linkages, through which they are transmitted effects between different CI sectors and its elements:

• Physical,

The state of the CI sector is dependent on the material output of other CI sectors.

• Cybernetic,

The state of the CI sector is dependent on information linkage to other CI sectors.

• Geographical,

The state of the CI sector is dependent on emergencies arising in the territory.

• Logic,

The CI sector is dependent on the status of a second CI sector, and the linkage mechanism is not physical, cybernetic or geographical (dependence transmitted via streams, which are for example legislation, financial instruments).

The same linkages typology was presented by Peerenboom et al. [13] or Chien-Cheng & Ssu-Min [14]. Dudenhoeffer, Permann & Boring [15] present their own interdependence linkages typology, which, however, only slightly differs from the classification referred by Rinaldi et al. [7]. Dudenhoeffer, Permann & Boring [15] distinguishe the following types of linkages:

• Physical,

Direct linkages between the CI sectors affecting the flow of supply - consumption - production.

• Information,

Direct linkages between the CI sectors are given by the information flow. An example might be the SCADA systems.

• Geospatial,

Linkages between the CI sectors spatially tied.

• Political,

Linkages between the CI sectors affect decisions framework.

Physical, geospatial and information linkage can be considered equivalent to physical, cyber and geographic linkages. Political linkage can be described in terms of content meaning linked with subordinated logical linkage featured by Rinaldi et al. [7], which has a more general meaning.

The typology by Dudenhoeffera, Permanna & Boring [15] extends Pederson's et al. [16] typology by the type of social linkages, which they perceive as the influence of factors (public opinion, public trust, and sharing cultural values) able to transfer to other CI sectors. In terms of content focus, it can again be social linkage subsume, as in the previous case by political linkages, under the logic linkage.

In comparison with previously presented approaches, Zhang & Peeta [17] present a completely different concept of CI sectors linkages typology definition. According to this concept the following types of linkages are proposed:

• Functional,

System functionality requires outputs from the other system or it possibly can be substituted by a different system.

• Physical,

Some systems are connected by physical attributes. Strong linkage, therefore, exists when systems jointly share the right to flow, leading to the mutual capacity constraints.

• Budget,

Systems functionality is largely influenced by the flow and distribution of public funds, especially in the context of centrally controlled economies or in the recovery phase after crisis or a disaster.

• Market,

The existence of shared market sources indicates that all systems interact in the same economic environment. It means that the systems always serve the same end-users, who determine the final consumption of the commodity / services - according to market opportunities.

A possible example of practical application of the mentioned approaches to the linkages classification between the CI sectors is also published in the defence research project dealing with the so-called Location - Based Critical Infrastructure Interdependence [8]. In this research, the dependencies identification were reflected by Rinaldi et al. [7] presented concept and consider the possible impact of interdependence between various important CI sectors through physical, cyber, geographical and logical linkages. Within the model, some scenarios were simulated. One scenario was the simulation of a shallow earthquakes with an intensity of 7.3 modified Mercalli scale (scale was compiled and based on observations of the earthquake effects and is used to measure macro-seismic intensity) in a seismically active region situated in the Strait Georgia, British Columbia, Canada.

The functional earthquake effect was spatially visualized in the project. High risk has been identified or a total of 23 objects important to the water infrastructure sector near Vancouver, Canada. Severe damage is also expected near Vancouver airport. Spatial analysis helped identify the level of risk with regard to population density. Simulations showed that, due to electricity supply failure, the functionality of another important CI will be disrupted.

According to the findings above, high pressure will be faced from the part of emergency services, as an element of one CI sectors (class no. 9 - Safety). Significant impact in this field is also foreseen to the transport sector.

III. SYNTHESIS OF ANALYSED APPROACHES

An overview of the approaches discussed for the linkages type's classification between different CI sectors is presented in Table. 1.

TABLE 1. OVERVIEW OF SELECTED APPROACHES TO LINKAGES CLASSIFICATION

Author	Linkages types
Rinaldi et al.	a) Dependency b) Interdependency 1. Physical, 2. Cybernetic 3. Geographical, 4. Logic,
Bühne et al.	• Requirements, • Exclusivity, • Help / advice, • Obstacles,
Dudenhoeffer, Permann & Boring	• Physical, • Information, • Geospatial, • Political,
Pederson et al.	• Physical, • Information, • Geospatial, • Political, • Social,
Zhang & Peeta	• Functional, • Physical, • Budget, • Market,

The classifications are generalized expression of the possible types of addictions and transmission effects between the CI sectors.

Current literature offers several possible approaches to classifying linkages between the CI sectors and their elements. From selected international sources as well as from the Czech Republic, we conclude that the most frequently cited classification is the one presented by Rinaldi et al. [7]. This classification distinguished the linkages as physical, cyber, geographic and logical. This is developed not only in the theoretical research, but it is also used for practical applications needs and the assessment of CI individual relations.

IV. CONCLUSION

This article has possible applicability in the project RESILIENCE 2015. Dynamic resilience evaluation of interrelated critical infrastructure subsystems should be through the prism of this classification in order to see how the flows within important CI sectors, particularly in the sectors of energy, transport and information and communication technologies affect each other and how they affect the other important CI sectors through interdependencies. The recommended theoretical concept of reflection on the issue of CI sectors interdependence is also used in the strategy plan of the new approach to the critical infrastructure sectors protection at EU level [11]. The article goal is to identify basic understanding of linkages type modelling in the context of critical infrastructure. Linkage type's definition is seen as a significant input to the security research project RESILIENCE 2015, mostly in relation to functional parameters identification for the domino and synergy effect assessment process. This article outcome provides a philosophical and theoretical framework and analysis implementation in the context of interdependencies impact in connection with critical infrastructure resilience assessment.

ACKNOWLEDGMENT

This work was supported by the research project VI20152019049 "RESILIENCE 2015: Dynamic Resilience Evaluation of Interrelated Critical Infrastructure Subsystems", supported by the Ministry of the Interior of the Czech Republic in the years 2015-2019.

REFERENCES

[1] CR. decree no. 432, 2010 on criteria for determining critical infrastructure element. In Collection of Laws of the Czech Republic. 2010 amount 149th

[2] CR. Law no. 240 dated 28.6. 2000 on crisis management and amending certain Acts (Crisis Act). In Collection of Laws of the Czech Republic. 2000 amount 73rd,

[3] D2.9 - State-of-the-art literature review of methodologies to assess the vulnerability of a "system of systems". [online]. [cit. 2015-11-30]. http://www.vce.at/SYNER-G/pdf/deliverables/D2.09_State-of-the-art%20literature%20review%20of%20methodologies%20to%20asse.pdf

[4] J., Markuci, P., Rostek, and M., Dopaterová, correspondence analysis as a tool for evaluation of interdependence. In. Protecting the population - Hazardous substances 2015. Ostrava: Association of Fire and Safety Engineering, 2015, p. 95 – 99. ISBN 978-80-7385-158-3.

[5] J., Markuci, and D., Řehák, Interdependencies of critical infrastructure. In: Fire Protection 2014. Ostrava: Association of Fire and Safety Engineering, 2014, p. 207 – 210. ISBN 978-80-7385148-4.

[6] P., Rostek, J. Markuci, and V. Adamec, The issue of dependency when assessing the criticality of an item of infrastructure. The Science for Population Protection [online]. 2014, roč. 6, č. 1 [cit. 2015-11-14]. http://www.population-protection.eu/prilohy/casopis/27/175.pdf

[7] S. M., Rinaldi, J. P. Peerenboom, & T. K. Kelly, Identifying, Understanding, and Analyzing Critical Infrastructure Interdependencies. IEEE Control Systems Magazine. 2001, p. 11- 25.

[8] M. R. Abdalla, and K. K. Niall, Location-Based Critical Infrastructure Interdependency (LBCII). [online]. [cit. 2015-11-30]. www.dtic.mil/cgi-bin/GetTRDoc?AD=ADA526442

[9] J. M., Hyeung-Sik, et al. Toward modeling and simulation of critical national infrastructure interdependencies. IIE Transactions. 2007, vol. 39, Issue 1, p. 57-71.

[10] S. Folga, et al. A systems-level methodology for the analysis of inland waterway infrastructure disruptions. Journal of Transportation Security. 2009, vol. 4, Issue 2, p. 121-136.

[11] Commission staff working document on a new approach to the European Programme for Critical Infrastructure Protection, Making European Critical Infrastructures more secure. [online]. [cit. 2015-11-30]. http://ec.europa.eu/dgs/home-affairs/what-we-do/policies/crisis-and-terrorism/critical-infrastructure/docs/swd_2013_318_on_epcip_en.pdf

[12] S., Bühne, G., Halmas, and K., Pohl, Modelling Dependencies between Variations Points in Use Case Diagrams. In: Pre - Proceeding of 9th International Workshop on Requirements Engineering – Foundations for Software Quality (REFSQ'03). Klagenfurt/Velden: 2003. p. 43 – 54.

[13] J., Peerenboom, R., Fisher, and R., Whitfield, Recovering from disruptions of interdependent critical infrastructures. In: Workshop on Mitigating the Vulnerability of Critical Infrastructures to Catastrophic Failures, 2001.

[14] Ch. Chien-Cheng, and T. Ssu-Min, Collection and Analysis of Critical Infrastructure Interdependency Relationships. Jornal of Computing in Civil Engineering. 2010, Issue. 24, Issue 6.

[15] D., Dudenhoeffer, M. R., Permann, and M., Manic. CIMS: A Framework for Infrastructure Interdependency Modeling and Analysis. In: Proceedings of the 2006 Winter Simulation Conference. Monterey: IEEE, 2006, p. 478 – 485.

[16] P., Pederson, et al. Critical Infrastructure Interdependency Modeling: A Survey of U.S.and International Research. Idaho: Idaho National Laboratory, Critical Infrastructure Protection Division, Idaho Falls, August 2006.

[17] P. Zhang., and S. A. Peeta, generalized modeling framework to analyze interdependencies among infrastructure systems. Transportation Research: Part B. 2011, vol. 45, Issue 3. p. 553 - 579.

Security and Safety Processes in Czech Republic Universities

Lucia Duricova, Martin Hromada, Jan Mrázek
Faculty of Applied Informatics
Tomas Bata University in Zlin
Zlin, Czech Republic
E-mail: {duricova, hromada, jmrazek}@fai.utb.cz

Abstract— **This paper focuses on security and safety requirements and processes to help universities in developing more effective security and safety risks management system. The proposal is based on management techniques and on understanding primary processes in university buildings. The solution proposes a system which is integrated as a management system in the commercial sector. However, this proposal only takes in account special conditions, such as requirements for students, which are present in the university buildings. The proposed system helps enforce more effective security and safety measures in school facilities and in universities.**

Keywords- Law Requirements; Risk Management; Safety; Security; Soft Targets.

I. INTRODUCTION

The aim of this paper is the proposal of a security and safety management system in universities with software support. Safety and security in academic institutions is a common topic, especially with school buildings being the target of different attacks [10] [11] [12]. The objects, that need to be under the security and safety management system, include structures or facilities that are visited daily by hundreds or thousands of students. The paper is focused on understanding the processes and also on the specification of security and safety risks.

This research concentrates on the system integration which has been applied into school facilities and universities. The current situation could be different in other countries. In the Czech Republic, the current state could be presented as a system without any special security requirements. The school facilities have problems with financial resources that could be used towards security techniques and with knowledges about efficient measures. These statements are based on studies which have been done in school facilities such as kindergartens, primary schools and secondary schools [1] [2] [3].

University management faces to a different problem. Universities want to be more open towards their surroundings for students and potential students. This is the reason why security attacks have happened at Czech Republic Universities [10] [12]. This statement resulted from interviews with management at Czech Universities.

Universities could apply basic principles of management to manage processes because the structure is similar as a commercial organization aiming to gain/earn a profit. Risk is a subjective concept that needs to be viewed and quantified on an individual basis [4].

This research defines processes which could be implemented into software. The level of security and safety situation at universities depends on the correct setting of measures. The software has to know the processes that occur at the university on daily basis and also the ideal situation. The ideal situation is represented by the values that are used for the fuzzy statements. The fuzzy statements are used for the decision making process [3].

The reminder of this paper is organized as follows. In Section 2, we defined the elementary law requirements which have to be integrated into the software. This had been done in order to simplify requirements for the management of school facilities and universities. In Section 3, we defined the categorization of the physical structure of a university building. The categorization could have an impact on security and safety incidents. In Section 4, we described the classification of each building or part of the building by the impact to emergency incidents. The aims of access are classified in section 5. According to the aim of access, the system should define the typical behavior and then identify NOK (Non-conformity) of process. In section 6, the impact of risk sources is defined. In section 7, special events are identified. Software solution must identify special events by values that represents it; for example, planning in calendar (user define special event in application). After that, the software will propose special conditions that have to be fulfilled before action. In the section 8, the proposal of security and safety solution is explained. This part describes system realization (the processes have been already specified in the previous section 2-8). The real life case study is expressed in section 9. The last section concludes this research paper.

The paper proposes one system solution that could effectively manage security and safety situation in the school facilities and the universities. The software could supply missing knowledges to management of the school facilities and universities. The research relates to the smart home security and intelligent management system that could support school facilities. The fuzzy logic is the modern theory which belongs to artificial intelligence field [5].

II. Laws Requirements Was Integrated to School Facilities in Czech Republic

Law requirements are aimed to security and safety requirement that are integrated into school facilities and also universities, but it is not limited to this kind of facilities. In Czech Republic, two groups of universities are defined. Institution, which belongs to the first level of university, can perform role of a researcher (development and innovation). Each student must respect internal directives at university and at other buildings that are part of the campus. It is the first requirement that should be followed. In the proposal, it could be utilized as implementation support [3].

The internal directives are defined for appropriate behavior in object and also there is applied in educational system. If these directives have special security and safety option, it could be called as security and safety directives; however, it must be applied into other processes and also into related directives.

In safety solution, Czech Republic has two groups of requirements. The first is an Occupational Health and Safety (OHS). These requirements do not affect only employees and also students [8]. On the other hand, Czech Republic has specified requirements for Fire Protection (FP). This second group is based on primary firefighting building technical solution which is designed in project plan by authorized engineer. This solution is implemented to project in the preparatory development phase. Other fire requirements are derived from this solution which is implemented in operation of facilities. The special safety conditions for primary, secondary, and high school are specified in Czech law; however, these conditions are not established for universities. It could be utilized for definition of primary requirements for this type of objects. That means, it could be specified for schools, universities, theatres, shopping centers and other objects which fall into soft targets category.

III. Physical Structure of University Buildings

This section considers the division of parts of university. University buildings are used to educational process or to other supported processes. This categorization is important for the proposal of software solving. The proposal of software has implemented this structure into the main program.

A. *Size and Separation University Building*

The university consists of educational buildings, individual faculties, and other buildings. The number of visitors is closely related to the location and territorial jurisdiction. There is a relevant assessment of objects whose activities are closely related to the processes in the university. The building or premises separation should be evaluated mainly from two perspectives, namely the distribution of individual objects and their connectivity with a university.

B. *Distribution of Relevant Faculties and Buildings*

The dislocation of individual objects should be addressed by linking effectiveness ties and with location of the object. This aspect should be examined in the relation to the transport or access of individuals into the object, and also due to the timetable of the teaching process and other aspects. A parts of the university are defined as the basic building block.

The map of dislocation helps visitors to familiarize with the localization of individual rooms or increase the degree of orientation of the building. The software support will define requirements for the parts of university, and it could help to solve incidents quickly and effectively. An expert who will make decisions could see the structure of building and the number of persons in object. It could be useful for emergency. The main reason is to use the plans for solving incidents and security and safety situations. The proposal of the system security and safety integration implements plans for support into decision making process. Experts can offer effective and smart solutions if they are informed about the dislocations and security devices layout [2].

In individual building complex, where the systematic solution is implemented, the efficiency of safety and security is lower than in the whole area. In the second case, the distance between university buildings is different in each educational institution. Therefore, this is the one of many inputs that is supplied to the decision making process.

While the student is moving between buildings, there is higher probability of safety and security emergency incidents. In the software solution, this could be represented by numerical value. Due to this value, the expert is aware about the current situation.

This is important fact, especially, if we are talking about the possibility of the injury risks and also repeated controls on re-entry to another parts of the university [4].

IV. Definition of University Buildings

This section deals with specifications for each kind of university building (see Figure 1). This definition considers three parts:

- Complex structure,
- the main and supported aim of the object,
- the primary visitors aim.

In this section, primary options are presented. These options can improve security and safety situations at universities.

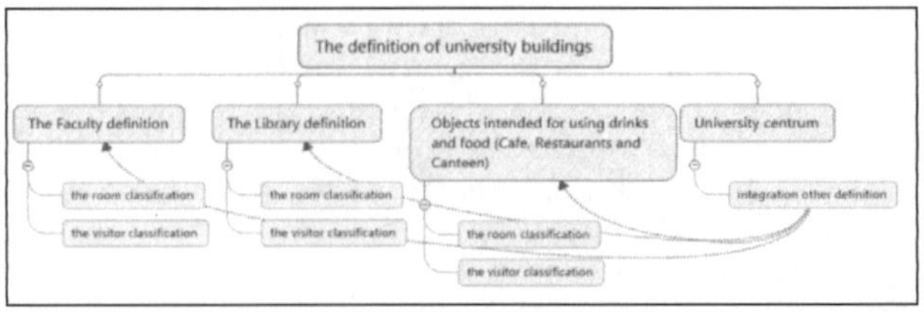

Figure 1. Definition of university buildings.

The definition of university buildings is the first part of object categorization. According to the building categorization, the software can identify input requirements.

If several objects are located in one central place, there is a need to consider their purposes. Individual components should be analysed as an individual unit.

This part of paper has been reflected physical structure of university buildings. After this analytical process, the analyses of visitors are followed. The next process examines the ties between visitor aim and operation requirements. This process will be applied in software. When the evaluation is negative, then the visitor aim is different than university aim. The management should implement security and safety rules into this process. These rules have to be implemented into process, have to be documented and also controlled. The main aim of the University building is education. Another object aims are supporting and the object have to be adapted to these requirements. In this situation, there are reciprocity ties. It could be utilized to achieve greater safety and security situation.

V. Evaluation of User Access

Each category of the school facility is specified by the aim and function rules which are closely related to the person who sets the access to the facilities. For the effective security and safety options, the study and evaluation of these ties and its attributes is important. The intersection of the attributes should be used for effective decision-making in the crisis situations; for example: public course and common classes.

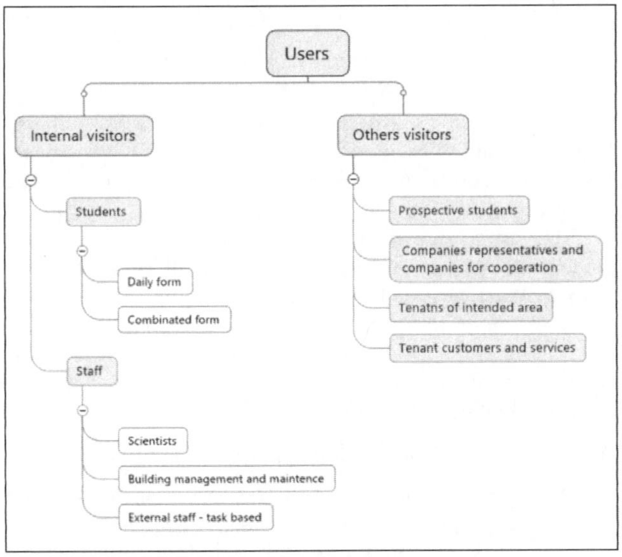

Figure 2. The definition of users.

According to the specification (primary building, second visitors), the management should define the security and safety requirements and furthermore system options. The effective measures should set up rules for visitors in building and manage their movement. The measures have an impact on incident probability. The software will monitor visitors by the effective measures. The visitor has to apply for access by an assigned card. The assigned card has given rules that correspond with the visitor aim. The categorization of visitor with assigned card is depicted in Figure 2. This solution could be implemented into a program and transferred into the soft targets net. The management of solution could be faster and more effective. The software will replace expert knowledges and then the manager of the object can specify the internal object knowledges.

VI. Impact of Risk Sources

This part of the paper will describe causes of the incidents that could happen in university buildings. In case, that the management of university will know root cause of incident, then the setting of permanent measures will be more effective, because the measures will be implemented for specific event. In the paper, two primary groups of risk sources are defined (human factors, technical factors). These two factors are represented in software by numerical value. In each category, whole range of the values that represents status of these factors is defined.

A. Impact and context with measures - Human factors

The factors, which are described in this section, are resulted of survey in educational buildings. This factor also occurs in commercial building; however, the management coordinates it with ISO standard. The human factors are important for definition of typical human behavior and it could be implemented to software solving. In the next part, the main points of human factors are defined.

- Cause of security incident by inappropriate behaviour (unwanted conduct).
- Occurrence of human error negligence, ignorance - without the presence of variations in operational practices.
- Lack of definition and application of security measures in operation.
- Establishment of internal procedures and rules with the help of guidelines that define the desired conditions and the required visitor behaviour.
- The implementation of measures and procedures of the directives in the actual operation of the facilities.
- Monitoring compliance with the security measures binding to the desired level.

It is only the first part of risks. The second part is connected to the technical factors.

B. Impact and context with measures - Technical factors

The technical components are used to security measures and also for other use. The technical components, which are used to other use, could have impact to security and safety situation in object. Security technical components are used to achieve more effective monitoring and permanent controlling in object [4]. The security components are designed to support managers and experts. The causes of technical difficulties are defined:

- Improper installation of equipment - technical failure of the device or other parts.

- The failure of the technical component caused by its use.
- Short circuit was caused by other activities.
- Closely related to the definition of procedures for the installation of technical equipment and functional tests and more.
- Closely related to the defined intervals to check the technical component devices.
- Specification of the possible effects of the above mentioned equipment.

The risk sources are implemented to the proposal as inputs for the analytical processes. The proposal of software solving is based on the object characteristics and the sources of risks.

VII. Special Events in Universities

In the research, each process is implemented into a flowchart. It should be integrated to security and safety solution. For integration, primary Deming's cycle (PDCA model) is chosen. Table I. defines events that can occur at the University and educational objects. The next part of the proposal will define the preventive actions in event planning.

TABLE I. THE CHARACTERISTIC OF SEPARATION IN PROCESSES [2]

Num.	The separation in university processes		
	The Process	***The Separation***	***Groups of person***
1.	Educational	Admission process	Prospective students
		Enrolment to studies	Acceptance of candidates
		The beginning of the semester – full-time study	Enrolled students
		The beginning of the semester – correspondence course	Enrolled students
		Exam period	Students who have been granted credits (full-time and correspondent).
		Final exam	Students who graduated and fulfil student's requirements.
2.	Public events	Conference, workshops and other regulate actions.	Invited guests, acceptable reservations, payments.
		Open door day and other actions.	Public actions.
3.	Commercial sector	Operation of commercial sector.	Clients and business partners.
		Meetings and workshops organized by the commercial sector.	Clients and business partners (it could be public action).

This part of paper defines primary events in educational processes; however, behavior and interest of students in free time period is not presented in these analyses. Free time period is period between two teaching units or two groups of activities.

VIII. The Proposal of Security and Safety Solution

The proposal has been implemented to two groups of university buildings. In the new buildings or facilities, the proposal should be included in plan documentation for construction. In existing buildings, the application of this proposal is more demanding because of the processes must not be suspended. Both categories are based on similar principle. For the proposed application, fuzzy logic was chosen. The processes definitions are demonstrated in Figure 3.

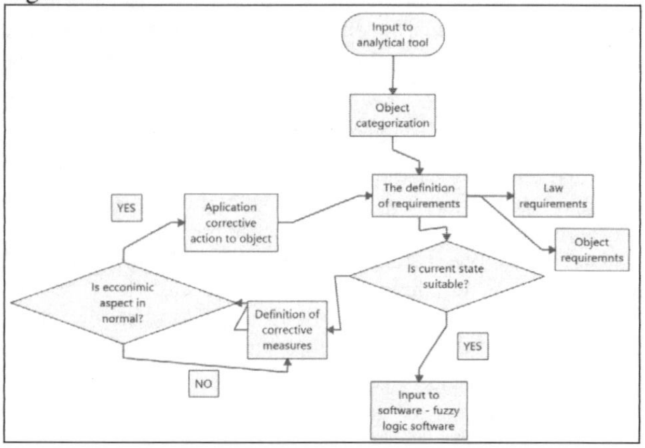

Figure 3. Analytical process and software integration.

Fuzzy logic is based on analysis of real numbers between 0 and 1. Fuzzy logic works with fuzzy statements that are constructed from expert experiences and knowledges.

The first analytical part is based on the object categorization. The software inputs are objects that have defined characteristic properties and measures. The software analyzes the current state in the object and also the control statements. If the current state does not correspond with the required state, the software defines immediate actions or decision making actions [3].

A. *The proposal for educational object integration*

- Analysis the current state (definition of buildings aim, visitors aim, events, categorization of teaching units and processes and definition of acceptable and unacceptable risks).
- The definition of root causes (safety and security solution and suggestibility of other processes in the objects).
- The definition of permanent corrective actions (PDCA model).
- The repeated security and safety analysis (law requirements and management requirements).

Figure 4. shows designed ties between measures in educational objects. The measures are defined in planning process and also in operator process. Users should define input attributes and this attributes could be set by experts or by building documentations.

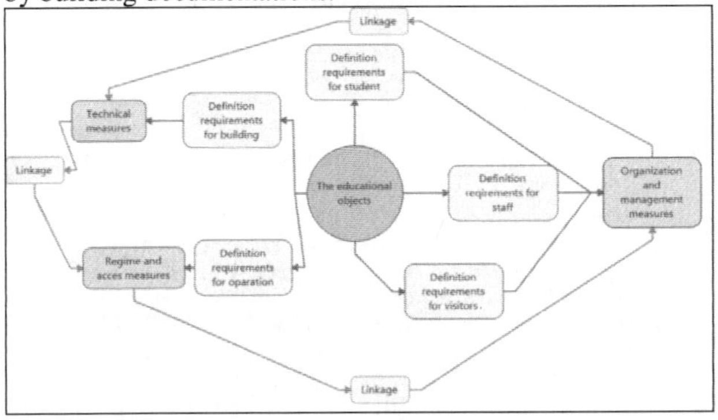

Figure 4. Integration into educational objects.

The next part defines proposal for the division of educational rooms.

- Specific places in object – define the requirements to the access, the requirements for the manipulation with the materials and the machines, definition of the safety procedures for working process, the definition of room aim and definition of risk attributes.
- Non-public space object - these spaces belong to group premises accessible to the public; however, the access control does not require a high level of management. The management defines the same attributes as previous. In these places, specific objects (machine and materials) should not be placed.
- The public space at university – it is not public for everyone (only on Open day door or other specific events); however, the management defines public space as a space, where every person who has aim to be in university can move.

Access to university facilities should be managed and monitored. In case, that the part of the building is used for commercial purposes, the rules for the minimization of possible creation of security incidents should be defined. These rules cannot influence the main activities of the university and supported processes.

B. The categorization of system layout

- University areal - defined territory forms a single unit. The university areal consists of several buildings with undeveloped land between them. The complex should be bordered.
- The simple structure of the university buildings – the university is formed by one or more connected buildings (mostly faculties).
- The complex structure of the university buildings - multiple buildings with different distance between them that are in competence of university (located at the site of one city or the structure also affects flights to another city) [2].

Those types of structures guaranties safety and security procedures which are specified especially in their dislocation. In the case of the complex there is a possibility of managing the entry and exit of the building. The categorization will be set in software. It means, we must use description that is written above for the implementation in a school facilities and a university.

Other approaches are defined separately and it causes that measures are not as effective as can be. The software support will economize financial support and reduces requirements for security operators. These are the main two reasons why the managers and directors do not want to invest money to security solutions.

IX. REAL-LIFE CASE STUDY

The software could help the academic objects. If a university campus is included into the software, an expert can see where people are and what they are doing. If some incident threatens, the expert could have a number of people in the building immediately.

A. The fire in the building

In the software we can see, where the fire is, what cause it, who is threaten and what decision expert should do.

Without the software, we could lose time. We could see where the fire is; for example, fire control panel, but we cannot see other information as access, number of visitors, the position of the resources for extinguishing. Other information could be integrated to one system that could provide the expert decision making. Nowadays, the universities integrate more systems in an object; however, the management is different for each other. This proposal could integrate it together. The aim is to unite each output from central unit that manage these components. If the software knows the visitor aim, the expert also knows that visitors are not able to orient in the building.

The reasoning is based on fuzzy rule in the software. The fuzzy rules use the linguistic variables. The form of fuzzy rule is:

If $x \in A$ and $y \in B$ then $z \in C$, where A, B, and C are fuzzy sets.

B. Example for fuzzy reasoning

If (security coefficient of events 1 is medium) and (number of visitors is high) then (security measures are medium).

The degree of support for the variable “security measures” is defined by fuzzy set “medium”. The degree of support for the variable “security coefficient” is defined by fuzzy set “medium” and the degree of support for the variable “number of visitors” is defined by fuzzy set “high”. The underlying idea is with increasing number of checks of propositions in premise; the more suggestions could be derivate. For the degree of support for the truth of the fuzzy proposition "security measures are medium", the fuzzy implication must be defined. The fuzzy statement defines the degree of support for the fuzzy rule. The defuzzification is process in which the one shape value is determined from the interval [5].

C. *The software solution*

The access for visitors is monitored by a card. They will obtain cards in registration process. Management rules are defined with an event plan. After the software is familiarized with the plans, the measures will be done.

This part of paper applies the application into processes in the universities and the school facilities. The measures will be supported by the expert groups. The expert groups are represented by fuzzy statements in software. That is the main reason why this solution could be effective and the management does not need to know any special knowledges about security and safety decision making. The research is aimed to software support; however, we still need the support of training for effective decision making; for example: employee training. The employee training is aimed on a crises situation. They will manage crises situations; for example: attack in a school.

X. CONCLUSION

The main advantage is the system approach which should manage security and safety situation at universities. The system integration could increase effectivity of all processes. In this paper, the security and safety proposal was presented as a system solution which is used in World Corporation, and also companies and it is called management systems with software support. This paper describes primary processes and identifies possible weaknesses in processes which could be used as an opportunity for improve. These methods are certificated by authorized subject and the effectiveness is verified every day.

ACKNOWLEDGMENT

This work was supported by Internal Grant Agency of Tomas Bata University in Zlin under the project No. IGA/FAI/2016/012.

REFERENCES

[1] L. Fennely and M. Perry, " The Handbook for School Safety and Security," 1st ed., Elsevier, 2014, ISBN: 978-0-12-800568-2.

[2] L. Prochazkova and M. Hromada, " The Proposal System for the Safety Assesment of Soft Targets with Focus on School Facilities," Proceeding of 3rd CER Comparative: SCIEMCEE Publishing, Vol. II, pp.: 30-34, ISBN: 978-0-9928772-6-2.

[3] L. Duricova Prochazkova and M. Hromada. "The Proposal of the Soft Targets Security". Advences in Intelligent Systems and Computing, Automation Control Theory Perspectives in Intelligent Systems. Proceedings of the 5th Computer Science On-line Conference 2016 (CSOC2016), Vol3, Springer, pp.: 337-345. ISSN 2194-5357, ISBN 978-3-319-33387-8, DOI 10.1007/978-3-319-33389-2.

[4] Ch. Sennewald, and C. Baillie, "Effective Security Management," 6th ed.,Amsterdam: Elsevier, 2016, ISBN: 978-0-12-802774-5.

[5] T. J. Ross, "Fuzzy logic with engineering applications" 3rd Edition, John Wiley & Sons, Ltd. ISBN: 978-0-470-74376-8.

[6] ISO 31000:2009, Risk management – Principles and guidelines.

[7] ISO/IEC 27001:2013, Information Technology- Security Techniques- Information Security Management Systems – Requirements.

[8] British Standard BS OHSAS 18001/2007, Occupational Health and Safety Management Systems- Requirements.

[9] ISO 9000:2005, Quality Management Systems- Fundamentals and Vocabulary.

[10] http://www.bdlive.co.za/national/education/2016/05/16/arson-attack-at-university-of-johannesburg-caused-damage-estimated-at-r100m-university-says

[11] http://www.dailymail.co.uk/wires/ap/article-2792116/1-killed-knife-attack-Czech-school.html

[12] http://edition.cnn.com/2016/02/29/us/ohio-school-incident/

Comprehensive System of Intense Convective Precipitation Forecasts for Regional Crisis Management

David Šaur, Lucia Ďuricová
Tomas Baťa University in Zlín
Faculty of Applied Informatics
Zlín, Czech Republic
e-mail: saur@fai.utb.cz, duricova@fai.utb.cz

***Abstract*— This paper focuses on the contemporary possibilities of predicting intense convective precipitation and the utilization of this information in Crisis Management procedures of the Zlin Region in the Czech Republic. The first part describes the Information, Notification and Warning System of the Zlin Region, which ensures comprehensive forecasts of convective precipitation. The outputs from the convective precipitation forecast system and the mobile meteorological radar (MMR50) are part of a comprehensive forecast. Both of these predictive tools are analyzed in this paper. The first principles of complex prediction are demonstrated in a case-based study involving the local flash floods that affected the Zlin Region on July 24th, 2015. The main contribution of the paper is unique information on the use of mobile meteorological radar (MMR50) to forecast thunderstorms and flash floods formation in the Zlín Region.**

Keywords-Flash Floods; Weather Forecast; Thunderstorms; Crisis Management

I. Introduction

In the last decade, flash floods have been one of the most abundant types of flooding in the Czech Republic. Despite the fact that large sum of money are being spent on flood prevention measures, effective protection against this type of flooding is almost nonexistent.

The main reason for this situation is the character of torrential floods and the possibility of their prediction. Flash floods are caused by intense convective precipitation over a very small area - in the order of kms^2 in a relatively short time (several dozen of minutes). The consequence of flash floods is a very steep rise in the level of the affected watercourse [1].

The main problem is the insufficient amount of ground meteorological stations including aerological stations that provide input data for Numerical Weather Prediction (NWP) models. Another shortcoming is insufficient resolution, which cannot affect the size of the convective cells. The use of NWP models for the prediction of intense convective precipitation has been investigated in many studies [2][3][4].

The second system used for predicting convective precipitation is "nowcasting" which calculates the shift of precipitation fields in the order of 30-60 minutes in advance. However, nowcasting systems cannot predict the dynamic development of convective precipitation in time. Nowcasting is combined with the outputs of NWP models [5][6][7].

The forecasting of intense convective precipitation is implemented by expert meteorological systems that combine the characteristics of NWP models, meteorological radars and satellites; including meteorological nowcasting in foreign meteorological services. The disadvantages of expert systems result from the forecasting systems´ deficiencies [8][9].

The fundamental problems reside in forecasting for a specific location and time of occurrence of intense convective precipitation; including sufficient lead-time ahead of the forecast.

The Czech Hydrometeorological Institute is the only institution in the Czech Republic that provides forecasts and warning information on the occurrence of dangerous atmospheric phenomena. However, this information is not of sufficient quality and accuracy - precisely because of the complicated temporal and spatial occurrence of these phenomena. Therefore, the Zlín Region is the only region in the Czech Republic that has decided to create its own complex system for forecasting torrential rainfall. One justifying reason for the design of this system is to provide another alternative that would support the decision-making processes of the regional crisis management of the administrative authorities before the occurrence and while finding a solution for flash floods.

In Section 3, the graphical and tabular expression of the probability of occurrence of convective precipitation will be the output for individual Municipalities with Extended Powers (MEP) in the Zlin Region. The information will be available, not only for the region, but also for MEP mayors including other municipalities and institutions.

The main objective of the comprehensive forecasting system will be to provide timely and high-quality information on the occurrence and development of future weather for crisis management and civil protection purposes. This information will then be used for preventive measures against the occurrence of flooding; for example, preventive inspections control of flood defenses, material and other resources.

II. The Complex Forecasting of Convective Precipitation

The complex of forecasting of convective precipitation is based on a sequence of activities necessary to ensure timely and high-quality information regarding the likely formation of flash floods:

- Monitoring of forecasting and warning information from the Czech Hydrometeorological Institute.
- Information from the convective precipitation forecast system outputs for the next 24 hours.
- Very short prediction times (i.e., nowcasting) by the mobile meteorological radar (MMR50) for 30 to 60 minutes.
- Verification of radar data through an observation network of professional and amateur meteorologists in the Zlín Region.

The comprehensive forecast implementation tool is the Information, Notification and Warning System of the Zlin Region (further only INWS ZR), which consists of information support for crisis management and population protection for extraordinary events, for example, floods, technological accidents, etc.

As can be seen in Figure 1, the backbone of the system is a robust and secure communication infrastructure (a fiber optic cable), which interconnects 11 municipalities with extended powers and other municipalities with the Zlín Region Crisis Staff regional controlling centre. The Zlín Region´s Information, Notification and Warning System is also used to communicate with the public administration sector, the Fire Rescue Services of the Zlín Region and the other municipalities' warning information systems [10][11].

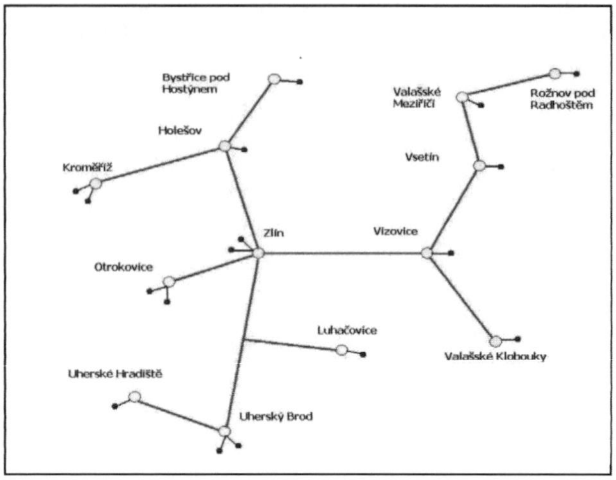

Figure 1. Structure of the INWS ZR [10].

INWS ZR consists of the following major components:

- Central Dispatch.
- Warning Information Systems (WIS).
- WIS Server.
- Videoconferencing systems.
- Municipal Closed-Circuits Television (CCTV) surveillance systems.
- Meteorological sensors and stations.
- Information and bulletin boards.
- Environmental and chemical detection elements.
- Mobile meteorological radar (MMR50).
- Alternative energy resources [12].

The forecasting of dangerous atmospheric phenomena has become a part of this system. The main component of this system is the control application of the INWS ZR. Simultaneously, control applications include outputs from:

- Convective precipitation forecasting system.
- Mobile meteorological radar (MMR50)

The comprehensive prediction of convective precipitation is comprised of the output control application of the INWS ZR that distributes data from radar measurements as well as the convective precipitation forecast system for authorities and other crisis management participants.

A. *The INWS ZR control application*

The INWS ZR control application is a user interface that enables the collection, analysis and evaluation of data for crisis management purposes in the Zlin Region. This application consists of two software components:

- The INWS ZR server application, connected to the data network with the individual clients of the INWS ZR under one municipality of extended powers.
- The INWS ZR applications client that runs on PCs in the individual departments and MEPs of the Zlin Region.

Access to the control applications of the INWS ZR is secured by logging into the INWS server. If the user is logged in, then they get permission to read and modify individual work sheets. The work sheets contain crisis management data and information about objects, documents, history, traffic, water courses, radar outputs from the mobile meteorological radar (MMR50) and other forecasting information [11].

B. *The convective precipitation forecasting system*

The core of the convective precipitation forecast system is an algorithm based on the principle of analyzing and evaluating the output of meteorological variables and the parameters of numerical weather prediction models; especially regional NWP model ALADIN [13]. The main research hypothesis is to assess the impact of the relief of the terrain on the development of convective precipitation in the target area. Because of this, one has to use an analysis of historical weather events and selected floods caused by torrential rainfall in order to produce supplementary, more accurate, warning information from the Czech Hydrometeorological Institute.

The main outcomes of the report are:

- The spatial and temporal occurrence of convective precipitation.
- The lead-time ahead of forecasts for the next 6-24 hours.

The "Place of occurrence" means the territory of the municipality with extended powers. The time occurrence forecast is set at the three-hour time interval.

The main method is a Multi-Criteria Assessment (MCA) whose basis is the selection criteria of the meteorological variables and the setting of the weights for these criteria.

The criteria weights were determined by analyzing the aerological data of 70 meteorological situations in 2007-2015.

The Convective Precipitation Forecast Algorithm (CPFA) operates in seven phases:

I. General characteristics of the predicted weather situation.
II. The forecasted time of the convective precipitation occurrence.
III. The air masses forecast conditions.
IV. The forecasted probability of dangerous accompanying phenomena (e.g., torrential rainfall, hail, strong wind gusts and tornadoes).
V. The forecasting of local conditions between the surface and the lift condensation level.
VI. The comparison of air masses´ forecast conditions and the local conditions with historical weather situations statistics.
VII. The main output of the forecast.

The first phase shows the basic characteristics of predicted weather conditions; such as date, flow direction at 700 hPa (i.e., precipitation movement direction), the type of weather situation, the triggering factor of convection and warning information by the Czech Hydrometeorological Institute. The second phase is focused on the prediction time occurrence of convective precipitation (i.e., 3-hour period). The forecast is based on the penetration of the NWP models ALADIN CHMU, ALADIN SHMU, GFS, GEM, UKMET, EURO4 outputs. The selection of these NWP models is based on an analysis of 50 weather situations with which these models have achieved the highest success rate of forecasting of convective precipitation.

Table I provides information about the weather conditions of air masses and the corresponding meteorological elements and convection indices:

TABLE I. AIR MASS CONDITIONS.

Meteorological condition	Meteorological elements, convection indices
Atmospheric instability	CAPE, Lifted Index, Showalter Index, K-Index, TT index, temperature gradient 2m-925,850, 500-850 hPa, Wetbulb temperature 0-1 km, Mixing ratio 1000 hPa
Triggering convection factors	Convective Inhibition, Relative Humidity 1000-500 hPa, Precipitable Water, Relative voriticity 850 hPa, Moisture Convergence, Frontogeneze 850 hPa, Temperature 850 hPa, Orographic Lift and Changing wind direction
Wind shear	Deep Layer Shear 0-6 km, Low Layer Shear 0-1 km, Storm Relative Helicity 0-3 a 0-1 km, SWEAT index
The organization and movement of storms	Jet Stream (300 hPa), Low Level Jet (850 hPa), Motion Convective Storm Propagation Vector, Wind 700 hPa

Each criterion (meteorological element, index convection) is classified according to the degree of intensity and probability of occurrence of convective precipitation clouds:

TABLE II. COEFFICIENTS OF THE INTENSITY AND PROBABILITY OF THE OCCURRENCE OF CONVECTIVE PRECIPITATION.

Coefficients	0	1	2	3
Thunderstorm instensity	Weak	Strong	Very strong	Extremely strong
Rainfall intensity (mm/hours)	0-29	30-49	50-89	>90
Propability of occurrence (%)	0-24	25-49	50-74	75-100

Tables II implies that the intensity of precipitation coefficients is related to the instability of the atmosphere, wind shear and the organization of the storms. The convective precipitation probability coefficients are used to trigger convection factors.

The intensity or probability of the convective precipitation occurrence is calculated according to this equation:

$$(\Sigma n/\Sigma m*3)*100(\%) = P . \quad (1)$$

where n is the sum of the forecast coefficients, e.g. forecasts of atmospheric instability, and m is the total number of predicted meteorological variables.

Fourthly, the probability of occurrence of dangerous atmospheric phenomena is defined as an intersection of selected meteorological variables defining the conditions of air masses.

In the fifth phase, the forecast of local conditions was calculated as the intersection of ALADIN meteograms meteorological variables and the morphometrical characteristics of relief:

- The air temperature at 2 meters above ground.
- The relative humidity 2 meters above ground.
- The difference of mean sea level pressure.
- The wind direction and speed at 10 meters above ground.
- The degree of cloud cover.
- The characteristics of terrain relief affecting the thermal conditions, e.g. orientation and slope of the terrain, the degree of vegetation coverage, the heat contrast of the Earth's surface, the Z-factor and the altitude and ridge parameters.
- The characteristics terrain relief influencing windy conditions; for example, settlement, valley parameters and wrapping obstacles.

In the sixth phase, the outputs of the first to third stages forecasts are compared with the historical statistics of meteorological situations. The main criteria are the direction of the precipitation movement, the synoptic situation and selected meteorological elements. The aim of this phase is to determine the degree of similarity between the predicted and historical meteorological situations.

The last phase is the final forecast of future occurrences of convective precipitation, which will include maps of the Zlin Region, including municipalities with extended powers for forecast purposes:

- The probability of time and place occurrence of precipitation for 6 to 24 hours in advance.
- The intensity of convective precipitation.
- The probability of the occurrence of dangerous atmospheric phenomena (e.g., heavy rainfall, hail, strong gusts and tornadoes).

This predictive information will be important in terms of its preventive nature for the region´s Crisis Management authorities and other participants.

C. *The MMR50 Meteorological Rradar*

The mobile meteorological radar (MMR50) is a device for detecting precipitation and other nonmeteorological targets within a radius of 60 km.

TABLE III. PARAMETETRS OF THE MMR50 METEOROLOGICAL RADAR.

Technical parameters	**The MMR 50 Mobile Meteorological Radar**
Location	The town Holešov Industrial Zone in the Zlín Region
Frequency	9,41 GHz
Wavelength/band	3 cm/ X-band
Transmitter power peak	50 kW
Maximum theoretical range	100 km

Table III presents the technical specification of the mobile meteorological radar (MMR50), which provides detailed information and the current state of precipitation through six radar products (i.e., Plan Position Indicator, Constant Altitude Plan Position Indicator, Range height indicator, ECHO TOP, Vertically Integrated Liquid). Very short-term forecast (Nowcasting) is secured by means of the Nowcasting TITAN forecasting software with forecasts for 30-60 minutes.

The fundamental radar quantity is the Radar Reflectivity Z in the dBz unit, which is converted from the rainfall intensity I:

$$10^{\wedge}(Z-10\log(a)/10b) = I. \qquad (2)$$

where the values of a and b are experimentally determined constants (a = 16, b = 200) [1].

III. CASE STUDY OF THE FLASH FLOOD ON 24.7.2015

The principle of the complex forecast of convective precipitation is shown with a case study of the flash flood that occurred on July 24th, 2015.

The main cause of the flash floods was a cold front, which ensured the emergence of sufficient atmospheric instability, combined with a moderate wind shear. This situation was characterized by the continuous emergence of new precipitation – and, its stationary movement.

This torrential rainfall, in combination with hail and strong wind gusts, caused material damage amounting to tens of millions Czech crowns. The most affected villages were Slušovice and Fryšták in the central part of the Zlin Region, where cellars and houses were flooded.

A. *Convective Precipitation Forecasting System*

The weather situation forecast was very complicated due to the uniqueness of the formation and development of the intensive convective precipitation.

In the previous section, the convective precipitation forecast was dealt with in several stages. The outcomes of a brief analysis of the predicted weather conditions were:

- The direction of precipitation movement from the southwest, with a speed of 9 m / s.
- The type of weather situation - an area of low pressure associated with a cold front over western Slovakia.
- Warning information from the Czech Hydrometeorological Institute was not released.

The Czech Hydrometeorological Institute did not issue predictive warning information on thunderstorms for the entire Czech Republic. Nevertheless, the forecast was calculated for 24 hours in advance, which found the likely occurrence of intense convective precipitation.

Subsequently, the interval occurrence of intense convective precipitation was determined - based on the outputs of the NWP models for 24 hours in advance:

TABLE IV. FORECAST OF PRECIPITATION TIME OCCURRENCE.

NWP models	**Time period (3 hours)**
ALADIN CHMU	12:00-15:00, **15:00-18:00**
ALADIN SHMU	12:00-15:00, **15:00-18:00**, **18:00-21:00**
GFS	**15:00-18:00, 18:00-21:00**
GEM	06:00-09:00, 09:00-12:00, 12:00-15:00, **15:00-18:00, 18:00-21:00,** 21:00-24:00
UKMET	12:00-15:00, **15:00-18:00, 18:00-21:00,** 21:00-24:00
EURO4	**15:00-18:00**

As shown in Table IV, times in bold typeface indicate those time intervals for which the predictions were calculated. The interval 15:00-18:00 is identified as 15 hours. The interval 18:00-21:00 is 18 hours.

The third phase involves the calculation of air mass conditions. Air mass includes the part of the atmosphere which is defined by the difference between the lift condensation level and the lower boundary of the troposphere.

The formation of strong and very strong thunderstorms was caused by a combination of sufficient atmospheric instability and a moderate wind shear in the central and northeastern parts of the Zlin Region.

TABLE V. AIR MASS FORECAST CONDITIONS.

Municipality with Extended Powers in the Zlin Region	Atmospheric instability		Convection trigger		Wind shear		Organization and motion of storm	
	15	*18*	*15*	*18*	*15*	*18*	*15*	*18*
Uherské Hradiště	1	2	2	2	0	1	1	1
Otrokovice	1	2	2	2	0	1	1	1
Kroměříž	1	2	2	2	0	**1**	1	1
Holešov	1	2	2	2	0	**1**	1	1
Zlín	1	2	2	2	0	**1**	1	1
Bystřice	1	2	2	2	0	**1**	1	1
Val. Meziříčí	1	2	2	2	0	**0**	1	1
Rožnov	1	2	2	2	0	**0**	1	1
Vsetín	1	2	2	2	0	**0**	1	1
Vizovice	1	2	2	2	0	**1**	1	1
Val. Klobouky	1	2	2	2	0	**1**	1	1
Luhačovice	1	2	2	2	0	**1**	1	1
Uherský Brod	1	2	2	2	0	**1**	1	1

Table V shows that the air mass conditions were more favorable after 18:00 hours.

TABLE VI. FORECAST OF LOCAL CONDITIONS.

Municipality with Extended Powers in the Zlin Region	Orographic effect		Thermal effect		Convergence effect		Resulting forecast	
	15	*18*	*15*	*18*	*15*	*18*	*15*	*18*
Uherské Hradiště	0	0	2	2	1	1	1	1
Otrokovice	0	0	1	1	2	2	1	1
Kroměříž	1	1	2	2	1	1	1	1
Holešov	1	0	2	2	2	2	2	1
Zlín	1	1	2	2	2	2	2	2
Bystřice	1	1	2	2	1	1	1	1
Val. Meziříčí	1	1	2	2	2	2	2	2
Rožnov	1	1	2	2	2	2	2	2
Vsetín	1	1	2	2	2	2	2	2
Vizovice	1	1	2	2	2	2	2	2
Val. Klobouky	1	1	1	1	2	2	1	1
Luhačovice	1	0	2	2	2	2	2	1
Uherský Brod	1	1	2	2	2	2	2	2

Table VI demonstrates the probability of formation of convection affected by the local weather conditions which are orographic, thermal and wind conditions of terrain relief for a specific time interval. The most favorable conditions for the initial formation of convection above the Earth's surface were predicted for the northeastern and central parts of the Zlin Region.

The sixth and seventh phases were consolidated for the clarity of the main output. The resulting forecast is a combination of air mass conditions and the local conditions, combined and compared with selected historical weather precipitation statistics.

TABLE VII. RESULTING FORECAST.

Municipality with Extended Powers in the Zlin Region	6th and 7th phases of predicted convective precipitation			
	23.7	*11.7.2011*	*7.8.2011*	***Resulting forecast***
Uherské Hradiště	0	0	0	0
Otrokovice	0	0	0	0
Kroměříž	1	0	2	**1**
Holešov	1	0	1	**1**
Zlín	1	1	0	**1**
Bystřice	1	2	1	**1**
Val. Meziříčí	1	0	1	**1**
Rožnov	1	0	0	**1**
Vsetín	1	0	0	**1**
Vizovice	1	0	0	**1**
Val. Klobouky	0	0	0	**0**
Luhačovice	0	0	0	**0**
Uherský Brod	0	0	0	**0**

Table VII summarizes the facts the outputs from statistics only confirm or complement the new convective precipitation locations. The resulting forecast only changes if the statistics concur on the occurrence of precipitation outside the forecast of conditions of air masses and the local conditions. In this case, the resulting forecast remains unchanged.

B. Nowcasting by the mobile meteorological radar (MMR50)

Very short-term forecasting was performed using the mobile meteorological radar (MMR50).

TABLE VIII. OUTPUTS OF NOWCASTING ON 24.7.2015.

Locations	**Time**	**Intensity (mm)**	**Air flow direction/ nowcasting**
Vsetín-Huslenky	17:15	25	SW/Vsetín-Cáb, Uherský Brod

Locations	Time	Intensity (mm)	Air flow direction/ nowcasting
Vsetín	17:30	30	SE/Vsetín-Hošťálková
Vsetín-Hošťálková	17:45	40	SE/Zlín-Fryšták
Zlín-Fryšták	18:00	50	SE/Holešov

As revealed in Table VIII, the most intense rainfall occurred in the village of Fryšták between 17:00 and 18:00 hours, at an average intensity of 37 mm / hour. Residents of Fryšták registered the occurrence of severe hail, combined with torrential rainfall, which caused considerable damage to property. The nowcasting method provided accurate predictions in terms of the place of occurrence of convective precipitation.

C. *Verification of the forecast on 7/24/2015*

Verification of comprehensive convective precipitation forecasts was performed using the outputs of ground –based meteorological stations.

The most intense rainfall occurred at stations:

- Zlín-Štípa - with 43 mm (Zlín); forecast 30-50 mm
- Huslenky - with 34 mm (Vsetín); forecast 30-50 mm
- Hošťálková - with 33 mm (Vsetín); forecast 30-50mm

The success of the prediction of precipitation locations is 81% for Municipalities with Extended Powers in the Zlin Region for both time periods. The success rate of forecasted precipitation occurrence time was 100%.

IV. CONCLUSION

The aim of this article was to provide information about the comprehensive forecasting of convective precipitation in the Zlín Region. The first section mentioned the importance of the Information, Notification and Warning System of the Zlín Region; and, especially in the Crisis Management field. The main focus was on the outputs of the convective precipitation forecast system.

The principle of complex predictions was described in the case study of 7/24/2015, when there was a local flash flood in the central part of the Zlin Region. The success rate of comprehensive predictions reached 81%, whereby, it met the condition predictions of success rate by more than 50%.

Future research will focus on optimizing the limits of the meteorological elements and the search for similar historical events. The main objective will be to continually refine and improve predictions of the place and time of occurrence of convective precipitation in order to provide preventive measures and improve the preparedness of Crisis Management authorities against the occurrence of flash floods.

ACKNOWLEDGMENT

This article was supported by the Department of Security Engineering under TBU in Zlín´s Internal Grant No.: IGA/FAI/2016/023 "Optimization of the System of Convective Precipitation Forecasts for Increase its Success Rate".

REFERENCES

[1] D. Řezacová, et al. "Physics of clouds and precipitation". Prague: Academia, 2007. 574 pp. with. Fig.Gerstner; sv. 2. ISBN 978-80-200-1505-1.

[2] M. Kaspar. "Analyses of gust fronts by means of limited area NWP model outputs". [cit. 2016-04-05]. doi: 10.1016/S0169-8095(03)00066-8.

[3] K. Lagouvardos, V. Kotroni, E. Defer and O. Bousquet. "Study of a heavy precipitation event over southern France, in the frame of HYMEX project: Observational analysis and model results using assimilation of lightning". [cit. 2016-04-05]. doi: 10.1016/j.atmosres.2013.07.003.

[4] G. Wang, W. Wai-Kin, Y. Hong, L. Liu and J. Dong. "Improvement of forecast skill for severe weather by merging radar-based extrapolation and storm-scale NWP corrected forecast: Observational analysis and model results using assimilation of lightning". [cit. 2016-04-05]. doi: 10.1016/j.atmosres.2014.10.021.

[5] P. Novak. "The Czech Hydrometeorological Institute's severe storm nowcasting system". [cit. 2016-04-05]. doi: 10.1016/j.atmosres.2005.09.014.

[6] S. Kolios and H. Feidas. "An automated nowcasting system of mesoscale convective systems for the Mediterranean basin using Meteosat imagery". [cit. 2016-04-05]. doi: 10.1002/met.1282.

[7] C. E. Pierce, P. J. Hardaker, C. G. Collier and C. M. Haggett. "GANDOLF: a system for generating automated nowcasts of convective precipitation". [cit. 2016-04-05]. doi: 10.1017/S135048270000164X.

[8] L. Panziera, U. Germann, M. Gabella and P. V. Mandpaka. "NORA-Nowcasting of Orographic Rainfall by means of Analogues: the COALITION approach. Quarterly" Journal of the Royal Meteorological Society" 2011, [cit. 2016-04-05]. s. 2106-2123 doi: 10.1002/qj.878.

[9] R. Lee and a J. E. Passner. "The development and verification of TIPS: An Expert System to Forecast Thunderstorm Occurrence". [cit. 2016-04-05]. Avalaible at: http://journals.ametsoc.org/doi/pdf/10.1175/1520-0434%281993%29008%3C0271%3ATDAVOT%3E2.0.CO%3B2

[10] M. Kucera. "Information, Notification and Warning System of the Zlin Region and MEP Uherské Hradiště". [cit. 2016-04-04]. Avalaible at: https://digilib.k.utb.cz/bitstream/handle/10563/34416/ku%C4%8Dera_2015_dp.pdf?sequence=1&isAllowed=y

[11] "Information, Notification a Warning System of the Zlín Region", Integrated project, Zlín Region [online]. 2012 [2014-03-31]. [cit. 2016-04-04]. Available: http://www.kr-zlinsky.cz/-informacni-vyrozumivaci-a-varovaci-system-zlinskeho-kraje-integrovany-projekt-cl-1392.html

[12] INWS Zlín Region - Information, Notification and Warning System". [cit. 2016-04-04]. Avalaible at: http://www.colsys.cz/novinky/detail/ivvs-zlinskeho-kraje.htm

[13] Czech Hydrometeorological Institute - Model predictions ALADIN. [cit. 2016-04-04]. Available at: http://portal.chmi.cz/files/portal/docs/meteo/ov/aladin/results/ala.html#nebul

Insight into Contemporary Dissemination Techniques of Mobile Botnet Clients (Bots)

Milan Oulehla
Faculty of Applied Informatics
Tomas Bata University in Zlin
Zlin, Czech Republic
oulehla@fai.utb.cz

David Malanik
Faculty of Applied Informatics
Tomas Bata University in Zlin
Zlin, Czech Republic
dmalanik@fai.utb.cz

Abstract— **Currently, smartphones and tablets offer a wide range of functionalities, such as Web browsing, social networking, as well as using banking applications. This has resulted in s constant increase in popularity of mobile devices connected to the Internet 24/7. In the 2nd quarter of 2015, the Android operating system has dominated the market with an 82.8% share, which makes it the most widespread mobile operating system in the world. However, this popularity is double-edged, including both users and botnet creators. The research papers "Android Botnets on the Rise: Trends and Characteristics and How Can Botnets Cause Storms?" as well as "Understanding the Evolution and Impact of Mobile Botnets" imply urgent need for additional research into this field. Therefore, the research described by this article includes not only a theoretical study into the ways of delivering the botnet command and essential botnet knowledge based on published research, but also provides a practical investigation into the ways of infecting smartphones and tablets with botnet clients (bots). Special tools have been developed for performing certain malicious actions enabling real testing of safety mechanisms of the Google Play. These tools have also been used in combination with other useful techniques such as social engineering and deceitful actions trying to get users to unintentional cooperation. Finally, some challenging results and security vulnerabilities have been raised by the research.**

Keywords- Android permission analysis; bot (client of botnet); bot dissemination, C&C server; Google Play; mobile botnet

I. INTRODUCTION

Mobile devices, such as smartphones, tablets and wearable devices are able to perform a whole range of features resulting in their utilization for both personal purposes, such as Web browsing, social networking, using banking applications, etc. [11][10], and for business purposes, including continuous access to corporate mailbox and real-time file sharing [11]. Besides these functionalities, most of the mobile devices are connected to the Internet 24/7 and unlike personal computers they can use different connections to the Internet using technologies such as EDGE[1], 3G[2], HSDPA[3], Wi-Fi[4], etc. [12]. All these factors cause continuous growth in the popularity of mobile devices. This research focuses on Android because it is one of the most popular mobile operating systems in the world, which had over 1 billion active users in 2014 [24]. One year later, in the 2nd quarter of 2015, the Android operating system had 82.8% market share [14]. The research papers "Android Botnets on the Rise: Trends and Characteristics" [20] and "How Can Botnets Cause Storms? Understanding the Evolution and Impact of Mobile Botnets" [25] suggest that popularity of mobile devices is double-edged, including both users and botnet creators. The findings published in [21] are alarming. The researchers examined 1,632 popular applications published on Google Play. They employed methods of static analysis, which contribute to the revelation that 151 applications represent a potential security threat. The investigation published in [15] has also brought concerning results: 93% out of 1,260 tested mobile malware samples contained patterns of botnet behavior. Such situation is as serious as the one similar to mobile antivirus field. In [19], a prototype of hybrid command and control mobile botnet has been created and subsequently tested by four mobile antivirus programs with worrying results: "All the anti-viruses were active during the execution of the prototype but failed to identify any malicious activities". All facts stated above imply the urge for further research into the field of mobile botnets. This paper contributes to the mobile platform security improvement.

II. INSIGHT INTO BOT DISTRIBUTION ISSUES

A. *Principal terms*

In order to better understand mobile bot distribution issues, with emphasis on the Android platform, seems useful to introduce some main terms used in this field.

- Google Play is a software distribution platform for mobile devices. Google Inc. has developed an automated antivirus system, called Google Bouncer with the purpose of finding and removing malicious software published on Google Play [16].

[1] Enhanced Data rates for GSM Evolution (EDGE)

[2] third generation of mobile telecommunications technology

[3] High-Speed Downlink Packet Access (HSDPA)

[4] wireless local area network

- Bot (also known as agent or zombie) is a piece of malicious software installed on the mobile devices of victims [11]. Bots are clients of botnet network and botmaster can control them via C&C server[5] [3].
- AndroidManifest.xml is a file, which is an inseparable part of every Android application. "The manifest file presents essential information about a described app to the Android system; the system requires this information before it can run any of the app's code. It describes the components of the application including activities, services, broadcast receivers, and content providers as well as declares, which permissions the application must have in order to access protected parts of the API[6] and interact with other applications." [6]
- Dynamic application analysis is concentrated on application patterns of behavior. Inspected applications are executed in controlled environment and their running is logged and subsequently evaluated (e.g., analysis of captured *.pcap files). Methods of dynamic analysis try to find certain anomalies in network traffic, battery consumption, CPU[7] utilization, etc.
- Static application analysis, unlike dynamic application analysis, focuses on inspection of the source code. "An application is analyzed without its executing." [1]. It typically consists of a decompilation phase and a code analysis. The tools including Dex2Jar [1], JD-GUI [1], Apktool [13] and Virtuous Ten Studio (VTS) [13] are employed during the process of static analysis. In the cases of Smali, Java and XML code analysis, pieces of malicious code are searched for. Nevertheless, there are certain techniques, which make the accurate automatic code analysis more difficult for example code obfuscation or harmful intention camouflaged by a programming style. It is also quite difficult to programmatically decide whether it is malicious intent or just badly written part of code. All these pitfalls result in the fact that the static analysis methods cannot be easily converted to the automated code analyzer.
- BroadcastReceiver [9] is an Android Java class, which does not have any user interface and therefore it can run silently in the background. From this place it processes events from the system or other applications including: SMS[8] has been received, a device is connected via Wi-Fi, certain custom application events, etc. All these features make BroadcastReceiver convenient for performing harmful actions of mobile malware. Google, the creator of Android operating system has realized threats resulting in using of BroadcastReceivers. For this reason starting from Android 3.1 and higher, every application, which wants to use BroadcastReceiver requiring certain permissions also has to have an Activity [7]. This measure caused that malware creators have focused on techniques allowing camouflage of malware Activities.
- "PUSH" is the way of botnet command delivering, during which commands are sent from the C&C server to bots [12].
- "PULL" is the way of botnet command delivering, during, which bots periodically send requests to the C&C server. Then server sends commands as responses [12].

B. Android permission analysis

Google Play as well as anti-viruses analyze permissions from AndroidManifest.xml file [20]. From the Android applications' point of view, there are two kinds of permissions: function permissions and actually requested permissions (see Figure 1, set A and B). However, there is another point of view, which is represented by Android system permissions [8]. From this perspective, normal and dangerous permissions exist (see Figure 1, set C and D) [8]. Function permissions represent a group of permissions which are legitimate. Function permissions represent a group of permissions which are legitimate because this application is not able to perform its function without RECORD_AUDIO permission. set of all permissions an application asks for is called requested permissions. It can contain both functional (legitimate) and illegitimate requests. Normal permissions form a static list of permissions, which are not considered to be dangerous. It also surprisingly contains permissions such as INTERNET, ACCESS_NETWORK_STATE and RECEIVE_BOOT_COMPLETED.

These permissions are particularly suitable for communication with C&C servers. Dangerous permissions consist of permissions by, which serious harm could be caused e.g., RECORD_AUDIO or READ_CONTACTS and more. Because of this, the set of functional and requested permissions differs in most applications. Compared to the sets of normal and dangerous permissions, which are static and always have the same elements. The system of dynamic and static permission sets helps to improve accuracy of Android permission analysis. The analysis process tries to find permission discrepancies, which could be expressed as: $A - B \neq \emptyset$. According to [8] the emphasis is put on: $(A - B) \cap D \neq \emptyset$. For example, a real voice recording application could ask for functional permission such as above-mentioned RECORD_AUDIO, however, it can request for any Android permission e.g., READ_CONTACTS, RECEIVE_BOOT_COMPLETED and INTERNET. Permissions analyzers try to find the discrepancy between function permissions and requested permissions. Permissions READ_CONTACTS, RECEIVE_BOOT_COMPLETED and INTERNET represent searched contradiction where READ_CONTACTS permission is the most significant security risk. Our preliminary research of Google Play

---

[5] Command-and-control server

[6] Application Programming Interface

[7] Central processing unit

[8] Short message service

applications suggests that the phenomenon of excessive permissions is mainly concerns free of charge applications.

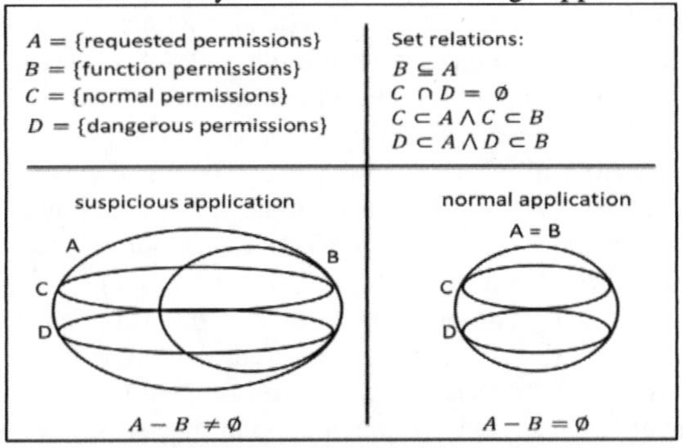

Figure 1. Android permission analysis

III. MEANS OF CONTEMPORARY MOBILE BOT DISSEMINATION

There is a whole range of ways how mobile bots can be distributed into mobile devices:

- Third Party Application Markets are a traditional place where mobile malicious applications have occurred [20]. There is a wide range of mobile malware starting from suspicious applications collecting Web browser history for targeted advertising and ending with sending text messages to premium-rate numbers owned by cyber criminals without user's knowledge [5].
- Android applications, which represent a repackaged version of legitimate applications as were described in [20]. Here is a typical scenario: the paid version of a popular Android game (e.g., Minecraft: Pocket Edition) is decompiled. Then certain malicious code is included. Finally from infected code, APK[9] package is again built. Nevertheless the repackage experiments, which have been carried out during our research suggest that not all repackage APK applications have the same functionality and stability as original APK applications.
- Mobile versions of worms are used for the bot distribution to the mobile device. Worms are able to replicate themselves to other mobile devices using typical security vulnerabilities on the host mobile operating system to infect them [1], [17]. For example, first well known mobile worm was Cabir, which used to spread through Bluetooth technology [26].
- Spam and phishing use sending out emails containing either a hypertext link to infected Web page for downloading bot APK application or an attachment with a bot software, which pretends to be useful in some way [11].
- Malware application for bot dissemination placed on Google Play. As was mentioned earlier, the Android operating system reached over 1 billion active users in 2014 and almost everybody is able to install software from Google Play, except users with inexpensive smartphones or tablets which are not Google certified Android devices. Thus, there is an extremely huge number of potential victims, which transforms Google Play into extremely promising distribution platform for botnet creators. This is probably the most dangerous way of bot spreading because users of Android running devices are used to trust Google Play and they are not alert as during installations from different software sources. Nevertheless, Google Play store has security mechanisms trying to detect and ban malicious applications.

[9] Android application package

IV. CHARACTERISTICS OF MODERN ANDROID MALWARE

There is a range of factors, which should be taken into account by contemporary malware creators because their ignorance could lead to a disclosure by antivirus programs or by users themselves. There is a list of activities, which well written modern malware should never do:

- Unnecessarily running malware starting from boot of an Android operating system and ending with switching off mobile device since permanent or long-term running of malware results in high battery consumption. Atypical battery consumption can attract user's attention and it can lead to the revelation of malware [19][11].
- Malicious actions demanding high computing power, which could lead to excessive CPU utilization. This phenomenon can be detected by machine learning anomaly detectors [1].
- Sending of stolen data, attack performing (e.g., DDoS attack) and communication (e.g., mobile bot – C&C server) via cellular network using technologies such as EDGE, 3G or LTE. There are several issues: Mobile networks have limited bandwidth and generation of high traffic volumes may quickly consume the available bandwidth [11]. A lot of bots are identified and controlled by IP addresses. Incessant switching between cellular and Wi-Fi network could lead to ambiguous bot identification and subsequent malfunction of botnet as a whole [3].

Communication between mobile malware applications and the servers of attackers is realized via TOR[10] network. Plenty of security scans perform routine network traffic inspection of tested applications and each anonymous communication through TOR network using Onion routing is generally considered suspicious. It could cause employing of more thorough analyses.

V. BOT DISTRIBUTIONAL APPLICATION PUBLISHED ON GOOGLE PLAY STORE

"Malware, packaged within an Android game app called BrainTest, had been published on Google Play twice. Each instance had between 100,000 and 500,000 downloads according to Google Play statistics, reaching an aggregated infection rate of between 200,000 and 1 million users." [22]. These findings are alarming and they imply that despite

[10] The Onion Router https://www.torproject.org

Google Bouncer, it is possible to publish application containing malware. In addition, as mentioned above, the research published in [21] has revealed that 9.25% of examined popular applications published on Google Play had a potential security threat. These results have been achieved by employing methods of static analysis. It indicates a hypothesis that Google Bouncer primarily focuses on dynamic analysis and inspection of AndroidManifest.xml file, whereas static analysis is underestimated. This claim is also supported by research, which was carried out by ESET Security Company: "Another interesting issue is why Bouncer didn't statically analyze the executable file inside the assets of the uploaded game. For that reason, the Trojan horse stayed undetected and was freely provided to users." [23]. The target of our research has been influenced by the facts stated above. However, a different approach has been employed. Unlike previously published papers, our research has not concentrated on inspection of existing suspicious applications published on Google Play. In contrast it has been focused on creation of two different bot distributional applications with the same purpose, which should practically prove or disprove a hypothesis about insufficient static analysis of Google Bouncer by using the same scenario:

- the experimental bot distributional applications can be successfully published on Google Play bypassing security mechanisms of Google Bouncer;
- the experimental bot distributional applications can deliver an installation file of bot application to mobile device of victim;
- the experimental bot distributional applications can prepare fraudulent installation of bot application on mobile device of victim.

A. *The common basis of experimental bot distributional applications used*

Despite the fact that bot distributional applications employing different principles of bot infection, both of them take into account findings of Android permission analysis and characteristics of modern Android malware (discussed in detail above), which can lead to their disclosure. They have also been developed with the purpose to camouflage malicious intentions during dynamic analysis and inspection of AndroidManifest.xml. On the contrary, harmful actions of the experimental applications have been presented in uncovered form in the code of applications, which have even not been obfuscated. It means that both of them have a common base,, which will be described in the following section. The first bot distributional application is called "Spennymoor Weather" (see Figure 2) and the second is called "Meadowfield Weather" (see Figure 4). The target bot application, which should be fraudulently installed by SpennymoorWeather as well as Meadowfield Weather is called "bot application" in this paper. The bot distributional applications have legitimate and illegitimate parts. The legitimate part is an ordinary weather forecast application for Spennymoor and Meadowfield towns. It shows usual meteorological information such as picture of current weather, present temperature, humidity etc. The illegitimate part is designed with emphasis on findings stated in detail above. It makes use of the fact that probably the best form of bot distributional application is a mixture of a bot and a Trojan horse. The illegitimate part has also been created to be able to perform every malicious action only by function permissions of a legitimate part of the application. Due to the lack of IP address, most cellular phones use NAT[11] gateway and thus the devices are not directly reachable [12]. In addition, IP addresses are changed frequently [3] because of incessant switching between cellular and Wi-Fi network. It causes inconvenience in using "PUSH" based communication mechanism. On the other hand, bots employing "PULL" style, regularly establish connection with C&C servers, which could generate additional network traffic. As mentioned in the Insight into bot distribution issues section, anomalies in network traffic can be detected by methods of dynamic analysis. That is the reason why the "PULL" based communication mechanism used by this research has led to the improvement of the mechanism. Illegal part of bot distributional applications has been implemented as background thread with the intention to be operational for as short a time as possible. Unlike classical "PULL" scenario, illegal part of bot distributional applications is not periodically triggered and it does not try to connect to C&C server with request for installation commands. It has been inconspicuously launched by successful downloading of JSON (JavaScript Object Notation), which contains both weather forecast information and control commands for installation of bot application. Once the illegal part is started, a command from JSON is assessed using command evaluate mechanism, which pretends that it is SHA256[12] protection against modification of weatherenginesupportlibrary, an internal component placed in ../res/raw directory of bot distributional application. The weatherenginesupportlibrary is an encrypted array of bytes and thus nobody can investigate its content and purpose. SHA256 value of weatherenginesupportlibrary represents the order for installation of the bot application: The value from downloaded JSON and calculated SHA256 value of weatherenginesupportlibrary are compared. If the values are not equal, it means that command for installation of bot application has not been issued and illegitimate part of application is immediately terminated. Otherwise the process of fraudulent installation continues. The bot distributional applications Spennymoor Weather and Meadowfield Weather employ different methods, which are described separately in the following subsections.

---

[11] Network Address Translation

[12] Secure Hash Algorithm 256bit

VI. FINDINGS AND RESULTS

A. *Spennymoor Weather – an experimental bot distributional application*

In order to be approved by Google Bouncer, Spennymoor Weather has been designed as inconspicuous as possible. That is the reason why Spennymoor Weather application contains within itself encrypted array of bytes. In fact, it is a bot application, which should be fraudulently installed on the mobile device of a victim. In fact it is an anonymous array of bytes, which was encrypted using AES[13] algorithm with 256-bit key. This measure prevents Google Bouncer from inspecting contents of array and getting results in weakly polynomial time. Spennymoor Weather is a mixture of a bot and a Trojan horse, which is considered to be particularly suitable for bypassing security tests. Since the application has a legitimate purpose and at the same time it is controlled by botmaster, there is no standard observable algorithmic pattern of malicious behavior. Botmaster is a human being whose administration can be quite random. Spennymoor Weather also does not perform any typical malicious actions as memory access violation, gathering/sending users' information or remote code execution. All above mentioned facts resulted in publishing Spennymoor Weather on Google Play store (see Figure 2 and Figure 3/1) so Android users can install it. Once it is installed, the decryption uses a password taken from a variable stored in weather forecast JSON, saves malicious APK in a persistent memory of a device. Subsequently, the fraudulent installation of bot application, which looks like a legitimate update can be performed by order of botmaster (see Figure 3/2). This way, a mobile device can be infected by a bot application, which has not been inspected by any security mechanisms (see Figure 3/3).

Figure 2. Spennymoor Weather – an experimental bot distributional application on Google Play

[13] Advanced Encryption Standard

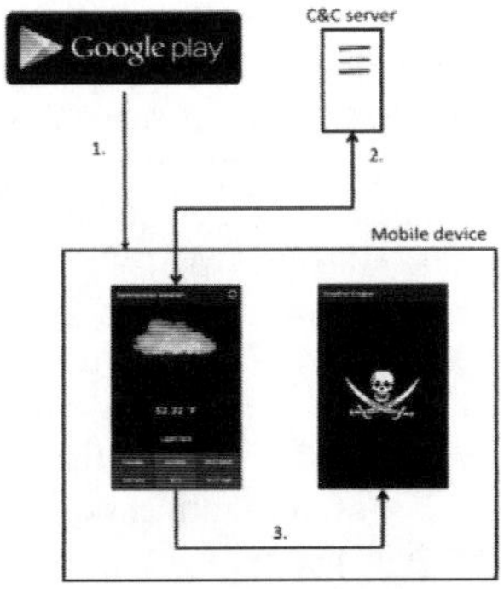

Figure 3. Mechanism of bot dissemination employed by Spennymoor Weather

B. *Meadowfield Weather – an experimental bot distributional application*

The fact that Google Bouncer has allowed publishing Spennymoor Weather containing within itself an encrypted bot application on Google Play, has influenced additional direction of our research in designing Meadowfield Weather application, which is also a mixture of bot and a Trojan horse but has more dangerous features and its malicious intention has been more obvious than in case of Spennymoor Weather application. Despite these facts, Meadowfield Weather has been successfully published on Google Play too, as can be seen from Figure 4 and anybody of more than billion active users is able to download and install it directly from Google Play to her/his mobile device (see Figure 5/1). Moreover it does not include any additional malicious software instead; it is designed to employ two different servers. The first is a C&C server and it is used for controlling bot application installation (see Figure 5/2). The second is a file server, which is designed to offer downloading of bot application to Meadowfield Weather (see Figures 5/3 and 5/4). It means that bot application can be regularly changed according to varying cyber-criminal intentions without the need of code adjusting of Meadowfield Weather. There is a measurement preventing security tests to scan bot application:

- Bot application published on file server is encrypted by AES cipher with complex password [4]. Meadowfield Weather contains fast, single-purpose deciphering subsystem but it does not include a password. This password is sent by a botmaster via C&C server in weather forecast JSON only on condition that an order for installation of bot application was issued. It means that only a combination of Meadowfield Weather deciphering subsystem, encrypted application from file server and password from JSON downloaded from C&C server can lead to decryption of bot application.
- A pair of encrypted bot application and a password can be periodically changed without any code editing of Meadowfield Weather.

- The encrypted application does not have a file extension *.apk in any phase of the installation process, which makes explanation of its purpose more unclear and even if the *.apk file extension is missing; the installation works reliably on Android operating system.

Once the bot application is downloaded on the mobile device, Meadowfield Weather performs decryption using password from weather forecast JSON in a way described above. Then Meadowfield Weather tries to carry out a fraudulent installation employing a method of social engineering by which it attempts to persuade the user to finish this installation of bot application (see Figure 5/5). Meadowfield Weather pretends that the bot installation process is an update of Weather Engine, which is necessary for operation of Meadowfield Weather. The moment the bot application is installed on the mobile device, there is a whole range of techniques, which could be used for its camouflage e.g., [18].

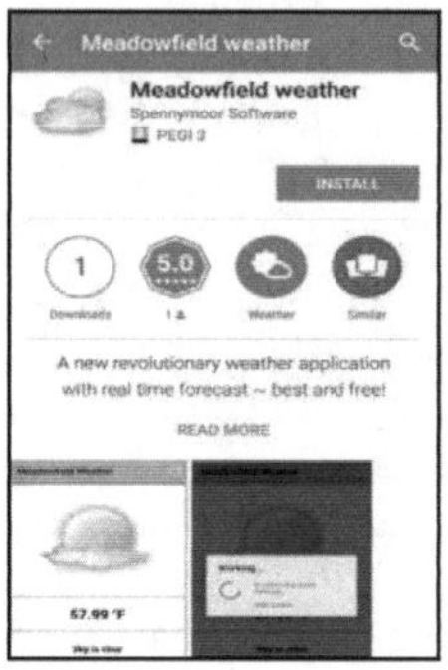

Figure 4. Meadowfield Weather – an experimental bot distributional application on Google Play

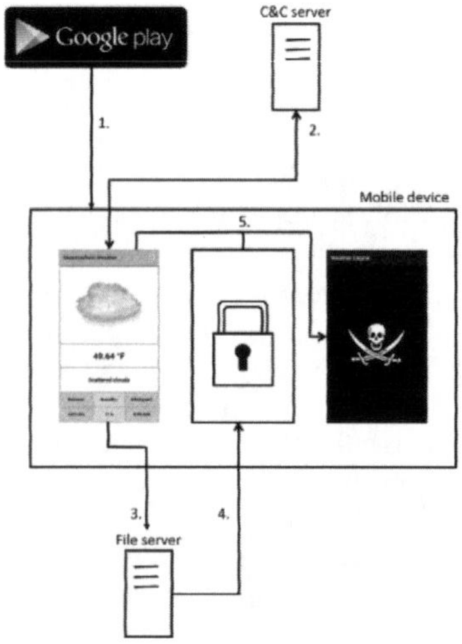

Figure 5. Mechanism of bot dissemination employed by Meadowfield Weather

VII. CONCLUSION

This article deals with dissemination techniques of modern mobile bots. Due to better understanding to the research described in this paper, certain main terms have been explained primarily. Means of contemporary mobile bots dissemination have been described on the basis of preliminary research carried out and published papers in the corresponding field. The study of Android permission analysis and characteristics of modern Android malware have enabled to design Spennymoor Weather and Meadowfield Weather applications. These two pieces of experimental bot distributional software represent a mixture of a bot and a Trojan horse and they have been created as inconspicuously as possible. They have a legitimate part, which is a weather forecast application for Spennymoor and Meadowfield towns. The illegal part does not perform any typical malicious actions as is gathering sensitive personal information or periodical connecting to C&C server. It has only one purpose, which is a fraudulent installation of bot application. These features resulted in a fact that both of them have been able to bypass Google Bouncer security mechanisms. Moreover, they enabled the installation of apk bot application both from internal resource (Spennymoor Weather) and from file server (Meadowfield Weather). The main finding reveals that it is possible to deliver APK bot application, which has not been tested by any security scans to the mobile device of the victim. What is more Google Play could be employed for this purpose. This seems to be an alarming and obviously a really dangerous behavior, which indicates that the Spennymoor Weather and Meadowfield Weather should never pass through Google Bouncer security scan. Our results also confirmed research findings published in [21] and [23]. Research carried out together with papers listed above also imply that Google Bouncer security tests are solely focused on dynamic application analysis and inspection of AndroidManifest.xml whilst static application analysis is being underestimated. Limitation of the research: current research has been focused on qualitative analyses of Google Bouncer security mechanisms while quantitative analysis has not been performed. Research carried out as a basis of this study has mostly concentrated on techniques allowing bypassing security scans based on dynamic application analysis resulting in the fact that only some aspects of Google Bouncer security mechanisms have been examined. For this reason, it would be beneficial to carry out research of applications published on Google Play focused on automated testing with emphasis on static analyses, which represents at the same time our recommendation for future research. Nevertheless, on the basis of findings published in this article, examination of APK applications published on unofficial sources as file share servers seems to be promising as well.

VIII. DISCLOSURE

During the performed research any data from users has not been collected. All malicious actions were performed only on devices owned by Tomas Bata University in Zlín, Faculty of Applied Informatics. The C&C server and its botmaster interface have been developed by independent offensive security researcher Kamil Vávra (contact: @vavkamil). The botmaster interface has been designed for executing malicious actions based on IP addresses, which ensured that all active targets were devices exclusively owned by Faculty of Applied Informatics. Currently both bot distributional applications published on Google Play are clean, there is no illegitimate part. The Spennymoor Weather and Meadowfield Weather are available and free of charge for everyone. It is our courtesy, how to give warm thanks to users of Google Play.

ACKNOWLEDGMENT

This work was supported by the Ministry of Education, Youth and Sports of the Czech Republic within the National Sustainability Programme project No. LO1303 (MSMT-7778/2014) and by the European Regional Development Fund under the project CEBIA-Tech No. CZ.1.05/2.1.00/03.0089 and also by Internal Grant Agency of Tomas Bata University under the project No. IGA/FAI/2016/016.

REFERENCES

[1] Z. Abdullah, M. M. Saudi, and N. B. Anuar, Mobile botnet detection: Proof of concept. s.l., IEEE 5th Control and System Graduate Research Colloquium, 2014.

[2] M. Boodaei, Mobile Malware: Why Fraudsters Are Two Steps Ahead. [Online]. Available at: http://www.trusteer.com/blog/mobile-malware-why-fraudsters-are-two-steps-ahead, 2011.[Accessed 2016 5 10].

[3] B. Choi, et al., Detection of Mobile Botnet Using VPN. s.l., Seventh International Conference on Innovative Mobile and Internet Services in Ubiquitous Computing, 2013.

[4] I. Cornell, How to Create a Complex Password. [Online] Available at: http://www.it.cornell.edu/services/managed_servers/howto/passwords/complexity.cfm, 2012. [Accessed 2016 5 20].

[5] Department of Homeland Security, DHS-FBI Bulletin: Threats to Mobile Devices Using the Android Operating System. [Online]. Available at: https://publicintelligence.net/dhs-fbi-android-threats/, 2013.[Accessed 2016 5 10].

[6] Developers, App Manifest. [Online]. Available at: http://developer.android.com/guide/topics/manifest/manifest-intro.html, 2015. [Accessed 2016 5 9].

[7] Developers, Activity. [Online]. Available at: http://developer.android.com/reference/android/app/Activity.html, 2015. [Accessed 2016 5 15].

[8] Developers, Normal and Dangerous Permissions. [Online]. Available at: http://developer.android.com/guide/topics/security/permissions.html#normal-dangerous, 2015. [Accessed 2016 5 7].

[9] Developers, n.d, Application Fundamentals. [Online]. Available at: http://developer.android.com/guide/components/fundamentals.html, 2015. [Accessed 2016 5 9].

[10] M. R. Faghani, U. T. Nguyen, Socellbot: a New Botnet Design to Infect Smartphones via Online Social Networking. s.l., IEEE Canadian Conference on Electrical and Computer Engineering (CCECE), 2012.

[11] P. Farina, E. Cambiaso, G. Papaleo, and M. Aiello, Mobile Botnets Development: Issues and Solutions. International Journal of Future Computer and Communication, 12, 2014.

[12] G. Geng, et al., The Design of SMS Based Heterogeneous Mobile Botnet. Journal of computers, 1, 2012.

[13] A. Gupta., Learning Pentesting for Android Devices. s.l.:Packt Publishing, 2014.

[14] IDC, 2015, Smartphone OS Market Share, 2015 Q2. [Online]. Available at: http://www.idc.com/prodserv/smartphone-os-market-share.jsp. [Accessed 2016 5 8].

[15] X. Y. Z. S. Jiang, Android Malware. New York, NY: Springer, 2013.

[16] H. Lockheimer, Android and Security. [Online]. Available at: http://googlemobile.blogspot.co.uk/2012/02/android-and-security.html, 2012. [Accessed 2016 5 10].

[17] M. M. Saudi, A new model for worm detection and response : development and evaluation of a new model based on knowledge discovery and data mining techniques to detect and respond to worm infection by integrating incident response, security metrics and apoptosis. Bradford: University of Bradford, 2011.

[18] M. Oulehla, D. Malanik, Techniques Allowing Broadcast Receiver Malware on Android Platform.. Zakynthos, Proceedings of the 19th International Conference on Systems, 2015.

[19] H. Pieterse, M. Olivier, Design of a Hybrid Command and Control Mobile Botnet. The Journal of Information Warfare, 2013.

[20] H. Pieterse, M. Olivier, Android botnets on the rise: Trends and characteristics. s.l., Information Security for South Africa. IEEE, 2012.

[21] S. Poeplau, et al., Execute This! Analyzing Unsafe and Malicious Dynamic Code Loading in Android Applications. s.l., NDSS Symposium, 2014.

[22] A. Polkovnichenko, A. Boxiner, BrainTest – A New Level of Sophistication in Mobile Malware. [Online]. Available at: http://blog.checkpoint.com/2015/09/21/braintest-a-new-level-of-sophistication-in-mobile-malware/, 2015. [Accessed 2016 5 14].

[23] L. Stefanko, Android trojan drops in, despite Google's Bouncer. [Online] Available at: http://www.welivesecurity.com/2015/09/22/android-trojan-drops-in-despite-googles-bouncer/, 2015.[Accessed 2016 5 15].

[24] C. Trout, Android still the dominant mobile OS with 1 billion active users. [Online] Available at: http://www.engadget.com/2014/06/25/google-io-2014-by-the-numbers/, 2015. [Accessed 2016 5 8].

[25] Z. L. W. Wang, C. Wang, How Can Botnets Cause Storms? Understanding the Evolution and Impact of Mobile Botnets. s.l., IEEE INFOCOM 2014 - IEEE Conference on Computer Communications, 2014.

[26] T. Zhao, G. Zhang, and L. Zhang, An Overview of Mobile Devices Security Issues and Countermeasures. s.l.:International Conference on Wireless Communication and Sensor Network, 2014.

Innovation Standard Methods of Evaluating the Results of Shooting

Zdeněk Maláník
Faculty of Applied Informatics
Tomas Bata University in Zlin
Zlin, Czech Republic
malanik@fai.utb.cz

David Malanik
Faculty of Applied Informatics
Tomas Bata University in Zlin
Zlin, Czech Republic
dmalanik@fai.utb.cz

***Abstract*—This article deals with a new method of theoretical and practical training for professional qualification examination to obtain a gun license in the Czech Republic. When using the new method of teaching and training, the shooting accuracy is assessed as one number; this number contains the information of the capability of a shooter to hit the assigned part of a target from the short-term perspective as well as from the long-term perspective.**

Keywords—Series Shooting Capability Index; Process Shooting Capability Index; Time Shooting Capability Index.

I. INTRODUCTION

Shooting a firearm is a test of a shooter's sensor and motor performance; the shooter is required to accurately hit an assigned target. Trained shooters are able to fulfill such a task due to their ability to attain an appropriate shooting pose, to concentrate sufficiently, to aim the firearm accurately and to master the finger movement while pulling the trigger and during the shot itself. Hit accuracy is a suitable criterion for the assessment of the shooter's success.

A number of methods for hit accuracy assessment have been described in available literature. Such methods use, for example, average radius, R50 circle, R100 circle, 2R100 circle, plain sum of values, standard deviation and, eventually, estimated universe standard deviation, the ellipsis of dispersion, probability of the hit, etc.

The method introduced in this article is a suitable supplement for the above mentioned traditional methods of assessment for the needs of the Firearm License applicants training. It is a method of shooting accuracy assessment where one number rates the ability to hit the assigned part of a target (for the purpose of the competence test training, in particular) and to hit the scoring rings; all of it from the short-term (immediate) as well as from the long-term perspective. The method it based on specification of the Series Shooting Capability Index (SSCI) and the Process Shooting Capability Index (PSCI).

II. SHOOTING CAPABILITY

A. The Competence Test

While sitting for the competence test, the applicant is required to hit the assigned target with the assigned number of hits. The hit must be aimed and carried out within the previously specified part of the target. For example, the international pistol target 50/20 is being used while handguns are being fired; shooting is carried out from the distances of 10 or 15 meters. A great number of forces influence the bullet trajectory; this shows in fact, that the hit points are variable and do not exactly correspond to the point being aimed at. Thus, every process of shooting shows a certain degree of consistency (or inconsistency).

B. The Variability

The term shooting process capability represents the shooters' ability to consistently hit the assigned target. Three capability indices are proposed for the use of the shooting capability evaluation:

- The Series Shooting Capability Index (SSCI) ${}^{d}C_{s}$, which evaluates the capability in the process of shooting one series; the conditions of shooting do not change during the course of the series;
- The Process Shooting Capability Index (PSCI) ${}^{d}C_{p}$, which assesses the shooters' ability to hit the assigned target from the long-term perspective. The Process Shooting Capability Index must be set on the basis of the results of several series (minimum of 25 series). The conditions of shooting change in an anticipated way (for example the time devoted to shooting a single series, temperature and other characteristics of the environment, etc.) within the time when the minimal number of series will be carried out.

The Process Shooting Capability Index (PSCI) ${}^{d}C_{t}$ (assessed from several series) evaluates the shooters' permanent (long-term) ability to fulfil the given shooting performance in a given time (minimal permissible time span of shooting).

III. SERIES SHOOTING CAPABILITY INDEX

We suggest using the capability index C_s for evaluation of the shooting process within one series; that is a short-term process shooting capability. The above mentioned index may be expressed as a ratio of requirement for a target and the consistency within the shooting process

$$C_s = \frac{\text{requirement for target}}{\text{consistency within a process}} \qquad (1)$$

Requirement for a target represents the required outcome of the shooting process, that is, usually the type of target and its size. Consistency of the shooting process is defined by an interval which includes all the shots' scores. In case the consistency is subject to a normal dispersion, such intervals may be defined as a multiple of standard deviation s. If we were to evaluate the consistency of the shooting process using the interval ± 1.s (standard deviation), 68.27 % of hits' scores would fall within this interval. If the interval was ± 2.s, the consistency of the shooting process would be related to 95.45 % of all the hits' scores. If the interval was ± 3.s, the consistency of the shooting process would be related to 99.73 % of all the hits' scores. The interval (± 3. s) is suggested to become a standard for the consistency evaluation of the shooting process. Such intervals represent the measure which may be perceived as accurate enough for the evaluation of the shooting process quality (that means a sure target hit). The term process shooting capability in one series represents the shooters' ability to hit the required target with all shots within the given series.

A statistical data normality check must be carried out after the adjustment of all hits' scores acquired from the performed shots (concordance of the measured data with the normal dispersion test). In case of non-refusal of the hypothesis that the consistency of the shots is a subject of normal dispersion, we may define the estimate of the Process Shooting Capability Index C_s for the assessed series by the following formula

$$\hat{C}_s = \frac{\text{requirement}}{6s} \qquad (2)$$

where s represents the standard deviation within the shooting process of one series. The requirement for hits may be expected to have the shape of a circular scoring ring with the diameter T. If the coordinates of the hits being shot from the distance d are marked with the symbols ${}^d x$ and ${}^d y$, the value of the hit radius ${}^d r$ may be determined according to formula (3). The hit radius represents the distance of a given hit from the target point (decision point specified in the certain part of a target, in this case, in the center shooting ring).

$${}^d r = \sqrt{{}^d x^2 + {}^d y^2} \qquad (3)$$

While calculating the Series Shooting Capability Index, the standard deviation of the radius within the given series ${}^d s$ (shooting from the distance d) may be defined by the formula

$${}^d s = \sqrt{\frac{\sum_{j=1}^{n} ({}^d r_j - {}^d \bar{r})^2}{n-1}} \qquad (4)$$

where n represents the number of shots (and hits) in the relevant series. Shooting capability index ${}^d C_s$ in the relevant series shot from the assessed distance "d" (the only number relevant for the evaluation the process shooting capability) is defined by the formula

$${}^d C_s = \frac{0{,}5.T - {}^d \bar{r}}{3.{}^d s_r} \qquad (5)$$

where ${}^d \bar{r}$ is the median of the radius of the hits which was achieved while shooting from a given distance d; it is defined by the formula (6).

$${}^d \bar{r} = \frac{\sum_{j=1}^{n} {}^d r_j}{n} \qquad (6)$$

and ${}^d s_r$ is the standard deviation of the radius of the hits for the relevant series for shooting from the distance d. In the denominator of the formula (5) calculating the capability index ${}^d C_s$ the value of the three standard deviations is 3. ${}^d s_r$; this represents the interval of the estimate of the consistency in the shooting process from the given firearm. The probability is 99.73 % (on condition of normal dispersion). Basic criteria for evaluation of short-term shooting process capability are introduced in Table I. These criteria are based on the value of the Series Shooting Capability Index.

TABLE I. CRITERIA FOR EVALUATION THE SERIES SHOOTING CAPABILITY INDEX

Series Shooting Capability Index	Evaluation of the Shooter in the Series	Verbal Evaluation of the Shooter's Capability
${}^d C_s < 1{,}00$	*Incompetent*	The shooter either has not achieved satisfactory consistency in shooting or the median of the radius of the hits is too high
${}^d C_s = 1{,}00$	*Competent with condition*	Terminal value of the short-term capability
${}^d C_s > 1{,}00$	*Competent*	Shooter is very consistent in the shooting process in the given series and the median of the radius of the hits is also very good

I. PROCESS SHOOTING CAPABILITY INDEX

The Process Shooting Capability Index (established on the basis of several series) evaluates the ability of the shooter to permanently (in the long-term) hit the assigned target and abide by the imposed features of the shooting process

$${}^d C_p = \frac{0{,}5.T - {}^d \bar{\bar{r}}}{3.{}^d s_p} \qquad (7)$$

The Process Shooting Capability Index is defined by formula (7) where $^{d}\overset{=}{r}$ is the median of the radius of the hits achieved from a given distance *d*; it is calculated from "m" series (each of the series consists of an identical number of shots) by the formula

$$^{d}\overset{=}{r} = \frac{\sum_{i=1}^{m} {^{d}\bar{r}_i}}{m} \tag{8}$$

and $^{d}s_p$ is the standard deviation of the radius of the hits in the shooting process; the shooting is carried out from the distance *d*. To enumerate the standard deviation of the shooting process from the distance *d*, formula (9) is used

$$^{d}s_p = \frac{^{d}\overline{R}}{k} \tag{9}$$

where $^{d}\overline{R}$ is the average dispersion of the values in the radius of hits; it is calculated from all evaluated series. *k* is the statistical constant number dependent on the number of executed shots *n* in the given series (number of shots in the series). The values of constant *k* are stated in Table II. These are valid for 2 -15 shots in an individual series.

TABLE II. THE VALUES OF THE STATISTICAL CONSTANT K

Number of Shots in a Series	k	Number of Shots in a Series	k	Number of Shots in a Series	k
2	1,128	**7**	2,704	**11**	3,173
3	1,693	**8**	2,847	**12**	3,258
4	2,059	**9**	2,970	**13**	3,336
5	2,326	**10**	3,078	**14**	3,407
6	2,534	**11**	3,173	**15**	3,472

Table III contains of basic criteria for evaluation of the shooting process based on the value of the Process Shooting Capability Index (long-term capability).

V. Time Shooting Capability Index

When sitting for the competence test, the ultimate time span for shooting a particular kind of firearm is specified for each group of Firearm License; the lengths of the time spans may be found in Table III.

May the symbol ^{d}t represent the time of shooting (given in seconds) carried out from the distance *d*. We may assume that the time span for the shooting performance of a particular shooter, carried out from the distance *d*, will have normal placement with the median $^{d}\bar{t}$ and the standard deviation $^{d}s_t$. The Time Shooting Capability Index is defined by the formula

$$^{d}C_t = \frac{t_{\max} - {^{d}\bar{t}}}{3.{^{d}s_t}} \tag{10}$$

where $t_{\max}$ is the ultimate time span for shooting, as indicated in Table III.

TABLE III. The Ultimate Time Span for Shooting a Particular Kind of Firearm when Sitting for the Competence Test

Firearms License Category				
A	**B**	**C**	**D**	**E**
5 minutes (Small-bore rifle, handgun) **3 minutes** (scatter gun)	**5 minutes** (Small-bore rifle, handgun) **3 minutes** (scatter gun)	**5 minutes** (small-bore rifle) **3 minutes** (scatter gun)	**2 minutes** (handgun)	**3 minutes** (handgun)

The so-called moving range for the time spans of individual shootings $^{d}R_{k_i}$ is used to calculate the standard deviation $^{d}s_t$ The moving range $^{d}R_{k_i}$ is defined by the formula

$$^{d}R_{k_i} = |t_i - t_{i+1}| \tag{11}$$

where t_i is the time span of shooting *i*,

t_{i+1} is the time span of shooting *i*+1.

This means that, first of all, after the second shot (within the training) we subtract the time span of the second shot from the time span of the first shot; then we subtract the time span of the third shot from the time span of the second shot, etc. Having used the average moving range, we may estimate the standard deviation of the time span of shooting for all assessed series and the particular shooter from the evaluated *m* series according to the formula

$$^{d}s_t = \frac{^{d}\overline{R_k}}{d_2} = \frac{^{d}\overline{R_k}}{1{,}128} \tag{12}$$

where d_2 is a constant number – 1,128 – this number represents the moving range for two values $^{d}\overline{R_k}$ represents the average moving range which may be defined by the formula

$$^{d}\overline{R_k} = \frac{\sum_{i=1}^{m-1} {^{d}R_{k_i}}}{m-1} \tag{13}$$

where m represents the number of series. For example, the Time Shooting Capability Index for Firearms License Category D is defined by the following formula

$$^{15}C_t = \frac{120 - {}^{15}\bar{t}}{3.{}^{15}s_t} \quad (14)$$

Basic criteria for the shooting process evaluation (shooting being carried out from a particular kind of firearm) based on the values of the Time Shooting Capability Index may be found in Table IV.

TABLE IV. CRITERIA FOR THE TIME SHOOTING CAPABILITY INDEX ASSESSMENT

Time Shooting Capability Index	**Shooting Process Evaluation from the Ti Span Perspective**	**Verbal Evaluation of the Shooters' Capability**
$^dC_t < 1{,}00$	*Incompetent*	The shooter either has not achieved long-term satisfactory consistency in time span of shooting or the median of the radius of the hits is too high
$^dC_t = 1{,}00$	*Competent on Condition*	Terminal value of the shooting capability from the time span perspective
$^dC_t > 1{,}00$	*Competent*	In long-term, the shooter has consistent time span in the shooting process and the shooting time median

VI. Capability Indices Interpretation

The statistical importance of the capability indices is that every single value of the index represents the probability of a shot being placed within the assigned area (as long as shooting time span being evaluated does not exceed the assigned time). First of all, the importance of the capability index with the value being equal to 1 will be clarified (^dC_s = 1,00, or ^dC_p = 1,00). It means that, in the given example, we place exactly 3 standard deviations of the shooting process to the formula $0{,}5.T - {}^d\bar{r}$ (T represents, for example, the diameter of the largest ring of the pistol target 50/20.)

In this case, the probability of the target miss equals to 1-F(3) = 0.00135, where F(3) represents the value of the distribution function of the standardized normal dispersion in three standard deviations.

In other words, the probability that the radius of the hits will be larger than 0.5T is 0.135 %. This means that only one hit out of one thousand hits (thirteen out of ten thousand, etc.) will not fall within the scoring rings of the 5/20 target.

In general, the procedure of interpretation is as follows. We ask: what multiple of the standard deviation of the radius of the hits may be placed within the space $0{,}5.T - {}^d\bar{r}$? The symbol u represents such a multiple and it is defined by one of the following formulas

$$p({}^dr \le 0{,}5T) = F(u) = \int_{-\infty}^{u} f(u)du = \frac{1}{\sqrt{2\pi}}\int_{-\infty}^{u} e^{-\frac{u^2}{2}}du \quad (17)$$

The probability of the target miss will thus be equal to

$$p({}^dr > 0{,}5T) = 1 - F(u) \quad (18)$$

In the case of the interpretation of the Time Shooting Capability Index, we ask: what multiple of the standard deviation of the shooting time span may be placed within the time span $t_{\max} - {}^d\bar{t}$? The symbol u represents this multiple and it is defined by the following formula

$$u = 3.{}^dC_t \quad (19)$$

The probability of the shooting carried out from the distance d being finished within the assigned time span $t_{\max}$ equals to the distribution function of the standardized normal dispersion

$$p({}^dt \le t_{\max}) = F(u) \quad (20)$$

The probability of exceeding the assigned time span$t_{\max}$ equals

$$p({}^dt > t_{\max}) = 1 - F(u) \quad (21)$$

VII. Main Factors And Shooting

There are seven crucial factors essentially influencing the professional defense solution. (Figure 1.)

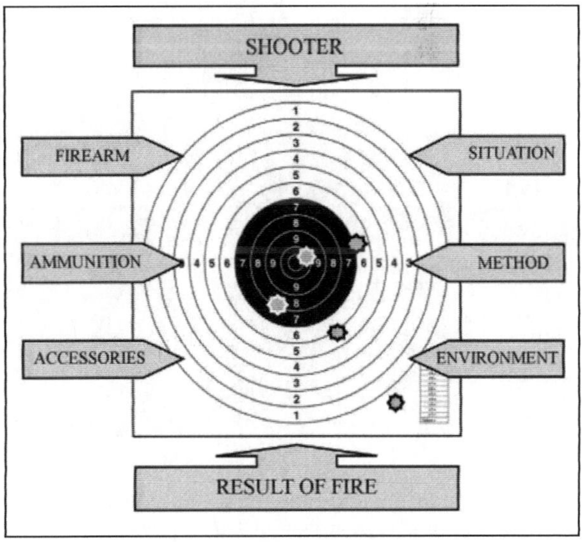

Fig 1: *The factors influencing the results of shooting* [6]

These are: shooter, firearm, ammunition, accessories, situation, method and the environment [6]. These factors determine the outcome of the shooting. The shooter is a main critical element of the shooting result [7]. His mental and physical condition, level of knowledge and training decides.

Fig 2: *Method of training* [7]

Important properties of the weapon are its purpose, size, weight, magazine capacity, user simplicity. Ammunition must meet the characteristics such as security, reliability, quality of processing and efficiency. Basic equipment for the shooter is as holster, belt, eye and ear protection, clothing, etc. (Figure 2.)

Fig 3: *Method of shooting* [8]

Each training situation may be different. The first time it is important to practice on site. Next step is changing of the shooting position and movement. There are many ways and methods of shooting [8]. Some examples of shooting methods include: two-handed, one-handed, with use of cover, etc. (Figure 3.) The environment influences the solution of the situation in professional defense in the form of location (city, apartment, park, crowd, public transport, restaurant, etc.), season and time of the day (snow, rain, wind, ice, dawn, fog, etc.) and inspection (witnesses, cameras, media, etc.) (Figure 4.) [9]. These basic elements of professional defense work together; the orders may change in each situation.

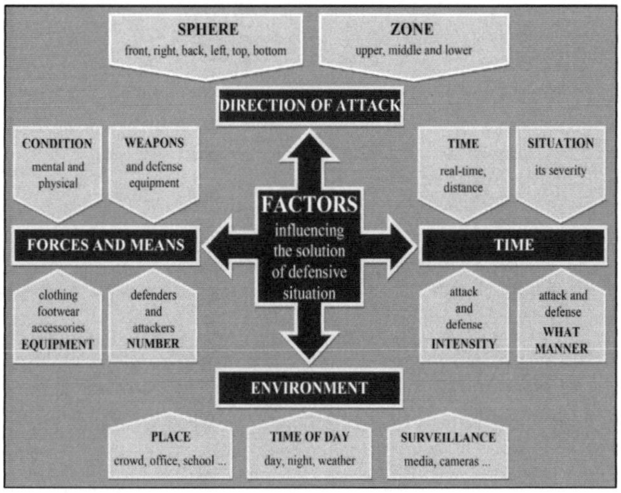

Fig 4: *Factors influencing the solution of defensive situation* [9]

To successfully meet the objectives of professional defense, one needs to be part of the Commercial Security Industry workers (hereinafter CSI). This special requirement includes broadband knowledge and skills. Part of the remit employee CSI who use a weapon for their work is defined in terms of reliability in hitting the target. To evaluate the success of hitting, only three classic ways are currently used. Due to both current and prospective conditions of using weapons in defense, it is appropriate to supplement a new method of evaluation, focusing primarily on reliability intervention. This method allows for assessment in terms of a single intervention or series of interventions, as well as the short and long terms, or in terms of time. Everything is expressed by a single number. The new evaluation of competence of shooting will be useful both for regular staff evaluation, eventually for the appropriateness of including them to task or job. The industry of commercial security services includes a range of security nature, which includes personnel performing duties with a gun. Currently, training with weapons is implemented according to the law on weapons and, beyond the law, training is left to the discretion of private security service or to the self-employed. Evaluation of shooting is currently being carried out by the basic methods of evaluation. A new method for evaluating the reliability of the shooting using an eligibility index leads to increase quality of service and enhanced professionalism in the use of weapons in the CSI.

I. CONCLUSION

This article presents one way of evaluating the shooting success. The method may be used while evaluating the competence tests of the Firearm License applicants. The method is based on calculation of the Series Shooting Capability Index and Process Shooting Capability Index. These two indices are further complemented by the Time Shooting Capability Index. This method is suitable for the evaluation of individual shooting series as well as for the long-term evaluation of the competence test training. The above described method represents a brand new complex attitude to the evaluation of the shooting process. Such a method has already been used in the industrial field, but it has never been applied to the field of firearms shooting evaluation. The shooting evaluation method (using the three capability indices) widens the range of other, already existing, methods of evaluation. Its viability may only be verified by the actual use of the method.

REFERENCES

[1] S. Beer, R. Jankových, J. Komenda, and F. Racek "Firing ranges and training in shooting"Univerzity of defense, Brno, pp. 117, 2010.

[2] D. Lapková, and Z. Maláník "Dividing of weapons and personal defense equipment". Security technologies, systems and management II.: Theory and practice of asset protection and physical security. Zlín: VeRBum, 2012, pp. 142-155. ISBN 978-80-87500-19-4.

[3] Z. Maláník"Preliminary issue of professional defense". Security technologies, systems and management I.: Theory and practice of asset protection and physical security. Zlín: VeRBuM, 2011, pp. 247-259. ISBN 978-80-87500-05-7.

[4] J. Tošenovský, and D. Noskievičová, "Statistical methods for quality improvement". Ostrava: Meontanex 2000.

[5] R. Jankových, "Barrel guns and ammunition". [on line]. Brno, 2012, ISBN 978-80-260-2385-5. Available form www.vutbr.cz.

[6] Z. Maláník, "The factors influencing the results of shooting".Own source. Brno: 2012.

[7] Z. Maláník, "Method of training". Own source. Zlín: 2013.

[8] Z. Maláník, "Method of shooting". Own source. Brno: 2012.

[9] Z. Maláník, "Factors influencing the solution of defensive situation". Own sourece, Brno: 2013.

Possibilities of the Search Engine Shodan in Relation to SCADA

Jan Vávra, Martin Hromada
The Department of Security Engineering
Tomas Bata University in Zlín
Zlín, Czech Republic
e-mail: {jvavra, hromada}@*fai.utb.cz*

Abstract— **Recently isolated Industrial Control System (ICS) became accessible and interconnected with Information and Communication Technology (ICT). Nowadays, the ICS is considered as the target of a considerable number of cyber-attacks. Moreover, the contemporary development of the ICS indicates its growing availability over the Internet. There are a few methodologies how to find Internet-connected devices. However, there is one well-known search engine for Internet-connected devices. The Shodan is a widely used tool that provides an enormous capability for targeting Internet-connected devices. In this article, we examine the current state of the ICS availability via the Internet. Therefore, we evaluate the possibility of exposing the vulnerable ICS systems in order to specify their relations to SCADA cyber security. Finally, we identify 974 vulnerable SCADA devices via the Shodan.**

Keywords-Shodan; Cyber Security; Industrial Control System; Vulnerability; Supervisory Control and Data Acquisition.

I. INTRODUCTION

An enormous number of the cyber-attacks relating to the ICS and its main subgroup Supervisory Control and Data Acquisition (SCADA) systems have the eminent influence on the SCADA cyber security. Moreover, the disruption of the SCADA services could have a significant impact on the population, environment or the state itself.

The SCADA was designed as an isolated system. However, the recently isolated system has become more interconnected with external technologies like Information and Communication Technologies (ICT). The evolution of the SCADA has led to a production of new vulnerabilities, which are significant threats to SCADA. Furthermore, Pollet [8] predicted an increasing dependency of the SCADA systems on IT; therefore, the percentage of industrial companies utilizing cyber security solutions will rapidly grow.

There is a considerable number of search engines for Internet-connected devices. Patton et al. [9] have investigated some of the emerging vulnerabilities that exist. Moreover, they give us examples on how dangerous Shodan[3] can be even with a small subset of devices. Markowsky et al. [10] demonstrated how simple can the Internet of Things (IoT) be reachable via Shodan. In addition, Bodenheim et al. [11] investigated the capabilities of the Shodan in relation to SCADA. The authors conclude that Shodan should be categorized as a threat to Internet-facing SCADA.

The Shodan project is highly interested in searching for SCADA devices. Therefore, the ICS radar was created in order to present the results to the public. However, the previous research has not fully addressed all cyber security aspects, especially vulnerable SCADA devices. Moreover, the cyber security of SCADA communication protocols is discussed in the article.

The rest of the article is organized as follows. Section II presents basic information about SCADA systems. The search engine for Internet-connected devices Shodan is analyzed in Section III. Section IV gives an overview of Industrial Control Systems Cyber Emergency Response Team. In Section V, the industrial communication protocols are described. The next Sections (VI and VII) include methods and results. Finally, Section VIII provides the discussion of the article.

II. SUPERVISORY CONTROL AND DATA ACQUISITION SYSTEM

SCADA is a main subgroup of the ICS. Moreover, it can be described as data gathering, remote and centralized system. It is also used for monitoring, management and control of industrial processes. Therefore, the public and private organizations use them as a means to improve efficiency of the industrial system. Moreover, the SCADA is an internal part of the Critical Information Infrastructure (CII) [12]. Nowadays, the CII has enormous influence in almost every sector of the critical infrastructure (transportation systems, power plants, dams, water treatment, oil production, chemicals, gas distribution, etc.). Therefore, every cyber-attack on the CII systems must be considered as a critical threat, which can result in a fatal impact on the environment, population or a country [12].

The SCADA have a positive influence on contemporary society; nevertheless, these systems are under increasing pressure to improve connectivity via the Internet [12]. Thus, the recently isolated systems are becoming more dependent on interconnection with external technologies [1]. This recent evolution of industrial systems resulted in productions of new vulnerabilities. Thus, the protected system becomes more vulnerable to new cyber-attacks.

III. SHODAN

Shodan is a robust search engine for Internet connected devices. The engine was developed by John Matherly. Moreover, he launched it in 2009. Shodan has capabilities to find and collect important information about Internet-connected devices. The main source of information comes from banners. The engine uses a banner grabbing technique in order to find specific devices like servers, routers, printers, ICS, etc. Shodan is continuously searching for the technology accessible from the Internet. Furthermore, it is able to index the devices and investigate available services. This information is collected and stored in the main Shodan database. As a result, there is a highly valuable database with thousands of the records. The database is free to use, moreover, there are no restrictions for users. They can easily use one of the filters in order to find valuable information. The basic filters are focused on these fields:

- Product name
- Product version
- Port
- Operating system
- Country or city
- Specific IP address

Shodan is able to track most of the Internet-connected devices. Moreover, it includes SCADA. The SCADA systems are based on specialized technology and protocols. The uniqueness of the SCADA creates new opportunities for the attackers. Shodan provides unique ability to find and scan industrial devices. The representation of SCADA devices connected to the Internet can be seen in Figure 1. Thus, they are accessible around the World especially in the United States of America and Europe. As a result, there are a considerable number of vulnerable devices connected to the Internet.

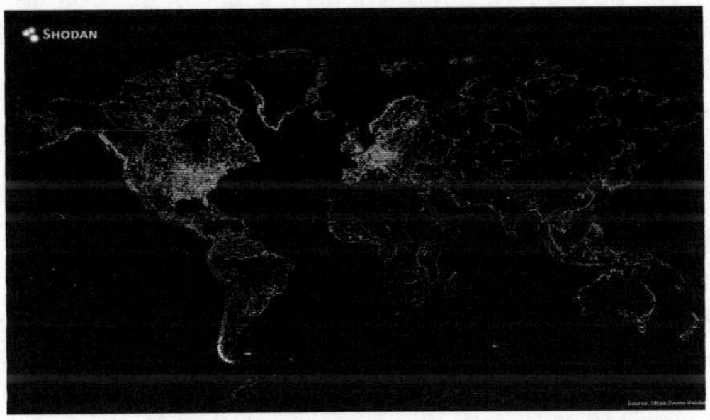

Figure 1. The SCADA map created by Shodan. (adapted from [3])

Reconnaissance and data gathering is the first step of every cyber-attack. Moreover, the attacker can focus on important information about the targeted organization. They are looking for vulnerable elements of the system which can be exploited. For example: the information about SCADA assets, ICT assets, partners, services, protective measures and even employees themselves [2].

A. *Banner Specification*

The banners are metadata about the system. They are highly useful for administrators to manage and categorize their networks. However, the banners are the main type of information for Shodan. Besides, there is the technique called banner grabbing. It is used to identify the information like services, operating system, open ports, communication protocol name or information about product and its version in order to find a vulnerable system [4]. A partial example of the banner is shown in Figure 2. This is real example acquired from the Shodan. There is a lot of information about the system; however, only some information is really important. The important information includes: port, longitude, latitude, area_code, dma_code, and ip.

- **Port** – This segment represents the end point of network communication. Furthermore, it has close relationship with IP address and communication protocol. Each port is developed for different services.
- **Longitude** – The longitude is a geographic coordinate. Moreover, it defines east-west geolocation of the device.
- **Latitude** – The latitude is a geographic coordinate. Moreover, it defines north–south geolocation of the device.
- **Area_code** – The area code is a special identifier for the location where the device is located. However, it is only available in the USA [3].
- **Dma_code** – The DMA code is an acronym for designated market area code. It is a specific group of counties covered by television stations.
- **IP** – It is designed as a unique identifier for every device connected to a global or local network.


```
{
  "timestamp": "2014-01-16T08:37:40.081917",
  "hostnames": [
    "99-46-189-78.lightspeed.tukrga.sbcglobal.net"
  ],
  "org": "AT&T U-verse",
  "guid": "1664007502:75a821e2-7e89-11e3-8080-808080808080",
  "data": "NTP\nxxx.xxx.xxx.xxx:7546\n68.94.157.2:123\n68.94.156.17:123",
  "port": 123,
  "isp": "AT&T U-verse",
  "asn": "AS7018",
  "location": {
    "country_code3": "USA",
    "city": "Atlanta",
    "postal_code": "30328",
    "longitude": -84.3972,
    "country_code": "US",
    "latitude": 33.9335000000001,
    "country_name": "United States",
    "area_code": 404,
    "dma_code": 524,
    "region_code": null
  },
  "ip": 1664007502,
  "domains": [
    "sbcglobal.net"
  ],
  "ip_str": "99.46.189.78",
  "os": null,
```


Figure 2. The real example of the banner. (adapted from [3])

Figure 2 shows the other important information such as organization name, Internet Service Provider (ISP), country code or city. The information extracted from the banners is very useful for administrators. However, it is also helpful to hackers.

IV. Industrial Control Systems Cyber Emergency Response Team

Industrial Control Systems Cyber Emergency Response Team (ICS-CERT) is a division of the Department of Homeland Security. The objective of the ICS-CERT is to create a reliable system for one main purpose. The ICS-CERT designed a complex system in order to manage the risk of the ICS. The database of ICS vulnerabilities was developed. Furthermore, the ICS-CERT provides important services for ICS cyber security [5]. Figure 3 illustrates the essential ICS-CERT services.

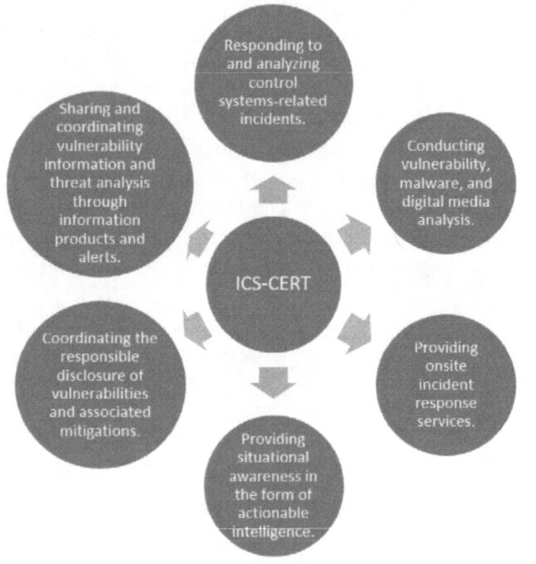

Figure 3. The essential ICS-CERT services. (adapted from [5])

The information published by ICS-CERT has significant influence in risk reduction in relation to the SCADA system. Nevertheless, it has a high value for the attackers. The database of ICS vulnerabilities can be used for targeting and exploiting of the vulnerable system. Furthermore, the SCADA has enormous problems with the updates. The updates implementation is a time consuming process because of testing. The time gap between publication of the vulnerability and updating of the system is the target for the attacker.

V. Industrial Communication Network Protocols

Industrial networking is essential for every SCADA system. Moreover, it is responsible for establishing and maintaining industrial communication between controls, supervisory or even business devices. This section is designed as a theoretical basis which describes industrial communication network protocols.

A. *Modbus*

It is one of the most widely used industrial communication protocol. It can be described as a serial communication protocol which is robust, open and simple. It was designed in 1979 by Modicon [2]. This communication protocol commonly uses port 502 in order establish communication.

B. *DNP3*

Distributed Network Protocol (DNP3) is an extensively used industrial communication protocol which is designed to establish traffic between master station and slave stations. In addition, it is widely used in the water and electric sectors of the critical infrastructure [2]. It is common knowledge that DNP3 uses port 20000 for communication.

C. *IEC-104*

This standard for industrial communication was created by the International Electrotechnical Commission (IEC). The whole name of the standard is IEC 60870-5-104. Moreover, the standard enables communication between control station and remote sites via TCP/IP [6]. The standard usually uses port 2404.

D. *EtherNet/IP*

This application layer protocol is based on Ethernet technologies and Common Industrial Protocol [6]. The protocol can be used for information exchange or controlling of processes. It was developed by Rockwell Automation [6]. In addition, it is mostly used in the USA. EtherNet/IP establishes the communication based on port 44818.

E. *EtherCAT*

This Ethernet based Fieldbus was invented by Beckhoff Automation. This protocol excels in short time cycle, low jitter and low hardware costs. The EtherCat is applicable for hard and soft real-time requirements in automation technology; it was introduced in 2003 [7]. This communication protocol commonly uses 34980 port in order establish communication.

VI. Methods

The research presented in this paper is entirely focused on a process of identification of the SCADA via the Internet. Therefore, the search engine for Internet-connected devices Shodan was used. This research can be divided into two main parts.

The first objective of the research is to evaluate the current state of vulnerable SCADA devices which are accessible via the Internet. To fulfill this goal of the research we used Shodan and ICS-CERT database of vulnerabilities. Our primary aim is the time gap between publication of the vulnerability and updating of the system in order to eliminate the vulnerability. The SCADA updates cannot be implemented on a daily basis due to updates testing. Therefore, every update can be considered as critical. Thus, this interval is extensive in case of SCADA. We used ICS-CERT database in order to identify potential vulnerable devices. Moreover, we focused especially on devices which must not be accessible via the Internet due to the mitigation strategies. Thus, the research is concentrated on the product name and its version in order to detect vulnerable systems. Furthermore, the product name and version is collected as a result of banner grabbing technique. Thereafter, we identify and uncover vulnerable devices via Shodan. A considerable number of devices were collected. The total sample consists of almost one thousand devices which were collected in the first three months of 2016. In the follow-up phase of the study, we evaluated the data in order to obtain crucial information for the purpose of the article. In addition, each device was evaluated and classified.

The second goal of the research is to specify the current state of cyber security in relation to industrial communication protocols. Five industrial communication protocols were chosen. They are main representatives of the industrial protocols. Furthermore, we identified their commonly used communication ports. As a result of this knowledge, we were able to find these devices via Shodan. Moreover, the operating system of each device was tested in order to find devices based on industrial communication protocol with vulnerable operating system like Windows XP.

TABLE I. SCADA PORTS

Industrial Communication Protocol	Port
Modbus	502
DNP3	20000
IEC-104	2404
EtherNet/IP	44818
EtherCAT	34980

Table 1 presents the tested industrial communication protocols with their ports. In the interest of determining the relationship between industrial communication protocols and operating systems, a quantitative data analysis was used. Each rule was evaluated and classified.

VII. RESULTS

The aim of the article is the evaluation of the cyber threats in relation to the SCADA systems. In order to evaluate the SCADA cyber security, we determined two main objectives. The first objective of the research was to evaluate the data in term of vulnerability distribution and the influence on the countries. The second objective focused on the cyber security in relation to industrial communication protocols. The cyber security specification of industrial communication protocols and their vulnerabilities was developed.

The first goal of the research can be divided into two main parts. The first of them is aimed on a specific group of vulnerabilities. They are published by ICS-CERT. Therefore, they are considered as a serious threat. Moreover, all the collected vulnerabilities cannot be accessible via the Internet due to mitigation strategies. However, we found 974 devices with vulnerability registered in ICS-CERT database. The distribution of the devices collected via Shodan is shown in Figure 4.

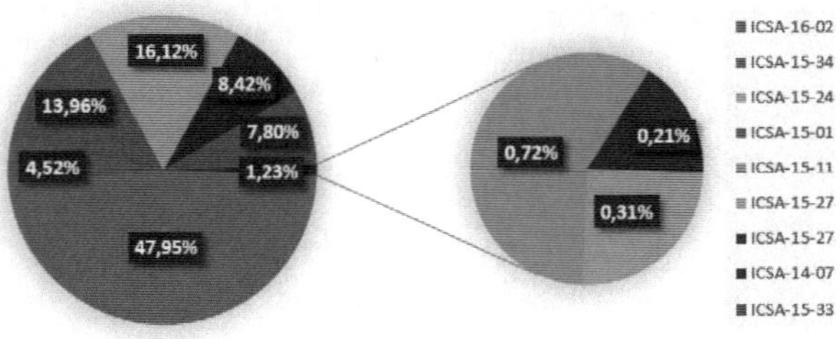

Figure 4. Vulnerable devices collected via Shodan.

As can be seen, the largest percentage of cases represents vulnerability with name ICSA-16-026-02 with almost 48% of all cases; following ICSA-15-274-01 with 16,12% and ICSA-15-013-03 with 13,96% of all cases.

The second part of the first objective is based on the previous part. Furthermore, we wanted to find the answer to the question: "Which country is the most affected by the vulnerabilities from the previous section." The result can be seen in Figures 5 and 6.

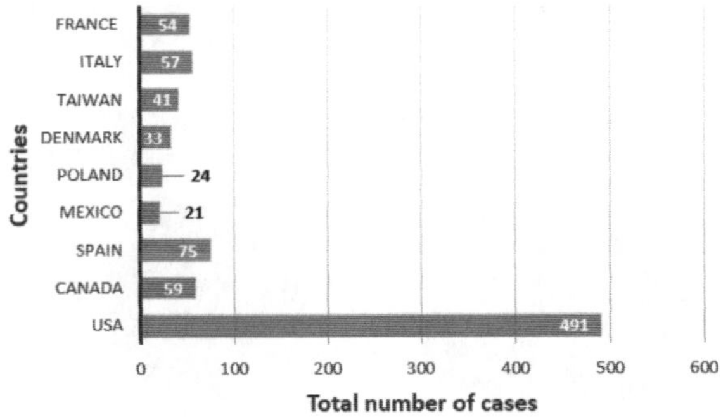

Figure 5. Affected countries due to the vulnerabilities - high impact.

Due to a considerable number of affected countries, the sample was divided into Figure 5 and Figure 6. As can be seen in Figure 5 the most affected country is the USA with almost 50% of all affected devices. On the other hand, we cannot omit Spain with 75 affected devices and Canada with

59 affected devices. In addition, even in the case of Europe, there are only 291 affected devices in comparison with the USA.

Figure 6 shows us the countries which were affected less than the countries in Figure 5. However, Figure 5 shows us that even relatively small countries like Lithuania, Netherlands or Austria were affected by the vulnerabilities.

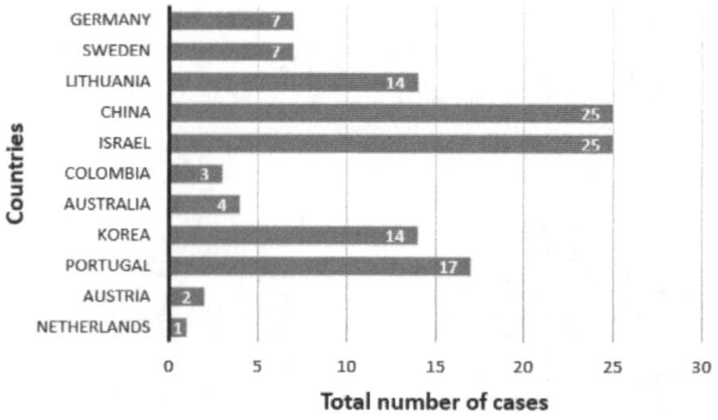

Figure 6. Affected countries due to the vulnerabilities - low impact.

The second objective of the research was to evaluate the current state of industrial communication protocols. Five industrial control protocols were evaluated. The main idea of the research was to find and identify vulnerable points in relation to industrial communication protocols. Therefore, we focus on an operating system of the devices. Thus, the SCADA devices were identified via an industrial communication protocol; moreover, the sample was classified by operating system due to find vulnerable devices. We consider Windows XP as vulnerable against cyber-attacks. Therefore, every system running on Windows XP is not reliable compared to others operating systems.

According to the research, we examined 317 891 Internet-connected SCADA devices. The distribution of the devices is shown in Figure 7.

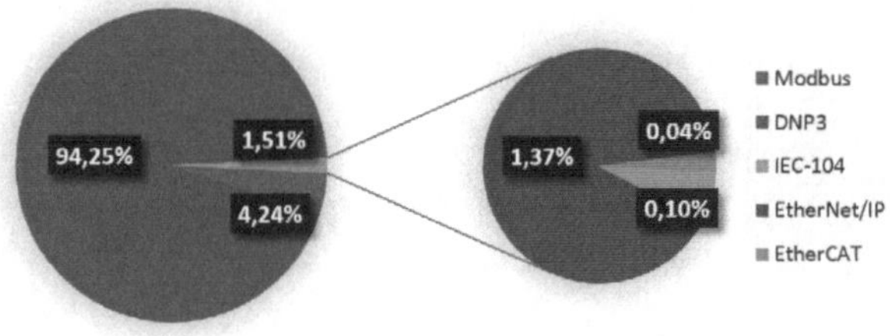

Figure 7. The distribution of the Internet connected SCADA devices.

This considerable number of the Internet-connected SCADA devices is mostly represented by the devices with the DNP3 communication protocol (94.25% of all devices). It is noticeable that the other SCADA protocols contain only 5.75% of all devices. They consist of 18 275 devices.

The second part of the objective was to evaluate the SCADA devices according to their operating system. For the purpose of the research; the data from the previous section were used. We added a new query which led to information selection. The results can be seen in Figure 8.

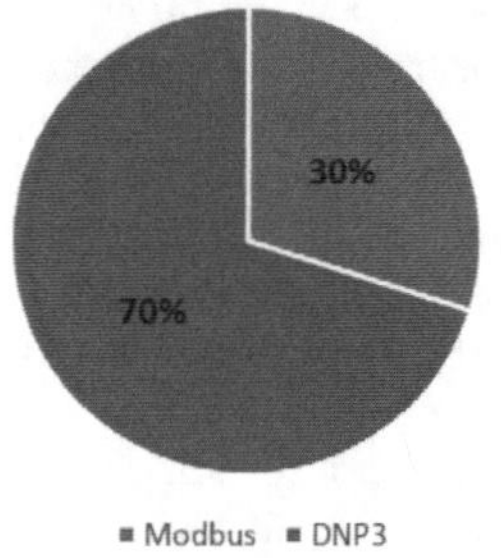

Figure 8. The distribution of the internet connected SCADA devices based on Windows XP.

The total number of affected devices was 188. In addition, it is important to notice that only devices based on Modbus (30% of all devices) and DNP3 (70% of all devices) communication protocol use Windows XP as an operating system. As a consequence, there are 56 potentially vulnerable Modbus devices in the USA. Furthermore, there are 132 potentially vulnerable DNP3 devices divided between the USA, Serbia, Croatia, the United Kingdom and the Russian Federation.

VIII. Discussion

The objective of the article was to evaluate the SCADA cyber security. Therefore, this case study was based on search engine Shodan and ICS-CERT database. The results are in relation with earlier studies conducted with Shodan (Patton et al. [9]; Markowsky et al. [10]; Bodenheim et al. [11]. However, the results indicate the enormous number of vulnerable devices accessible via Shodan.

Contemporary trends show us the imminent interest in identifying of Internet connected devices like IoT or SCADA. However, the results show us that there is a group of potentially vulnerable devices. Moreover, there must be noted that every SCADA vulnerability can be considered as a critical threat.

Our research is concentrated primarily on a time gap between publication of the vulnerability and updating of the system in order to eliminate the vulnerability. Once the information about vulnerabilities is published, every attacker may exploit it for cyber-attack.

The first objective of the research showed us that 974 SCADA devices can be accessible via the Internet although it is not allowed. Furthermore, almost 50% of all devices were affected by the ICSA-16-026-02 vulnerability. In addition, the most affected country was the USA with 491 devices. It is 50% of all affected devices due to the highest density of SCADA devices. Furthermore, it is noticeable that all of the affected countries are considered technically advanced with the relatively high density of SCADA devices.

The second objective of the research showed the cyber security comparison between industrial communication protocols. Thus, five protocols were tested. Almost 320 000 devices were collected. 94% of all collected devices operated via the DNP3 communication protocol.

Even though DNP3 is one of the most widely used communication protocols, the current state of the DNP3 devices density does not match the results of this research. Therefore, we can conclude that devices communicating via DNP3 are vulnerable against search engines like Shodan.

In addition, we used the collected data in order to find SCADA systems operating with Windows XP, which is not considered as a trustworthy operating system. It should be noted that 188 devices were affected. 70% of all devices operate with the DNP3 protocol and the rest with the Modbus protocol. The collected SCADA devices can be vulnerable against cyber-attacks focused on the exploitation of the operating system. Furthermore, the rest of protocols seem to be secured against banner grabbing technique.

It should be noted that this study has been primarily concerned with SCADA-specific devices. Although we examined an enormous amount of SCADA devices, we must consider that only a few of them can be exploited. However, we tried to make the sample as accurate and credible as possible. Thus, the necessary extension of the state of the art was fulfilled. Nonetheless, more research is required in this area in order to determine the reliable cyber defense of the critical information infrastructure.

ACKNOWLEDGMENT

This work was funded by the Internal Grant Agency (IGA/FAI/2016/014) and supported by the project ev. no. VI20152019049 "RESILIENCE 2015: Dynamic Resilience Evaluation of Interrelated Critical Infrastructure Subsystems", supported by the Ministry of the Interior of the Czech Republic in the years 2015-2019. Moreover, this work was supported by the Ministry of Education, Youth and Sports of the Czech Republic within the National Sustainability Program project No. LO1303 (MSMT-7778/2014) and also by the European Regional Development Fund under the project CEBIA-Tech No. CZ.1.05/2.1.00/03.0089.

REFERENCES

[1] K. Stouffer, J. Falco, and K. Scarfone, Guide to Industrial Control Systems (ICS) Security, National Institute of Standards and Technology, 2011.

[2] E. Knapp, Industrial network security: securing critical infrastructure networks for Smart Grid, SCADA, and other industrial control systems. Waltham, 2011.

[3] Shodan: The search engine. [Online]. Available from: https://www.shodan.io/ 2016.03.01

[4] T. S. Kondo and L. J. Mselle, "Penetration Testing With Banner Grabbers and Packet Sniffers," Journal of Emerging Trends in Computing and Information Sciences, vol. 5, no. 4, Apr. 2014, pp. 321-327.

[5] Industrial Control Systems Cyber Emergency Response Team. ICS-CERT. [Online]. Available from: https://ics-cert.us-cert.gov 2016.03.16

[6] B. Galloway and G. P. Hancke, "Introduction to industrial control networks," Communications Surveys & Tutorials, vol. 15, no. 2, Jul 2013, pp. 860-880.

[7] EtherCat: Technology Group. [Online]. Available from: https://www.ethercat.org/en/technology.html 2016.03.18

[8] J. Pollet, SCADA 2017: The Future of SCADA Security. [Online]. Available from: https://files.sans.org/summit/euscada12/PDFs/RedTigerSecurity_SCADA_2017.pdf 2016.03.15

[9] M. Patton, E. Gross, R. Chinn, S. Forbis, L. Walker, and H. Chen, "Uninvited Connections: A Study of Vulnerable Devices on the Internet of Things (IoT)," IEEE Joint, Intelligence and Security Informatics Conference (JISIC 2014), Sept. 2014, pp. 232-235, doi: 10.1109/JISIC.2014.43.

[10] L. Markowsky and G. Markowsky, "Scanning for vulnerable devices in the Internet of Things," Intelligent Data Acquisition and Advanced Computing Systems: Technology and Applications (IDAACS 2015), Sept. 2015, pp. 463-467, doi: 10.1109/IDAACS.2015.7340779.

[11] R. Bodenheim, J. Butts, S. Dunlap, and B. Mullins, "Evaluation of the ability of the shodan search engine to identify internet-facing industrial control devices," International Journal of Critical Infrastructure Protection, vol. 7, no. 2, Jun. 2014, pp. 114-123.

[12] J. Vávra and M. Hromada, "Comparison of the intrusion detection system rules in relation with the SCADA systems," 5th Computer Science On-line Conference (CSOC 2016), vol. 465, Apr. 2016, pp. 159-169, doi: 10.1007/978-3-319-33622-0_15.

The Configuration of Alarm Systems during the Measurement of Electromagnetic Interference

The Analysis of the Requirements of Legislation and Technical Standards

Jan Valouch, Stanislav Kovář
The Faculty of Applied Informatics
Tomas Bata University in Zlin
Zlin, Czech Republic
e-mails: {valouch,skovar}@fai.utb.cz

***Abstract*–Alarm systems shall meet the requirements of electromagnetic compatibility. This is one of the basic prerequisites for their successful application, and thus, the quality of security of buildings. The article analyzes the configuration requirements of security alarm systems during a measurement of radiated electromagnetic interference. Requirements for configuration and operation are not uniform. Inconsistent and unclear requirements of technical standards may result in the differences in measurement results.**

Keywords-electromagnetic compatibility; alarm systems configuration; equipment under test; alarm security systems.

I. INTRODUCTION

Requirements for electromagnetic compatibility of products (in the European Union) are regulated by relevant documents, which are issued as directives of the European Parliament and the Council of the European Union. Currently, *Directive 2014/30/EC on the harmonization of the laws of the Member States relating to electromagnetic compatibility* regulates the electromagnetic compatibility (EMC) requirements of products.

Verification of compliance with the electromagnetic interference (EMI) requirements is realized in the form of standardized tests - measuring the levels of electromagnetic emissions. Components of alarm systems (control panel, detectors, keypad, power supply, access module, communicator, etc.) as electronic or electrical equipment are products which are the source and receiver of electromagnetic interference too [1].

The intention of EMI standards is to establish requirements for methods of measurement, to fix limits of disturbance, to describe general measurement conditions, recording and interpretation of measurement results, etc. Requirements for measurement conditions include in particular configuration, arrangement, installation and operation of the Equipment Under Test (EUT). Requirements for configuration and operation are not uniform. This may result in differences in measurement results.

A. Basic definitions

EUT-representative equipment or functionally interactive group of equipments (system) which includes one or more host unit(s) and is used for evaluation purposes.

Configuration - mode of operation and other operational conditions of the EUT.

Arrangement - physical layout of the EUT that includes connected peripherals/ associated equipment within the test area [2][3].

An analysis of requirements that are applicable to the configuration of intrusion and hold-up alarm system (IHAS) when measuring the radiated electromagnetic disturbances is presented in Section 2. Section 3 presents a comparison of requirements for EUT configuration.

II. CONFIGURATION REQUIREMENTS FOR EQUIPMENT UNDER TEST

Configuration of the EUT within the verification of EMC parameters represents the determination of the manner of its operation and the determination of next operating conditions. EUT configuration requirements are set forth in the relevant legislation, but especially in the technical standards EMC (basic, generic and product) for different types of tests.

A. EU Legislation – Directive 2014/30/EU

The currently valid EMC Directive 2014/30/EU on the harmonization of the laws of the Member States relating to electromagnetic compatibility sets out in particular the following configuration requirements for EUT:

- The electromagnetic compatibility assessment shall take into account all normal intended operating conditions,
- The equipment shall meet the essential requirements in the configurations foreseeable by the manufacturer as representative of normal use in the intended applications,
- During the test it is sufficient to perform an assessment on the basis of the configuration most likely to cause maximum disturbance [2].

1) Historical EU requirements according to Directive 2004/108/EC

The directive, which applied from 2005 to 2016, includes almost the same configurations requirements as a currently valid Directive 2014/30/EU. In 2007, the manual was published Guide for the EMC Directive 2004/108/EC. Guide explains and clarifies some of the most important aspects related to application of the directive (including EUT configuration requirements).

The basic requirement is an assessment on the basis of the configuration most likely to cause maximum disturbances. This method is often referred to as the "worst case" scenario [4].

Previous Directive 1989/336/ EEC (valid 1992-2007) not describe issues of the configuration of the EUT within the parameters of EMC verification. EMC Directive 76/889/ EEC was valid during the period 1976-1992. This directive has set out the following configuration requirements:

- apparatus is to be operated under normal operating conditions as indicated in the manufacturer's instructions,
- for individual types of products directive sets out a standardized load.

B. National legislation - Govermment Decree No. 616/2006 Coll. on technical requirements for products in terms of electromagnetic compatibility

The electromagnetic compatibility assessment shall take into account all normal intended operating conditions. EMC test shall confirm whether the EUT meets the essential requirements in all the possible configurations identified by the manufacturer as representative of its intended use.

C. Basic standard EN 55016-2-3

The standard EN 55016-2-3 ed. 3 (Specification for radio disturbance and immunity measuring apparatus and methods, Part 2-3: Methods of measurement of disturbances and immunity- Radiated disturbance measurements) represents the basic standard for the implementation of the radiated disturbance measurement (regardless of the type of EUT). This standard sets out particular, the following EUT configuration requirements:

- the testing of equipment shall satisfy the following conditions:

a) EUT is configured for use of typical manner,

b) EUT is configured is a manner that will maximize disturbance,

- During measurement, the configuration of EUT shall be adjusted so that the above two conditions, the conditions a) being satisfied first and followed by conditions b),
- Interface cables shall be connected to each interface port on the EUT,
- The normal load conditions shall be as defined in the product specification,
- EUT should be tested in different modes of operation [7].

D. Generic standard EN 61000-6-3

Standard EN 61000-6-3 ed. 2 (Emission standard for residential, commercial and light-industrial environments) specifies requirements for products and systems operating in residential or industrial environments. This standard in particular sets out the following EUT configuration requirements:

- EUT operation mode must be selected in relation to the highest expected emissions,
- All types of input/output ports shall be tested,
- In the case where the EUT may be part of another system, it must be tested in a minimum configuration of auxiliary equipments necessary for the operation of its inputs,
- EUT configuration shall be varied in order to find the maximum emissions (within the typical applications and installation) [8].

1) Historical configuration requirements according to EN 50081-1

In the past, previous technical standard EN 50081-1 (valid from 1994 to 2004) has set the following requirements, for example:

- If the EUT has a large number of terminals, it is necessary to select their sufficient number so as to simulate actual operating conditions,
- The operating mode of EUT corresponds to the normal use [9].

The configuration requirements of EUT are described very briefly.

E. Product family EMC standard EN 55022

European standard EN 55022 ed. 3 Information technology equipment- Radio disturbance characteristics - Limits and methods of measurement sets out limits and procedures for the measurement of the levels of spurious signals generated by the Information Technology Equipment (ITE). These requirements are also applied to components of alarm systems. The measurement conditions include, in particular:

- The EUT shall be configured, installed, arranged and operated in a manner consistent with typical applications,
- The operational conditions of the EUT shall be determined by the producer according to the typical use of the EUT with respect to the excepted highest level of emission,
- Interface cables, load and devices shall be connected to at least one of each type of port of the EUT,
- Multifunction equipment shall be tested with each function operated in isolation,
- A system that consist a number of separate units shall be configured to form a minimum representative configuration [3].

Where there are multiple interface ports of the same type, additional cables, loads or devices may have to be added to the EUT depending upon the result of preliminary tests (the actual number of additional cables may be limited to the condition where the addition of another cable does not significantly affect the emission level, i.e. varies less than 2 dB, provided that EUT remains compliant).

Figure 1 shows an example of pre-compliance measurement of electromagnetic emission of the alarm system component (relay module). The differences in measured values are due to differences in the number of connected electrical load.

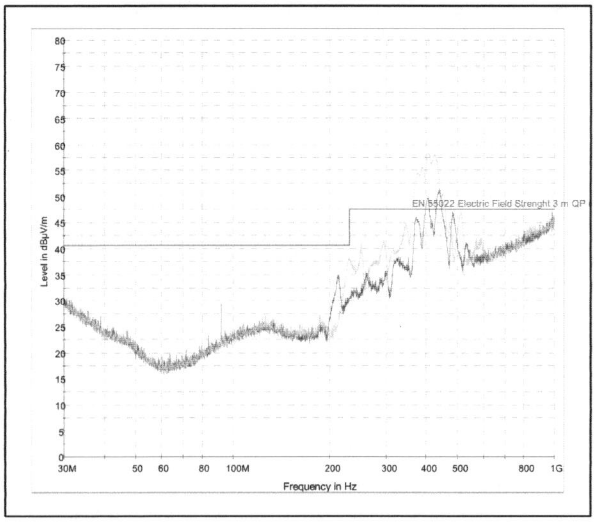

Figure 1. The results of measurements of electromagnetic radiation

Blue values indicate EMI of relay module with electrical load 20 W, green value - electrical load 50 W.

F. Military standards

Military standard MIL STD 461 establishes requirements for the control of the electromagnetic compatibility of electronic, electrical, and electromechanical equipments and subsystems designed or procured for use by activities and agencies of the Department of Defense (DoD) [10]. In the Czech Republic, these requirements are implemented in a defense standard COS 599902. Standard sets out the following configuration requirements of the EUT:

- During emission measurements, the EUT shall be placed in an operating mode which produces maximum emissions.
- For EUT with several available modes, a sufficient number of modes shall be tested for emissions such that all circuitry is evaluated,
- All electrical input and output interfaces shall be terminated with either the actual equipment from the platform installation or loads which simulate the electrical properties (impedance, grounding, balance, etc.) present in the actual installation,
- When variable electrical loading is present in the actual installation, testing shall be performed under expected worst case conditions [5].

A prerequisite for maximum emission levels are the conditions under which the EUT draws the highest primary supply current. The result is the highest activity of interface circuits and generating the maximum current consumed for the digital signals internal time base.

III. COMPARISON OF REQUIREMENTS FOR CONFIGURATION EQUIPMENT UNDER TEST

Legal and technical regulations set out many operational variants (EUT configurations).

Table I. presents application possibilities of EUT configuration during EMC measurements. Configuration options correspond and can be met in accordance with the standard technical thinking. Test engineer configures EUT in cooperation with the manufacturer. For normal products (e.g., personal computer) is not a problem to determine the representative configuration (PC, monitor, keyboard, mouse, loud-speakers, etc.), but opinions may differ on the configuration of specific products (e.g., IHAS). The notion "normal operating conditions" may be understood differently for IHAS (status arm, disarm status, alarm status, fault status, service mode). From a technical perspective, variants of configuration that are set by regulations can be regarded as comparable, so as synonyms. Variants can be divided into several groups:

a) **typical application** (foreseeable configurations, usual usage, common operating conditions, normal operating conditions, standardized load, normal installation practice, normal composition of system, typical installation, typical mode, typical load condition, configuration according to manufacturer, active mode),

b) **worst operating conditions** (worst case, expected worst case conditions, experimental configuration changes, maximum current consumption of EUT, expected highest emission levels),

c) **actual usage** (simulation of the actual operating conditions, operating mode according to the acquisitions requirements),

d) **minimum configurations** (minimum representative configurations, configuration with one of each type module, at least one cable for each type of interface, gradual addition of cables and modules

e) **maximum configuration** (all representative configurations, operation using test programs, test for each function operated in isolation, all possible configurations according to producer, cables connected to each port of the EUT),

f) **standby mode**

We distinguish typical and actual use. Actual use may not always be typical, e.g., in a situation where the user uses only additional functions of the product (e.g., IHAS may be utilized to control a large number of non-alarm applications and alarm functions will be utilized at a minimum). We distinguish the concepts of maximum configuration and "worst case". EMI of EUT at maximum configuration may not always be the highest [6].

This classification does not solve the problem of practical measurement EMI in terms of configuration settings EUT. There still remain a few other different configurations.

TABLE I. THE EUT CONFIGURATION VARIANTS

Legislation and EMC technical standards / Variant of Configuration of equipment under test	Directive 2014/30/EU	Directive 2004/108/ES	Directive 76/889/EHS	GD No. 616 / 2006 Coll.	EN 55016-3-2	EN 61000-6-3	EN 50081-1	EN 55022 ed. 3	MIL STD 461F	AECTP-500
Typical application						x		x		
Foreseeable configurations	x	x								
Usual usage					x					
Common operating conditions				x						
Normal operating conditions			x							
Standardized load			x							
Normal installation practice								x		
Normal composition of system								x		
Typical installation								x		
Typical mode								x		
Typical load condition								x		
Configuration according to manufacturer	x	x		x	x			x		
Active mode										x
Worst case		x								
Expected worst case conditions									x	x
Experimental configuration changes					x		x			
Maximum current consumption of EUT									x	x
Expected highest emission levels	x	x			x	x	x	x	x	x
Actual usage					x					
Simulation of the actual operating conditions						x	x			
Operating mode according to the acquisitions requirements									x	x
Minimum representative configurations						x	x	x		
Configuration with one of each type module								x		
At least one cable for each type of interface								x		
Gradual addition of cables and modules								x		
All representative configurations	x	x								
Operation using test programs								x		
Test for each function operated in isolation								x		
All possible configurations according to producer				x						
Cables connected to each port of the EUT					x				x	x
Standby Mode										x

During a test, a manufacturer or a testing engineer does not always know exactly:

- The environment where the product (EU) is used,
- The real production version of the EUT (risk of additional production adjustments and changes),
- The real configuration in practice,
- The real types of connected peripherals,
- The distance between the EUT and peripherals,
- The range of EUT integration with other devices or systems,
- The typical operating mode in practical application,
- The installation technology, etc.

A Testing engineer searches the maximum levels of EMI (usually by changing the orientation of the EUT, changing adjustable operating modes, height and polarization of measurement antennas). Actual installation and operating conditions of EUT can be different in a practical application.

IV. DISCUSSION OF RESULTS

The most common laws and standards set the following configurations:

- The typical applications (33% of total recommendations),
- The worst operating conditions (29%),
- The maximum configuration (16%),
- The actual usage (10%),
- The minimum representative configurations (10%).

Most often, technical standards specify configuration according to typical applications or configuration with the expected highest emission levels. However, often also they recommend other operating modes and configurations (maximum configuration, minimum configuration, actual usage, etc.). Requirements vary widely. This situation is not ideal within the the measurement of electromagnetic radiation disturbances. It would be appropriate that the EUT configuration requirements were precisely defined for individual EMC tests. The opposite situation may result in the divergent interpretation of the provision of technical standards.

V. CONCLUSION AND FUTURE WORK

The article analyzes the configuration requirements of security alarm system during a measurement of radiated electromagnetic interference. Legal and technical regulations set out the many operational variants of EUT configuration. Requirements for configuration and operation are not uniform. This may result in differences in measurement results. Most often, the technical standards recommended configuration according typical applications or configuration with the expected highest emission levels. However, often also they recommend other operating modes and configurations (maximum configuration, minimum configuration, actual usage, etc.). These terms can be interpreted differently. Requirements analysis forms the initial part of the research, which will continue by thorough experimental measurement and evaluation of electromagnetic radiation of the security alarm systems, including an optimization proposal of configuration requirements. A thorough comparison between the proposed requirements and related standards will be done. This is essential for determining the exact requirements for changes in standards. Currently, a separate technical standard for EMI measuring of alarm systems is missing.

REFERENCES

[1] J. Valouch, Technical requirements for Electromagnetic Compatibility of Alarm Systems. In: International Journal of Circuits, Systems and Signal Processing, vol. 9. USA, Oregon: North Atlantic University Union, 2015, pp. 186–191. ISSN: 1998-4464.

[2] European Parliament and of the Council. Directive 2014/30/EC on the harmonisation of the laws of the Member States relating to electromagnetic compatibility. Official Journal of the European Union, L 96. Luxembourg: Publications Office of the European Union, p. 28 , 2015.

[3] EN 55022 ed. 3 Information technology equipment - Radio disturbance characteristics - Limits and methods of measurement. Brussels: CENELEC, CISPR SCI, 2010. p. 72. < http://www.unmz.cz/office/standards> [accessed June 2016].

[4] Guide for the EMC Directive 2004/108/EC. Brussel: European Commission, p. 66, 21 May 2007.

[5] ČOS 599902. Requirements for the control of electromagnetic interference characteristic of subsystem and equipment. 3. ed. Praha: Defence Standardisation, Codification, and Government Quality Assurance Authority, p. 204, 2012.

[6] J. Valouch, Electromagnetic Compatibility of Machinery for Sugar Production. Czech Sugar and Beet Journal. No. 9 – 10, 131, 2015. Praha: VUC, 2015, pp. 306–310. ISSN 1210-3306 (Print).

[7] EN 55016-2-3 ed. 3 Specification for radio disturbance and immunity measuring apparatus and methods - Part 2-3: Methods of measurement of disturbances and immunity - Radiated disturbance measurements. Brussels: CENELEC, CISPR,2010. p. 102. < http://www.unmz.cz/office/standards>. [accessed June 2016].

[8] EN 61000-6-3 ed. 2 EMC: Generic standards- Emission standard for residential, commercial and light-industrial environments. Brussels: CENELEC, CISPR SC H, 2006. p. 20. < http://www.unmz.cz/office/standards>. [accessed June 2016].

[9] EN 50081-1 EMC: Generic emission standard. Part 1: Residential, commercial and light industry. Brussels: CEN, 1992.p. 12.<http://www.unmz.cz/office/standards>. [accessed June 2016].

[10] MIL-STD-461-G Requirements for the control of electromagnetic interference characteristic of subsystem and equipment. USA: DoD, 2015. p. 255 < https://assist.dla.mil>. [accessed June 2016].

Comparison of Security Devices in Terms of Interception

Stanislav Kovář, Jan Valouch, Hana Urbančoková and Milan Adámek
Department of Security Engineering, Faculty of Applied Informatics
Tomas Bata University in Zlin
Zlin, Czech Republic
E-mail: {skovar, valouch, urbancokova, adamek}@fai.utb.cz

Abstract— **Currently, electromagnetic interference presents a major problem in the design of electronic and electrical equipment and systems. Equipment must be designed to ensure that its operation does not negatively affect itself or the devices in its vicinity. To demonstrate how this can be achieved, the paper aims at comparing the electromagnetic interference generated by analog and IP cameras where the measurement fulfils the strict requirements described in the ČSN EN 55022 ed. 3 standard.**

Keywords-electromagnetic interference; semi-anechoic chamber; closed circuit television; transmission path; far-field.

I. INTRODUCTION

Electromagnetic compatibility (EMC) continues to be a current research topic, especially in today's world where the number of electronic items in homes and workplaces have significantly increased. EMC is defined as the ability of electronic or electrical devices or systems to work correctly in an environment where other sources of electromagnetic signals operate. Devices or systems, for example Closed circuit television (CCTV), can be perfectly reliable, but they are not usable if they cannot work in the electromagnetic environment. In the case of CCTVs, the system consists of multiple devices (security camera, monitoring unit, control unit, etc.) each of which generates a different frequency range.

Electromagnetic compatibility [4] is typically classified into two categories namely electromagnetic susceptibility (EMS) [9] and electromagnetic interference (EMI) [3]. Electromagnetic interference is a process wherein the signal generated by the source of interference is transmitted via electromagnetic constraints to disturbed systems. EMI is concerned with identifying causes of disturbance. On the other hand, EMS is set up to remove the effects of EMI. In effect, EMS tasked to establish a limit in which the device can operate without failures, which potentially can adversely affect its function [1][9]. There is a limited number of research publications that deal with the interception of the video signal, and this is the reason why this contribution exists.

The purpose of this research is to investigate whether the cameras generate a sufficient level of interference that could be eventually exploited to acquire the transmitted information.

Sections 2 and 3 clarify what kinds of devices were used for the experiment. Section 4 defines the process of measurement followed by the configuration of an equipment under test during the analysis. In Section 6, the results are shown. The contribution of the paper is described in Section 7.

II. EQUIPMENT UNDER TEST

CCTV is defined as an information technology equipment used to obtain, transmit, display and store video information. Basically, the camera captures the image of a scene. The information captured by a camera is transmitted via a transmission medium to a control unit (notebook, Network Video Recorder). Subsequently, the control unit displays the information in the display unit (monitor). Finally, the information can be stored (memory disks, cloud computing) with strict adherence to privacy and data protection laws governing the area of operation.

For the purpose of this paper, a CCTV consists only of a control / display unit (notebook) sensing unit (IP and analog camera) and communication medium (twisted-pair cable). Cameras intended for the test are IP camera VIVOTEK FD8136B F3 and analog camera HIKVISION DS-2CE56C5T-AVPIR3.

III. MEASURING EQUIPMENT

The electromagnetic interference testing was performed in the laboratories of electromagnetic compatibility at the University of Tomas Bata in Zlin. The equipment under test (EUT) was placed in a semi-anechoic chamber equipped with pyramidal absorption materials. The absorbers eliminate internal reflections in the chamber, which could cause deformation of the results of the measuring. The bilogarithmic-periodic antenna, as shown in Figure 1, measures the equipment in the chamber and operates over a wide frequency range of 30MHz - 2GHz. Concurrently, another measuring equipment is placed outside the semi-anechoic chamber. The testing of the security cameras was performed using the following techniques of measurement:

- CBL 6112 - bilogaritmic-periodic antenna,
- ESU8 (Rohde & Schwarz) - EMI test receiver which is operating in the range from 20 Hz to 8 GHz,
- EMC32 (Rohde & Schwarz) - EMC measurement software,

- OSP 130 (Rohde & Schwarz) - switch and control unit,
- OSP 150 (Rohde & Schwarz) - switch and control unit.

IV. PROCESS OF MEASUREMENT

The CCTV used to perform the testing included an analog or IP camera. Most parts of the CCTV were moved outside the semi-anechoic chamber to avoid a large distortion of the electromagnetic interference of the cameras. Power over Ethernet (POE) adapter was placed inside and outside the semi-anechoic chamber, in order to determine its influence on the level of EMI. Similar tests under the same conditions were carried by the authors in another research publication [2].

The standard [3] requires a changing polarization (horizontal and vertical) and an antenna height (from 1m to 4m - the possibilities of testing the workplace) during the measurement. A peak detector was used to measure the interference of the cameras. The peak detector helps to evaluate the maximum level of EMI for each frequency value. Contrariwise, the quasi-peak detector evaluates several samples of interference for each frequency value within the specified frequency range. In this case, the frequency range of the measurement is set from 30MHz to 1GHz, which covers a working frequency of both cameras.

The measurement process was conducted according to standard EN 55022 ed. 3 [3], which defines the procedure for measuring a test equipment. The entire process can be summarized in the following steps.

A. *Preparing the workplace*

Selection and preparation of measuring equipment suitable to perform the measurement were first carried out. These techniques of measurement involved the preparation of bilogaritmic-periodic antenna, switching and control unit, receiver and computer with the measuring software.

B. *Configuration of EUT*

To avoid distortion during the measuring process, the device to be tested has to be properly configured for the task. In this case, the tested security camera was placed in the semi-anechoic chamber. The entire configuration is shown in Figures 1 and 2.

C. *Wiring of EUT*

The test devices must be connected in accordance with the requirements set out in the proposal. The function must be thoroughly tested to ensure that the measurement results would be relevant.

D. *Configuration changes*

CCTV always consists only of one camera (IP or analog) to avoid interference between each of them; one camera was exchanged for another. Additionally, the location of the POE adapter was also placed outside the semi-anechoic chamber.

E. *Evaluation of results*

The final step involved the processing and evaluation of measurement results.

V. DISPOSITION OF EUT

The equipment must be connected to its functional state. Standard EN 55022 requires that the testing devices are placed on an insulated (non-metallic) support. Subsequently, all cables must be routed over the rear edge of the insulated surface (in this case, it is a wooden table), ie over the edge which is farthest from the measuring antenna. The standard also requires the distance between adjacent devices to be at least of 0.1m. All surplus parts of cables, which are longer than 0.4 m must be folded.

The security camera was placed in the semi-anechoic chamber on a wooden table and the distance of measuring device from the antenna was 3m, according to standard recommendations. The IP and analog cameras were powered by the POE adapter. The effect of POE adapter on the overall level of interference was also researched during the testing. Therefore, several measurements were performed with POE adapter located inside and outside the chamber. The first variant is shown in Figures 1, 2.

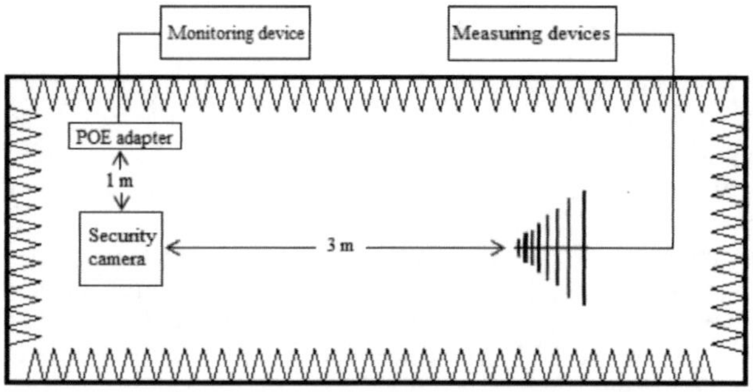

Figure 1. POE adapter placed inside the semi-anechoic chamber.

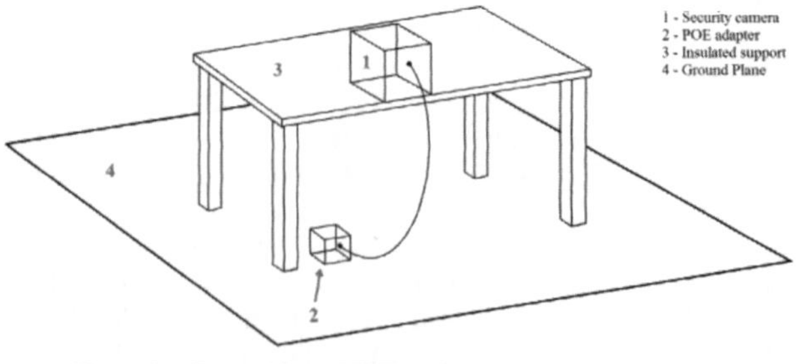

Figure 2. Disposition of EUT in the semi-anechoic chamber.

The POE adapter as shown in Figure 2, is positioned so that the effects on the measurement are minimized.

VI. RESULTS OF MEASUREMENT

This part of the paper is devoted to the presentation of results obtained through the measuring process. Measurements were performed in accordance with the requirements of EN 55022 ed. 3. The antenna changed the height and polarization during the testing to determine the conditions of the EMI in different situations. The progress of radiation was stated in a horizontal and vertical polarization of antenna for each change of the position during the testing procedure.

The x-axis always describes the frequency in Hz in the following figures and the y-axis shows the level of electromagnetic interference in dB/m. The frequency range is displayed from 30MHz to 1GHz and EMI range is displayed from 0 to EMI 80dBμV/m. The limit within which the level of EMI should not be exceeded is around the value of 41dBμV/m.

A. *Analog camera*

The analog camera was connected as shown in Figure 1 and Figure 2. The Hikvision camera was set in an active mode throughout the time of measurements. The camera transmitted data based on the condition of the scene into the laptop, which displayed it. This operation was carried out to verify the functionality of the device. The distance between the security camera and the antenna was 3m.

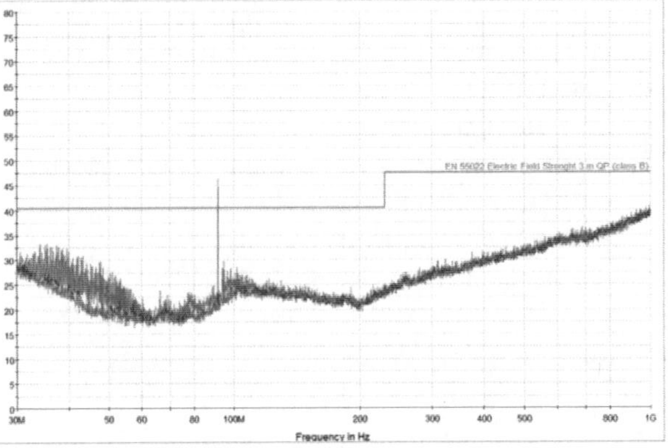

Figure 3. Waveform of EMI in horizontal and vertical polarization.

The most interesting results were reported at the location with the antenna height of 2.5 m and that is why the results presented in this entire section were measured under the same conditions. The changing of the height of the antenna detected no significant differences. The blue color depicts the horizontal polarization of antenna whiles the red shows the vertical polarization. This marking is valid for the entire section. The differences between the max and min values are given below. The maximum and minimum values of electromagnetic interference generated by the analog security camera are as follows:

a) Horizontal polarization of antenna

- maximum level: 45.987dBμV/m (91.711MHz),
- minimum level: 16.389dBμV/m (63.868MHz).

b) Vertical polarization of antenna

- maximum level: 39.938dBμV/m (995.701MHz),
- minimum level: 16.726dBμV/m (74.645MHz).

The peak which originated in the frequency point of 91.711MHz is caused both by an unattached Bayonet Neill Concelman (BNC) connector (Composite Video Blanking and Sync (CVBS) output) and twisted pair which received a radio signal (outside the semi-anechoic chamber). In other words, nothing was connected to the BNC connector, which remained free. Connecting only one connector was done for testing purposes in order to compare EMI of the coaxial cables (CVBS output, HD video output). For comparison, Figure 4 describes the process of EMI with attached CVBS output, but the HD video output was not connected to the laptop. In both cases, the free BNC connector acts as an antenna; therefore, a fluctuation arose in the waveforms of the EMI.

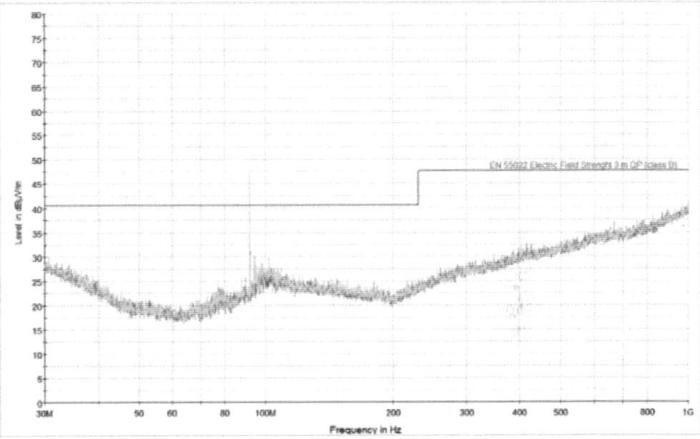

Figure 4. EMI waveform of the analog camera with the CVBS output.

In Figure 4, the waveform of interference with the connected CVBS output represented by green color is shown. The previous measurement (horizontal polarization) is also shown in the figure; however, it is largely hidden by the new green waveform. The measurement makes sense only for the horizontal polarization of the antenna because the camera did not record any significant changes in vertical polarization. The maximum and minimum values of the new measurement recorded are:

- maximum level: 47.005dBμV/m (91.711MHz),
- minimum level: 16.437dBμV/m (60.633MHz).

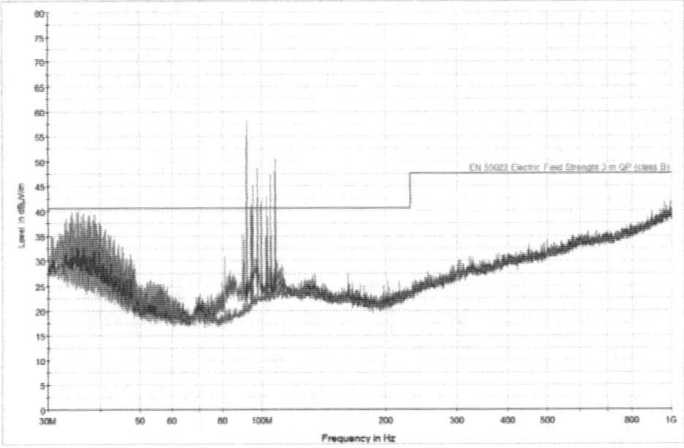

Figure 5. Waveforms of EMI with POE adapter outside the measuring chamber.

Figure 5 shows the state of the EMI analog cameras. The POE adapter which supplies energy to the security camera is located outside the measuring chamber. The differences which resulted during the comparison of waveforms with the adapter (Figure 3), and without the adapter (Figure 5) are immediately visible. Figure 5 displays an increase of interference in the frequency range from 30 to 70MHz in the vertical polarization, and in the range from 90 to 115MHz in horizontal polarization. The maximum and minimum values for horizontal and vertical polarizations were the following:

c) Horizontal polarization of antenna

- maximum level: 58.242dBμV/m (91.711MHz),
- minimum level: 16.873dBμV/m (60.391MHz).

d) Vertical polarization of antenna

- maximum level: 41.767dBμV/m (992.719MHz),
- minimum level: 16.548dBμV/m (72.151MHz).

B. IP camera

The measurement procedure is the same as with the analog camera.

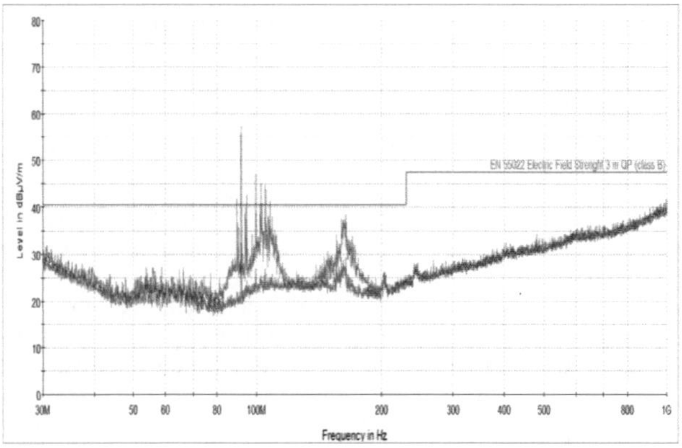

Figure 6. Waveform of EMI.

Figure 6 describes the course of electromagnetic interference generated by IP cameras, where the height of the antenna is set at 2.5m. The color-marking of waveforms is the same as in the previous cases. The undesirable influence of radio interference is especially visible in the frequency range from 50 to 250MHz. Radio frequencies were transmitted via unshielded twisted-pair cable. The influence of interference is mainly evident in the blue course of the measurement. This case was observed in analog cameras and similar waveforms can be expected in the following measurements.

a) Horizontal polarization of antenna

- maximum level: 57.539dBμV/m (91.711MHz),
- minimum level: 17.821dBμV/m (51.466MHz).

b) Vertical polarization of antenna

- maximum level: 32.444dBμV/m (91.711MHz),
- minimum level: 16.772dBμV/m (78.392MHz).

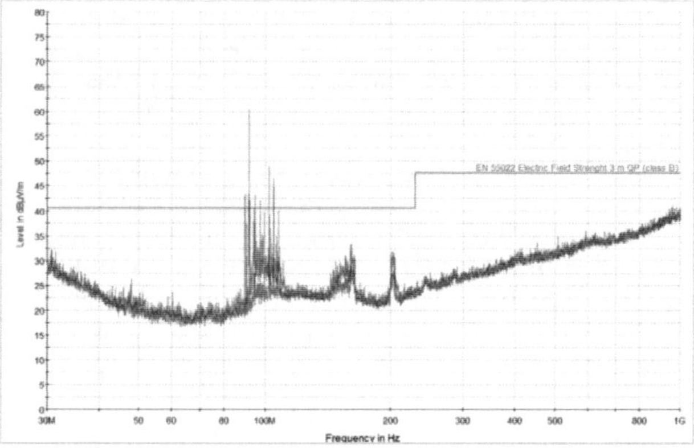

Figure 7. Waveform of EMI with POE adapter outside of semi-anechoic chamber.

Figure 7 compares the state of EMI of IP cameras with POE adapter outside of the semi-anechoic chamber. According to the figure, it is evident that changes are mainly in the blue (horizontal) waveform. The change of height of the antenna is mainly seen in the maximum values of EMI. This fact was ascertained by comparing the results of several measurements. The shape of the curve remains almost the same and the values of EMI are as follows:

c) Horizontal polarization of antenna

- maximum level: 57.132dBμV/m (91.711MHz),
- minimum level: 17.552dBμV/m (67.275MHz).

d) Vertical polarization of antenna

- maximum level: 40.880dBμV/m (980.884MHz),
- minimum level: 16.772dBμV/m (78.392MHz).

C. Electromagnetic background

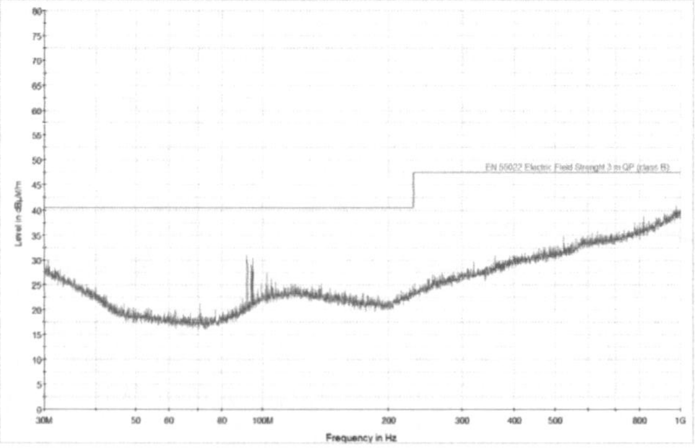

Figure 8. Electromagnetic background.

As seen in Figure 8, the electromagnetic background depicts the fluctuations in the frequency range from 80 to 100MHz, which must affect the resulting value of EMI obtained in this frequency band during the measuring. Interference in this band corresponds to radio waves. This fact must be taken into account in the analysis.

VII. CONCLUSION AND FUTURE WORK

The paper described the state of electromagnetic interference generated by IP and analog cameras. It was observed that measurement is influenced by radio signals, which are commonly encountered in each environment. This unwanted radio interference had a significant impact on the results of the measurement because interference exceeded the desired limit of 41dBμV/m set in the standard CSN EN 55022 ed.3. This problem can be eliminated by using another transmission medium (fiber optic cable, shielded twisted pair). The use of an analog camera is better able to handle the disturbance which also is as shown in the results of the measurements. The reason may be a converter that converts digital information into analog. Conversely, IP camera generates higher interference in the larger frequency range (about 80 to 250MHz), and this fact may be exploited to acquire the transmitted information.

To ensure the required level of electromagnetic interference, it is necessary to pay attention to all parts of the system (CCTV). This is because each weakness in the system can have a congruent effect on the level of interference generated by the system or more precisely its parts.

The main purpose of this paper was to prepare a basis for further research aimed at obtaining information via electromagnetic radiation. As shown in this investigation, cameras provide a sufficient amount of data that can be analyzed in detail. The results suggest that further research should be focused on the use of IP cameras which produce more unwanted information.

ACKNOWLEDGMENT

The work was funded with the support of the Internal Grant Agency of Tomas Bata University under the project No. IGA/CebiaTech/2016/005, and support of research project No. LO1303 (MSMT-7778/2014) by the Ministry of Education, Youth and Sports of the Czech Republic within the National Sustainability Programme and also by the European Regional Development Fund under the project CEBIA-Tech No. CZ.1.05/2.1.00/03.0089.

REFERENCES

[1] J. Svacina, “Electromagnetic compatibility: principles and notes”, Issue No. 1. Brno: University of Technology, 2001, 156 p, ISBN 8021418737. (in Czech).

[2] S. Kovar, J. Valouch, H. Urbancokova, and M. Adamek, "Electromagnetic interference of CCTV," in the International Conference on Information and Digital Technologies 2015, Slovakia, Žilina, 2015, pp. 161-166.

[3] ČSN EN 55022 ed. 3. Information technology equipment - Characteristics of high-frequency disturbance - Limits and methods of measurement. Prag: Czech office for standards, metrology and testing, 2011. (in Czech)

[4] Encyclopedia electromagnetic compatibility [online]. 2009 [cit. 2016-05-15]. Available from: http://www.radio.feec.vutbr.cz/emc/. (in Czech)

[5] J. Valouch, “Electromagnetic Compatibility of Alarm Systems - Legislative and Technical Requirements,” in Security Magazin, Issue No 106, 2/2012, Praha: Security Media, 2012, pp. 32-36, ISSN 1210- 8273.

[6] J. Valouch, “Electromagnetic Compatibility of CCTV,” in Alarm Focus, Issue. No 2, 2/2013. Brandýs nad Labem: Orsec, 2013, p. 22- 23, ISSN 1805-9007. (in Czech)

[7] J. Valouch, “Technical requirements for Electromagnetic Compatibility of Alarm Systems,” in the International Journal of Circuits, Systems, and Signal Processing, Volume 9, USA, Oregon: North Atlantic University Union, 2015, pp. 186 – 191, ISSN: 1998-4464.

[8] J. Valouch, “Integrated Alarm Systems,” in the Computer Applications for Software Engineering, Disaster Recovery, and Business Continuity, Series: Communications in Computer and Information Science, Vol. 340, 2012, XVIII. Berlin: Springer Berlin Heidelberg, 2012. Chapter, pp. 369 - 379. ISSN 1865-0929.

[9] D. Kovac, I. Kovacova, and J. Kanuch, “EMC in terms of theory and application,” Issue No. 1. Prag: BEN, 2006, 216 p., ISBN 80-7300-202-7. (in Czech)

[10] H. Ott, “Electromagnetic Compatibility,” USA, Hoboken: WILEY, 2009, 844 p., ISBN: 978-0-470-18930-6.

Theoretical Sources for a Theory of Safety and Security

Ludek Lukas
Department of Security Engineering
Tomas Bata University in Zlín
Zlín, Czech Republic
email: lukas@fai.utb.cz

***Abstract*—Safety and security are top priorities in our society and addressing problems in these areas is crucial. Several different kinds of safety or security exist today, such as international security, cyber security, physical security, fire safety, and so on. The scientific community is starting to address the creation of a theory of safety and security. The theory of safety and security will be followed by a series of default theories. This paper discusses the concepts and theoretical sources we can draw from for the theory of safety and security, as well as subsequent knowledge.**

Keywords-theory of safety and security; risk theory; crisis theory; causality.

I. Introduction

Nowadays, a mostly pragmatic approach prevails in the safety and security research [1]. Currently, safety and security research is realized independently, with each sector addressing its own kind of safety or security. Each kind of safety or security mostly creates its own professional conceptual apparatus.

Many specialists think that it is not possible to connect problems of international security, fire safety, information security or work health safety in one unit because they do not have a collective content. There are obvious reasons for that. Until now, no comparison was done between the different kinds of safety and security; in addition, no generalization was attempted.

Specialists in each field work on and develop their own kind of safety or security measures independently. Each kind of safety or security is solving its own specific problems of that field, which are meant to prevent danger or negative consequences. Because of this reason, each kind of safety or security was created by taking into account measures that make a reference object safe or secure. The different kinds of safety and security were researched and evolved separately. Until now, there is no common theoretical basis for safety or security.

Many scientific disciplines like informatics or electronics have their own theory. There also should be the theory of safety and security. The theory of safety and security should evolve from each kind of safety or security. This theory should reflect the existing theoretical knowledge in the area of safety and security research and other disciplines which have relations to safety and security.

The theory of safety and security can draw mainly from the following sources:

- Copenhagen school of security studies,
- risk theory,
- crisis theory,
- causality.

The following section analyzes the above mentioned sources and their impact on the theory of safety and security. The last part of the article discusses the starting points which should be respected in the theory of safety and security.

II. Copenhagen School of Security Studies

Theoretical security research exists for a long time. The main research was done in the field of international security and military. The specialists who researched this field had mostly political science education. They researched the security from the political science and governance point of view. The aim of their research was to solve mainly military problems between states. The Copenhagen School of Security Studies (CSSS) had a significant position in this field. During the 90s of 20th century, the CSSS focused on the research into other sectors of security. In their work [1], they emphasized security research not only in area of military security, but in human security, environment and other sectors. The specification of security sectors and securitization process are the main benefits of CSSS for security research. There are three main questions about security:

1. Whose security?
2. Security of which values?
3. Security against what?

Answers to these questions should help analyze the security reality. They define what the reference object is, what protects it, and what the threats are. Answers to these questions allow specifying the basic elements and interactions in the analyzed kind of security. The situational analysis is the result of this process. This analysis is the basis for solving security problems and choosing of the appropriate security methods, measures and resources.

The representatives of the CSSS emphasize that security is ensured primarily in the military area. They also recommended to make the research and to solve the security problems in the political, social, economic and environmental sectors. Through this, they developed from the security discipline the transdisciplinary scientific field. The creation of the security sectors meant a top-down approach for solving the security problems in society.

The identification of the securitization process was the last contribution of the CSSS. The securitization is speech act. Its aim is to transform the political problem into security problem. The securitization actor identifies some political problem, and after that he emphasizes the needs of solution as the security problem. This problem gets into the security agenda and has high priority of solution.

The specifications of a formal frame for security and securitization process are basic benefits of the CSSS for the theory of safety and security. The main drawback of this school is a lack of a solution for a security situation.

III. The Risk Theory as a Base for the Theory of Safety and Security

Risk theory is a widely used scientific discipline, based on the identification of a threat, the specification of risk and the specification of how to overcome the risk. The essence of risk lies in the objective existence of threats. The risk comes from consciously controlled acting, or chaotic and uncontrolled acting of each part of a complex. In the behavior of elements, moments may arise when the elements, whether intentionally or randomly, are getting into direct interaction (collision, impact).

Many interactions are negative, with devastating impact. This impact is proportional to the magnitude and direction of the action (measure), where the individual reference objects are involved in negative interactions. This negative interaction is named "security incident". The application of the risk theory evaluates which threats (or negative acts) affect the reference object, and which ones have more or less significant impact. The purpose of risk identification is to identify the worst possible impact of threats and prepare measures to counteract these threats. The proposed measures should prevent the effects of threats or prevent negative impacts on the reference object.

The aim of risk is to express how probable and how large the negative impact will be on the reference object. The risk can be determined quantitatively as well as qualitatively. Its size has more variables. There is currently no definition of risk that is clearly defined and accepted. Usually, the risk is characterized by the size of the negative impact or the harm and by the probability of threat exposure. Some authors have added the vulnerability of the reference object into the risk definition [5]. The question of vulnerability is purposeful. The vulnerability emphasizes the threats to which the reference object is prone. This parameter is involved in specification of probability of exposition. If it is not prone to threat exposition, the exposure probability, and also vulnerability, will be lower.

The method of risk management is used in many fields. These include project management, investment, economics, and so on. It is also always part of the management. The goal of the risk management is not to find a way to efficiently fulfill the objective function of the reference object. Its aim is to determine the negative impact, which can affect the reference object, how the reference will be affected, how it acts or how to minimize the impacts.

Risk management has an important position in the field of safety and security. It is focusing on minimization of damage or impact. The risk theory could be used as methodology for specification of possible negative impacts, which could harm the reference object. Due to this fact, risk management is used in many fields, in which significant theoretical development and practical applications were developed. Methods of risk analysis have been elaborated. Nowadays, we have many methods of risk analysis. These methods allow quantifying the level of risk. Depending on the approach and nature of the application, different risk analysis methods could cause different results, which were obtained during the analysis of one specific security problem.

Risk management prefers the repressive manner for ensuring the safety or security. It defines for what risk and how the reference object should be prepared. The disadvantage of the risk management is that it does not find out the causes of threats. Threats are taken as a fact and it only focuses on what they can cause. Unacceptable risk is solved by appropriate measures. The solution comes as acceptance of risk, risk retention, risk transfer and risk avoidance.

Despite this disadvantage, risk theory creates the basis of the theory of safety and security. The main contribution is its well developed methods of risk analysis. The risk theory is well applied in kinds of safety or security that protect the conditions of reference object (physical security, information security, administrative security and so on). Risk theory is less suitable for the kinds of safety or security that govern the reference object (international security, homeland security and so on). In these cases, it is about creating the secure of safe environment as the result of synthesis.

IV. The Crisis Theory and Its Relation to the Theory of Safety and Security

A crisis is an important phenomenon, which has negative influence on human society. The negative effect is a common sign of security breach and crisis. For the safety and security research, it is important to determine what is the reason and nature of safety and security problems. Moreover, we need to examine what is the relation between the theory of safety and security and the crisis theory.

Crisis theory is a scientific discipline focused on the theoretic aspects of crisis research, mainly on nature and causes of crisis. The basics of crisis prevention and its handling are based on the crisis theory.

The crisis theory has systems and a dynamic character. The crisis theory is independent from a concrete reference object; it also researches the basic aspects of the creation and development of crisis. The crisis theory is the basis for successful management of a crisis. Nowadays, the crisis is understood as:

- time when contradictions culminate,
- or as a complicated situation.

These terms are similar. They are appropriate for designation of a time period when existential complications arise. The crisis is considered as a state or period when danger is coming out and simultaneously the aim function of the reference object is threatened. The crisis arises when there is a significant change in conditions for the reference object. Changing conditions occurs due to the chaotic or uncoordinated behavior of each part of the system. During this time period, the configuration of conditions and environment are changing. It could be caused by a lack of inputs, a fault in the power supply or production elements, or escalation of electric voltage, and so on. Each change requires an adequate system reaction to provide adaptation. If the changes are expected, the system can be prepared for them and after that; it also can have a suitable reaction. The situation is different when a rapid change has a higher than expected value. During this situation, the system can have an inappropriate reaction and, following that complications or crisis may arise. Basically, the crisis is created due to:

- unexpected and large negative situation,
- unmanaged control.

A. *Unexpected and Large Negative Situation*

An unexpected situation is a situation which cannot be predicted. The complications are created by a negative event of large scale (for example, natural disasters, the sharp fall in the price of the shares on the stock exchange, large-scale attack of an unknown computer virus, and so on). The system is not prepared for these changes, because they are not frequent and the prevention is economically unbearable. The system should be prepared for these negative situations. Managing the crisis is based on minimization of the influence of the negative situation and also on system recovery. Crisis management is a special kind of management created for managing and overcoming the crisis. The activation of new forces and equipment is a basic crisis measure.

B. *Unmanaged Control*

The nature of the crisis arising is based on the unmanaged control. The crisis usually includes periods (stages) of latent symptoms, acute, chronic and resolved/unresolved crisis. In the stage of latent symptoms, the accumulation of unresolved problems happens. If the managing system is not catching up or is not solving the crisis symptoms, the crisis comes out. In the acute stage, problems culminate. The unsolved problems accumulate, too. The control system should start solving these problems slowly. A breakpoint of the situation is then reached. This breakpoint is based on the capacity of the system, especially on the control system. The crisis is eliminated if the system is capable of activating and ensuring plenty of resources for appropriate measures. The crisis management has been activated, too. The crisis management has to act fast and has to be effective enough to solve the crisis without harming the elements of the complex. In crisis, we usually do not have enough relevant information. So, crisis solving must be done during an unclear situation. Knowledge and experience, obtained from previous crisis, plays a key role in managing complicated situations. Decisions usually have irreversible implications. The systems have to be prepared for crisis and also have to make the plans for eliminating the crisis situation. At the same time, they should solve the crisis immediately in the stage of latent symptoms. This ensures avoidance of crises.

C. *Relations between Crisis and Safety and Security*

The crisis theory and the theory of safety and security represent the common form of scientific knowledge, which gives the systematic view about laws and main substantial relations, reasons and conclusions of special types of negative effect affecting reference objects. These negative effects are crisis and security incidents. Both of them have negative effects for the reference object. The reason why negative effects happen is different in each case. The key reason of crisis is the unmanaged control and the key reason of security incident is the objective existence of danger and intentional, unintentional or accidental emergence of safety and security incidents. The common signs of crisis and safety and security incidents include:

- a negative effect for the reference object,
- arising due to changes in the reference object and its inputs,
- the fact that overcoming of complications requires a specific type of management,
- the fact that the size of the impact can be minimized by prevention and repression,
- the usage of the risk theory as the basic theory for its managing and overcoming.

The different signs are:

- difference in the nature of arising,
- security incidents happens suddenly, but a crisis usually comes gradually.

Disclosure of security breaches lies in the objective existence of threats and intentional, negligence or accidental exposure. The security incident emerges due to the chaotic evolution. It can be a cause of negative interaction and also as creation of damage. The crisis is based on an unmanaged control of changed conditions. Both theories have many common points, but their basics are different. Crisis can cause security incidents and also security incidents can cause crisis. On one side, the economic crisis leads to increasing criminality and also, on the other side, a security incident such as an attack on oil pipeline can cause an energy crisis, for example. There are relations between them. In practice, the safety or security is ensured continuously. On the other hand, the crisis is solved only at the time it arises.

Also, there are applied relations between superiority and subordination. The security manager provides measures in each kind of safety or security. The physical security, personal security or information security are basic kinds of safety or security in a manufacturing company, for example. If the crisis begins, the crisis manager takes care of management. His task is to lead the organization out of the crisis. The crisis manager must understand the fulfillment of objective function of the organization. By his actions, he tries to make the organization become fully operational. The security manager helps the crisis manager especially with prevention of crisis by minimizing security incidents in the field of property, staff or information. During the crisis, the crisis manager is superior to security manager.

V. Causality and Its Relation to the Theory of Safety and Security

The causality is a scientific discipline which researches relations between cause and effect. The term causality has evolved from the Latin word „causa". The cause is relation, where cause and effect are mutually connected. The law of causality determines that anything that happens has at least one cause, and also any cause has future consequences. The same causes create the same effects. It is structured by a causal relationship (causal nexus). Causality is an expression of the relationship between two events, where one of them raises and the second is called the "cause". Basically the reason is the term, which causes effect.

Causality is key for the theory of safety and security. It allows establishing a logic chain of causes of security or safety violation. From this point of view of safety or security, there is inadequate position of causality. A role of causality is neglected. It is important to focus on this problem.

VI. Background for the Theory of Safety and Security

The theory of safety and security should specify the basic concepts and knowledge in the field of safety and security in the most general context. The Czech concept of the theory of safety and security will be different from the English concept. The security identifies security incidents caused intentionally. The safety identifies safety incidents caused by negligence or accidentally.

The Czech language, contrary to the English language, uses the terms "safety and security" as one term "bezpecnost". The Czech language does not distinguish between intentional and accidental incidents. Therefore, the Czech concept of the theory of safety and security will be in certain aspects different from the English concept of the theory of safety and security.

The theory of safety and security should follow up to the crisis theory, the risk theory, the causality and the CSSS. Based on the analysis of the above mentioned theories, the theory of safety and security exploits the following findings and conclusions:

A. The Copenhagen School of Security Studies

The CSSS' benefit is a conceptual security framework which gives the answers to basic questions: "Whose security?", „Security of which values?", „Security against what? " The response is the notion of a" reference object ", which refers to an object whose security is assessed. Another benefit is the list of threats affecting the reference object.

A sector approach to decomposition of the security environment is another benefit. Sectors refer to areas where security issues should be identified and addressed. If there is an accumulation and a repetition of security problems, a new kind of security is created for its solution.

The last benefit is specifications of the securitization process. This concept shows how the problem becomes a security issue. The problem then comes to the security agenda. Security issues are those that have to reference the object's existential influence and impact.

B. Risk Theory

The risk theory offers to the theory of safety and security a basic methodological approach to the identification and assessment of safety and security problems by identifying threats, risk analysis and the choice of method of risk management. Risk theory gives to theory of safety and security the basic terms. Basic terms are a threat, risk, damage and impact.

C. Crisis Theory

The crisis theory is closely linked to the theory of safety and security by managing the breach consequences. Most security breaches get a reference object into a crisis and it is important to overcome it.

D. Causality

The causality deals with the causes of safety and security breaches. The theory of safety and security can utilize the types of causes of safety and security breaches. It is the intent, negligence and chance.

The above described theories offer to the theory of safety and security new knowledge and themes. The newly created theory of safety and security can draw from this knowledge. The theory of safety and security can be created in several ways. Based on the conclusions, the theory of safety and security will be established by generalization and induction.

Such a theory should be created in the form of postulates creating a systematic, generalized picture of the essential patterns and contexts of safety and security, its breaching and ensuring.

TABLE I. Usable Knowledge From The Analysed Sources

Source	Usable Knowledge
Copenhagen school of security studies	• answers for situation analyses, • sector approach, • securitization.
risk theory	• basic methodological approach: • threat – risk – measure.
crisis theory	• solution of safety or security event.
causality	• causes of safety or security event.

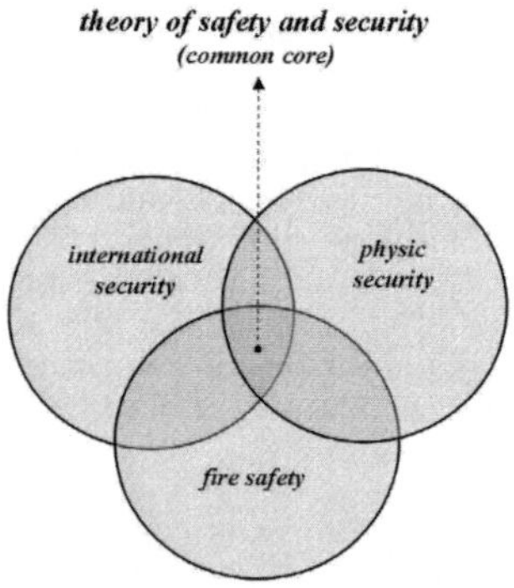

Figure 1. Induction of the kinds of safety or security

Then, the theory of safety and security could clarify the issue of safety and security in the whole range of the most general aspects. Fig. 1 depicts the generalization and induction of the selected kinds of safety or security as a way for creating the theory of safety and security.

VII. Conclusion

Nowadays, there is an effort to create the theory of safety and security. The newly created theory of safety and security would provide a common framework for all kinds of safety and security. The problem of safety and security has been addressed for a long time, and a theory of safety and security should utilize already established theories and theoretical discipline. Based on long-term research, we identified fundamental theories which should establish a background for the theory of safety and security. These theories can be used as source for creating the theory of safety and security. The theories discussed include the Copenhagen school of security studies, risk theory, crisis theory and causality. The newly created theory of safety and security is based on a generalization of the findings from the already established kinds of safety and security. This theory will be realized in the form of postulates. It can be assumed that the Czech version of the theory will be different from the English version. Czech language and other Central European languages do not distinguish between intentional and unintentional threats, like English language does. The substance of the theory of safety and security, however, remains the same. It will focus on clarification of the issue of safety and security in the most general aspects.

Acknowledgment

This work was supported by the Ministry of Education, Youth and Sports of the Czech Republic within the National Sustainability Programme project No. LO1303 (MSMT-7778/2014).

References

[1] B. Buzan, O. Weaver, J. de Wilde, Security: New Framework for Analysis. London: Lynne Rienner Publishers, 1998.

[2] B. Buzan, L. Hansen, The evolution of international security studies. Cambrige: Cambrige University Press, 2009.

[3] M. McDonald, “Securitization and the Construction of Security”. In: European Journal of International Relations December 2008, vol. 14 no. 4563-587.

[4] L. Lukas, “On theory of security”. In: Kosicka bezpecnostna revue, vol. 2015, no. 2, pp. 187 – 192, ISSN 1338 -6956.

[5] M. Hromada, “Security Models.” In: Kosicka bezpecnostna revue, vol. 2015, no. 2, pp. 118 – 127, ISSN 1338 -6956.

[6] C. Smith, D. Brooks, Security science: the theory and practice of security. Walthman, MA: Butterworth-Heimann, 2013.

Comparison of Various Encryption Techniques Based on Deterministic Chaos

Miroslav Popelka
Faculty of Applied Informatics
Tomas Bata University
Zlín, Czech Republic
e-mail: popelka@fai.utb.cz

Abstract—**In this paper, six image encryption algorithms were considered in order to compare the influence of data shifting on encrypted data. Presented algorithms are based on a deterministic chaotic logistic map and shift the individual components of a pixel RGB (Red, Green, Blue) or complete color of the pixel to secure given input. The algorithms have been written in C# language and were adjusted to encrypt an image, nevertheless, they can be easily modified for any other multimedia file. Furthermore, two C# applications have been created. Chaos - Statistical testing application was created to evaluate histogram, sensitivity, correlation, entropy, and time consumption of the original and encrypted images. Additionally, another C# windows application was developed for the visualization and presentation of the generated chaotic data; furthermore, it provides basic encryption with various types of chaotic maps and dimensions.**

Keywords-Chaos; Chaotic Deterministic Map; Image Encryption; Pixels Shifting.

I. INTRODUCTION

Like many other great inventions, encryption was created in wartime in order to make a message impossible to read without some specific knowledge. Over time, many encryption techniques were developed to reach this goal with various mathematical and statistical knowledge. One of the interesting techniques for an image encryption in these days is chaotic encryption. In particular, discrete chaotic encryption is a widespread technique which uses a variety of deterministic map and differential equations.

Many technical papers were published on this topic. Discrete chaotic encryption algorithms for encryption of different types of multimedia files were published, for instance in [1], [2], and [3]. In these papers, multiple discrete chaotic maps were combined or chained in order to encrypt a required multimedia input file. For instance, L. Zhang et al. [1] present an image encryption algorithm based on "XOR plus mod" operation. The algorithm is designed to increase resistance in comparison with previously designed algorithms. Also, C. Li et al. [2] mention a chaotic image encryption algorithm using XOR operation; furthermore, they implement a circular bit shifting of image data. Total shuffling algorithm for image encryption is described in [3], where presented encryption algorithm combines two chaotic systems to improve the security level. To achieve this, the authors used a matrix in order to shift the position of image pixels. In [13], [14], and [15] the authors are using dispersion matrix to disperse data and provide more secure algorithms.

The purpose of all the mentioned algorithms was to improve the encryption process in terms of speed and security. In this paper, six algorithms with data shifting were developed.

Furthermore, two windows based applications for binary data sequence generation of the selected chaotic map and for analytical and statistical testing were created. The first application can encrypt or decrypt three types of multimedia files (image, text and binary file). Moreover, the encryption method can be selected from the list offered by the deterministic chaotic map; in addition, the initial condition parameters can be set up as well. The second application is used for the statistical evaluation of encrypted multimedia files in various tests (correlation, histograms, sensitivity, entropy, and time consumption).

In this paper, six image encryption methods using deterministic chaotic map are presented, especially a logistic map. These encryption algorithms can be easily transformed to encrypt any multimedia file.

The rest of the paper is structured as follows. Section II presents basic information about the logistic chaotic map. In Section II, we describe our proposed algorithms based on this logistic map. In Sections IV and V, two C# applications are presented. In Section VI, we evaluate and compare the data obtained in testing the proposed algorithms. Section VII provides a discussion of the results, and we conclude in Section VIII.

II. DETERMINISTIC CHAOTIC MAPS

The main property of chaotic dynamic systems is the sensitivity of initial conditions and control parameters and encryption algorithms benefit from this advantage. Discrete systems are mainly described by discrete formulas or differential equations, which represent their behavior in a short time period. In this paper, a basic deterministic logistic map is used.

A. *Logistic map*

This is one of the simple dynamical nonlinear systems, which shows chaotic behavior. A mathematical model of this map is described in (1) and a bifurcation diagram is shown in Figure 1.

$$x_{n+1} = r\, x_n\, (1-x_n). \tag{1}$$

Where "xn" and "xn+1" are numbers between zero and one. "xn" has an initial value usually set to 0.1. A parameter "r" is in the interval (0, 4]. The "r" parameter has a value equal to 1 at the start.

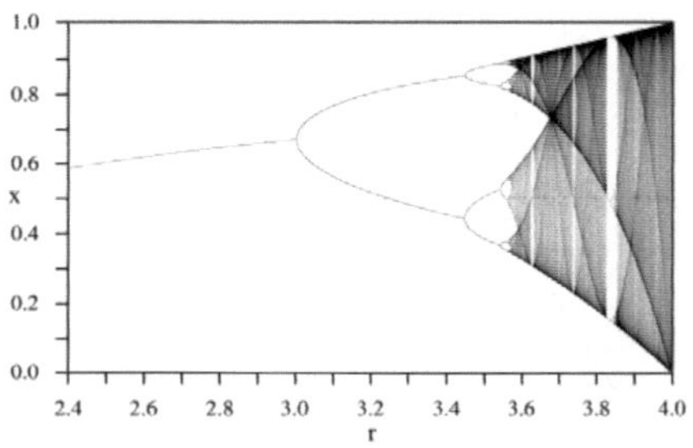

Figure 1. Bifurcation diagram of a logistic map [9]

III. ENCRYPTION APPLICATION

In this section, six encryption algorithms are described. Each algorithm is written in C# language and has this structure, which is described in Figure 2.

```
for (int i = 0; i < image.Height; i = i + 1)
{
  for (int j = 0; j < image.Width; j = j + 1)
  {
    original_pixel = image.GetPixel(i, j);
    byte R_component = (byte)(original_pixel.R ^ Ch_pole[ch_i]);
    byte G_component = (byte)(original_pixel.G ^ Ch_pole[ch_i + 1]);
    byte B_component = (byte)(original_pixel.B ^ Ch_pole[ch_i + 2]);
    byte A_component = (byte)(original_pixel.A ^ Ch_pole[ch_i + 3]);
    encrypted_pixel = Color.FromArgb(A_component, R_component,
    G_component, B_component);
    image.SetPixel(i, j, myRgbColor);
    ch_i = ch_i + 4;
```

Figure 2. A general structure of the encryption algorithms

The middle section is shown in Figure 2. It is different for all presented algorithms. This section is important for every algorithm which is described in the following sections.

A. *Simple algorithm with XOR*

The first algorithm performs only simple XOR operation with a binary data. This operation takes each pixel red, blue, green and alpha component and performs XOR operation with generated binary chaotic data. The individual value obtained is placed in the same pixel position where it was before. This algorithm can be seen in Figure 2.

B. *Algorithm with a basic data shifting*

The second presented algorithm described in Figure 3, is based on pixel shifting. The position of each pixel is given by original pixels position in X-th row and Y-th column. If pixel positions and generated chaotic data are known XOR operation is done for every single pixel. The foregoing implies that the final image will be reconstructed with the same pixels as in the original image, although their position will be changed.

```
new_row = (Ch_pole[ind] ^ lower_k) *
      (Ch_pole[ind + 1] ^ upper_k) % (image.Height);
new_col = (Ch_pole[ind + 2] ^ lower_l) *
      (Ch_pole[ind + 3] ^ upper_l) % (image.Width);

myRgbColor = image.GetPixel(new_col, new_row);

Encr_image.SetPixel(new_col, new_row, pixelColor);
Encr_image.SetPixel(l, k, myRgbColor);
```

Figure 3. An encryption algorithm with the basic data shifting

C. *Algorithm with an advanced data shifting*

In Figure 4 the third algorithm based on pixel shifting is described. In contrast with the previous shifting algorithm, where pixels are shifted, in this algorithm, positions of individual components (R, G, B, A) of all encrypted data are shifted. Exclusive disjunction of specific components and generated chaos is calculated and encrypted image is provided.

```
int new_row_red = (Ch_pole[ind] ) *
      (Ch_pole[ind + 3]) % (image.Height);
int new_col_red = (Ch_pole[ind]) *
      (Ch_pole[ind + 1]) % (image.Width);
int new_row_green = (Ch_pole[ind] ) *
      (Ch_pole[ind + 1] ) % (image.Height);
int new_col_green = (Ch_pole[ind] ) *
      (Ch_pole[ind + 2]) % (image.Width);
int new_row_blue = (Ch_pole[ind + 1] ) *
      (Ch_pole[ind + 3]) % (image.Height);
int new_col_blue = (Ch_pole[ind + 2] ) *
      (Ch_pole[ind + 3] ) % (image.Width);
int new_row_a = (Ch_pole[ind] ) *
      (Ch_pole[ind + 3]) % (image.Height);
int new_col_a = (Ch_pole[ind] ) *
      (Ch_pole[ind + 2] ) % (image.Width);
```

Figure 4. An encryption algorithm with a circle data shifting

D. *Algorithm with a circle data shifting*

The fourth tested algorithm, which can be seen in Figure 5, changes the position of pixels in circles with specific radius and angle. To deploy individual pixels in a circle, it is important to determine the radius and the angle from the generated chaotic data.

```
radius = ((int)angle * radius);
angle =( angle * ch_l )% 360;

Point circle_point = new Point(0, 0);
circle_point.X = (int)(x + radius * Math.Cos(angle * (Math.PI / 180.0)));
circle_point.Y = (int)(y + radius * Math.Sin(angle * (Math.PI / 180.0)));
```

Figure 5. An encryption algorithm with a circle data shifting

Centers of the circles are located into a position of every pixel in the rectangular arrangement. After evaluating an angle and radius of the circle, it is necessary to define the new position and provide a completely encrypted image.

Due to the rectangular data arrangement in the original image, the algorithm had to deal with overflow. The overflow led to unwanted results. The solution how to compensate overflow can be seen in Figure 6.

```
if (Math.Abs(circle_point.X) >= image_height)
{
   int dif = ((Math.Abs(circle_point.X)) % image_height);
   if (dif == 0) { dif = 1; }
   if (ch_1 > 127)
   circle_point.X = dif;
   else
      circle_point.X = image_height-dif;
}
```

Figure 6. An overflow compensations for x coordinates

E. *Algorithm with a polynomial data shifting*

The fifth algorithm, displayed in Figure 7, also used the analytical mathematical function in order to change the position of pixels in the encrypted image. In this case, a polynomial function of a second degree was applied on the position of the individual pixel.

```
integers[0] = ch_pole[0] * x * x * x +
              ch_pole[1] * x * x +
              ch_pole[2] * x +
              ch_pole[3] ;
integers[1] = ch_pole[3] * y * y * y +
              ch_pole[2] * y * y +
              ch_pole[1] * y +
              ch_pole[0] ;

Point new_spot= new Point(0,0);

new_spot.X = (Math.Abs(integers[0])) % image_height;
new_spot.Y = (Math.Abs(integers[1] ))% image_width;
```

Figure 7. An encryption algorithm with a polynomial data shifting

In this algorithm, an overflow needs to be reckoned. The solution is very similar to the previous one, although the overflow compensation is slightly more often applied due to polynomial function characteristic. The overflow compensation can be seen on the last two lines in Figure 7.

F. *Algorithm with change color/position*

Finally, this encryption algorithm combines a position shifting with pixel R, G, B and A components of the color, in order to change the position of given pixel. This algorithm can be seen in Figure 8.

The first step was to decompose pixel colors into R, G, B and A components.

Two components and a number of rows (X) are XORed and used for determination of the new X position.

Two other parts of the pixel color are processed in the same way to obtain a new column number (Y).

```
    byte red = (byte)(pixelColor.R ^ Ch_pole[ind]);
    byte green = (byte)(pixelColor.G ^ Ch_pole[ind + 1]);
    byte blue = (byte)(pixelColor.B ^ Ch_pole[ind + 2]);
    byte alpha = (byte)(pixelColor.A ^ Ch_pole[ind + 3]);

pixelColor = Color.FromArgb(alpha, red, green, blue);
myRgbColor = image.GetPixel(new_col, new_row);

    byte red_n = (byte)(myRgbColor.R ^ Ch_pole[ind+3]);
    byte green_n = (byte)(myRgbColor.G ^ Ch_pole[ind + 2]);
    byte blue_n = (byte)(myRgbColor.B ^ Ch_pole[ind + 1]);
    byte alpha_n = (byte)(myRgbColor.A ^ Ch_pole[ind]);

myRgbColor = Color.FromArgb(alpha_n, red_n, green_n, blue_n);
```

Figure 8. An overflow compensations for x coordinates

IV. APPLICATION DESCRIPTION

The main window of this application was designed to generate chaotic pseudo-random data. This data were used together with the original data to perform an encryption. The main window of the application is divided into three main control parts.

A. *Settings section*

The most important part of the main window is the settings section, which is situated on the very left side of the main window. Selectors and two text boxes can also be found. Selectors are designated to select the dimension of the chaotic map and for selection of the specific deterministic chaotic map in the second selector. According to the previous selections, texts in text boxes below are dynamically updated and they contain parameters and initial conditions according to the selected dimension and type of deterministic chaotic map. Part of this setting section can be seen in Figure 9.

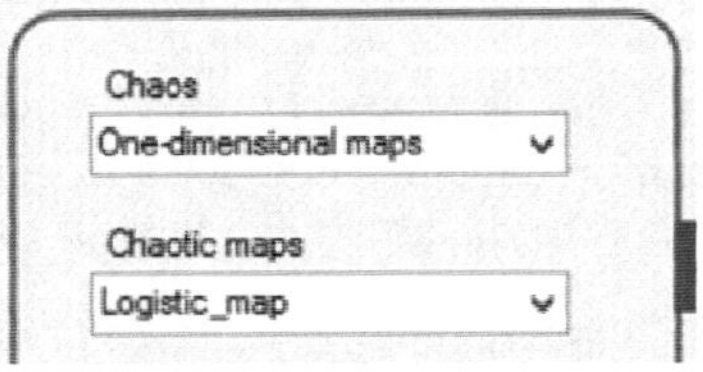

Figure 9. Selection of dimension and type of chaotic map

B. *Control section*

The application control elements are placed in the middle between settings and the results section. This middle control section contains buttons to change the content of the results section. There are a decryption, an encryption and also a visualization data buttons. Figure 10 shows the main control buttons in the application.

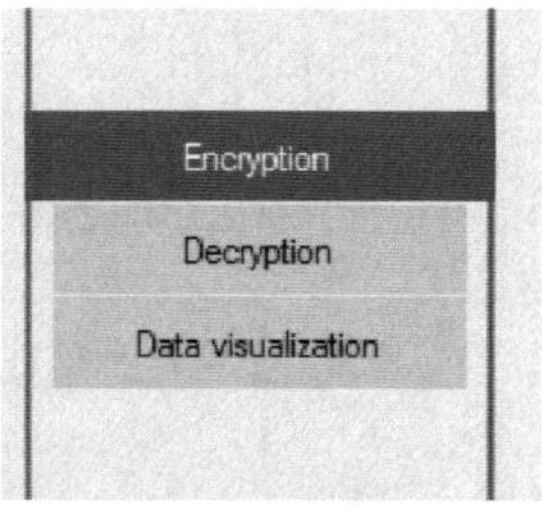

Figure 10. Control buttons

C. *Results section*

In terms of displaying the results, this section is the most important of all. In the result section, decrypted files, images, and text files can be encrypted. The results obtained are displayed in appropriate form for observation. An example of the obtained result is shown in Figure 11.

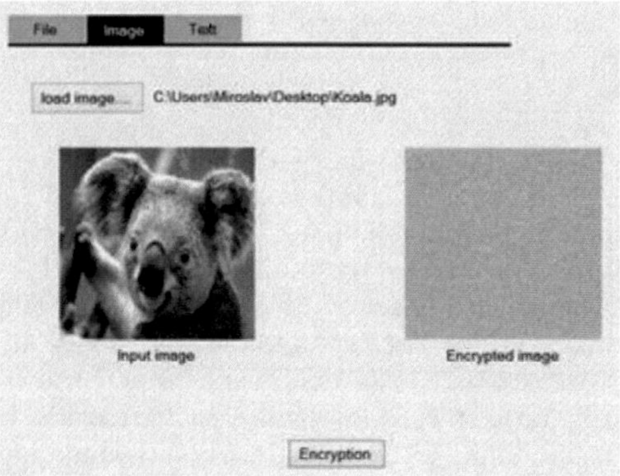

Figure 11. Example of application results section

Naturally, this application does not serve only for the generation of chaotic data. In addition, it can be used for encryption of different multimedia files. It is necessary to attach a list of parameters and initial conditions to the encrypted file. These items are needed for successful decryption.

Of course, the parameters and the initial conditions cannot be transported non-encrypted. On this attached information is applied well-known RSA encryption algorithm, which works with the public and private key.

V. TESTING APPLICATION

Analytical and statistical tests are an integral part of the development of encryption algorithm. For these reasons, the testing application was created in order to complete all mentioned tests.

In this test application, it is possible to test input non-encrypted and encrypted file in various tests such as histogram, image entropy, sensitivity and correlation of every pixel. The Chaos - Statistical testing application can be seen in Figure.12.

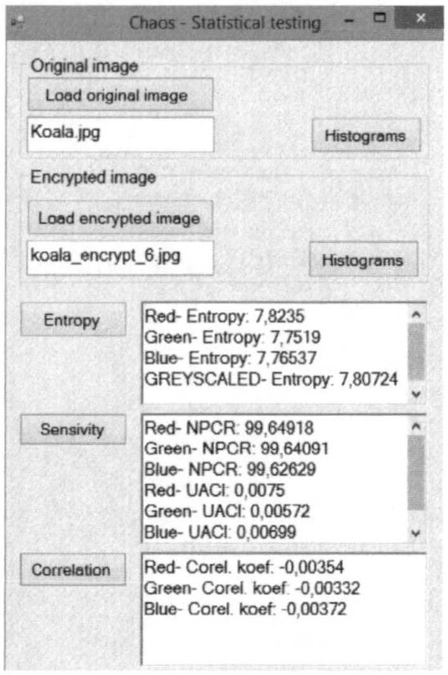

Figure 12. The Chaos - Statistical testing

Moreover, the disturbance of specific color in an original and in an encrypted image can be estimated in this application. Time consumption of each presented algorithms can be also measured by the application. The encryption time depends on an image size, although images must have the same resolution, otherwise, the result will not be possible to compare. Furthermore, comparison of a color and a grayscale image is not relevant and the given result will not be definitive.

The technique of time measurement will start at the beginning of the encryption algorithm itself, after producing of the chaotic data. All measurements were performed on the same computer with the same hardware equipment to prevent a hardware performance error.

VI. RESULTS

The input data for all six methods were an identical collection of images. This image collection covers both a grayscale and color images with various resolutions ranging from 50 x 50 pixels to 1024 x 768 pixels. The chosen resolution range is sufficient to show dependency on the number of pixels.

The image collection was divided into three equal parts by the image resolution. Every collection part contains ten color and ten grayscale images with the corresponding resolution. The comparison of obtained results from an individual algorithm can be seen in following Figure 13. and tables (Table I – Table VI).

A. Time consumption comparisons

Figure 13. represents time consumptions of every presented encryption algorithm in the selected image collection.

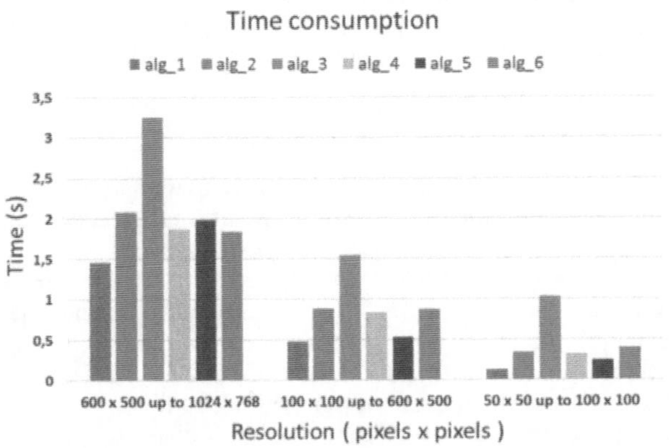

Figure 13. The average time consumption for each algorithm

B. Statistical comparisons

The statistical results were estimated for the color and grayscale images within the specific collection and these results are averaged and displayed in the tables (Table I – Table VI). Individual statistical test and their formulas are described in this section.

1) Image entropy

It denotes the probability of the single pixel color in the encrypted image (2).

The ideal image entropy for one color image is 8. In this paper, the individual color components (R, G, B) are averaged into a single value in order to compare with results obtained from grayscale images.

$$H(s) = -\sum_{i=0}^{2^n-1} P(s_i)\log_2[P(s_i)]. \tag{2}$$

2) Sensitivity analysis

To test the influence of the change of image pixel on the encrypted image, two statistical coefficients are often used. The first coefficient is net pixel change rate (NPCR) (3).

$$NPCR = \frac{\sum_{ij} D(i,j)}{M \times N} \times 100\% . \tag{3}$$

and the second is the unified average changing rate (UACI) (4).

$$\mathrm{UACI} = \frac{1}{\mathrm{M} \times \mathrm{N}} \cdot \Sigma_{\mathrm{ij}} \frac{|\mathrm{c}_1(\mathrm{i},\mathrm{j}) - \mathrm{c}_2(\mathrm{i},\mathrm{j})|}{255} \times 100\,\% \tag{4}$$

These two coefficients state for an encrypted image pixel sensitivity on the original image pixels.

3) Correlation

The correlation is the dependency between a pixel in the original and encrypted image. The ideal value is 0. The correlation can be calculated by (5).

$$\gamma_{xy} = \frac{Conv(x,y)}{\sqrt{D(x)} \cdot \sqrt{D(y)}} . \tag{5}$$

4) Measured and averaged statistical results

This section displays Table I – Table VI in order to compare individual results in the individual statistical tests.

TABLE I. RESULTS FOR GRAYSCALE IMAGES WITH RESOLUTION (600 X 500) UP TO (1024 X 768) PIXELS

Algorithm No.	Grayscale			
	Entropy	*NPCR*	*UACI*	*Correlation*
1	7.8472	99.4948	0.0089	-0.0003
2	7.7072	99.5967	0.0285	0.0077
3	7.7861	99.6149	0.0045	0.0144
4	7.5999	99.6351	0.0065	-0.0010
5	7.6098	99.6063	0.0052	-0.0052
6	7.9132	99.7198	0.0061	-0.0035

TABLE II. STATISTICAL RESULTS FOR COLOR IMAGES WITH RESOLUTION (600 X 500) UP TO (1024 X 768)PIXELS

Algorithm No.	Color			
	Entropy	*NPCR*	*UACI*	*Correlation*
1	7.7862	99.4968	0.0085	-0.0002
2	7.7339	99.5899	0.0254	0.0058
3	7.7874	99.6086	0.0040	0.0134
4	7.6011	99.6337	0.0061	-0.0021
5	7.5998	99.5979	0.0058	-0.0061
6	7.9298	99.7301	0.0065	-0.0039

TABLE III. STATISTICAL RESULTS FOR GRAYSCALE IMAGES WITH RESOLUTION (100 X 100) UP TO (600 X 500) PIXELS

Algorithm No.	Grayscale			
	Entropy	*NPCR*	*UACI*	*Correlation*
1	7.7482	99.5238	0.0085	-0.0005
2	7.6972	99.5836	0.0294	0.0076
3	7.8001	99.6259	0.0037	0.0140
4	7.5874	99.6201	0.0073	-0.0009
5	7.7001	99.6086	0.0043	-0.0048
6	7.8513	99.7205	0.0055	-0.0033

TABLE IV. STATISTICAL RESULTS FOR COLOR IMAGES WITH RESOLUTION (100 X 100) UP TO (600 X 500) PIXELS

Algorithm No.	Color			
	Entropy	*NPCR*	*UACI*	*Correlation*
1	7.7663	99.5337	0.0071	-0.0004
2	7.6881	99.5741	0.0282	0.0088
3	7.8555	99.5993	0.0039	0.0190
4	7.6577	99.6009	0.0066	-0.0014
5	7.7305	99.6255	0.0050	-0.0050
6	7.9012	99.7318	0.0056	-0.0048

TABLE V. STATISTICAL RESULTS FOR GRAYSCALE IMAGES WITH RESOLUTION (50 X 50) UP TO (100 X 100) PIXELS

Algorithm No.	Grayscale			
	Entropy	*NPCR*	*UACI*	*Correlation*
1	7.7919	99.4819	0.0080	-0.0010
2	7.7872	99.5954	0.0304	0.0084
3	7.7189	99.5949	0.0063	0.0159
4	7.5867	99.6256	0.0085	-0.0008
5	7.6672	99.6163	0.0054	-0.0059
6	7.9624	99.7298	0.0070	-0.0031

TABLE VI. STATISTICAL RESULTS FOR COLOR IMAGES WITH RESOLUTION (50 X 50) UP TO (100 X 100) PIXELS

Algorithm No.	Color			
	Entropy	*NPCR*	*UACI*	*Correlation*
1	7.8211	99.4997	0.0075	-0.0006
2	7.7344	99.5954	0.0259	0.0083
3	7.7299	99.5925	0.0056	0.0136
4	7.5616	99.6311	0.0093	-0.0006
5	7.7493	99.6327	0.0033	-0.0070
6	7.9338	99.7213	0.0064	-0.0039

VII. DISCUSSION

In this paper, six shifting chaotic encryption techniques have been presented. Every algorithm was tested under various tests, such as correlation, image sensitivity, and time consumption. All algorithms are based on the pixel shifting and XOR operation with the chaotic data. The results obtained from six image encryption algorithms were compared and the differences between these results were negligible. All six algorithms provide the same level of security. This fact is supported by Tables I – VI. Especially, correlation coefficients display the most accurate information about the individual pixel similarity of the original and encrypted image. Nevertheless, an entropy in the last presented algorithm is about 7.9, which means, how many pixels have a random color. In other words, how much from the encrypted image is similar to the original. As can be seen from presented results these techniques provided adequate results according to their complexity. The results from statistical tests and the time consumption of an individual test were not as expected. Especially, results of entropy, NPCR and UACI did not provide such results in comparison with [1], [2] and [3]. However, the last presented algorithm showed that a position shifting combined together with the color components can produce satisfactory results in a reasonable time. This algorithm and its variation will be examined in future research.

VIII. CONCLUSION

The main aim of this work was to compare and evaluate position shifting algorithms. Six different image encryption algorithms based on the chaotic discrete logistic map were created. Each algorithm was tested in various tests (correlation, histograms, sensitivity, image entropy, and time consumption). These tests were performed on the collection of the test images with a resolution of 50 x 50 pixels up to 1024 x 786 pixels and results were shown in tables for every presented algorithm. In addition, the time consumption has been measured for every algorithm. The last presented algorithm has most significant results from all the created algorithms.

ACKNOWLEDGMENT

This work was supported by Internal Grant Agency of Tomas Bata University under the project No. IGA/FAI/2016/024.

REFERENCES

[1] L. Zhang, X. Liao and X. Wang, "An image encryption approach based on chaotic maps" Chaos, Solitons & Fractals, May 2005, pp. 759-765, doi: 10.1016/j.chaos.2004.09.035.

[2] C. Li, S. Li, G. Alvarez, G. Chen and K. T. Lo,"Cryptanalysis of a chaotic encryption system" Physics Letters A, Sept. 2007, pp. 23-30, doi: 10.1016/j.physleta.2007.04.023.

[3] T. Gao and Z. Chen,"Image encryption based on a new total shuffling algorithm" Chaos, solitons & fractals, Oct. 2008, pp. 213–220, doi: 10.1016/j.chaos.2006.11.009.

[4] S. Fu-Yan, L. Shu-Tang and L. Zong-Wang "Image encryption using high-dimension chaotic system" Chinese Physics, Dec. 2007, pp. 3616 - 3624, doi: 10.1088/1009-1963/16/12/011

[5] C. Y. Chee and D. Xu, "Chaotic encryption using discrete-time synchronous chaos" Physics Letters A, Dec. 2006, pp. 284-292, doi: 10.1016/j.physleta.2005.08.082

[6] Zhang, W., Wong, K. W., Yu, H., & Zhu, Z. L. (2013). An image encryption scheme using reverse 2-dimensional chaotic map and dependent diffusion. Communications in Nonlinear Science and Numerical Simulation, 18(8), 2066-2080.

[7] S. El Assad, M. Farajallah, "A new chaos-based image encryption system", Signal Processing: Image Communication, vol. 41, 2016, pp. 144-157.

[8] M. Farajallah, S. El Assad, O. Deforges, "Fast and secure chaos-based cryptosystem for images", International Journal of Bifurcation and Chaos, IJBC, February 2016, Vol. 26, No. 02, pp. 1650021-1 1650021-21. DOI: 10.1142/S0218127416500218.

[9] Zhang, X., Zhao, Z., & Wang, J. (2014). Chaotic image encryption based on circular substitution box and key stream buffer. Signal Processing: Image Communication, 29(8), 902-913.

Using Ethical Hacking to Analyze BYOD Safety in Corporations

Roman Jašek, Jakub Nožička
Faculty of Applied Informatics
Tomas Bata University in Zlín
Zlín, Czech Republic
e-mail: {jasek, nozicka}@fai.utb.cz

***Abstract*—Tablets and smart phones using the Android platform are still more popular for the general population than devices using operating system Microsoft Windows or iOS. This fact is useful for hackers. For hackers, it is important to always carry with them tools to scan the network traffic in a manner that is not obvious to others. It may be difficult, and sometimes impossible, to connect to a network that the hacker wants to attach using metallic cable. Hackers are less striking in scanning network traffic on the wireless network and even less striking in scanning when using tablets. For this purpose, is perfect to use tablet with Kali Linux (Android platform). Such a tablet can be modified to be used for attacks on corporate wireless network and potential hacker becomes even less striking. Kali Linux distribution does not have high hardware department, therefore can be used at tablets with basic hardware equipment.**

Keywords- hacking; tablet; android; Kali Linux; wireless network.

I. Introduction

The aim of the work was to demonstrate that BYOD (Bring Your Own Device), which is becoming still more popular in organizations and can provide security weakness in organization. Percentage of organizations that use BYOD is unstoppably growing every year. Potential hacker, who wants attacking on wireless networks in organization that using BYOD tablets will be conspicuous with using of notebook. This problem can be solved with using of tablet for this purpose. Also was proved that tablet is a universal tool, which can be used for penetration testing of wireless networks, and also that this solution is low cost while maintaining all its functions, compared with a laptop.

Some technical papers were published with this aim. Security of Tablets in BYOD Programs are published, for instance in [4] and [5]. These papers are describing present security of tablets, and forecasting how many tablets will be using in next years. Aim of this paper were verify, than tablet can be suitable tool for hacking of wireless networks in corporations. Some technical papers were published with this aim. Security of Tablets in BYOD Programs are published, for instance in [4] and [5]. These papers are describing present security of tablets, and forecasting how many tablets will be using in next years. In [7] and [8] the authors are describing just possibilities of sending secure data from BYOD devices to public cloud or to private server.

Firstly, basic information about hardware which was used for this research. In next section software which was used for hacking are described. In section IV and are presented how to install Kali Linux in to tablet and how can be executed attack to wireless network via tablet. There were created two testing tablets, which can be using for penetration of wireless network in corporations.

II. Hardware Description

A partial goal of research was to prove that the tablet is a suitable and low cost solution for penetration testing of wireless networks. For verification of the solution, Kali Linux was installed on 2 tablets. As a representative of tablets with the lowest price, was used tablet Prestigio multipad 7.0 ultra duo. And as a tablet, which have better HW (hardware) equipment was chosen Lenovo Yoga 2.

A. Tablet Prestigio multipad 7.0 ultra duo

As already mentioned above, the tablet Prestigio multipad 7.0 ultra duo was chosen as a representative of tablets with the lowest price. The goal was to verify that the hacking can be done on this type of device. The device has a processor DualCore ARM A9 (RK3066) with 1.6GHz, 1GB RAM (Random-access memory) memory and 8 gigabytes of storage. This configuration is the minimum required to ensure all functions of Kali Linux.

B. Tablet Lenovo Yoga 2

Tablet Lenovo Yoga 2 was chosen as the representative of popular tablets. Compared with the tablet Prestigio multipad 7.0 ultra duo, it has better technical parameters and is therefore more suitable for hacking. The device has a processor Intel Atom Z3745, 4 x 1.86 GHz, 2GB of RAM and 32 GB storage. This HW configuration gives Kali Linux better support and faster response of system.

C. Antenna

For better reaction radius of hacking of wireless networks is needed to enhance the reach of the antenna. This can be ensured by using the external antenna. Android does not support all standard architectures chipsets used in antennas. Android supports just antennas with architecture realtek, as an example can be used popular antenna Alfa AWUS036H.

III. Software Description

Kali Linux is a Linux distribution derived from Debian. Kali Linux is designed for digital forensics and penetration testing. Before Kali Linux was widely used Linux distribution BackTrack. However, that did not fully support tablets architecture, despite modifications to the tablet were not fully stable. Kali Linux can be installed on a computer hard drive or it can run without installation from Live CD (Compact Disc). Kali Linux is distributed in 32 and 64 bit version. Kali Linux is even available for ARM processors used in Raspberry Pi computers. Kali Linux is available in versions for i386 and amd64 architectures, where is minimal configuration needed: 1GHz CPU (Central processing unit), 8GB HDD (hard disk drive), 300 MB of RAM.

Kali Linux contains a lot of selected applications designed for penetration testing. An attacker would likely begin at application EvilAP. EvilAP is application for creating a false Wi-Fi hotspot, which is ready for eavesdropping. EvilAP can know how to redirect all requests from the surroundings at the same time; because of that hotspot with the client (another phone, tablet, and laptop) can connect without their owner knowing. Once that happens, all communications can be monitored. If this attacker fails to create a fake hotspot, Aircrack-ng remains the most important application for network injection which is used to crack passwords of secured wireless networks using WEP (Wired Equivalent Privacy) or WPA-PSK (Wi-Fi Protected Access). This application requires Wi-Fi card or Wi-Fi adapter, which can be switched into monitoring mode, connecting the wireless adapter is possible on tablet. Application Wireshark (formerly Ethereal) is a protocol analyzer and packet sniffer. Among the most common applications is included analysis and debugging problems in wireless networks, software development, development of communication protocols and scanning network communication. Another useful tool for hackers is Wireshark application that allows setting the network interfaces to various modes, allowing seeing all the traffic on these interfaces, including broadcast and multicast. Wireshark has collected a lot of raw data and hackers then use many filters and select just data which are important. Default version of Kali Linux is provided with more than 300 security tools for hacking and penetration testing. If it still misses some application, user can instantly install it from the repositories of Linux. Kali Linux contains every tool, which hacker needs and expects from Linux distributions.

As it is written below Kali Linux is a Linux distribution, which is free and easy to HW, also there exists images for small computers ranging from the popular Raspberry Pi and ending by some Chromebooks, this fact makes Kali Linux even more useful for low costs projects.

A phenomenon known as BYOD, is increasing worldwide. Solution where employees use their private device is used in foreign countries and in the Czech Republic by more and more companies. BYOD solution has many advantages and disadvantages. The primary advantage for the company is economic saving, saving of the acquisition of working devices and software, employee together do not have to carry more equipment and working with it, to which they are accustomed. On the other side, this solution has many disadvantages, main disadvantage is security.

BYOD in organizations is increasingly common, at present 38 percent of organizations does not provide employees with working IT (Information technology) equipment. According to a global survey by Gartner CIO (Chief information officer) is expected that by the end of the year will exceed the number of steps minded companies 40 percent. The main reason why more and more organizations are thinking this way, is economic fact. But apart from the costs which organizations save on IT devices and the renewal of IT devices, employees are also more satisfied if they can work on their devices. BYOD also supports organization's innovation by increasing the number of users of mobile applications in the organization's environment. When BYOD is most prevalent in medium and large organizations, it is suitable for smaller business that can help development of organizations without large investments. BYOD is widespread throughout the world; however, the organizations in the United States use BYOD more than organizations in Europe. Not surprisingly, the highest safety arouses interest in using the technology BYOD. Risk of data lost on mobile platforms is particularly urgent. Some security policy organizations using BYOD are designed to share data taking place only in the cloud, which generally reduces the risk of safety.

Since 2012, tablets have become a phenomenon in organizations, the organization overwhelmingly reaching for tablets running Android and iOS, tablets with Windows OS (operating systems) and other, occupy at market a negligible 2% popularity. BYOD tablets were at the beginning of 2012, the domain of iOS, which occupied a market of over 60%, but by 2013 this number is reduced when Android gets to the forefront. According to analysts, this is due to one thing and that is the economy, the cheapest devices which use iOS participate at the market price of 250 USD (United States dollar), while the price of useful Android devices start at US (United States) $ 100. Currently, the difference is clearly noticeable, tablets running Android, with nearly 70% share of installations in organizations; clearly defeats tablet devices running iOS.

This fact is playing right into potential hackers hands for attacking wireless networks using tablets running Android. Hacker who uses attack tablets must use the Android system, as shown by surveys, most organizations use precisely the Android device and the attacker becomes less conspicuous for the neighborhood [1]-[6].

IV. KALI LINUX INSTALLATION FOR ANDROID

For Kali Linux developers, it was firstly important to make their products work seamlessly even on devices that are using Android. Currently, Kali Linux distribution can be installed on devices with Android 4.4 and above. Installation requires at least 5 GB of free memory in the internal memory or external storage and a fast Internet connection [3].

A. Configuring Kali Linux for Android

To install Kali Linux user must do a few basic things. The user can select their architecture to verify that the downloaded distribution Kali Linux is genuine; set the type and location of the installation on the device. In Figure 1 are all necessary settings for the installation of Kali Linux [3].

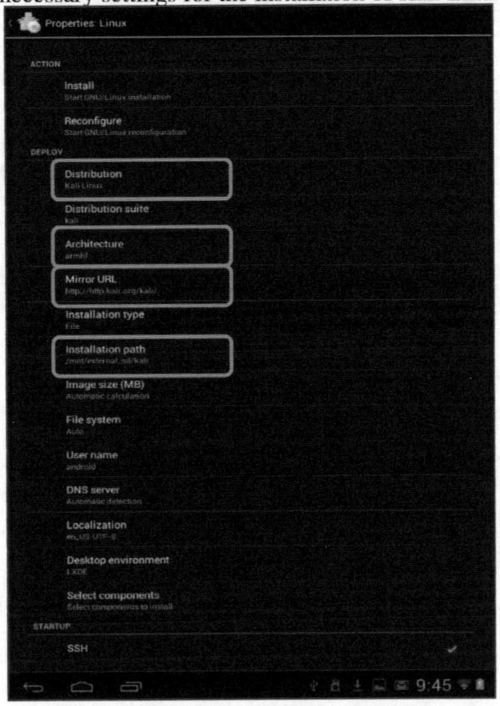

Figure 1. Linux Deploy properties.

B. *Downloading Kali Linux image*

Once the user makes all settings as you can see in Figure 2, Kali Linux begins to download image from Linux servers. This process is directly dependent on the speed of your Internet connection.

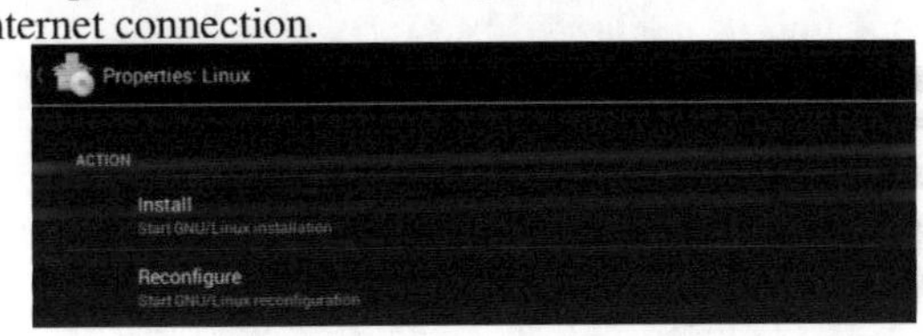

Figure 2. Linux Deploy properties.

C. *Starting chroot Kali Linux*

Once the user makes all settings, as you can see in Figure 3, Kali Linux begins to download image from Linux servers. This process is directly dependent on the speed of your Internet connection.

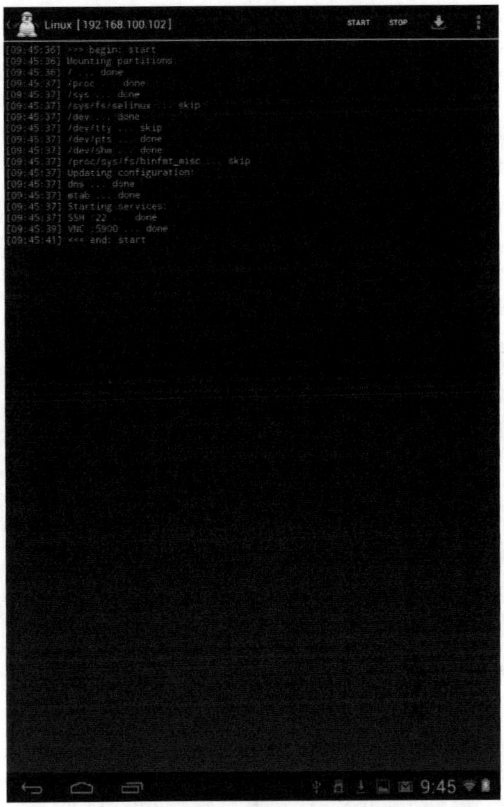

Figure 3. Starting Linux Deploy properties.

D. *Login to chroot Kali Linux*

After installing and starting Linux Kali user must login into the GUI (Graphical User Interface), to begin working in Kali Linux. For this purpose were used androidvnc. Android browser VNC (Virtual Network Computing) needs to set just a few trinkets, first he selects the new connection type, enters a nickname, enters a password changeme, and 5900 as a port. After this is all filled in, just click a button to connect, as you can see in Figure 4. [3].

Figure 4. Android VNC properties.

After logging in to the tablet version of Kali Linux users will work with the same graphical interface as in classical version of the desktop Kali Linux.

V. KALI LINUX ENVIRONMENT

After successful installation of Kali Linux, users will see graphic environment of Kali Linux. As seen in Figure 5, Kali Linux distribution has the same graphical environment both on a tablet and a laptop; moreover tablet version of Kali Linux offers the same features as the live version that runs on a laptop.

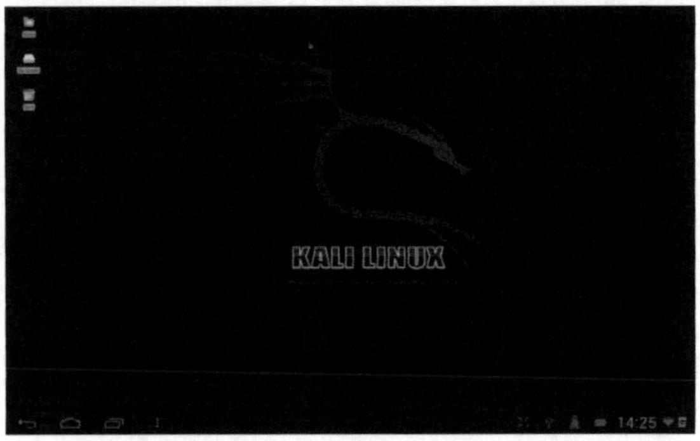

Figure 5. Linux Deploy environment.

For hacker is most important to connect to the organization's wireless network. Depending on the used device, networks can be scanned by device's internal antenna, or by external antenna connected to the tablet as seen in Figure 6.

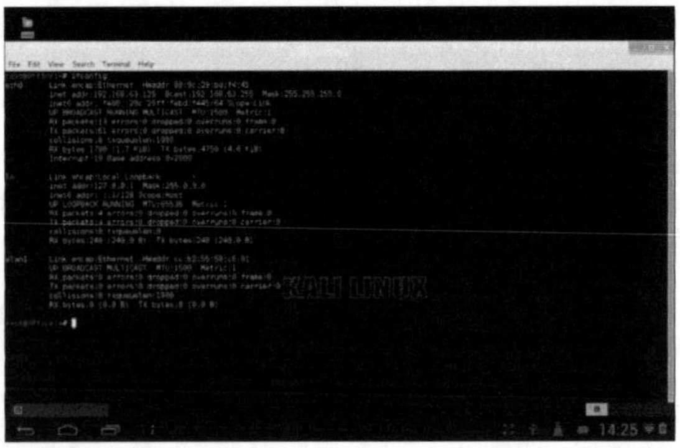

Figure 6. Kali Linux ethernet settings.

In case it is possible to scan wireless network, so for sniffing passwords is ideal tools Aircrack-ng, as shows Figure 7.

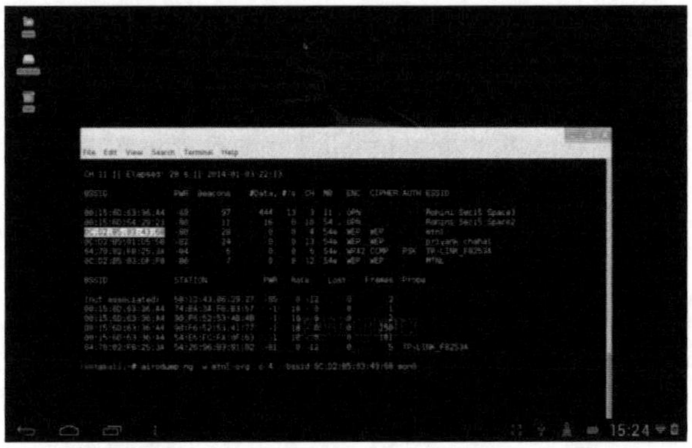

Figure 7. Kali Linux Aircrack-ng.

After connecting to wireless network hacker is already able to do all sorts of network security tests or security attacks. It is important to hacker to monitor network traffic, for this purpose it is suitable Wireshark, Dsniff, TShark, through which hacker can capture passwords, for example passwords from POP3 (Post Office Protocol) email accounts. Furthermore hacker can use Nmap tool, which enables it to obtain information about the computers on the network, what services are available in the network, what types of network firewalls and uses and much more. Hacker can also forge AP (access point) in an organizationn and can use the tablet as a fake AP, on which the other users can connect. Except of attacks on organizations network, attacks can be realized via tablet bluetooth attacks on mobile phones in the organization.

VI. CONCLUSION

In this work, we described security risks of BYOD solution when using a tablet. The main advantage of this BYOD solution is another chance for security attack by an organization, which organizations often ignore. Tablet as a penetration tool provides same value as a notebook, but with less cost and far less conspicuous for the surroundings. It was closely examined that the tablets with the installation of Kali Linux provide the same attacks as a full-fledged notebook. The motivation for the approach that was outlined in work is absolutely inconspicuousness of attacker in an organization which uses BYOD for their employees. Popularity of BYOD is still growing, organizations says, that primary advantage is economic savings compared to buying your own equipment. Organizations are aware of security risks of BYOD and primary separate corporate and user's private data. If an employee uses a BYOD tablet in organization, so in most cases employee works with corporate data in the cloud, on remote desktop, which is connected to the tablet. Proposed solution provides hacker more anonymity, because attacker with the tablet in an organization which uses BYOD tablets becomes even more unobtrusive than attacker who uses a laptop.

ACKNOWLEDGMENT

This work was supported by Internal Grant Agency of

Tomas Bata University under the project No. IGA/FAI/2016/026.

References

[1] B. Hayes and K. Kotwica, “Bring Your Own Device to Work: Trend Report,“ Oxford: Newnes, 2013.

[2] D. Assing S. Calé, “Mobile Access Safety: Beyond BYOD, “ London: John Wiley & Sons, 2013.

[3] M. Alamanni, “Kali Linux Wireless Penetration Testing Essentials, “ Birningham: Packt Publishing Ltd, 2013.

[4] M. Karch, “Android for Work: Productivity for Professionals,“ New York: Apress, 2010.

[5] Gartner, “Gartner Predicts by 2017, Half of Employers will Require Employees to Supply Their Own Device for Work Purposes. “ [Online]. Available from: http://www.gartner.com/newsroom/id/2466615

[6] Gartner. Gartner Says Tablets Are the Sweet Spot of BYOD Programs. “ [Online]. Available from: http://www.gartner.com/newsroom/id/2909217.

Article in a journal:

[7] U. Vignesh and S. Asha, “Modifying Security Policies Towards BYOD” Procedia Computer Science, vol. 50, May 2015, pp. 511 – 516, doi:10.1016/j.procs.2015.04.023

[8] M. Olalere, M. Abdullah, R. Mahmod and A. Abdullah, “A Review of Bring Your Own Device on Security Issues” Volume 4, No. 4, April 2015, pp. 62-73, doi: 10.1177/2158244015580372

Critical Infrastructure Protection – Modeling of Domino and Synergy Effects

Martin Hromada
Department of Security Engineering
Faculty of Applied Informatics, Tomas Bata University in Zlin
Zlin, Czech Republic
email: hromada@fai.utb.cz

Abstract—**Critical infrastructure protection is presently seen as an important aspect of society's maintenance of functional continuity from an economic and social perspective. This fact is seen as a motivation for the development of relevant approaches and methodologies, which have significant impact to the critical infrastructure protection and resilience level. The interactions of various critical infrastructure subsystems have a major relation to the domino and synergy effect assessment and on the overall critical infrastructure protection resilience level. The domino and synergy effect impact to critical infrastructure resilience will therefore be described in the article by a selected mathematical model. The model will present the assessment approach of inter-connections modeling between critical infrastructure subsectors, allowing the evaluation of the potential domino effect in the context of Czech Republic critical infrastructure.**

Keywords- critical infrastructure; model; domino effect; resilience; protection; leontief's economy model;

I. INTRODUCTION

Increasing technological dependence increased the need to identification and designation of elementary State system, whose malfunction will have a major impact on the society functional continuity maintenance in all its social aspects. In the context of the previous argument, the elementary State system is considered critical infrastructure. Perceptions of critical infrastructure are not a modern phenomenon, although it can be stated that there is an increased attention on the protection of critical infrastructure since 2001, which is strongly influenced by the turbulence in the security environment. Influences in the security environment crate a discussion about relevancy of modeling of domino and synergy effects. There are many relevant research works which are addressing topics and issues of modeling, where the most proper were presented by Y., Haimes, and P., Jiang, (2001) [9], R. Santos, (2006) [10], Y., Haimes, (2015) [11], Rehak [12], T., Macaulay (2008) [13]. Relevant outcomes of above mentioned research works include developing the theoretical and, in some cases, also practical framework for modeling and simulation of critical infrastructure in a wider context. The framework was filled in this article by practical application of selected methodologies and models in connection with the Czech Republic critical infrastructure. The second part of the article discusses about theoretical baseline of structures and principles of modeling. The third part therefore theoretically explains the selected model's possibilities and application potential. The practical use and application of selected mathematical model is presented in the fourth section.

II. STRUCTURES AND BASIC PRINCIPLES OF MODELING

In everyday language, the term modelling has different meanings and interpretations. It depends on the nature of the expertise, the degree of knowledge and education, culture, purpose, and many other attributes. Usually, in the model we are developing a kind of reality copy, or create a "prototype", or simulation, how something should be. Always we observe "something" from a certain point of view or interest for a purpose. It is essential to correctly define the elements of interest, abstracted from the whole and develop a system where the basic elements are incorporated together with the key factors influencing the elements. Relations between elements should be clearly visible, quantifiable so we can say that the elements of the system are structured. This structure "links tightness" between the elements is the criterion which defines whether the element is included or not in a given system and it is essential for the identification of impacts, and their level decides the success or failure of the system understanding. Ultimately, this leads to the abstraction of the real nature of the elements in their formal substitution variables and maintaining the relations between them have been observed in the corresponding real elements, i.e. developing a mathematical model. The model is already formal relations between quantities expressed by features, causes and consequences dependent respectively independent variables that come into corresponding quantitative values. This means that the real system is represented in a different form, which is clearer, simpler and more understandable and should give an idea about the future direction of the system. The model is in a way a copy of reality to which it corresponds (it is isomorphic) [1].

The explanation of the model can be expressed in two aspects. In particular, the model provides the knowledge of necessary consequences. What will be, how it will be, what, can be expected if "nothing" affects the system from outside we call this projection. The second aspect is that the model presents an idea of the direction. That is, the model gives an answer for a possible state in the future, provided that "now" is something that happened. We call this prediction. The theoretical basis will then be applied in the context of the mathematical modelling in a broader context.

III. LEONTIEF'S ECONOMY MODEL, STATIC INTERPRETATION

An extensively studied model applied to the problem of Critical Infrastructure is based on Leontief's economic model that addresses the description of the n companies' production steady state X 1, X 2. . . Xn of the selected system. If Xi company for its 1 dollar production needs from Xj company to purchase production worth ai, j, dollar and the matrix A = (i, j) n degree represents the supplier - customer companies relations X1, X2,. . . Xn (Leontief's matrix of technical coefficients, which sum's in each column are less than or equal to 1). Let U = [U1, U2 . . . UN] be the vector of external requirements for final consumption for customers outside the system. The question is, how much every company must make in order to satisfy the requirements with external customers (external, consumption outside the system) and the supplier - customer organizations requirements of the system (internal, consumption system). If we searched the entire output denoted x = [x1, x2...Xn], then it is obviously that x - for the internal consumption (production for the system). It can however also be expressed by the product Ax. Then the equation x - u = Ax describes the equilibrium between production companies. It describes their mutual requirements and the requirements of external customers (produced just as much as they need. They do not overproduction or deficiency). Since the totals of each column of the matrix A are less than or equal to 1, the equation always has the only solution as x = (I - A) -1U where I is the identity matrix. The diagram for the three companies is presented in Figure 1. [2][3][4].

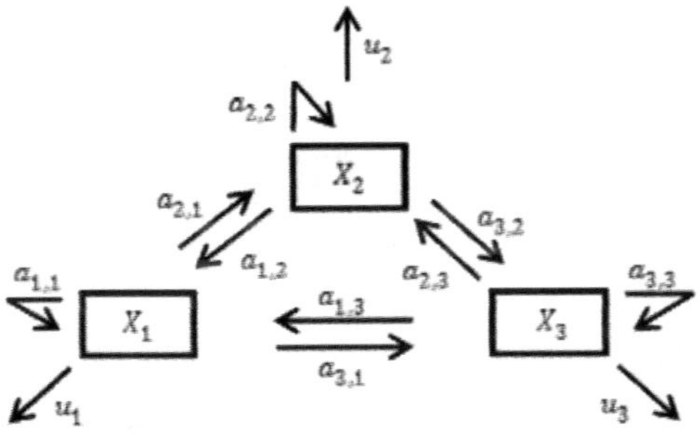

Figure 1. Diagram for three Critical Infrastructure elements [8]

A. *Domino and synergy effect and Critical Infrastructure elements degradation spread*

To describe the internal state, we take into account the relationships between elements of the system, their response to input u and momentary state x. If the system is linear, status change can be described by the equation

$$dx/dt=Ax+Bu \tag{1}$$

or in the discrete form by the equation

$$x(k+1)=Ax(k)+Bu(k). \tag{2}$$

Leontief's economic model can be used in the context of Critical Infrastructure, wherein x is a Critical Infrastructure element degradation importance, u is an input variable to cause a primary Critical Infrastructure element degradation, A is a matrix of pairwise dependence, which features describe the tag container relation between two elements, and reflect the transfer of degradation from first element to second. Let paired relationship between elements Xi and Xj be expressed graphically Xi → Xj with transfer coefficient ai,j. If the value of the element degradation XJ is xj, its transfer to the element Xi is the value of ai, j · xj. This is a first degree transfer Figure 2.

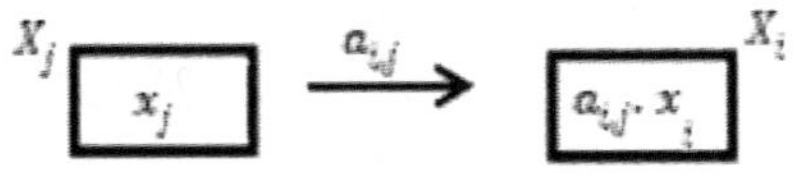

Figure 2. First degree transfer [4]

The value ai,j·xj spreads from Xi element to another and the second degree transfer is created. Next transfer creates a third transfer and so on. The following figure 3 shows the pair dependence of 5 Critical Infrastructure elements, which defines the first degree transfer. Second degree transfers are for example X1 → X2 → X3, X1 → X2 → X4, X2 → X3 → X5, X2 → X4 → X5. Third degree transfers are for example X1 → X2 → X3 → X5, X1 → X2 → X4 → X1, Fig. 3. For example, if the element X1 was degraded, the transfer X1 → X2 → X4 → X1 increase its degradation.

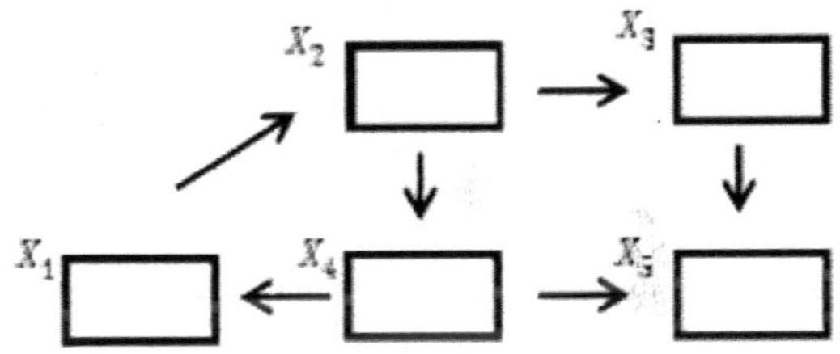

Figure 3. Third degree degradation [8]

The mentioned transfers are only possible passage as degradation can spread. It depends which element has been degraded, which element is "active" at being degraded and which way the degradation will spread. Figure 4 shows the initial degradation of the first element with the value x1 = 0:15 ("active element").

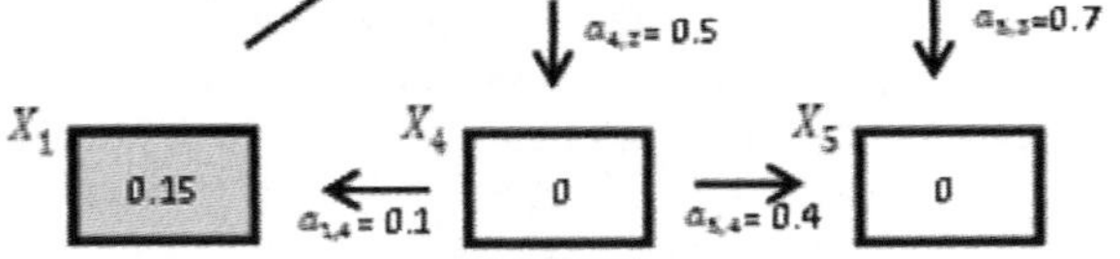

Figure 4. First degree degradation [8]

From Figure 5, the first degree transfer degradation is transferred to the second element in the 0.03 value. The other elements degradation did not transfer to and for the next transfer will be "active" second element.

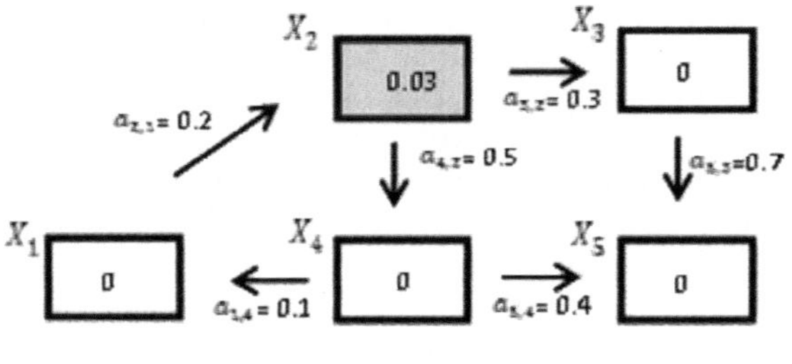

Figure 5. Second element degradation [8]

The second element delegate the second-degree transfer to third element degradation in the value of 0:03 · 0.3 = 0.009 and the fourth element transferred degradation in the value of 0:03 · 0.5 = 0015th "active" elements are X3 and X4 (see Figure 6).

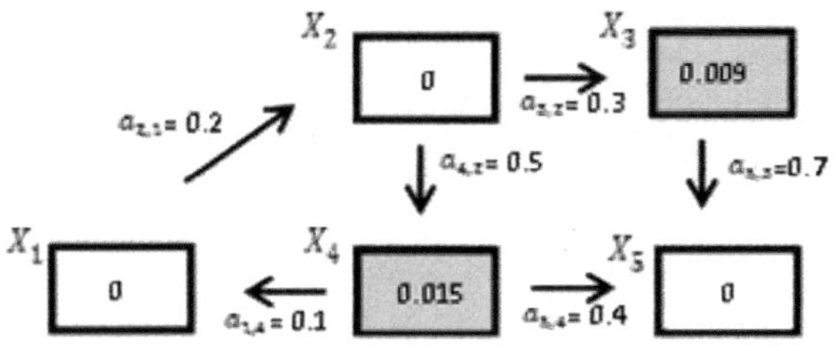

Figure 6. Degradation to third element [8]

From the third and fourth element is third degree degradation transferred to the elements X5 and X1 in the values 0009 · 0015 · 0.7 + 0.4 = 0.0123 to the element X5 valued at 0.015 · 0.1 = 0.0015 to X1. "Active" elements are X1 and X5 but the transfer from X5 does not exist, and the cycle is repeated with the "active" element X1. Figure 7.

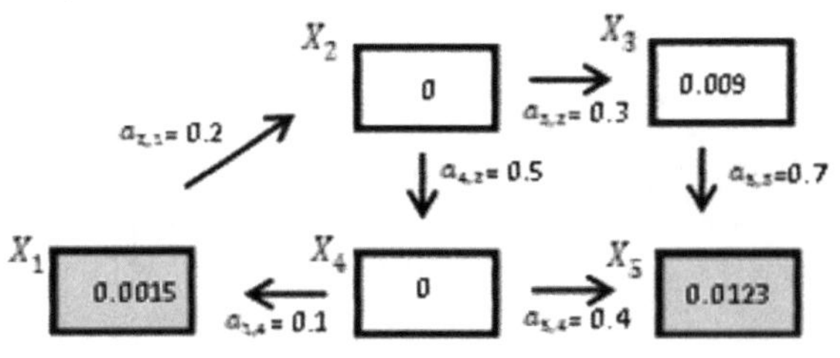

Figure 7. Third degree degradation [8]

In general, the input to the system resulting to primary elements degradation and by their mutual linkage spreading from one element to the other, from the second to the third and so on. The way degradation spreads through the system can be called a domino effect. If x0 = u is the first degree degradation, then by paired dependence will be extended to subsequent degradation, which increased by Δ1 = Ax0, which generates the subsequent amendment of Δ2 = AΔ1 = A (Ax0) = A2x0, etc. After n steps we get an increased value Dn = A (Dn-1) = Anx0. As with Leontief's economic model it forms the analogous question of whether the transfer of degradation would settle to the final value x, which will also vary, e.g. or reaches a steady state. That occurs when the resulting value of the degradation x is decomposed into the sum of the initial input degradation and degradation generated by domino effect. This is represented by equality x = Ax + u. In this case, the totals of each column of the matrix A may be greater than 1 and the equation may not have a solution. When equilibrium occurs, the resulting degradation is x = ((I-A)^τ)U [5], [6], [7].

For the above example, the pair-wise dependency matrix has the form:

$$A = \begin{pmatrix} 0.0 & 0.0 & 0.0 & 0.1 & 0.0 \\ 0.2 & 0.0 & 0.0 & 0.0 & 0.0 \\ 0.0 & 0.3 & 0.0 & 0.0 & 0.0 \\ 0.0 & 0.5 & 0.0 & 0.0 & 0.0 \\ 0.0 & 0.0 & 0.7 & 0.4 & 0.0 \end{pmatrix}$$

and input degradation is given by the vector x0 = u = [0.15,0,0,0,0]. Additions degradation from "zero" (initial) to ninth are equal to:

Δ0 = A0x0 = Ix0 = x0 = [0.15,0,0,0,0],

Δ1 = Ax0 = [0,0.03,0,0,0],

Δ2 = AΔ1 = A(Ax0) = A2x0 = [0,0,0.009,0.015,0],

Δ3 = AΔ2 = A(A(A(x0)) = A3x0 = [0.0015,0,0,0,0.0123],

Δ4 = AΔ3 = A(A(A(A(x0))) = A4x0 = [0,0.0003,0,0,0],

Δ5 = AΔ4 = A5x0 = [0,0.00009,0.00015,0,0],

Δ6 = AΔ5 = A6x0 = [0.000015,0,0,0,0.000123],

Δ7 = AΔ6 = A7x0 = [0,0.000003,0,0,0],

Δ8 = AΔ7 = A8x0 = [0,3x10-6,0,0,0],

Δ9 = AΔ8 = A9x0 = [0,0,9x10-7, 1.5x10-6,0].

The resulting value of elements degradation is given by the n matrix equations solution Ax = ax + u as x = (I - A) - 1U = [0.151, 0.030, 0.009, 0.151, 0.012] T, Figure 8 - Graph 1.

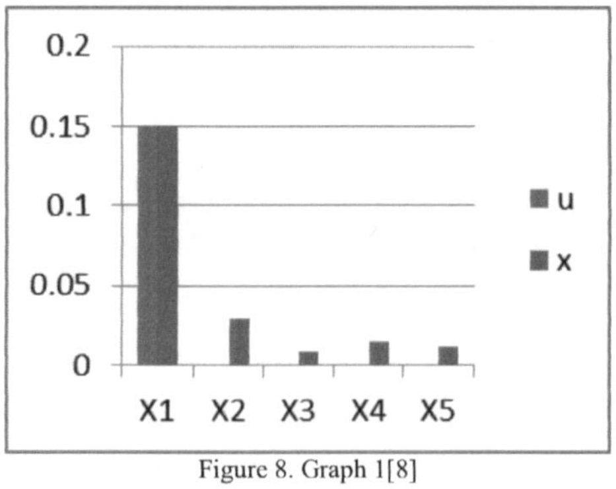

Figure 8. Graph 1[8]

For the input of degradation of the first and second elements in the values ul = 0:15, 0:25 u2 = (vector u = [0.15, 0.25, 0, 0, 0]), the resulting degradation of the components of the vector x = (I - A) = -1U are [0.164, 0.283, 0.085, 0.141, 0.116] Figure 9 - Graph 2.

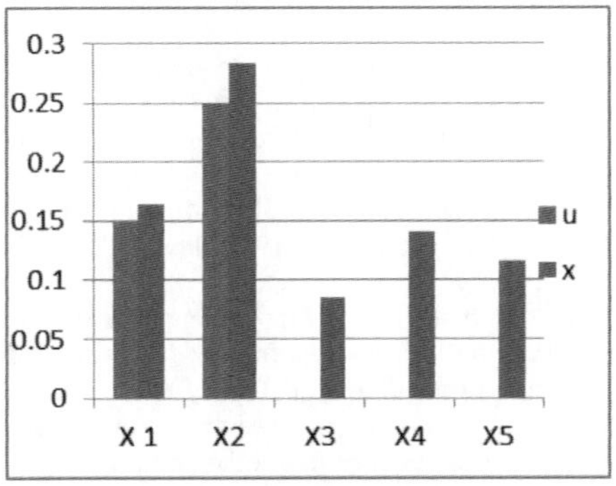

Figure 9. Graph 2 [8]

If all the elements are equally degraded, for example to 0.15 (vector u = [0.15, 0.15, 0.15, 0.15, 0.15] T) and the resulting degradation is given by the vector x = (I - A) -1U = [0.174, 0.185, 0.205, 0.242, 0.391] T. The percentage of degradation increased in steps of 16%, 23%, 36%, 61% and 160%. From these values it is clear that the most vulnerable elements are X3, X4, X5. X5 is the element which should to be protected as much as possible, Figure 10 [8].

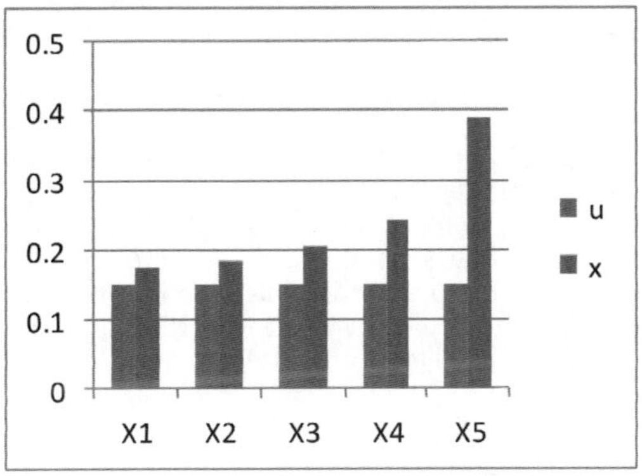

Figure 10. Graph 3 [8]

The theoretical framework will then be applied to the critical infrastructure protection in the Czech Republic. Within the scope of application model will be used in practical knowledge of individual sub-systems (the areas) of the Czech Republic critical infrastructure linkages assessment.

IV. OUTPUTS OF THE CZECH REPUBLIC CRITICAL INFRASTRUCTURE PRACTICAL MODELLING

The critical infrastructure in the Czech Republic is divided into the 27 areas (sectors) that have significant input into societal functions. Within the modelling they were established reciprocal links in terms of the coefficient of activity and passivity, which allows to determine the linkage value Activity coefficient expresses the potential of a critical infrastructure area affecting the other areas (electricity for district heating) and the passivity coefficient ex-pressed the impact of other areas to selected critical infrastructure area (electricity) - (district heating - electricity). The quantitative expression of these coefficients is implemented through Qualitative Risk Correlation Analysis [8]. Determination of linkages has been implemented through the 27x27 matrix. After determining the values of linkages, Leontief's model was applied up to the third degree of degradation, which expresses dominoes and then synergistic effects in three time intervals 24, 48, 72h for 25% of an electricity power failure (see Figure 11) .

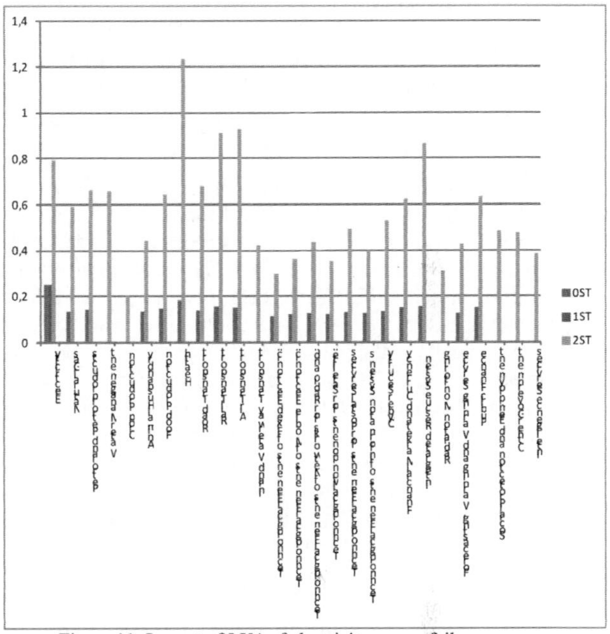

Figure 11. Impact of 25% of electricity power failure

For a better illustration, a 3D graph was generated, which expresses the impact of electricity power failure to the other areas of the Czech Republic critical infrastructure. From the graph you can read the most vulnerable areas of critical infrastructure and the overall spread of dominoes and synergistic effects. This approach allowed us to identify secondary and tertiary linkages below the area of the electricity power failure in the context of the time frame. These facts will then be implemented in the process of crisis preparedness of critical infrastructure operators. Another benefit will be the use of the conclusions in the project Security Research Project - VI20152019049 - RESILIENCE 2015 Dynamic Resilience Evaluation of Interrelated Critical Infrastructure Subsystems.

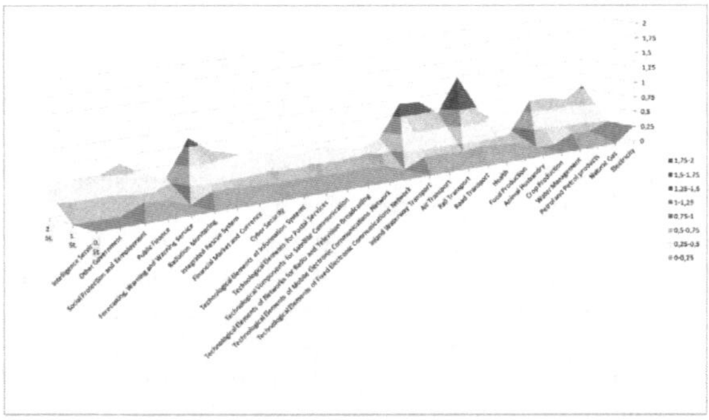

Figure 12. Impact of electricity power failure on other critical infrastructure subsystems

Figure 12 shows the impact o 25% electricity power failure on other critical infrastructure subsystems.

V. CONCLUSION

The facts and knowledge presented in this paper pointed to the possibilities of mathematical modelling in the context of the needs of critical infrastructure protection and resilience. The first section of the article presented a definition of critical infrastructure as a fundamental system affecting the society functional continuity.. Another part of the text dealt with the general approach to the model development that has been further developed within the application of Leontief's economic model to the issues of determining the interactions and evaluation of domino and synergy effect within the system elements. In the end of this publication, we present partial results from the application of the model for Czech Republic critical infrastructure system and security research project RESILIENCE 2015 issues.

ACKNOWLEDGMENT

This work was supported by the research project VI20152019049 "RESILIENCE 2015: Dynamic Resilience Evaluation of Interrelated Critical Infrastructure Subsystems", supported by the Ministry of the Interior of the Czech Republic in the years 2015-2019.

REFERENCES

[1] P., Brunovský, Mathematical theory of optimal managemet, ALFA, Bratislava, 1980.

[2] V.,Havlena, J., Štecha, Dynamical systems theory, ČVUT, 2005, Praha

[3] W. W., Leontief, Input-Output Economics, Second Edition, 1986, Oxford university press, New York.

[4] M., Matejdes, Applied mathematics, 2005, Matcentrum Zvolen.

[5] R. E., Miller, and P. D., Blair, Input-Output Analysis: Fundations and Extensions, 1985, Prence-Hall, Englewood Cliffs, NJ.

[6] G., Oliva, S., Panzieri, R., Setola, Agent-based input–output interdependency model, International Journal of Critical Infrastructure Protection, 3(2010), 79-82.

[7] J. R., Santos, Inoperability input-output modeling of disruptions to interdependent economic systems, Systems Engineering 9 (1) (2006) 20-34.

[8] M., Hromada et all, Critical infrastructure protection in Czech republic energy sector, 1. vydání, Ostrava: Sdružení požárního a bezpečnostního inženýrství, 2014. 272 s. ISBN 978-80-7385-144-6

[9] Y., Haimes, and P., Jiang, (2001). Leontief-based model of risk in complex interconnected infrastructures. Journal of Infrastructure systems, 7(1), 1-12.

[10] J. R. Santos, (2006). Inoperability input-output modeling of disruptions to interdependent economic systems. Systems Engineering, 9(1), 20-34.

[11] Y., Haimes, (2015). Risk modeling, assessment, and management. Sage, A. P. (Ed.). John Wiley & Sons. (CHAPTER 18)

[12] D., Rehak P., Senovsky Preference Risk Assessment of Electric Power Critical Infrastructure. Chemical Engineering Transactions, 2014, Vol. 36, pp. 469-474. ISSN 1974-9791. DOI: 10.3303/CET1436079

[13] Chemical Engineering Transactions, 2014, Vol. 36, pp. 469-474. ISSN 1974-9791. DOI:

[14] 10.3303/CET1436079 T., Macaulay, Critical infrastructure: understanding its component parts, vulnerabilities, operating risks, and interdependencies. CRC Press.

Towards Extensible Signature Policies in Brazil: A Case Study

Maurício de Oliveira, Martín Vigil, Marcelo Carlomagno Carlos, and Ricardo Custódio
Federal University of Santa Catarina
Florianópolis 88040-900, Brazil
Email: mauricio.so@posgrad.ufsc.br, martin.vigil@ufsc.br, me@marcelocarlos.com, custodio@inf.ufsc.br

***Abstract*—Signature policies are a set of rules to create and verify signatures. For example, they specify the signature algorithm that a signer should employ and the evidence a verifier must use to verify a signature. Brazil has adopted signature policies to regulate legally binding signatures. Our contribution is to analyze and improve the use of signature policies in Brazil. Our analysis shows that the current policies present a serious issue in situations where the requirements of a signature change. A practical example is when the validity of a signature needs to be extended, e.g., to guarantee non-repudiation time-stamps become required. To address this issue, we propose the *extensible signature policies* which, in addition to the definition of how a signature is created and verified, specifies which further policies can be applied to the signature. We demonstrate the efficacy of our solution by performing new signature policies and developing a prototype. Furthermore, we argue that our *extensible signature policies* solution does not require significant changes on existing signature methods and infrastructure.**

Keywords–Signature Policy; Digital Signature; Public Key Infrastructure; Time-Stamp.

I. Introduction

Digital tools and solutions are becoming a more constant part of our routines. For instance, people are increasingly engaging in e-commerce, whose size has doubled from 2011 to 2014 in the world [1]. However, despite the evolution of security mechanisms, frauds are still increasing. For instance, retailers and buyers have to deal with the risk of fraudulent e-commerce transactions, which has increased by 30% in 2015 in the United States [2].

To address these issues, digital signatures [3] pose an interesting solution. The reason is that signatures can provide integrity, authenticity, and non-repudiation. Integrity means one can check whether a piece of data has been unexpectedly altered. Authenticity allows identifying who originated a signature on the data. Non-repudiation prevents the originator of this signature from denying that he or she is the originator. Therefore, digital signatures are useful to prevent criminals from manipulating data or transactions without being noticed. Moreover, signatures are legally accepted to establish commitments in several countries, e.g., Brazil [4].

When using signatures, the involved parties need to agree beforehand how signatures are created and verified. This is needed because there are several options for creating and verifying signatures. For example, a party may prefer a specific signature algorithm to others, e.g., the *Elliptic Curve Digital Signature Algorithm*[5] rather than RSA[5]. Moreover, when signing a document, further data can be signed together with the document. For instance, the certificate containing the signer's public key. This certificate and the corresponding revocation status can be also attached to the signature to help verifiers to check the signature. Still, without knowing the parameters used for generating the signature, verifiers may not be able to verify it.

A solution for the issue above is the adoption of signature policies. They have been proposed by the European Telecommunications Standards Institute [6][7] and are a set of rules for creating and verifying signatures. Brazil has adopted signature policies to regulate the use of legally binding signatures. The adopted policies can be used to generate the *basic*, *dated*, *complete*, and *archival* signatures [8]. The basic signatures are for authenticating data and no additional information is attached to the signatures. The dated signatures have a time reference provided by a time-stamp. This time-stamp is attached to the signatures. The complete signatures have the signer's complete certificate chain, the corresponding revocation statuses, and a time-stamp. The archival signatures are used for archiving and have the signer's chain, the corresponding revocation statuses, and one or more time-stamps. After signing a document, the used policy cannot be changed because signing parties sign the document and the used policy together.

In this paper, we analyze the use of signature policies in Brazil and propose improvements. Our analysis identified a serious issue when using signature policies. Consider that one party created a basic signature to indicate his or her commitment to a transaction with a second party. Some time later, the second party opens a dispute in court providing the signature as a proof of the commitment. The problem is that the signature can become invalid before the dispute starts. This can happen because the validity of a signature ends when the signer's certificate expires or is revoked, e.g., due to private key compromise. In this case, the non-repudiation property of the signature is lost because one cannot prove that the signature was created *while* the signer's certificate was valid. A straightforward solution would be attaching a time-stamp to prove that the signature existed *before* the signer's certificate became invalid. However, the basic signature policy does not allow the use of time-stamps, preventing the addition of new times-stamps. Similar problem also affects dated and complete signatures. Although they allow using a time-stamp to extend the validity of a signature, the time-stamp itself has limited validity since it also relies on a signature. Note that one could apply a second time-stamp on the first time-stamp to extend the validity of the first time-stamp, but this is only allowed by the archival signature policy.

Solutions for this issue would be to identify the required validity time of signatures before creating them or using the signatures with the longest validity, i.e., archival signatures. However, these are not good solutions. Parties may not always be able to identify the required validity time of their signatures in advance. If an archival signature is used, the policy requires certificates, revocation statuses, and time-stamps to be added even when they are not necessary, e.g., at the beginning of the signature validity. These initially unnecessary data require approximately 6 times as much space as a basic signature. Moreover, this overhead is magnified in repositories containing several signatures, because the Brazilian signature policies require that each signature contains its own copy of certificates, revocation statuses, and time-stamps.

To solve this issue properly, we propose the *extensible signature policies*. Similarly to the existing state-of-the-art policies, extensible policies are a set of rules for creating and verifying signatures. However, extensible policies allow for applying additional and more evolved policies to a signature. For example, a *basic extensible signature policy* could permit users to add a time-stamp to the signature by applying a *dated* or *archival signature policy* if necessary. Hence, parties need not know in advance the expected validity of their signatures. Also, parties avoid the overhead of using a time-stamp when it is not necessary.

Our proposal is compatible with the signature policy standard, since we use the extensions feature of this standard. We demonstrate the efficacy of our solution by implementing signature policies and developing a prototype. This prototype is based on a signature software provided by the Brazilian Public Key Infrastructure. Moreover, we demonstrate that Brazil could employ our solution without significant impact on signature users and existing infrastructure.

The remainder of this work is organized as follows. We introduce signatures, time-stamps, and policies in Section II. In Section III, we analyze the case of signature policies in Brazil. Section IV presents our solution, the extensible signature policies. Section V describes how we implemented the extensible policies and developed a prototype. In Section VI, we evaluate our solution. Finally, we draw our conclusions and plan future work in Section VII.

II. DIGITAL SIGNATURES, TIME-STAMPS, & SIGNATURE POLICIES

This section presents the background necessary for this work. We first introduce the parties involved when digital signatures, time-stamps, and signature policies are used. Then, we explain signatures, time-stamps, and policies.

The parties that can be involved in the use of digital signatures, time-stamps, and signature policies are called *signers*, *verifiers*, *signature policy issuers*, and *judges*. Assuming a scenario where a *signer* and a *verifier* are participating in a transaction involving digital signatures, e.g., a seller signing a receipt stating that the payment from a buyer has been received and the purchase will be delivered, the steps to create the digital signature are: i) the two parties agree on a signature policy, issued by a signature policy issuer, establishing how this signature should be created and verified; ii) the signer creates a signature according to the chosen policy; and iii) if the signature may be needed after its validity ends, the signer or verifier can apply time-stamps to it.

Considering the same scenario mentioned before, when verifier needs to check the digital signature, the verification is performed using the policy initially defined. If there are time-stamps, they are also checked. The verifier performs the verification to be convinced that the signature is a proof of the signer's commitment. When there is a dispute between a signer and a verifier, a judge may be necessary. For example, when the signer wants to repudiate his or her commitment by claiming that he or she has not created that particular signature. In this case, the judge checks whether the signature is indeed a valid signature from the repudiating party in order to decide in favor of the signer or verifier. To do this, the judge also uses the policy and time-stamps.

Digital signatures guarantee integrity, authenticity, and non-repudiation of data [9]. Integrity allows to check whether the signed data has been modified. Authenticity allows identifying who created the signature on the data. Non-repudiation prevents the originator of the signature from claiming that he or she has not generated the signature. Because of these guarantees, signatures are useful to prevent frauds and to enforce commitments. Frauds are prevented because signatures allow users to notice when data has been modified (integrity) or forged (authenticity). Commitments can be enforced because signatures prevent a user from denying that he or she has acknowledged some data by signing it (authenticity and non-repudiation).

We now explain how digital signatures work. They can be generated using asymmetric cryptography [3], which provides three algorithms. First, a signer uses the *key generation algorithm* to generate his or her key pair (k_s, k_p), where k_s is the secret signing key and k_p is the public verification key. Next, given a piece of data d, the signer uses the signing key k_s and the *signature generation algorithm* to create a signature σ on d. Finally, given the public key k_p, the signature σ, and the signed data d, a verifier uses the *signature verification algorithm* to check whether σ is a valid signature.

The public key k_p is usually distributed in the form of a public key certificate [9]. This certificate is issued by a certificate authority (CA), which authenticates the signer's identity. Moreover, a certificate is only valid for a limited period of time. During this period, the CA can revoke the certificate if needed, e.g., when the corresponding private key is compromised. After a certificate expires or is revoked, a digital signature no longer provides the non-repudiation property. This is because the verifier cannot check whether the signature was generated by the signer *before* the certificate expired or was revoked, or by a forger *after* the expiration or revocation.

Time-stamps are a well-known solution for the above issue. They are issued by trusted time-stamp authorities (TSAs) as follows. Assume a piece of data d is to be time-stamped. A TSA time-stamps d by creating signature σ on d together with the current date and time τ, i.e., τ is the moment when σ is created. The signature σ is stored together with the date and time τ in a time-stamp t.

A party can use a time-stamp to guarantee the non-repudiation of a signature even after the public certificate necessary to verify this signature is no longer valid. More precisely, *before* this certificate expires or is revoked, the party requests a time-stamp on that particular signature together with the certificate and revocation status showing that the certificate is still valid. Later, if the certificate expires or is revoked, the time-stamp can be used to demonstrate that the signature *already existed* when the certificate was valid and, therefore, that the signature was created at a time when only the legitimate signer could have produced it [10]. Note that this time-stamp is not intended to demonstrate the exactly time when the signature was created, but rather to show that the signature was created at some point in time *before* the certificate containing the verification public key expired or was revoked.

However, since time-stamps also rely on signatures, they have a limited validity period. Consequently, further time-stamps are needed, yielding the time-stamp sequence found in Figure 1. In this sequence, the first time-stamp extends the validity of the document signature. The subsequent time-stamp extends the validity of the previous time-stamp signature and so on. The last time-stamp should have a valid signature at the moment the verifier checks the document signature [11].

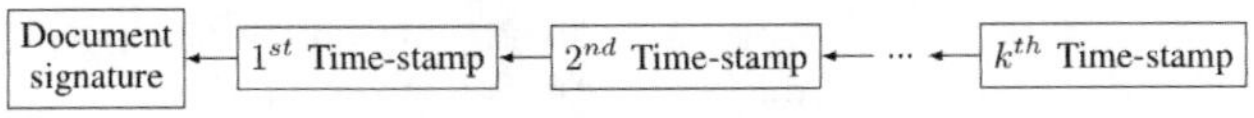

Figure 1. A document signature and a sequence of time-stamps.

Digital signatures are often distributed in a single file which includes their corresponding time-stamps. More precisely, this file contains the digital signature and the so-called *signed* and *unsigned attributes*. Signed attributes are additional data that the signer signs along with the document. For example, the certificate that verifiers must use to verify the digital signature. By contrast, unsigned attributes are not signed together with the document. Therefore, any party can append to or remove them from the digital signature without corrupting it. Examples of unsigned attributes are time-stamps and evidence showing that the certificate needed to verify the signature was not revoked (e.g., certificate revocation lists). The definition of the file containing a digital signature and the corresponding signed and unsigned attributes is provided by the so-called *Advanced Electronic Signatures* [12][13]. We will refer to this file simply as a *signature*.

Because signatures can be created using distinct signature algorithms and containing several attributes, signers and verifiers should agree beforehand how these signatures must be. To this end, signature policies have been proposed and standardized [6][7]. They are a set of rules for creating and verifying signatures. A signature policy has a unique identifier provided by the signature policy issuer. When signing a document d using a policy identified by i, signers create a digital signature σ on d together with i. Moreover, they provide σ together with i in the form of a signature (i is a signed attribute). Thus, verifiers and judges can identify the used policy and verify the signature accordingly.

III. Signature Policies in Brazil

This section describes how signature policies have been implemented by the Brazilian Public Key Infrastructure (PKI). We start by detailing the implemented signature policies. Next, we explain how they are distributed. Then, we analyze their limitations and implications.

In Brazil, people can use signatures to establish a legally binding commitment only if these signatures fulfill specific signature policies. More precisely, the Brazilian PKI created four signature policies. The policies are defined as follows.

1) The *basic signature policy* can be used for short-term authentications, e.g., to authenticate wire transfers.
2) The *dated signature policy* can be used when the creation time of a signature is needed, e.g., to authenticate auction bids. It contains a time-stamp computed on the digital signature as an unsigned attribute.
3) The *complete signature* can be used when the signer's certificate chain and revocation statuses may not be available for verifiers. It also provides a time-stamp on the digital signature together with the chain and revocation statuses. This time-stamp prevents that the signature becomes invalid if any certificate in the chain is revoked or expires. This policy can be used, for example, to authenticate contracts.
4) A *archival signature* is used for long-term archiving, e.g., to guarantee the integrity of electronic land records. It contains the signer's certificate chain and revocation statuses, and one or more archival time-stamps. An archival time-stamp is applied on the whole content of a signature, including previous archival time-stamps.

TABLE I. Signature policies created by the Brazilian PKI.

Features	Signature Policies			
	Basic	Dated	Complete	Archival
Policy identifier	✓	✓	✓	✓
Time-stamp on the digital signature	x	✓	x	x
Complete certificate chain & revocation statuses	x	x	✓	✓
Time-stamp on the dig. signature, chain & rev. statuses	x	x	✓	x
Archiving time-stamp	x	x	x	✓
Maximal validity (years)	6	6	6	x

Signatures must explicitly identify the fulfilling policy as a signed attributed. Moreover, signatures are valid for up to six years, which is the maximum validity of certificates in the Brazilian PKI. By contrast, this does not apply to archival signatures because their validities can be extended indefinitely by using further time-stamps. Table I summarizes the four presented policies.

The Brazilian PKI distributes these policies as follows. First, the policies are described in the form of machine-readable files using (i.e., using the ASN.1[14] and XML languages) following the signature policy standard [6][7]. Next, the hash of each of these files is included together with the corresponding policy identifier in a list. This list is also in the ASN.1 and XML forms and is signed by an authority. Finally, the policies and the signed list are published in a public repository. Signature softwares can verify the authenticity of the list and use signature policies with minimal user interaction.

We now analyze the limitations and implications of the presented approach. The limitations are two fold. First, the policies themselves prevent the signature verification from using any data that is not defined in the policies. For example, the basic signature policy allows using no time-stamps. Second, the policy used to create a signature cannot be later changed. This is because the digital signature fixes the identifier of the used signature policy. Changing the signature policy identifier corrupts the digital signature. It is worth to mention that these limitations apply not only to the Brazilian signature policies but also to any implementation using signature policies.

TABLE II. THE SIZES OF BASIC, DATED, COMPLETE, AND ARCHIVAL SIGNATURES IN KILOBYTES.

	Signature type			
	Basic	Dated	Complete	Archival
Size (kB)	2.96	5.76	18.40	18.40

The implication of using the presented approach is that the validity of signatures other than archival signatures cannot be extended. To illustrate this in practice, assume the following scenario. A seller used the *dated signature policy* to sign a receipt saying that he or she has sold some goods to a buyer. However, the goods have not been delivered and the buyer wants to open a dispute at a court. If the dated signature is about to become invalid because, for example, the time-stamp issuer's certificate will expire soon, then the buyer may have no time to submit the signature as valid evidence to the court. In this case, adding further time-stamps to extend the signature validity does not help the buyer, since the used signature policy establishes that only a single time-stamp is verified. Moreover, re-signing the receipt is of no use because the seller may not want to re-sign it or may have even passed away.

Therefore, the parties using signatures to establish commitments should know in advance the required validity for signatures or select the signature policy with the longest validity time, namely the archival signature policy. Both approaches have shortcomings. Knowing the required validity time for signatures before creating them may not be always possible. Selecting the archival signature policy to guarantee the longest signature validity is inefficient. More precisely, an archival signature must contain the signer's chain, the corresponding revocation statuses, and an archival time-stamp even if they are not necessary.

To illustrate this overhead, Table II compares the sizes of basic, dated, complete, and archival signatures soon after they are created. In the case of the archival signature, it contains only one archival time-stamp. To generate the signatures we used real certificates and time-stamps from the Brazilian PKI.

As it can be seen from the table, the overhead of using an archival signature policy to ensure the longest possible signature validity time is significant. More precisely, the archival signature is approximately 6 and 3 times as big as the basic signature and the dated signatures, respectively. Compared to the complete signature, there is no overhead.

Therefore, it would be desirable that parties first create small signatures with simple policies, e.g., the basic or dated signatures, and then add time-stamps or further data (e.g, certificate chains and revocation statuses) by using more evolved policies only when necessary. The next section shows how this can be done.

IV. EXTENSIBLE SIGNATURE POLICIES

As we have seen, signature policies have shortcomings. For instance, if a policy allows applying no time-stamps to a signature, then the validity of this signature cannot be extended beyond the lifetime of the signer's certificate. To address these shortcomings, we propose the *extended signature policies*. We first introduce our approach and then detail how parties can use it.

An extended signature policy is a policy that not only defines how a signature is created and verified, but also explicitly specifies which additional policies can be applied to this signature. These policies can be applied at any moment during the signature validity. More precisely, the additional policies allow including further information as unsigned attributes in the original signature when necessary. In this way, time-stamps in the form of unsigned attributes can be applied only when the signer's certificate is about to become invalid. Note that, when parties select an extensible policy, they agree not only on the selected policy, but also on the additional policies that the selected policy identifies.

We now detail how such policies are used. Assume that two parties participating in a transaction want to create a digital signature to establish one party's commitment. To do that, they select an extensible signature policy. Then, one party performs the signature, e.g., by signing a digital document. The signing process is the same as when using the state-of-the-art signature policies. The signer selects an extensible policy and creates a signature following the rules of the selected policy. He or she signs the document together with the identifier of the selected policy and provides this identifier as a signed attribute within the signature. Note that the only difference now is that the signer uses an extensible instead of a state-of-the-art signature policy.

When an additional operation needs to be performed over an existing signature that supports extensible policies, e.g., extending the validity of the signature, the following steps are required:

1) Select an additional policy to be applied to the signature. For example, a policy that provides certificate chains, revocation statuses, and time-stamps.
2) Check that the initial policy allows the selected policy to be applied.
3) Apply the selected policy to the signature by including the necessary information, e.g., time-stamps, as unsigned attributes in the signature.
4) Add the identifier of the selected policy as an unsigned attribute to the signature.
5) Optionally, apply a time-stamp on the signature to demonstrate when the additional policy was applied. Add this time-stamp also as an unsigned attribute to the signature.

The signature verification is also different in our approach. Now it is necessary to check not only whether the signature is valid, but also whether the additional policies applied are allowed. Assume that a signature was created using the policies $p_1, p_2, \ldots, p_k$, where p_1 is the initial policy and $p_2, \ldots, p_k$ are the additional policies. Additionally, assume that an authentic copy of these policies is provided. Then, the following steps should be executed:

1) For $j = 2, \ldots, k$, check that policy p_{j-1} allows policy p_j to be used. This is done by verifying that p_{j-1} explicitly specifies the identifier of p_j.
2) For $j = 1, \ldots, k$ verify the signature using the verification rules specified by policy p_j. For example, check that the time-stamp sequence is valid. For performance reasons, we suggest verifying the digital signature with the signature verification algorithm

(see Section II) only at the first iteration. The reason is that this algorithm is usually time-consuming.

V. Implementation

In this section, we demonstrate our solution by implementing the extensible signature policies and a prototype needed to create and verify signatures.

A. *Extensible Signature Policies*

We defined three new signature policies, namely, the *basic extensible signature policy*, *dated extensible signature policy*, and *complete extensible signature policy*. They are similar to the existing *basic*, *dated*, and *complete* signature policies found in the Brazilian PKI. The difference is that the new policies specify which additional policies can be applied to a signature. More specifically, the *basic extensible signature policy* allows to add a time-stamp to the signature by applying the *dated extensible signature policy* or the *archival signature policy*. The *dated extensible signature policy* permits to add the signer's certification path, revocation statuses, and a time-stamp to a signature by applying the *complete extensible* or *archival signature policies*. The *complete extensible signature policy* allows to add an archival time-stamp to the signature by using the *archival signature policy*. An oriented graph is provided in Figure 2 to illustrate the signature policies found in the Brazilian Public Key Infrastructure and our extensible signature policies. An edge from policies p to p' indicates that p' can be applied to signatures generated under p. Note that we have not exhausted the possible relations between policies in the graph.

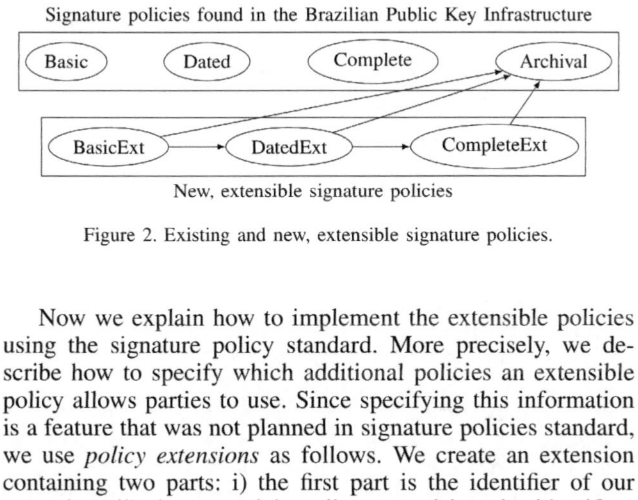

Figure 2. Existing and new, extensible signature policies.

Now we explain how to implement the extensible policies using the signature policy standard. More precisely, we describe how to specify which additional policies an extensible policy allows parties to use. Since specifying this information is a feature that was not planned in signature policies standard, we use *policy extensions* as follows. We create an extension containing two parts: i) the first part is the identifier of our extension; ii) the second is a list comprising the identifiers of the additional policies. In this list, we also include a hash computed from each additional policies in the ASN.1 or XML format. For example, in the case of the signature policy *basic extensible* (see *BasicExt* in Figure 2), this list includes the *archival signature policy*. Since this extension needs to be checked during the signature verification, we place it in the section *Verification Rules* of the signature policy standard. We present our extension in ASN.1 and XML in Figures 3 and 4, respectively, since the standard uses ASN.1 and XML.

```
AddSignPolicies ::= SEQUENCE OF
 AddSignPolicy
AddSignPolicy ::= SEQUENCE {
signPolicyIdentifier
        OBJECT IDENTIFIER,
signPolicyHash   SignPolicyHash }
```

Figure 3. The new policy extension written in ASN.1.

```
<xsd:complexType
        name="AddSignPoliciesType">
 <xsd:sequence maxOccurs="unbounded">
  <xsd:element name="AddSignPolicy"
   type="AddSignPolicyType"/>
 </xsd:sequence>
</xsd:complexType>
<xsd:complexType name="AddSignPolicyType">
 <xsd:sequence>
  <xsd:element name="SignPolicyIdentifier"
   type="XAdES:ObjectIdentifierType"/>
  <xsd:element name="SignPolicyDigest"
   type="ds:DigestValueType"/>
 </xsd:sequence>
</xsd:complexType>
```

Figure 4. The new policy extension described in XML.

B. *A Prototype for Creating and Verifying Signatures*

We developed a prototype by extending the software provided by the Brazilian PKI for creating and verifying signatures. The original software is open-source and can be requested to the National Institute of Information Technology, the agency running the Brazilian PKI.

Our modifications to the original software were minimal. The signing process remains unchanged. The only difference now is that users can also select the new policies we introduced in Section V-A. For example, in Figure 5, we use our prototype to select the file *test_file.txt* to be signed and the XML file *basic_policy_v2.2_ext.xml* providing the *basic extensible policy*. From the XML file, the prototype extracts and shows the description of the selected policy. This description is presented in Portuguese and shows the scenarios where the signer can make use of this policy. When we click on the button *Next*, the prototype asks for the private key and signs the selected file *test_file.txt*. This is not illustrated due to space restrictions.

Most of the changes on the verification process remain hidden from the users perspective in our prototype. As in the original software, they select the signature they want to verify, and the software automatically checks the signature and provides the verification status. For example, in Figure 6, we use our prototype to select the signature found in the file *basic_signature_ext.xml*. The prototype verifies and shows that the selected signature is valid. Moreover, if additional policies had been used, then the prototype would also check whether their use is allowed. If the signature is valid and the used policies are allowed, then the user can apply an additional policy to this signature. To this end, our prototype first reads the most recent policy applied to the signature, obtains the list of allowed policies (see Section V-A), and shows this list to the user. Next, the user selects an additional policy

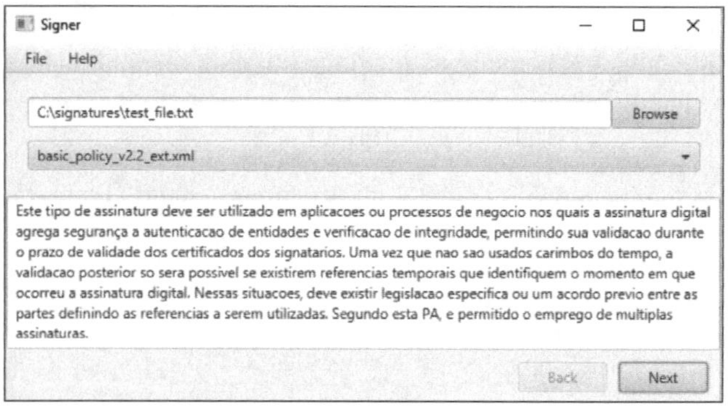

Figure 5. The prototype being used to sign a file.

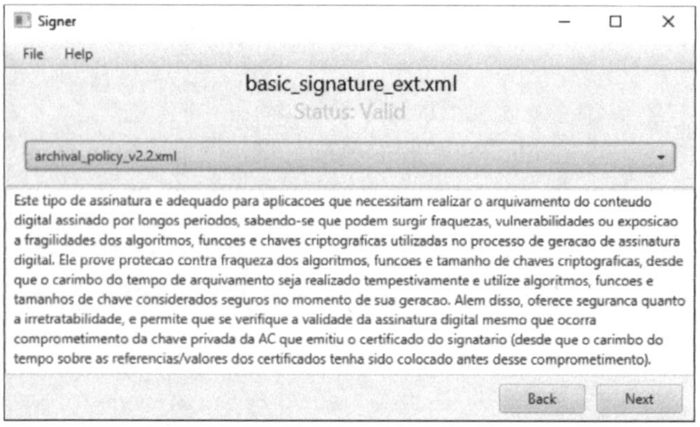

Figure 6. The prototype being used to verify and extend the validity of a signature.

from the list and clicks on the button *Next*. For example, in Figure 6 we apply the allowed policy *archival signature policy* found in the file *archival_policy_v2.2_ext.xml* to the *basic extensible signature* found in *basic_signature_ext.xml*. Finally, the prototype proceeds according to the selected policy.

VI. Evaluation

We demonstrated that the new, extensible policies are practical because the overall effort to replace the state-of-the-art policies by extensible policies is not significant for the involved parties. Our implementation used the existing infrastructure in Brazil as a study case to validate our proposal's applicability and compatibility with existing methods.

For the parties using signatures to perform commitments, deciding which signature policy to select becomes more complex in our proposal. More precisely, they should consider not only how signatures should be created and verified, but also whether they want to allow the validity of these signatures to be extended. Note that making our approach simpler by ruling out all policies that cannot be extended is not desirable. This is because in some scenarios participants may indeed want to select policies that prevent extending the validity of signatures. For example, electronic voting schemes might require that signatures used for short-term authentication expire in order to protect voters' privacy.

For a signing party, the signature process is the same when using extensible or state-of-the-art policies. Verifying parties should notice no differences between extensible and state-of-the-art policies when checking signatures with time-stamps. This is because extensible policies require more verifications than state-of-the-art policies, but these verifications consume negligible running time. More precisely, the additional verifications are checking whether an additional policy applied to the signature is allowed by the previously used policy, e.g., the initial policy employed to generate the signature. This operation consists of checking whether the identifier of the additional policy is specified by the previously used policy (see Section V-A). This simple operation should be negligible if compared to the signature verification algorithm, which consumes significant running time to verify the digital signatures on documents or time-stamps [11].

The impact on the existing infrastructure is not significant. We created the new policies by using the policy extensions feature provided by the signature policy standard (Section IV). The impact of this is that only the verification procedure of signature softwares needs to be adapted to support extensible policies. This adaption is not significant, as we showed by using our prototype in Section V. The signing procedure of these softwares remains compatible with extensible policies. Likewise, the software that policy issuers use to issue policies needs to be adapted to use our policy extension. By contrast, the procedures for signing and publishing the policies remain unchanged.

VII. Conclusion and Future Work

Digital signatures are useful to prevent frauds and create commitments between parties involved in a transaction. Since signatures can be used in several ways, e.g., by employing distinct signature algorithms, the parties involved need to agree beforehand how their signatures should be created and verified. To address this need, signature policies have been proposed and standardized. Those policies are a set of rules to create and verify signatures. To date, Brazil has adopted signature policies to regulate legally binding signatures.

Our contribution includes the analysis and improvement of signature policies in Brazil. Nevertheless, this work is not restricted to the Brazilian signature policies, but it is applicable to any scenario using the signature policies standard. Our analysis shows that signature policies can limit the practical use of signatures. The reason is that, if a signature policy allows for no time-stamps, i.e., signed evidence showing when some data existed, then users cannot extend the validity of a signature beyond the expiration or revocation of the certificates needed to verify the signature. Note that this is necessary in several scenarios, e.g., when a party wants to extend the validity of a signature in order to provide it as valid evidence to a court. Conversely, if a signature policy requires time-stamps, their use can be unnecessarily inefficient. More precisely, the signature can only be validated accordingly if it contains a time-stamp, even though this time-stamp is not needed yet because the signature will expire in the far future.

Our solution is the *extensible signature policies*. These policies allow additional policies to be applied to a signature. Therefore, parties can select a policy that fulfills their current requirements. If the requirements change in the future, e.g., time-stamps become necessary, parties can apply an additional policy that addresses the new requirements without invalidating the previously used policy. Verifiers check the signature according to the initial and additional policies.

Finally, we demonstrate the applicability of our proposal by implementing the new policies on the Brazilian PKI and adapting an existing signature software. More precisely, we have shown that the changes required to put our solution into practice do not cause a great impact on signature users and existing infrastructure.

Future work. We plan to allow signers to select not only an initial signature policy that can be extended, but also the rules that any additional policy should contain. For example, a signer may want that any additional signature policy applied to his or her signature prevents verifiers from using Certificate Revocation Lists when verifying his or her signature.

Moreover, further work needs to be done to allow for an archival signature policy that can be extended. This is necessary in particular situations, for example, when signatures must remain valid for several decades. Our approach cannot be used in such cases because, when creating an archival signature policy, the additional policies that can be applied to this archival signature policy may not yet exist. To address this issue, we plan to use the so-called *chameleon hash functions* [15]. These function can be used to precompute references to additional signature policies that will be created and include these references in the archival signature policy.

VIII. Acknowledgments

This work has been funded by CAPES, Brazil.

References

[1] R. van Welie, R. Willemsen, J. Abraham, and B. Nagelvoort, "Global B2C E-commerce Report 2015," Ecommerce Foundation, Tech. Rep., 2014.

[2] N. Bose and M. Potter, "Fraud rates on online transactions seen up during holidays: study," 2015, http://www.reuters.com/article/us-retail-fraud-idUSKCN0T611T20151117 [retrieved: June, 2016].

[3] W. Diffie and M. E. Hellman, "New directions in cryptography," IEEE Transactions on Information Theory, vol. 22, no. 6, 1976, pp. 644–654.

[4] Presidency of the Republic, "Interim Measure n. 2.200-2, August 24, 2001," Official Diary of the Union, aug 2001, p. 65.

[5] J. A. Buchmann, Introduction to Cryptography. Springer, 2002.

[6] ETSI, "Electronic Signatures and Infrastructures (ESI); ASN.1 format for signature policies," Tech. Rep. ETSI TR 102 272, 2003.

[7] ——, "TC Security - Electronic Signatures and Infrastructures (ESI); XML format for signature policies," Tech. Rep. ETSI TR 102 038, 2002.

[8] R. S. Martini, "Signature Policies Requirements for the Brazilian PKI," Information Technology Institute, Tech. Rep. 7, 2015.

[9] C. Kaufman, R. Perlman, and M. Speciner, Network Security: Private Communication in a Public World (2nd Edition). Prentice Hall, 2002.

[10] D. Bayer, S. Haber, and W. S. Stornetta, Improving the Efficiency and Reliability of Digital Time-Stamping. New York, NY: Springer New York, 1993, pp. 329–334.

[11] M. Vigil, J. A. Buchmann, D. Cabarcas, C. Weinert, and A. Wiesmaier, "Integrity, authenticity, non-repudiation, and proof of existence for long-term archiving: A survey," Computers & Security, vol. 50, 2015, pp. 16–32.

[12] ETSI, "Electronic Signatures and Infrastructures (ESI); CMS Advanced Electronic Signatures (CAdES)," Tech. Rep. TS 101 733, 2012.

[13] ——, "XML Advanced Electronic Signatures (XAdES)," Tech. Rep. ETSI TS 101 903, 2009.

[14] O. Dubuisson, ASN. 1: communication between heterogeneous systems. Morgan Kaufmann, 2001.

[15] H. Krawczyk and T. Rabin, "Chameleon signatures," in Proceedings of the Network and Distributed System Security Symposium. San Diego, CA: The Internet Society, 2000.

Information Support System Development in Relation to Critical Infrastructure Element Resilience Evaluation

Martin Hromada
Department of Security Engineering
Faculty of Applied Informatics, Tomas Bata University in Zlin
Zlin, Czech Republic
email: hromada@fai.utb.cz

Abstract— **Evaluating and ensuring the resilience of critical infrastructure is essential in terms of maintaining vital societal functions. This fact increases the importance of developing relevant mathematical models and their implementation to software tools. This article therefore discusses the development process of a critical infrastructure resilience evaluation mathematical model as a basis for information support system development. The article addresses both the description of selected resilience evaluation attributes as well as the possible structure of the information support system.**

Keywords- critical infrastructure; resilience evaluation; information support system.

I. INTRODUCTION

Critical infrastructure as a system is an essential part of society functional continuity, its economic or social structure and systems. In relation to this fact, approaches and tools were proposed, which reflect the above mentioned essentiality and create the framework for a risk assessment system, which should positively affect the functionality and resilience. Critical Infrastructure Protection in the Czech Republic is regulated by Act no. 430/2010 Coll., which can be seen as an implementation of Council Directive 2008/114/EC on the identification and designation of European Critical Infrastructures and the assessment of the need to improve their protection, which provides a framework for creating a common European access to Critical Infrastructure Protection. This Directive establishes certain instruments for the identification and designation of an European and national infrastructure (sector and cross-cutting criteria), as well as instruments for increasing the protection of Critical Infrastructure in the context of the need to maintain functional continuity of the society (Operator Security Plan, Security Liaison Officer, Public Private Partnership and etc.). These instruments can also be seen from the resilience evaluation perspective, where, as it was said, resilience is seen as an indicator that quantifies the ability to provide functionality in terms of internal and external factors negative effects, provided to the need of establishing the limits, when degradation of system functionality is acceptable and when it is not [3]. Relevant approaches which were the philosophical baseline and the concept for security research project were presented in several articles. The most appropriate are RAMCAP Plus Approach [2] or D., Rehak P., Senovsky [10]. The rest of the paper is structured as follows. The first section provides the theoretical input to the resilience evaluation process in the context of information support. The second part is focused on resilience terminology specification. The third part then discusses and presents the security research outcome – Methodology for the Resilience Evaluation System of the Critical Infrastructure Elements and Networks in Selected Areas in Czech Republic as a unique and new approach to resilience evaluation and its implementation to decision support calculator as a relevant information support system.

II. RESILIENCE

"System resilience" in relation to critical infrastructure is a relatively new term, but, in principle, there are some accepted definitions:

Resilience is the „ability to resist, absorb, recover from or successfully adapt to adversity or a change in conditions" according to the U.S. Department of Homeland Security Risk Steering Committee [1].

Resilience is „both the inherent strength and ability to be flexible and adaptable after environmental shocks and disruptive events"according to Tierney and Bruneau [1].

Resilience is understood as „the ability of systems, infrastructures, government entities, businesses, and society to adapt to adverse events, to minimize the impact of such events (keeping the system running), and also to anticipate future adverse events and be able to prevent them"according to the CRN Report, Focal report 6, Risk Analysis, Resilience – trends in Policy and Research [1] [2].

III. CRITICAL INFRASTRUCTURE ELEMENT RESILIENCE EVALUATION METHODOLOGY ALGORITHMS

One appropriate approach, which was a philosophy baseline for our new approach for resilience evaluation was All-hazard risk and resilience: Prioritizing Critical Infrastructures Using the RAMCAP Plus Approach [2]. The RAMCAP Plus process avoids unnecessary detail, precision and cost by focusing on the most critical assets at a facility and keeping the approach relatively simple and intuitive. There are numerous other risk methodologies in use by specific industries, but their results are generally not comparable with other industry sectors or, in some cases, with other facilities within the sector. Many are qualitative, producing relative results that can be compared only locally, if at all. Moreover, several of the available methods require the assistance of specialized consultants and/or considerable amount of time, money and personnel resources, which discourages their use and makes them costly to use on a regular basis. The RAMCAP Plus process – through the cost-effective application of common and consistent terminology and metrics – provides a basis for using existing data and reporting results in a consistent, quantitative, directly comparable manner [2]. Depending on the purpose, the resilience of critical infrastructure element or elements evaluation should be done as an external or internal evaluation. It should be based on knowledge of nature and basic functional, technological and spatial attributes of the evaluated critical infrastructure elements. Next, we will therefore present a unique approach which reflects actual security, safety and resilience issues in Czech Republic in relation to critical infrastructure stability and functional continuity.

Multi-criteria evaluation is one of the appropriate methods for evaluating the resilience of critical infrastructure element and system. This method allows implementation of a comprehensive evaluation of relatively independent indicators and parameters. It uses a semi-quantitative expression of the individual indicators value. Its disadvantage is a lower resilience level performance. It allows to rate a critical infrastructure element in an appropriate range of resilience levels. The result of evaluation unfortunately does not specify how long the element of critical infrastructure can withstand the influence of negative factors. The advantage is the evaluation of the protection measures quality in relation to identified threats and risks [3].

It is obvious that the multi-criteria evaluation should be related to the security areas, which have a positive impact on the resilience level (robustness and preparedness), including their components. Every area of security and safety should have a positive impact on the robustness and preparedness level. The assessment should therefore establish standards (criteria) for the selected security and safety areas, through checklists. A comprehensive evaluation requires the expression of the risk value (coefficient) and its relationship and impact on the selected element or sector of critical infrastructure resilience. This highlights the fact that the final system resilience level is the average value of resiliencies related to selected risks. For complex multi-criteria critical infrastructure element or sector resilience evaluation, a mathematical relationship was established, represented by following equation:

$$ODP = \frac{\sum OD_i}{x_i} \qquad (1)$$

where:

ODP - is the resilience value of the evaluated critical infrastructure elements,

OD_i - is the resilience value of the critical infrastructure element in relation to the selected (i-th) risk

x_i - is the number of selected risks [4].

The mathematical expression of critical infrastructure elements resilience in relation to the i-th risk is:

$$OD_i = \frac{(1 - H_{RZi}) + (1 - K_S) + (K_{RO} * V_{RO} + K_{PR} * V_{PR})}{3} \qquad (2)$$

where:

H_{RZi} - is the risk value of i-th risk
K_S - is correlation coefficient,
K_{RO} - is the robustness coefficient,
V_{RO} - is the weight of robustness,
K_{PR} - is the preparedness coefficient,
V_{PR} - is the weight of preparedness [2][3].

A. *Analysis and Risk assessment*

Analysis and risk assessment in the context of the above-mentioned methodology is based on a two steps process:

1. Semi-quantitative risk analysis,
2. Qualitative risk correlation analysis (QARS)

In the first instance, the risk is semi-quantitatively expressed by the relationship:

$$R = P * N \qquad (3)$$

where:

R - Risk value,
P - The probability of threats application,
N - Impact value

In risk and vulnerability evaluation process is necessary to use relevant methodology for the expression of the mutual relationships and interdependencies between identified risks. For this purpose, the (QARS) methodology was selected.

The importance of this methodology is especially in connection with the diversification of risk based on level of risk activity (the risk ability or potential to cause further risks) and passivity evaluation (possibility that the risk may be caused by other risks) in relation to other risks.

The process of implementation of the QARS analysis is a multi-steps process, with the first step being the creation of a list of possible risks.The next step is focused on the expression of importance relations and interdependencies between the identified risks in the form of spreadsheet correlation Table 1.

TABLE 1. LIST OF RISKS

Index		1	2	3	4
Index.	The Threat Of	High temperature	Lightning	Tree fall	Operating error of third parties
1	High temperature	x			
2	Lightning	1	x	1	0

x - Reflects the fact that the risk itself cannot cause,
1 - Is the real possibility that the risk Ri may cause risk Rj,
0 - Expresses a condition where there is no real possibility that the risk Ri may cause risk Rj
Coefficients of the correlation and interdependencies calculation are based on the equations:

$$C_A R_i = \frac{\sum R_i}{x-1} \qquad C_P R_i = \frac{\sum R_i}{x-1} \tag{4}$$

where:
$C_A R_i$ is the value of activity coefficient,
$C_p R_i$ is the value of passivity coefficient,
$\sum R_i$ is the sum of risks,
x - total number of risk.

After adding values to the correlation table for the tree fall risk, the horizontal axis (activity coefficient) and vertical axis (passivity coefficient), and after using the above equations, we have the following parameters (presented in Table 2):

TABLE 2. COEFFICIENTS AND RISK INDEX

The Risk Index	1	2	3	4	5	6	7	8	9	10
Activity Coef.	0,00	0,22	0,44	0,44	0,56	0,56	0,67	0,56	0,11	0,11
Pasivity Coef.	0,67	0,00	0,11	0,44	0,67	0,00	0,44	0,33	0,44	0,33

Subsequently, the coefficient values are plotted on a graph, which ultimately enables the identification of the most significant risks in terms of their potential (high activity and passivity potential).

For the risk evaluation or for the process of determinig the most significant risks, the graph must be divided into segments that differentiate risks according to their significance. To divide the graph into 4 segments, it is necessary to define S1 and S2 lines that divide the graph itself and the risks to the segments where it is assumed that in the first segment will be 80% if major risks.

To express the parameters for lines S1 and S2, we use the equations:

$$S_{1/2} = C_{A/P\max} - \frac{(C_{A/p\max} - C_{A/P\min})}{100} * 80 \tag{5}$$

where:
$C_{A\max}; C_{A\min}$ - minimum and maximum values of activity coefficient,
$C_{P\max}; C_{P\min}$ - minimum and maximum values of passivity coefficient,

Then, the lines are implemented and divide the risks in 4 segments (Figure 1) that represent the level of risks:

1. I. Segment - Primarily significant risks – the highest activity and passivity coefficients,
2. II. and III. Segment – Secondary significant risks,
3. IV. Segment – Tertiary significant risks – low value of activity and passivity coefficients,

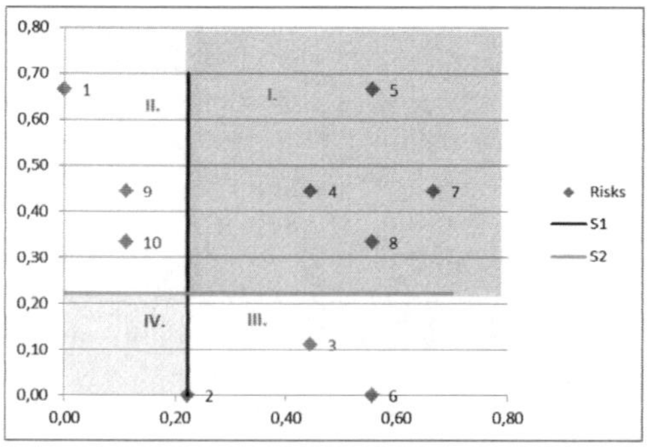

Figure 1. Division into 4 risk segments

This process allows us to divide risks by the highest potential in relation to system functionality degradation due to domino efect, which can be seen as an expression and evaluation of the vulnerability parameter (Vi) [3][4].

B. *Software application*

In relation to above-mentioned procedure, the second step of risk analysis and assessment is the risk list creation. This method is based on the use of simple mathematical equations. In connection with this fact, the excel calculator was selected, mostly because it provides easy editing and graph work. The resulting Table 3 was:

TABLE 3. RISKS CORRELATION TABLE

i	Table of correlations	1	2	3	4	5	6	7	8	9	10	11	12	13	14	15	16	17	18	19	20	21	22	23	24	25	26
	Energetics																										
1	Short-term electricity outage	✚	☐	☑	☐	☐	☐	☐	☐	☐	☐	☐	☐	☐	☐	☐	☐	☐	☐	☐	☐	☐	☐	☐	☐	☐	☐
2	Long-term electricity outage	☐	✚	☐	☑	☐	☐	☐	☐	☐	☐	☐	☐	☐	☐	☐	☐	☐	☐	☐	☐	☐	☐	☐	☐	☐	☐
3	Outage of water supply	☐	☐	✚	☐	☑	☐	☐	☐	☐	☐	☐	☑	☐	☐	☑	☐	☑	☐	☐	☐	☐	☐	☐	☐	☐	☐
4	Outage of gas supply	☐	☐	☐	✚	☐	☐	☑	☐	☐	☐	☐	☐	☐	☐	☐	☐	☐	☐	☐	☐	☑	☐	☐	☐	☐	☐
	Natural impacts																										
5	Flood	☐	☐	☐	☐	✚	☐	☐	☐	☐	☐	☐	☐	☐	☐	☐	☐	☐	☐	☐	☐	☐	☐	☐	☐	☐	☐
6	Prolonged drought	☐	☐	☐	☐	☐	✚	☐	☐	☐	☐	☐	☐	☐	☐	☐	☐	☐	☐	☐	☐	☐	☐	☐	☐	☐	☐
7	Extreme heat and drought	☐	☐	☐	☐	☐	☐	✚	☐	☐	☑	☐	☐	☐	☐	☐	☐	☐	☐	☑	☐	☐	☐	☑	☐	☐	☐
8	Thick frost	☐	☐	☐	☐	☐	☐	☐	✚	☐	☐	☐	☐	☐	☑	☐	☐	☐	☐	☐	☐	☐	☐	☐	☐	☐	☐
9	Pandemic, epidemic	☐	☐	☐	☐	☐	☐	☐	☐	✚	☐	☐	☐	☐	☐	☐	☐	☐	☐	☐	☐	☐	☐	☐	☐	☐	☐
	Risks associated with the human factor																										
10	Conflagration	☐	☐	☐	☐	☐	☐	☐	☐	☐	✚	☐	☐	☐	☐	☐	☐	☐	☐	☐	☐	☐	☐	☐	☐	☐	☐
11	Explosion	☐	☐	☐	☐	☐	☐	☐	☐	☐	☐	✚	☐	☐	☐	☐	☐	☐	☐	☐	☐	☐	☐	☐	☐	☐	☐
12	Robbery	☐	☐	☐	☐	☐	☐	☐	☐	☐	☐	☐	✚	☐	☐	☐	☐	☐	☐	☐	☐	☐	☐	☐	☐	☐	☐
13	Leaks of pollutants in the area	☐	☐	☐	☐	☐	☐	☐	☐	☐	☐	☐	☐	✚	☐	☐	☐	☐	☐	☐	☐	☐	☐	☐	☐	☐	☐
14	Outage in logistics	☐	☐	☐	☐	☐	☐	☐	☐	☐	☐	☐	☐	☐	✚	☐	☐	☐	☐	☐	☐	☐	☐	☐	☐	☐	☐
15	The virtual attack	☐	☐	☑	☐	☑	☐	☐	☐	☐	☐	☐	☑	☐	☐	✚	☐	☐	☐	☐	☐	☐	☐	☐	☐	☐	☐
16	The terrorist attack	☐	☐	☐	☑	☐	☐	☐	☐	☐	☐	☐	☐	☑	☐	☐	✚	☐	☐	☐	☐	☐	☐	☐	☐	☐	☐
17	Disruption of public order	☐	☐	☐	☐	☐	☐	☐	☐	☐	☐	☐	☐	☐	☐	☐	☐	✚	☐	☐	☐	☐	☐	☐	☐	☐	☐
18	Unavailability of staff	☐	☐	☑	☐	☐	☐	☐	☐	☐	☐	☐	☐	☐	☐	☐	☐	☐	✚	☐	☐	☐	☐	☐	☐	☐	☐
19	Sudden rush of patients	☐	☐	☐	☐	☐	☑	☐	☐	☐	☐	☐	☐	☐	☐	☐	☐	☐	☐	✚	☐	☐	☐	☐	☐	☐	☐
20	Technical failures	☐	☐	☐	☐	☐	☐	☐	☐	☑	☐	☐	☐	☐	☐	☐	☐	☐	☐	☐	✚	☐	☐	☐	☐	☐	☐
21	Sabotage	☐	☐	☑	☐	☐	☐	☐	☐	☐	☐	☐	☐	☐	☐	☐	☐	☐	☐	☐	☐	✚	☐	☐	☐	☐	☐
22	Violent criminal activity	☐	☐	☐	☐	☐	☐	☐	☐	☐	☐	☐	☐	☑	☑	☐	☐	☐	☐	☐	☐	☐	✚	☐	☐	☐	☐
23	Acts of vandalism	☐	☐	☐	☐	☐	☐	☐	☐	☐	☐	☐	☐	☐	☐	☐	☐	☐	☐	☐	☐	☐	☐	✚	☐	☐	☐
24	Plundering	☐	☐	☑	☑	☐	☐	☐	☐	☐	☐	☐	☐	☐	☐	☐	☐	☐	☐	☐	☐	☐	☐	☐	✚	☐	☐
25	Reserve 1	☐	☐	☐	☐	☐	☑	☐	☐	☐	☐	☐	☐	☐	☐	☐	☑	☑	☐	☐	☐	☐	☐	☐	☐	✚	☐
26	Reserve 2	☐	☐	☐	☐	☐	☐	☐	☑	☐	☐	☐	☐	☐	☐	☐	☐	☐	☐	☐	☑	☐	☐	☐	☐	☐	✚

Reset

After inputting the values in the table and using appropriate mathematical background, the resulted graph (Figure 2) and risks segmentation was:

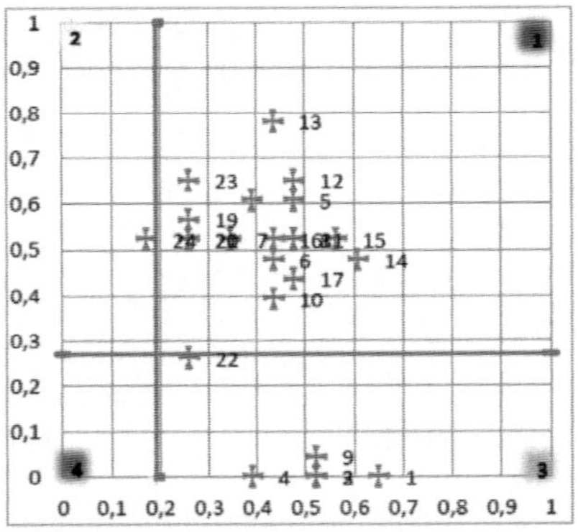

Figure 2. Risks correlation graph

where the segment properties presented in Figure 3 are:

S	Segment properties
1	Areas of primary and secondary dangerous risks
2	Areas of secondary dangerous risks
3	Areas of primary dangerous risks
4	Relatively safe area

Figure 3. Segment properties

For the process of determining the value of the risk coefficient/parameter HRzi, we select risks which can be considered critical - located in I. quadrant of QARS. These risks values are seen through first phase of risk assessment and analysis, which takes into account the degree and significance of the selected risks impact to the system. For the determination of the risk value the following equation was applied:

$$H_{RZi} = \frac{H_{Ri}}{H_{Ri\max}} \tag{6}$$

where:
H_{RZi} - is the risk value of i-th risk in range <0,1>
H_{Ri} - is the original risk value expressed in the first phase of the risk analysis
H_{Rimax} - the maximum attainable risk value within the value range.

The final list for evaluation of critical infrastructure element risk value is presented in the Figure 4:

i	Risks	Active	Passive	S
	Energetics			
1	Short-term electricity outage	0.04	0.00	2
2	Long-term electricity outage	0.04	0.00	2
3	Outage of water supply	0.17	0.22	1
4	Outage of gas supply	0.09	0.13	1
	Natural impacts			
5	Flood	0.00	0.09	2
6	Prolonged drought	0.00	0.04	4
7	Extreme heat and drought	0.13	0.04	3
8	Thick frost	0.04	0.00	2
9	Pandemic, epidemic	0.00	0.04	4
	Risks associated with the human factor			
10	Conflagration	0.00	0.04	4
11	Explosion	0.00	0.00	2
12	Robbery	0.00	0.09	2
13	Leaks of pollutants in the area	0.00	0.09	2
14	Outage in logistics	0.00	0.09	2
15	The virtual attack	0.13	0.04	3
16	The terrorist attack	0.09	0.00	1
17	Disruption of public order	0.00	0.04	4
18	Unavailability of staff	0.04	0.00	2
19	Sudden rush of patients	0.04	0.04	4
20	Technical failures	0.04	0.00	2
21	Sabotage	0.04	0.04	4
22	Violent criminal activity	0.09	0.00	1
23	Acts of vandalism	0.00	0.04	4
24	Plundering	0.09	0.00	1

Figure 4. Risks assessment list

C. *Correlation value*

Determination of correlation coefficient K_s is an important aspect that expresses the position of the linkages and dependencies within the critical infrastructure system. Generally, the main linkages and dependencies areas are:

a) Logical linkages and dependencies,
b) Physical linkages and dependencies,
c) Territorial linkages and dependencies.

To determine the value of correlation parameter the following equation is applied:

$$K_s = \frac{\sum Si}{S_{\max}} \tag{7}$$

where:
K_s - correlation parameter value
Sum Si - the sum of the dependence degree of the i-th CI elements groups to other CI areas
S_{max} - is the maximum value of correlation

After the mathematical expression of correlation value parameter, the final list for critical infrastructure element correlation value calculation was (Figure 5):

Product or Service	Is the element Hospital care dependent on another product		Dependency
Electricity supply	( ) yes	(•) no	0
Gas supply	( ) yes	(•) no	0
Water supply	(•) yes	( ) no	8
Food supply	(•) yes	( ) no	6
Functionality of communication networks	(•) yes	( ) no	4
Access to data services	( ) yes	( ) no	0
Availability of staff	( ) yes	(•) no	0
Supply of medical materials	(•) yes	( ) no	7
Forecasting and warning service	(•) yes	( ) no	1
Public Administration	(•) yes	( ) no	3
Transportation	( ) yes	(•) no	0
	Reset	Ks	0.26

Figure 5. Correlation value

D. Robustness coefficient evaluation

The robustness expressed by $K_{RO,}$ represents strength, durability, resistance to deformation. It is the ability to resist and withstand the effects of negative events without significant function degradation. In this methodology, the CI element robustness is divided into structural robustness and security robustness. These two areas, respectively, their expressions, form a relationship for the evaluation of the system robustness:

$$K_{RO} = K_{RZ} * K_{SR} \quad (8)$$

where:

K_{RO} - is the robustness coefficient,
K_{RZ} - is the structural robustness coefficient,
K_{SR} - is the security robustness coefficient.

The evaluation of security robustness coefficient K_{RZ} in relation to the resilience evaluation is seen from a wider context. The security robustness coefficient expresses the extent and quality of the critical infrastructure element security in connection with identified risks. Individual measures, according to their nature and effect, are divided into specific security areas. There are areas of physical security, information security, administrative security, personnel security, etc. For each type of critical infrastructure element, different security areas should be defined. The security robustness coefficient basically consists of:

- level of physical security M_{FB} - which is an expression of the extent and quality of the measures taken in the critical infrastructure element physical security,
- level of information security M_{IB} - which is an expression of the extent and quality of the measures taken in the critical infrastructure element information security,
- level of administrative security M_{AB} - which is an expression of the extent and quality of the measures taken under the critical infrastructure element administrative security,
- level of personal security M_{PB} - which is an expression of the extent and quality of the measures taken in the critical infrastructure element personnel security.

The importance (weight) of individual security area components of the security robustness is as individual as the status and importance of robustness and preparedness in relation to the selected critical infrastructure element resilience. The importance determination, that is, the weights determination of security robustness for individual components, is realized using pair wise comparison (Fuller triangle).

In the case of any two security robustness components comparison of the n components, we select all combinations of two elements of n, where the total number of combination is equal to (figure 6):

$$K = \frac{n * (n-1) * (n-2)!}{2!\,(n-2)!} = \frac{n * (n-1)}{2} \quad (9)$$

1	1	1	1	1	1	1	1
2	3	4	5	6	7	8	9
2	2	2	2	2	2	2	
3	4	5	6	7	8	9	
3	3	3	3	3	3		
4	5	6	7	8	9		
4	4	4	4	4			
5	6	7	8	9			
5	5	5	5				
6	7	8	9				
6	6	6					
7	8	9					
7	7						
8	9						
8							
9							

Figure 6. Example of Fuller triangle

Therefore, weights assessment may be calculated by the following equation:

$$V_i = \frac{m_i}{\sum_{i=1}^{k} m_i} = \frac{m_i}{K} \quad (10)$$

Mathematical expressions of weights determine the safety and security areas that are relevant for the evaluation process which influence the final value of the resilience (in the case that the weight of administrative security is 0, it is clear that we would not evaluate the measures provided by this security area).

For security robustness evaluation, a process has been formulated following the relationship:

$$K_{RZ} = M_{FB} * V_{FB} + M_{IB} * V_{IB} + M_{AB} * V_{AB} + M_{PB} * V_{PB} \quad (10)$$

where:

V_{FB} - is the weight of physical security,
V_{IB} - is the weight of information security,
V_{AB} - is the weight of administrative security,
V_{PB} - is the weight of personal security,
M_{FB} - concerns the determination of the physical security measures quality,
M_{IB} - concerns the determination of the information security measures quality,
M_{AB} - concerns the determination of the administrative security measures quality,
M_{PB} - concerns the determination of the personal security measures quality [3].

Regarding the software application of security robustness expression, we used selected security areas importance comparison by Fullers triangle (Figure 7.):

Compare the importance of individual areas			
Physical and object security	○	◉	IT security
Physical and object security	◉	○	Business continuity management
Physical and object security	◉	○	Administrative security
IT security	◉	○	Business continuity management
IT security	○	◉	Administrative security
Business continuity management	○	◉	Administrative security

Figure 7. Security areas importance comparison

and the selected security areas checklist fulfilment is represented in Figure 8:

IT security	Yes	No
Antivir	◉	○
Firewall	○	◉
Identification and authentication	○	◉
RAID	◉	○
Access control	○	◉
Traffic Control	◉	○
256-bit encryption	○	◉
Ensuring sterility of environment	◉	○
Staff training	◉	○
Prevention	◉	○

Figure 8. Selected security areas checklist

E. *Structural robustness coefficient evaluation*

Resilience of critical infrastructure element is the ability to ensure functionality in terms of external and internal factors effects. Each resilience value should have a point featured element (building, room), surface element (agricultural fields, complex reservoirs), line element (pipeline, pipeline) and element with the network characteristics (Radiation Monitoring Network). The level of element resilience is related to the security measures, but also reflects the systemic, structural and technological characteristics. A critical infrastructure element with network character structure will be able to withstand the effects of natural disasters without serious function degradation, if it will be able in terms of its structure, redirect the flow of technology and alternative way to bridge the shortfall of transit components. To determine the degree of influence, it is necessary to reflect those characteristics that are part of normal operation and are immediately available to use and do not require extensive activation of forces and means. These characteristics determine the structural robustness of a critical infrastructure element.

In the process of assessing structural robustness, it is possible to use the so-called macro-view approach. Widely distributed critical infrastructure element deployed on a large territory (region, country) is more vulnerable than a point element (Department Building). The probability that it will deal with the effects of natural disasters is higher, also has given his blanket deployment of more vulnerabilities.

Structural robustness of critical infrastructure element expresses the ability to withstand the effects of negative factors due to its structure, system and technology properties. It also includes the ability to withstand the effects of negative factors without function degradation, potential of deploying the redundant subsystems to isolate the failure (to prevent their spread) and flexibility to redirect service. In relation to this fact, the critical infrastructure elements have the character of the building, technological unit, staffed technical system, processes, systems or services, the assessment of structural robustness should be determined by a multi-criteria evaluation.

The evaluation process is represented by scoring of the main attributes that determine the magnitude of the structural robustness. The structural robustness coefficient K_{SR} varies in the interval 0.8 – 1. Structural robustness coefficient K_{SR} expresses the influence of topological structure, complexity and other properties or characteristics of the deterioration of protective measures effect of evaluated critical infrastructure element. If the coefficient of structural robustness K_{SR} is lower, the more attention should be paid to emergency preparedness. The main attributes by which the evaluation of the structural robustness should be performed include:

- type of topological structure,
- complexity,
- number of key technologies
- flexibility
- redundancy
- perimeter protection.

Topological structure type of element is a topological expression of its physical appearance. The type of topological structure is evaluated by the topology index value I_t. Determination of the topological structure type is carried out by using the system architecture, implemented in the system analysis. Based on the analysis of sectoral criteria, we distinguish between four types of topological structures of the critical infrastructure elements. These include point, area, line and network structures. Topological structure type is reflected in the range of elements, the degree of centralization and density of components of critical infrastructure elements, etc. Index topology I_t has values in the range 0 – 3. Value of I_t is determined by identifying the type of evaluated element topology (point, area, line and network) and the specifications of its size. The network character elements I_t are determined by using partial methods. Next, we characterize all four types of topological structures.

The point structure element is an element that forms a centred closed unit, located on a small area. Usually, it may be protected as a whole against external events. This category includes critical infrastructure elements represented by building, group of buildings, building with mast etc. The closeness and separation from the outside boundary elements improves the conditions for the functioning and reduces its vulnerability. For such elements, structural robustness may not be in high demand. Index topology I_t of elements with an area up to 1000 m^2 takes the value 3, with area over 1000 m^2 has a value of 2, and the maximum size of the point element is 1 hectare.

The surface structure element has the character of surface unit. The dimensions of element length and width are comparable in size. The geometric shape is not clear, it may take the form of rectangles, squares, triangles and polygons, etc. Such an element occupies a large and geographically compact area. Element target function is associated with a wide area of space. The surface dimensions are so large, and it usually means that the physical security provided around the perimeter is difficult to achieve, but not always. Examples of surface structure element with ensured physical security may be airports, especially international flights. An example of element which is not ensured by physical security is an important agricultural field. Elements topology index I_t of area to 1 km^2 takes the value 2, the area between 1-10 km^2 has a value of 1 and a surface of 10 km^2 has a value of 0.

The line structure element is characterized by a line arrangement. It represents an element which ensures transmission, supply or transport between two physically separate locations. This kind of element is not usually possible to protect as a whole. Its interruption causes degradation of transmission, delivery or transportation. Only local points on the line should be protected, such as compressor stations, booster stations, etc. In terms of its nature it is the most vulnerable category of critical infrastructure elements and ensuring their resilience requires high preparedness to function restoration. Structural robustness coefficient should reduce the overall resilience value of the element represented by the protective measures and preparedness to restore function. Linear character element topology index I_t with a length of 10 km takes the value 1, with a length of 10 km has the value 0.

The network structure element is characterized by a network structure. It consists of several components (nodes) which are interconnected. The network is characterized by a topological structure that expresses the nature and type of interconnection nodes. We distinguish between tree, star, polygon and bus structures. If the network is dense, it is less vulnerable and can better adapt to the failure of one of the nodes or edges. Element resilience significantly reflected the ability of technologies in the area of routing. If the technology in the network allows automatically or at least automated forwarding, element resilience is greatly increasing. Resilience is also affected and have irreplaceable role in relation to the importance of each node in the network. A key role in these elements plays a central node, which collects data, evaluates and presents it for further use. Failure of the central node can mean functionality disruption of the whole critical infrastructure element. Therefore, it is important that the network functions of the central node are backed up. Another structural robustness characteristic of the network is the uniformity of edges distribution. If there are nodes in the network with the number of edges significantly higher than the rest, the failure of nodes should significantly degrade the quality of the provided function of evaluated critical infrastructure element than the other. Index I_t of network topology structure element is determined by the partial multi-criteria methodologies. Depending on the type of network topology, the number of core nodes, the total number of nodes and the average number of edges per node should the topology index I_t takes values from 0 - 3.

Element complexity integrates a number of categories (types) of components and their total number. The level of complexity is evaluated using the complexity index value I_s. If the system is complicated, it is more vulnerable and less resilient. A number of complications may occur at the interfaces between the components and technologies. A complex system also requires a higher degree of specialization of the individual components, which degrade the interchange ability of components. Extensive systems tend to be prone to restructured complexity. Simple systems take the complexity index I s value 2, medium (medium complexity) systems take value 1 and 0 value is for complex systems. The criterion for determining the degree of complexity can also be the number of employees.

In addition to the complexity of critical infrastructure element, the resilience is significantly affected by the number of key and support technologies that ensure the fulfilment of its key function. For example the key technology of electricity production dispatching is an information technology as a Local area network. The number of key technologies is identified in the system analysis in the specification of technology architecture. Generally, the more complex systems are more vulnerable. Mostly the technological dependence of society, forced the establishment of critical infrastructure protection. Just a limitation of raw materials for key technology elements of critical infrastructure is degrading its functionality. Similarly, the failure of one technological unit should spread failures by domino effect in other technological units. The increasing number of technologies leads to increased vulnerability and limited element resilience. Technological complexity of evaluated critical infrastructure element is evaluated using the key technologies index I_{kt}. If the element contains less than 2 key technologies take the key technologies index I_{kt} value 2, when the number of technologies is 3-4 is an index of key technologies I_{kt} assigned with value of 1, and if the number of key technologies is 5 and more the index value is 0.

Flexibility as a general feature means adapting of the building operations in relation to changes in conditions, the input variables and its structure and other key features. Flexibility is reflected by critical infrastructure elements adaptation to new conditions. It ensures the implementation of the target element function and in the case of breakdown or failure of some critical infrastructure elements component. It provides flexibility in redirecting the flow in case of failure of one of its nodes. Flexibility properties should be considered to technologies ensuring the fulfilment of the objective function. For example the high voltage transmission system ability is to bridge the section shortfall by redirection and the use of other sections for power transmission. The ability of critical infrastructure flexibly is evaluated by the flexibility index I_f. If key technologies allow the flexibly adaptation of their activities, the flexibility index If is assigned the value 2, in the absence of flexibility potential, flexibility index I_f takes the value 0.

Redundancy generally means excrescence. In the field of critical infrastructure elements, redundancy means the extension of the structure of the key components backup. The purpose of redundancy is to create the conditions where the failure of a key component will be immediately substituted by using redundant (backup) components. Implementation of redundancy principle can be seen through a backup operation control, which assumes the management after failure of the main control room. Applying the principle of redundancy is an important characteristic to ensure structural robustness of critical infrastructure element. Using redundant principal components is expressed by the redundancy index I_r. Redundancy index I_r takes the value 1, when the redundancy principle is applied. In the case when element does not have any redundant key technologies, redundancy index I_r is assigned by the value 0.

The geographic scope of the evaluated critical infrastructure elements translates into the possibility of ensuring the physical security by perimeter protection. If there is a feature on a relatively small area, it is economically viable to ensure the physical security as a whole. In the case where the element is located on a large area or a long line, it is not economically viable to protect it as a whole. The monitoring networks elements can be protected by local perimeter protection. The structure and use of perimeter protection is evaluated by a perimeter protection index I_{po}. If the critical infrastructure element does not build the perimeter protection, the perimeter protection index I_{po} is assigned by the value 0. If is the perimeter protection is local,, the perimeter protection index I_{po} takes the value 1, and in case of a complete perimeter protection, the index value is 2.

The values of topology index I_t, complexity index I_s, key technologies index I_{kt}, flexibility index I_f, redundancy index I_r and perimeter protection index I_{po} are listed in following Equation 11 [3].

$$K_{SR} = 0{,}8 + \frac{I_t + I_s + I_{kt} + I_f + I_r + I_{po}}{60} \qquad (11)$$

K_{SR} - structural robustness coefficient[5]

Software application of structural robustness evaluation is divided into two parts. The first part is the highest hierarchical level and it is presented in Figure 9:

Type of topology	point		area		
	> 1000 m2	< 1000 m2	> 1 km2	1 – 10 km2	< 10 km2
Complexity	simple (under 10 employees)			medium (10-100 em	
Number of core technologies	0-2 of technology			3-4 of technol	
Flexibility	no				
Redundancy	no				
Perimetric protection	unprotected			local	
				K_{SR}	0.93

Figure 9. Structural robustness evaluation

In the case when the topological type is a network, it is necessary to fulfil additional information, as shown in Figure 10:

Type of topology	bus	star / circle
Number of core nods	1 node	2 nodes
The number of nodes	to 5 nodes	6 - 15 nodes
The average number of edges per node	to 1,5 edge	1,6 - 2,2 edges

Figure 10. Additional table for network structural robustness evaluation

F. Preparedness coefficient evaluation

Preparedness of critical infrastructure element expresses its ability to restore its function after its degradation by the effects of negative factors (risks). Preparedness is evaluated through the preparedness parameter/coefficient K_{PR}, which can be understood as an expression of the ability to adequate reaction respectively response to the outbreak of an emergency or incident as well as the ability to recover and return to desired system functionality.

The mathematical expression of preparedness of the selected critical infrastructure (CI) element is given by:

$$K_{PR} = \frac{K_r + K_p + K_i}{3} \tag{12}$$

where:

K_r - coefficient of identified risks accuracy,
K_p - CI subjects crisis preparedness plan quality coefficient,
K_i - CI subjects crisis preparedness plan implementation quality coefficient,

Each part (defined coefficients) of the preparedness coefficient has a different check list. For this reason, we presented the example of a selected one (Figure 11) and the final software application of critical infrastructure element preparedness coefficient evaluation.

Crisis preparedness	Yes	No
Security audit	○	◉
Identification of possible events	◉	○
Contact Information	◉	○
Organization structure	◉	○
Insurance contracts	◉	○
Description of the main activities	○	◉
Probability of events occurrence	◉	○
List of procedures	◉	○
List of needs and resources	○	◉
Determination of responsible persons	○	◉

Figure 11. Crisis preparedness plan quality coefficient

The final software application of critical infrastructure element, the preparedness coefficient evaluation, is as an important aspect of specific critical infrastructure resilience evaluation (Figure 12):

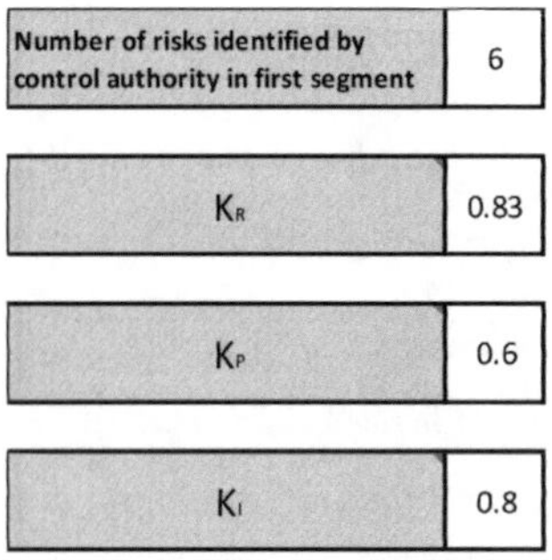

Figure 12. The final preparedness coefficient evaluation

G. Critical infrastructure element resilience evaluation

It is obvious that the multi-criteria evaluation should relate to the areas of security, which have a positive impact on the level of resilience (robustness and preparedness), including their components. Each area of security, having a positive impact on the robustness and preparedness should be assessed in relation to the established standards (criteria), for selected area through checklists. A comprehensive evaluation requires expressing the value (coefficient) of the risk and its relationship and impact to the value of resilience in relation to selected element or sector of critical infrastructure. This highlights the fact that the total value of resilience under evaluated system is the average value of resilience in relation to i-th risk. For a complex multi-criteria evaluation of selected CI element or elements the resilience was established by the following mathematical relationship:

$$ODP = \frac{\sum ODi}{xi} \tag{13}$$

where:

ODP - selected CI element resilience value
ODi - CI element resilience value in relation to selected i-th risk
xi - number of selected risks

The mathematical expression of CI elements resilience in relation to the i-th risk is:

$$ODi = \frac{(1 - H_{RZi}) + (1 - K_S) + (K_{RO} * V_{RO} + K_{PR} * V_{PR})}{3} \tag{14}$$

where:

H_{Rzi} - the value of i-th risk,
K_s - correlation parameter,
K_{RO} - robustness parameter,
V_{RO} - robustness weight,
K_{PR} - preparedness parameter,
V_{PR} - preparedness weight,

Equations (1- H_{Rzi}) and (1- K_s) reflect the fact that risk and correlation value negatively affect the value of the critical infrastructure element resilience.

The presented facts are the basis for the final evaluation of the critical infrastructure element or group of elements resilience in the relevant sector.

The final qualitative evaluation will be presented in the software application part of final critical infrastructure element resilience evaluation.

For final critical infrastructure element resilience evaluation, we used the above-mentioned facts and mathematical expressions and they are presented in Figure 13:

i	Risks	S	P	N	H_{RZi}	Odi
	Energetics					
1	Short-term electricity outage	1	3	1	0.12	0.77
2	Long-term electricity outage	1	2	3	0.24	0.73
3	Outage of water supply	1	3	1	0.12	0.77
4	Outage of gas supply	1	3	2	0.24	0.73
	Natural impacts					
5	Flood	1	2	2	0.16	0.76
6	Prolonged drought	2	3	2	X	X
7	Extreme heat and drought	3	1	0	X	X
8	Thick frost	2	2	0	X	X
9	Pandemic, epidemic	2	2	0	X	X
	Risks associated with the human factor					
10	Conflagration	2	0	0	X	X
11	Explosion	2	0	0	X	X
12	Robbery	1	2	1	0.08	0.78
13	Leaks of pollutants in the area	1	2	3	0.24	0.73
14	Outage in logistics	2	0	0	X	X
15	The virtual attack	1	3	2	0.24	0.73
16	The terrorist attack	1	3	1	0.12	0.77
17	Disruption of public order	2	0	0	X	X
18	Unavailability of staff	1	0	0	0	0.00
19	Sudden rush of patients	1	0	0	0	0.00
20	Technical failures	1	0	0	0	0.00
21	Sabotage	3	0	0	X	X
22	Violent criminal activity	1	3	4	0.48	0.65
23	Acts of vandalism	2	0	0	X	X
24	Plundering	1	3	1	0.12	0.77

ODP	0.59

Figure 13. Final resilience evaluation

Qualitative expression of critical infrastructure element resilience evaluation is represented by Figure 14:

Resilience evaluation	Value of ODP	Verbal rating	The minimum value of the robustness	The minimum value of the robustness of security	The minimum value of preparedness
Great (A)	0,8– 1	system is ready for all identified risks, none risks was neglected	0.5 as a result of the relationship $K_{RO}*V_{RO}$	Is given by the weights of individual parameters V_{FB}, V_{IB}, V_{AB}, V_{KO}	0.5 as a result of the relationship $K_{PR}*V_{PR}$
Very good (B)	0,6 – 0,8	system is ready for all of the important identified risks	0.4 as a result of the relationship $K_{RO}*V_{RO}$	Is given by the weights of individual parameters V_{FB}, V_{IB}, V_{AB}, V_{KO}	0.4 as a result of the relationship $K_{PR}*V_{PR}$
Good (C)	0,4 – 0,6	systém is ready for the most of important identified risks	0.3 as a result of the relationship $K_{RO}*V_{RO}$	Is given by the weights of individual parameters V_{FB}, V_{IB}, V_{AB}, V_{KO}	0.3 as a result of the relationship $K_{PR}*V_{PR}$
Enough (D)	0,2 – 0,4	system is ready for the most of the identified risks	0.3 as a result of the relationship $K_{RO}*V_{RO}$	Is given by the weights of individual parameters V_{FB}, V_{IB}, V_{AB}, V_{KO}	0.3 as a result of the relationship $K_{PR}*V_{PR}$
Unable to resist (E)	0 – 0,2	system is not ready for the majority (more than half) of the identified risks	0.2 as a result of the relationship $K_{RO}*V_{RO}$	Is given by the weights of individual parameters V_{FB}, V_{IB}, V_{AB}, V_{KO}	0.2 as a result of the relationship $K_{PR}*V_{PR}$

Figure 14. Qualitative expression of resilience evaluation

Figure 14 presents the qualitative expression of resilience evaluation as a final step of comprehensive approach for resilience evaluation. The approach was validated in selected critical infrastructure element as a reflection to practical model implementation ambition.

IV. CONCLUSION

As it was stated in the introduction, the resilience of critical infrastructure is a major aspect of critical infrastructure protection level improvement and assurance and maintenance of functional continuity. The paper presented selected facts and knowledge of the evaluation process in connection with selected attributes of methodological resilience evaluation. The evaluation process was followed by the software application and implementation of the presented mathematical relations. These facts should allow and provide a basis for information support system development. The presented model and resilience evaluation methodology was an outcome of security research project, where the main aim is to develop an unique and new approach and model to define and evaluate the critical infrastructure resilience. In relation to this fact, it is necessary to mention that resilience evaluation methodology was certified by Ministry of Trade and Business and Ministry of Interior of Czech Republic. The above mentioned model presents the mathematical modelling which is presently the framework for Dynamic Resilience Evaluation in new security research project RESILIENCE 2015.

ACKNOWLEDGMENT

This work was supported by the research project VI20152019049 "RESILIENCE 2015: Dynamic Resilience Evaluation of Interrelated Critical Infrastructure Subsystems", supported by the Ministry of the Interior of the Czech Republic in the years 2015-2019.

REFERENCES

[1] CRN Report, Focal report 6, Risk Analysis, Resilience – trends in Policy and Research, Commisioned by the Federal Office for Civil Protection Zurich, pp.25. April 2011

[2] ASME Innovative Technologies Institute, LLC,. All-hazard risk and resilience : Prioritizing Critical Infrastructures Using the RAMCAP Plus Approach. 1. New York : ASME, 2009. 155 p. ISBN 978-0-7918-0287-8

[3] M., Hromada, L., Lukas Conceptual Design of the Resilience Evaluation System of the Critical Infrastructure Elements and Networks in Selected Areas in Czech Republic, The twelfth annual IEEE Conference on Technologies for Homeland Security (HST '12), will be held 13-15 November 2012 in Greater Boston, Massachusetts. Pp. 353-358, ISBN 978-1-4673-2707-7

[4] M., Hromada Knowledge sharing in the risk analysis proces in energy sector, 3rd EU-US-Canada Expert Meeting on Critical Infrastructure Protection (CIP) May 22nd – 23rd 2012, Brussels

[5] M., Hromada, L., Lukas, The Status and Importance of Robustness in the Process of Critical Infrastructure Resilience Evaluation, The 13th annual IEEE Conference on Technologies for Homeland Security (HST '13), held 12-14 November 2013 in Greater Boston, Massachusetts. Pp. 589-594, ISBN 978-1-4799-1533-0

[6] E. G., Vugrin, D.E., M. A., Warren Ehlen, R. C., Camphouse A Framework for Assessing the Resilience of Infrastructure and Economic Systems, In: Sustainable and Resilient Critical Infrastructure Systems, 1st Edition, pp. 84-85,April 2010,ISBN 978-3642114045

[7] M., Hromada, L., Lukas Critical Infrastructure Protection and Resilience as an Actual Challenge of Security Education,

Computers and Technology in Modern Education, Kuala Lumpur, Malaysia, April 23-25, 2014, p. 62-69, ISBN: 978-960-474-369-8

[8] L., Lukas, M., Hromada, Simulation and Modelling in Critical Infrastructure Protection, In: International Journal of Mathematics and Computers in Simulation, Issue 1, Volume 5, p. 386-394, 2011, ISSN: 1998-0159, http://www.naun.org/journals/mcs/

[9] L., Lukas, M., Hromada, Resilience as Main Part of Protection of Critical Infrastructure, In: International Journal of Mathematical Models and Methods in Appliad Sciences, Issue 1, Volume 5, p. 1135-1142, 2011, ISSN: 1998-0140, http://www.naun.org/journals/m3as/

[10] D., Rehak P., Senovsky Preference Risk Assessment of Electric Power Critical Infrastructure. Chemical Engineering Transactions, 2014, Vol. 36, pp. 469-474. ISSN 1974-9791. DOI: 10.3303/CET1436079

Strengthening Software Diversity Through Targeted Diversification

Vipin Singh Sehrawat[1]
VipinSingh.Sehrawat@utdallas.edu

Yvo Desmedt[1,2]
Yvo.Desmedt@utdallas.edu

[1]Department of Computer Science,
The University of Texas at Dallas, Richardson, USA

[2]Department of Computer Science,
University College London, London, UK

***Abstract*—Code reuse attacks use snippets of code (called gadgets) from the target program. Software diversity aims to thwart code reuse attacks by increasing the uncertainty regarding the target program. The current practice is to quantify the security impact of software diversity algorithms via the number/percentage of the surviving gadgets. Recent attacks prove that only reducing the number of surviving gadgets does not add any security against code reuse attacks. We propose the use of the count/percentage of usable and surviving gadgets as the metric to quantify the security impact of software diversity algorithms. We present a novel software diversity algorithm, named *NOP4Gadgets*, that leaves 0.012% and 14.35% surviving and usable gadgets, respectively. NOP4Gadgets performs targeted diversification, concentrated around the potential Return Oriented Programming (ROP) gadgets. The performance overhead of NOP4Gadgets is 1% for the SPEC CPU2006 benchmark suite.**

Keywords–Software diversity, Return Oriented Programming, Code reuse attack, Targeted diversification.

I. INTRODUCTION

Code reuse attacks use snippets of code (called gadgets) from the target program and libraries. They allow the attacker to bypass the modern defence mechanisms like Data Execution Prevention (DEP) and Address Space Layout Randomization (ASLR). ROP [1] and Jump Oriented Programming (JOP) [2] are two forms of code reuse attack. Since the introduction of code reuse attack with return-to-libc [3], numerous defense mechanisms and tools have been proposed for its detection and/or prevention [4]–[12].

Code reuse attacks are facilitated by "Software Monoculture", that is the practice of running the same software on a large number of machines. So, if an attack is successful against the software then it can be used to compromise all machines which run that software. Software monoculture and the over-reliance on certain pieces of software, whether they are operating systems or applications, have been cited [13], [14] to increase the likelihood and severity of widespread security compromises.

Cohen [15] proposed *program evolution* as a solution to software monoculture. Program evolution implies that a program should evolve into different but semantically similar versions of itself. The primary goal of software diversity techniques is to achieve efficient (with minimum overhead) program evolution. Larsen et al. [16] provide a detailed survey of the known software diversity techniques. The common approach to quantify the security impact of software diversity techniques is by counting the number of surviving gadgets, which are the functionally similar gadgets present at the same positions within the diversified copies of an executable. Recent attack by Snow et al. [17] shows that only reducing the number of surviving gadgets does not add any security against code reuse attacks. In this paper, we propose a new metric to quantify the security impact of software diversity techniques. Our approach is to use the count/percentage of both, usable (intended and unintended ROP gadgets that can be used in an attack) and surviving gadgets to better quantify the security impact. Section III explains our metric and its advantages in detail.

In this paper, we present a novel software diversity algorithm, called NOP4Gadgets, that performs targeted diversification. Unlike existing no-op insertion implementations [18]–[21] NOP4Gadgets decides the type(s) of no-op(s) and the probability of no-op insertion based on the current and previous machine instructions, written by the compiler. By virtue of targeted diversification, NOP4Gadgets successfully reduces the number of both surviving and usable gadgets. Note that there are known techniques like G-Free [6] and Return Less Kernels [7] that target usable gadgets, but those are not software diversity techniques as they are not geared towards producing large numbers of diverse versions of the given executable. Existing no-op insertion based software diversity techniques do not perform targeted diversification, instead they all rely only on randomized no-op insertion. Also, none of the known implementations provides any analysis about its security impact in terms of the usable gadgets' statistics.

NOP4Gadgets leaves less than 0.80% surviving gadgets, and incurs a negligible overhead of 1% for the SPEC CPU2006 benchmark suite. Unlike existing no-op insertion implementations NOP4Gadgets focuses only on the potential ROP gadgets, thus avoiding unnecessary work. Goktas et al. [22] showed that gadgets with more than 30 instructions are also usable. So, while measuring the security impact of NOP4Gadgets we fixed the maximum gadget length to 200 bytes. We also developed a stronger version of NOP4Gadgets, which on average leaves

0.012% surviving gadgets and 14.35% usable gadgets, and incurs a negligible additional overhead of 0.651%. A drawback of software diversity is that it offers multiple attack surfaces. This provides the attacker with the option to attack the more vulnerable version(s). NOP4Gadgets leaves similar number of surviving and usable gadgets in each diverse version of an executable. Hence, no version is 'weaker' than the other.

The rest of the paper is organized as follows. Section II gives a background on code reuse attacks and no-op insertion. In Section III, we present and discuss our metric for quantifying the security impact of software diversity algorithms. In Section IV, we present our software diversity algorithm, named NOP4Gadgets, that performs targeted diversification, concentrated around the potential ROP gadgets. Section V gives the detailed security impact and performance overhead analysis of NOP4Gadgets. Section VI and Section VII give the future work and conclusion, respectively.

II. Background

A. *Code Reuse Attack*

Code reuse attacks use snippets of code (called gadgets) from the target executable/library. Return-to-libc [3] is the early form of code reuse attack in which the attacker reuses entire functions of `libc`. Code reuse attacks allow the attacker to defeat DEP by avoiding direct code injection. ROP and JOP are the two classes of code reuse attack. The gadgets used in ROP and JOP end with return and jump instructions, respectively.

Checkoway et al. [23] demonstrated the effectiveness of code reuse attack by successfully compromising a Direct Recording Electronic (DRE) voting machine by using ROP gadgets. An ROP attack uses buffer overflow to overwrite the stack with a series of return addresses that point to known ROP gadgets. By carefully positioning data on the stack the attacker can execute the gadgets in any desired order. A sequence of ROP gadgets that are executed in a predetermined order is called ROP chain. Table I shows an example ROP chain that adds the contents of two memory addresses and stores the result at a third memory address.

TABLE I. ROP CHAIN EXAMPLE

Address	**ROP Gadget**
0x00401077	pop eax pop ebx ret
0x00400795	mov eax, [eax] ret
0x00400ef6	mov ebx, [ebx] ret
0x0040136c	add eax, ebx pop ecx ret
0x004011ad	mov [ecx], eax ret

The general steps of an ROP attack are:

1) Analyze the code of the target executable and related libraries for aligned or unaligned instruction sequences, that end with a return instruction.
2) Filter the discovered ROP gadgets according to the desired attack.
3) Use buffer overflow to inject the starting addresses of the gadgets, as well as the addresses of any required data onto the stack.
4) Overwrite the return address with the address of the first gadget of the ROP chain.

Once the return instruction of the first gadget gets executed, the value stored in the instruction pointer, `eip`, is updated to the address of the first gadget. After the initial gadget is executed, its return instruction updates the value of `eip` to the address of the second gadget in the chain. In this manner, each gadget returns control to the next gadget in the chain. Automated tools like "Return-Oriented toolkits" [24] can be used to construct arbitrary attack codes using ROP gadgets.

JOP is more subtle than ROP, a jump instruction only performs an unidirectional control flow transfer. To manipulate the control flow the attacker uses a special gadget called the *dispatcher gadget*. To initiate the attack, a buffer overflow is used to jump to the dispatcher gadget. After executing, each gadget returns the control back to the dispatcher gadget which forces a jump to the next gadget in the JOP chain.

Code reuse gadgets can be divided into two broad classes, intended and unintended. Intended gadgets are the ones that consist of proper, aligned instructions, generated by the compiler. On the other hand, the instructions in unintended gadgets start somewhere within the proper instructions. On x86, the number of unintended gadgets always exceeds the number of intended gadgets. But it is harder to use the unintended gadgets because they may include infrequently used instructions and complicated addressing modes. Therefore, only the unintended gadgets of short lengths are considered usable.

B. *No-op Insertion*

No-ops are short code sequences that when executed have no effect on the registers or the memory. The processor fetches and executes these instructions without any change in the program state. Compilers insert no-ops in the object code to fulfill alignment constraints, and to add timing delays to code fragments [25]. No-op insertion has also been used as a software diversity technique with the aim to reduce the number of surviving gadgets [18]–[21].

No-op insertion can also break existing ROP gadgets, especially the unintended ones. The x86 instruction set is very irregular and the lengths and formats of the instructions depend on the first byte (opcode). Even a single byte inserted inside the byte array of a gadget can significantly alter it. Our algorithm, NOP4Gadgets, uses this property of no-op insertion and targets all potential ROP gadgets. NOP4Gadgets performs targeted diversification, the bulk of which is done within the potential ROP gadgets. Therefore, even if the attacker jumps into the binary at an arbitrary point and executes some unaligned instructions, before reaching the return instruction she encounters the no-ops inserted by NOP4Gadgets. Hence, the execution is forced to realign with the actual code. Figure 1 shows how inserting a no-op instruction at the right position can break an existing ROP gadget.

ROP gadget before no-op insertion:

03 3B	89 E1	89 C3
ADD edi, [ebx]	MOV ecx, esp	MOV ebx, eax

Gadget removed after no-op insertion:

03 3B	89 E1	90	89 C3
ADD edi, [ebx]	MOV ecx, esp	NOP	MOV ebx, eax

Figure 1. Removing ROP gadget by using no-op insertion

1) Why was the gadget removed: Inserting no-op before the return instruction changes the length and decoding of the instruction. For example, the no-op(s) inserted before a return opcode 'C3' may cause it to be decoded as an operand of the preceding instruction. This removes the gadget as now the sequence of instructions does not end with the return instruction. This gadget removing effect is more profound with the x86 instruction set because of the higher number of unintended gadgets.

III. Our Approach to Quantify the Security Impact

All known software diversity techniques quantify their security impact via the number/percentage of surviving gadgets present in the diverse versions. The purpose of software diversity is to produce diverse versions of the given program. The diversity achieved by any technique can be measured by recording the disparities in the diverse versions. Thus, counting the number of surviving gadgets is the correct method of quantifying the diversity. But when it comes to measuring the security impact against specific class(es) of attack(s), it is pivotal that we take into account the nature and various components of the attack. Snow et al. [17] showed that concentrating only on reducing the number of surviving gadgets does not add any security against ROP attacks. Therefore, using only the number of surviving gadgets is not the right method to quantify the security impact against code reuse attacks.

We propose the count/percentage of usable and surviving gadgets as the metric to quantify the security impact of software diversity algorithms. The following list gives the various advantages of our approach over the current approach.

1) Sophisticated attacks [17] do not make any assumptions about the surviving gadgets, but all attacks need some minimum number of usable gadgets. Therefore, the number of remaining usable gadgets must be a prime criterion in measuring the security impact against code reuse attacks.
2) We know that surviving gadgets are a good measure of diversity, but the count of the usable gadgets gives the exact number of gadgets available to the attacker.

IV. Our Algorithm (NOP4Gadgets)

We present a novel software diversity algorithm, named NOP4Gadgets, that performs targeted diversification, focused on the potential ROP gadgets. Unlike existing no-op insertion implementations [18]–[21] NOP4Gadgets decides the type and number of no-op(s), along with the probability of no-op insertion, based on the current and previous machine instructions, written by the compiler. Any set of harmless (which do not create new gadgets) no-op instructions can be

```
- I: MachineBasicBlock Iterator
- BB: MachineFunction Iterator
- MI: MachineInstr pointer to I
- NopTable: Table of candidate no-ops (Table II)
- bool pre1 ← false, pre2 ← false
procedure NOP4Gadgets
    if (MI->getOpcode() == ret) then
        call PrecedingInstNOP(BB, I)
        call CandidateInstNOP(BB, I)
    else
        call RandomInstNOP(BB, I)
procedure PrecedingInstNOP(BB, I)
    if (I > BB->begin()) then
        I ← I-1
        pre1 ← true
        if (I > BB->begin()) then
            I ← I-1
            pre2 ← true
    call PrecedingNOPs(pre1, pre2, BB, I)
procedure PrecedingNOPs(pre1, pre 2, BB, I)
    if pre2 == true then
        With probability p2 call insertRandom(BB, I)
        I ← I+1
    if pre1 == true then
        With probability p1 call insertSpecific(BB, I)
        I ← I+1
procedure CandidateInstNOP(BB, I)
    with probability q1 call insertSpecific(BB, I) once
                        OR
    with probability q2 call insertSpecific(BB, I) twice
                        OR
    with probability q3 call insertSpecific(BB, I) thrice
    I ← I+1
procedure RandomInstNOP(BB, I)
    with probability p call insertRandom(BB, I)
procedure insertSpecific(BB, I)
    insert a random 2 byte no-op instruction
procedure insertRandom(BB, I)
    insert a random no-op instruction
```

Figure 2. NOP4Gadgets as an LLVM pass

used to implement NOP4Gadgets. But as we compare the performance overhead of our algorithm with "Profile-guided NOP insertion" (PNOP) [18], we used the same set of no-ops as used in the PNOP implementation. Table II lists the no-op instructions used in the implementation.

We implemented NOP4Gadgets as a *MachineFunctionPass* of Low Level Virtual Machine (LLVM 3.5). Our backend pass identifies the return instructions as they are being written by the compiler and invokes the appropriate no-op insertion function(s) accordingly. Figure 2 gives the pseudocode of NOP4Gadgets. NOP4Gadgets examines the two instructions that immediately precede the return instruction. The user can customize this process to examine any number of preceding instructions. This feature of NOP4Gadgets can be used to identify the type of the potential ROP gadget and then configure the

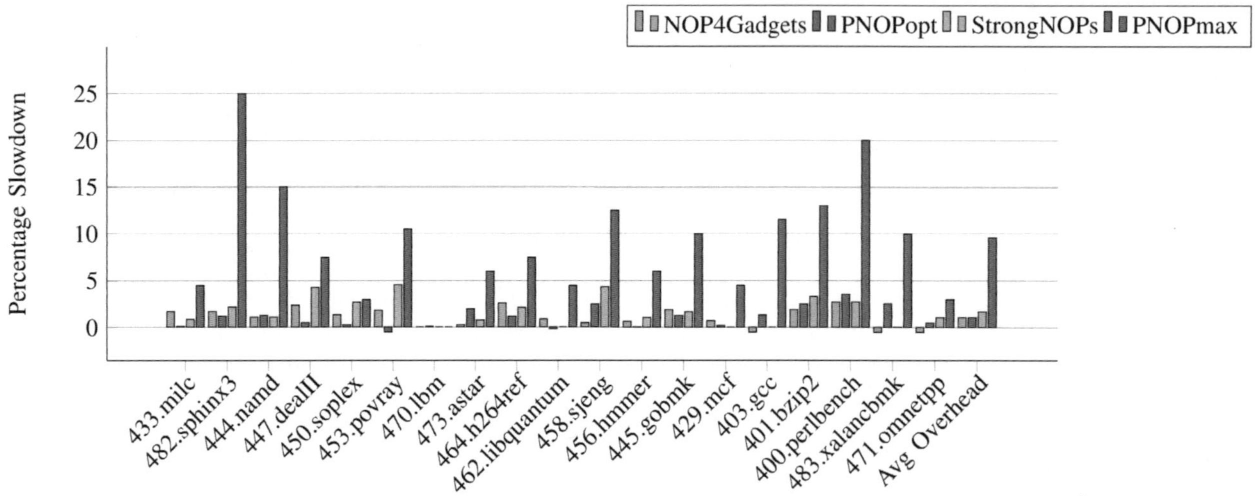

Figure 3. SPEC CPU2006 runtime overhead comparison of NOP4Gadgets with Profile-Guided NOP insertion (PNOP)

***PNOPopt:* Minimum overhead version of PNOP | *PNOPmax:* Maximum diversity/security version of PNOP**

behaviour accordingly. For example, if the user wants to target only the LOAD (gadgets that loads value to register) type ROP gadgets then he can configure the algorithm to perform no-op insertion only within the LOAD type gadgets, and ignore the others. NOP4Gadgets uses two functions, *insertSpecific*, which inserts a random two byte no-op and *insertRandom*, which inserts a no-op instruction, randomly selected from Table II. These features provide flexibility and control over the kind and level of security, and enables the user to optimize the performance overhead.

TABLE II. CANDIDATE NO-OP INSTRUCTIONS

Instruction	Opcode
mov esp, esp	89 E4
mov ebp, ebp	89 ED
lea esi, [esi]	8D 36
lea edi, [edi]	8D 3F
no-op	90

Our test results showed that for removing/breaking the existing ROP gadgets, 2 byte long no-ops are more effective than 1 byte no-ops. Thus, if the current instruction is a return instruction `ret`, then NOP4Gadgets inserts random 2 byte no-op(s) before it and the preceding instruction. The number of 2 byte no-ops inserted before `ret` can be one, two or three, and is governed by the probabilities q_1, q_2 and q_3, respectively. The instruction (`pre`) preceding `ret` gets one 2 byte no-op inserted before it with probability p_1. A randomly selected no-op is inserted with probability p_2 before the instruction that precedes `pre`. A randomly chosen no-op is inserted with probability p before the rest of the instructions. The (security impact)/(performance overhead) ratio can be altered by adjusting the various probabilities. For NOP4Gadgets, the probabilities governing no-op insertion are set as: $q_1 = .85$, $q_2 = .05$, $q_3 = 0$, $p_1 = .05$, $p_2 = .05$, $p = .04$.

TABLE III. PERCENTAGE OF SURVIVING GADGETS IN THE SPEC CPU2006 BINARIES BUILT BY NOP4Gadgets COMPILER

Benchmark	Original binary	Surviving %
483.xalancbmk	522681	0.31%
401.bzip2	1425	2.38%
403.gcc	90056	0.58%
429.mcf	1421	4.22%
433.milc	11729	0.86%
444.namd	10487	0.68%
445.gobmk	38927	0.30%
447.dealII	37432	0.89%
450.soplex	28612	0.37%
473.astar	4340	3.68%
482.sphinx3	6509	1.46%
464.h264ref	33763	0.25%
470.lbm	816	6.7%
400.perlbench	39699	0.27%
471.omnetpp	27918	0.49%
456.hmmer	17881	4.25%
458.sjeng	28612	1.29%
462.libquantum	3096	2.90%
453.povray	57208	1.08%
Average	-	0.78%

V. EVALUATION OF NOP4GADGETS

We also developed a stronger version of NOP4Gadgets, named *StrongNOPs*. The various no-op insertion probabilities for StrongNOPs are: $p = 0.05$, $p_1 = 0.5$, $q_1 = 0.10$, $q_2 = 0.55$, $q_3 = 0.35$. This section gives a detailed analysis of the performance overhead and security impact of NOP4Gadgets and StrongNOPs.

TABLE V. USABLE AND SURVIVING GADGETS PRESENT IN THE BINARIES BUILT BY StrongNOPs COMPILER

Program	Usable Gadgets	Surviving Gadgets	Size Increase
Advancemame-1.2	12.96%	0.011%	7.8%
Inkscape-0.48.5	34.68%	0%	2.1%
Scummvm-1.7.0	7.915%	0.033%	5.1%
Ghostscript-9.09	27.56%	0%	6.21%
Wesnoth-1.12.1	17.49%	0%	3.2%

Average Usable Gadgets	Average Surviving Gadgets	Average Size Increase
14.35%	0.012%	4.81%

A. *Performance Evaluation*

We used SPEC CPU2006 benchmark suite to compute the performance overhead of NOP4Gadgets and StrongNOPs. The average performance overhead of NOP4Gadgets is 1.069%, which is similar to the performance overhead of the minimum overhead version of PNOP [18]. Average performance overhead of StrongNOPs is 1.72%, which much smaller than the 9.5% performance overhead of the maximum diversity/security version of PNOP. Figure 3 shows a comparison of PNOPopt (minimum overhead version of PNOP), NOP4Gadgets, PNOPmax (maximum security/diversity version of PNOP) and StrongNOPs in terms of the percentage slowdown for the SPEC CPU2006 benchmarks.

B. *Security impact*

We quantified the security impact of NOP4Gadgets and StrongNOPs by using our new metric, that is by using the count/percentage of both usable and surviving gadgets. Goktas et al. [22] showed that ROP gadgets with more than 30 instructions are also usable. So, we set the maximum gadget length to 200 bytes. To count the number of surviving gadgets we wrote a program called *Discoverer*, that uses *ROPgadget* [26] to discover ROP gadgets within the `.text` section of the given executable. It then removes all the no-op instructions from the discovered gadgets and searches for identical gadgets present at the same location within different binaries.

We built 20 copies of the SPEC CPU2006 benchmarks using the NOP4Gadgets compiler. For each benchmark we took the two copies that share the maximum number of surviving gadgets between them. The average percentage of surviving gadgets found in the SPEC CPU2006 binaries was 0.78%. Table III shows the percentage surviving gadgets for each benchmark.

We built five popular open source programs using our StrongNOPs compiler. Table V gives the statistics about the surviving and usable gadgets found in the diversified versions of the programs. Note that in three out of the five programs StrongNOPs left no surviving gadgets. On average, StrongNOPs left only 0.012% surviving gadgets and removed over 85% of the usable ROP gadgets.

VI. Future Work

Current software diversity mechanisms primarily focus only on reducing the number of surviving gadgets. With NOP4Gadgets, we presented a novel approach of combining software diversity with gadget removal. Concentrating on removing/breaking the gadgets naturally reduces the number of surviving gadgets. Table VI lists the five broad categories of ROP gadgets. We plan to extend NOP4Gadgets or devise a similar software diversity technique that removes all gadgets of some specific type(s).

TABLE VI. TYPES OF GADGETS

Gadget type	Semantic	Example
ADJUST	adjust reg./mem.	add eax, 2
CALL	call a function	call [esi]
LOAD	load value to reg.	mov eax, [ebx]
STORE	store to mem.	mov [eax], ebx
SYSCALL	systemcall	sysenter

VII. Conclusion

The current approach to quantify the security impact of software diversity algorithms relies only on the number/percentage of the surviving gadgets. Recent attack by Snow et al. [17] shows that only reducing the number of surviving gadgets does not add any security against code reuse attacks. Hence, the current approach of measuring the security impact is flawed. In this paper, we proposed the use of the count/percentage of usable and surviving gadgets as the metric to quantify the security impact of software diversity algorithms. We argued that the proposed metric has several advantages over the current practice. We also presented a novel software diversity algorithm, named *NOP4Gadgets*, that performs targeted diversification, concentrated around the potential ROP gadgets.

NOP4Gadgets performs the bulk of the diversification within the potential ROP gadgets. It allows the user to target specific class(es) of ROP gadgets, and ignore the others. NOP4Gadgets uses different no-op insertion functions, that are configured to use specific type(s) of no-op instructions. NOP4Gadgets leaves less than 0.80% surviving gadgets, and incurs 1% performance overhead for the SPEC CPU2006 benchmark suite. The stronger version of NOP4Gadgets, named *StrongNOPs*, breaks more than 85% of the usable ROP gadgets, and incurs a negligible additional performance overhead of 0.651%. On average, StrongNOPs leaves only 0.012% surviving gadgets and 14.35% usable gadgets. We also presented a detailed comparison of NOP4Gadgets with the existing no-op insertion implementations [18]–[21]. Software diversity algorithms that follow our approach of focusing on both usable and surviving gadgets can prove to be a powerful tool against code reuse attacks, especially when combined with other defense mechanisms like G-Free [6] and Control Flow Integrity [8].

REFERENCES

[1] H. Shacham, "The geometry of innocent flesh on the bone: Return-into-libc without function calls (on the x86)," in Proceedings of the 14th ACM conference on Computer and communications security, 2007, pp. 552–561.

[2] T. Bletsch, "Code-Reuse Attacks: New Frontiers and Defenses," Ph.D. dissertation, North Carolina State University, 2011.

[3] S. Designer, "Return-to-libc attack," Bugtraq, 1997.

[4] P. Chen, H. Xiao, X. Shen, X. Yin, B. Mao, and L. Xie, "DROP: Detecting Return-Oriented Programming Malicious Code," in 5th International Conference on Information Systems Security, 2009, pp. 163–177.

[5] L. Davi, A. R. Sadeghi, and M. Winandy, "Dynamic integrity measurement and attestation: towards defense against return-oriented programming attacks," in ACM workshop on Scalable trusted computing, 2009, pp. 49–54.

[6] K. Onarlioglu, L. Bilge, A. Lanzi, D. Balzarotti, and E. Kirda, "G-Free: Defeating Return-Oriented Programming through Gadget-less Binaries," in ACSAC, 2010, pp. 49–58.

[7] J. Li, Z. Wang, X. Jiang, M. Grace, and S. Bahram, "Defeating Return-Oriented Rootkits with Return-less Kernels," in EuroSys, 2010, pp. 195–208.

[8] M. Abadi, M. Budiu, U. Erilingsson, and J. Ligatti, "Control-flow integrity principles, implementations, and applications," in ACM Transactions on Information and System Security (TISSEC), Volume 13, Issue 1, October 2009.

[9] M. Prasad and T. Chiueh, "A Binary Rewriting Defense against Stack-based Buffer Overflow Attacks," in USENIX Annual Technical Conference, 2003, pp. 211–224.

[10] C. Zhang, T. Wei, Z. Chen, L. Duan, L. Szekeres, S. McCamant, D. Song, and W. Zou, "Practical Control Flow Integrity and Randomization for Binary Executables," in Proceedings of IEEE Symposium on Security and Privacy, 2013, pp. 559–573.

[11] Y. Cheng, Z. Zhou, Y. Miao, X. Ding, Huijie, and R. Deng, "ROPecker: A Generic and Practical Approach For Defending Against ROP Attack," in 21st Annual Network and Distributed System Security Symposium, 2014.

[12] I. Fratric. (2012, September) ROPGuard: Runtime Prevention of Return-Oriented Programming Attacks. [retrieved: May, 2016]. [Online]. Available: http://www.ieee.hr/_download/repository/Ivan_Fratric.pdf

[13] D. E. Geer, "Monopoly considered harmful," in IEEE Security & Privacy, 2003, pp. 14–17.

[14] M. Stamp, "Risks of monoculture," Communications of the ACM - Homeland security, 2004, vol. 47, p. 120.

[15] F. Cohen, "Operating system protection through program evolution," Computers and Security, 1993, vol. 12, pp. 565–584.

[16] P. Larsen, A. Homescu, S. Brunthaler, and M. Franz, "Sok: Automated software diversity," in SP '14 Proceedings of the 2014 IEEE Symposium on Security and Privacy, 2014, pp. 276–291.

[17] K. Z. Snow, F. Monrose, L. Davi, A. Dmitrienko, C. Liebchen, and A. R. Sadeghi, "Just-In-Time Code Reuse: On the Effectiveness of Fine-Grained Address Space Layout Randomization," IEEE Symposium on Security and Privacy, pp. 574–588, 2013.

[18] A. Homescue, S. Neisius, P. Larsen, S. Brunthaler, and M. Franz, "Profile-guided Automated Software Diversity," in Proceedings of the IEEE/ACM International Symposium on Code Generation and Optimization, 2013, pp. 1–11.

[19] T. Jackson, B. Salamat, A. Homescu, K. Manivannan, G. Wagner, A. Gal, S. Brunthaler, C. Wimmer, and M. Franz, Moving Target Defense. Springer New York, 2011, vol. 54, ch. Compiler-Generated Software Diversity, pp. 77–98.

[20] T. Jackson, "On the Design, Implications, and Effects of Implementing Software Diversity for Security," Ph.D. dissertation, University of California Irvine, 2012.

[21] T. Jackson, A. Homescu, S. Crane, P. Larsen, S. Brunthaler, and M. Franz, Moving Target Defense II. Springer New York, 2013, vol. 100, ch. Diversifying the Software Stack Using Randomized NOP Insertion, pp. 151–173.

[22] E. Goktas, E. Athanasopoulos, M. Polychronakis, H. Bos, and G. Portokalidis, "Size does matter: Why using gadget-chain length to prevent code-reuse attacks is hard," in USENIX, 2014.

[23] S. Checkoway, A. J. Feldman, B. Kantor, J. A. Halderman, E. W. Felten, and H. Shacham, "Can DREs provide long-lasting security? the case of return-oriented programming and the AVC advantage," in Electronic voting technology/workshop on trustworthy elections, USENIX, 2009.

[24] R. Hundt, E. Raman, M. Thuresson, and N. V. Mao, "An extensible micro-architectural optimizer," in Proceedings of the 9th IEEE/ACM International Symposium on Code Generation and Optimization, CGO, 2011, pp. 1–10.

[25] L. Tang, J. Mars, and M. L. Soffa, "Compiling for niceness:mitigating contention for QoS in warehouse scale computers," in Proceedings of the 10th IEEE/ACM International Symposium on Code Generation and Optimization, 2012, pp. 1–12.

[26] J. Salwan. (2012) ROPgadget - Gadgets finder and auto-roper. [retrieved: May, 2016]. [Online]. Available: http://shell-storm.org/project/ROPgadget/

APPENDIX A
LLVM BACKEND PASS IMPLEMENTATION

We implemented our algorithm as an LLVM MachineFunctionPass. MachineFunctionPass is part of the LLVM code generator that executes on the machine dependent representation of each LLVM function in the program. The next step was to write two no-op insertion functions and add them to LLVM. In the beginning of the MachinFunctionPass we inspect the current machine instruction and depending on whether it is a return instruction or not, we call different function(s). In order to correctly identify the machine instructions the target architecture(s) must be fixed. As NOP4Gadgets is most effective with x86 instruction set, we set x86 as the architecture.

Once it is verified that the current machine instruction is a return instruction, we proceed to the next step that is to move back by one or two instructions, if possible. This is done by comparing the current value of "MachineBasicBlock iterator" with the "MachineFunction iterator" and if possible the MachineFunctionPass moves one or two steps back to the previous instruction(s). Finally, we call one or both no-op insertion functions (insertSpecific and insertRandom).

A. X86::Return Instructions

Below is the list of *LLVM's x86 return instructions*, used in the implementation of NOP4Gadgets.

```
RETQ, IRET64, IRET32, IRET16, LRETQ, RETW,
RETL, RETIL, RETIQ, RETIW, EH_RETURN,
EH_RETURN64, LRETIL, LRETIQ, LRETIW,
LRETL, LRETQ, LRETW
```

Education System in Commercial Security

Vladislav Stefka
Faculty of Applied Informatics, Department of Security Engineering
Tomas Bata University in Zlin
Zlin, Czech Republic
stefka@fai.utb.cz

Abstract— **This paper addresses the preparation of the new Law on private security services in the Czech Republic, pitfalls and possibilities of practical use in the field of security work. This new law should adjust the position of private security services in their business, but also the opportunity for involvement in the Integrated Rescue System of the Czech Republic.**

Keywords- Commercial Security, Detective Activities, Property Protection and Security.

I. INTRODUCTION

The Czech Republic - as perhaps the only country in the European Union, does not have a law that would comprehensively regulate Commercial Security proceedings. On the one hand, this situation is seen as a particular example - because it is a business that should not be constrained by other actors, especially actors in the Executive Powers sphere; on the other hand, the fact is that most security services employees only have very low qualifications - which is reflected in the fact that staff salaries are on the lower end of the wage curves.

Despite these and other problems in connection with Private Security Services´ activities and working in the Private Detective trade, a number of changes in this area have been recently made.

The amendment to the Trade Act - in the area of Security Services, which came into effect on 1, January, 2009, modified the conditions of doing business in the Security Guard and Private Detective fields. Given that earlier adaptation of the contents of individual trades was contained in the Government regulations, it can be assumed that the adjustment made by the Small Business Act - a superior rule of law, will contribute to improve and provide a higher social status of these activities.

The great development of PSS finally occurred after the fall of the Communist regime, i.e. from the early 90s. Regarding their legal basis, their activities were cancelled in 1991 by the Decree of the Federal Ministry of the Interior; but, a new trade law - ranked them among the Licensed Trade sector and the "Private Eyes Service" as follows, "undertakings providing for the security of property and persons", (later referred to as "the Security of Property and Persons", and later again, under the "Provision of Technical Services for Persons and Property", and created a new legal basis for this kind of business. At the same time however, dating back to 1992, the introduction of special treatment for the PSS area was mooted, as was the need for a separate law; however, these efforts were unsuccessful, and ended there. The last attempt to create such a special act was seen in the Spring of 2011; in June, 2011 - but interdepartmental commentary procedures were terminated, and there was not much time for further noticeable developments. According to information from the Ministry of the Interior, they were still "working hard" on the Bill and it was planned to send this to the Government to 31. 12. 2012.

The amendment to the Trade Act itself includes newly specified conditions for Security and Private Detective services - which refers to the fact that the required professional competence for these trades, inter alia, is evidenced by a Professional Qualification Certificate for the relevant work activities, which will be issued by an authorized body established under special regulations of the Ministry of Education, Youth and Sports. This is actually the accreditation process based on the authorisation by the Ministry of the Interior.

This otherwise set the conditions for implementing the Ministry of Interior Decree No. 16/2009 Coll., "On the Content and Scope of Qualifications for Security and Private Detective Services". The decree was published in Volume No. 6 of the Collection of Laws of the Czech Republic, which was distributed on January 16, 2009, and came into force on its publication in the Official Gazette.

The content of this ordinance is to establish the conditions for the acquisition of competence in operating a licensed Security Guards trade and licensed Private Detective trade services and for them to become proficient employees and for entrepreneurs operating a licensed Security Guards trade and licensed Private Detective trade services, as well as the method for the implementation of proficiency tests in order to acquire professional qualifications for the above activities and the content of the test.

The condition for obtaining such expertise is to create a Qualification Standard - which consists of upgrading proficiency and the development of criteria and evaluation methods.

II. THE NATIONAL SYSTEM OF QUALIFICATIONS FOR THE LICENSED TRADE

1. Guarding Property and Persons; and...
2. Private Detective Services

This established the qualification standards with effect from June 19, 2009 as follows:

A. Guards (Code 68-008-E)

Where, for competence standards, this implies training of at least 20 hours, followed by an examination before a three-member expert committee composed of duly authorised people.

The Training Content is primarily:

- The implementation of protection and security of persons and property
- Manipulating technical security systems
- The application of the principles of interaction with the Integrated Rescue System - especially the Police, and other defined entities
- The application of the legal basis of security activities
- The control of persons and vehicles at personnel gates and other gates
- The control of guarded object activities
- The surveillance of buildings and public spaces
- Implementing simple actions to ensure and restore security and to reduce losses to property and human health
- The use of physical security funds
- The documentation of surveillance controls and services provided

B. Detective Trainee (Code 68-009-M)

Where, to obtain proficiency training, it is expected to cover at least 20 hours, followed by an examination before a three-member expert committee of duly authorised persons.

The content of this training is primarily:

- Orientation in the basic legal standards and provisions with emphasis on security
- Legal issues and the protection of personal data
- Readiness to apply the basic forms and methods of Private Detective duties, and for their practical implementation
- The principles of the operation and control of basic private detective resources and aids
- Other activities
- Documenting and evaluating information, and their registration and preparation for handover to the client
- A readiness to use Informatics

Based on the evaluation standard, they then have to show the extent of the requirements and evaluation criteria in the form of written, oral and practical examinations.

Both of the above-mentioned tests include a written exam, in the form of test questions that are randomly generated from a set of questions - which is an examination system available on a data-carrier. The test results are validated by the test board, as are the oral and practical exams, which are designed to address particular situations.

The final evaluation is carried out by the Examination Committee, which evaluates the fulfilment of the professional competence and conduct requirements and the outcome of the tests and these are entered into the record during the test.

A candidate who satisfies the conditions set out in the criteria and evaluation method is evaluated such that the Commission issues a final "Pass" rating. Otherwise, the rating "Failed" is recorded; while the evaluation is carried out by means of commission members′ votes, and the result is then communicated to the Commission Chairman.

The test is performed on the basis of a written application. The applicant for consideration′s preparation time is 20 minutes, while the written exam can take up to 45 minutes, and the oral and practical exams that follow-on may last 30 minutes.

An applicant who passes the exam shall be issued a Certificate of Professional Qualification by the duly authorised person(s); among other things, this must include the Certificate′s Registration Number and the name of the appropriate scope of business activities for which the professional qualification certificate is issued.

The decision to grant accreditation from the Ministry of Education, Youth and Sports to an organisation is authorised in accordance with: § 108, Para. 2, Act No., 435/2004 Coll., "On Employment", as amended; as well as Decree No. 524/2004 Coll., on "Providing Retraining to Applicants and Applicants for Employment"

The original intention, in terms of this certificate was that it will be valid for five years from the date of its issue.

C. Security Services Handlers, (Code: 68-001-H)

Other professional qualifications have been established for this licensed trade; they must be able to:

a) Demonstrate their knowledge of Dog Handling (K9, Cynology) Methology and explain the difference between tame and domesticated animals
b) Explain the concept of the instinctive conduct of dogs/K9s, and the importance for the survival of the individual as and when this arises, and to cite two examples
c) Explain the Conditioned Response (Behaviour) concept for dogs, and the importance for the survival of the individual as and when this arises, and to cite two examples
d) Explain the Habituation (loosely - adaptation) Concept, and the importance for the survival of the individual as and when this arises, and to cite two examples
e) Divide dogs by type of Higher Nervous Activity into four groups (i.e. IP Pavlova distribution), and each type simple way to characterize and explain the appropriateness of different types of dogs for guard duty,
f) Describe the expression f (threat) confident aggressive dog ready to attack (describe position, ruff, the position of the ears, tail, revealing teeth, view dog, sound speech)

g) Describe the expression (threat) dog for aggressive behaviour, which is caused by a sense of danger and fear of the dog (describe position, ruff, the position of the ears, tail, revealing teeth, view dog, sound speech),
h) Describe the expression obeying dog (especially in active and passive subordination) - describe the attitude, the movement of the dog, the position of the ears, tail, facial expressions, audible speech and specify the territorial negotiations dog, the reason for this behaviour, speech, application and use of security service,
i) Describe the defensive reaction of the dog - especially active (escape, attack) and especially passive, explain the reason for this behaviour and explain the use of active defence reaction of the dog in the direct attack on the dog and handler,
j) Shall be determined by lot three of the criteria that the applicant meets the test.

Orientation in laws and regulations relating to the possession, training and use of dogs/K9s to protect the health and property of persons

In your own words, explain: a) § 1, Para. 1 of Act no. 409/2008 Coll., on the Protection of Animals against Cruelty; b) in your own words - explain: § 4, Para. 1, Points a), b), d), h), s) of Act No. 409/2008, Coll., "On Protection of Animals against Cruelty; in connection with § 4, Para. 1, Point a) to § 4, Para., 3; c) In your own words, explain: § 28 of the Criminal Code, No. 40/2009 Coll. (Destitution); d) Cite the wording of § 29 of the Penal Code, No. 40/2009 Coll. (Necessary Defence) and explain and introduce the main principles of Health and Safety in the use of a dog to protect the health and property of persons; In your own words, explain: 1) § 76, Para., Detention of a Suspected Person. 2) ...and of the Criminal Code (Limiting Personal Freedom), and give a practical example of the application of this section during Guard Duty.

Practical demonstration of Dog/K9 Training (Cynology) - Handler Defence

a) Demonstrate "field screening" – the dog/K9, on command, runs to the handler - once to the right, and once to the left of the handler´s axis; procedure will be repeated, but withdrawn at least twenty steps and examine a shelter
b) Demonstrate "finding and exposure" (marking) a hidden person – they must find a hidden person and indicate the place by persistent barking
c) Demonstrate "guarding suspect" during the tour – the dog lies at a distance of about five steps from the handler and inspects the suspect(s) as to whether they are carrying a concealed weapon – or not; the dog demonstrates how it controls each suspects´ and perpetrators´ behaviour in an attack on the handler - and is ready to effectively prevent injury to the handler
d) Demonstrate the Dog/K9´s defence of the handler – i.e. "Dribbling", thereby effectively helping the dog handler in averting an attack by perpetrators
e) Demonstrate the skill of Escorting Suspects – how a handler with a dog must accompany the suspect to a designated place and transfer them into the custody of a responsible person. Handlers escort suspects as follows: "Rear Escort" – involves accompanying a suspect at a distance of about five paces, while the dog is kept by the handler´s left leg, and is ready to defend effectively.

D. Supervision Centre Worker, (Code: 68-003-H)

The Maintenance of Technical Security Systems oriented on a Receiving Device and Signal Evaluation from security systems; they must be able to:

a) Describe the principles, design, use and operation of Technical Security Systems with a focus on the Receiving Device
b) Evaluate signals from security systems in the monitoring centre
c) Describe the principles of personal data protection when processing and evaluating technical security systems
d) Describe the principles of protection of information received in the monitoring centre
e) They must meet all the criteria

a) They must applying the principles of co-operation with the Integrated Rescue System, and especially with the Police and other defined entities and to characterise the principles of cooperation with Police and Municipal Police operations at the monitoring centre under the applicable provisions of the relevant laws; b) Characterise the principle of consultation with Fire-fighting Units, and the Ambulance and Emergency Services, in averting damage to property and the health of persons, under the provisions of the relevant laws in the operations of a Monitoring Centre, as well as State Emergency Telephone Numbers. They must meet both criteria.

E. The Head Detective Code, (68-002-T)

They must know how to:

a) Apply legal standards with an emphasis on Safety and the legal issues of Privacy; and understand the Constitutional Law - with an emphasis on the activities of Private Detective services
b) Apply the Civil and Commercial Law with an emphasis on typical contractual relationships in the Private Detective Business
c) Apply Trade Law, Labour Law, and Tax Law
d) Apply Criminal Law and Criminal Procedure, Administrative Law and Administrative Procedure - with an emphasis on Administrative Offences and the Law on Weapons and Ammunition

e) Apply the Law on the Free Access to Information Act and the Data Protection Act
f) Understand the Act on the Czech Police and Municipal Police and explain its use in the performance of their work.

They must meet all the criteria.

III. Conclusion

The introduction of mandatory training and testing in personnel security agencies and private detectives – apart from its positive aspects, also has its practical shortcomings. The number of employees in these services range from a sober estimate of 50,000 workers. This raises the question as to whether it is possible for authorised persons to handle such numbers of people and to train and test them - and it is thus necessary to consider the Economic Impact on businesses in this field, and especially, during the current economic crisis.

Another unresolved issue so far, is just how far the extension of both programmes for authorisation - and even Accreditation. Granting authorisation is a five-year period, and accreditation requires another three years.

Furthermore, the logical question arises as to whether it would be appropriate to amend that part of the Evaluation Standard that would deal with the need to commission three-member examination committees, comprised of the duly authorised persons.

References

[1] BAHYLOVA, L., PHILIP, J., MOLEK, P. et al. Constitution of the Czech Republic: comment. Prague: Linde, 2000

[2] BARTA, M. et al. Private security services: general concepts. Prague: Czech Police Academy Republic, Prague, 2011.

[3] MACEK, P. NOVAK, F.: Private security services. Police History 2005

[4] KINCL, J. : Professional qualifications in commercial security. Professional Publishing , Prague 2010

[5] FRYSAR, M. : Safety managers, businessmen and politicians, Public history 2016 Prague

[6] PROTIVINSKY, M. : Crime prevention, ARMEX, Prague 2009

[7] STRADAL , J. : Qualification based on practice, NUOV Prague 2014

[8] VYSKOCIL, K. : Management support processes , Professional Publishing , Prague 2014

[9] STEFKA, V. : Handbook for training employees in security services Zlin 2012 . Internal syllabi – unpublished

[10] HUNTINGTON, S. 2008 Political Order in Changing Societes. Yale University Press ISBN 0300001717.500 s.

[11] PASHA,M.K., Globalizarion,Difference und Human Security, Florenc,Routlege 2014 ISBN 978-04157065

[12] TOLK, A., NABIL, R.A., : Defense And Security Berlin 2012 ISBN 978-4673-4781-5

Possibilities of Technical Security of Elementary Schools

Rudolf Drga
Tomas Bata University in Zlin
Faculty of Applied Informatics
Zlin, Czech Republic
e-mail: rdrga@fai.utb.cz

Hana Charvatova
Tomas Bata University in Zlin
Faculty of Applied Informatics
Zlin, Czech Republic
e-mail: charvatova@fai.utb.cz

Abstract— **This paper presents the technical security of elementary schools as one of the possible targets for terrorist attacks or unstable individuals. It explores the organizational structure of large and small schools, their regime precautions, the current level of technical support and possible options for improvement, both in the field of communication, and especially in the full utilization of existing security systems.**

Keywords-Elementary school; technical security; organizational structure.

I. INTRODUCTION

Nowadays, elementary schools represent one of the possible soft targets for terrorist attacks or unstable individuals who themselves want to attract media attention. With regards to the mentioned second group of terrorists, some countries have a set of specific rules indicated by law, which prohibit broadcasting of such cases in public media. This constitutes a failure of attacker's goal (see. Anders Behring Breivik, a Norwegian far-right terrorist who committed the 2011 Norway attacks [1]. He is an idol for similar individuals, where media worldwide has broadcasted the case.)

For the evaluation of schools, it is necessary to divide them according to their size. We use the number of attending students as the most important parameter, as it affects the internal organization of the school. A clear division is shown in Table 1.

TABLE I. DIVISION OF ELEMENTARY SCHOOLS ACCORDING TO SIZE

Size of school	*Number of students*	*Basic activities*	*Other activities*
small	up to 100	Elementary school 1st to 5th grade, kindergarten, after-school club	irregular activities
medium	100-400	Elementary school 1st to 9th grade, kindergarten, after-school club, school canteen	regular activities - reduced range
large	over 400	Elementary school 1st to 9th grade, kindergarten, after-school club, school canteen	large regular activities

A small school, mainly located in a village, has up to 100 students. Its basic activities are teaching students of grade 1 to 4 or 5, running kindergarten and after-school clubs. Various other activities, which do not have regular character, such as competitions, carnivals, etc., are organized on its premises or on the public ones.

A medium school teaches approximately 100 to 400 students. It is located in the catchment villages or small towns. Their activities include teaching of students of grade 1 to 9. Furthermore, there is one kindergarten, after-school clubs and other activities are run on a limited scale.

A large school has over 400 students, teaches grades 1 to 9, runs kindergarten, after-school clubs and the school canteen is open even to the public. Regular large-scale activities and events are organized by people who are not employees of the institutions, but have access to the premises.

II. SMALL SCHOOL

The organizational structure of a small school is shown in Figure 1. Its organizational structure is relatively simple and the possibility of penetration of potential perpetrators is relatively low in compliance with basic safety precautions. The regular daily schedule starts in the morning by bringing students to school. They are mostly accompanied by parents, siblings, grandparents or friends in order to be there by a certain time.

There is always a janitor at the entrance to the building. He guards the entrance and checks all the people coming to the school premise. He knows most of them personally and can thus let them into the cloakroom where students can change their shoes and leave some coats in the winter time. This is important at the beginning of the school year when new 1st grade students do not know the school rules and need the support of their loved ones. When the arrival time is over, the janitor makes sure there is nobody around the cloakroom and locks the entrance door. Furthermore, students will sit at their desks in classrooms and have their classes. The teacher checks the number of students. In case someone is missing, he checks if the child is excused. If not, he sends SMS to parents asking about the absence of the student and the child should be traced.

The situation is relatively simple, because parents and acquaintances are identifiable and know each other personally, so the penetration of strangers is rarely possible. Furthermore, the control of the number of students is easy. School employees are: a director, teachers, cooks and cleaners. With all those employees the work and psychological characteristics can be easily verified. School staff represents a small team. Interpersonal issues can arise rather than an attack on the children by a staff member. The director is fully responsible for employees and internal organizational management. Other entities who cooperate with a small school are municipal offices and suppliers of services and materials to the kitchen. A special door with bell is used for the entrance of third parties. Every such person is then met by a school employee and thus a safe movement of a stranger in the school building is ensured.

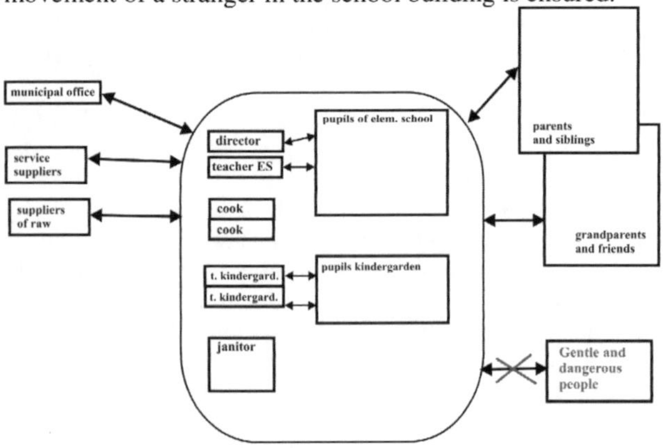

Figure 1. Organizational structure of small school.

The following Figure 2 shows an example of technical security of the small school object. The school is situated in a building with adjacent land for outdoor activities of students. The yellow line indicates perimeter protection, blue line protective shield of building and the red line the entrances for students and the suppliers of goods or services. After students and staff leave the building, arming of the building is set by the janitor. This starts the sheath and the inner protection of the building for the protection of property inside the building.

Figure 2. Technical security of small schools.

As explained above, the current security status of small school is very good due to good regime precautions. For communication with inputs, basic bells without a direct call to the recipient are used. So it is time consuming to handle the arrival of a stranger. Therefore, an internal communicator for the elementary school is proposed. It would have direct key presses for specific employee. Using a video phone has a great advantage in the visual inspection of anyone entering. After verifying a person, we can remotely let her/him inside the building if she/he belongs to the circle of known people. On the other hand, if the person is unknown, we can provide a guide or meet her/him personally. The problem of current video communicators is that they do not offer a great variety of target recipients, optional by simple function keys. Another advantage would be if communication devices would be portable (mobile) and the staff would always have them with them. The second option would be a stable device in every classroom and different places all over school premises.

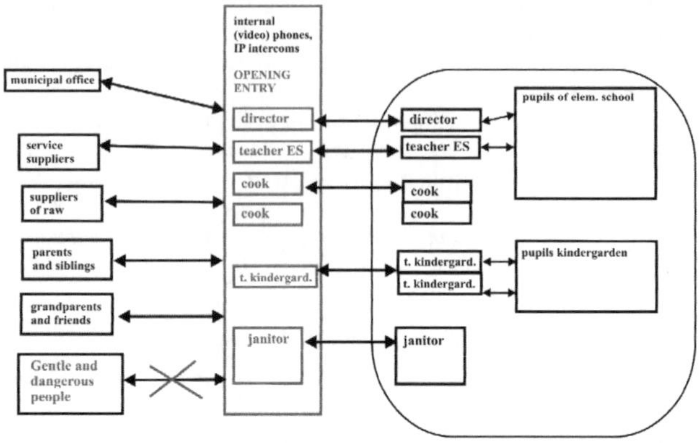

Figure 3. Addressed internal communication to specific individuals using videophones.

For monitoring of students on their way to and from school, a simple and fast tool for sending SMS and e-mail placed on a server (Figure 4) where every teacher would have their client access would be suitable. The advantage of this solution is that the information concerning the exchange of information with those responsible people for the students would have been clearly concentrated in one place, which would allow sharing among teachers, and also parents, after the definition and implementation of access rights. Even these small schools now have their websites to provide information to the public about the activities of teaching, but also for various events.

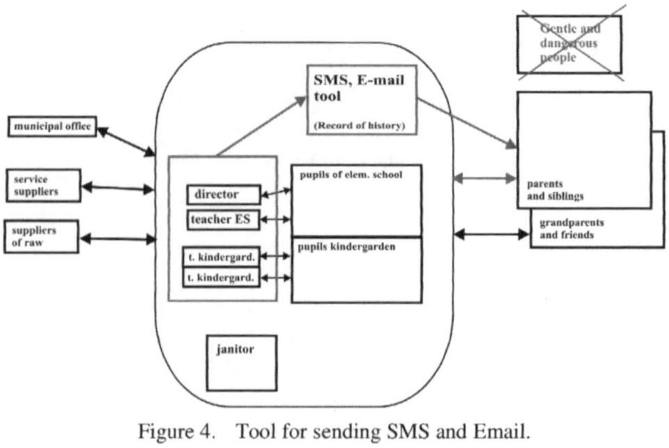

Figure 4. Tool for sending SMS and Email.

I&HAS (Intruder and Hold Up System) is used as a default system in small schools. Only after all students and employees leave the building, it works and guards in full mode. In the event that there would be arming the perimeter (yellow line) or shell (blue line) to protect the building envelope, the daily regime I&HAS is not used. In this case, the system protects the lives of persons who are inside the building.

Another feature that can extend this system is usage of emergency buttons. Mainly, teachers or school staff members who come into contact with the public and students would have them. The lowest level of distress would mean calling the school director, a higher degree would mean calling the emergency squad ARC (alarm receiving centre) and the highest grade then calling the state police. This is shown in Figure 5.

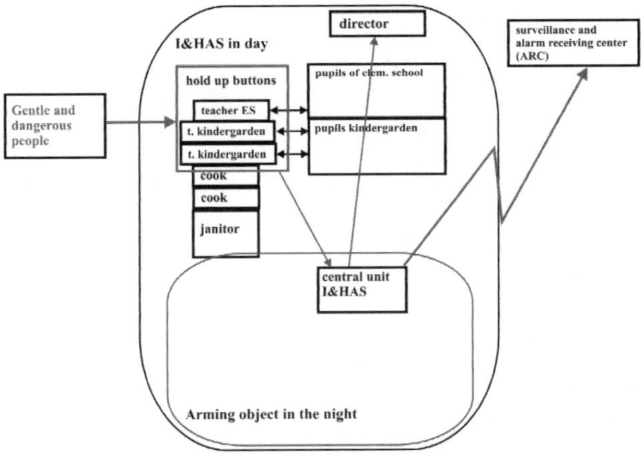

Figure 5. Modernization of technical security small school.

III. LARGE SCHOOL

The situation in the large school in comparison with a small school is completely different, as shown in Figure 6. Teachers do not know personally all the students, neither their families and friends. The arrival procedures of students to school are similar, but a janitor or supervising teacher is not able to memorize hundreds of students and identify among them a new student. The most difficult situation is in the beginning of the year when new parents accompany first-graders to the cloakroom and help them with changing clothes. After the arrival of students to school, the janitor locks the main door. Any stranger that comes to the school building from the outside either rings the bell to the janitor or the school office.

In the case when a student does not come to school, the absence is written to the class register and must be settled within the next day, not immediately. Also, an excuse of the student is realized through the school office and it is not processed until the next day. So, that there is always a delay.

Other school services in areas such as catering, schools have secured such a manner that external boarders have their own entrance to the dining room with a simple access system, where they are using an identification element - the card – that opens the entrance door. Under normal circumstances, these people have no access to the rooms outside of dining area.

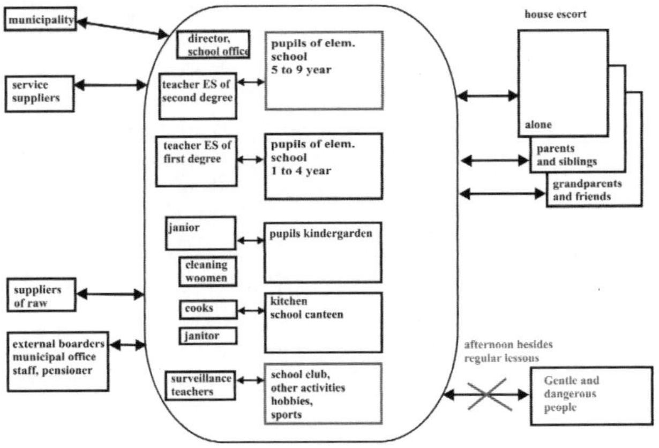

Figure 6. Organization structure of large schoool.

Technical support of school is done mechanically by securing the building envelope on the ground and indoor space with I&HAS, as shown in Figure 7. The electronic security system is only used at the time when all the students and staff leave all objects, without connection to ARC, with only alarm reporting to the director and his assistants.

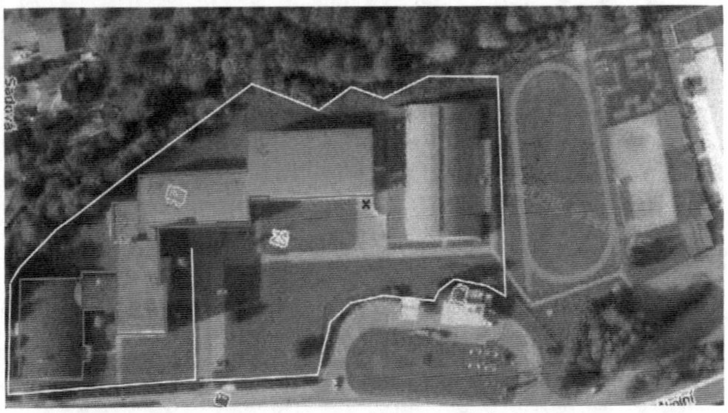

Figure 7. Technical security of large school.

In order to improve an internal communication and to increase the visibility of strangers in all objects, systems should be installed, as is shown in Figure 8. In the areas of movement of people and potentially the possible intrusion of unknown and dangerous people, access points with a capacity of passages appropriate to the specific use must be installed. In addition to the record of the people who passed through the gates, it is appropriate to supplement those places on internal communicators that allows direct connection between the visitor and the specific person. In large schools, the main entrance is directly connected to the director's. For suppliers of raw materials, it should be directly linked to the kitchen. For the access of external diners to the dining room, just an access point using a proximity card and a video recording of individual passages is needed.

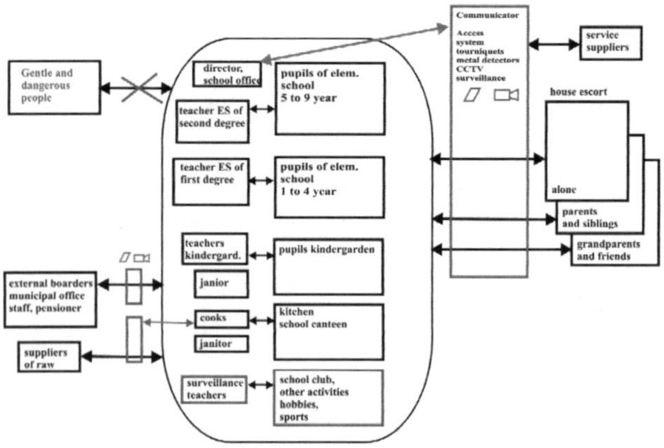

Figure 8. Access system with CCTV surveillance.

For the main entrance, which is used for the arrival and departure of students from school, it is necessary to use such a system approach, which has high passages. If we want to have maximum security, they must be installed turnstiles that cannot be skipped, or otherwise scour and students are identified individually, not in groups. In this case, there would have to be turnstiles installed in parallel in a number of 5-10 pieces to increase the capacity of passages, or the students would have come at a precise time and walk in groups, which is, with the number of more than 400 students, a fairly challenging task. In this case, an access server that accurately records the comings and goings of individual students can be installed and problems with attendance or truancy can be better traced. Another advantage would be that the class teacher would have a day by day overview of students who did not arrive to school and are unexcused.

Figure 9 shows a wider usage of I&HAS. The basis is the use of the system in day and night mode. In night mode, the system would work the same way as it works now, when students and staff are not at schools. In day mode, at least the emergency buttons should be available to all teachers. In case of emergency they would call to the director's office, at a higher level of distress then ARC and, in the case of a critical event then directly to the police.

Other function would be full roofing of the building shell (Figure 7 - blue line) except the access points. Last usable functions are guarding of the perimeter (Figure 7 - yellow line) in day mode. This is in practice very difficult to implement as the regular maintenance necessary to the surrounding vegetation is costly, especially on the banks of the river flowing around.

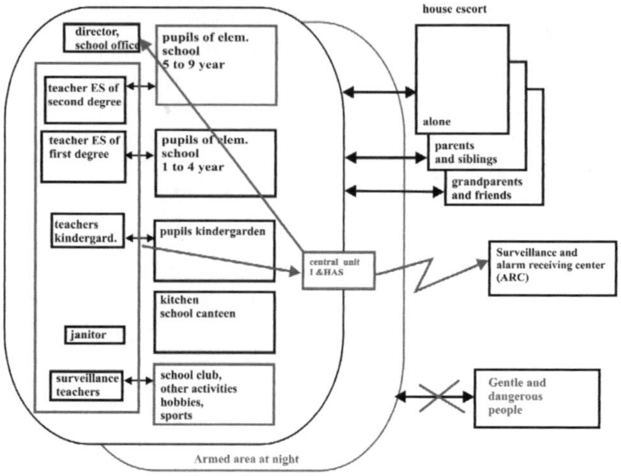

Figure 9. Modernization of technical security of large school.

As it is evident from the previous procedure, security systems I&HAS, ACCESS (Access System) and CCTV (Close Circuit Television) cooperate here. Therefore, the best solution is the realization of an integrated security system. For the realization we can use systems which are commercially available, where it is necessary to respect the extensiveness of the system.

IV. CONCLUSION

Currently, it can be stated that Czech society is very calm. Compared to other European countries or the world, the local crime rate is low. There is as well an important fact, that guns and weapons are not owned in large quantities, as is very common for example in the USA.

The disadvantage of our society is that we are naive and not trained to security risks. The citizen does not know how to take care of their own safety and security in their neighbourhood. They expect everything from government and state security forces.

Currently, great emphasis is placed on prevention against various threats. The goal should be education for active, mature multicultural society, as the current word is globalized.

It is possible to use standard regime precautions and regular technical support against the attacks of criminals. Against the threat of terrorists and unpredictable individuals, costly technical support (X-rays, metal detectors, drug detectors) and demanding regime precautions could be used.

Generally, the particular security level of an elementary school should be tailored to the criminality level of the specific location.

REFERENCES

[1] The Guardian: *Anders Breivik*. [Online]. Available from: https://www.theguardian.com/world/anders-behring-breivik

[2] L. Lukas, M. Adamek, R. Drga, A. Velas, T. Lovecek, J. Reitspis et al., "Security Technologies, Systems and Management I." (in Czech). Zlín: VeRBuM, 2011. ISBN 978-80-87500-05-7.

[3] L. Lukas, M. Adamek, F. Brabec, Z. Dvorak, M. Kelemen, Z. Malanik et al., „Security Technologies, Systems and Management II." (in Czech). Zlín: VeRBuM, 2012. ISBN 978-80-87500-19-4.

[4] L. Lukas, M. Adamek, F. Brabec, R. Drga, M. Hromada, V. Laucky et al., "Security Technologies, Systems and Management III." (in Czech). Zlín: VeRBuM, 2013. ISBN 978-80-87500-35-4.

[5] L. Lukas, R. Drga, M. Hromada, J. Kamenik, S. Lichorobiec, J. Sevcik et al., "Security Technologies, Systems and Management IV." (in Czech). Zlín: VeRBuM, 2014. ISBN 978-80-87500-57-6.

Resistance of Passive Security Elements as A Quantitative Parameter Influencing The Overall Resistance and Resilience of A Critical Infrastructure Element

Tomáš Loveček
Faculty of Security Engineering/Department of Security Research
University of Zilina
Zilina, Slovakia
e-mail: Tomas.Lovecek@fbi.uniza.sk

Anton Šiser
Faculty of Security Engineering/Department of Security Management
University of Zilina
Zilina, Slovakia
e-mail: Anton.Siser@fbi.uniza.sk

David Řehák
Faculty of Safety Engineering/Department of Public Safety
VŠB – Technical University of Ostrava
Ostrava, Czech Republic
e-mail: david.rehak@vsb.cz

Martin Hromada
Faculty of Applied Informatics/Department of Security Engineering
Tomas Bata University in Zlín
Zlín, Czech Republic
e-mail: hromada@fai.utb.cz

***Abstract*— The character of protection and resilience of critical infrastructure is an important parameter, which directly affects the functioning and operational status of modern states. This article specifies the meaning of resistance indicator within the overall resilience of critical infrastructure element. In this paper, resistance indicator expresses the resistance of mechanical barriers and building construction and it is useful in creating a model of quantitative assessment of the level of protection of critical infrastructure elements.**

Keywords- resistance; resiliance; delay time; barriers; indicator.

I. INTRODUCTION

According to the 2007 decree of the European Council, critical infrastructure has to include primarily such physical resources, services, IT equipment and communication networks damage to or destruction of which would severely influence the critical social functions including the supply chain, healthcare, security, safety, economic and social well-being of the population or functioning of the European Union (EU) or its member states [1]. Protection of these elements or objects, deemed strategic for the state, is dealt with through individual solutions in various legal regulations but with different approaches to their protection. Such objects include nuclear plants, objects and areas for storage and manipulation with state secrets or objects housing financial institutions [2].

However, the critical infrastructure can include other elements/objects, the specific protection of which has not yet been covered by laws (such as line and node objects and elements of road, air, water or rail transport, chemical plants, suppliers of various forms of energy, hydraulic engineering objects, food and grocery businesses, industrial companies, mobile network providers, hospitals and other providers of care, etc.); the responsibility for their protection should be on the shoulders of the public sector, as well as the owners and managers of the individual elements of critical infrastructure [3] [5].

The paper structure includes 8 important sections. After the introduction, Section II focuses on assessing the current state, reviewing laws and European standards. Section III defines the relation between the terms "resistance" and "resilience". Section IV defines the options for evaluation of security systems and Section V then expands on the properties of passive barriers. Sections VI and VII are focused on collecting delay time data using a matrix, statistics and operation analysis. The final section summarizes the possible future developments in this area.

II. PROTECTION OF CRITICAL INFRASTRUCTURE – LEGISLATION AND STANDARDS

The existing EU standards approach the physical and object protection of the elements of the critical infrastructure through proclamations and do not specify specific proposals for its solutions. The Green Book document [2] states several possible means (tools) of improving preventive measures, security, preparedness and response in terms of the protection of the critical infrastructure within the EU conditions, but does not specify them further. This approach is similar on the national level, where according to [3] [4] [5], tools which can be used to lower the endangerment of the critical infrastructure can be technical elements for discouragement, detection, verification, signalization and elimination of the violator (mechanical and electronic) as well as the activity of security services (such as an intervention by a security force or the military); there is no further specification however what the resulting level of protection should be.

The analysis of the legal regulations of both the European and national levels of individual member states of the EU shows that the main focus is placed on implementing safety measures against anthropogenic threats (threats sources caused by person acting to damage or destroy an element of critical infrastructure), which are classified as tools increasing the resistance of the elements of critical infrastructure.

III. Resistance and Resiliance

The Resistance of a system can be understood as the ability of the system to resist the effect of negative factors, which do not lead to the change in the ability of the system to function. It is an ability of the system to resist changes that would lead to the system itself visibly changing. The resistance of a system is one of the many factors influencing the system's overall resilience. System resilience can be understood as the ability of a system to secure and maintain its functionality under the effects of negative factors as well as retain the functions of the system if changes to the system do occur.

The resistance of a system can be divided into structural and safety resistance. Structural resistance is the ability of a system to withstand the effects of negative factors based on the construction of its various elements, their placement in the system and the technologies utilized. Security resistance is the ability of a system to withstand the effects of negative factors using a system of security measures (Security Resistance) with minimal impact on the public safety (Safety Resistance).

IV. Evaluation Of Security Resistance Level

The existing tools, which evaluate the necessary or existing security resistance level use one of the two main approaches [6]:

- qualitative approach,
- quantitative approach.

There are several tools around the world using one of the aforementioned approaches [6] [11]:

- tools using the qualitative approach: RiskWatch (USA), CRAMM: CCTA Risk Analysis and Management Method (Great Britain),
- tools using the quantitative approach: SAVI: Systematic Analysis of Vulnerability to Intrusion, ASSESS: Analytic System and Software for Evaluation of Safeguards and Security (Sandia National Laboratories, USA), Sprut (Scientific and Production Enterprise ISTA SYSTEMS JS Co., Russia), SAPE (Korea Institute of Nuclear Non-proliferation and Control, South Korea), SATANO: Security Assessment of Terrorist Attack in a Network of Objects, (University of Žilina, Faculty of Security Engineering Slovakia, TLP spol. s r.o., Czech Republic).

Tools utilizing the qualitative approach are based on the evaluators' expert estimates when it is not possible to confirm the exact security resistance level and it is necessary to rely on the expert skills of the authors of these approaches. In such case it is impossible to verify whether the protection system is understated or overstated from in terms of the proposed protective measures.

Tools based on the quantitative approach allow the exact evaluation of the proposed protective measures based on measurable input and output parameters. In such cases, in contrast to the qualitative approach, the adequacy of a proposed solution can be confirmed. The basic parameter of the quantitative approach to resistance evaluation is the object protection level, which is judged based on structural and security resistance.

Structural resistance is evaluated separately by means of evaluation the individual elements of the object protection system such as the breakthrough resistance of a given object, i.e., the resistance of such object to various ways and methods of unwanted breakage [7]. The safety resistance is evaluated by evaluating the overall object protection level [8]. Figure 1 shows the visual classification of the basic evaluation parameters of critical infrastructure object resistance.

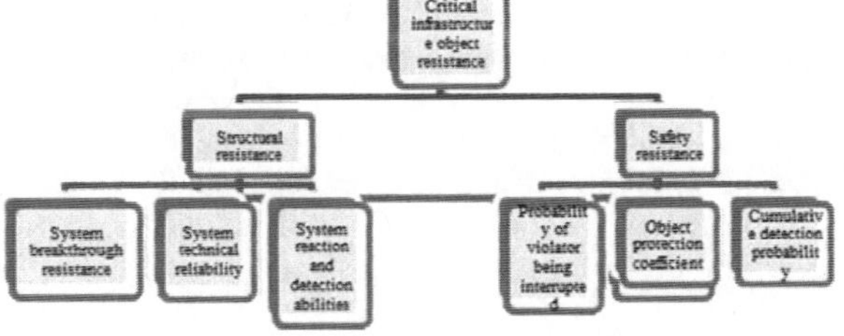

Figure 1. Basic evaluation parameters of a critical infrastructure resistance

The advantage of the quantitative approach is that subjectivity and influence of the evaluator is minimized and such amount and structure of protective measures is used so that the violator is detected and apprehended by a response unit before reaching his goal. Ironically, this approach is least used in practice.

The main reason for not using the quantitative approach is the fact that the evaluation tools do not have access to a basis of probability and temporal parameters of two main factors, which are the vector of approach and the protection system, both of which influence the overall required level of protection.

Other missing bases on parameters of factors influencing the overall protection level include:

- times of breakthrough resistance of passive protection elements, which change based on the type of tools used to break through them,
- the likelihood of being detected by active protection elements, which changes based on the violator's knowledge of the technology utilized (such as the way physical changes are evaluated as a result of a protected area being broken into) [10],
- reaction times of response units, changing based on the strategy of the response,
- reliability of the technical protection elements,
- reliability of the human factor.

The reason for the absence of these bases of input probability and temporal parameters is the fact that there are no methodical approaches specifying a simple way of acquiring them and up until recently, there was no research infrastructure, which would allow the creation of polygons and their subsequent filling with relevant data.

V. Delay Time Of Passive Barriers

Upon closer examination of the selected indicators influencing the resilience and general level of protection of an object, there are several links emerging that lead to the used mechanical security measures and structural barriers. The main task of these systems is to discourage, set back or completely prevent a potential violator reaching the protected object. The common element of all mechanical security systems and structural barriers is their attribute known in professional literature as delay time. This variable expresses the time in which a passive protective elements (such as doors, vaults, locks, etc.) has the ability to resist any tool or applied physical strength and depends on the mechanical properties of the materials used, abilities, skills and knowledge of the violator, effects of weather and other factors. The delay time value is expressed mathematically as:

$$DT = T_2 - T_1 \quad (1)$$

i.e., the subtraction of T_1 – which is the time at which the violator began penetrating the passive protective element from, T_2 – which is the time at which the passive protective element has been penetrated.

The emphasis placed on studying the delay time of passive elements is rendered necessary by the fact that it is the only measurable attribute, which can also be used in the process of qualitative evaluation of the level of protection of an object. With the knowledge of exact values of delay time of each individual obstacle placed on the critical path we can - with a high degree of precision – determine whether a task force or a response team is able to act against a potential threat in time, whether it is caused by natural processes or is anthropogenic in its nature before this threat reaches its ultimate goal, i.e., the object under protection; this can be represented by tangible assets, intangible assets or human resources. In case of a standard violator interested in stealing valuables or some other form of property with high liquidity, the time of this theft path will consist of the studied delay time values of all existing passive security elements, the time of transitioning between them, but also the time necessary for retreat.

If the overall theft path is T_A – the time of action – then this value represents the maximum time within which the response team must perform a successful intervention against the violator. This time for intervention can be expressed as T_R – the reaction time – and will include the time from the first detection, evaluation, verification of the alert message and also the time necessary for transit and apprehension of the suspect through the means of the response unit. By comparing the times T_A and T_R we can then evaluate the level and effectiveness of the physical protection system. It can be concluded that for an effective case of property protection, the following must be true [9]:

$$T_A > T_R \quad (2)$$

i.e., the action time - T_A, which the violator needs to reach the protected object must always be longer than T_R necessary to apprehend the violator. For more precise quantitative evaluation of the level of protection, it is necessary to return to the delay time value of passive protection elements and structural barriers in relation to the tools or means utilized.

VI. Delay Time Data Matrix

As part of the professional and publishing activities of the Faculty of Security Engineering, University of Zilina, a new method of evaluation for the effectiveness and level of physical protection of systems is being developed; this method would be based on exact time values expressed as delay time presented in a matrix using the 'tool versus the passive security element' relation. Part of the matrix proposal is represented in Figure 2.

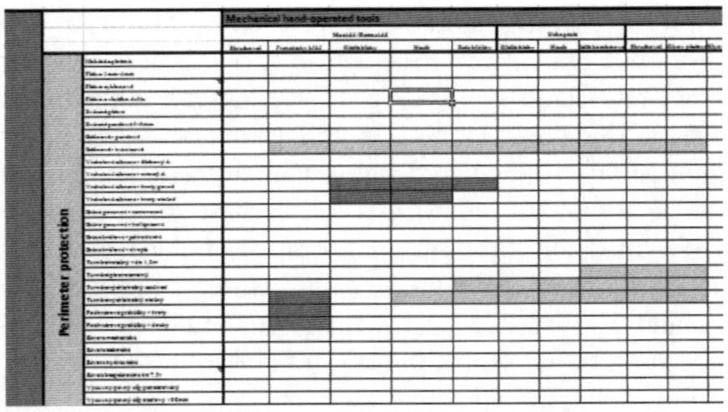

Figure 2. Proposal of delay time data matrix

In compiling and completing this matrix, several issues arise. Before we get to the most important one, which is the great amount of missing data, let us begin with the complications related to the selection of suitable representatives, both on the side of passive security elements and structural barriers, as well as on the side of tools used to breach them.

Since it is impossible to take into account the existence of all available security systems and the tools to break them, it proved necessary to divide them into categories from which the following elements best represent the overall character of their respective categories. This step simplified the entire process significantly and did not, in fact, decrease the quality of the end result. The current state of categories is not final and requires further modifications alongside continuous updates concurrent with the market development.

The first axis of the matrix consists of passive security elements divided into groups based on its location:

- perimeter protection (different types of fences, gates, turnstiles, ramps, etc.),
- outer protection (security doors, locks, windows, grilles, shutters, gates, security window films, etc.),
- object protection (safes, cabinets, boxes, etc.).

This axis also contains a separate group consisting of the most popular structural barriers.

The second axis focuses on tools, means and resources used to overcome passive security elements. They are divided into the following groups:

- physical load (breakage, kicking, etc.),
- improvised tools (ladder, rock, pole, etc.)
- mechanical hand-operated tools (axes, hammers, crowbar, screwdriver, etc.),
- motor tools (electric saw, drills, grinders, petrol saws, special hydraulic tool, etc.),
- thermal tools (liquid nitrogen, hot-air pistols, oxy-acetylene tools, etc.),
- firearms (.22LR, 9x19 Luger pistols, 5.56x45 rifles, etc.),
- explosives,
- means of transport (cars, trucks and special vehicles),
- specialized tools developed specifically to negotiate locks, doors, etc.

After the axes have been finalized, the matrix needs to be completed with specific values using all the currently known data accumulated in technical standards as well as resulting from tests performed. Where technical standards are concerned, it is necessary to point out their norms are not synchronized due to various reasons. There are several technical commissions and approval boards working in the field of development of technical standards focused on passive security elements. Some of these organizations have members who are also producers of such elements, which open up the potential for lobbying as well as directly influencing the normalization process for personal gains. As such, the delay time value may be skewed by testing parameters being set up in a way that is more suitable for certain products or in favour of their manufacturers.

Another problem found in detailed study of European standards is performing the tests in ideal conditions, which do not take into account real effects of the environment as well as the use of a limited amount of tools, as it is with the EN 1627 standard. This standard for penetration tests only involves some types of widely available tools. The use of specialized tools or high-performance thermal tools is not included in this case.

There is a specific issue in cases where the standard does not show resistance of passive security elements, as is the case in glass panes, against the effects of explosives or firearms using a measure of time but rather the maximum pressure or number of repeated impacts that the element is able to successfully resist. In case of explosives, the effects are shown immediately, therefore the only temporal value that can be measured is the time necessary to prepare and set the charge. The effects themselves on the passive security elements can only be assumed in realistic conditions, because all values listed in the standards have been measured in open areas or using pressure tubes and only using TNT-based explosives. The effects of other explosives will likely have to be calculated using the actually known coefficients [12]. Additionally, influence of the environment on the propagation of a pressure wave in real conditions will have to be taken into account. The largest task in the process of filling in the values of delay time is acquiring the missing data, which cannot be found in the norms or were not processed in any other way.

VII. COLLECTING DATA METHODS

A big contributing factor in collecting the data is selecting a method, which will lead to this data in the most effective way possible.

A. Expert opinions and valuation

Currently, the Faculty of Security Engineering of the Zilina University is focused on studying various approaches. One of them is using expert opinions. For this approach to be feasible, a larger number of professionals have to be selected, specialists in specific fields with extensive practical experience; they would then be answering prepared and unambiguous questions. Based on the responses and after their subsequent evaluation, relevant values could be achieved. The disadvantage of this approach is its organizational and managerial complexity as well as a large number of persons involved.

B. Fuzzy logic application

A second approach of gathering usable data for the delay time value is the use of fuzzy logic. Fuzzy logic is a system in mathematical theory, which uses the many-valued logic containing real values from the <0 ; 1> interval and elements of approximate deduction based on the rules of human logic. The term fuzzy logic came to be in 1965 based on scientific activities of a mathematician and scientist of Azerbaijani descent, L.A. Zadeh at the University of California, Berkeley. The first indications of this theory can be found in the early 20th century and it found its use in the subsequent years in various fields such as engineering, logistics, economics and computer sciences. Similarly, it can be used in risk analysis and evaluating the physical protection systems and their level of effectiveness. The advantage of fuzzy logic je its simple application to any values with no regard as to whether they are expressed as time, pressure or otherwise. The entire process takes place in mutually related steps, which are shown in Figure 3.

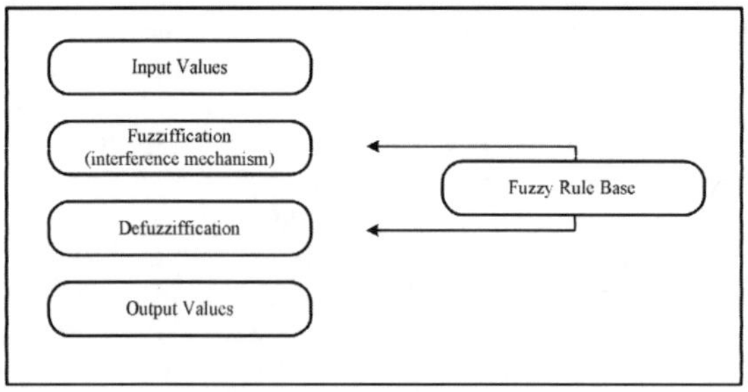

Figure 3. Fuzzy logic application steps

Entry data of random nature are assigned a level of adjacency through the use of evaluation language operators based on the regulation strategy defined by the rule base. Through the process of defuzzification, we create quantifiable results and obtain output values. This entire process seems simple, but each step allows for use of several methods. This puts high demands on the knowledge of the field of general logic, mathematics and statistics.

For a higher evaluation of accuracy of results obtained with the use of fuzzy logic, verification is needed, e.g., in the form of case studies, which would simulate realistic conditions and their influence on a real object. Penetration tests of selected passive security elements with the use of specific tools may serve as another kind of verification tool. The Faculty of Security Engineering at the Zilina University has performed similar tests as part of the PACITA and VEGA projects focused on acquiring delay time values of the most often used fences, safety walls, and other security elements. All missing delay time data could be acquired this way though this seems unrealistic due to high financial cost of the process. Therefore, the verification through selected tests is the biggest asset of the process.

VIII. CONCLUSION

Creating a database that would exactly present the quality of security elements based on their delay time values when being negotiated by a specific set of tools means a huge advancement in the abilities of quantitative evaluation of the quality of physical protection systems. In terms of evaluating resilience, i.e., the ability of an object or system to maintain its functionality against the influence of negative factors, the process of determining delay time values offers possibilities to highlight links to other indicators of resilience, specifically in case of structural resistance. Relations are, however, also clear in case of other indicators such as readiness, security or safety; and as was previously mentioned, it has a considerable importance when determining the reaction time. All acquired data will serve as an important step forward in the field of object security, especially in the application of quantitative evaluation of the physical protection systems.

ACKNOWLEDGMENT

This work was supported by the research project VI20152019049 "RESILIENCE 2015: Dynamic Resilience Evaluation of Interrelated Critical Infrastructure Subsystems", supported by the Ministry of the Interior of the Czech Republic in the years 2015-2019.

REFERENCES

[1] Council Decision 2007/124/EC, Euratom, Council decision of 12 February 2007, establishing for the period 2007 to 2013, as part of General Programme on Security and Safeguarding Liberties, the Specific Programme Prevention, Preparedness and Consequence Management of Terrorism and other Security related risks,

Accessed on 15 Feb. 2016, Available at: http://eur-lex. europa.eu/LexUriServ/LexUriServ.do?uri=OJ:L:2007:058:00 01:0006:EN:PDF.

[2] Green paper on a european programme for critical infrastructure protection.

Accessed on 30 March 2016, Available at: http://eur-lex.europa.eu/legal-content/EN/TXT/PDF/?uri=CELEX:52005DC0576&rid=8

[3] National concept of protection and defense methods of critical infrastructure in the Slovak Republic, Accessed on 18 April

2016, Available at: http://www.economy.gov.sk/narodny-program-pre-ochranu-a-obranu-kritickej-infrastruktury-v-slovenskej-republike--pdf-/136156s

[4] National program of protection and defense of critical infrastructure in the Slovak Republic

Accessed on 18 March 2016, Available at: http://www.rokovania.sk/File.aspx/ViewDocumentHtml/Mater-Dokum-186499?prefixFile=m_

[5] L. Simak, J. Ristvej, (2009). The Present Status of Creating the Security System of the Slovak Republic after Entering the European Union, Journal of Homeland Security and Emergency Management: Vol. 6 : Iss. 1, Article 20, ISSN: 1547-7355. DOI: 10.2202/1547-7355.1443

[6] T. Lovecek, at al. Qualitative approach to evaluation of critical infrastructure security systems. In: European journal of security and safety. ISSN 1338-6131. - Vol. 1, no. 1

[7] M. Hromada et al. The system and method of resilience evaluation of critical infrastructure / Systém a způsob hodnocení odolnosti kritické infrastruktury. Ostrava, 2014. 177 p. ISBN 978-80-7385-140-8.

[8] D. Řehak, L. Hadacek. Uniform methodology for determining the equipment for the production, transmission and distribution of national and european critical infrastructure and physical protection of these devices / Metodika jednotného určování zařízení pro výrobu, přenos a distribuci elektřiny národní a evropskou kritickou infrastrukturou a zajišťování fyzické ochrany těchto zařízení. [certified methodology]. Prague, 2013. 51 p. Č.j.: MV-104188-1/PO-OKR-2013

[9] M. L. Garcia, The design and evaluation of physical protection systems. USA: Elsevier. (2001). ISBN 0-7506 – 7367 – 2.

[10] G. Honey, Intruder alarms. 3rd edition. USA: Elsevier. (2007). ISBN – 13: 978-0-7506-8167-4

[11] T. Lovecek, J. Reitspis, Design and evaluation of physical protection systems / Projektovanie a hodnotenie systémov ochrany objektov. Žilina: EDIS- University of Žilina. (2011). ISBN 978-80-554-0457-8

[12] V. Kavicky, L. Figuli, S. Jangl, Z. Zvakova, Analysis of the field test results of ammonium nitrate: fuel oil explosives as improvised explosive device charges. In: Structures under shock and impact XIII: (13th international conference, SUSI 2014: New Forest, United Kingdom, 3 June 2014 through 5 June 2014). – Southampton, Boston: WITpress, 2014. – ISBN 978-1-84564-796-4. – P. 297-309. – (WIT Transactions on the Built Environment, Vol. 141. – ISSN 1746-4498). Available online with ISBN 978-1-84564-797-1.

Electromagnetic Compatibility and Power-Line Quality

Frantisek Hruska
Tomas Bata University in Zlín
Faculty of Applied Informatics
Zlín, Czech Republic
e-mail: hruska@fai.utb.cz

Milan Navratil
Tomas Bata University in Zlín
Faculty of Applied Informatics
Zlín, Czech Republic
e-mail: navratil@fai.utb.cz

***Abstract* — The quality of power-line nets is very closely related to electromagnetic compatibility, so several quality parameters need to be evaluated to take this into consideration. Quality parameters are generally measured with the help of analyzer devices. There are standard quantities and parameters - as well as special data relating to the metering of dynamic behavior consumption, or harmonic frequency actions, etc. The basic parameters are analyzed in accordance to the different factors and coefficients of active and reactive processes. Electromagnetic Compatibility Evaluation makes use of results gained from the analysis of power-line quality. The electromagnetic compatibility evaluation results are then more accurate and predictive regarding the actual state and its influence over a distribution network from third-party consumption. This ensures that reliable operations to consumers are maintained and that any negative interaction of the supply network is minimalized.**

Keywords-EMC; power-line quality; consumer net parameters; harmonic frequency; dynamic system

I. INTRODUCTION

Electro-Magnetic Compatibility (further only EMC) is a significant system for the preservation of power-line nets and their operations, for immunity and for the economy of states. Its determination and observance is subject to lawful procurement and standards [1] [10]-[14][16].

The term "power-line quality" is involved in several heterogeneous areas of the distribution network structures connected to appliances that demand energy. The user is closely linked to EMC problems, and the solutions require specific access to low-net frequency (50 Hz and harmonics) and to heavy currents and strong magnetic fields [2][3].

The stability of power-line parameters within tolerance limits is given by legal regulations and standards which provide for electric-power distribution in transmission systems. The energy consumer generally influences issues by connecting to a network - according to the kind and type of arrangement back to a distribution network and next - other neighboring consumers [4].

EMC deals with the ability of each electric or electronic device to work, fault-free, in an electromagnetic field (i.e. electromagnetic susceptibility) and do not generate a disturbance field into its surroundings (i.e. electromagnetic interference).

The problem of EMC is ever-more topical as a consequence of the extensive use of low-current electronic devices on one hand, while, on the other hand, there are ever more numbers of power-semiconductor converters that generate interferential disturbances. These disturbances extend through space and in the ambient environment. The rest of the paper is structured as follows. Section II presents basic power-lines parameters. The following sections address interactions in a power line, periodic voltage fluctuation, voltage asymmetry, harmonics and, finally, power line quality measurement.

II. POWER-LINE NET PARAMETERS

The basic parameters of a power-line network include:

- Supply frequency
- Net voltage
- Supply network voltage difference
- Rapid dynamic voltage changes
- Short-term voltage drops
- Power-line voltage asymmetry
- Harmonic and inter-harmonic voltage
- Short-term or long-term breaks in power supply
- Overvoltage between live conductor and earth

The measured values for each parameter have Root Mean Square (RMS) data, peak data, and given-limit data. The limit data relates to the agreements or contracts between partners. Frequency and voltage parameters are system data based on the distribution system and supply demands. The electrical energy power producers assure these parameters at the production point [5][8].

III. INTERACTIONS IN A POWER-LINE

Electromagnetic Interferences (further only EMI) Sources are generally established by the electrical arrangement (e.g. generators, transformers, changers, switches) or electrical-devices (e.g. sources, LV consumers, automation elements, light sources, etc.). An EMI source can also be a system that produces electrostatic charges. Other specific EMI sources include radio and television transmissions, wireless communications and nets [9].

The coupling between EMI elements is realized by cable as a galvanic structure, or in capacitive or inductive structure environments. A general view of EMI is shown in Figure 1.

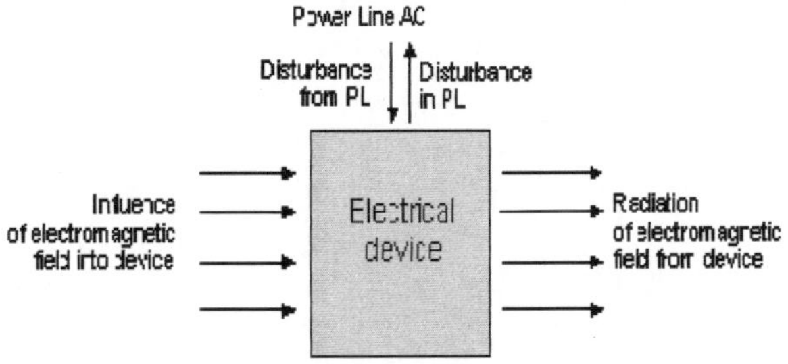

Figure 1. EMI Inter-connection Scheme

The retro-interaction of a connected consumer is always displayed in a real supply network. The current consumption from nets causes voltage change at impedances over time and according to the connection distance. These processes have a stochastic character. A chart showing supply network and consumer connections is shown in Figure 1 [5]-[7].

For example, it is possible to show this in the incidence of disturbing influences from light sources. All sources except light bulbs without regulation react specifically, according to the time behavior of voltage in the network. The process is represented by the following characteristics: the effective value of the voltage; its drift; and changes in the harmonics and inter-harmonics of voltage; etc.

IV. Periodic Voltage Fluctuation

Periodic Voltage Fluctuation over a longer time-frame is called flicker. It is visible - without measurement, in light sources - displayed as optic reception alterations.

Flicker is induced in appliances by switching on some big power-loading, by starting-up some heavy-duty motors, by some form of variable power-loading, or by dynamic behavior at current consumption levels.

Flicker is also negatively expressed as a magnetic arrangement, when it can shut-off switch elements. Its negative incidence and disturbances are also displayed in the information technology arrangements, or by computation techniques, or measurement and actuator techniques.

V. Voltage Asymmetry

Multi-phase systems use an Asymmetry Classification system. Asymmetry means that all three voltage and currents phases have the same amplitude and the phase shift is 120°. This is valid for a system where effective pressure is associated with tension between successive phased tensions. In order to classify asymmetry, there is a need to speculate about the partition of a system into consecutive (d), backward (e) and zero (h) systems.

The main source of asymmetry is the asymmetry of current-loading. There are many appliances that draw heavy power-loads from one or two phases and on the high voltage side (e.g., train traction, electrical ovens). Low-voltage loading is usually single-phase and here, the situation is without guarantee of asymmetry.

VI. Harmonics

The harmonic frequencies for EMC in a power-line network can be observed up to the fiftieth harmonics scale. Inception of harmonics is an arrangement which distorts the sinusoidal wave. Devices - such as frequency converters rectifiers and units that transact phase-angle control of sinus traces induce a very strong rise in harmonics and have a very strong influence that is possible to follow for the third harmonics scale (150 Hz), the fifth (250 Hz) scale, and the seventh harmonic scale (350 Hz) [5][6][8]-[11].

A description of the real process of harmonics scales: x(τ) is possible with the help of the Fourier Function:

$$x(\tau) = a_0 + \sum_{1}^{n} \left[a_k . \cos(k.\overline{w}.\tau) + b_k . \sin(k.\overline{w}.\tau) \right] \quad (1)$$

where,

$$\overline{w} = \frac{2\pi}{T} = 2\pi f , \quad (2)$$

$$a_0 = \int_{-T/2}^{+T/2} x(\tau).d\tau = \frac{1}{2\pi} \int_{-\pi}^{\pi} w.\tau.d(w.\tau) \quad (3)$$

$$a_k = \frac{1}{\pi} \int_{-\pi}^{\pi} x(w.\tau).\cos(k.w.\tau).d(w.\tau) \quad (4)$$

$$b_k = \frac{1}{\pi} \int_{-\pi}^{\pi} x(w.\tau).\sin(k.w.\tau).d(w.\tau) \quad (5)$$

The total harmonic content is assessed in accordance with the Total Harmonic Disturbance (THD) parameter - it is a total distortion of the harmonics or of a total harmonic factor. Its formula is given by:

$$THD_1 = \frac{\sqrt{\sum_{2}^{n} I_k^2}}{I_1} \quad (6)$$

Voltage spikes and related disturbances are negative and have backward effects on the power-line network from the harmonics. Different processes are the source of harmonics and at the connection point of devices. The harmonic currents flow from a nonlinear arrangement to the networks and change the impedance of the network.

VII. POWER-LINE QUALITY MEASUREMENT

A demo-measurement was performed using a FLUKE 437 device [12].

The wiring of the device for a three-phase system is shown in Figure 2. It is possible to parameterize this to various kinds of networks (e.g.TN S, TN C).

Measurement is performed using an embedded micro-computer system, programmed for the automatic metering of concrete functions.

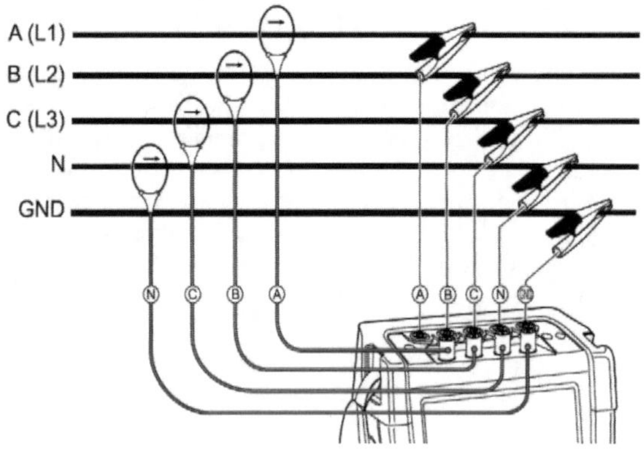

Figure 2. Scheme of connection on a three-phase network

The basic metering is transformed using algorithms for the parameters mentioned below:

- The measurement time-window (Tw) is 10/12 cycles in accord with the frequency - (i.e. 50/60 Hz), IEC 61000-4-30
- It uses 5 samples per 10 cycles
- The sampling of metering using a Fluke 437 device is 100 kHz (10 mm), and is derived from the frequency of sinusoids.
- The accuracy of measurements is for voltage of 0.1% from V_{nom} for a near entrance; for a current of 0.5% out of the read values
- The resolution is 0.01V; for flows within an i430flex TF cable is 1x 1A; for 10x greater sensitivity, it is 0.1A
- A 16-bit ADC on 8 channels is employed
- The frequency accuracy and resolution is 90.001 cps
- Effective Voltage: $Urms = \sqrt{\frac{1}{T_w}\sum_{n=0}^{T_w} u_n^2}$

  (7)
- Effective Current: $$Irms = \sqrt{\frac{1}{T_w}\sum_{n=0}^{T_w} i_n^2} \qquad (8)$$
- Effective Power (W):

$$P_x = \frac{1}{N}\sum_{n=K}^{K+N} u_x(n).i_x(n) \qquad (9)$$

- Basic Effective Power of Phases (W) :

$$P_{1X} = U_{1x}.I_{1x}.\cos(\varphi u_{1x} - \varphi i_{1x}) \qquad (10)$$

- Apparent Power (S):

$$S_X = U_x.I_x, \qquad (11)$$

- Reactive Power (only basic) (Q):

$$Q_{1X} = U_{1x}.I_{1x}.\sin(\varphi u_{1x} - \varphi i_{1x}) \qquad (12).$$

A. Examples of Measurements on Devices

The model measurements were performed for selected appliances – namely, for a small Voltcraft 2256, 60VA power supply; for an IR radiator like a typical ohmic appliance, and for an ETATOOL 930W impacted drilling machine as an inductance appliance.

B. Measurement Results

The results of sample measurements are presented in Figure 3, here below. As a demonstration, it shows metering of U – voltage; I – current; and f – frequency, for an IR radiator:

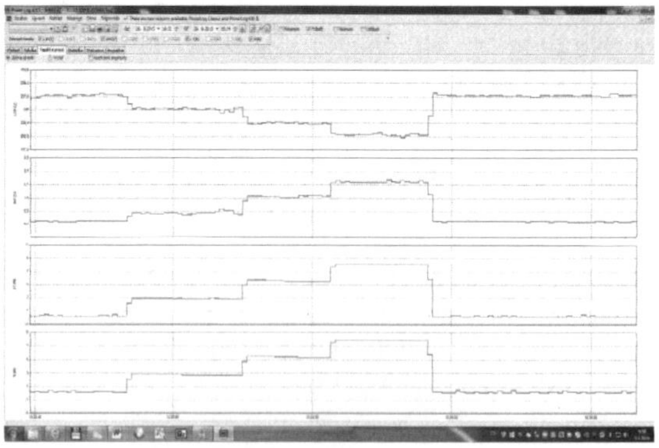

Figure 3. Graphs of MEAS42 Measurements

Another demonstration shown in Figure 4, is the measurement falls and over-swings for a drilling machine:

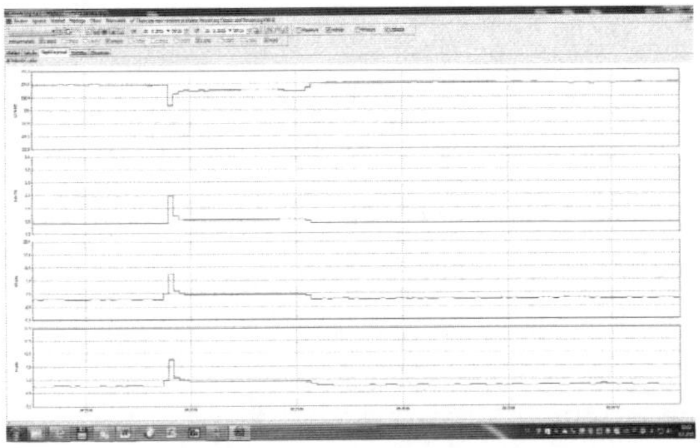

Figure 4. Graphs of MEAS44 Measurements

The measurement of harmonics is depicted in Figure 5 and Figure 6 for voltage, and subsequently - for the THD coefficient:

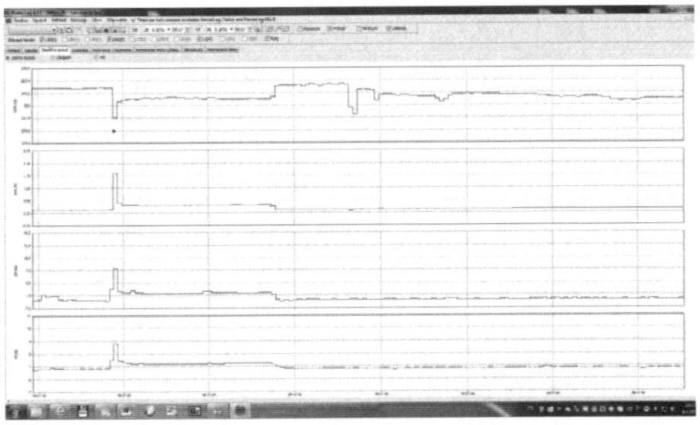

Figure 5. Liner Graphs of MEAS79 Measurements

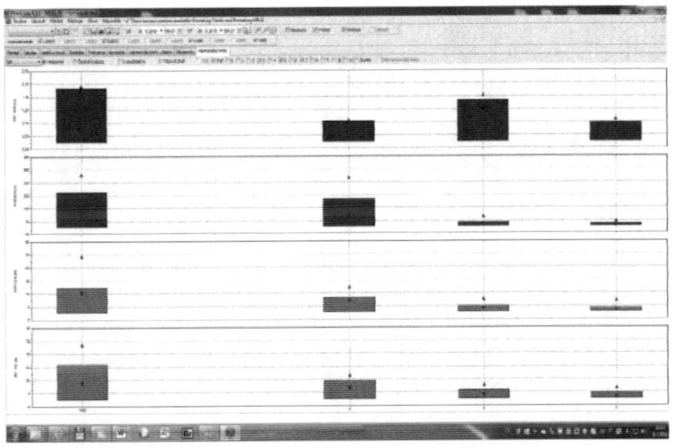

Figure 6. Column Graphs of MEAS79 Measurements

The measurement of asymmetry and impacts on voltage and current is shown in Figure 7:

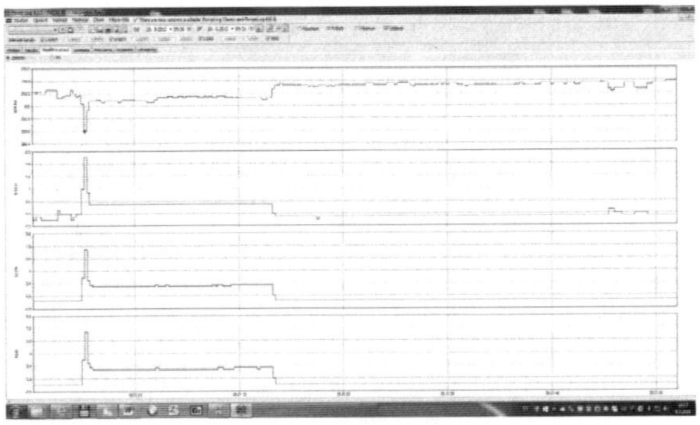

Figure 7. Graphs of MEAS85 Measurements

VIII. CONCLUSION

This contribution shows the significance and impacts of connections with power-line quality. It presents all the problems that it solves – i.e. common main problems like for instance – the generation of harmonics, and the impacts of fast changes – i.e. "flicker" and "voltage asymmetry". It also goes on to show examples of the measurement of power-line quality by the help of modern devices - for three sample appliances. At the same time, there is an accent on the structure relating to electromagnetic compatibility questions.

REFERENCES

[1] R. C. Dugan, Mark McGranaghan, Surya Santoso, H. Wayne Beaty, Electrical Power Systems Quality. McGraw-Hill, 2003.

[2] A. Baggini, Handbook of Power Quality. Wiley, 2008

[3] A. Kusko, T. Marc, Power Quality in Electrical Systems. McGraw Hill, 2007.

[4] Rules of operation of distribution systems. Quality of voltage in distribution system, ways of its detection and evaluation. (Pravidla provozování distribučních soustav. Kvalita napětí v distribuční soustavě, způsoby jejího zjišťování a hodnocení.). Prague – ERU, 2011. PPDS.

[5] A. Dán, P.Santarius, Quality of supplied energy in nets of low voltage (Kvalita dodávané energie v sítích nízkého napětí). Ostrava – VSB-TU a Hungarian Copper Promotion Centre.

[6] P.Mindl, Problems of EMC in operation of electric arrangement and instruments of low voltage (Problémy EMC v provozu elektrických zařízení a přístrojů nízkého napětí). Prag – CVUT, 2001

[7] P. Marek, Measurement and analyse of quality of power-line nets. (Měření a analýza kvality napájecí sítě). BRNO-VUT, 2013

[8] W. Langguth, Quality of electric energy – guide. Grounding and EMC. Principles of electromagnetic compatibility (EMC) (Kvalita elektrické energie – Průvodce. Uzemnění a EMC. Základy elektromagnetické kompatibility (EMC)). Leuven-Hungarian Copper Promotion Centre. Translate Ostrava-VSB-TU, 2006

[9] J. Driesen, T. CraenenBroeck, Quality of electric power – guide. Interference voltage. Introduction to the asymmetrically (Kvalita elektrické energie – Průvodce. Rušivé napětí. Úvod do nesymetrie). Leuven-Hungarian Copper Promotion Centre . Překlad Ostrava-VŠB-TU, 2005

[10] V. Hašpl, Higher harmonics and its incidence on power-line net (Vyšší harmonické a jejich působení na síť). Elektro 6/2008, pp. 32-33

[11] ČSN IEC 1000-2-1 (33 3431) Electromagnetic compatibility (EMC). Part of 2: Environment. Chaptert of 1: Description of environment - electromagnetic environment of low - frequency conducted by disturbance and signals in public distribution power-line nets. (Elektromagnetická kompatibilita (EMC). Část 2: Prostředí. Díl 1: Popis prostředí - elektromagnetické prostředí pro nízkofrekvenční vedené rušení a signály ve veřejných rozvodných sítích.). Czech Office for standards, metrology and Testing, Prague, 1993

[12] ČSN IEC 1000-2-2 (33 3431) Electromagnetic compatibility (EMC). Part 2: Environment. Chapter 2: Compatibility levels of low-frequency disturbing conducted by disturbance and signals in public distribution power-line nets. (Elektromagnetická kompatibilita (EMC). Část 2: Prostředí. Díl 2: Kompatibilní úrovně pro nízkofrekvenční rušení šířené vedením a signály v rozvodných sítích nízkého napětí). Czech Office for standards, metrology and Testing, Prag, 1995.

[13] ČSN EN 61000-2-4 (33 3432) Electromagnetic compatibility (EMC). Part of 2: Environment. Chapter of 4: Compatibity levels of low-frequency disturbing conducted into industrial fabrics. (Elektromagnetická kompatibilita (EMC) - Část 2: Prostředí - Oddíl 4: Kompatibilní úrovně pro nízkofrekvenční rušení šířené vedením v průmyslových závodech). Czech Office for standards, metrology and Testing, Prag, 2003.

[14] ČSN EN 61000-4-11:1996(33 3432) Electromagnetic compatibility (EMC). Part of 4: Environment. Chapter of 11: .Short - period of drops of voltage, short interrupts and slow voltage change - examination immunity. (Elektromagnetická kompatibilita (EMC) - Část 4: Zkušební a měřicí techniky - Oddíl 11: Krátkodobé poklesy napětí, krátká přerušení a pomalé změny napětí - Zkoušky odolnosti.). Czech Office for standards, metrology and Testing, Prag, 2005.

[15] Fluke Corporation. Three - phase analyzer of quality of electric energy (Třífázový analyzátor kvality elektrické energie.) Fluke 437-II. User guide. 2012.

[16] IEEE Standard 519 Recommended Practices and Requirements for Harmonic Control in Electrical Power Systems section 10.5 Flicker

Interception Methods and GSM

Michal Sustek, Miroslav Marcanik, Milan Oplustil, Pavel Tomasek, Zdenek Urednicek
Faculty of Applied Informatics
Tomas Bata University in Zlin
Zlin, Czech Republic
Email: {sustek, marcanik, moplustil, tomasek, urednicek}@fai.utb.cz

***Abstract*— Nowadays, eavesdropping is a real problem, whether it is about the interception of personal or corporate information. Current technologies enable us to use a wide variety of listening devices and methods. It may not be just a recording on a dictaphone, but also the use of vibration. The issue of eavesdropping is very popular today and many people and organizations work on solutions to prevent it. The work of these companies is mostly successful, but a problem still remains related to GSM (Groupe Special Mobile) interception. This contribution provides an insight into the principles of defense against the complex problem of eavesdropping. In any case, people have to be careful and consider what kind of information is communicated using cell phones and other technologies and what are the possibilities of their interception.**

Keywords-eavesdropping; interception; GSM; 5G; wire-tracking.

I. INTRODUCTION

Today, the boom of information and communication technologies contributes to an increasingly connected society. Modern technology surrounds us and it is, therefore, not surprising that almost every one of us owns a cellular phone. We all use it to communicate information. GSM phones are often used to communicate corporate information of critical importance. With the development of technology on transmission, we can see the development options of technologies on sound capturing and interpreting this information back [1]. It leads to a risk of using interception devices. Therefore, it is necessary to know what principles and technologies are used in the implementation of the interception, but also how to prevent it [2]. Eavesdropping can affect everybody in the world.

Countermeasures exist for most eavesdropping methods. However, GSM interception presents a specific issue It is difficult to identify an offender performing the passive form of eavesdropping. It forms part of the problem which must be dealt in the future.

Defense-technical inspection is the primary method [4] used to detect interception devices in a room or on other devices. This method is nondestructive for the device itself. Inspection is performed on suspicion of eavesdropping occurrence. An authorized person performs an initial analysis of space aimed at identifying possible risks and the type of interception device. In an organization, the inspection can be made visible, so that the employees of the company knew, but it can also be done discreetly, outside office hours, in which case the employees are unaware. This systematic inspection is supported by technical facilities [4], both for the detection of interception and subsequent security premises and equipment.

In some areas, it is mandatory to have devices for protecting against interception. Nowadays, with compelling interception devices, it is possible to see several technologies used in wiretaps. These technologies include a contact or non-contact scanning of information from windows, or the use of GSM phones, radio interception, direct recording on a recording unit, as well as passive and active GSM interception.

We should pay attention to protect relevant information, whether by technical means and/or by using common sense.

This contribution presents the basic outline of eavesdropping. It presents some methods of interception and countermeasure. That contains technical, regime measures and identification method including the defense-technical inspection.

Section 1 presents the GSM technology in general including mobile stations, the next generation 5G networks, and their architecture. Section 2 focuses on interception methods and protection methods against interception. The primary part of defense against eavesdropping is a defense-technical inspection. This inspection contains physical control, radio analysis, detection of nonlinearity and other measurements. It is used in protection of meeting places. The main goal is an identification of interception devices and defense against them. Devices against which one must protect are contact and contactless devices, unauthorized use of GSM phones, radio interception and record unit. GSM interception is divided into active and passive form. The active form is reliable, but it is easier to identify. On the other hand, the passive version of GSM interception is almost invisible, but it is not as reliable and it is useless in case of a moving device. The resources, which are used for defense, are GSM jammers, security wallpaper, radio analyzers and more.

II. GSM TECHNOLOGY

GSM technology is based on ETSI (European Telecommunications Standards Institute) standards [8]. The primary document is standard "GSM - Phase first". In the development of this technology, these were several GSM phases until today's generation was created (Long Term Evolution, hereinafter, the LTE [8]) and for future generations 5G. The GSM network consists of mobile stations, the base station subsystem, a network and switching subsystem and operational subsystems. Subsequently, we will define several types of GSM services, such as telematics services, advanced services, additional services, the Subscriber Identity Module (SIM) card and phone.

GSM coverage area is divided into bundles. Each bundle consists of 7 cells. Inside each cell, there is a base station assigned to a particular group of channels and provides communication with mobile subscribers. In the event when the area of all the cells is equal to at least the interference area, it is possible to use the same channel group in all cells [6].

To obtain better properties of the system it is possible to use sectorization. The entire GSM area is divided into a smaller number of cells. This leads to the need to increase the number of base stations because the cells are smaller, but the covered area has the same size.

The number of required channels is not changing but the number of base stations growths from 7 to 21. Their number can be reduced again to 7 by placing three separate directional antennas at the intersection of three neighboring cells.

A. Mobile station

The GSM user communicates using mobile stations, which means not only the receiver/transmitter (cell phone), but also a SIM module. The SIM card is used as unique identifier for user within the network.

Source coding performs of the encoder source, which digitizes the analog signal and the digital side eliminates redundant data contained in the audio. The main goal of this step is to reduce the data flow to a minimum since each channel has its limitations. For removing these frequencies, a parametric method is used. The signal is divided into 20 msec segments. Then it is used to each segment LPC (Linear Predictive Coding) filter and LRP (Long-Range fading Prediction) to encryption.The resulting signal is composed of 188 bits, which carry information about calling and 72 bits, which carry information about filters. These two parts make up the frame of length 260 bits. There are 50 of these frames in one second, therefore, the bit rate is 13kbps.

To minimize unwanted signals, such as noise, interference, and scattering, channel coding is used, which adds additional bits to the colloquial frame which are used in the decoder to remove and reduce errors. In essence, it is a block of convolution codes that divide the 260-bit blocks colloquial framework into 3 classes (50 major, 132 minor and 78 less important). Based on these codes, it is possible to nearly double the signal and the speed.

The signal is magnified with redundant bits which are added to information binary string. It leads to increasing error detection and correction capabilities. A block, the size of which is 456 bits, is divided into 8 groups of size 57 bits each. These groups are interleaved with the last four groups of the previous block and with the first four groups of the following block.

B. 5G Architecture

One of the main ideas of designing 5G networks [6] is a separation of internal and external users into two segments. This approach aims to avoid losses resulting from signal passing through the walls, or at least minimize it. It will be realized with a complex antenna system and massive Multiple Input/Multiple Output (MIMO) technology, which will be deploying large antenna arrays with tens or hundreds of antenna segments. While the most common MIMO technologies serve 2 to 4 antennas, the goal of massive MIMO systems is to increase user options by using antenna arrays. Outdoor base stations will be equipped with an extensive antenna array of antenna elements around the cells. These cells will be connected by optical fibers with base stations. Outdoor users are equipped with a limited number of antenna elements, but they can work with others in an extensive virtual network. An antenna array will be installed outside buildings and will communicate with external base stations.

One can use a mobile architecture where internal users need to communicate only with the internal access points with antenna arrays; then, one can use technologies for short-range communication (Wi-Fi [6], the ultra-wide band [6], mm-wave communications [6]).

5G network architecture should also contain heterogeneous macrocells, microcells, small cells, and transmitters. To ensure adequate coverage for users who move too quickly, it will also work with mobile femtocells, which combine the concept of mobile relays and femtocells [6]. In Figure 1, one can see the planned architecture for 5G networks.

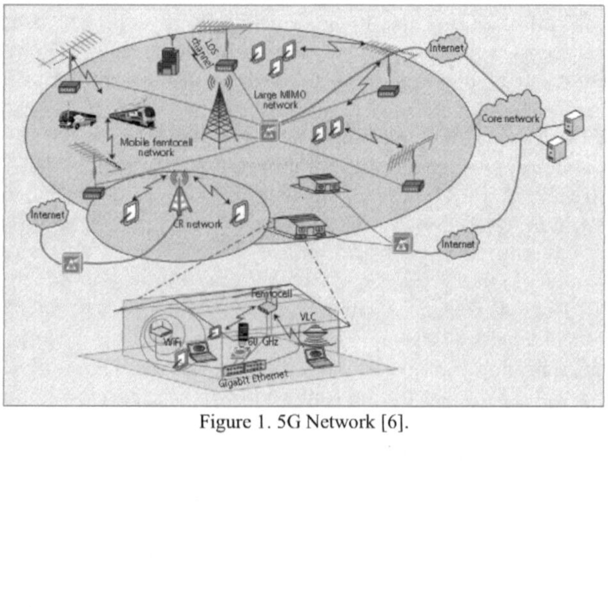

Figure 1. 5G Network [6].

C. Encryption for data protection

Current encryption is used to protect against unwanted eavesdropping. The GSM network calculates the secret key, which length is 64 bits, after verifying the mobile phone in the mobile station. A key figure of TDMA (Time Division Multiple Access) frame lengths of 22 bits is input to the cipher algorithm A5 [6]. The A5 algorithm generates a pseudo-random sequence which, along with 114-bit bursts used XOR function. It leads to data encryption. The A5 algorithm is relatively fast and it establishes a 228-bit sequence during TDMA frame.

After encryption, the modulation signal has a carrier wave using GMSK (Gaussian Minimum Shift Keying) modulation. GMSK is two-state modulation which is based on the frequency keying stroke.

III. INTERCEPTION

Interception of mobile phones and monitoring the flow of information are current topics of great interest. With the available technologies, it is possible to eavesdrop on almost any form of communication. On the other hand, however, it remains the issue of cryptography and steganography [1]. Wiretapping is usually conducted by a third party (i.e., not the operator, but he can know about eavesdropping and allow it). Wiretapping is divided into active and passive forms. The operator knows about the active form and sees it in the system, however, a passive form is not known to the operator. The passive form is based on the capture of radio signals and then decoding them.

The passive way has very significant limits in terms of reach and effectiveness, because, when the phone is in motion, these interceptions have problems with receiving the signal. For this type of interception, a computer equipped with a GSM antenna, receiver, and special software is used. This software enables the device to identify all phones within range and can focus on one or multiple phones. Then, it can record, decode and eavesdrop the cell phones (in the case of short message service and multimedia messaging service). The interception of conversation is not possible to find or identify. Consequently, it is necessary to focus on defense rather than detection.

A. Defense-technical inspection

Defense-technical inspection is the basic form for detecting interception devices in a room and also it is not destructive to the device. The inspection is conducted on the grounds of suspicion. An authorized person performs an initial analysis of the room aimed at identifying possible risks of the type of interception, determination of inspection techniques and inspection frequency. As with all steps, it is necessary to select the date, time, method and inspection techniques themselves. The inspection can be made visible, so that the employees of the company knew, but also discreetly outside office hours, by which employees are not aware [4].

Most companies that provide the inspection to be carried out require the constant presence of a responsible person from the part of the applicant, which is to prevent further irregularities and accusations that might occur. Once an interception is found in an area, there are basically three options to deal with it. These options are its liquidation, inform the police or use it for disinformation the offender. The inspection consists of four steps:

- Physical control
- Radio Analysis
- Detection of nonlinearity
- Other measurements

1) Physical control

In the first step of defense-technical inspection, all the equipment and other resources, which could contain the interception, will be disassembled. Examples include outlet detectors, telephones, lights, switches, and other similar devices.

2) Radio Analysis

The second step performs spectral analysis [3] in the room. It scans all frequencies that occur at that place and subsequently verifies if each frequency has a reason for its existence. The principle of this method is to detect the presence of radio equipment which is designed for the interception. Figure 2 shows the radio analysis output. Each frequency indicates radio signals of potential interception hardware.

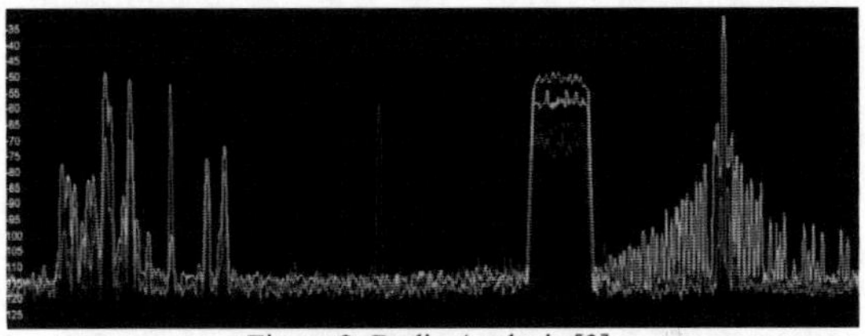

Figure 2. Radio Analysis [3].

3) Detection of nonlinearity

After identifying the presence of a radio detector, the inspection checks nonlinearities. The method is based on the fact that each intercepted device includes semiconductor components. It allows the discovery of semiconductors in the transmitted electromagnetic field. This detection method is used for walls, construction equipment etc.

4) Other measurements

The last step is to check the other elements, such as telephone lines, checking in infra-specter, control of leadership in the over-voice band.

Due to a large amount of work, it is an approximate speed of inspection 10 m^2 per hour for a couple of technicians. After the inspection is completed, the authorized person of the contracting authority receives a verbal report follows by a written report on the results of the inspection and the list of used methods. Of course, as in all sectors of security, the best protection is a combination of technical means to human disturbance, because the technology is not always reliable and can be a failure [4].

B. *Technique for protection meeting places*

With the increasing diversity of eavesdropping devices also grows a diversity of protection devices against the interception. These safeguards are mandatory in some areas. Today, after the expansion of eavesdropping devices it is possible to see several technologies that are used for wiretapping (contact or contactless sensing information from windows, the use of GSM phones, the radio interception, direct recording on the recording unit).

1) Protection against contact and contactless information gain from windows or walls of the building

The interception is performed on the basis of vibration of the glass panel or the wall of a building. The method/devices used to protect these surfaces are white noise generators [4]. The white noise vibrates on the window panels and in the walls. Optionally, one can add speakers, from which the noise is able to superimpose a recording of the voice recorder. Due to the frequency range of the white noise, it is clear that it passes all frequencies of human speech. The white noise is a mechanical wave. It leads to interference with the signal and then it cannot be deleted with the available technology. It protects reliably before interception using stethoscopic and laser microphones. Despite all the advantages it also has one major disadvantage, especially for the comfort of the people on negotiations. The frequencies are in the audible spectrum and can thus interfere with the comfort of each person in the room [4].

2) Protection for unauthorized use of GSM phones

Under this type of protection, it is possible to use two devices (Identification GSM operation and the GSM jammer). The identification of the GSM operation uses sensitive devices that detect signals in the GSM band, and inform both acoustically and visually about the unauthorized transmissions. The disadvantage is the necessity to set it to a sensitivity to avoid false alarms announcement [4].

The second option is a GSM jammer, which operates in the GSM phones. GSM jammers jam the receiver, which subsequently cannot log into the network. There are many types of jammers, which vary in reliability. However, the problem remains that, in fact, it is illegal to interfere with the operators signal [4].

3) Protection against radio interception

The most common type of interception is radio interception [10]. It has good possibilities for capturing and sending the signal. However, as in all other cases, these are ways to prevent it. For protection, they are used in radio analyzer, jammer, safety foil, and wallpapers.

Radio analyzer saves all radio frequencies, which are active in the area. After subsequent scanning of the radio spectrum, the results can be compared with the new scan and the error detected. This deviation indicates a new radio receiver/transmitter that can be tapped in space and display the field strength (relative distance of the transmitter). These devices have a difference in bandwidth with which they are able to operate and control the speed. Like with all other devices, there are also certain disadvantages. In particular, these disadvantages include the relatively high demands on the operation and the high coverage area of different radio signals. Only in London, the scan of a single site can detect 600 active frequencies. That is the reason why is it necessary to carefully adjust the sensitivity of these because not of all the disturbing frequencies comes from listening devices [4].

The second possibility is a jammer; whose function is very similar to GSM jammers. The main advantage is the fact that they produce no false signals. But, as with the GSM version, there is questionable legality and yet unknown effects on human health by prolonged exposure. Some types of jammers are nowadays used as protection against remotely charge attacks that have initiated igniter radio signal.

The third measure, which operates on the principle of Faraday's cage (inhibits the passage of radio signals from the protected area) are security stickers, wallpapers, and foils. Its application is technically very demanding. Wallpaper itself contains a copper layer. It is necessary to completely cover each element of the room (doors, windows, line filters for 230 V line). The use of a protective element is rather rare due to the complexity [4].

4) Protection from obtaining information direct entry to the recording unit

In the context of digitization, it is no longer possible to use some methods for protecting before recording the acoustic signal to a recording device, which was used earlier. Today's equipment for direct recording does not radiate. It is necessary to choose methods that have an effect on the quality of recorded sound. The solution is the noise generator with speakers. The noise binds to the signal and degrades it. Nowadays, there are no technical possibilities to effectively eliminate the noise from the recording [4].

C. *Techniques to protect communications media*

The advent and subsequent development of GSM technology have created a new risk, which involves interception of mobile phones and information communication in this way. It is important to recognize that the GSM network protects information with encryption only on the way to a GSM cell and back to the phone, the rest is unprotected.

Currently, there is a wide variety of devices that are able to decrypt the signal in real time and perform it in this way of the interception. These elements can be active or passive.

1) Active

Active devices are essentially fake GSM cells. The device convinces its target that the device is the best cell, which should be used with the cell phone. The signal is duplicated. One copy is forwarded to a GSM network and the second copy is decrypted. These systems are active and they are detectable on the side of the operator. By default, this method is used in urban residential areas, approximately 500 meters from their target. Generally, these methods are more reliable than passive methods of eavesdropping [4].

2) Passive

The capturing signal takes place on the side of the cell phone. The attacker must be in urban areas about the same distance. The main advantage of this method is "invisibility". On the other hand, if the target moves, the interception is essentially impossible because the device is not able to quickly re-tune the frequency in order to capture the tapped signal.

The best method of defense of communications equipment is their encryption. Therefore, many cell phone manufacturers have started to produce versions of their phones, which are equipped with encryption devices. The basis is the principle on which the information is digitized, encrypted and in such form goes with the device. On the receiver side, one must also use an encrypted phone for which it is possible to decrypt the information [4].

3) GSM interception

As in the case of radio interception, it is a small device that senses ambient sounds, but, unlike classical radio interception, it does not intercept the broadcast signal locally on discrete frequency, but it is transmitted using the same principle as talking on a cell phone. Actually, the interception is logged into base transceiver station as well as cell phone and from a signal transmitted. Nowadays, this type of interception is widespread for several reasons. First, it has a virtually unlimited range; the attacker can be anywhere there is a phone signal coverage. Second, the main supply is operating almost unlimited. The last point is called costs. The costs are minimal (advantageous monthly fee) and it is almost impossible to capture the conventional methods for detecting interception (Radio frequency detectors, radio spectrum analyzers). The findings of this type of the interception device are problematic for several reasons. First, the signal is not transmitted on a usual frequency and analog modulation, but it uses GSM network infrastructure itself with FDMA/TDMA (Frequency Division Multiple Access/ Time Division Multiple Access). The entire eavesdropping is not conducted continuously, but it is invoked to "request" call on the device. In principle, the device is logged into the network. The device is hidden, if it does not launch an active interception, it looks like others cell phones.

Although finding of these devices is difficult it is not impossible. One can use a spectrum analyzer and a strict adherence to procedures. If one wanted to avoid installation of interception device, one must have 24-hour control over all daily routines in the room. This approach is costly and unsustainable.

IV. CONCLUSION AND FUTURE WORK

Nowadays, the interception issue affects all people, even if they do not realize it. Due to the technical progress of society, there are many means of communicating information, but also a lot of resources for their capture.

This technology creates a risk of misuse of critical information. Currently, there is a large amount of communication through people's cell phones. Cell phones are often used to communicate critical corporate information. Fortunately, despite the technical capabilities of the attacker, there are countless ways to resist interception.

Defense-technical inspection is the basic form for detection of interception devices in a room and that is also non-destructive to the device. The inspection is conducted on the grounds of suspicion. An authorized person performs an initial analysis of the room aimed at identifying possible risks of the type of interception, determination of inspection techniques and inspection frequency. As with all steps, it is necessary to select the date, time, method and inspection techniques themselves. The inspection can be made visible, so that the employees of the company knew, but also discreetly outside office hours, by which employees are not aware.

For technical resources, in addition to physical control, spectral analysis is also performed. This is a scan of all frequencies and their subsequent comparison with a reference measurement. Based on this comparison, it is possible to identify suspect signals that could potentially come from interception devices. Another method that is used is the control of nonlinearities. The method is based on the fact that each previously produced interception includes semiconductor components. The nonlinearities detection method can detect the presence of semiconductors in a sensing area because the electromagnetic field in the area is affected by these semiconductors. The authorized person must not forget to check the other elements, such as telephone lines, checking in infra specter, control of the over-voice band.

Defense against GSM interception is difficult because its identification is not easy. Its signal is not broadcasted on a frequency and analog modulation but uses GSM network infrastructure itself with FDMA/TDMA access. The entire interception is not carried out continuously, but it is invoked to "request" call on the device. In principle, the device is logged into the network. The device is hidden, if it does not launch an active interception, it looks like others cell phones.

The next steps of research will lead to a deeper understanding of wiretaps in terms of features and options for defense against them. Following this understanding will be appropriate to conduct a testing and measuring for available wiretaps. On the other hand, the most interesting methods of interception, the GSM interception is probably the best option for a creation of any external encryption applications.

ACKNOWLEDGMENT

This work was supported by Internal Grant Agency of Tomas Bata University under the project No. IGA/FAI/2016/25.

REFERENCES

[1] S. Fisman, Wiretapping, and Eavesdropping. Clark Boardman Callaghan, 1978. ISBN 068559856X.

[2] J. Losert, Infosafe - Protection against eavesdropping, special technology [Online]. Olomouc:, 2016. Available from: http://www.infosafe.cz/ 2016.5.17

[3] J. Mudroch, Mudroch Labs s.r.o [Online]. Bánská Bystrica, Available from: http://www.triangulace.cz/ 2016.5.17

[4] F. Kucera, Mobile interception. Android World [Online]. Praha: VSHosting, 2012 Available from: http://www.svetandroida.cz/mobilni-odposlechy-jak-funguji-a-lze-se-jim-branit-201201 2016.5.17

[5] N. Kokesova, Principles of operations of contemporary mobile communication networks . Brno, 2006. Supervisor Doc. Ing. J. Saudek, CSc.

[6] Ch. Wang and F. Haider, "Cellular Architecture and Key Technologies for 5G wireless Communication Networks" IEEE Communications Magazine. 2014, (2): 9. Available from: http://cms.comsoc.org/SiteGen/Uploads/Public/Docs_TC_5GMWI/Cellular_Architecture_and_Key.pdf 2016.5.17

[7] I. Poole, 5G Mobile / Cellular Technology. Radio-Electronics [Online] Available from: http://www.radio-electronics.com/info/cellulartelecomms/5g-mobile-cellular/technology-basics.php 2016.5.17

[8] J. Kacerovsky, GSM Networks. Semestral paper, Communication systems and services, Brno, 2002. Available from: http://www.uai.tode.cz/stud_mat/GSM/it420_gsm.pdf 2016.5.17

[9] M. D. Renzo et al., "Spatial Modulation for Generalized MIMO: Challenges, Opportunities, and Implementation," Proc. IEEE, vol. 102, no. 1, Jan. 2014, pp. 56–103.

[10] C.-X. Wang and S. Wu, "Massive MIMO Channel Measurements and Modeling: Advances and Challenges", IEEE Wireless Communication.

[11] WWRF, L. Sorensen and K. E. Skouby, User Scenarios 2020, report, July 2009; http://www.wireless-world-research.org. 2016.5.29

[12] N. Jamaly., A. Derneryd and Rahmat-Samii, Y. "Spatial Diversity Performance of Multiport Antennas in the Presence of a Butler Network", Antennas and Propagation, IEEE Transactions on, On page(s): 5697 - 5705 Volume: 61, Issue: 11, Nov. 2013.

[13] Kempe D. and F. McSherry, A decentralized algorithm for spectral analysis, Journal of Computer and System Sciences, v.74 n.1, p.70-83, February 2008

[14] X. Li, H.-N. Dai, Q. Zhao and Q. Wang. "Eavesdropping Attacks in Wireless Ad Hoc Networks under a Shadow Fading Environment" Proceedings of the 2014 International Conference on Internet of Vehicles (IOV 2014)

Preliminary Study of Shielding of 802.11ah

Pavel Tomasek

Tomas Bata University in Zlin,
Faculty of Applied Informatics,
Zlin, Czech Republic
Email: tomasek@fai.utb.cz

Abstract—**This work is a preliminary study aimed at discussion and simple comparison of two ways of shielding against eavesdropping of wireless communication under new standard IEEE 802.11ah between electrical devices included in the rapidly growing Internet of Things. This security problem could be solved with a special selective surface which is proposed in this document.**

Keywords–IEEE 802.11ah; Internet of Things; Shielding; Eavesdropping

I. INTRODUCTION

The standard from the Institute of Electrical and Electronics Engineers (IEEE) with the label of 802.11ah [1] is a quite hot topic in the field of the Internet of Things (IoT). For the purpose of communication between even very small electrical appliances this represents a very new and efficient way of communication [2].

The world of IoT is full of electrical sensors, accessories, wearables, security elements, various appliances utilizable in Smart Home (for instance lighting, cooking, heating) and also agriculture monitoring, industrial automation and smart metering. The number of mentioned devices is supposed to raise rapidly in the near future what is related with significant security risks.

Therefore, the main goal of this preliminary study is aimed at analysis of possible ways of shielding communication under this standard against eavesdropping outside a room or a building.

This study is partially based on the previous work [3] where the goal was to reflect wireless communication under standard IEEE 802.11b,g. The final computed results of the optimized structure reflecting 2.4 GHz wireless communication are presented in Fig. 1.

This article includes the following content: Section II contains a brief description of IEEE 802.11ah. In Section III, some possible ways of shielding of this type of wireless communication are described. Finally, Section IV concludes ideas and ways mentioned in this preliminary study.

II. IEEE 802.11AH

The IEEE standard of 802.11ah, also called "Wi-Fi HaLow", has a great potential of usability in the area of IoT because of two main reasons [4]:

- Low power consumption thanks to a native power saving mechanism with sleep modes (should consume much less energy than Bluetooth or Wireless-Fidelity (Wi-Fi) of earlier standards b, g, a or n)

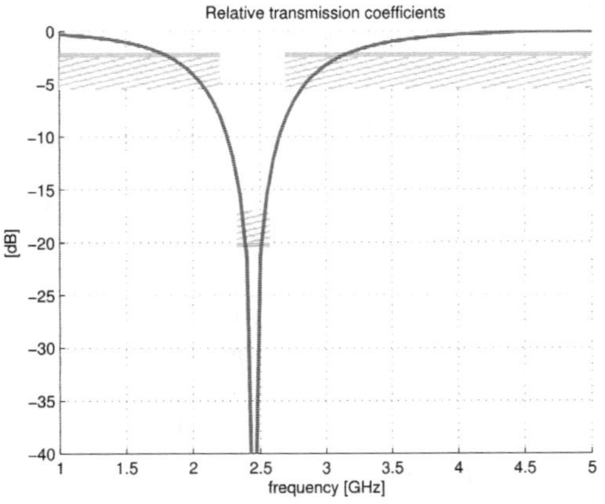

Figure 1. Transmission coefficients of the optimized FSS Wi-Fi filter [3].

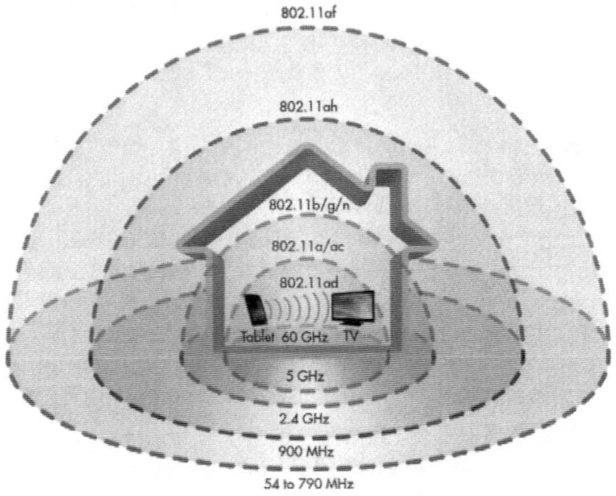

Figure 2. Comparison of different Wi-Fi ranges [2].

- Long range (can penetrate walls much more easily), the penetration and range of various Wi-Fi standards is depicted in Fig. 2.

Both items mentioned above are based on the key technological features of IEEE 802.11ah [5]:

- Sub 1 GHz frequency
- Design of new Physical Layer (PHY layer) and Media Access Control Layer (MAC layer). These new layers

include several modifications with respect to consolidated IEEE standards. The IEEE 802.11ah MAC layer incorporates most of the main IEEE 802.11 characteristics, adding some novel power management mechanisms.

- Typical range of IEEE 802.11ah is 100 – 1000 m
- Transmission power is <10 mW – <1 W (depending on the country's regulations)
- Battery operation should be from months to years (also thanks to long sleeping periods)

The mentioned standard is very new. It was standardized and introduced only few months ago, in January 4 2016 [1] (the first IEEE 802.11 standard was released in June 1997). The first certified devices should come soon (probably in 2017 or 2018). Due to these data, the topic of this study is unique and potentially very important and interesting from the point of view of secure communication.

III. Shielding

Considering wireless communication between electrical sensor or general devices using IEEE 802.11ah, the first idea of how to shield a communication in a room, in a small building or area is to use

A) A Faraday cage or
B) A wallpaper reflecting only a specific frequency range.

A. *Faraday Cage*

Faraday cages are named after the English scientist Michael Faraday. Faraday shield (cage) is an enclosure made from a conductive material or by a mesh of such material to block electric fields.

These shields – cages can be used to protect different kinds of electronic equipment from electrostatic discharges. They cannot block magnetic fields like Earth's magnetic field, but they can protect the interior from electromagnetic radiation coming from the outside. An external electrical field leads to rearrangement of the charges, and this cancels the field inside. Electric fields (applied externally) create forces on electrons in the conductor, creating a current, which will further result in charge rearrangement. The current will cease when the charges rearrange and the applied field inside is cancelled [6].

This approach is cheap but has several very negative side effects. First of all, whole frequencies coming to or from a cage are reflected, generally:

- Global System for Mobile (GSM) [7]
- Universal Mobile Telecommunications System (UMTS) [8]
- Long-Term Evolution (LTE) [9]
- 2.4 and 5 GHz Wi-Fi [4]
- Bluetooth [5]
- and possibly also the visible light if not using a mesh

This approach may go against the original aim to use IEEE 802.11ah in longer distances.

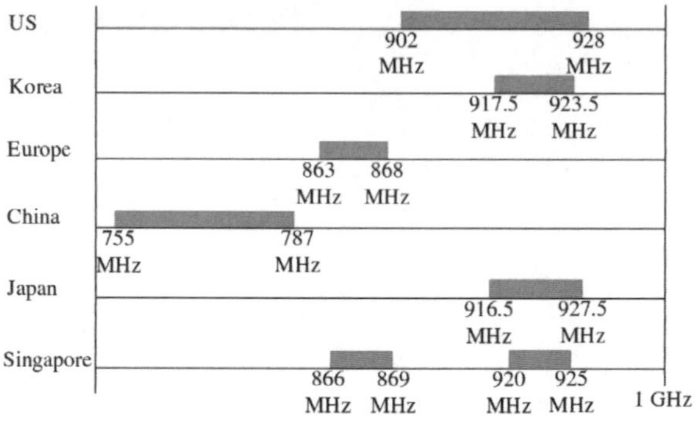

Figure 3. Sub 1 GHz spectrum specified in the IEEE 802.11ah channelization [16].

B. *FSS*

Frequency Selective Surfaces (FSSs) [10] are important spatial filters, which can efficiently filter desired band of frequencies. Therefore, these can play a significant role in electromagnetic related problems.

Frequency selective surfaces can be used and adjusted to prepare a structure reflecting just a desired narrow range of a spectrum.

To briefly sketch the history, the beginning of FSS relates to Ben A. Munk who was the guru of this approach [10]. In the last decade, the idea of FSS has spread out into many applications. Example of a band-pass FSS is in [11] where the goal was to transmit GSM signals through energy efficient windows. One of the first FSS absorbers was presented by Salisbury and Jaumann [12]. Great research has been already done in the field of FSS including also the analysis of frequency characteristics of dielectric period structures [13] and another analysis of characteristics of dielectric grating of left-handed and right-handed materials [14]. FSS are also used in the antenna theory and experiments like analysis of ultra wide band planar monopole antenna and its design [15].

This second idea of how to shield the communication is to use a special pattern/wallpaper selectively attenuating just the frequency range used in IEEE 802.11ah.

With respect to the design, rules and law of various countries the frequency range for Europe is 863 – 868 MHz (for example in USA it is 902 – 928 MHz and in China it is 755 – 787 MHz) [16]. Fig. 3 presents the ranges in more detail.

The standard of IEEE 802.11ah is operating in sub-gigahertz frequencies in comparison with traditional IEEE 802.11b or IEEE 802.11g working at 2.4 GHz and IEEE 802.11a working at 5 GHz.

The schema of a typical FSS structure: simple cross and a Jerusalem-cross is presented in Fig. 4. Both models consist of simple rectangular elements. Theoretically, the second geometry may have better reflection. Moreover double-layer should provide a more narrow band-stop filter.

In Fig. 4, a and a_j represent the width and height of a cell (a cell is just one square element of the whole structure of FSS; index j relates to the structure depicted on the right: the Jerusalem-cross), l and l_j is the total width and height of

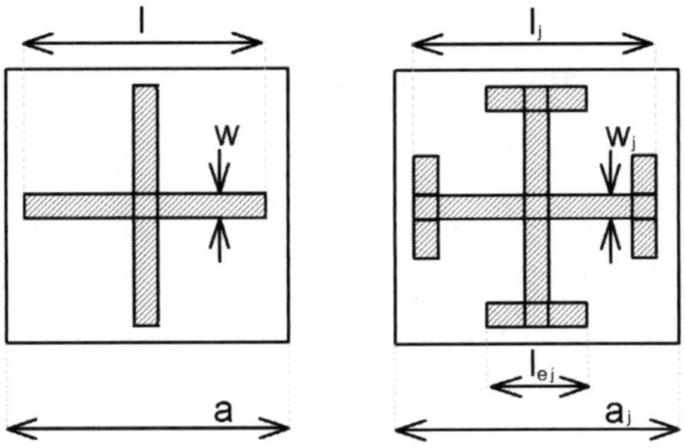

Figure 4. Schema of a cell containing the simple cross (on the left) and the Jerusalem-cross (on the right).

the cross, w and w_j is the width of an arm and l_{ej} represents the length of the bar connected to the end of an arm of the Jerusalem-cross.

There is also a special software suitable for optimization of FSS elements. It is FSSMR software [17], which was developed at Tomas Bata University in Zlin and which analyses the planar periodic structures and tries to optimize them with respect to the optimization goals. Therefore, this software is suitable for estimation of proper values of design variables (a, a_j, l, l_j, w, w_j, and l_{ej}) to meet the optimization goals (and thus to reflect the desired frequency band in this case of IEEE 802.11ah).

There are also some shortages in this approach. One of the most questionable aspects of the FSS approach is the influence of the angle of incidence which must be also examined. Another problem is with windows when attempting to secure a room against transmitting sub 1 GHz frequencies outside the room.

IV. CONCLUSION

A very new standard for wireless communication suitable for the Internet of Things, IEEE 802.11ah, has been introduced in this preliminary study together with possible ways of how to shield communication under mentioned standard. A theoretical concept of a wallpaper with a deep practical impact has been revealed. Also, some shortages of this approach have been described.

The boom of Internet of Things is coming. It can make life simpler (like other technologies in the history), but it also contains a great portion of a threat of abuse. This article points this out.

Further analysis, design of FSS filter with adaptation to the narrow specific range of frequencies and also practical experiments should be processed in further work.

ACKNOWLEDGMENT

This work was partially supported by Internal Grant Agency of Tomas Bata University under the project No. IGA/CebiaTech/2016/004. This work was supported by the Ministry of Education, Youth and Sports of the Czech Republic within the National Sustainability Programme project No. LO1303 (MSMT-7778/2014).

REFERENCES

[1] "Wi-Fi Alliance(R) introduces low power, long range Wi-Fi HaLow(TM)," 2016, URL: http://www.wi-fi.org/news-events/newsroom/wi-fi-alliance-introduces-low-power-long-range-wi-fi-halow [accessed: 2016-03-30].

[2] J.-J. DeLisle, "What's the Difference Between IEEE 802.11af and 802.11ah?" Microwaves and RF, vol. 54, 2015, pp. 69–72, ISSN: 0745-2993.

[3] P. Tomasek and S. Gona, "Automated Design of Frequency Selective Surfaces with the Application to Wi-Fi Band-Stop Filter," in Progress in Electromagnetics Research Symposium. Electromagnetics Academy, Cambridge, 2013, pp. 221–224, ISBN: 9781934142264.

[4] E. Khorov, A. Lyakhov, A. Krotov, and A. Guschin, "A survey on IEEE 802.11ah: An enabling networking technology for smart cities," Computer Communications, vol. 58, 2014, pp. 53–69, ISSN: 0140-3664.

[5] T. Adame, A. Bel, B. Bellalta, J. Barcelo, and M. Oliver, "IEEE 802.11ah: The WiFi Approach For M2M Communications," IEEE Wireless Communications, vol. 21, 2014, pp. 144–152, ISSN: 1536-1284.

[6] "Faraday Cage," 2016, URL: http://www.faradaycage.org/ [accessed: 2016-03-30].

[7] M. Y. Rhee, Global System for Mobile Communications. Wiley-IEEE Press, 2009, ISBN: 9780470823392. [Online]. Available: http://ieeexplore.ieee.org/xpl/articleDetails.jsp?arnumber=5628374

[8] A. Samukic, "Umts universal mobile telecommunications system: development of standards for the third generation," in Global Telecommunications Conference, 1998. GLOBECOM 1998. The Bridge to Global Integration. IEEE, vol. 4, 1998, pp. 1976–1983 vol.4, ISBN: 0-7803-4984-9.

[9] W. C. Lai, "Long term evolution antenna design by fdtd for femto communication on tablet application," in RF and Wireless Technologies for Biomedical and Healthcare Applications (IMWS-BIO), 2015 IEEE MTT-S 2015 International Microwave Workshop Series on, Sept 2015, pp. 120–121, DOI: 10.1109/IMWS-BIO.2015.7303807.

[10] B. Munk, Ed., Frequency selective surfaces – theory and design. New York, USA: Willey & Sons, 2000, ISBN: 978-0-471-37047-5.

[11] G. Kiani, L. Olsson, A. Karlsson, K. Esselle, and M. Nilsson, "Cross-Dipole Bandpass Frequency Selective Surface for Energy-Saving Glass Used in Buildings," IEEE Transactions on Antennas and Propagation, vol. 59, 2011, pp. 520–525, ISSN: 0018-926X.

[12] R. Haupt, "Scattering from Small Salisbury Screens," IEEE Transactions on Antennas and Propagation, vol. 54, 2006, pp. 1807–1810, ISSN: 0018-926X.

[13] R. Mehrnejad and R. Razmjoueian, "Frequency characteristics of dielectric periodic structures," in ACMIN'12 Proceedings of the 14th international conference on Automatic Control, Modelling & Simulation, and Proceedings of the 11th international conference on Microelectronics, Nanoelectronics, Optoelectronics. WSEAS, Stevens Point, Wisconsin, USA, 2012, pp. 187–190, ISBN: 978-1-61804-080-0.

[14] R. Mehrnejad and R.Razmjoueian, "Characteristics of Dielectric Grating of Left Handed and Right Handed Materials," in ACMIN'12 Proceedings of the 14th international conference on Automatic Control, Modelling & Simulation, and Proceedings of the 11th international conference on Microelectronics, Nanoelectronics, Optoelectronics. WSEAS, Stevens Point, Wisconsin, USA, 2012, pp. 205–208, ISBN: 978-1-61804-080-0.

[15] M. Rahim, T. Masri, H. Majid, O. Ayop, and F. Zubir, "Design and analysis of ultra wide band planar monopole antenna," WSEAS Transactions on Communications, WSEAS, vol. 10, 2011, pp. 212–221, ISSN: 1109-2742.

[16] W. Sun, M. Choi, and S. Choi, "IEEE 802.11ah: A Long Range 802.11 WLAN at Sub 1 GHz," Journal of ICT Standardization, vol. 1, 2013, pp. 83–108, ISSN: 2246-0853.

[17] S. Gona and V. Kresalek, "Development of a Versatile Planar Periodic Structure Simulator in MATLAB," COMITE, vol. 14, 2008.

Authentication of Czech Banknotes using Raman Microscopy

Hana Vaskova, Pavel Valasek
Department of Electronics and Measurements
Faculty of Applied Informatics, Tomas Bata University in Zlin
Zlin, Czech Republic
vaskova@fai.utb.cz, p_valasek@fai.utb.cz

Abstract—**At the present time, all modern banknotes contain security features to prevent their counterfeiting. Some of these features include special paper and inks with a specific composition as well as tints that are hard to reproduce by commercial copiers and printers. Current availability of digital technologies makes it much easier to produce higher quality counterfeits than in the past. This paper is focused on systematical experimental examination of paper and inks used on Czech banknotes to obtain characteristic Raman spectra that serve for the authenticity assessment. Raman spectroscopy is a powerful method for material identification and meets requirements of the forensic examination. This method has the potential to recognize various substances, even their structural modification. On the basis of Raman spectra, it is possible to determine whether the questioned banknote is genuine or a forgery, even though the specific composition of inks is a manufacturing secret. Raman spectral data of the investigated Czech banknotes were used for creation of a spectral library for the purpose of further verification of questionable banknotes.**

Keywords-authenticity; Czech banknotes; Raman sepctra; inks; spectral library.

I. INTRODUCTION

Banknotes are used worldwide as universal mean of payment. Also, the desire of self-enrichment is a sentiment found all over the world. The desire to become rich is sometimes accompanied by illegal activities, including forgery of money. Creating and using counterfeit money is one of the oldest crimes in history. Current popularization and availability of digital technology shifts the level of counterfeits at a higher level and it is much easier to produce counterfeit money than it was in the past.

To prevent counterfeiting banknotes, all the modern banknotes contain different amounts of more or less successfully falsifiable security features. Many of them are recognizable to the naked eye as safety watermarks, key register line or hidden diagram. Some can be verified using ultraviolet (UV) light or chemical reaction of a special pen with the banknote paper, but some require more advanced analytical tools where a naked eye is not sufficient as a detector. Understandably, it is much more difficult and demanding to falsify these kinds of advanced security features.

In this paper, the term "banknote" refers to currency bills i.e. money, but could also be used in a broader sense, to include different valuable documents, cheques, travel tickets, stamps, vouchers, shares, etc.

Raman spectroscopy/Raman microscopy is an innovative analytical tool that has become a valuable part of laboratories all over the world lately [1]. This potential method allows an insight into the structure of materials on a molecular level and enables evaluation of their composition based on the characteristic molecular vibrations caused by incident monochromatic light. Raman spectroscopy is a powerful tool for material identification. Applications of Raman spectroscopy comprise increasing number of scientific and technical fields in recent years. We mention some examples in the following fields: material sciences [2], nanotechnology [3], chemistry [4], pharmaceutical industry [5], food technology [6], biology [4], medicine [7], arts and cultural heritage [8], as well as forensic analysis [9] and security [10].

Raman spectroscopy is an effective tool for rapid identification [9]. The key importance for the identification is a highly specific chemical "fingerprint" in form of Raman spectrum for every individual chemical element or its modification. Raman spectra reflect vibrations of bonding in the structure after laser irradiation and are unique. Essentially, it is analogical to the human fingerprints. The method fulfils the requirements for forensic examination. It is also non-destructive, non-invasive and applicable to a wide range of substances. Specifically, for the application presented in this paper it means, that researched banknotes may be after analyzing, if genuine, return back into circulation.

Apart from the common methods used for counterfeits detection suggestions for other innovative approaches to banknotes control and confirmation of their authenticity have been proposed in the recent years. L.S. Eberlin et. al. [11] use ambient mass spectrometry for chemical analysis of banknotes to obtain characteristic chemical profiles for genuine banknotes and for counterfeits. This method meets requirements of non-destructive, instantaneous, reproducible measurements. G. S. Spagnolo et. al. [12] use a new approach to verify banknotes originality based on the idea of hylemetry, a methodology conceptually similar to biometry applied to non-living matter. Specifically, the random distribution pattern of the metallic security fibres set into the paper pulp is dealt in the paper. C. Nastoulis et. al. [13] propose a new method useful for banking systems around the world for the different banknote recognition using probabilistic neural network.

The rest of the paper is structured as follows. The scope of the research is outlined in Section 2. In Section 3, the Czech banknotes are introduced together with some statistics of counterfeits since 2008 and brief overview of the methods used for counterfeits detection. Section 4 describes the fundamental principle and features of Raman microscopy, the studied method applied to detect counterfeit banknote. The results of Raman analyses are then discussed in Section 5. The conclusion and future work is presented in Section 6.

II. Scope Of The Research

The possibility of the authenticity assessments of Czech banknotes has been investigated using fundamental features and advantages of Raman microscopy. Both genuine Czech banknotes and their counterfeits were studied on the basis of the material composition characteristic for their manufacture. Analysis of the used materials can be conducted in order to confirm counterfeit currency. For the purpose of relatively rapid evaluation of spectral data of examined banknotes the database of Raman spectra of paper and inks used on Czech banknotes was created.

III. Czech Banknotes

There are six banknotes currently in circulation in the Czech Republic, valid since 1993 when Czechoslovakia was separated into two individual countries.

Figure 1. Overview of the valid Czech banknotes.

The nominal value of these banknotes are 100 Czech koruna / crown (CZK), 200 CZK, 500 CZK, 1000 CZK, 2000 CZK and 5000 CZK, all the banknotes are displayed in Figure 1. In addition, there used to be two other valid banknotes, in the value of 20 CZK and 50 CZK, which were withdrawn from circulation in 2008 and 2011, respectively, and were replaced by coins only. The author of all Czech banknotes is Oldrich Kulhanek (1940 - 2013), Czech painter, graphic and stage designer, illustrator and pedagogue.

Czech banknotes and coins are very safe in comparison with other international currency. The development and application of protective elements on Czech banknotes are some world leaders. The 1000 CZK banknote with innovative security features was awarded the title Banknote of the Year in 2008 [14] by The International Association of Currency Affairs. This was an acknowledgment of the quality of Czech banknotes as being among the highest in the world, not only in terms of artwork but also in the technical level of protective elements applied. This was the third award of the Czech currency since 1993.

A. *Statistics of Counterfeits*

The occurrence of counterfeits of Czech Banknotes has been decreasing since 2008 according to the Czech National Bank (CNB) and as seen in the graph in Figure 2. Nevertheless, 2,383 banknotes in the cash value 2,355 million CZK were captured in 2015. The most often faked in recent years are 1000 CZK (57.2 % in 2015) and 500 CZK (17.89 % in 2015) banknotes [15].

Absolutely predominant (96.6 % in 2015) forgery technique for the Czech currency in a long term is inkjet print. Colour copying was used for 3.3 % of fakes revealed last year. On the other hand, the most often forgery technique used on Euro banknotes captured in the Czech Republic in 2015 was offset print for 52.8 %, which is not almost used on CZK banknotes fakes (only 0.1 %), followed by inkjet print for 46.6 % of counterfeited Euro. The situation was similar with the US dollars, with 98.3% of counterfeits using offset print.

On a five-grade scale of danger (1 very dangerous - 5 primitive) the highest degree for CZK banknotes (89 %) is

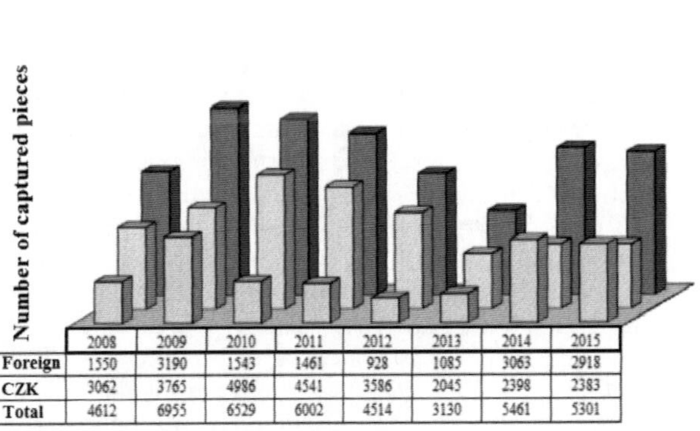

	2008	2009	2010	2011	2012	2013	2014	2015
Foreign	1550	3190	1543	1461	928	1085	3063	2918
CZK	3062	3765	4986	4541	3586	2045	2398	2383
Total	4612	6955	6529	6002	4514	3130	5461	5301

Figure 2. Occurrence of counterfeits of Czech Banknotes and EURO banknotes in the Czech Republic from 2008 to 2015 [8].

4th degree (less successful), 5th degree (6 %) followed by 3rd (4 %). Even the number of counterfeit banknotes of 2nd degree (dangerous) decreased from 21.8 % for all Czech falsified banknotes in 2011 to 0.1 % in 2015 [15]. Counterfeits of Euro banknotes seized in the Czech Republic are much more likely (than Czech banknotes) to be ranked 2nd (6 %) and 3rd (51 %) degree of danger. Counterfeit US dollar banknotes seized in the Czech Republic mainly fall into the 3rd degree of danger category (98 %) [16]. The quality of CZK counterfeits compared to Euro and US dollar counterfeits underlines good technical quality of protective elements of Czech banknotes.

B. Methods for counterfeits detection

There are various methods and techniques known for testing authenticity of banknotes. Firstly, simple methods to verify visible elements are used, such as watermark lamps, intaglio print, microtext, UV luminescence or holograms. Secondly, more sophisticated methods are used, which require special equipment for verification, not only naked eye, and are usually based on the colour response of banknote's features analysis. These methods include Magnetic Ink Scanners, isocheck, Fibre-Based Certificates of Authenticity or colour analyses.

Generally, it is not possible to say which method is the best. Usually, a combination of more methods gives better results and confirmation.

Generally the process of control of the authenticity of banknotes could be summed up into four steps:

1. checking of the paper – unique feel of the paper
2. checking of the print quality – sharp and clean lines
3. checking security features on the banknote
4. comparing with the banknotes of the same series

IV. RAMAN MICROSCOPY

Raman spectroscopy, as a modern spectroscopic method, has, in principle, the potential to answer a number of questions concerning chemical details of a molecular structure. This feature makes Raman spectroscopy suitable for material identification [1].

The method is based on the Raman effect, an inelastic scattering of photons on molecules. The majority of incident photons is scattered elastically (Rayleigh scattering), only a very small part (approximately 1 of ten million photons) needful for origin of Raman spectra is scattered inelastically. This fact requires precise instrumentation to ensure conditions for accurate measurements. Analysis possibilities are extended when using the advantages of optical microscopy via a coupled microscope.

Raman spectroscopy brings advantages over other techniques as non-destructiveness, no special requirements for sample preparation, rapidity, applicability to all states of matter and different forms, measurements through covering layers or contactless measurements. The listed features make this analytical tool convenient, attractive and participating on the growth of its popularity and applicability worldwide.

The greatest drawback of the method is occurring of luminescence which as much stronger quantum effect may overlap Raman spectra and mask spectral information. Another disadvantage is eventual degradation of a sensitive sample when using intense laser beam [17], [18].

V. EXPERIMENTAL PART

All types of Czech banknotes were analyzed by Raman microscopy. The procedure is demonstrated on 200 CZK banknote in this paper, however the same routine was applied on all banknotes. On each banknote, 23 points were picked, both on the face and the reverse side. The performance criterion consisted in a color layout and also in the distribution of different printing techniques used during the production of the banknotes and the application of protecting elements.

The most important aspects of the banknotes analyses using Raman spectroscopy were the used inks and paper. To study the diversity of the results two types of banknotes imitation were created – by the inkjet printer and by color copier. These are the most often used methods in the Czech banknotes counterfeiting.

A. Inks

For obvious reasons, the specific composition of inks used on banknotes is not publically known. Using Raman microscopy does not suffer from an absence of this specific information although this manufacturing secrets. Original banknotes provide corresponding data which serves as the standard for comparison. Colours occurring on all banknotes together with the number of protective elements are listed in Table 1.

TABLE I. INKS AND SECURITY FEATURES ON BANKNOTES

Value [CZK]	*No. of measured points*	*Inks - colours*	*No. of security features*
100	23	green, red, yellow, black	6
200	23	brown, orange, green, black	6
500	23	brown, yellow, red, ochre, green, black	7
1000	23	violet, ochre, pink, blue, black	8
2000	23	green, violet, yellow, pink, black	8
5000	23	blue, red, yellow, pink, black	8

B. Paper

Banknotes are printed on special high quality paper. This paper is based on cotton, contains a mixture of chemical additives, also characteristic fibers (several mm long) and watermarks to prevent the imitation. More stringent requirements are laid on this paper in comparison with ordinary consumer paper made of wood fibers. Banknote paper must have greater strength and flexibility, must be resistant to bending, breaking and tearing. Czech banknotes are printed on natural colored paper. This means that the paper is not pure white, but has a very light ochre tint.

One of the easiest ways of fake's recognition is its sound of wrinkling or friction (the acoustic safety feature). It is influenced by appropriate composition of the paper fibers. The paper banknotes sounds differently than writing paper, the sound is tougher.

C. Measuring Device

InVia Basis Raman microscope from Renishaw was used for recording all Raman spectra. Argon ion laser with the excitation wavelength 514 nm in visible area (VIS) and maximum output power of 20 mW and 785 nm near infrared (NIR) diode laser with maximum output power 300 mW were used as light sources. A Leica DM 2500 confocal microscope with the resolution up to 2 μm was coupled to the Raman spectrometer.

All measurements were collected at magnification 20x or 50x, with 15 s exposure time, 10 accumulations. Powers of lasers were from 0.1 % to 5 % of the output laser power. The samples were scanned in range 200 to 3200 cm^{-1} with 2 cm^{-1} spectral resolution.

D. Results

Czech banknotes and their imitations were measured using both lasers (VIS and NIR). Some of the inks exhibited luminescence and their Raman spectra were poor quality or were not possible to acquire by laser from the visible region. Therefore, most of spectra were acquired by NIR laser. High level of luminescence was also present at imitations. This behavior is also a partial result indicating the presence of luminescent element which is missing in the spectra of original banknotes.

The layout of the inks is typical to the used printing method hence microscope view can satisfactorily prove the forgery in many cases.

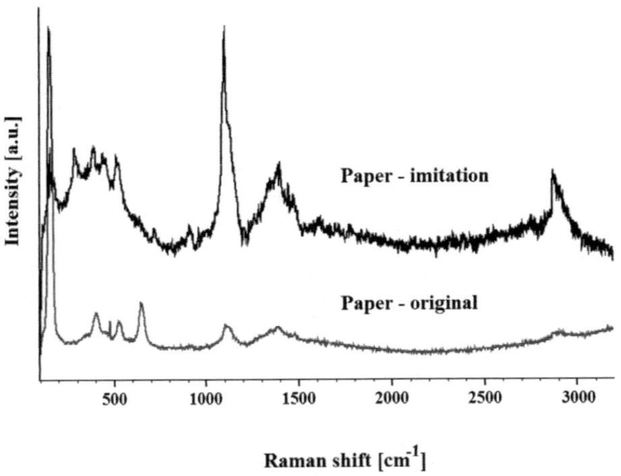

Figure 3. Raman spectra of banknote and ordinary office paper.

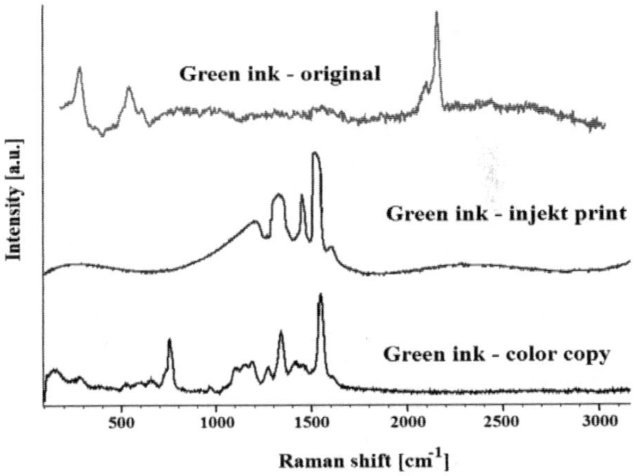

Figure 5. Raman spectra of green ink on genuine 200 CZK banknote and its two imitations.

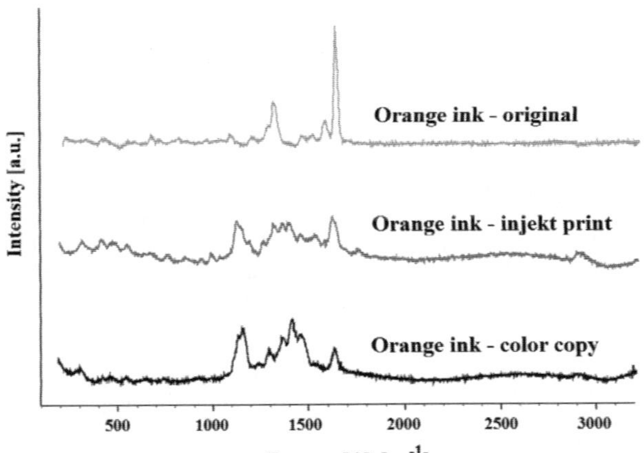

Figure 4. Raman spectra of orange ink on genuine 200 CZK banknote and its two imitations.

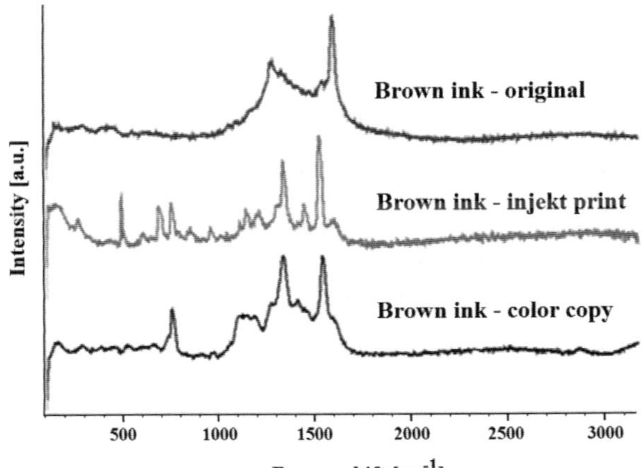

Figure 6. Raman spectra of green ink on genuine 200 CZK banknote and its two imitations.

Spectrum of paper confirms the presence of viscose fibers recovered from cellulose that are similar in structure to fibers of cotton from which are divergent mainly by the presence of the peak at 650 cm^{-1} for C-S-C vibrations [19]. This peak is missing from the spectrum of ordinary paper. Raman spectra of banknote paper and ordinary office paper used for imitations are displayed in Figure 3.

In some measured points not only a spectrum of an ink but also spectral response of the paper can be observed. In these cases the spectrum of paper of the banknote is for further processing of spectral data in spectral library subtracted from the measured Raman spectrum.

The diversity in layout of characteristic peaks for different colours can be seen in Figure 4 to Figure 6.

Noticeable differences in Raman spectra are recorded for genuine banknotes and reproductions as is shown in Figure 4 to Figure 6 for orange, green and brown ink on 200 CZK banknotes. Different layout of Raman peaks and their intensities clearly demonstrate various compositions of used inks.

VI. Conclusion and Future Work

Based on characteristic Raman spectra of banknote materials, paper and inks, the authenticity assessment of Czech banknotes was presented. Raman spectroscopy was used as an innovative tool for analyzing Czech banknotes in this sense. The features examined have characteristic Raman spectra and provide information about the authenticity of banknotes and point out any successful forgeries, which are not possible to distinguish with the naked eye. For the purpose of further verification of banknotes, the Raman spectral library of inks measured on all Czech banknotes using lasers from visible and near infrared region was created.

A similar routine was applied on selected Euro banknotes and the results show universality of the use of Raman microscopy for the purpose of banknotes originality assessment.

The future work within the research will be focused on measurement of Czech banknotes issued in all the years to have a complete reference data for the Raman spectral library.

Acknowledgment

This work was supported by the Ministry of Education, Youth and Sports of the Czech Republic within the National Sustainability Program project No. LO1303 (MSMT-7778/2014) and also by the European Regional Development Fund under the project CEBIA-Tech No. CZ.1.05/2.1.00/03.0089.

References

[1] R. S. Das, Y. K. Agraval, "Raman spectroscopy: Recent advancements, techniques and applications," Vibrational Spectroscopy, vol. 57, is. 2, pp. 163-176, 2011.

[2] W.H. Weber, and R. Merlin, Raman scattering in materials science. Springer Science & Business Media, 483 p. 2013.

[3] A. C. Ferrari, and D. M. Basko, "Raman spectroscopy as a versatile tool for studying the properties of graphene," Nature nanotechnology, vol. 8, no. 1, pp. 235-246, 2013.

[4] E. Smith, and G. Dent, Modern Raman spectroscopy: a practical approach. John Wiley & Sons, 2013.

[5] Y. S. Li, and J. S. Church, "Raman spectroscopy in the analysis of food and pharmaceutical nanomaterials," Journal of food and drug analysis, vol. 22, no. 1, pp. 29-48, 2014.

[6] H. Vaskova, and M. Buckova, "Thermal degradation of vegetable oils: spectroscopic measurement and analysis," Procedia Engineering, vol. 100, pp. 630-635, 2015.

[7] P. Matousek, and N. Stone, "Recent advances in the development of Raman spectroscopy for deep non-invasive medical diagnosis, " vol. 6, no. 1, pp. 7-19, 2013.

[8] H. Gomes, P. Rosina, P. Holakooei, T. Solomon, and C. Vaccaro, "Identification of pigments used in rock art paintings in Gode Roriso-Ethiopia using micro-Raman spectroscopy," Journal of Archaeological Science, vol. 40, no. 11, pp. 4073-4082, 2013.

[9] J. M. Chalmers, G. H. Howell, and M. D. Hargreaves, Infrared and Raman spectroscopy in forensic science. 1st pub. Chichester, West Sussex, UK: Wiley, 618 p. 2012.

[10] M. López-López, and C. García-Ruiz, "Infrared and Raman spectroscopy techniques applied to identification of explosives," TrAC Trends in Analytical Chemistry, vol. 54, pp. 36-44, 2014.

[11] L. S. Eberlin et al., "Instantaneous chemical profiles of banknotes by ambient mass spektrometry," Analyst, vol. 135, is. 10, pp. 2533 – 2539, 2010.

[12] G. S. Spagnolo, L. Cozzella, and C. Simonetti, "Banknote security using a biometric-like technique: a hylemetric approach," *Measurement Science and Technology*, vol. 21, pp. 1 – 8, 2010.

[13] C. Nastoulis, A. Leros, and N. Bardis, "Banknote recognition based on probabilistic neural network models," WSEAS Transactions on Systems, pp. 802-805, 2006.

[14] Central Banking: Czech banknote wins prize. [Online]. Available from: http://www.centralbanking.com/centralbanking/news/1425097 /czech-banknote-wins-prize/ 2016.04.11

[15] Ceska narodni banka: Padelky 2011. [Online]. Available from: http://www.cnb.cz/ 2016.04.11

[16] Ceska narodni banka: Padelky 2015. [Online]. Available from: http://www.cnb.cz/ 2016.04.11

[17] N. B. Colthup, H. D. Lawrence, and S. E. Wiberley, Introduction to infrared and Raman spectroscopy. 3rd ed. San Diego: Academic Press, 547 p. 1990.

[18] H. Vaskova, "A powerful tool for material identification: Raman spectroscopy," International Journal of Mathematical Models and Method in Applied Science, vol. 5, pp. 1205-1212, 2011.

[19] L. L. Cho, "Identification of textile fiber by Raman microspectroscopy," Forensic Science Journal, vol. 6, no. 1, pp.55-62, 2007.

An Efficient Pseudo Chaotic Number Generator Based on Coupling and Multiplexing Techniques

Ons Jallouli*, Safwan El Assad*, Mohammed Abu Taha *, Maryline Chetto†, René Lozi‡, Daniel Caragata§
*Institut d'Electronique et de Télécommunications de Rennes, UMR CNRS 6164, Université de Nantes, France,
Emails: {ons.jallouli, safwan.elassad, mohammad.abu-taha}@univ-nantes.fr
†Institut de Recherche en Communications et cybernétique de Nantes, UMR 6597, Université de Nantes, France,
Email: maryline.chetto@univ-nantes.fr
‡Laboratoire J.A. Dieudonné, UMR CNRS 7351, Université de Nice Sophia-Antipolis, France
Email:Rene.LOZI@unice.fr
§ Universidad Tecnica Federico Santa Maria, Department of Electronic Engineering, Av. Espana 1680, Valparaso, Chile
Email:daniel.caragata@usm.cl

***Abstract*—Cryptosystems require a very good and secure source of randomness for their security. Such a source is extremely difficult to obtain in practice. Hence, developing a secure pseudo-random number generator reveals necessary. In this paper, we propose a new pseudo chaotic number generator. The proposed structure integrates three discrete chaotic maps: Piece Wise Linear Chaotic (PWLCM), Skewtent and Logistic maps, which are weakly coupled and implemented with finite precision N=32 bits. It also includes a chaotic multiplexing technique. The experiment results and statistical analysis prove the robustness of the proposed generator as well as its efficiency in terms of computation time in comparison with know chaotic generators of the literature. Based on the previous structure, a random number generator that uses Linux generator has been designed : `"/dev/urandom"`.**

Keywords–Pseudo-chaotic number generator; Weakly Coupling; Chaotic multiplexing technique; Random numbers; Security analyses.

I. INTRODUCTION

Random numbers generators are useful for a variety of purposes in various contexts including statistical mechanics, gaming industry, cryptography and communications, etc. There are two basic types of random number generator: True Random Number Generators (TRNGs) and Pseudo-Random Number Generators (PRNGs). TRNGs produce a random bit stream from a non-deterministic natural source. They extract randomness from certain physical phenomena such as thermal and atmospheric noises. TRNGs are characterized by a higher security. However, their implementation requires additional devices, which make them inconvenient (cost and slow) [1]. A PRNG is a deterministic algorithm that produce numbers whose distribution is uniform, by inputting an initial seed (often generated by a TRNG). PRNGs are important in practice for their rapidity in number generation, reproducibility of the pseudo-random sequences and requiring less memory for storage [2].

Over the past years, many researchers have been attracted to chaos in the design of PRNGs, due to its intrinsic properties such as ergodicity, randomness and high sensitivity to initial conditions and parameters [3]. Several PRNGs have been proposed in the literature. Shujun et al. [4] presented a novel pseudo-chaotic bit generator based on a Couple of Chaotic Systems called CCS-PRBG. Analyses show that it has good cryptographic properties, but the speed of the proposed generator is not high enough for real time applications. Lozi [5] introduced new models for very weakly coupled logistic and tent maps using single or double precision numbers. Also, he used a double threshold chaotic sampling and mixing in weakly coupled tent maps [6]. This technique improves randomness of the generated sequence but causes a decrease in the speed performance. In [7], we proposed a Pseudo Chaotic Number Generator (PCNG) based on three weakly-coupled discrete skewtent maps and uses a chaotic multiplexing technique. This structure is very secure but its implantation was not optimized.

In this paper, we present an efficient PCNG based on three weakly coupled discrete chaotic maps namely PWLCM (Piece-Wise Linear Chaotic Map), Skewtent and Logistic maps. Besides, the structure uses a chaotic switching technique that increase the security performance. In addition, based on the proposed PCNG and Linux generator "/dev/urandom". The paper is organized as follows: the architecture of the proposed PCNG is described in Section II. In Section III, we give its performance in terms of security and computation time. Then, we present in Section IV the proposed RNG. Finally, we conclude our work in Section V.

II. STRUCTURE OF THE PROPOSED PCNG

The scheme of the proposed PCNG is presented in Fig. 1. It is based on iterating three chaotic maps, namely, Pwlcm, skewtent and logistic maps, which are weakly coupled by a coupling matrix. It also includes a chaotic multiplexing technique [6], [8]–[13] .

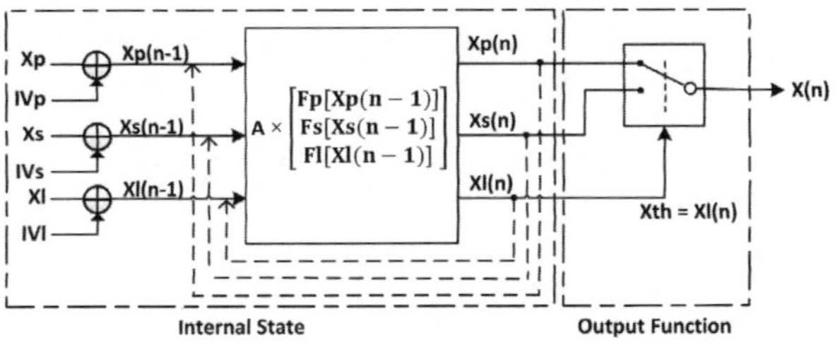

Figure 1: Structure of the proposed chaotic generator.

The generated samples X(n) are quantified on N = 32 bits.

The secret key of the system consists of:

- The initial conditions Xp, Xs and Xl of the three chaotic maps: Pwlcm, Skewtent and Logistic respectively, ranging from 1 to 2^N-1.
- The control parameter Pp and Ps of Pwlcm and Skewtent maps, where $1 \leq Pp \leq 2^{N-1}$ and $1 \leq Ps \leq 2^N - 1$.
- The parameters of the coupling matrix A, ε_{ij}, ranging from 1 to 2^k with k ≤ 5.

The chaotic system uses three initial vectors IVp, IVs and IVl, each quantified on 32 bits.

All the initial conditions, parameters and initial vectors are chosen randomly from file "`/dev/urandom`", interfaces to the entropy pool sources on the Lunix kernel.

The functionality of the chaotic generator is as follows:

Step1: It calculates the initial values Xp(0), Xs(0) and Xl(0) as follows:

$$\begin{cases} Xp(0) = Xp \oplus IVp \\ Xs(0) = Xs \oplus IVs \\ Xl(0) = Xl \oplus IVl \end{cases}$$

Step2: The chaotic maps are weakly coupled by a coupling matrix A, as indicated by (1):

$$\begin{bmatrix} Xp(n) \\ Xs(n) \\ Xl(n) \end{bmatrix} = A \times \begin{bmatrix} Fp[Xp(n-1)] \\ Fs[Xs(n-1)] \\ Fl[Xl(n-1)] \end{bmatrix}. \quad (1)$$

where A is given by:

$$A = \begin{bmatrix} \varepsilon_{11} & \varepsilon_{12} & \varepsilon_{13} \\ \varepsilon_{21} & \varepsilon_{22} & \varepsilon_{23} \\ \varepsilon_{31} & \varepsilon_{32} & \varepsilon_{33} \end{bmatrix} \quad (2)$$

with

$$\begin{cases} \varepsilon_{11} = 2^N - \varepsilon_{12} - \varepsilon_{13}. \\ \varepsilon_{22} = 2^N - \varepsilon_{21} - \varepsilon_{23}. \\ \varepsilon_{33} = 2^N - \varepsilon_{31} - \varepsilon_{32}. \end{cases}$$

Fp[X(n-1)], Fs[X(n-1)] and Fl[X(n-1)] are the discrete PWLCM, Skewtent and Logistic maps functions respectively [7].

$$Fp[X(n-1)] =$$

$$\begin{cases} \left\lceil 2^N \times \frac{X[n-1]}{P} \right\rceil & \text{if } 0 < X[n-1] \leq P \\ \left\lceil 2^N \times \frac{X[n-1]-P}{2^{N-1}-P} \right\rceil & \text{if } P < X[n-1] \leq 2^{N-1} \\ \left\lceil 2^N \times \frac{2^N-P-X[n-1]}{2^{N-1}-P} \right\rceil & \text{if } 2^{N-1} < X[n-1] \leq 2^N - P \\ \left\lceil 2^N \times \frac{2^N-X[n-1]}{P} \right\rceil & \text{if } 2^N - P < X[n-1] \leq 2^N - 1 \\ 2^N - 1 - P & otherwise \end{cases} \quad (3)$$

$$Fs[X(n-1)] =$$

$$\begin{cases} \left\lfloor \frac{2^N \times X[n-1]}{P} \right\rfloor & \text{if } 0 < X[n-1] < P \\ 2^N - 1 & \text{if } X[n-1] = P \\ \left\lfloor \frac{2^N \times (2^N - X[n-1])}{2^N - P} \right\rfloor & \text{if } P < X[n-1] < 2^N \end{cases} \quad (4)$$

$$Fl[X[n-1]] =$$

$$\begin{cases} \left\lfloor \frac{X[n-1] \times [2^N - X[n-1]]}{2^{N-1}} \right\rfloor & \text{if } X[n-1] \neq [3 \times 2^{N-2}; 2^N] \\ 2^N - 1 & \text{if } X[n-1] = [3 \times 2^{N-2}; 2^N] \end{cases} \quad (5)$$

Step3: The output samples X(n) are controlled by a threshold T and a chaotic sample Xth which is equal to Xl(n):

$$X(n) = \begin{cases} Xp(n), & \text{if } 0 < Xth < T \\ Xs(n), & \text{otherwise} \end{cases} \quad (6)$$

Notice that at the end of each execution, a new IV is generated. This allows to produce a new key stream for the next execution (using the same secret key).

III. Simulation Results and Analysis

A. Security Analysis

1) Key space analysis: A PCNG should have a large key space in order to make brute-force attacks infeasible. It is generally accepted that a key space of size equal or greater to 2^{128} is secure. The size of the secret key of the proposed system is:

$$|K| = (|Xp| + |Xs| + |Xl|) + (|Pp| + |Ps|) + 6 \times |\varepsilon_{ij}|. \quad (7)$$

where $|Xp| = |Xs| = |Xl| = |Ps| = 32$ bits ; $|Pp| = 31$ bits and $|\varepsilon_{ij}|$ is equal to 5 bits. Therefore $|K| = 189$ bits.

The size of the secret key is large enough to resist any brute-force attacks. Such a large space of keys is a necessary condition, but not sufficient. Indeed, the generated sequences must be cryptographically secure.

2) Key Sensitivity: The sensitivity on the key is an essential property for any PCNG. Naturally, a small change in the secret key causes a large change in the output sequences. In order to verify this characteristic, we calculate the Hamming Distance of two sequences generated with only one bit change (lsb bit) in the parameter Pp. We calculate the average Hamming Distance $D_{Hamming}$ between two sequences S_1 and S_2, over 100 random secret keys. The $D_{Hamming}(S_1, S_2)$ is defined by the following equation:

$$D_{Hamming}(S_1, S_2) = \frac{1}{Nb} \times \sum_{K=1}^{Nb} (S_1[K] \oplus S_2[K]) \quad (8)$$

where Nb is the number of bits in a sequence. The obtained average value of Hamming distance is equal to 0.499988. This value is close to the optimal value of 50%. This result illustrates the heigh sensitivity on the secret key of the proposed PCNG.

B. Statistical Analysis

To test the statistical properties of the proposed PCNG, we used several known statistical tests. They concern mapping, auto and cross-correlation, histogram, chi square and NIST test.

1) Phase space trajectory or mapping analysis: The mapping or the phase space trajectory of the generated sequences reflects the dynamic behaviour of the system. In Fig. 2, we give a zoom of the obtained mapping. It is messy due to the used chaotic coupling and switching techniques. Therefore, it is impossible to identify the type of the used chaotic maps.

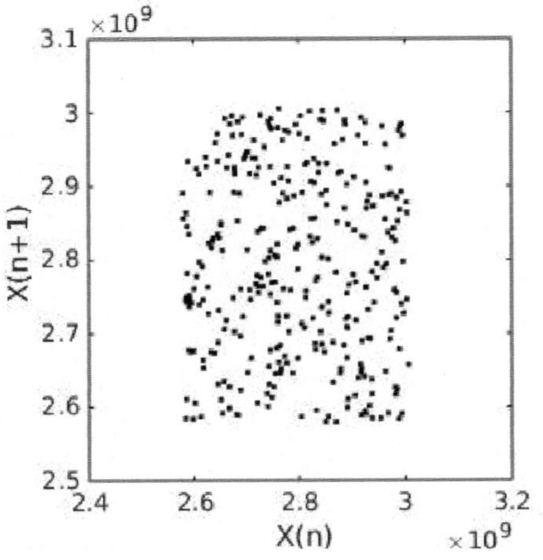

Figure 2: Mapping of the sequence X.

2) Histogram and Chi-square analysis: We study the distribution uniformity of the generated sequences. A PCNG must provide a uniform distribution in the whole phase space. We give in Fig. 3 the histogram of a generated sequence, by our PCNG, formed by 10^7 samples.

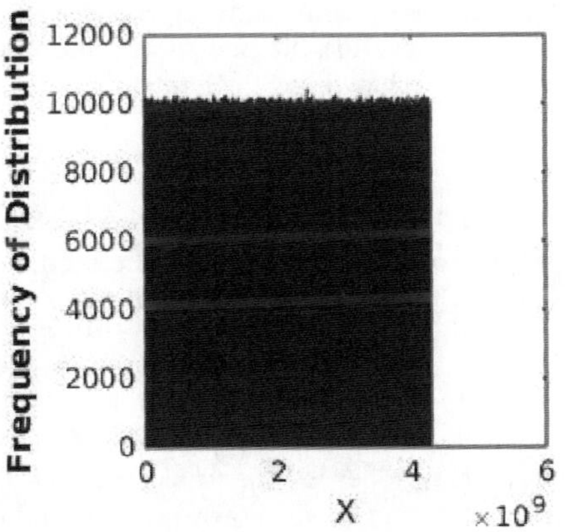

Figure 3: Histogram of a generated sequence X.

Visually, we observe that the generated sequence is nearly uniformly distributed. We then apply the chi-square test to assert the uniformity of the sequence [14]. The experimental Chi-square χ^2 value is given by:

$$\chi^2_{\text{exp}} = \sum_{i=0}^{K-1} \frac{(O_i - E_i)^2}{E_i}. \tag{9}$$

where K is the number of classes (sub-intervals) chosen in our experiment equal to 1000, O_i is the number of observed (calculated) samples in the i-th class and E_i is the expected number of samples of a uniform distribution, $E_i = 10^7/K$.

We compare the experimental value given by (9) with a theoretical value obtained for a threshold α=0.05 and a degree of freedom K-1=999. The experimental value of chi-square is equal to 1027.26. This value is lower than the theoretical one which is equal to 1073.64. These results confirm the uniformity of the generated sequence.

3) Correlation analysis: Correlation reflects the intensity of connection which may exist between two random variables. In PCNG, the values in the sequences must not be repeated nor correlated. To avoid the statistical analysis, the correlation coefficients of two sequences X and Y, computed with nearby initial conditions, should be close to zero.

The correlation coefficient is calculated by the following equation:

$$\rho_{XY} = \frac{\sum_{i=1}^{N}(x_i - \bar{X})(y_i - \bar{Y})}{[\sum_{i=1}^{N}(X_i - \bar{X})^2]^{1/2} \times [\sum_{i=1}^{N}(Y_i - \bar{y})^2]^{1/2}}. \tag{10}$$

where $\bar{X} = \frac{1}{N}\sum_{i=1}^{N} x_i$ and $\bar{Y} = \frac{1}{N}\sum_{i=1}^{N} Y_i$ are the mean values of two sequences X and Y respectively.

The calculated correlation coefficient ρ_{XY} is equal to 0.0022 (close to zero). Also, in Fig. 4 we give a zoom of the cross-correlation function of sequences X and Y, and the auto-correlation of sequence X. Results clearly show the negligible correlation between the generated sequences X and Y.

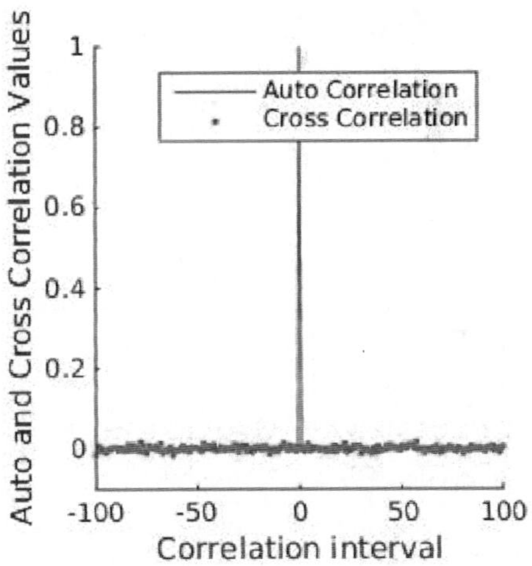

Figure 4: Cross-correlation of sequences X and Y, and auto-correlation of sequence X.

4) NIST test: We apply the NIST statistical test, which presents one of the most popular standard test for analysing randomness of binary data. The STS 2.1.2 version statistical test suite published in [15] is used. It consists of a battery of

188 tests (globally 15 different tests) to conclude regarding the randomness or non-randomness of binary sequences. For each test, a set of m P-values are expected to indicate failure. Indeed, an α = 0.01, indicates that 1% of the m sequences are expected to fail.

- A $P - value \geq \alpha = 0.01$ would mean that the sequence would be random with a confidence of $(1 - \alpha) = 99\%$.
- A $P - value < \alpha = 0.01$ would mean that the conclusion was that the sequence is non-random with a confidence of $(1 - \alpha) = 99\%$.

In our experiments, we generate m = 100 sequences, each of length 10^6 bits, and $\alpha = 0.01$.

The results are given in Fig. 5 and Table I. It can be seen that the bit-sequences pass all tests and fulfil the hypothesis of randomness. Therefore, the proposed chaotic generator is robust against statistical attacks.

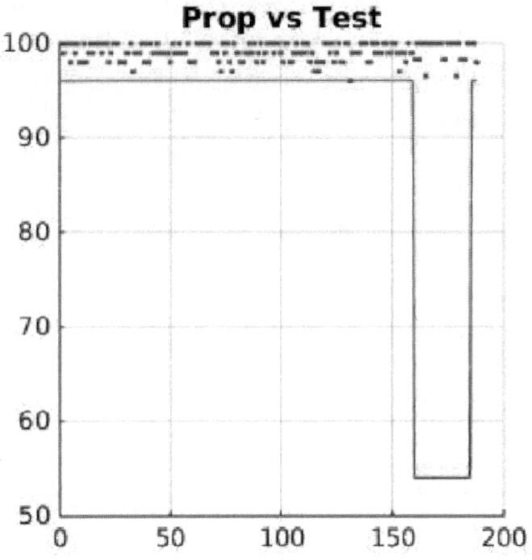

Figure 5: NIST tests results.

TABLE I: P-VALUES AND PROPORTION RESULTS OF NIST TEST.

Test	*P-value*	*Proportion*
Frequency test	0.972	99
Block-frequency test	0.055	99
Cumulative-sums test	0.834	98.5
Runs test	0.534	100
Longest-run test	0.290	99
Rank test	0.964	97
FFT test	0.384	97
Non periodic-templates	0.482	98.939
Overlapping-templates	0.637	98
Universal	0.237	98
Approximate entropy	0.936	99
Random-excursions	0.314	99.364
Random-excursions-variant	0.295	99.435
Serial test	0.606	100
Linear-complexity	0.290	99

C. Speed Performance

Speed is an important factor for evaluating the performance of a PCNG. For the proposed PCNG, we calculate the bit rate (in Mega bits per second) and the number of needed cycles to generate one byte. All experiments are performed on a personal computer with Intel(R) Core(TM) i5-4300M CPU @2.60GHz and memory 15,6 GB and the operating system is Ubuntu 14.04 Trusty Linux distribution, using GNU GCC Compiler. In tableII, we give, over 100 different secret keys, the average Bit Rate in Mbps and the average number of needed cycles to generate one byte (NCpB) for the proposed PCNG to generate 31250 samples. And we compare the obtained results with some known generators. The Bit Rate and NCpB are calculated respectively as follows:

$$Bit\ Rate(Mbps) = \frac{Generated\ data\ size(Mbits)}{Average\ generation\ time(s)} \quad (11)$$

$$NCpB = \frac{CPUspeed(Hz)}{Bit\ Rate(Byte/s)} \quad (12)$$

TABLE II: COMPUTING PERFORMANCE OF SOME KNOWN PCNGS.

Pseudo chaotic generator	*Bit Rate (Mbps)*	*NCpB*
Proposed PCNG	514.73	41
Jallouli et al. [7]	138	151
Shujun et al. [4]	9	711

We notice that the proposed chaotic generator is faster than the following known pseudo random number generator of the literature: Francois et al. [16], QUANTIS [17] and Blum Blum Shub [18].

IV. Design of a Random Number Generator

The ability to generate random numbers is important for many applications including cryptographic ones and others applications that do not require deterministic sequences when using the same secret key. For that, we adapt our PCNG, to be used as a random numbers generator. The proposed random numbers generator has the same structure of Fig. 1, but includes a refresh process repeated every R% samples, for generating a sequence X(n) of length n, to update the values of Xp(R), Xs(R) and Xl(R). The refresh process uses random values from the file "/dev/urandom" [19], interface to the Linux kernel's random number generator. For example, when using R = 50%, the bit rate of the proposed random numbers generator is equal to 397 Mbits/s.

V. Conclusion and Future Work

In this paper, we reported a work on the design, realization and test of a new pseudo chaotic number generator. This one is based on three discrete chaotic maps: PWLCM, Skewtent and Logistic that are weakly coupled. The proposed PCNG also includes a chaotic switching technique. Results of the statistical analysis show that the proposed PCNG has very good cryptographic properties due to its structure. In addition, it runs faster than other well known pseudo random number generators. Furthermore, the structure of the PCNG is updated to be used as a RNG for various applications that need random numbers such as generation of cryptographic keys, computer games and some classes of scientific experiments.

Our future work will focus on a software realization of chaos-based stream ciphers and the measurement of their energy consumption.

VI. Acknowledgement

The authors would like to thank the European Program Erasmus Mundus E-GOV-TN.

References

[1] B. Sunar, W. J. Martin, and D. R. Stinson, "A provably secure true random number generator with built-in tolerance to active attacks," IEEE Transactions on computers, vol. 56, no. 1, 2007, pp. 109–119.

[2] H. Karimi, S. Morteza Hosseini, and M. Vafaei Jahan, "On the combination of self-organized systems to generate pseudo-random numbers," Information Sciences, vol. 221, 2013, pp. 371–388.

[3] L. Kocarev and S. Lian, Chaos-based cryptography: Theory, algorithms and applications. Springer, 2011, vol. 354.

[4] L. Shujun, M. Xuanqin, and C. Yuanlong, "Pseudo-random bit generator based on couple chaotic systems and its applications in stream-cipher cryptography," in Progress in CryptologyINDOCRYPT 2001. Springer, 2001, pp. 316–329.

[5] R. Lozi, "Giga-periodic orbits for weakly coupled tent and logistic discretized maps," Modern Mathematical Models, Method and Algorithms for Real World Systems, A.H. Siddiqi, I.S. Duff and O.Christensen Editors, Anamaya Publishers, New Delhi India, 2006, pp. 80–124.

[6] ——, "Emergence of randomness from chaos," International Journal of Bifurcation and Chaos, vol. 22, no. 02, 2012, p. 1250021.

[7] O. Jallouli, S. El Assad, M. Chetto, R. Lozi, and D. Caragata, "A novel chaotic generator based on weakly-coupled discrete skewtent maps," in International Conference on Internet Technology and Secured Transactions, London, 2015, pp. 38–43.

[8] P. Amato, D. Mascolo, I. Pedaci, and D. Ruggiero, "Method of generating successions of pseudo-random bits or numbers," May 3 2006, uS Patent App. 11/381,474.

[9] R. Lozi, "New enhanced chaotic number generators," Indian Journal of Industrial and Applied Mathematics, vol. 1, no. 1, 2007, pp. 1–23.

[10] M. V. Petersen and H. M. B. Sørensen, "Method of generating pseudo-random numbers in an electronic device, and a method of encrypting and decrypting electronic data," Jan. 30 2007, uS Patent 7,170,997.

[11] S. El Assad, H. Noura, and I. Taralova, "Design and analyses of efficient chaotic generators for crypto-systems," in World Congress on Engineering and Computer Science 2008, WCECS'08. Advances in Electrical and Electronics Engineering-IAENG Special Edition of the. IEEE, 2008, pp. 3–12.

[12] S. El Assad, "Chaos based information hiding and security," in Internet Technology And Secured Transactions, 2012 International Conference for. IEEE, 2012, pp. 67–72.

[13] K. Desnos, S. El Assad, A. Arlicot, M. Pelcat, and D. Menard, "Efficient multicore implementation of an advanced generator of discrete chaotic sequences," in Internet Technology and Secured Transactions (ICITST), 2014 9th International Conference for. IEEE, 2014, pp. 31–36.

[14] L. Pace, "Chi-square tests," in Beginning R. Springer, 2012, pp. 217–228.

[15] B. Elaine and K. John, "Recommendation for random number generation using deterministic random bit generators," NIST SP 800-90 Rev A, Tech. Rep., 2012.

[16] M. François, T. Grosges, D. Barchiesi, and R. Erra, "A new image encryption scheme based on a chaotic function," Signal Processing: Image Communication, vol. 27, no. 3, 2012, pp. 249–259.

[17] A. K. Hartmann, Practical guide to computer simulations. World Scientific, 2009.

[18] L. Blum, M. Blum, and M. Shub, "A simple unpredictable pseudo random number generator," SIAM J. Comput., vol. 15, no. 2, May 1986, pp. 364–383. [Online]. Available: http://dx.doi.org/10.1137/0215025

[19] Z. Gutterman, B. Pinkas, and T. Reinman, "Analysis of the linux random number generator," in 2006 IEEE Symposium on Security and Privacy. IEEE, 2006, Berkeley/Oakland, CA, pp. 385 – 400.

A Novel Verifiable Multi-Secret Sharing Scheme Based on Elliptic Curve Cryptography

Nisha Patel, Prakash D.Vyavahare, Manish Panchal

Department of Electronics and Telecommunication Engineering
S. G. S. Institute of Technology and Science, Indore, India
Email: {nishapatel910622, prakash.vyavahare, hellopanchal}@gmail.com

***Abstract*—Multi-secret sharing schemes are used to protect multiple secrets by distributing them among many participants in such a manner that they can be reconstructed only by certain authorized group of participants. The scheme proposed by Lin-Yeh is one such method, which is based on Shamir's threshold scheme. In this paper a Verifiable Multi-Secret Sharing Scheme is proposed which is based on Shamir's threshold scheme, Elliptic Curve Discrete Logarithm Problem (ECDLP), and Double knapsack algorithm. The proposed scheme exhibits all the advantages of Lin-Yeh's scheme in which each participant has only one secret share for reconstructing multiple secrets. Additionally, the scheme does not require secure channel in secret share distribution phase since each participant's share is selected by participant himself. The scheme can also detect malicious participants during verification phase. The main advantage of ECDLP as compared to Rivest, Shamir and Adleman (RSA) and Discrete Logarithm Problem (DLP) is that it offers the same level of security for a smaller key size, thereby reducing processing overheads with lesser requirement of memory and bandwidth with faster implementation. Therefore, it can provide an efficient and secure mechanism for key management in public key systems.**

Keywords– Multi-Secret Sharing Scheme; Double Knapsack Algorithm; Shamir's Threshold Scheme; Malicious Participant Detection; ECDLP.

I. INTRODUCTION

Secret sharing schemes are important in protecting secret information from being lost, destroyed, modified and from unauthorized access. In a secret sharing scheme, the secret is distributed among the participants, and only an authorized group of participants can reconstruct the secret. In the case of (t, n) threshold secret sharing scheme, a secret is distributed to n participants and t (or more than t) participants can reconstruct the secret. The secret sharing schemes are used in different applications like image processing, bank vault opening, inter-continental ballistic missiles launch, and electronic transactions authentication.

In 1979, the secret sharing scheme was proposed independently by Shamir [1] and Blakley [2]. Blakley's scheme is based on the principle of linear projective geometry and Shamir's scheme is based on Lagrange interpolating polynomial. The common limitations of these schemes are: (i) At a time only one secret can be shared. (ii) To distribute the secrets, secure channel is needed. (iii) After the reconstruction of secret, the participant's share is disclosed to all. For sharing another secret, new secret share is redistributed to the participants over a secure channel. (iv) There is no mechanism to detect malicious participants. Shamir's scheme consumes lot of time and also costs for storage requirement. Therefore, it is used in sharing data of small size like the encryption key [3].

Several multi-secret sharing schemes based on strong mathematical structure are presented to remove these limitations, such as polynomial equations based Lin-Yeh method [4], secure one way function - He-Dawson method [5], matrix projection - Li Bai method [6] and many more. In Li Bai's method, the organization of secrets are in a square matrix. Therefore, the number of secrets must be a square of a number. If the number of secrets are not square, then the secret matrix is stuffed by dummy secrets.

He and Dawson [5] proposed a multi-secret sharing scheme based on one-way function, which uses successive one-way functions to share multiple secrets. Geng et al. [7] showed that He-Dawson scheme was actually one-time-use scheme and proposed a new multi-secret sharing scheme with multi-policy. The scheme proposed by Geng et al. is secure and multi-use system. Lin and Yeh [4] proposed a dynamic multi-secret sharing scheme, which is efficient than Geng et al. scheme in terms of computation complexity.

Lin-Yeh's proposed a scheme, which is based on One-way Hash Function (OHF) and the Exclusive OR (XOR) operation, in which multiple secrets can be reconstructed with only one secret share of each participant. Lin-Yeh's scheme is efficient and flexible multi-secret sharing scheme because each participant's share is unchanged even if the secrets to be shared are changed. The major issues with Lin-Yen's scheme are: it cannot detect malicious participants and requires a secure channel during secret distribution phase. The schemes mentioned in [8][9][10] have removed these limitations, but they need a secure channel for secret distribution and are inefficient in computation.

Several verifiable schemes have been proposed for multi-secret sharing [11][12][13], in which each participant needs to keep only one secret share, using which multiple secrets can be shared. Each participant submits a pseudo secret share which is calculated from the actual share of participant for reconstruction phase. Since participants themselves generate the secret share, it reduces the overhead on dealer and also removes the requirement of secure channel between dealer and participants. However, they are based on Discrete Logarithm Problem (DLP). In DLP-based schemes one needs more number of bits to achieve higher level of security and reliability than ECDLP, which increases the requirement of memory and bandwidth [14][15].

In this paper, we propose a scheme based on Shamir's threshold scheme, Elliptic Curve Discrete Logarithm Problem [16][17], the exclusive OR operation and Double knapsack algorithm [18]. The scheme provides the efficiency and flexibility similar to Lin-Yeh's scheme with advantages of malicious participant detection and without secure channel between the dealer and participants during secret share distribution phase. In the scheme proposed by us the participants, who will contribute in secret reconstruction, are decided by the dealer based on a proposed algorithm which uses the exclusive OR operation. Dealer sends this information to the combiner on public channel employing double knapsack algorithm. Elliptic curve cryptosystem provides the same level of security with smaller key size than other cryptosystems and offers lesser requirement of memory and bandwidth with faster implementation [19][20]. The security of scheme proposed by Hua and Aimin [21] is dependent on hash function. The scheme proposed by us does not have dependency on other cryptographic functions, such as hash function; so the scheme is efficient for threshold applications.

TABLE I. CONVENTION AND NOTATION

A	Group containing ID's of t participants
A'	Encoded form of A by double knapsack algorithm
C	Combiner
D	Dealer
E(F_p)	Elliptic curve E defined over F_p
F_p	Field with set (0, 1, 2, ..., p-1)
G	Generator point of prime order q
ID_j	Identifier of each participant $(1 \leq j \leq n)$
P_j	j^{th} Participant $(1 \leq j \leq n)$
R_j	Pseudo secret share of participant j
S_i	i^{th} Secret $(1 \leq i \leq k)$
S_l	l^{th} group secret in Lin-Yeh's method
U_j	Total number of participants in Lin-Yeh's method
Z_q^*	Field with set (1, 2, ... , q-1)
g	A primitive element over GF(p)
h	One-way hash function
n_1, n_2	Constants used in double knapsack algorithm
p	A large prime number
t	Number of participants required in secret reconstruction
x_j	Secret share of jth participant
$\oplus$	The exclusive OR operation
∞	Point at infinity on elliptic curve

The rest of this paper is organized as follows. In Section II, a review of Lin-Yeh's scheme is presented. In Section III, security weaknesses of Lin-Yeh's method are discussed, which is followed by brief description of Double knapsack algorithm in Section IV. In Section V, our proposed novel verifiable multi-secret sharing scheme based on elliptic curve cryptography is presented. The security features of the proposed scheme and its comparison with Lin-Yen method are presented in Section VI. Finally, the paper is concluded in Section VII.

II. REVIEW OF LIN-YEH'S DYNAMIC MULTI-SECRET SHARING SCHEME

There are three stages in Lin-Yen method [4], namely, (A) The system initialization stage, (B) Pseudo secret share generation stage and (C) Group secret reconstruction stage. They are explained as follows:

A. System Initialization Stage

The initialization of various public domain parameters and selection of their values is done by System Authority (SA) which is as follows:

1) p : a prime number which is large;
2) g : a primitive element over GF(p);
3) h(.) : a secure one-way hash function which produces a fixed length output for any arbitrary length of input;
4) ID_j : an identifier of the user U_j , for j = 1, 2, ... , n, where the secrets are to be shared among n participants.

Table I contains other notations and conventions.

B. Pseudo Secret Share Generation Stage

SA shares k group secrets S_i , where $1 \leq i \leq k$ among n users. Following steps are performed by the SA to produce pseudo secret shares and distribute master secret shares among the participants.

1) Corresponding to each participant j choose distinct $x_j \in Z_p^*$ for j = 1, 2, ... , n, as the master secret shares.
2) For i = 1, 2, ... , k, construct a polynomial f_i(x) of degree (i-1), as f_i(x) = S_i + d_1x + ... + $d_{i-1}x^{i-1}$ where $f_i(0)$ = S_i, d_1 to d_{i-1} are randomly selected integers.
3) For j = 1, 2, ... , n and i = 1, 2 ,... , k , compute V_{ij} = $f_i(ID_j)$, c_{ij} = $h^i(x_j) \oplus x_j$, R_{ij} = V_{ij} - c_{ij} mod p; Here $h^i(x_j)$ denotes i successive applications of h to x_j, symbol $\oplus$ denote the exclusive OR operation and c_{ij}'s are pseudo secret shares.
4) The master secrets x_j, for j = 1, 2, ... , n , are delivered by SA to each user U_j on secure channel and all R_{ij}'s are published.

C. Group Secret Reconstruction Stage

For reconstructing the lth group secret S_l , the following steps are performed by at least l participants out of n along with the group secret combiner:

1) For j = 1, 2, ... , l each U_j calculates his pseudo secret share as c_{lj} = $h^l(x_j) \oplus x_j$, and then sends it over secure channel to the group secret combiner.
2) After receiving all c_{lj}'s, for j = 1, 2, ... , l, the lth group secret is reconstructed by the group secret combiner as:

$$S_l = \left[\sum_{j=1}^{l} (c_{lj} + R_{lj}) \prod_{r=1, r\neq j}^{l} \frac{-ID_r}{ID_j - ID_r}\right] modp$$

III. SECURITY WEAKNESSES OF LIN-YEH'S METHOD

The multi-secret sharing scheme proposed by Lin-Yeh has following limitations:

1) Dealer selects the participant's secret share. Therefore, a dealer may become a cheater.
2) Secure channel is required between dealer and participants to distribute the secret share.
3) There is no mechanism to detect malicious participant.

IV. DOUBLE KNAPSACK ALGORITHM

Double knapsack algorithm is used to encode a message and make it secure over an insecure channel [18]. The algorithm is briefly described as follows:
Suppose there are two parties party 1 and party 2 who want to communicate securely.
Let r be the message to be encoded by party 1 and send to party 2.

Let l be the bit wise length of the message to be encoded. Let n_1 be a random number which is known only to sender and receiver. They calculate a series of vectors called a_i, as a_i = ${n_1}^i$, where i = 0, 1, 2, ... , (l-1). i.e.
a_i = 1, ${n_1}^1$, ${n_1}^2$, ${n_1}^3$, ... , ${n_1}^{l-1}$
Therefore $a_0 = 1$, $a_1 = n_1$, ... , $a_{l-1} = {n_1}^{l-1}$
First, r is converted into binary form as:
r = b_{l-1}, b_{l-2}, b_{l-3}, ... , b_2, b_1, b_0.
Where b_{l-1} is the Most Significant Bit(MSB) and b_0 is the Least Significant Bit(LSB).
Next r is encoded as:
$R = \sum a_i b_i$
and R is sent in place of r by party 1 to party 2.
Note that only sender and recipient know the series a_i.
The r value is recovered from R in an iterative fashion as follows:
STEP 1 let k = 1
STEP 2 R_1 = R - ${n_1}^{l-k}$
STEP 3 If $R_1 \geq 0$, Then a binary bit 1 is assigned to b_{l-k} and R = R_1.
STEP 4 If $R_1 < 0$, then a binary bit 0 is assigned to b_{l-k}.
STEP 5 Increase the value of k by one.
STEP 6 If $k \leq l$, go to STEP 2 and if $k > l$, then end the process.
Subsequently, if we repeat the above steps on R for a different value of n_1 like n_2 then it is called the double knapsack algorithm. Double knapsack algorithm has higher security than single knapsack algorithm.

V. PROPOSED SCHEME

The proposed scheme consists of three phases namely, (A). System initialization and secret share generation, (B). Secret construction and distribution, (C). Verification and secret reconstruction. These phases are described as follows:

A. System Initialization and Secret Share Generation

Let p be a prime number, and let F_p denote the field of integers modulo p. An elliptic curve E is defined over F_p. Let G be a point in E(F_p), and suppose that G has prime order q i.e. qG = ∞. Let P = (P_1, P_2, ... , P_n) denote the set of n participants and ID_j be the identification of jth participant. Let k (k ≥ 1) secrets to be shared be denoted by S = (S_1, S_2, ... , S_k). Let D be the trusted dealer.
Various steps involved in construction of shares are as follows:

1) The trusted dealer selects a generator G of prime order q. The dealer publishes the system parameters (p, E, q, G) on public channel.
2) Each participant P_j (1 ≤ j ≤ n) selects a random number $x_j \in Z_q^*$ as its own secret share and computes $R_j = x_j$ G mod p. The participant sends R_j to the dealer on public channel.
3) The dealer must ensure that for any values of i and j, $R_i \neq R_j$. If D finds that $R_i = R_j$ for some i and j then, D requests to participant j to send new R_j until D gets distinct values of R_j.
4) After collecting the R_j from all the participants the dealer chooses n distinct integers $ID_j \in Z_q^*$ (1 ≤ j ≤ n) as each participants identification. D will publish (R_j, ID_j) for all j = 1, 2, ... , n.

B. Secret Construction and Distribution

Secret construction and distribution is done as follows:

1) D randomly selects a number $b_0 \in Z_q^*$ and constructs a polynomial f(x) of degree k.
f(x) = $b_0 + S_1 x + S_2 x^2 + ... + S_k x^k$ mod p
Where $S_1, S_2, ..., S_k$ are k secrets to be shared.
2) For i = 1, 2, ... , k the dealer computes f(i).
3) D chooses another random number $x_0 \in Z_q^*$ and calculates $R_0 = x_0 G$ mod p and $I_j = x_o R_j$modp for j = 1, 2, ... , n. D computes the multiplicative inverse of x_0 as x_0^{-1} by using [($x_0 * x_0^{-1}$) mod p = 1] and by employing double knapsack algorithm encodes x_0^{-1} as y_0. D publishes R_0 and transmits y_0 to combiner on public channel.
4) D will select a group of participants t out of n, which is based on the number of secrets to be shared. The secret share of this group of participants will only be used by the combiner to reconstruct the secrets. Let the group be denoted as : A = $(ID_1, ID_2, ..., ID_t)$ where $t \leq n$.
5) D will observe the co-ordinates of I_t point for all ID_t, present in group A. Point I_t is represented as $(x, y)_t$ in co-ordinate form for t^{th} participant. Note that (x, y) is a point on elliptic curve E. The value of d is calculated by application of exclusive OR operation on the co-ordinates of I_t, in different ways in order to satisfy $d > k$, as mentioned below.
The algorithm known to both D and combiner has following steps:
   a) D will select minimum value from co-ordinate $(x, y)_t$ for all t and calculate d as:
   d = $[x_1 \oplus y_2 \oplus ... \oplus x_t]$ mod p
   where for ID_1 let min$(x, y)_1 = x_1$ (i.e. for ID_1 the x co-ordinate has minimum value) , for ID_2 let min$(x, y)_2 = y_2$ (i.e. for ID_2 the y co-ordinate has minimum value) , ... , and for ID_t let min$(x, y)_t = x_t$.
   If $d < k$ then D will change the A by increasing or decreasing the number of participants in A.
   b) If D will not get $d > k$ from step (a) then D calculates d by taking only x co-ordinates of I_t for all t present in A and calculates d as :
   d = $[x_1 \oplus x_2 \oplus ... \oplus x_t]$ mod p
   c) If D is again not able to get $d > k$ from step (b) then D calculates d by taking only y co-ordinates of I_t for all t ≤ n and calculates d as :
   d = $[y_1 \oplus y_2 \oplus ... \oplus y_t]$ mod p
   d) Till step (c) if D does not get desired value of d then D calculates d by taking sum of x and y co-ordinates of I_t for all t and calculates d as:
   d = $[(x_1 + y_1) \oplus (x_2 + y_2) \oplus ... \oplus (x_t + y_t)]$ mod p.
6) After getting d , D will compute f(d).
7) Using the double knapsack encoding algorithm the dealer will transmit the ID_t of the selected participants group A as A' and f(d) as f(d)' over a public channel. For using this algorithm the dealer and combiner agree on two random numbers n_1 and

n_2.

8) Then D will publish [f(1), f(2), ... , f(k), f(d)', A'].

C. *Verification and Secret Reconstruction*

Reconstruction of the secrets S_i (i = 1, 2, ... , k), and detection of cheater, is done by the combiner as follows :

1) Using the published information R_0 all the participants compute $W_j = x_j R_0$ and by employing double knapsack algorithm convert W_j in W_j'. Each participant delivers W_j' to the combiner on public channel. For this encoding the jth participant and combiner agree upon two random number.
2) The combiner decodes W_j from W_j' for all the participants, depending upon the knapsack constants on which the participant and combiner have agreed.
3) Now combiner decodes y_0 as x_0^{-1} by using n_1 and n_2 and checks whether $(x_0^{-1} * W_j) = R_j$ for all j = 1, 2, ... , n. If this is false then the malicious participant is detected.
4) Combiner gets [f(1), f(2), ... , f(k), f(d)', A'] from published information. Then it decodes the A' and f(d)' as A and f(d) respectively, by the knowledge of n_1 and n_2.
5) After getting group A, the combiner calculates d using the co-ordinates of W_j point of t participants by the same algorithm as used by dealer on the co-ordinates of I_j point for t participants present in group A, during secret construction phase.
6) After gathering the (k+1) data point [(1, f(1)), (2, f(2)), ... , (k, f(k)) and (d, f(d))] the combiner can reconstruct the k secrets using the following Lagrange interpolation:

$$f(x) = \left[\sum_{i=1}^{k+1} Y_i \prod_{j=1, j\neq i}^{k+1} \frac{x - X_j}{X_i - X_j}\right] modp$$

Where (X_i, Y_i) for i = 1, 2, ... , (k+1); denotes the (k+1) pairs respectively.

VI. SECURITY FEATURES AND COMPARISON OF THE PROPOSED SCHEME

A. *Security Features*

1) There is no role of dealer in selection of participant's secret share. Therefore, a dealer cannot become a cheater.
2) If an attacker attempts to get x_j from public information R_j, then the problem is equivalent to solving a discrete log problem on elliptic curves which is computationally hard.
3) The security of proposed scheme is based on the difficulty in solving the discrete logarithm problem on elliptic curves and finding double knapsack algorithm constants n_1 and n_2. In our scheme only D and combiner have the knowledge of A. Therefore, only the combiner can reconstruct the secrets using the Lagrange interpolation.

B. *Malicious Participant Detection*

The participants themselves generate the secret share x_j, so only the participant can calculate W_j using the published information R_0. The product of x_0^{-1} and W_j ensures that W_j belongs to the jth participant only. If any malicious participant tries to give false value as W_j" then it is easily caught by verifying that $x_0^{-1} * W_j'' \neq R_j$. This is achieved by the use of a integer x_0^{-1}.

Theorem : If $(x_0^{-1} * W_j = R_j)$, then P_j is true; otherwise P_j may be a cheater.

Proof : $x_0^{-1} * W_j = x_0^{-1} * (x_j R_0) = x_0^{-1} * x_j * (x_0 * G) modp = (x_j G) modp = R_j$.

C. *Performance Comparison*

The performance comparison of the proposed scheme with the Lin-Yeh's scheme is shown in Table II. The Lin-Yeh's multi-secret sharing scheme is based on OHF and XOR operation, successive use of hash function in the scheme contributes great complexities [22]. Lin-Yeh's scheme

TABLE II. COMPARISON OF PROPOSED SCHEME WITH LIN-YEH'S SCHEME

S.No	Characteristics	Lin-Yeh's Scheme	Proposed Scheme
1	Mathematical structure used	OHF	ECDLP
2	Detection of malicious participant	No	Yes
3	Dependent on security of other cryptographic function such as hash function	Yes	No
4	Participant selects his secret share	No	Yes
5	Secure channel requirement during share distribution	Yes	No
6	Parallel secret reconstruction	No	Yes
7	Cryptanalytic strength	Less	More
8	Computation time	Less	Comparable

uses $(k(n + k))$ one-way hash functions and $(k(k - 2))$ modular multiplication computations [4]. As compared to the other operations, the time for performing the modular addition and the XOR operation is ignored, because they are negligible. The proposed scheme's complexity is mainly based on polynomial interpolation and the point multiplication computation on elliptic curve. The proposed scheme uses $(4n + 1)$ point multiplication computation on elliptic curve. Point multiplication is the most important and most basic operation in elliptic curve cryptosystem, and we have methods to speed up the computation [23]. Interpolation operations are the common property in the schemes, which are based on Shamir's secret sharing scheme. we have efficient algorithms [24], using them the performance of our proposed scheme is improved largely. Especially, when the degree of the polynomial f(x) is only 1, only two pairs of (1, f(1)) and (d, f(d)) are required to reconstruct the secret S, which largely reduces the computational complexity. The complexity due to double knapsack algorithm is acceptable, because it is important in order to detect the malicious participant. In addition, the proposed scheme does not need secure channel. Therefore, proposed scheme has more cryptanalytic strength and offers higher security.

VII. CONCLUSION AND FUTURE WORK

In this paper, a verifiable multi-secret sharing scheme, which is based on Shamir's threshold scheme and elliptic curve discrete logarithm problem is proposed. The scheme offers the advantages over Lin-Yeh's scheme with verification feature of given shares and reduction in the cost of secure communication channel, required during secret distribution phase. The increase in computational complexity due to ECDLP is acceptable due to various advantages of Elliptic Curve Cryptosystem over other Cryptosystems. Therefore, the proposed scheme provides an efficient and secure mechanism for key management in public key systems. Key recovery mechanisms, distributed information storage and secure protocols, such as access control can be efficiently implemented by the proposed scheme.

The scheme proposed in this paper requires a trusted combiner during secret reconstruction and verification phase to detect malicious participants. The scheme can be modified in future, such that it does not require a trusted combiner.

REFERENCES

[1] A. Shamir, "How to share a secret?" Communication of the ACM, vol. 22, pp. 612-613, 1979.

[2] G. Blakley, "Safeguarding cryptographic keys," Proc AFIPS 1979 Nalt Conf, New York: AFIPS Press, vol. 48, pp. 313-317, 1979.

[3] A. Abdallah and M. Salleh, "Secret sharing scheme security and performance analysis," International Conference on Computing, Control, Networking, Electronics and Embedded Systems Engineering, pp. 173-180, 2015.

[4] H. Y. Lin and Y. S. Yeh, "Dynamic multi-secret sharing scheme," International Journal of Contemporary Mathematical Sciences, vol. 3, pp. 37-42, 2008.

[5] J. He and E. Dawson, "Multistage secret sharing based on one-way function," Electron. Lett., Vol. 30, pp. 1591-1592, 1994.

[6] L. Bai, "A strong ramp secret sharing scheme using matrix Projection," Proceedings of the 2006 International Symposium on a World of Wireless, Mobile and Multimedia Networks, pp. 652-656, 2006.

[7] Y. J. Geng, X. H. Fan, and F. Hong, "A new multi-secret sharing scheme with multi-policy," The 9th International Conference on Advanced Communication Technology, Vol. 3, pp. 1515-1517, 2007.

[8] F. Wang, L. Gu, S. Zheng, Y. Yang, and Z. Hu, "A novel verifiable dynamic multi-policy secret sharing scheme," Advanced Communication Technology (ICACT), The 12th International Conference, Vol. 2, pp. 1474-1479, 2010.

[9] D. Zhao, H. Peng, C. Wang, and Y. Yang, "A secret sharing scheme with a short share realizing the (t, n) threshold and the adversary structure," Computers and Mathematics with Applications, Vol. 64, Issue 4, pp. 611-615, August 2012.

[10] H. Pilaram and T. Eghlidosy, "An efficient lattice based multi-stage secret sharing scheme," in press, IEEE 2015.

[11] J. J. Zhao, J. Z. Zhang, and R. Zhao, "A practical verifiable multi-secret sharing scheme," Computer Standards and Interfaces, vol. 29, pp. 138-141, 2007.

[12] J. Qu, L. Zou, and J. Zhang, "A practical dynamic multi-secret sharing scheme," Information Theory and Information Security (ICITIS), pp. 629-631, 2010.

[13] A. Nalwaya, P. D. Vyavahare, and M. Panchal, "Veriable dynamic multi-secret sharing scheme," International Conference on Security and Management (SAM), pp. 186-188, 2013.

[14] M. Amara and A. Siad, "Elliptic curve cryptography and its applications," 7th International Workshop on Systems, Signal Processing and their Applications (WOSSPA), pp. 247-250, 2011.

[15] L. D. Singh and T. Debbarma, "A new approach to elliptic curve cryptography," International Conference on Advanced Communication Control and Computing Technologies (ICACCCT), pp. 78-82, 2014.

[16] D. Hankerson, A. Menezes, and S. Vanstone, "Guide to Elliptic Curve Cryptography," Springer, 2004.

[17] B. Qing-hai, Z. Wen-bo, J. Peng, and L. Xu, "Research on design principles of elliptic curve public key cryptography and its implementation," International Conference on Computer Science and Service System, pp. 1224-1227, 2012.

[18] R. R. Ramasamy, M. A. Prabakar, M. I. Devi, and M. Suguna, "Knapsack based ECC encryption and decryption," International Journal of Network Security, vol. 9, pp. 218-226, Nov. 2009.

[19] W. Stallings, "Cryptography and Network Security," Pearson, 2012.

[20] R. Markan and G. Kaur, "Literature survey on elliptic curve encryption techniques," International Journal of Advanced Research in Computer Science and Software Engineering, vol. 3, pp. 906-909, 2013.

[21] S. Hua and W. Aimin, "A multi secret sharing scheme with general access structures based on elliptic curve," 3rd International Conference on Advanced Computer Theory and Engineering (ICACTE), vol. 2, pp. 629 632, 2010.

[22] A. Das and A. Adhikari, "An efficient multi-use multi-secret sharing scheme based on hash function," Applied Mathematics Letters, vol. 23, pp. 993-996, April 2010.

[23] R. M. Avanzi, H. Cohen, and C. Doche, "Handbook of Elliptic and Hyperelliptic Curve Cryptography", Chapman and Hall/CRC Press, 2005.

[24] K. H. Rosen, "Elementary Number Theory and Its Applications", Addison-Wesley, MA, 1993.

An Improved ID based Proxy Signature Scheme based on Elliptic Curve Cryptography

Deepa Mukherjee
Electronics and Telecommunication
SGSITS
Indore, India
Email: dmukherjee1991@gmail.com

Prakash Vyavahare
Electronics and Telecommunication
SGSITS
Indore, India
Email: prakash.vyavahare@gmail.com

Manish Panchal
Electronics and Telecommunication
SGSITS
Indore, India
Email: hellopanchal@gmail.com

Abstract—**Proxy signature schemes allow the original signer of a message to delegate his signing capability to a proxy signer to generate a valid proxy signature on behalf of the original signer. One such scheme is proposed by Zhang and Kim which is based on Elliptic Curve Cryptography and Identity based Signature. However, Zhang's scheme requires secure channel for transmission of private key, has no provision of private key revocation and signature verification by any user. In this paper, we propose an improved ID based proxy signature scheme based on bilinear pairing. The scheme employs Knapsack algorithm for key distribution which eliminates the need for secure channel for sending the private keys from Private key generator (PKG) to respective users. The scheme also supports private key revocation by concatenating time parameter with public key of proxy signers. The signature can be verified only by a designated verifier. It is shown that the proposed proxy signature scheme satisfies all security requirements. Finally, the proposed proxy signature scheme is compared with that of Zhang and Kim's scheme and is shown to have merits over the latter one. Therefore, the proposed scheme can be a potential candidate for implementation of future proxy signature schemes.**

Keywords–Proxy Signature Scheme; ID based Cryptography; designated verifier scheme; ECC; Knapsack Algorithm;

I. INTRODUCTION

Digital Signatures are used in a wide variety of modern cryptographic systems that support data integrity and authentication. In public key cryptography, prior to any communication, each user should obtain a certificate from the Certificate Authority validating their public-private key pair. Proxy signatures schemes are one of the variety of digital signatures. Proxy signature schemes are required when the original signer is not available for some duration due to some reasons. Proxy signature scheme can be of two types depending on the signing authority. In full delegation scheme, signing rights are given permanently to the proxy signer. In partial delegation, signing right is delegated for a fixed period of time. The period of delegation and the type of messages that can be signed is usually specified by message warrant issued by the original signer at the time of delegation of signing authority.

In public key cryptography, the users must obtain their public-private key pair from the Certificate Authority prior to message communication [1]. In case of ID based cryptography, a trusted third party called as Private Key Generator (PKG) generates public-private key pair for the signers and transmits it to them via secure channel [2] [3]. In the recent proposals of proxy signatures, the public key of the signers is based on their popular public IDs (such as email id, telephone number etc).

Mambo [4] has described a proxy signature scheme based on Discrete Logarithm Problem (DLP). Recently, an improved proxy signature scheme based on RSA algorithm was proposed by Akanksha et. al [5] in Secureware 2015. The first ID based proxy signature scheme was proposed by Zhang and Kim, which requires a secure channel for transmission of private keys to the respective signers. Zhang and Kim [6] have described an identity based proxy signature scheme based on Elliptic Curve Cryptography. SK Hafizul [7] has described a designated verifier proxy signature scheme. This scheme [6] requires a secure channel for transmission of private key from PKG to user. It has no provision for private key revocation and the signature can be verified by any unknown verifier. The proposed proxy signature scheme attempts to overcome the drawbacks of this particular scheme.

In this paper, we have proposed an ID based proxy signature scheme that eliminates the requirement of a secure channel for transmission of secret key from PKG to signer. It also allows for changing the private key from time to time or when it is compromised to avoid its misuse for a long time. The proposed signature scheme has a designated verifier for verification of the signature created by the signer.

The rest of the paper is organized as follows. Section 2 decribes the Zhang and Kim's scheme. In Section 3, an improved ID based proxy signature scheme is proposed with its security analysis presented in Section 4. Finally, the paper is concluded in Section 5.

II. ZHANG AND KIM'S SCHEME

Let PKG be the private key generator. It generates public-private key pairs for the original and proxy signer. Let, Alice (A) be the alias name for original signer and Bob (B) be the alias name for proxy signer. Let Z_p be a field of order p. Let P be an element of Z_p having order p. Let p be a primitive element of Z_p. G_p be an additive cyclic subgroup of Z_p generated by P and G_M be a multiplicative group obtained by bilinear pairing of G_p and $e : G_p \times G_p \rightarrow G_M$ be a bilinear map that maps an element in G_p to an element in G_M. Table 1 summarizes the list of conventions and notation used in paper. The scheme advances as follows:

1) **Setup Phase**
In setup phase, Private Key Generator(PKG) generates its own public/private key pair. Let P_{pub} be

TABLE I. **LIST OF SYMBOLS**

SYMBOL	SIGNIFICANCE
A	Original Signer
B	Proxy Signer
C	Verifier
$C_{1,i}$, $C_{2,i}$	Encrypted r_i
G_p	Additive group over Z_p
G_M	Multiplicative Group obtained by Bilinear Mapping of G_p
H_1, H_2	Publicly Known Hash function
ID	Identity of the user e.g. email.
P	Generator element of Z_p
PKG	Private Key Generator
P_{pub}	Public key of PKG
Q_A, S_A	Public-private key pair of original signer
Q_B, S_B	Public-private key pair of proxy signer
Q_C, S_C	Public-private key pair of verifier
Q_W, S_W	Public-private key pair of proxy signer in proposed scheme to sign any message
Q_i'	Intermediate Public Key of the User i in the proposed scheme
S_1'	Signature of original signer on message warrant m_w in proposed scheme
S_g	Signature of proxy signer on message m in proposed scheme
U_A, c_A	Signature of original signer on message warrant mw in Zang and Kim's scheme
U_B, c_B	Signature of proxy signer on message m in Zang and Kim's scheme
Z_P	[0,p-1]
Z_p*	(1,p-1]
$Z \in_R [1, p-1]$	Random Number (Nounce) selected from Z_P
e	Bilinear map which maps an element in G_M to an element in G_P
k_A	Random number generated by original signer in Zang and Kim's scheme
k_B	Random number generated by proxy signer in Zang and Kim's scheme
l	Bitwise length of private key S_i of user i in proposed scheme
m_w	Message warrant
p	Number of elements in field Z_p
r_i	Point on elliptic curve randomly selected by user i for Knapsack algorithm
s	Master key or secret key of PKG
t_i	Time for which the generated public key in proposed scheme is valid

the PKG's public key that is generated using PKG's master key s as follows:

a. Let G_P be an additive cyclic subgroup of Z_p and G_M be a multiplicative cyclic group obtained by bilinear mapping of G_p each of prime order p.
b. Let P be the generator element of G_p
c. Define a bilinear map $e : G_p \times G_p \rightarrow G_M$.
d. PKG selects a random number $s \in_R Z_p^*$ and
e. PKG calculates its own public key Ppub as follows
f. $P_{pub} = sP$

The system public parameters are $params = (G_p, G_M, e, p, P, Ppub, H_1, H_2)$, where H_1 and H_2 are publicly known hash functions.

2) **Extract Phase**
In Extract phase, PKG calculates public and private key pairs (Q_A, S_A) and (Q_B, S_B) based on ID_A and ID_B for original and proxy signer respectively. Let ID be the public identity of the user such as telephone number or email id, etc.

a. Let ID_i is the public ID of i where $i \in (A, B)$
b. For the given identity ID of a signer(telephone number, email id, etc), PKG computes the public key Q_i as for ID as follows:
$Q_i = H_2(ID)$
c. The private key S_i is calculated by PKG as
$S_i = sQ_{ID}$
where s is the private key of PKG $s \epsilon Z_p$

Then, Q_{ID_i} is the public key of i where $i \in (A, B)$
S_{ID_i} is the private key of original signer where $i \in (A, B)$
PKG sends S_A and S_B to A and B respectively on secure channel.
Note that ID_A and ID_B i.e. IDs of original and proxy signers are publicly known
Since H_2 is public function, anyone can calculate Q_A and Q_B

3) **Proxy Key Generation**
To delegate his signing capability to a proxy signer, the original signer A makes signed warrant m_w that consists of public IDs of A and B, type of messages that can be signed by proxy signer (B) and validity period of proxy signer's signatures.
To delegate the signing capacity to the proxy signer, the original signer (Alice) makes the signed warrant m_w consisting of public IDs of original and proxy signer, type of messages that can be signed and valid time period for proxy signature. The proxy key S_{Bm} is generated by Bob as follows:

a. A randomly selects $k \in_R Z_p^*$ and computes
$r_A = e\,(P, P)^k$
$c_A = H_1\,(m_w \parallel r_A)$
$U_A = c_A S_A + kP$
b. A then sends (m_w, c_A, U_A) to B on secure channel.
Note that S_A and P lie on elliptic curve on Z_p and c_A and k_A are scalar quantities. and r_A is not sent explicitly from A to B
c. On receiving the above information from A, proxy signer B computes the following:
$r_A = e\,(U_A, P)\, e\,(Q_A P_{pub})^{-c_A}$
and accepts the signature to be valid if and only if
$c_A = H_1\,(m_w \parallel r_A)$
This validates that B has received information from A only(authentication).
d. If the signature on message warrant is valid, B computes his private proxy key as follows:
$S_{Bm} = c_A S_B + U_A$ where S_{Bm} is a modified proxy key created by proxy signer using the original proxy key sent by PKG to user.

4) **Proxy Signature Generation**
The message m is signed by proxy signer B using his proxy key S_{Bm} as follows:

a. Proxy signer B selects a random number $k_B \epsilon Z_p*$
b. B computes $r_B = e\,(P, P)^{k_B}$
c. B computes the proxy signature on message m using his proxy signature key S_B as follows:
$c_B = H_1\,(m \parallel r_B)$
$U_B = c_B S_{Bm} + k_B P$
d. B broadcasts (m, c_B, U_B).
where m is the message, r_B is an intermediate value and (c_B,U_B) is the signature of B

on message m.
The signature generated by this scheme is proxy protected as it can be created by the proxy signer only.

5) **Verification Phase**
Any verifier can verify signature on message m to be valid as follows:
   a) Verifier computes
   $r_B = e(U_B, P)\left(e(Q_A + Q_B, P_{pub})^{H_1(m_w \| r_A)} r_A\right)^{-c_A}$
   b) Verifier accepts signature to be valid on message m if and only if
   $c_B = H_1(m \| r_B)$

A. Security Analysis of Zhang and Kim's scheme

The security analysis of Zhang and Kim's scheme is as follows:

1) Secure channel is needed for transmission of secret key from PKG to original signer A and proxy signer B.
2) If the private keys of original signer A and proxy signer B has been compromised, even then since people use their popular public IDs as public key, the system is no longer secure.
3) Validity of generated signature can be verified by anyone which may not be desirable in some situations.

III. PROPOSED SCHEME

In previous section, the Zang and Kim's ID based proxy signature which did not fulfill all the security requirements. An ID based proxy signature scheme has been proposed that overcomes some of the shortcomings pointed out in the previous section. The given scheme consists of seven phases namely, 1. Setup phase, 2. Public Key Generation phase, 3. Private Key Generation phase, 4. Secret Key Sharing Phase 5. Proxy Key Generation Phase, 6. Proxy signature generation, and 7. Proxy signature verification.

Let PKG be the private key generator. It generates public-private key pairs for the original and proxy signer and verifier. Let Z_p be a field of order p. Let P be an element of Z_p having order p. Let G_p be an additive cyclic subgroup of Z_p generated by P and G_M be a multiplicative group obtained by bilinear pairing of G_p and $e : G_p \times G_p \rightarrow G_M$ be a bilinear map that maps an element in G_p to an element in G_M.

The various steps involved in the proposed proxy signature scheme are as follows:

1) **Setup phase**
In this phase, the PKG generates its own public private key pair(P_{pub}, s) as follows:
   a. PKG selects an elliptic curve E over Z_p and broadcasts it.
   PKG randomly selects $s \in Z_p$ where s is the private key of PKG.
   b. Let P be a point on elliptic curve. PKG generates its public key P_{pub} as follows:
   $$P_{pub} = sP \quad (1)$$
   where s is the private key of PKG
   PKG then broadcasts P_{pub} and P.

2) **Public Key Generation**
In this phase, PKG generates public keys of original signer A, proxy signer B and verifier C as follows:
   a. PKG calculates intermediate public key Q_i' using public ID of signer(such as email ID, telephone number etc) and a publicly known hash function H_1.
   $Q_i' = H_1(ID_i)$
   b. The intermediate public key Q_i' is concatenated with time parameter t_i which indicates the validity period of proxy signature key.
   $Q_i = Q_i' \| t_i$
   Q_i is the public key for entity where $i \in (A, B, C)$
   Note that public key is changed by PKG from time to time so that even if the private key is compromised, it cannot be misused for a longer time.

3) **Private key generation phase**
PKG computes each user i's private key as follows:
$S_i = sQ_i$
where
s is the secret key of PKG
Q_i is the public key of user i and
S_i is the secret key of user i

4) **Secret Sharing Phase**
   a. To obtain its private key, each user i selects a random point r_i on elliptic curve where $i \in (A, B, C)$
   Let $r_i = (r_{ix}, r_{iy})$ where r_{ix} and r_{iy} are the x and y coordinates of r_i respectively.
   b. User then computes $n_i = |r_{ix} + r_{iy}|$
   c. User i then selects another random number $k_i \in Z_p$.
   d. Each user i then encrypts the point r_i using PKG's public key according to the following equations [8]:
   $C_{1,i} = k_i P$
   $C_{2,i} = r_i + k_i P_{pub}$
   Where P_{Pub} is the public key of PKG.
   Note that P, r_i, $C_{1,i}$, $C_{2,i}$ and P_{pub} are points on an elliptic curve over Z_p and k_i is a scalar quantity
   e. User i then sends $C_{1,i}$ and $C_{2,i}$ to PKG on public channel.
   f. The PKG then decrypts $C_{1,i}$ and $C_{2,i}$ and obtain r_i as follows
   $r_i = C_{2,i} - sC_{1,i} = C_{2,i} - sk_iP = r_i + k_iP_{pub} - k_iP_{pub} = r_i$
   g. PKG then computes $n_i = |r_{ix} + r_{iy}|$
   h. PKG calculates a series N_i using number n_i as
   $N_i = (1, n_i, n_i^2, ...n_i^j, n_i^{l-1})$
   where $i \in (A, B, C)$ and $j \in (0, 1, 2....., l-1)$
   where l is the bitwise length of the private key.
   i. PKG converts S_i into binary form as $S_i = (b_{l-1}, b_{l-2}, ..., b_1, b_0)$
   Where b_{1-1} is the Most Significant

Bit(MSB) and b_0 is the Least Significant Bit(LSB)

j. PKG computes R_i for each user i using KNAPSACK algorithm [9]
$R_i = \sum n_i^j b_j,\ 0 \leq j \leq l-1$

k. Then PKG sends R_i to the signer on public channel.

l. Signer i recovers $S_i = (b_{l-1}, \ldots\ldots, b_0)$ as follows:
Let R_I be an intermediate value derived from R_i

I $k = 1$.
II $R_i' = R_i$
III $R_I = R_i' - n_i^{l-k}$.
IV If $R_I < 0$
$b_{l-k} = 0$
IV If $R_I \geq 0$
$b_{l-k} = 1,\ R_i' = R_I$
V $k = k + 1$
VI If $k \leq l$, go to step III
If $k > l$, then end the process

In this way user i recovers his secret key S_i.

5) **Proxy Key Generation**
Original signer creates a message warrant m_w specifying public identities of original and proxy signer, validity period of signing of the proxy signature and type of messages that can be signed.

a. The original signer computes

$$S_1 = H_2 (m_w \parallel S_A) \tag{2}$$

Where H_2 is publicly known hash function. and sends (m_w, S_1) to B on public channel.

b. B computes

$$S_1{}' = H_2 (S_1 \parallel S_B) \tag{3}$$

and sends $(m_w, S_1{}')$ to PKG on public channel.

c. PKG accepts $(m_w, S_1{}')$ if the following equation holds true:

$$S_1{}' = H_2 (H_2 (m_w \parallel S_A) \parallel S_B) \tag{4}$$

This verification can be done by PKG since S_A and S_B are known to PKG only

d. Then, PKG finally computes public key (Q_w) and private key (S_w) of proxy signer for signing a message.

$$Q_w = H_1 (m_w) \tag{5}$$

$$S_w = sQ_w \tag{6}$$

e. PKG then sends S_w to B on public channel using Knapsack algorithm. PKG also broadcasts the public key Q_w.

f. B accepts (S_w, Q_w) only if the following equation holds true:

$$e(S_w, P) = e(H_1 (m_w), P_{pub}) \tag{7}$$

This step ensures data integrity of S_w and Q_w.

6) **Proxy Signature Generation**
In this phase, proxy signer (B) generates proxy signature on message m in following manner:

a. B computes

$$T = e(S_w, Q_C) \tag{8}$$

where Q_C is the public key of verifier.

b. B then computes

$$S_g = H_2 (m \parallel m_w \parallel T) \tag{9}$$

c. B sends (m_w, m, S_g) to the verifier for verification

7) **Proxy Signature Verification**
To accept the signature is accepted by the verifier by calculating the following:

a. PKG calculates an intermediate value $\bar{T}$ as follows:

$$\bar{T} = e(H_1 (m_w,), S_C) \tag{10}$$

Where S_C is the private key of verifier given by following equation:

$$S_C = sQ_C \tag{11}$$

Where s is the private key of PKG and Q_C is the public key of verifier.

b. PKG calculates an intermediate variable s' as follows:

$$s' = H_2 \left(m \parallel m_w \parallel \bar{T}\right) \tag{12}$$

c. The signature is accepted by PKG if the following equation holds true:
$s' = S_g$

As the proxy signer B uses his own private key S_W, neither the original signer nor PKG can create a valid proxy signature.

Only a designated verifier can verify the proxy signature as the designated verifier's public key (Q_C) is also involved in creating the signature for message m and it can be verified by the designated verifier only by using his own private key.

A. An Implementation Example of the Proposed Scheme

The scheme can be implemented using an example given below. The elliptic curve considered is $E : y^2 = x^3 + 4x + 20$ and the calculations have been done using elliptic curve calculator [10]. The various steps of the proposed scheme can be exemplified as follows:

a **Setup Phase**
Let $E : y^2 = x^3 + 4x + 20$ be an Elliptic Curve defined over $Z_{29} = (0, 28)$.
Let P=(1,5) be a point on E over Z_p.
We assume that the order of P in 29.
Let the private key of PKG, s=3.
The public key of PKG P_{pub} is calculated as follows:
$P_{pub} = sP = 3(1,5) = (20,3)$

b **Public Key Generation Phase**
Let ID_i be the publicly known ID of user i.
Let H_1 be a hash function that maps ID_i to a point on E.
$Q_i{}' = H_1 (ID_i)$

The intermediate public key $Q_i{}'$ is concatenated with time parameter t_i which indicates the validity period of proxy signature key.
$Q_i = Q_i' \parallel t_i$
Q_i is the public key for entity where $i \in (A, B, C)$ where Q_i is the public ID of user i where $i \in (A, B, C)$
Where A is the original signer, B is the proxy signer and C is the verifier.
Let $Q_A = (20, 3)$, $Q_B = (4, 19)$ and $Q_C = (15, 27)$.

c **Private Key Generation Phase**
Private key of A i.e. S_A is calculated as follows:
$S_A = sQ_A$=$S_A = 3(20, 3)$=(14,23)
Similarly, $S_B = (17, 19)$ and $S_C = (19, 13)$

d **Secret Key Sharing Phase**
Let user A selects $r_A = (3, 1)$.
Therefore n_A = $|3 + 1|$=4
The generated series N_A = 1, 4, 16,........
A selects a random number k_A=2
A encrypts r_A as follows:
$C_{1,A} = k_A P$ = 2(1, 5) = (4, 19)
$C_{2,A} = r_A + k_A P_{pub}$ = (3,1) + 2(20,3) = (0, 7)
(4, 19) and (0, 17) is sent by A to PKG instead of (3, 1) on public channel.
PKG recovers r_A as follows:
$r_A = C_{2,A} - sC_{1,A}$ = (0, 17) - 3(4,19)= (3,1)
PKG calculates n_A = $|3 + 1|$ = 4
PKG generates N_A = 1, 4, 16,........
PKG converts S_A = (14, 23), the private key of A into binary form (01110, 10111).
14 is encrypted as follows:
$(14)_{10}$ = $(01110)_2$ = (0x256) + (1x64) + (1x16) + (1x4) + (0x1) = 84.
Similarly 23 is encrypted as 277.
PKG sends (84, 277) instead of (14, 23) to A on public channel.
84 is decrypted as follows:
Let R_I be an intermediate variable.
R_I = 84 - 4^4 = -172 which is negative, hence $b_4 = 0$.
R_I = 84 - 4^3 = 20 which is positive, hence $b_3 = 1$.
R_I = 20 - 16 = 4 which is positive, hence $b_2 = 1$.
R_I = 4 - 4^1 = 0 which is 0, hence $b_1 = 1$.
R_I = 0 - 1 = -1 which is negative, hence $b_0 = 0$.
Hence, 84 is decrypted into $(01110)_2$ = $(14)_{10}$.
Similarly, 277 is decrypted into $(10111)_2$ = $(23)_{10}$.
In this way, A recovers its private key S_A = (14, 23).
Similarly, B and C receive their private key S_B = (17, 19) and S_C = (19, 13).

e **Proxy Key Generation**
Original signer selects a message warrant m_w = 6.
The original signer computes
$S_1 = H_2(m_w \parallel S_A) = H_2(3 \parallel (14, 23))$
Where H_2 is publicly known hash function that gives a point S_1 on elliptic curve E.
Let S_1 = (10, 4)
and sends $(6, (10, 4))$ to B on public channel.
B computes
$S_1{}' = S_1{}' = H_2(S_1 \parallel S_B) = H_2((10, 4) \parallel (17, 19))$
Let $S_1{}'$ = (1, 24)
and sends $(6, (1, 24))$ to PKG on public channel.
PKG accepts $(6, (1, 24))$ if the following equation holds true:
$H_2(H_2(6 \parallel (14, 23)) \parallel (17, 19))$ = (1, 24).
PKG computes public-private key pair (S_w, Q_w) of proxy signer B as follows:
$Q_w = H_1(6)$
Where H_1 is a publicly known hash function that maps m_w to a point Q_w on elliptic curve E
Let Q_w be (8, 10).
The private key S_w is calculated as follows:
$S_w = sQ_w$ = 3(8, 10) = (16, 2).
PKG sends (16, 2) to B on public channel using Knapsack algorithm.
PKG also broadcasts the public key Q_w.
B accepts $(16, 2)$ only if the following equation holds true:
$e((16, 2), (1, 5)) = e(H_1(6), (20, 3))$, where e is a bilinear pairing that maps a pair of elements in additive cyclic group G_p to an element in multiplicative group G_M.
The above condition holds true if S_w is valid.
This step ensures data integrity of S_w and Q_w.

f **Proxy Signature Generation**
Let the message to be signed by proxy signer be m = 8.
(B) generates proxy signature on message m = 8 in following manner:
B computes
$T = e(S_w, Q_C) = e((16, 2), (15, 27))$
where Q_C is the public key of verifier. e is a bilinear pairing that maps a pair of elements in additive cyclic group G_p to an element in multiplicative group G_M.
Let us assume that bilinear pairing e maps (16, 2) and (15, 27) to an element (20, 26).
$e((16, 2), (15, 27))$ = (20, 26)
B then computes $S_g = H_2(8 \parallel 6 \parallel (20, 26))$
Assuming that the hash function gives (13, 6) as output, we obtain the following equation:
$S_g = H_2(8 \parallel 6 \parallel (20, 26))$ = (13, 6)
B sends $(6, 8, (13, 6))$ to the verifier for verification.

g **Proxy Signature Verification**
To accept the signature is accepted by the verifier by calculating the following:
PKG calculates an intermediate value $\bar{T}$ as follows:
$\bar{T} = e(H_1(6,), (19, 13))$
Let us assume that $H_1(6)$ = (2, 6).
We also assume the following:
$\bar{T} = e(H_1(6,), (19, 13))$ = (2, 6)
Where (19, 13) is the private key of verifier.
PKG calculates an intermediate variable s' as follows:
$s' = H_2(6 \parallel 8 \parallel (2, 6))$
The signature is accepted by PKG if the following equation holds true:
$s' = S_g$
The above equation holds true if the authorized proxy signer B signs the message m = 8 and designated verifier C verifies the signature.

B. Security Analysis of the Proposed Scheme

In this section we discuss about the security aspects of the proposed scheme such as trusted PKG, proxy key revocation, designated verifier, proxy protected, unforgability, non repudiation and secure channel. They are as follows:

1) **Trusted PKG**
The security of ID based signatures is based on the fact that PKGs should be trusted. If the PKG is not trusted then the scheme is not secure. However, given a trusted PKG, the scheme is secure.
2) **Private key revocation**
Even if private key of user is compromised, it cannot be misused for a long time as public key is valid only for particular time for which the time parameter t_i remains unchanged.
3) **Designated verifier**
Only designated verifier C can verify the proxy signature which is desirable in some situations.This is done by using the public key of verifier Q_C in creating the signature S_g which can be verified only if the verifier has the corresponding private key S_C. This happens because the designated verifiers public key is also involved in signing the message m and it can be verified by the designated verifier using his own public key.
4) **Proxy protected**
Only the proxy signer should be able to create a valid proxy signature, not the original signer. In this scheme, the secret key of the proxy signer S_w is calculated by PKG using his own secret key s which cannot be calculated by the original signer due to Elliptic Curve Discrete Logarithm Problem(ECDLP). Hence the proposed scheme is proxy protected.
5) **Unforgability**
Only the proxy signer should be able to create a valid proxy signature. In the proposed scheme, as the proxy signer creates the signature S_g using his own private key S_w, no one else can sign on behalf of proxy signer, neither the original signer himself nor a third party.
6) **Non-repudiation**
The proxy signer should not be able to deny his signature later on. In this scheme the proxy signer creates signature S_g by using his private key S_w and is verified by verifier using proxy signer's public key Q_w using his public key. Hence, the proxy signer cannot deny his signature.
7) **Secure channel**
In Zang and Kim's scheme, a secure channel is required for transmission of secret key from PKG to signers. In our proposed scheme, the PKG uses KNAPSACK algorithm to encrypt the secret keys and signers use reverse knapsack to extract back the keys. Therefore communication can take place on insecure channel.

TABLE II. **COMPARISON BETWEEN ZHANG AND KIM's SCHEME AND PROPOSED SCHEME**

Parameters	Zhang and Kim's Scheme	Proposed Scheme
Number of Steps	5	7
Secure channel requirement	Yes	No
Proxy key revocation	No	Yes
Designated verifier	No	Yes

The proposed scheme eliminates the need for a secure channel for transmission of private key from PKG to signers. It also provides the feature of private key revocation as per the need. The scheme has a provision for designated verifier only. Table 2 summarizes the comparison between Zhang and Kim's scheme and proposed scheme.

IV. CONCLUSION

In this paper, we have proposed a new ID based proxy signature scheme. The scheme has eliminated the use of secure channel for transmission of private key from PKG to original signer, proxy signer and verifier using KNAPSACK algorithm. This scheme also exhibits Private key revocation feature such that if a private key is exposed, it cannot be used for a long time. This scheme allows the proxy signature to be verified by a designated verifier only. As it satisfies all security requirements, it can be used in future proxy applications. This scheme is designed for a single proxy signer only, which can be extended to multiple proxy signers. However, the proposed needs a trusted PKG. This condition can be removed as part of future work.

REFERENCES

[1] D. Hankerson , D. Menezes and D. Vanstone, Guide to Elliptic Curve Cryptography, Springer, 2004
[2] https//courses.cs.washington.edu/courses/csep590/06wi/finalprojects
[3] A. K. Kommera , K. Kommera and P. K. Gunda, A Closer Look at ECC and RSA, "International Journal of Computer Science and Information Technologies", 2011, pp. 2220–2224
[4] M. Mambo , K. Usuda and E. Okamoto, Proxy signatures:Delegation of the power to sign messages, IEICE Transactions Fundamentals E79-A9, 1996, pp. 1338–1353
[5] A. Gupta , P.D. Vyavahare and M. Panchal, An Improved Threshold Proxy Signature Scheme, "SECURWARE: The Ninth International Conference on Emerging Security Information, System and Technologies", 2015, pp. 49–54
[6] F. Zhang and Kim, Efficient ID-based blind signature and proxy signature from bilinear pairings, Proceedings of the "8th Australasian Conference on Information Security and Privacy", 2003, pp. 312–307
[7] S.K. Hafizul and G.P. Biswas, Design of an Efficient ID-based Short Designated Verifier Proxy Signature Scheme, "Conference on Recent Advances in Information Technology", 2012, pp. 64–72
[8] W. Stallings, Cryptography and Network Security: Pearson, 2012
[9] R.R. Rajaram , M.A. Prabakar , M.I. Devi and M. Suguna, Knapsack based ECC encryption and decryption, "International Journal of Network Security", 2009, pp. 218–226
[10] http://www.christelbach.com/ECCalculator.aspx

Selective Hybrid Chaotic-Based Cipher for Real-Time Image Application

Moussa Farajallah
College of Information Technology and Computer Engineering
Palestine Polytechnic University
Hebron, Palestine
Email: mousa_math@ppu.edu

Rawan Qumsieh
Master of Informatics
Palestine Polytechnic University
Hebron, Palestine
Email: Rawan.iq@gmail.com

Samer Isayed
Master of Informatics
Palestine Polytechnic University
Hebron, Palestine
Email: samers@ppu.edu

***Abstract*—Confusion and diffusion are the two main principles in encryption. Confusion is a process that drastically changes data from the input to the output. In order to make it right, we have to make the relation between the key and cipher-text as complex as possible. On the other hand, diffusion means that changing a single character of the input will change many characters of the output. In other words, we can say that the output bits should depend on the input bits in a very complex way, so if we change one bit in the plain-text, the cipher-text will change completely. Many chaos-based algorithms were implemented with a chaotic map called the Skew Tent Map (STM), which we address and evaluate in this paper. Our proposed hybrid encryption scheme combines both stream and block ciphering algorithms to achieve the required level of security with the minimum encryption time. The proposed chaos-based cryptosystem uses the STM as a substitution based on a lookup table and STM as a generator to change the byte position to achieve the required confusion and diffusion effects. There is no need to have the inverse or the reverse of the generator in our proposed cryptosystem. The robustness of the proposed cryptosystem was proven by the performance and security analysis, as well as the high encryption speed (throughput).**

Keywords–skew tent map; confusion; diffusion; chaos-based cryptosystem.

I. INTRODUCTION

Finding new channels to transmit data over the Internet is easy, but the main problem is how to ensure sending it safely. Cryptography is the way to transform data, so that it is hidden to all except those who are the intended recipients of the data. So, it mainly provides secure ways to exchange personal and secret information between others through the electronic world. Encrypting images in the electronic world is especially important, yet the basic way to encrypt an image is slow in comparison with other fields of encryption. Many researchers are working to find cryptosystems to transmit images in a secure and fast way. On the other hand, the redundancy between bytes of the images is higher than it is in texts, and so we need a strong encryption algorithm to remove this high correlation and all crypto problem resulting from this high redundancy. We chose to work with chaos theory as it has the most powerful and important property required in any cryptosystem that produces random behaviors. Also, chaotic maps can be used as symmetric or asymmetric encryption algorithms [1].

It has been shown by many researchers that chaotic cryptosystems are excessively sensitive to the changes of their control parameters. Furthermore they have a pseudo-random behaviour toward non-authorized parties [2]–[7], and depending on the experimental results in [8]–[12], chaos-based encryption achieved a better security than the classical encryption algorithms [8].

Fridrich introduced the first chaos-based encryption algorithm [13] [14]. In his algorithm, the diffusion effect was achieved by using a non-linear feedback register, while the confusion effect was achieved by using three different 2-D chaotic maps; the standard one, the Backer's and the 2-D cat map.

Masuda et al. [15] [16] considered two different chaotic maps, "key-dependent chaotic s-box and chaotic mixing transformation" [15]. To make their cryptosystem resident to differential and linear cryptanalysis, they estimated bounds for the differential and linear probabilities.

Chaos-based image encryption was proposed in [17], where the authors used two Piece Wise Linear Chaotic Map (PWLCM), the first during implementing the addition modulo 256 in the substitution process, and the second is used in the permutation process (degree of 8). The error propagation, the slow encryption speed were weaknesses in this algorithm.

Finally, a fast and secure cryptosystem was proposed by Zhang et al. [18], which appears to be robust and secure against attacks, and faster than other previously proposed cryptosystems .

Our paper is organized as follows: The directly relevant work is presented in the next section. Then our cryptosystem and the evaluation regarding the complexity of execution and the security is shown in Section 3 and Section 4. Finally, the conclusion is given in Section 5.

II. RELATED WORK

For real-time image encryption, being fast and secure is the most important thing to many scientists in the cryptanalysis field.

A. Fridrich Model

Fridrich proposed in 1997 a chaos-based encryption scheme [13]. This model of Fridrich became the core structure of most all chaos-based cryptosystems.

The Fridrich model as shown in Figure 1 is composed of two layers; the first layer is the confusion layer which uses the 2D Baker chaotic map to calculate the new positions of

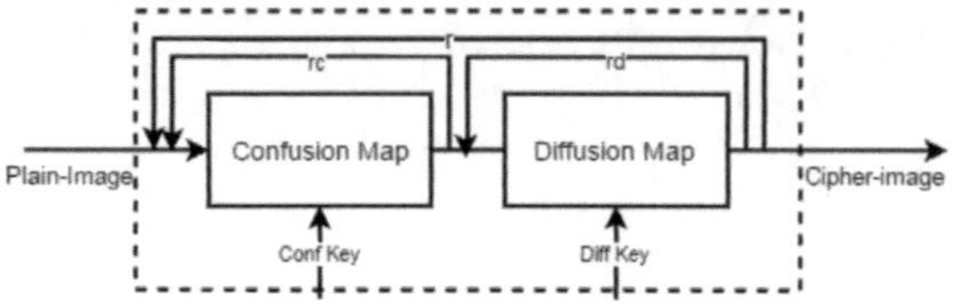

Figure 1. Fridrich image encryption architecture

each byte using(1)&(2), and the diffusion layer which is used to spread a single byte effect to the other bytes in the same block.

$$B(x,y) = (2x, \frac{y}{2}) \quad when\ 0 \leq x < \frac{1}{2} \tag{1}$$

$$B(x,y) = (2x-1, \frac{y}{2}+\frac{1}{2}) \quad when\ \frac{1}{2} \leq x \leq 1 \tag{2}$$

After calculating the new position of the byte, the x_1 position will be occupied with the value of the first shuffled position, while the second shuffled value will be in x_2, and so on. Solak [19] broke Fridrich's algorithm using a chosen cipher-text attack, as he revealed some secret permutation from the algorithm.

B. Masuda Model

Masuda et. al. in [15], introduced a cryptosystem which uses the Finite State Tent Map (FSTM), which encrypts as shown by (3), and decrypts as shown by (4).

$$F_A(X) = \begin{cases} \lceil \frac{256}{A} \times X \rceil + 1 & 1 \leq X < A \\ 256 & X = A \\ \left\lfloor \frac{256 \times (256-X)}{256-A} \right\rfloor & A < X \leq 256 \end{cases} \tag{3}$$

$$F_A{}^{-1}(X) = \begin{cases} X_1 & X_1 \times (256-A) > A \times (256 - X_2) \\ X_2 & X_1 \times (256-A) \leq A \times (256 - X_2) \end{cases} \tag{4}$$

where

$$X_1 = \left\lfloor \frac{A \times Y}{256} \right\rfloor \tag{5}$$

and

$$X_2 = 256 - \left\lfloor (1 - \frac{A}{256}) \times Y \right\rfloor \tag{6}$$

III. THE PROPOSED CRYPTOSYSTEM

Our proposed cryptosystem is based on a hybrid encryption scheme that combines both stream and block ciphering algorithms to achieve the required security level, with a minimum encryption time. Both stream and block ciphers in cryptography belong to the family of symmetric key ciphers in which we use the same key for both of the encryption and the decryption processes.

The stream cipher converts the plain-text bits directly into the cipher-text by XORing them with pseudo-random cipher bits, while block cipher encrypts fixed size blocks that contain a group of bits from the plain-text. Block encryption is more susceptible to cryptanalysis attacks than stream cipher because identical blocks of plain-text yield identical blocks of cipher-text [20]. The stream cipher has a higher speed of transformation and a low error rate, as an error that occurs in one bit will not affect the other bit. The block cipher has a high level of diffusion which any block effect will be spread into several blocks. On the other hand, the diffusion effect is low in the stream cipher, as all information of the plain-text is contained in a single cipher-text symbol. The block cipher has low encryption speed, as the entire block must be accumulated before the encryption or decryption process starts. Furthermore, the entire block here may corrupt due to an error in one bit.

A. Encryption Algorithm

Dividing the image into several numbers of blocks and encrypting block by block minimizes the error bits, so we divided our plain-text in the proposed algorithm into blocks with a predefined size of 256 bytes each (to use (3) in the permutation process as it does not map any block larger than 256 bytes). Our proposed algorithm encrypts the whole image using E_1 and E_2, where E_1 encrypts the odd blocks based on the FSTM proposed by Masuda et al. [15] as shown in Figure 1, while the diffusion and confusion effects are transferred between blocks using the Cipher-Block chaining mode (CBC) [21]. Equations (3) and (4) are implemented based on a look-up table to decrease the encryption time. The input of this look-up table will be the generated dynamic key from the implemented version of the used chaotic generator (see Section III-A) in addition to the byte from the plain-text as to be permuted or substituted.

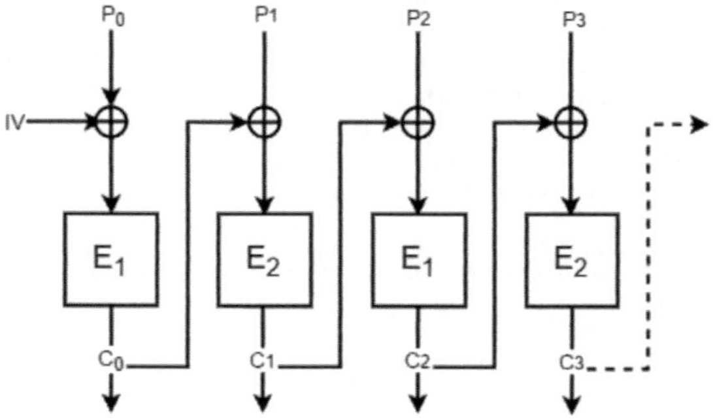

Figure 2. The proposed algorithm encryption process based on CBC mode

P_0 in Figure 2 represents the first plain block (B_0), while IV is the initial vector that is generated by the chaotic generator. C_0 is the resulting ciphered block that will be sent to the recipient side. E_1 is the proposed encryption algorithm which produces the confusion and diffusion based on slightly different look-up tables (LookupS to simulate (3) and (4) for substitution map, and LookupG to simulate (3) with small changes for the permutation map without needing the inverse map). Note that each map has different independent dynamic keys generated using the implemented chaotic generator:

- Substitution: our algorithm uses $C_{0,i} = LookupS(B_{0,i}, k_1)$ to encrypt the selected blocks from the plain image where $B_0 = B_{0,0}, B_{0,1}, B_{0,2}...B_{0,255}$ represents the first block pixels and $0 \leq i \leq 255$. While the decryption process of the ciphered block using the inverse look-up table as: $B_{0,i} = lookupS^{-1}(C_{o,i}, k_1)$.

- Permutation: it uses $C_{0,x} = lookupG(C_{0,i}, k_2)$ to change the ciphered byte position in the block during the encryption process and uses the same table in the decryption side. The generated pre-defined look-up table for the permutation map based on (3) with a small modification of the first part by converting the ceil operation into floor one to be used as the generator.

The second block (and all even blocks) will be encrypted in our algorithm based on a Selective Stream Cipher Algorithm (SSCA). The SSCA is proposed to speed up the encryption process and increase the throughput of the encryption under the required security level. The selected encrypted bit of each pixel (MSB) is chosen as its contribution from the total information in the pixel is 2^7 which means that it has an effect equivalent to the remaining bits in the pixel. This MSB is XORed with the generated key bits from the used chaotic generator which gives 32-bits for each sample. Dividing the block size (256 bytes) by the sequence length (32 bits) will give us 2^3 calls to the chaotic generator while encrypting each block, which means that we XOR the MSB without reusing any key bit.

B. Chaotic generator

In the proposed cryptosystem, we implemented the chaotic generator proposed by El Assad et, al. [22] to avoid the weakness in the chaotic systems regarding periodicity generating sequences. It consists of two chaotic maps, i.e., the Skew Tent Map (STM) and the discrete Piece-Wise Linear Chaotic Map (PWLCM), in which are connected in parallel to generate the sequence values of 32-bit samples.

IV. SECURITY AND COMPLEXITY ANALYSIS

A cryptosystem should be suitable and efficient for the target application, and it should offer the required security level. Analyzing the complexity of any cryptosystem is an important assessment factor, and researchers typically take this evaluation as the time of encryption/decryption. In this section we are using a more comprehensive measure to evaluate our proposed cryptosystem. The known theoretical attacks and the common statistical attacks are explained as well in this section.

A. Complexity analysis

The complexity of the algorithm used in the encryption method is an important factor which determines the time of performance. On the other hand, the performance can be determined by the running speed of the algorithm or the Encryption Throughput (ET) which can be calculated using (7), and the number of cycles needed to encrypt one byte, which is the CPU speed in Hertz divided by the ET in bytes as given in (8). The results for the encryption and decryption processes of our proposed cryptosystem are carried out using the Code::Blocks compiler of C programming on a PC with 2.30 GHz processor Intel $Core^{TM}$ i5-4200U CPU, 6GB RAM, and Windows 7, 64-bit operation system. Lena image (colored with the size of $512 \times 512 \times 3$ byte) is the image under test. The calculated time for the proposed cryptosystem is compared to the fastest chaos-based cryptosystems in the literature. To calculate the time, we calculated the average executions for the test images which are encrypted for 1000 different secret keys as shown in Table 1 for different image sizes 256, 512, and 1024, while Table 2 presents the running speed of the algorithm (throughput) in mega byte per second (MBps) and the number of cycles required to encrypt or decrypt one byte. Through those calculations, the number of encryption rounds is identified by the required security level.

$$ET = \frac{Image_{size}(Byte)}{Encryption_{time}(Second)} \quad (7)$$

$$Numberofcyclesperbyte = \frac{CPUSpeed_{(Hertz)}}{ET_{(Byte)}} \quad (8)$$

TABLE I. ENCRYPTION/DECRYPTION TIME OF DIFFERENT ALGORITHMS IN MILLISECOND

	Lena 256	Lena 512	Lena 1024
Proposed	1.385/1.315	4.965/5.009	18.845/19.256
Fouda [23]	3.98/4.19	15.58/16.77	62.32/67.08
Zhang 1 [18]	7.5/7.5	30/30	120/120
Zhang 2 [18]	7.5/8.25	30/33	120/132
Wang [24]	7.79/8.39	31.16/33.54	124.64/134.16
Akhshani [2]	14.4	57.6	230.4
Wong [25]	15.59/16.77	62.37/67.11	249.48/268.44
Kanso [26]	97.15	388	1554
Pareek [27]	160	920	5650
Farajallah [28]	6/5.8	24/23.2	96/92.8

As presented in Tables 1 and 2, our proposed cryptosystem is faster than other chaos-based cryptosystems, it is four times faster than the algorithms in [24] [18] and two times faster than [29]. As mentioned before, the cryptosystem had to achieve a high security level besides the encryption speed, so the speed isn't a sufficient assessment factor.

TABLE II. ENCRYPTION THROUGHPUT AND THE NUMBER OF CYCLES FOR EACH ENCRYPTED BYTE

	ET in MBps	Number of cycles per byte
Proposed	151.03	14.52
Fouda [23]	48.138/44.72	39.62/42.65
Zhang 1 [18]	25/25	122.07/122.07
Zhang 2 [18]	25/22.72	122.07/134.27
Wang [24]	24.06/22.35	122.85/132.24
Akhshani [2]	13.02	194.83
Wong [25]	12.03/11.18	245.7/26438
Kanso [26]	1.93	1121
Pareek [27]	0.39	2445
Farajallah [28]	31.25	94.60

B. Key space

Resisting brute force attack requires a large secret key, with at least 128 effective and independent bits. Depending on that fact, our proposed cryptosystem has a secret key with 169 bits. Moreover, the dynamic keys are changed for each new plain block for the substitution as well as the permutation in E_1. In E_2 all used dynamic bits are distinct and changeable for each new block.

C. Plain-text sensitivity attack

Depending on the diffusion definition, any change of a single bit of the plain-text, should statistically, change one bit out of two of the cipher-text, and similarly, if we change one bit of the cipher-text, then approximately one half of the plain-text bits should change.

In our proposed cryptosystem, two plain-text P_1 and P_2 were selected to be encrypted using the same secret key and have a difference in one bit in the first block. Most probably, the researchers chose the first bit in the image to be the different one, while in our scenario the chosen bit will be located in the beginning, in the middle, and at the end of the first block so as to get closer to the real application. The Unified Average Changing Intensity (UACI), which is calculated in (9) and the Number of Pixels Change Rate (NPCR) calculated using (10) are the two parameters used to measure any proposed cryptosystem's resistance to the plain-text sensitivity attack.

$$UACI = \frac{1}{L \times C \times P \times 255} \times \sum_{p=1}^{P}\sum_{i=1}^{L}\sum_{j=1}^{C} |C_1 - C_2| \times 100\% \quad (9)$$

$$NPCR = \frac{1}{L \times C \times P} \times \sum_{p=1}^{P}\sum_{i=1}^{L}\sum_{j=1}^{C} D(i,j,p) \times 100\% \quad (10)$$

where D(i,j,p) = 0 when it's the same value in C_1 and C_2 while it is 1 when it's different. And L is the height, C is the width and P is the depth of the image. Table 3 presents the results of the plain-text sensitivity attacks of our proposed cryptosystem, where the optimal value for UACI is 33.46% and for NPCR is 99.61% which are given in [30] [31].

TABLE III. THE UACI AND THE NPCR PLAIN-TEXT SENSITIVITY TESTS FOR THE PROPOSED CRYPTOSYSTEM

Image	UACI	NPCR
Lena 512	33.463968	99.605423
Baboon 512	33.462189	99.607487
Boat 512	33.462248	99.606874

D. Key sensitivity attack

Any slight change in the secret key will produce a completely different ciphered image [32], which means that any cryptosystem has to be resistant to this sensitivity attack. However, changing one bit in the key during decryption of the ciphered image will completely destroy the decryption process (it will completely fail). The testing scenario of the key sensitivity is similar to the plain-text sensitivity attacks: we have one plain-text P and two secret keys with a difference of one bit. First, P is encrypted using K_1 to obtain C_1. Then the same plain-text P is encrypted using K_2 to obtain C_2. Finally, previously mentioned equations for NPCR and UACI (9 and 10) are used to evaluate the key sensitivity attacks of the proposed cryptosystem. As shown in Table 4 which presents the average results of the key sensitivity attacks, our proposed cryptosystem results indicate that the proposed cryptosystem is very sensitive to one bit change in the secret key.

E. Histogram analysis

The graph which shows the number of pixels in an image at each different intensity value is called the histogram. For the encrypted image, it should be uniformly distributed as shown in Figure 3 to be strong against the statistical attacks, in which we can benefit from the most used bit in the image and its position. To ensure that the ciphered image pixels are

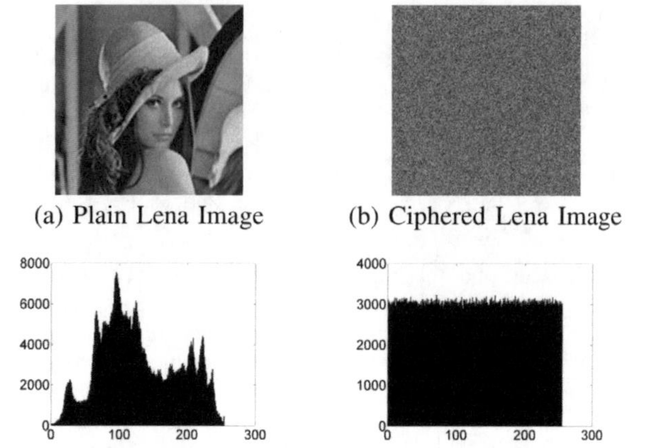

(a) Plain Lena Image (b) Ciphered Lena Image

(c) Histogram-plain image (d) Histogram-ciphered image

Figure 3. LENA IMAGE PLAIN AND CIPHERED WITH THEIR HISTOGRAM

TABLE IV. THE UACI AND THE NPCR KEY SENSITIVITY TESTS FOR THE PROPOSED CRYPTOSYSTEM

Image	UACI	NPCR
Lena 512	33.171848	99.609385
Baboon 512	33.343602	99.608161
Boat 512	32.531726	99.608082

uniformly distributed, we applied the chi-square test on the image histogram using (11).

$$\chi^2_{exp} = \sum_{i=0}^{Q-1} \frac{(o_i - e_i)}{e_i} \quad (11)$$

where Q is the number of levels (in this crypto is 256), o_i is the observed occurrence frequencies for each level in the ciphered image, while e_i is the expected one from the uniform distribution. Here $e_i = \frac{L \times C \times P}{256}$.

The obtained value of this test is close to 250, which meets the condition $\chi^2_{exp} < \chi^2_{th}(255, 0.05) = 293$. This result shows that the tested histograms are uniform and do not reveal any useful information for the statistical analysis.

F. Correlation analysis

The pixels in the encrypted image should have as low redundancy and correlation values as possible, even though the adjacent pixels in the plain images are very redundant and correlated.

To determine the correlation in encrypted images, we calculate the correlation coefficient (r_{xy}) as in (12) between two horizontally, vertically and diagonally neighboring pixels [33] for 10000 randomly pairs (N).

$$r_{x,y} = \frac{cov(x,y)}{\sqrt{D(x)}\sqrt{D(y)}} \quad (12)$$

where $cov(x,y) = \frac{1}{N}\sum_{i=1}^{N}([x_i - E(x)]\,[y_i - E(y)])$, $D(x) = \frac{1}{N}\sum_{i=1}^{N}(x - i - E(x))^2$, $E(x) = \frac{1}{N}\sum_{i=1}^{N}(x_i)$ and x,y are the pixel values of the two adjacent pixels in the tested image. Figure 4 shows the correlation results for the Lena

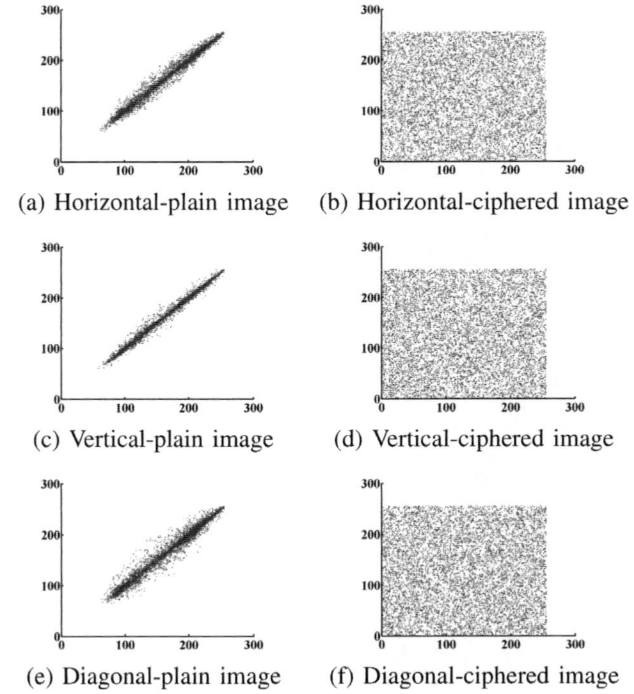

(a) Horizontal-plain image (b) Horizontal-ciphered image

(c) Vertical-plain image (d) Vertical-ciphered image

(e) Diagonal-plain image (f) Diagonal-ciphered image

Figure 4. Correlation analysis of the plain and ciphered Lena image. Plain-Image Correlation Values: Horizontal Correlation=0.993077; Vertical Correlation=0.996988; Diagonal Correlation=0.988087. Cipher Correlation Values: Horizontal Correlation=0.009019; Vertical Correlation=0.008971; Diagonal Correlation=0.010765.

image and its corresponding cipher image, which is encrypted by our proposed cryptosystem.

V. Conclusion and Future Work

In this paper, we proposed a hybrid encryption scheme that has both block and stream cipher algorithms. This combination achieved a faster cryptosystem than the existing ones, in addition to preserving the required security level. The proposed chaos-based encryption method is a hybrid of block and stream ciphers. The block cipher uses odd plain text blocks which are implemented by a substitution layer from the FSTM and a permutation layer that is achieved by using the (FSTM) as a generator. The stream cipher level is applied by a selective cryptosystem to encrypt the MSB of each byte in the even plain text blocks. Our modified version of the STM used a novel method designed with a confusion and a diffusion layer in order to be simple, fast and robust against known attacks. Our proposed cryptosystem is the fastest of all chaos-based cryptosystems known to us, which was proved in the section on the security and complexity analysis. The selective encryption of the MSB bit requires improvement in future work in order to increase the security level while constantly increasing the encryption time.

References

[1] R. Tenny and L. S. Tsimring, "Additive mixing modulation for public key encryption based on distributed dynamics," Circuits and Systems I: Regular Papers, IEEE Transactions on, vol. 52, no. 3, 2005, pp. 672–679.

[2] A. Akhshani, A. Akhavan, S.-C. Lim, and Z. Hassan, "An image encryption scheme based on quantum logistic map," Communications in Nonlinear Science and Numerical Simulation, vol. 17, no. 12, 2012, pp. 4653–4661.

[3] S. Behnia, A. Akhshani, H. Mahmodi, and A. Akhavan, "A novel algorithm for image encryption based on mixture of chaotic maps," Chaos, Solitons & Fractals, vol. 35, no. 2, 2008, pp. 408–419.

[4] G. Chen, Y. Mao, and C. K. Chui, "A symmetric image encryption scheme based on 3d chaotic cat maps," Chaos, Solitons & Fractals, vol. 21, no. 3, 2004, pp. 749–761.

[5] F. Chiaraluce, L. Ciccarelli, E. Gambi, P. Pierleoni, and M. Reginelli, "A new chaotic algorithm for video encryption," IEEE Transactions on Consumer Electronics, vol. 48, no. 4, 2002, pp. 838–844.

[6] M. Farajallah, S. El Assad, and M. Chetto, "Dynamic adjustment of the chaos-based security in real-time energy harvesting sensors," in Green Computing and Communications (GreenCom), 2013 IEEE and Internet of Things (iThings/CPSCom), IEEE International Conference on and IEEE Cyber, Physical and Social Computing. IEEE, 2013, pp. 282–289.

[7] F. Salam, J. E. Marsden, and P. P. Varaiya, "Chaos and arnold diffusion in dynamical systems," Circuits and Systems, IEEE Transactions on, vol. 30, no. 9, 1983, pp. 697–708.

[8] A. A. A. El-Latif, X. Niu, and M. Amin, "A new image cipher in time and frequency domains," Optics Communications, vol. 285, no. 21, 2012, pp. 4241–4251.

[9] B. Bhargava, C. Shi, and S.-Y. Wang, "Mpeg video encryption algorithms," Multimedia Tools and Applications, vol. 24, no. 1, 2004, pp. 57–79.

[10] J.-I. Guo et al., "A new chaotic key-based design for image encryption and decryption," in Circuits and Systems, 2000. Proceedings. ISCAS 2000 Geneva. The 2000 IEEE International Symposium on, vol. 4. IEEE, 2000, pp. 49–52.

[11] S. Li, G. Chen, and X. Zheng, "Chaos-based encryption for digital image and video," Multimedia Encryption and Authentication Techniques and Applications, 2006, p. 129.

[12] I. Mansour, G. Chalhoub, and B. Bakhache, "Evaluation of a fast symmetric cryptographic algorithm based on the chaos theory for wireless sensor networks," in Trust, Security and Privacy in Computing and Communications (TrustCom), 2012 IEEE 11th International Conference on. IEEE, 2012, pp. 913–919.

[13] J. Fridrich, "Image encryption based on chaotic maps," in Systems, Man, and Cybernetics, 1997. Computational Cybernetics and Simulation., 1997 IEEE International Conference on, vol. 2. IEEE, 1997, pp. 1105–1110.

[14] ——, "Symmetric ciphers based on two-dimensional chaotic maps," International Journal of Bifurcation and chaos, vol. 8, no. 06, 1998, pp. 1259–1284.

[15] N. Masuda, G. Jakimoski, K. Aihara, and L. Kocarev, "Chaotic block ciphers: from theory to practical algorithms," Circuits and Systems I: Regular Papers, IEEE Transactions on, vol. 53, no. 6, 2006, pp. 1341–1352.

[16] N. Masuda and K. Aihara, "Cryptosystems with discretized chaotic maps," Circuits and Systems I: Fundamental Theory and Applications, IEEE Transactions on, vol. 49, no. 1, 2002, pp. 28–40.

[17] D. Socek, S. Li, S. S. Magliveras, and B. Furht, "Short paper: Enhanced 1-d chaotic key-based algorithm for image encryption," in Security and Privacy for Emerging Areas in Communications Networks, 2005. SecureComm 2005. First International Conference on. IEEE, 2005, pp. 406–407.

[18] W. Zhang, K.-w. Wong, H. Yu, and Z.-l. Zhu, "An image encryption scheme using reverse 2-dimensional chaotic map and dependent diffusion," Communications in Nonlinear Science and Numerical Simulation, vol. 18, no. 8, 2013, pp. 2066–2080.

[19] E. Solak, C. Çokal, O. T. Yildiz, and T. Biyikoğlu, "Cryptanalysis of fridrich's chaotic image encryption," International Journal of Bifurcation and Chaos, vol. 20, no. 05, 2010, pp. 1405–1413.

[20] S. William, "Cryptography and network security: principles and practice," Prentice-Hall, Inc, 1999, pp. 62–90.

[21] W. F. Ehrsam, C. H. Meyer, J. L. Smith, and W. L. Tuchman, "Message

verification and transmission error detection by block chaining," Feb. 14 1978, uS Patent 4,074,066.

[22] S. El Assad and H. Noura, "Generator of chaotic sequences and corresponding generating system," 2011, uS Patent 8,781,116 B2.

[23] J. A. E. Fouda, J. Y. Effa, and M. Ali, "Highly secured chaotic block cipher for fast image encryption," Applied Soft Computing, vol. 25, 2014, pp. 435–444.

[24] Y. Wang, K.-W. Wong, X. Liao, and G. Chen, "A new chaos-based fast image encryption algorithm," Applied soft computing, vol. 11, no. 1, 2011, pp. 514–522.

[25] K.-W. Wong, B. S.-H. Kwok, and W.-S. Law, "A fast image encryption scheme based on chaotic standard map," Physics Letters A, vol. 372, no. 15, 2008, pp. 2645–2652.

[26] A. Kanso and M. Ghebleh, "A novel image encryption algorithm based on a 3d chaotic map," Communications in Nonlinear Science and Numerical Simulation, vol. 17, no. 7, 2012, pp. 2943–2959.

[27] N. Pareek, V. Patidar, and K. Sud, "Cryptography using multiple one-dimensional chaotic maps," Communications in Nonlinear Science and Numerical Simulation, vol. 10, no. 7, 2005, pp. 715–723.

[28] M. Farajallah, Z. Fawaz, S. El Assad, and O. Déforges, "Efficient image encryption and authentication scheme based on chaotic sequences," in The 7th International Conference on Emerging Security Information, Systems and Technologies, 2013, pp. 150–155.

[29] H. E.-d. H. Ahmed, H. M. Kalash, and O. F. Allah, "Encryption efficiency analysis and security evaluation of rc6 block cipher for digital images," in Electrical Engineering, 2007. ICEE'07. International Conference on. IEEE, 2007, pp. 1–7.

[30] Y. Wu, J. P. Noonan, and S. Agaian, "Npcr and uaci randomness tests for image encryption," Cyber journals: multidisciplinary journals in science and technology, Journal of Selected Areas in Telecommunications (JSAT), 2011, pp. 31–38.

[31] F. Maleki, A. Mohades, S. M. Hashemi, and M. E. Shiri, "An image encryption system by cellular automata with memory," in Availability, Reliability and Security, 2008. ARES 08. Third International Conference on. IEEE, 2008, pp. 1266–1271.

[32] J.-R. Ohm, G. J. Sullivan, H. Schwarz, T. K. Tan, and T. Wiegand, "Comparison of the coding efficiency of video coding standardsincluding high efficiency video coding (hevc)," Circuits and Systems for Video Technology, IEEE Transactions on, vol. 22, no. 12, 2012, pp. 1669–1684.

[33] R. Munir, "Security analysis of selective image encryption algorithm based on chaos and cbc-like mode," in Telecommunication Systems, Services, and Applications (TSSA), 2012 7th International Conference on. IEEE, 2012, pp. 142–146.

Seven Steps to a Quantum-Resistant Cipher

Julián Murguía Hughes
Independent Researcher
Montevideo, Uruguay
email: jmurguia@montevideo.com.uy

Abstract—**All cryptography currently in use is vulnerable and will become obsolete once quantum computing becomes available. Continuing the current path seeking for more and more complex algorithms cannot guarantee neither secrecy nor unbreakability. Increasing the complexity while it keeps being vulnerable does not seem to be the right approach. Thinking outside the box is not enough. We need to start looking from a different perspective for a different path to ensure data privacy and secrecy. In this paper, we share advances in searching for perfect secrecy instead of complexity and we try to light a path to a whole new quantum-resistant cryptography.**

Keywords-cipher; quantum-resistant; cryptography; secrecy; privacy; encryption; quantum; computing; resistant; data.

I. INTRODUCTION

In this work in progress, we show current achievements in the field of cryptography and present some future ideas in this area and their potential. No final results or final data is available at this time.

Since the beginning, cryptography has worked the same way; you take the original source of information (the plaintext), a key and a fixed algorithm and you apply the algorithm using the plaintext and the key as input to generate the cryptogram or cipher text as its output. And modern cryptography keeps working in the exact same way.

Although the first known evidence of some form of cryptography is almost four millennia old [1], one of the oldest known form of encryption is the Caesar's cipher. It was a substitution cipher where each character was replaced for the one located three places later in alphabetic order and considered the alphabet as a round circle where 'A' follows 'Z' and so, 'X' would be replaced by 'A', 'Y' would be replaced by 'B', 'Z' would be replaced by 'C', 'A' would be replaced by 'D' and so on. The Caesar's algorithm was just a shift by places process and the key used was just three, indicating the algorithm that each character in the plaintext needed to be shifted by three to generate the cryptogram.

Since then, algorithms have grown in complexity looking to enhance the security of the process and to make harder to recover the plaintext without knowing the key.

But what has not changed is the logic, i.e., the way it is done. Cryptography is still using an algorithm with a fixed set of instructions that will use the plaintext and the key as input to produce the cipher text. The same plaintext and the same key will always produce the same cryptogram.

There are two main attacks to try to get the plaintext without knowing the key: Cryptanalysis (analyze the process trying to find weaknesses or shortcuts that may allow to retrieve the original information without having the key) and Brute Force (try all possible keys).

Modern cryptography is not unbreakable and bases its security on two premises:

1) Cryptanalysis is not possible or too complex to be achieved.
2) Brute Force attacks require too much time.

It has been said and repeated that quantum computing will make obsolete all existing cryptography because it will allow brute force attacks to be completed in a short period of time.

All existing cryptography? No, there is an exception.

About a century ago, Gilbert Vernam invented an encryption technique [2] (Patent US 1310719 [3]) that thirty-something years later Claude Shannon proved [4] it was unbreakable and will remain unbreakable to quantum computing. It is not used because it requires the key to have the same length as the plaintext, to be random and not to be reused.

As today's information is always measured in bytes or multiple of bytes (Kilobytes, Megabytes, Gigabytes, Terabytes, etc.) for all the explanations and examples here, the byte as the basic unit of information will be used. Considering the byte as just a group of eight bits, being a bit a binary digit that can either be a zero (0) or a one (1).

A single byte can represent 256 different values, from 0 to 255 in decimal, from 00 to FF in hexadecimal and from 00000000 to 11111111 in binary.

For a byte, the Vernam cipher will use the XOR function between the plaintext byte and the key byte. The function will compare each bit within the first byte to the bit in the same position in the second byte and will generate a bit with a value of zero if both bits have the same value and one if they are different. The function will return the cryptogram byte as its result. For a specific plaintext byte value, each of the 256 possible values of the key will produce a different cryptogram byte value.

If you get the cryptogram byte and do not know the value of the key byte, every single possible value of the key byte has the exact same probability of being the right one and you have no way to decide which one of them is the right one and thus, which of the 256 possible values of the plaintext byte is the right one.

There is no possible cryptanalysis of this process and a brute force attack will end up with the plaintext mixed with a huge number of false positives (apparently valid results) with no way to tell which one is the original one.

Shannon proved that even knowing that the plaintext is just text, any possible text with the same length has the exact same probability of being the original plaintext [5].

In this paper, we will present our proposed encryption technique (patent pending [8]) and the seven steps to an unbreakable quantum-resistant cryptographic technique.

The rest of this paper is organized as follows. Section II describes the state of the art and the vulnerability to quantum attacks. Section III describes each of the seven steps of our proposed encryption technique. Section IV describes the analysis of a possible cipher based on those seven steps and compares it against Vernam's and other current standards. Section V describes the conclusions and Section VI describes the future work and goals.

II. STATE OF THE ART

According to the European Telecommunications Standards Institute (ETSI), "Without quantum-safe encryption, everything that has been transmitted, or will ever be transmitted, over a network is vulnerable to eavesdropping and public disclosure" [6].

Discussion and comparison between symmetric and public key cryptography currently in use becomes irrelevant once one understands that none of them is unbreakable.

Public key algorithms such as RSA (Rivest, Shamir and Adleman), ECC (Elliptic Curve Cryptography), Diffie-Hellman and DSA (Digital Signature Algorithm) will be easily broken by quantum computers using Shor's algorithms [7] and so, they are deemed to be insecure to quantum computing.

Symmetric algorithms as AES (Advanced Encryption Standard) are believed (but not proven) to be resilient against quantum attacks by doubling the key length.

Any cipher that bases its strength on its complexity and the computational power required for an attack will eventually be broken and persisting on this way will only provide a false sense of security that will last briefly.

Vernam's cipher and the one described in this paper make no computational assumptions and are both information-theoretically secure.

What we hope to achieve is to provide a cipher offering perfect unconditional security against eavesdroppers no matter how arbitrarily powerful they may be or become in the future and without the constraints the Vernam cipher has. Something none of the currently in use standards can offer.

III. THE SEVEN STEPS

A. *Step One (Use Multiple Encryption Functions)*

Vernam used a single function (XOR). Our approach will use many of them. Each function will take the plaintext byte and the key byte and will return a cryptogram byte and for each of the 256 possible key byte values will return a different cryptogram byte value.

Below, we will explain two of these functions that are similar and as unbreakable as the Vernam or XOR function; other functions with the same behavior will also be unbreakable.

- **Modular Addition:** Will add up the plaintext byte value and the key byte value wrapping up at 255. If the result is larger than 255 it will subtract 256 from the result. For a specific plaintext byte value, each possible key byte value will produce a different cryptogram byte value. If you get the cryptogram byte and do not know the value of the key byte, every single possible value of the key byte has the exact same probability of being the right one and you have no way to decide which one of them is the right one and thus, which of the 256 possible values of the plaintext byte is the right one.
- **Modular Subtraction:** Will subtract the key byte value from the plaintext byte value wrapping up at zero. If the result is negative it will add 256 to the result. For a specific plaintext byte value, each possible key byte value will produce a different cryptogram byte value. If you get the cryptogram byte and do not know the value of the key byte, every single possible value of the key byte has the exact same probability of being the right one and you have no way to decide which one of them is the right one and thus, which of the 256 possible values of the plaintext byte is the right one.

Using multiple functions provides additional security because, if one has the cryptogram byte, not only the key byte used is unknown, but also the function used.

For a given plaintext byte value, any valid function should return 256 different results based on the value of the key byte, so applying each function to the given plaintext byte value and for each key byte value from 0 to 255, will produce a list of 256 different results.

Each of those functions is as secure and unbreakable as Vernam's XOR and using many of them does not diminish either the security or the unbreakability of the process.

When the plaintext's length is larger than one byte we can use one function to process the first byte, another one to process the second byte and so on. That leads us to the following step.

B. *Step Two (Use a Second Parameter)*

A second parameter will be used to indicate which function to use on each instance.

A block from this second parameter will indicate which one of the many available functions will be used to process a byte from the plaintext and a byte from the key.

Let us say we decide to use only 256 different functions from all that can be created. In such case, we will only need one byte from this second parameter to indicate which of those functions will be used for this specific plaintext byte and key byte.

So far, the second parameter byte value x will trigger function z.

How do we know which of the available functions is function z, is explained in the next step.

C. *Step Three (Order of the Functions)*

When we have many different functions, we need to identify them somehow and make a list of them.

This list is what will be used to decide which function will be triggered by which value from the second parameter.

And this list is not unique, 256 different functions can be ordered in 256! (n! = 1x2x3x,...n) different ways (256! is a 507 digit decimal number with a value larger than 8.578 * 10^506 or about 2^1684), and a different function order will produce a different cryptogram for the same plaintext and key.

Now, an attacker not only needs to try every possible key, also needs to guess which functions were used and which function is triggered by each possible value of the second parameter. And that, assuming the selected function order is hardcoded within the process.

So far, parameter byte value x will always trigger function z, unless we can make parameter value x trigger function w in a different run.

The order of the functions can be changed, as explained in the next step.

D. *Step Four (Changing the Order of the Functions)*

How do we make second parameter byte value x to trigger a function different from function z?

The solution is both simple and elegant.

We add a third parameter. One of those 256! possible orders of the numbers from 0 to 255 is loaded into a 256 elements vector, and value x is used to point to the vector's element whose value will be used to trigger the function.

A different third parameter will provide a different function order.

As this third parameter is a sequence of 256 values, each between 0 and 255, it is possible to exclude certain values just by replacing them (i.e., if you want the value 14 not to be used, then replace the element with a value of 14 for a different value).

Now, second parameter byte value x will trigger a function depending on the xth element of the third parameter.

So far, any attacker would know that the first byte from the cryptogram corresponds to the first byte of the plaintext, the second byte from the cryptogram corresponds to the second byte of the plaintext, and so on.

Next step will show how to change that.

E. *Step Five (Block Processing)*

Let us take a block of bytes of a given length from the plaintext and process it in reverse order, starting from the last byte in the block, processing it and saving it as the first byte in the cryptogram. Then the previous to the last to be the second byte in the cryptogram and so on, until we end processing the block by processing its first byte and then continue with the next block.

The last block may be shorter but it is equally processed from last byte to first one as any other block without any need of any additional dummy information to be added.

Now, unless the attacker knows the exact length of the block used, there is no way to know from where to start to retrieve the original plaintext.

F. *Step Six (Key Length and Key Repetitions)*

So far, no mention has been made of the key length.

Vernam's cipher requires the key to have at least the same length as the plaintext. If the key is shorter, the process starts to repeat and it weakens its security.

If we use a key shorter than the plaintext it will wrap up at the end, but unless the key and the second parameter both have the exact same length, there will be no repetitions until we reach a position within the plaintext equal to the minimum common multiple of the lengths of both the key and the second parameter. And as it may eventually happen the whole process would be vulnerable unless we find a way to avoid repetitions.

The solution is, once again, simple and elegant.

When the end of the key is reached, before starting to repeat it, the process changes the function order by modifying the elements in the vector explained in step four.

Each time this happens, the change process behaves differently.

Now, even if the key and the second parameter have the exact same length and they start to repeat in the exact same order, the sequence of functions triggered will not be the same and so no repetitions will occur.

G. *Step Seven (Make Lengths Variable)*

Current encryption standards use fixed length blocks and fixed length keys (they may offer different key sizes but with very limited pre-defined fixed sizes).

Our solution allows for user selected lengths for the key, the second parameter and the processing block.

The key length may go from a single byte to any length, even the same length of the plaintext or longer.

The second parameter may go from a single byte to any length, even the same length of the plaintext or longer.

The processing block size may go from a single byte to any length up to the length of the plaintext and is limited only by the maximum size allowed by the system where the encryption is implemented.

When building up the application, different groups and number of functions may be used to create personalized non-standard versions.

IV. ANALYSIS

A. A cipher complying with these seven steps

If we build up a cipher complying with these seven steps, it may use up to four parameters:

- The key to be used.
  This key is just a sequence of bytes of any length and can be longer, equal in length or shorter than the plaintext.
- A second parameter defining which function to use on each instance.
  This second parameter is a sequence of bytes of any length and there is no relation between its length and the lengths of the plaintext or the key.
- An original function order.
  This is a 256 bytes string that will be used to define an initial order for the encryption functions to be used.
- A processing block size.
  This will define the number of bytes to be read at once from the plaintext and processed in reverse order (from the last byte to the first one) to generate the cipher text. A value of 1 (one) will make the plaintext to be processed straight from the first byte to the last one.

Depending on how the cipher is programmed and implemented, it can allow the user to manually type every parameter or to select or chose them.

The encryption process will work as follows:

1. The user may select the plaintext to process, the key, the second parameter, the initial function order and the processing block size.
2. The process loads the initial function order into a 256 element vector.
3. If the remaining of the plaintext is shorter than the processing block, the processing block size is adjusted accordingly.
4. The process reads a processing block from the plaintext. If the plaintext has been exhausted, the process ends.
5. The process takes the last byte from the processing block.
6. The process takes a byte from the key.
   If the key has been exhausted, reorder the original function order vector elements and read the first key byte again.
7. The process takes a byte from the second parameter.
   If the second parameter has been exhausted, start over from its first byte.
8. The process uses the byte from the second parameter to point to an element from the initial function order vector and uses its value to trigger an encryption function passing the plaintext and key bytes as parameters.
9. The function triggered returns a cipher text byte that is written to the cipher text output.
10. The process takes the previous byte from the processing block.
    If the processing block has been exhausted, jump to step 3.
11. Jump to step 5.

The decryption process will work the exact same way, using the cipher text instead of the plaintext and reversing the encryption process.

B. Comparing this cipher with Vernam's one

Is easy to see that if one of the possible encryption functions used is the XOR function and the initial function order vector elements all have the same value and that specific value triggers the XOR function, then and only then, this cipher will behave the same as the Vernam's one.

A text message properly ciphered through the Vernam Cipher gives absolutely no clue on the key used or the original plaintext and a brute force attack will end up with a huge number of false positives.

A brute force attack will return some invalid or unreadable results but will also return any possible message with the exact same length and there is no way to decide which one is the true original one.

The Vernam Cipher is not used because it has three requirements that need to be fulfilled to comply with Shannon's definition for Perfect Secrecy:

1) The key needs to have the same length as the plaintext.
2) The key must be random.
3) The key must not be reused.

These three requirements are mandatory because Vernam used a single encryption function (XOR) in the process.

With the Vernam Cipher, for any given cipher text byte, one needs to try any possible key byte value and you will end up with 256 different results, each one with the exact same probability of being the plain text byte value.

With our proposed encryption technique and even assuming the attacker knows the exact processing block size used for this specific cipher text, all the encryption functions used and can match each cipher text byte with the corresponding byte position in the plaintext; the attacker will still need to try each of the 256 possible key byte values with each of the encryption functions involved. So, if we used 256 different encryption functions, the attacker will end up with 65,536 possible values for the plain text byte, each one repeated many times and no way to decide which value is the original one.

If the attacker does not know the processing block size, it multiplies the effort required as the first byte from the plaintext may correspond to any of the bytes in the cipher text, the second one to any of the bytes except the last and so on, doing the math it means there are n! (n! = 1x2x3x,...n) possible orders for the cipher text to match the byte order of the plaintext, being n the length in bytes of both the plaintext and the cipher text.

Our proposed cipher does not have the same constraints as the Vernam one.

Figure 1 shows a comparison between Vernam's cipher and our proposed one:

	VERNAM	Our Proposed Cipher
Sample plaintext length	140	140
Processing block size	1	Variable
Key size	140	Variable
Key and plaintext length must match	Yes	No
Key must be true random	Yes	No
Key must not be reused	Yes	No
No. of functions	1	256
No. of possible results per function	256	256
No. of possible results per Byte	256	65536
Ciphertext to plaintext match	1	140!
No. of possible results per Byte from brute force attack	256	65536 x 140!
No. of possible results per Byte from brute force attack as power of 2	2^(8)	2^(809)
Probability of being the plaintext byte	0,39%	0,39%
Rounds	1	1
False Positives	Yes	Yes

Figure 1. Comparing Vernam's cipher to our proposal.

The key may have any length and it does not matter if it is shorter than the plaintext because we can assure the same key value-encryption function sequence will not be repeated.

As we use some additional parameters, does the key truly need to be random?

Leaving aside any discussion about what is truly random and what is not, anything can be used as a key; a text, a web page, a file from the Internet. As far as the key is kept secret, it really does not matter whether it is truly random or not.

What if the key is reused?

Using the same key again is irrelevant as far as we do not use the same processing block size, same second parameter and same initial function order altogether again.

C. *Comparing this cipher with currently used ciphers*

Due to their extreme complexity, none of the current encryption standards will produce a false positive when a wrong key is used and that is why they are vulnerable to brute force attacks.

All currently used encryption base their privacy and security on the unavailability of enough computational power required to try all possible keys in a short time and that is why they will all fail under a quantum attack capable of trying every possible key in very little time.

There is an old saying: "How do you hide an elephant on a beach? By filling the beach with elephants".

The strength of our proposed encryption technique relies not on the computational power required to try every possible key, second parameter, initial function order or function set; its strength relies on the fact that we assume it can be done but the real original plaintext will be hidden at plain sight within an immense sea of false positives with absolutely no indication on which one is the right one.

Figure 2 shows a comparison between our proposed cipher and other symmetric ciphers:

	Block Size	Key Size	Rounds	False Positives
DES [9]	64 bit	56 bit	16	No
3DES [10]	64 bit	128 bit	48	No
AES [11]	128 bit	128, 192, 256 bit	9, 11, 13	No
BLOWFISH [12]	64 bit	32-448 bit	16	No
Our Proposed Cipher	Variable	Variable	1	Yes

Figure 2. Comparison between this cipher and current symmetric standards.

Public-key cryptography currently in use (including RSA and ECC) relies on the presumption that some problems cannot be solved or would will require an extremely long time to be solved, and therefore, that it would take a very long time for their secured data to be decrypted. But as quantum algorithms can solve some of these problems with ease, that assumption is fatally challenged.

Picture 3 shows public-key key sizes broken in recent years and projections for the near future:

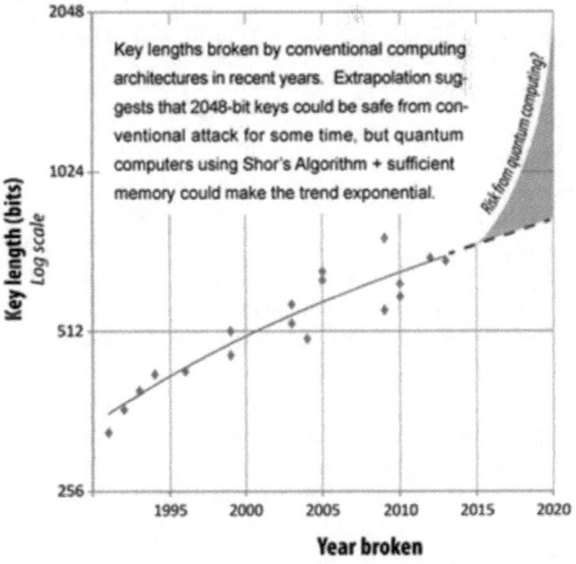

Figure 3. Breaks of the RSA cryptosystem in recent years using conventional computation [6].

D. *Attacking this cipher*

Trying to retrieve the plaintext from a cipher text created through an implementation of this cipher without having any additional information will be at least as difficult as trying to retrieve the plaintext from a cipher text created through a proper use of the Vernam cipher having only the cipher text.

Any attack must take into consideration that all the parameters are external to the process and they all may be different from one plaintext encrypted to the next and also the fact that the process may be used in reverse order. Decryption can be used to protect the plaintext and encryption with the same parameters used to retrieve the original plaintext.

Any possible attacker will need to face the following difficulties when attempting a brute force attack to break an encryption created with an implementation of this cipher:

- Which cipher text byte corresponds to each plain text byte.
- Which encryption functions exist and which of them were used.
- Which function was used on each instance.
- Which was the key used.

Let us give the attacker the advantage of knowing all the encryption functions involved, the specific set used to create the cipher text and the processing block size used. In such situation, for each byte in the cipher text, the attacker needs to try every possible function for every possible key byte value and so, instead of getting 256 possible values as with Vernam's cipher, the result will be 65536 possible values having every single one the exact same probability of being the plaintext byte value despite the repetitions.

And that is the best case scenario for the attacker.

If the processing block size is not known, the attacker will need to try any block size from a single byte to the length of the cipher text. While this adds time and difficulty to the attack, every possible outcome still has the exact same probability of being the original plain text despite the repetitions.

V. CONCLUSIONS

Assuming there is currently enough available computational power to try in a very short time every single key length and value, with every single processing block size and every single possible encryption function there still will not be possible to decide which one of the apparently valid results is the true original plaintext.

Even knowing that the plaintext is just plain text, any possible text with the same length or shorter (just filled with spaces at the end to reach the same length) has the exact same possibility of being the original plaintext. And that is the essence of perfect secrecy, something none of the currently in use encryption standards or solutions can offer.

We've seen here that this new encryption technique offers the same level of perfect secrecy guaranteed by the Vernam cipher without its constraints.

With billions and billions of files available through the internet and the capability of using any of them as a key, as a second parameter and even as the original function order, nobody needs to remember long keys, just needs to remember which files were used and how to reach them.

If one has enough computational power like quantum computing promises to offer when it becomes available, one may be able to break and read any file encrypted with any of the current standards, techniques and tools with two exceptions:

- Anything protected through the proper use of the Vernam cipher will remain secret.
- Anything protected through the use of our proposed cipher will remain secret.

VI. FUTURE WORK

This is a work in progress and there is still a lot of work ahead before it could be considered complete.

We have already implemented an encryption solution complying with the seven steps defined here. It is a Windows app programmed in Visual Basic 6.0 that uses 256 different encryption functions and is capable of encrypting and decrypting files up to about 900 TB (900,000,000,000,000 bytes long) and fast enough to cipher/decipher a 40 MB file in less than five seconds.

Future work will aim to validate the ideas presented in this paper by means of practical results, simulations, statistical analysis and practical performance comparisons with other ciphers.

Future work will also aim to test and evaluate the ideas presented in this paper and their application for Format Preserving Encryption.

REFERENCES

[1] H. Sidhpurwala, "A Brief History of Cryptography" redhat Security Blog, August 14th, 2013.

[2] G. S. Vernam, "Cipher Printing Telegraph Systems for Secret Wire and Radio Communications", Journal of the IEEE 55: 109-115.

[3] G. S. Vernam, Patent 1,310,719. "Secret Signaling System", Patented July 22, 1919. United States Patent and Trademark Office.

[4] C. E. Shannon, "A Mathematical Theory of Communication", The Bell System Technical Journal, Vol. XXVII, No. 3, July 1948, pp. 379-423 and October 1948, pp. 623-656.

[5] C. E. Shannon, "Communication Theory of Secrecy Systems", The Bell System Technical Journal, Vol. XXVIII, No. 4, pp. 656-715.

[6] ETSI, "Quantum Safe Cryptography and Security", ETSI Whitepaper No. 8, June 2015, ISBN No. 979-10-92620-03-0.

[7] P. W. Shor, "Polynomial-Time Algorithms for Prime Factorization and Discrete Logarithms on a Quantum Computer", SIAM J. Comput. 26 (5): 1484–1509.

[8] J. Murguia Hughes, "Poly-Algorithmic Encryption Technique", Patent Pending.

[9] "Data Encryption Standard (DES)", FIPS PUB 46, United States National Institute of Standards and Technology (NIST), January 15, 1977.

[10] W. C. Barker and E. Barker, "NIST Special Publication 800-67 Revision 1: Recommendation for the Triple Data Encryption Algorithm (TDEA)", NIST Special Publication 800-67, January 2012.

[11] "Announcing the ADVANCED ENCRYPTION STANDARD (AES)", FIPS PUB 197, United States National Institute of Standards and Technology (NIST), November 26, 2001.

[12] B. Schneier, "Description of a New Variable-Length Key, 64-Bit Block Cipher (Blowfish)", Fast Software Encryption, Cambridge Security Workshop Proceedings (Springer-Verlag): 191-204, 1993

Reflecting on the Use of Sonification for Network Monitoring

Louise Axon, Sadie Creese, Michael Goldsmith, Jason R. C. Nurse

Department of Computer Science, University of Oxford,
Parks Road, Oxford, UK
Email: {louise.axon, sadie.creese, michael.goldsmith, jason.nurse}@cs.ox.ac.uk

Abstract—**In Security Operations Centres (SOCs), computer networks are generally monitored using a combination of anomaly detection techniques, Intrusion Detection Systems (IDS) and data presented in visual and text-based forms. In the last two decades significant progress has been made in developing novel sonification systems to further support network monitoring tasks. A range of systems has been proposed in which sonified network data is presented for incorporation into the network monitoring process. Unfortunately, many of these have not been sufficiently validated and there is a lack of uptake in SOCs. In this paper, we describe and reflect critically on the shortcomings of traditional network-monitoring methods and identify the key role that sonification, if implemented correctly, could play in improving current monitoring capabilities. The core contribution of this position paper is in the outline of a research agenda for sonification for network monitoring, based on a review of prior research. In particular, we identify requirements for an aesthetic approach that is suitable for continuous real-time network monitoring; formalisation of an approach to designing sonifications in this space; and refinement and validation through comprehensive user testing.**

Keywords*–*Sonification; Network Security; Anomaly Detection; Network Monitoring; Research Agenda.

I. Introduction

The monitoring capabilities of the Security Operations Centres (SOCs) within and on behalf of organisations are vital to enterprise cybersecurity. SOCs are run by security analysts who monitor and aim to maintain network and systems security. In the face of a constantly evolving set of threats and attack vectors, and changing business operations, there is a requirement for effective monitoring tools in SOCs.

One of the key challenges that SOCs face in monitoring large networks is the huge volume of data that can be present on the network. This is both the data created by the day-to-day operations of the enterprise, and data created by security tools. For real-time monitoring, tools that present this data in a form that can be processed quickly are essential. Intrusion Detection Systems (IDS) and visualisations are general examples of classes of tools that are widely used to convey information pertaining to network security in a form that can be easily understood by analysts. The anomaly detection techniques that usually underlie such tools have certain limitations, and can produce false positive and negative results [1] [2]. Detecting attacks, and recognising which risks must be prioritised over other attacks and malign activities is difficult, and the degree of inaccuracy of detection systems can make it even more so.

Over the last two decades, the incorporation of sonification of network data into the monitoring activity of SOCs has been considered. Sonification is the presentation of data in a sonic (generally non-speech) form. Some of this prior work has provided sound evidence of the role sonification could play in improving SOC monitoring capabilities. It has already been shown, for example, that using sonification techniques enables users to detect false positives from IDS more quickly [3]. Based on the state of the art, there are, however, clear requirements for further research and testing to validate the usefulness of sonification for efficient network monitoring, and to develop appropriate and effective sonifications to enhance network monitoring capabilities.

In this paper, we review the major developments in sonification and multimodal systems for network monitoring over the last two decades. In particular, we consider approaches to design and user testing, since we have identified these as two areas in which further research is needed. A key contribution of this paper is a consolidation of existing work, and an analysis of the approaches taken thus far to sonifying network monitoring tasks. We also derive and outline a research agenda for advancing the field; specifically, we aim to highlight directions in which work is needed in order to validate and improve sonification techniques for network monitoring tasks in SOCs. We identify a requirement for comprehensive assessment of the extent to which, and ways in which, sonification techniques can be useful for network monitoring tasks in SOCs through extensive, in-context user-specific testing. We also identify a requirement for the development of aesthetic sonifications appropriate for use in continuous network monitoring tasks, and a requirement for a formalised approach to designing sonifications for network monitoring.

This paper is structured in four further sections to achieve the research aims set out above. In Section II, we present traditional approaches to network monitoring and detail their shortcomings. In Section III, we review prior work in using sonification for network monitoring, and highlight outstanding challenges in the field. Section IV presents a research agenda for sonification for real-time network monitoring. In Section V, we give our conclusions and future work.

II. Traditional Approaches to Network Monitoring

Network monitoring is generally conducted by security analysts, who observe activity on the network – usually using a variety of tools – in order to detect security breaches. According to the UK government's information security breaches survey for companies across the UK in 2015, 90% of large organisations reported that they had suffered a security breach, the median number of security breaches for a large organisation was 14, and the average cost to a large organisation for its worst security breach of the year was £1.46m–£3.14m [4]. In the face of such frequent and potentially costly breaches, network monitoring and attack detection capabilities are of extremely high importance.

A variety of tools are used in network monitoring: IDS, Intrusion Prevention Systems (IPS), visualisations, textual presentations, and firewalls are some of the tools with which analysts conduct their monitoring tasks. The subject of our research paper is primarily detection, rather than prevention capabilities. We therefore focus on two key approaches to the detection phase – IDS and visualisation – and on the anomaly detection techniques that often underlie these.

Anomaly detection techniques describe methods for the detection of changes in systems that may be of interest from a monitoring perspective. In anomaly detection, the state of the network is monitored and compared with a specified "normal" baseline. Anomalous activity is that which exceeds an acceptable threshold difference from this baseline. Anomaly detection often informs the output of IDS and visualisations. There are several reports reflecting on the state of the art in anomaly detection techniques: [1] [5] [6]. In general, we can divide anomaly detection methods into three categories [1] [7]: detection methods based on statistics, in which values are compared against a defined acceptable range for deviation [8] [9]; detection methods based on Knowledge Systems, in which the current activity of the system is compared against a rule-based "normal" activity [10]; and detection methods based on Machine Learning, automated methods in which systems learn about activities and detect whether these are anomalous through supervised or unsupervised learning [5] [11].

Network monitoring is largely based on alerts given by IDS. Many IDS have been based on Denning's model [12]. In general, there are two types of IDS. Statistical anomaly-based IDS monitor network traffic, and compare it against an established baseline (based on bandwidth, protocols, ports, devices, and connections that are "normal"). Signature-based IDS compare packets monitored on the network against a database of signatures/attributes from known malicious threats [1]. Leading SOCs typically craft their own signatures, defined by analysts in the form of rules. Recent advances automate the collection and analysis of data from a range of sources such as logs and IDS alerts using novel Machine Learning and Data Mining approaches.

Much of the presentation of network monitoring data is conveyed through visualisation systems. There are a number of recent surveys of the state of the art in visualisation techniques for security monitoring. Conti *et al.* in [13] and Zhang *et al.* in [14] present reviews as of 2007 and 2012 respectively, reporting research into improving graphical layout and user interaction techniques [15] [16]. Visualisations generally work by mapping network data parameters to visual parameters, such that analysts can observe the changes in the visualisation presented and from this deduce changes in, and information about, the network. The design of effective visualisation involves identifying mappings that represent the data in an intuitive way that can be understood by security and network analysts, in SOCs for example, without inducing cognitive overload, and can convey as effectively as possible any information pertaining to the security of the computer network.

There are certain drawbacks to current approaches to the monitoring and analysis of security data. Anomaly detection techniques can be unreliable or inaccurate, and may produce false positives and false negatives [1] [2]. A shortcoming of existing visualisation-based network monitoring systems is the requirement that operators dedicate their full attention to the display in order to ensure that no information is missed – for real-time monitoring especially – which can restrict their ability to perform other tasks. Furthermore, the number of visual dimensions and properties onto which data can be mapped is limited [17].

Based on these shortcomings in existing monitoring techniques, we identify ways in which monitoring capability in SOCs might be improved. While many promising advances have been made recently in novel data analytics approaches in particular, we highlighted that network monitoring systems do not always produce reliable outputs. It is, therefore, important that the human operator has situational awareness and an understanding of the network state, in order that he can interpret the alerts given by the detection systems used, and accurately decide their validity. Such awareness could also enable analysts to detect patterns, recognise anomalous activity and prioritise risks differently to their systems. Techniques that provide analysts with a continuous awareness of the state of the network require further investigation. Research is also needed into novel methods for improving the presentation of network data, the main technique for which is currently visualisation. In particular, it is important to design representations of large volumes of network data that are as easy as possible for analysts to use, understand and act on.

III. Network Monitoring Using Sonification

We believe that sonification could address the requirements with which we conclude Section II in a number of ways. Presenting network data as a continuous sonification may improve analysts' awareness of the network state, and furthermore may enable the analyst to detect patterns in the data, acting as a human anomaly detector of sorts. These are both areas for investigation and are detailed as research questions in Section IV. Sonification could also offer a solution to the shortcomings of visualisation techniques for network monitoring, as another human interface alongside the visualisation, using a different sense. Firstly, sound can be presented for peripheral listening – a secondary task – and, if designed appropriately, engage the listener's attention as required, allowing operators to perform other tasks in the meantime; secondly, using sound offers another set of dimensions in addition to visual dimensions to which data can be mapped.

In this section, we present background on sonification generally. Following this, we review prior work in the application of sonification to network security monitoring, and in multimodal systems (combining visuals and sound) for network monitoring.

A. Sonification: A Background

Sonification is used in numerous fields, such as financial markets, medicine (Electroencephalography (EEG) monitoring [18], image analysis [19]) and astronomy. User testing has validated that the presentation of sonified data can improve certain capabilities in a number of applications: improved accuracy in monitoring the movement of volatile market indices by financial traders [20], and improved capabilities for exploratory analysis of EEG data [21], for example.

A variety of techniques and guidelines have been developed for the design and implementation of sonification [22] [23] [24] [25]. Throughout sonification literature there are three main approaches recognised: earcons/event-based sonification (discrete sounds representing a defined event), parameter mapping sonification (in which changes in some data dimensions are represented by changes in acoustic dimensions), and model-based sonification (in which the user interacts with a model and receives some acoustic response derived from the data).

The current state of the art in sonification for network and server monitoring is summarised in Hildebrandt [17], in which systems for sonification of computer security data are identified, in various stages of maturity. It is concluded that there is a lack of formal user and usability testing, even in those systems that are already fully developed [26] [27] [28]. Our work differs from Hildebrandt in two key ways. Firstly, while Hildebrandt's survey gives an overview of the design approaches taken in some existing sonification systems, our survey provides much greater detail on the sonification design of existing systems in terms of sonification techniques, sound mapping types, the network data and attack types represented and the network monitoring scope. Secondly, we make recommendations in our research agenda for advancing sonification system design for the network monitoring context through aesthetics and formalisation, as well as defining the research questions to be answered through user testing.

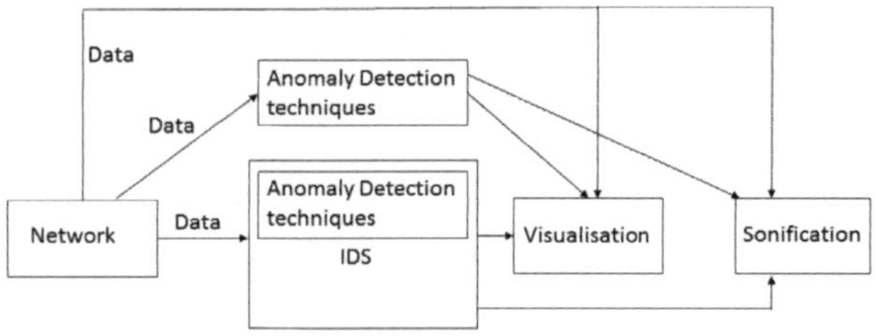

Figure 1. A summary of the existing relationship between traditional monitoring techniques and their potential relationship with sonification systems in SOCs.

Figure 1 shows the existing relationship between raw data, anomaly detection techniques, IDS and visualisations in SOC monitoring, and the position we envisage sonification might take in this setup.

B. Applications of Sonification to Network Monitoring

PEEP, a "network auralizer" for monitoring networks with sound, is presented in [26]. PEEP is designed to enable system administrators to detect network anomalies – both in security and general performance – by comparing sounds with the sound of the "normally functioning" network. The focus of PEEP is on the use of "natural" sounds – birdsong, for example – in sonifying network events. Recordings are mapped to network conditions (excessive traffic and email spam, for instance), and are played back to reflect these conditions. Abnormal events are presented through a change in the "natural" sounds. PEEP represents both network events (when an event occurs it is represented by a single natural sound) and network state (state is represented through sounds played continuously, which change when there is a change in some aspects of the state, such as average network load). There is, however, no validation of the performance of PEEP and its usefulness for monitoring networks.

The Stetho network sonification system is given in [29]. Stetho sonifies network events by reading the output of the Linux tcpdump command, checking for matches using regular expressions, and generating corresponding Musical Instrument Digital Interface (MIDI) events, with the aim that the system creates sounds that are "comfortable as music". The aim of Stetho is to convey the status of network traffic, without a specific focus on anomaly detection. The research includes an evaluation experiment in which the Stetho system is used – users' ability to interpret the traffic load from the sounds generated by Stetho is examined. The experiment shows that this monitoring information can be recognised by users from the sounds created by Stetho; however, only four users are involved in the evaluation experiment.

Network Monitoring with Sound (NeMoS) is a network sonification system in which the user assigns network events, and the system then associates these events with MIDI tracks [30]. The system is designed to allow monitoring of different parts of a potentially large network system at once, with a single musical flow representing the whole state of the part of the system the system manager is interested in. The focus is not on network security but on monitoring network performance in general; printer status and system load, for example, can be represented through two different sound channels.

More recently, Ballora *et al.* look to create a soundscape representation of network state which aids anomaly detection by assigning sounds to signal certain types and levels of network activity such as unusual port requests [31] ("soundscape" definition given by Schafer [32]). The concept is a system capable of combining multiple network parameters through data fusion to create this soundscape. The fusion approach is based on the JDL Data Fusion Process Model [33], with characteristics of the data assigned to multiple parameters of the sound. The authors aim, firstly, to map anomalous events to sound and, secondly, to represent the IP (Internet Protocol) space as a soundscape in which patterns can emerge for experienced listeners. No validation is carried out as to the usefulness of the system in network anomaly detection tasks.

Vickers *et al.* use a soundscape approach to sonify meta properties of network traffic data [34]. The aim of the system is to alert the system administrator of abnormal network behaviour with regard to both performance and security; it is suggested, for example, that a distributed denial-of-service (DDoS) attack might be recognisable by the system's representation of an increase in certain types of traffic. There is, however, no evaluation of users' ability to recognise such information using the system. Vickers *et al.* then extend that work to further explore the potential for using sonification for network situational awareness [35]. For this context, i.e., continuous monitoring for network situational awareness – it is argued that solutions based on soundscape have an advantage over other sonification designs in this context, and that there is a need for sonifications that are not annoying or fatiguing and that complement the user's existing sonic environment.

A soundscape approach is also adopted in the InteNtion system [27] for network sonification. Here, network traffic analysis output is converted to MIDI and sent to synthesisers for dynamic mixing; the output is a soundscape composed by the network activity generally rather than the detection of suspicious activity specifically. It is argued that the system could be used to help administrators detect attacks; however this is not validated through user testing. DeButts is a student project available online in which network data is sonified with the aim of aiding security analysts to detect anomalous incidents in network access logs [36].

García-Ruiz *et al.* investigate the application of sonification as a teaching and learning tool for network intrusion detection [37] [38]. This work includes an exploratory piece in which information is gathered regarding the subjects' preferred auditory representations of attacks. Sonification prototypes are given for the mapping of log-registered attacks into sound. The first uses animal sounds – auditory icons – for five different types of attack ("guess", "rcp", "rsh", "rlogin", "port-scan"); the second uses piano notes at five different frequencies as earcons to represent the five types of attack. Informal testing was carried out for these two prototypes, and suggested that the earcons were more easily identifiable, while the subjects could recall the attack types more easily using the auditory icons. While this is a useful start to comparing approaches to sonification design for network data, the mappings tested are limited, and further research is required into mappings involving other sound and data types.

Systems have been proposed to sonify the output of existing IDS, and to act as additions to the function of these systems. The CyberSeer [39] system uses sound to aid the presentation of network security information with the aim of improving network monitoring capability. Sound is used as an additional variable to data visualisation techniques to produce an audio-visual display that conveys information about network traffic log data and IDS events. The requirement for user testing to establish the most effective audio mappings is recognised, but no testing is carried out.

Gopinath's thesis uses JListen to sonify a range of events in Snort Network Intrusion Detection System to signal malicious attacks [3] (Snort is a widely used open-source network intrusion detection system for UNIX derivatives and Windows). The aim is to explore the usefulness of sonification in improving the *accuracy* of IDS; usability studies indicate that sonification may increase user awareness in intrusion detection. Experiments are carried out to test three hypotheses on the usability and efficacy of sonifying Snort. The findings are: musical knowledge has no significant effect on the ability of subjects to use the system to find intrusions; sonification decreases the time taken to detect false positives; immediate monitoring of hosts is possible with a sonified system. As noted in Hildebrandt [17], however, the comparison is somewhat biased since the control group without auditory support had to conduct the tasks by reading log files, without access to the visualisation-based tools to which those tested with auditory support had access.

Multimodal systems, that combine visualisation and sonification for network monitoring, have also been explored. Varner and Knight present such a system in [40]. Visualisation is used to convey the status of network nodes; sonification then conveys additional details on network nodes selected by the user. This multimodal approach is useful because it combines advantages of the two modalities – the spatial nature of visualisation, and the temporal nature of sonification – to produce an effective and usable system. García-Ruiz *et al.* describe the benefits and pitfalls of using multimodal human-computer interfaces for analysing intrusion detection in [41]. A sonification method is proposed for network intrusion detection systems (NIDS) as part of a multimodal interface, to enable analysts to cope with the large amounts of information contained in network logs.

Qi *et al.* present another multimodal system for detecting intrusions and attacks on networks in [42]; distinctive sounds are generated for a set of attack scenarios consisting of denial-of-service (DoS) and port scanning. The same approach is adopted by Brown *et al.* [43]: the bit-rates and packet-rates of a delay queue are sonified in a system for intrusion detection. The sounds generated by the system, which maps bit rate and packet rate to sound, are tested (not tested on users, but listened to by the authors) for DoS and port scanning attack scenarios. It is concluded that the sounds generated could enable humans to recognise and distinguish between the two types of attack. However, user testing is needed to validate this conclusion and investigate the extent to which this approach is effective.

NetSon [28] is a system for real time sonification and visualisation of network traffic, with a focus on large-scale organisations. In this work, there are no user studies, but the system is being used at Fraunhofer IIS, a research institution, who provide a live web stream of their installation [44]. Microsoft have a multimodal system, *Specimen Box*, for real-time retrospective detection and analysis of botnet activity. It has not yet been presented in a scientific publication, but description and videos of the functioning system are presented online [45]. The system has not been subject to formal evaluation, but is used in operations at the Microsoft Cybercrime Centre.

Mancuso *et al.* conduct user testing to assess the usefulness of sonification of network data for military cyber operations [46]. The aim of the testing, in which participants were tasked with detecting cyber attacks using either a visual display only, or both visual and sonified displays, was to assess the extent to which sonification can improve the performance and manage the workload of, and decrease the stress felt by, operators conducting cyber monitoring operations on military networks. The testing results show that the sonifications did not affect the performance, workload or stress. However, only one method of sonifying the data was tested, in which each possible source and destination IP address was represented by a different instrument and note, and the loudness increased if a threshold packet size was exceeded. The results do not, therefore, show that sonification does not affect performance, stress and workload in this context, but demonstrate only that this particular method of sonifying the data is ineffective.

C. Outstanding Challenges

In Table I, we summarise the sonification systems previously developed (solutions for which full systems or prototypes have been developed) for network monitoring; from this we have identified three key areas in which research is lacking: user testing, sonification aesthetics, and formalisation of an approach to designing sonification systems for network monitoring.

In general, a weakness in the articles in which user studies are conducted is the small number of users involved. Table I shows that little user testing has been carried out, and of that which has, none has specifically targeted security analysts, and none has been conducted in a SOC environment. Table I shows also that there has been little (and no comprehensive) evaluation of the usefulness of existing sonification systems for network security monitoring tasks. Extensive user testing is required in this field to validate the usefulness of the approach and of proposed systems, and to refine the sonification design.

The systems listed vary in the data they represent. Some map raw network data to sound, some map the output of IDS

TABLE I. REVIEW OF APPROACHES TO AND USER TESTING IN EXISTING SONIFICATION SYSTEMS FOR NETWORK MONITORING, ORDERED BY YEAR.

Author	Year	Sonification approach description	User testing	Number of participants	Nature of participants	Network data type mapped	Sound type	Sonification technique	Monitoring scope	Evaluates usefulness for security monitoring?	Multimodal
Gilfix [26]	2000	"Natural" sounds mapped to network conditions	N			Raw data	Natural (wildlife and nature) sounds	Parameter-mapping; soundscape	Anomaly detection: conditions such as high traffic load and email spam are mapped to sound	N	N
Varner [40]	2002	Multimodal system: visualisation conveys status of network nodes; sonification conveys additional details on network nodes selected by the user	N			Not specified	Not specified	Not specified	Network attack detection	N	Y
Kimoto [29]	2002	Maps parameters of sound to raw network data	Y	4	Subjects familiar with network administration	Raw data	Musical	Parameter-mapping	General network activity	N	Y
Malandrino [30]	2003	Associates MIDI tracks to user-defined network events	N			Raw data	Musical	Event-based	Network performance	N	N
Gopinath [3]	2004	Instrument and pitch mapped to IDS alert intrusion type	Y	20	Computer Science students and staff	IDS alerts	Real-world (man-made/natural) and musical	Parameter-mapping	Anomaly detection: used alongside IDS logs to improve detection capability	Y	N
Papadopoulos [39]	2004	Combines network events rendered as spatial audio with 3D stereoscopic visuals to form a multimodal representation of network information. Sounds are created in response to changes in data patterns using Gaussian Mixture Modelling	N			A variety	Real-world and musical	Parameter-mapping	Anomaly detection: network data presented for pattern recognition, and IDS output sonified	N	Y
Qi [42]	2007	Maps traffic pattern (based on a classification-based mitigation system) to audio; byte rate and packet rate mapped to frequency and intensity of audio respectively	N			Classification-based attack mitigation system	Musical	Parameter-mapping	Network attack detection (DoS, port scanning)	N	N
El Seoud [38]	2008	Auditory icons (non-instrumental) and earcons (instrumental) mapped to attack type	Y	29	Telematics Engineering students	Logged attacks	Real-world and musical	Event-based	Network attack detection	N	N
Brown [43]	2009	Maps raw network traffic to sound to convey information on network status	N			Raw data	Musical	Parameter-mapping	Network anomaly detection (increase in traffic; HTTP error messages; number of TCP handshakes)	N	N
Ballora [31]	2011	Parameter mapping-based soundscape for overall IP space; obvious sound signals for certain types of activity levels	N			Raw data	Musical	Parameter-mapping; soundscape	Anomaly detection: anomalous incidents sonified, and network state presented to enable human pattern recognition	N	N
Giot [27]	2012	MIDI messages mapped to data outputted by SharpPCap library network traffic analysis; MIDI messages mixed to produce a soundscape	N			Raw data	Musical	Event-based; soundscape	General network activity and attack detection	N	N
deButts [36]	2014	Maps distinct notification tones to anomalous network events; visualises network traffic activity (multimodal)	N			Raw (access logs)	Single tones	Event-based	Anomaly detection: anomalous incidents mapped to sounds	N	Y
Vickers [34]	2014	Parameters of each sound generator (voice) mapped to the log return values for the network's self-organised criticality	N			Network's self-organised criticality	Natural	Parameter-mapping	Network performance and attack detection	N	N
Worrall [28]	2015	Multimodal system for large-scale network data. Maps data parameters and events to sound; parameter mapping sonification approach using melodic pitch structures to reduce fatigue.	N			Raw data	Musical	Parameter-mapping	General network activity	N	Y
Mancuso [46]	2015	Multimodal system for representing data on military networks, in which each source and destination IP is mapped to an instrument and pitch, and the loudness is increased when a packet size threshold is exceeded.	Y	30	Local population and air force base personnel	Raw data	Musical	Parameter-mapping	Network anomaly detection (packet rate threshold, source and destination IPs sonified)	Y	Y

systems, while some aim to map attacks to sounds; however, there is no comparison of the efficacy of these approaches, or of the usefulness of sonic representations of different attack types. The sonification design approaches (event-based, parameter mapping, and soundscape-based) also vary, as do the sound types (natural sounds, sounds that are musically informed) but there is as yet no comprehensive investigation into, or comparison of, the usefulness of these methods. Based on this, we propose that comparative research into the sonification aesthetics most appropriate to the network monitoring context is crucial, in order to inform sonification design. We further identify a requirement for the development of a formalised approach to designing sonifications in this field, to underpin developments and enable comparison. Next, we outline our detailed research agenda to address these issues.

IV. Research Agenda

We present our research agenda in three parts: comprehensive user studies, improved aesthetics, and formalisation.

A. Comprehensive User Studies

Section III indicates that of the proposals made for sonification systems for network monitoring, very few have conducted any user testing, and none have conducted such testing to the extent required for an appropriate understanding of the use of such systems and their suitability for actual deployment in security monitoring situations. As such, we outline a requirement for significantly more in-context user testing of sonifications for network monitoring tasks, carried out with security analysts in SOCs, to inform the design and investigate the advantages and disadvantages of the approach. It is important that sonification systems are tested in the SOC environment, in order to investigate how well they incorporate with the particular characteristics of SOCs – a variety of systems running simultaneously, collaborative working practice, high levels of attention required from workers.

We will conduct user testing to investigate the hypothesis that sonification can improve the network monitoring capabilities of security analysts. This hypothesis is proposed in light of prior work in other fields in which it is proven that certain capabilities can be improved by the presentation of sonified data, as outlined in Section III, and of the limited experimental evidence that shows that sonification can be useful for tasks involving network data specifically [3] [29].

For the validation of sonification as a solution to improving network monitoring capabilities, there are certain key research questions that need to be answered through user testing.

1) **To what extent, and in what ways, can the use of sonification improve the monitoring capabilities of security analysts in a SOC environment?** User testing is required to establish, firstly, the extent to which the presentation of sonified network data can improve the analyst's understanding and awareness of the network, as mentioned in Section II. Secondly, the extent to which this awareness can improve the ability of analysts to interact with, and decide the accuracy of the output of, their existing monitoring systems. Further investigation is also needed to establish whether the presentation of network data through sonification can enable analysts to "hear" patterns and anomalies in the data, and in this way detect anomalies more accurately than systems in any cases. Given the strong human capability for pattern recognition in audio representations [47] [48], and for contextualising information, it is plausible that a system that presents patterns in network data may enable the analyst to detect anomalies with greater accuracy than the traditional rule-based systems.
2) **Are there certain types of attack and threat that sonify more effectively than others, and what implications does this have for the design of sonification systems for network monitoring?** It is important that user testing is carried out to establish the cases in which sonified network data is most useful for network monitoring tasks. For example, it may be the case that certain types of attacks are better-represented through sonification than others, and that some attacks sound anomalous in a way that is particularly easy for analysts to use while others do not sonify well. Findings on this subject should inform sonification system design by distinguishing the attacks and threats in relation to which sonification performs best, and the areas in which the technique therefore has the potential to be most effective.

Answers to these questions will provide a greater understanding of the role sonification can play in improving monitoring capabilities in SOCs, the limits of the approach, and the extent to which it can be reliable as a monitoring technique. In conducting this testing, we expect to draw from existing research on conducting user studies in general, and in a security context [49] [50].

B. Improved Aesthetics

While there has been some work in aesthetic sonification, as shown in Section III, it has not been heavily applied in the context of network monitoring. Prior work indicates that sonification aesthetic impacts on its effectiveness. In an experiment comparing sonifications of guidance systems, for example, it was shown that sonification strategies based on pitch and tempo enabled higher precision than strategies based on loudness and brightness [51]. It was also shown in [52] that particular sonification designs resulted in better participant performance in identifying features of Surface Electromyography data for a range of different tasks involved. The aesthetics of the design are an important factor in producing sonifications that are suitable for continuous presentation in this context. In particular, the sounds should be unfatiguing and should achieve a balance in which they are unobtrusive to the performance of other tasks while drawing sufficient attention when necessary to be suitable for SOC monitoring. While there are other techniques that may be useful, we propose an approach to this design that draws on techniques and theories of musical composition. We can draw on work in aesthetic sonification by Vickers [47], and on work in musification, i.e., the design of sonifications that are musical. Some key questions to be answered regarding sonification aesthetics for network security monitoring are given below.

1) **Can the development of aesthetic sonifications based on techniques of musical composition alleviate the fatiguing nature of sonifications previously reported, and, secondly, are such sonifications more appropriate for continuous network monitoring tasks?** A drawback to sonification for network monitoring is the fatigue or annoyance that listeners can experience as a result of long-term exposure to sonification [35] [47]. The question of how this can be prevented if sonifications are to be developed that are appropriate for continuous network monitoring, and the suitability of a sonification approach based on techniques of musical composition for the network monitoring context requires investigation.
2) **To what extent does musical experience affect the ability of security analysts to use musically-informed sonification systems in network monitoring tasks?** The effect of users' musical experience on their ability to understand and make use of the sonification systems design will require investigation. Here, musical experience refers to the level of prior theoretical and aural musical training attained by the user. For this SOC monitoring context, analysts' use of the systems should not be impaired by a lack of musical experience.

Besides aesthetics, aspects of human perception must influence the design: the prior associations sounds may hold for users and the way in which this affects interpretation; the effect of musical experience on perception. It is important that the design takes into account factors in perception such as cross-field interference (in which different parameters of sound – pitch and tempo, for example – interact in a way that affects perception of either) and does not induce cognitive overload for the user.

C. Formalisation

To address the requirements above we need an underpinning framework which enables us to architect and experiment with sonifications in a flexible way, utilising heterogeneous models alongside each other in order to compare performance. No such framework currently exists, and we therefore identify that there is a need for a formal grammar for designing sonification for network monitoring. We propose the mathematical definition of a grammar for the representation of network data through parameter-mapping sonification that is derived from the results of user testing in a network monitoring context, techniques of musical composition, and the science of auditory perception.

A formal grammar for designing sonifications for use in the network monitoring context could tailor aspects of sonification design such as cross-field interference to produce sonifications that are appropriate for network monitoring tasks. A simple example is a simultaneous change in two network parameters: a statistically significant increase in traffic load, and messages received from an IP address that is known to be malicious (these two changes would generally be found by the statistical anomaly-based IDS and signature-based IDS, respectively, described in Section II). This could be the result of a DoS attack, and the sonification system should therefore attract the attention of the analyst. Cross-field interference could be leveraged in this case (with a mapping to higher pitch and increased tempo – two sound parameters which interact such that each appears more increased that it really is – for the two data parameters respectively) to ensure that the attack is highlighted by the sonification.

In order for the representation to be unfatiguing, we propose that a rule-based approach to aesthetic sound generation may be appropriate. In particular, a defined formal grammar for representing network data as sound could be applied to a variety of genres of music to generate a set of different-sounding sonifications of the same network data. We hypothesise that with this approach, users could be allowed to move between a set of musical genres at choice, all of which would sonify the network data according to the same grammar, and this could reduce the fatigue caused by the sounds. Below, we give the key questions to be investigated on formalising sonification systems for network monitoring.

1) **To what extent can a defined formal grammar produce sonification systems that improve network monitoring capabilities in SOCs?** We believe that a combination of factors, including human sound perception, sonification aesthetics and intuitiveness of mappings, will affect and, if addressed correctly, improve the usability of the sonifications designed. A formal grammar can, if designed correctly, combine the solutions to these requirements in a thorough and considered manner and we therefore hypothesise that such an approach may produce highly usable and useful sonification systems for network monitoring. The extent to which this is the case requires investigation through user testing of the systems produced according to the grammar.
2) **Is a rule-based approach to generating a set of different-sounding sonifications of the network data, which enables users to change between musical preferences, appropriate for a network security monitoring context?** This question is in two main parts. Firstly, does the presentation of a choice of different-sounding sonifications alleviate the fatigue induced by continuous sonifications, as reported in prior work? Secondly, does such a presentation affect the usefulness of the sonification for network monitoring tasks in any way? For example, it is viable that the presentation of a number of different-sounding sonifications may cause more confusion for users than the presentation of a single sonification, and that this may detract from the usability of the systems designed. If this is found to be the case, then methods for mitigating this effect, or other approaches to designing unfatiguing continuous sonification systems, will need to be investigated.

V. Conclusion and Future Work

We conclude that there is a growing requirement for the validation of using sonification in SOCs as a means of improving certain monitoring capabilities. The current state of the art provides evidence of the potential of sonification in advancing network security monitoring capabilities. Systems proposed and in use have been shown to be as effective as, or more effective than, other network monitoring techniques insofar as a limited amount of testing has been performed [17].

We recognise a requirement for development of the field in three main directions. Firstly, the performance of extensive user testing to validate claims about and show the extent of the suitability of sonification for network monitoring. Secondly, the need for aesthetics of the sonification design for continuous network monitoring, and the development of methods for generating sonifications that are unfatiguing, unobtrusive, and yet convey the data to an appropriate extent. Lastly, the formalisation of a design approach – a formal grammar that is defined by the requirements: representation of data, perception of sound, and aesthetics.

As future work, we intend to research the potential for sonification to match, or improve on, the performance of current monitoring systems in the SOC context. We will also define a formal grammar for the design of sonification for network monitoring, based on the results of user testing of mappings; in particular, this grammar will enable the design of rule-based aesthetic sonification for this context by drawing on music theory.

References

[1] P. Garcia-Teodoro, J. Diaz-Verdejo, G. Maciá-Fernández, and E. Vázquez, "Anomaly-based network intrusion detection: Techniques, systems and challenges," computers & security, vol. 28, no. 1, 2009, pp. 18–28.

[2] S. Axelsson, "The base-rate fallacy and its implications for the difficulty of intrusion detection," in Proceedings of the 6th ACM Conference on Computer and Communications Security. ACM, 1999, pp. 1–7.

[3] M. Gopinath, "Auralization of intrusion detection system using Jlisten," Development, vol. 22, 2004, p. 3.

[4] PWC, "2015 Information Security Breaches Survey," 2015, PWC in association with Infosecurity Europe.

[5] A. Lazarevic, L. Ertöz, V. Kumar, A. Ozgur, and J. Srivastava, "A comparative study of anomaly detection schemes in network intrusion detection." in Proceedings of SIAM International Conference on Data Mining, 2003, pp. 25–36.

[6] V. Chandola, A. Banerjee, and V. Kumar, "Anomaly detection: A survey," ACM Computing Surveys (CSUR), vol. 41, no. 3, 2009, p. 15.

[7] V. Kumar, J. Srivastava, and A. Lazarevic, Managing cyber threats: issues, approaches, and challenges. Springer Science & Business Media, 2006, vol. 5.

[8] D. E. Denning and P. G. Neumann, "Requirements and model for ides—a real-time intrusion detection expert system," Document A005, SRI International, vol. 333, 1985.

[9] N. Ye, S. Emran, Q. Chen, and S. Vilbert, "Multivariate statistical analysis of audit trails for host-based intrusion detection," IEEE Transactions on Computers, vol. 51, no. 7, 2002, pp. 810–820.

[10] D. Anderson, T. F. Lunt, H. Javitz, A. Tamaru, and A. Valdes, Detecting unusual program behavior using the statistical component of the Next-generation Intrusion Detection Expert System (NIDES). SRI International, Computer Science Laboratory, 1995.

[11] C. Tsai, Y. Hsu, C. Lin, and W. Lin, "Intrusion detection by machine learning: A review," Expert Systems with Applications, vol. 36, no. 10, 2009, pp. 11 994–12 000.

[12] D. Denning, "An intrusion-detection model," IEEE Transactions on Software Engineering, no. 2, 1987, pp. 222–232.

[13] G. Conti, Security data visualization: graphical techniques for network analysis. No Starch Press, 2007.

[14] Y. Zhang, Y. Xiao, M. Chen, J. Zhang, and H. Deng, "A survey of security visualization for computer network logs," Security and Communication Networks, vol. 5, no. 4, 2012, pp. 404–421.

[15] R. F. Erbacher, K. L. Walker, and D. A. Frincke, "Intrusion and misuse detection in large-scale systems," Computer Graphics and Applications, IEEE, vol. 22, no. 1, 2002, pp. 38–47.

[16] B. Shneiderman, "Dynamic queries for visual information seeking," IEEE Software, vol. 11, no. 6, 1994, pp. 70–77.

[17] S. Rinderle-Ma and T. Hildebrandt, "Server sounds and network noises," in Cognitive Infocommunications (CogInfoCom), 2015 6th IEEE International Conference on. IEEE, 2015, pp. 45–50.

[18] Z. Halim, R. Baig, and S. Bashir, "Sonification: a novel approach towards data mining," in Proceedings of the International Conference on Emerging Technologies, 2006. IEEE, 2006, pp. 548–553.

[19] T. Hinterberger and G. Baier, "Parametric orchestral sonification of EEG in real time," IEEE MultiMedia, no. 2, 2005, pp. 70–79.

[20] P. Janata and E. Childs, "Marketbuzz: Sonification of real-time financial data," in Proceedings of the International Conference on Auditory Display, 2004.

[21] T. Hermann, "Sonification for Exploratory Data Analysis," Ph.D. dissertation, 2002, Bielefeld University.

[22] G. Kramer, Auditory display: Sonification, audification, and auditory interfaces. Perseus Publishing, 1993.

[23] A. de Campo, "Toward a data sonification design space map," in Proceedings of the International Conference on Auditory Display, 2007, pp. 342–347.

[24] S. Barrass and C. Frauenberger, "A communal map of design in auditory display," in Proceedings of the International Conference on Auditory Display, 2009, pp. 1–10.

[25] S. Barrass et al., "Auditory information design," Made available in DSpace on 2011-01-04T02: 37: 33Z (GMT), 1997.

[26] M. Gilfix and A. Couch, "Peep (the network auralizer): Monitoring your network with sound." in Proceedings of the Large Installation System Administration Conference, 2000, pp. 109–117.

[27] R. Giot and Y. Courbe, "Intention–interactive network sonification," in Proceedings of the International Conference on Auditory Display. Georgia Institute of Technology, 2012, pp. 235–236.

[28] D. Worrall, "Realtime sonification and visualisation of network metadata," in Proceedings of the International Conference on Auditory Display, 2015, pp. 337–339.

[29] M. Kimoto and H. Ohno, "Design and implementation of stetho—network sonification system," in Proceedings of the International Computer Music Conference, 2002, pp. 273–279.

[30] D. Malandrino, D. Mea, A. Negro, G. Palmieri, and V. Scarano, "Nemos: Network monitoring with sound," in Proceedings of the International Conference on Auditory Display, 2003, pp. 251–254.

[31] M. Ballora, N. Giacobe, and D. Hall, "Songs of cyberspace: an update on sonifications of network traffic to support situational awareness," in SPIE Defense, Security, and Sensing. International Society for Optics and Photonics, 2011, pp. 80 640P–80 640P.

[32] R. Schafer, The soundscape: Our sonic environment and the tuning of the world. Inner Traditions/Bear & Co, 1993.

[33] O. Kessler et al., "[functional description of the data fusion process]," 1991, Office of Naval Technology Naval Air Development Center, Warminster PA.

[34] P. Vickers, C. Laing, and T. Fairfax, "Sonification of a network's self-organized criticality," arXiv preprint arXiv:1407.4705, 2014.

[35] P. Vickers, C. Laing, M. Debashi, and T. Fairfax, "Sonification aesthetics and listening for network situational awareness," in Proceedings of the Conference on Sonification of Health and Environmental Data, 2014.

[36] B. deButts, "Network access log visualization & sonification," Master's thesis, Tufts University, Medford, MA, US, 2014.

[37] M. Garcia-Ruiz, M. Vargas Martin, B. Kapralos, J. Tashiro, and R. Acosta-Diaz, "Best practices for applying sonification to support teaching and learning of network intrusion detection," in Proceedings of the World Conference on Educational Multimedia, Hypermedia and Telecommunications, 2010, pp. 752–757.

[38] S. El Seoud, M. Garcia-Ruiz, A. Edwards, R. Aquino-Santos, and M. Martin, "Auditory display as a tool for teaching network intrusion detection," International Journal of Emerging Technologies in Learning (iJET), vol. 3, no. 2, 2008, pp. 59–62.

[39] C. Papadopoulos, C. Kyriakakis, A. Sawchuk, and X. He, "Cyberseer: 3d audio-visual immersion for network security and management," in Proceedings of the ACM workshop on Visualization and data mining for computer security. ACM, 2004, pp. 90–98.

[40] P. Varner and J. Knight, "Monitoring and visualization of emergent behavior in large scale intrusion tolerant distributed systems," Technical report, Pennsylvania State University, 2002.

[41] M. García-Ruiz, M. Martin, and M. Green, "Towards a multimodal human-computer interface to analyze intrusion detection in computer networks," in Proceedings of the First Human-Computer Interaction Workshop (MexIHC), Puebla, Mexico, 2006.

[42] L. Qi, M. Martin, B. Kapralos, M. Green, and M. García-Ruiz, "Toward sound-assisted intrusion detection systems," in On the Move to Meaningful Internet Systems 2007: CoopIS, DOA, ODBASE, GADA, and IS. Springer, 2007, pp. 1634–1645.

[43] A. Brown, M. Martin, B. Kapralos, M. Green, and M. Garcia-Ruiz, "Poster: Towards music-assisted intrusion detection," 2009, poster presented at IEEE Workshop on Statistical Signal Processing.

[44] "Fraunhofer IIS Netson," 2016, URL: http://www.iis.fraunhofer.de/en/muv/2015/netson.html [accessed: 21/03/2016].

[45] "Specimen Box, The Office for Creative Research," 2014, URL: http://ocr.nyc/user-focused-tools/2014/06/01/specimen-box/ [accessed: 21/03/2016].

[46] V. F. Mancuso et al., "Augmenting cyber defender performance and workload through sonified displays," Procedia Manufacturing, vol. 3, 2015, pp. 5214–5221.

[47] T. Hermann, A. Hunt, and J. Neuhoff, The sonification handbook. Logos Verlag Berlin, GE, 2011.

[48] E. Yeung, "Pattern recognition by audio representation of multivariate analytical data," Analytical Chemistry, vol. 52, no. 7, 1980, pp. 1120–1123.

[49] J. Rubin and D. Chisnell, Handbook of usability testing: how to plan, design and conduct effective tests. John Wiley & Sons, 2008.

[50] J. R. C. Nurse, S. Creese, M. Goldsmith, and K. Lamberts, "Guidelines for usable cybersecurity: Past and present," in Proceedings of the Third International Workshop on Cyberspace Safety and Security (CSS). IEEE, 2011, pp. 21–26.

[51] G. Parseihian, C. Gondre, M. Aramaki, S. Ystad, and R. K. Martinet, "Comparison and evaluation of sonification strategies for guidance tasks," IEEE Transactions on Multimedia, vol. 18, no. 4, 2016, pp. 674–686.

[52] S. C. Peres, D. Verona, T. Nisar, and P. Ritchey, "Towards a systematic approach to real-time sonification design for surface electromyography," Displays, 2016.

LoT: a Reputation-based Trust System for Long-term Archiving

Martín Vigil, Denise Demirel, Sheikh Mahbub Habib, Sascha Hauke,
Johannes Buchmann, and Max Mühlhäuser

Technische Universität Darmstadt
Hochschulstr. 10, 64289 Darmstadt, Germany
Email: {vigil, ddemirel, buchmann}@cdc.tu-darmstadt.de
{sheikh, hauke, max}@tk.tu-darmstadt.de

Abstract—**Digital archiving systems are necessary to store documents for several years, such as electronic health records. However, security breaches in these systems may allow attackers to tamper with archived documents without being noticed. To address this threat, standardized archiving systems require a public key infrastructure, where a time-stamp authority is trusted to date and sign stored documents periodically. However, in practice a time-stamp authority may not be fully trustworthy, allowing an attacker to forge documents. Thus, in this paper, we introduce a novel reputation-based trust system for time-stamping-based archiving called *Long-term evaluation of Trust* (LoT), which alleviates the required trust assumptions. This makes LoT an important contribution to realize trust and security management for digital archiving systems using public key infrastructures. We implemented LoT showcasing its applicability to electronic health records and demonstrate its efficacy by simulations.**

Keywords–Digital Archiving; Time-Stamping; Reputation System; Trust; Electronic Health Record.

I. INTRODUCTION

In the field of long-term archiving [1], an important goal is maintaining the integrity and authenticity of stored data over long periods of time. An example of long-term stored data are electronic health records (EHRs), which should be preserved for the entire lifetime of a patient. The deployment of EHRs is already in progress: by 2020, the British National Health Service plans to make their patients' health and care records digitally available as a part of their "Personalized Health and Care 2020" strategy [2].

In the long run, attackers can gain access to archiving systems and tamper with archived data without being noticed. This can cause serious issues, such as physicians using forged electronic health records to prescribe wrong treatments. To cope with this security threat, existing long-term archiving schemes assume the existence of a trusted third party. This party periodically checks and/or signs the documents. The only standardized long-term archiving solutions are the time-stamping-based schemes (e.g., [3]). These schemes require public key infrastructures, where a trusted time-stamp authority (TSA) dates and signs documents by time-stamping them. A time-stamp allows users to verify when a document existed and whether it has been modified since. For the purpose of verification, users are bound to *trust* that the TSA has provided the correct date and time in the time-stamp. Since time-stamps have limited lifetime, e.g., TSAs' signatures expire, a single time-stamp cannot guarantee integrity and authenticity of a document for an indefinite period of time. Therefore, a chain of time-stamps is necessary. The first time-stamp authenticates the document and the subsequent time-stamps authenticate the previous ones, i.e., expired time-stamps. In this case, users have to trust *every* TSA involved in constructing the time-stamp chain.

However, the assumption of the existence of fully trustworthy TSAs raises security concerns regarding time-stamping-based schemes if TSAs turn out to be untrustworthy. For instance, a malicious TSA can time-stamp a forged signature using a particular date in the past when the corresponding signature key was still valid. Also, a single suspicious TSA is sufficient to cast doubt on the correctness of a time-stamp chain and of the corresponding archived document. It is somewhat surprising that such an issue has not been addressed yet, although TSAs are key actors of long-term archiving solutions and can be targets of attacks similar to that of certification authorities (see [4] for an overview of these attacks).

In order to alleviate the need to assume fully trusted time-stamp authorities, in this paper we propose a novel reputation-based trust system for long-term archiving solutions that is called *Long-term evaluation of Trust* (LoT). LoT evaluates the trustworthiness of each and every TSAs along with their issued time-stamps. Our proposed system provides users of long-term archiving systems the power to assess how likely it is that the TSAs provide correct time-stamps, documents are uncorrupted and authentic, as well as to determine when the documents have to be re-authenticated.

More precisely, the main contributions of this paper are as follows:

- Mechanisms to collect and process experiences regarding the TSAs and their issued time-stamps.
- Extended mechanisms for trust evaluation of the TSAs and time-stamps.
- A decision mechanism based on trust scores.
- A trust resetting mechanism.

The contributions are evaluated by means of simulation using our implemented trust system. The goal of the evaluation is to showcase the applicability and efficacy of our proposed trust system in the context of archiving EHRs.

Digital archiving systems should also guarantee the confidentiality of stored documents. However, this security goal is not addressed in this work because the current archiving systems do not provide confidentiality in the long run. More precisely, there is no solution available that guarantees both long-term integrity and information-theoretic confidentiality.

Nevertheless, this is a vital research field, and we plan to address this security goal in future work (see [5] for preliminary results).

The remainder of this work is organized as follows. Related work is provided in Section II. The background for the reader to understand our contribution is provided in Section III. Our contributions are presented in Section IV and evaluated in Section V. In Section VI, we draw the conclusion and discuss our future work.

II. Related work

In this section, we briefly discuss the state-of-the-art regarding long-term archiving schemes and trust systems.

Long-term Archiving. Lekkas and Gritzalis [6] propose a long-term archiving scheme where digital signatures are used to guarantee that EHRs have not been forged. Moreover, the scheme assumes the existence of trusted third parties, the so-called notaries, that verify and renew these signatures regularly. Vigil et al. [7] soften this trust assumption by proposing a peer-to-peer network of notaries, where one notary checks that another notary verifies and renews signatures properly. However, the reputation of notaries is not available for users in the long term. Besides notary based solutions, the approaches using TSAs [8] are very promising and have been even standardized (e.g., [3]). However, for this type of archiving scheme no trust evaluation is available.

Trust & Reputation. Trust models and reputation systems have been proposed in various environments [9][10][11]. For instance, electronic marketplaces, peer-to-peer systems, and cloud computing. A number of commercial instances of such systems are also available, such as eBay and Amazon. Moreover, Braun et al. [12] propose a reputation system called CA-TMS to be used in public key infrastructures. More precisely, their system allows for assessing the trustworthiness level of certificate chains. However, none of the existing systems or models have been applied to long-term archiving schemes yet.

Our Scheme. To the best of our knowledge, our scheme is the first one to allow for trust evaluation when TSAs instead of notaries are used. Note that this significantly changes the archiving procedures and correspondingly how trustworthiness is evaluated. Moreover, our scheme provides a centralized reputation-based trust system where the reputations of TSAs and time-stamps are stored indefinitely. These reputations allow users to estimate the trustworthiness of TSAs and time-stamps even in the long run. In this work, we focus on classical time-stamping-based schemes where a time-stamp is signed by a single TSA as described in the standardized solution [3]. To analyze other approaches (e.g., a time-stamp is signed by multiple TSAs) is left for future work. Furthermore, we assume that the storage system stores the time-stamps generated. In addition, they can be published in a newspaper. However, note that this requires the existence of witnesses why a reputation system for the TSAs remains a useful tool.

III. Preliminaries

In this section, we explain how to use time-stamping to authenticate long-term data. Moreover, we present an adversary model for time-stamping and discuss the trust users put in digital signatures.

A. Long-term archiving of data

When using documents that already exist for long periods of time, it is necessary to check that these documents have not been forged since they were stored. To address this issue, several time-stamping schemes have been proposed with different security goals. In general, a time-stamping scheme generates an initial time-stamp to establish that a document and its signature existed at the date and time they were stored (proof of existence) and that they have not been changed since (integrity). Moreover, this time-stamp allows to verify the document authenticity even after the document signature becomes invalid or cryptographically insecure. However, the digital signature that guarantees the authenticity of the time-stamp is also valid and secure for a certain period of time only. After this period, the time-stamp and the document can be manipulated without being noticed. Therefore, it is necessary to renew the time-stamp timely. More precisely, before the time-stamp becomes insecure, the scheme generates a new one. This new time-stamp authenticates the old time-stamp. That is, the new time-stamp can be used to verify that the old time-stamp existed when the corresponding signature was valid and secure and that the old time-stamp has not been changed since. This process generates an endless time-stamp sequence which can be used to demonstrate that the document existed and was not changed since it was archived.

Fig. 1 illustrates an example of time-stamping. A signed document d is created at a time τ_0. This document is stored in an archive at a time $\tau_1 > \tau_0$. At this time, the signature on the document is still secure and a time-stamp s_1 is created. The time-stamp s_1 authenticates the document d, that is, s_1 can be used to verify that d existed at τ_1 and has not been changed since. The next time-stamps s_2 and s_3 are created at times $\tau_2 > \tau_1$ and $\tau_3 > \tau_2$, respectively. They authenticate the previous time-stamp before it becomes insecure. For example, s_2 authenticates s_1 at the time $\tau_2 < \tau_{2'}$, where $\tau_{2'}$ is when s_1 becomes insecure.

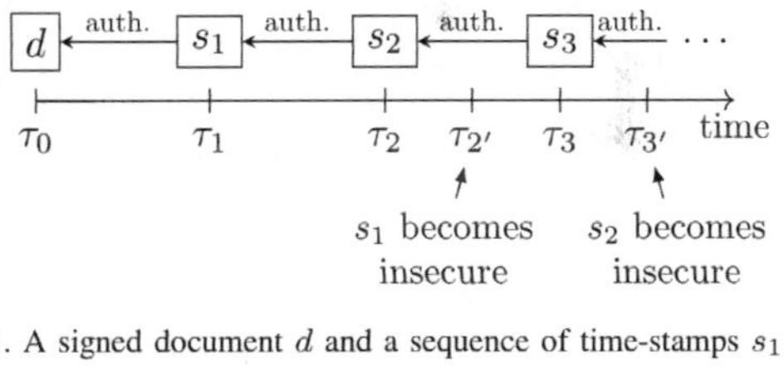

Figure 1. A signed document d and a sequence of time-stamps $s_1, s_2, \ldots$.

We now present the involved parties and procedures of time-stamping-based archiving schemes. The parties are *submitters*, *storage systems*, *TSAs*, and *retrievers*. *Submitters* send signed documents to storage systems. *Storage systems* store the submitted documents and can be realized, for instance, by building a cloud infrastructure. Additionally, storage systems request time-stamps to demonstrate that the submitted documents and their signatures have not been forged since their submission. Note that even if the document signature is no longer secure, the time-stamp ensures that neither the document nor the signature have been changed. *TSAs* are trusted third parties issuing the requested time-stamps. They are trusted to include the date and time when the time-stamps are issued in the time-stamps. *Retrievers* obtain signed documents and the corresponding time-stamps from the storage systems. They verify the time-stamps to ensure that the retrieved data is not a forgery.

The long-term archiving of signed documents comprises the procedures *initialization*, *renewal*, and *verification*. During the initialization, a first time-stamp s_1 is generated showing that the signed document d existed at the date and time τ_1. The procedure is detailed below and illustrated in Fig. 2.

1) A submitter sends a document d to a storage system.
2) The storage system requests the first time-stamp s_1 by sending d to a TSA. (To be precise, the hash of d instead of d itself is sent. Since hash functions are only computationally secure, time-stamps are also renewed when the hash function is about to become insecure. However, since this does not affect the reputation system we omit this detail for legibility.)
3) The TSA issues $s_1 = TS(d)$, where TS is a function that creates time-stamps on the given input. More precisely, TS creates a signature σ_1 on the input d together with the current date and time τ_1 and returns $s_1 = (\tau_1, \sigma_1)$.
4) The TSA returns s_1 to the storage system.
5) The storage system stores d together with s_1.

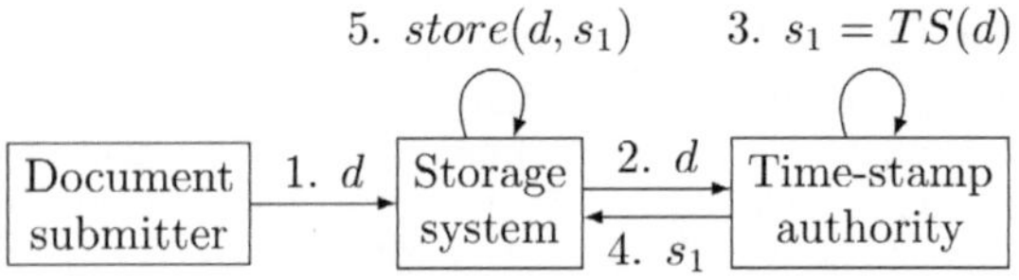

Figure 2. The initialization procedure.

The *renewal* procedure should be executed before the time-stamp s_1 becomes invalid. It generates a new time-stamp s_2 showing that s_1 existed at a date and time $\tau_2 > \tau_1$ when s_1 was still valid, and that s_1 has not been changed since. This procedure is explained next and depicted in Fig. 3.

1) The storage system requests s_2 by sending s_1 to a TSA.
2) The TSA issues $s_2 = TS(s_1)$. This time-stamp includes a signature σ_2 on s_1 together with τ_2, where $\tau_2 > \tau_1$ is the date and time when the TSA executed the function TS.
3) The TSA returns s_2 to the storage system.
4) The storage system stores d together with s_1 and s_2.

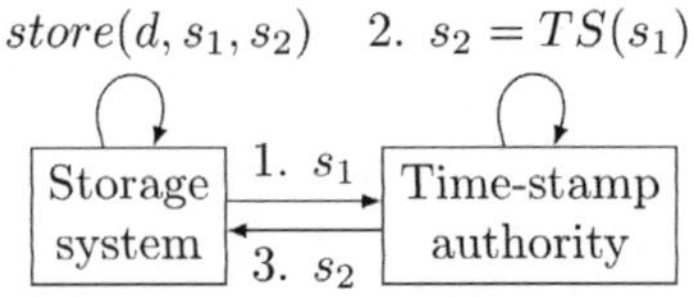

Figure 3. The renewal procedure.

The renewal procedure must also be performed for each time-stamp sequence $s_1, s_2, \ldots, s_k$ where the latest time-stamp s_k is about to become invalid. In this case, the storage system requests a time-stamp s_{k+1} by sending s_k to a TSA.

The *verification* procedure is executed by a retriever as follows. For $k > 1$, assume the retriever has obtained the signed document d and time-stamp sequence $s_1, \ldots, s_k$ from the storage system. Thus, he or she first verifies that s_k is a valid time-stamp using as time reference the date and time τ when he or she performs the verification. The verification includes checking that the signature σ_k contained in s_k is valid at the date and time τ. (Further properties are also verified, e.g., the security of key sizes, but we omit these details for ease of understanding and simplicity.) Similarly, for $j = k-1, \ldots, 1$ he or she verifies that s_j was a valid time-stamp at the date and time τ_{j+1} when the time-stamp s_{j+1} was generated. The date and time τ_{j+1} is found in the time-stamp s_{j+1}. Next, the verifier checks that the signature on d is valid at time τ_1 found in s_1. If the document signature and the k time-stamps are valid and the involved TSAs are trustworthy, then the retriever can be convinced that d is not a forgery, i.e., it existed on τ_1 and has not been changed since.

B. Adversary model

In this work, we will consider an adversary that is *active* and *mobile*. In the active adversary model, parties might deviate from the protocol. In addition, to meet long-term security, we assume that the attacker is mobile and might interact and corrupt different parties at different stages of the protocols' executions. Finally, we assume that the adversary can interact an unlimited time with the system but is computationally bounded each time he or she performs an attack (see [13] for a corresponding security model).

Long-term archiving comes with the following trust assumptions. First, the *TSAs* issue correct time-stamps, i.e., time-stamps containing the correct date and time. This must also be preserved at the presence of an attacker. More precisely, if there is an attacker who is able to control a *storage system*, then the TSAs do not collaborate with the attacker by issuing time-stamps containing the wrong date and time. Second, *certification authorities* issue correct certificates (proving the owner of a signature). In the following, we provide an example how a forgery could be carried out.

Assume our first trust assumption is not fulfilled and an attacker who gained access to the storage system is able to collaborate with a malicious TSA. In this case, the attacker can ask the TSA to issue time-stamps providing a date and time that is earlier or later than the date and time when the TSA in fact creates this particular time-stamp. This allows the attacker controlling the storage system to violate integrity and authenticity as follows. First, he or she takes a compromised signature key pair (e.g., of a doctor) and signs a forged document. Next, he or she requests a time-stamp containing a date and time from the malicious TSA, when the key pair of the signature was still secure and valid. This time-stamp can be used to convince a retriever that the attacker's document was signed by the corresponding doctor. However, such a back-dating attack needs the cooperation of a TSA, because the TSA is responsible for generating the evidence (i.e., time-stamps). Note that if an attacker controls a storage system, but there are no malicious TSAs that can collaborate with him or her, then the attacker can only forge time-stamps by using insecure and outdated signature keys and therefore will fail in generating an evidence that is valid at the current date and time. It follows that if all TSAs are trustworthy, not even a storage system that is controlled by an attacker is able to fake a time-stamp and violate integrity and authenticity. Therefore, a reputation-based trust system is required to deal with untrustworthy TSAs as well as time-stamps in long-term archiving solutions.

C. Trust Opinions on Signatures

Besides the correctness of a time-stamp, an important criterion to trust or distrust in the integrity and authenticity of a document is the correctness of the signatures. Each time the submitter or the TSA generates a signature, it is necessary to trust that the signature key pair used is indeed owned by the signer. In practice, public key infrastructures are used where certification authorities (CAs) issue digital certificates proving the ownership. Since these CAs are *assumed* to be fully trusted, the reputation system CA-TMS (see Section II) can be used in addition to our proposed system, LoT. Each time the storage system receives a signature, it sends the certificate chain and a security parameter to CA-TMS and receives a trust score. Depending on the application, it either rejects "untrusted" signatures or stores the trust score and leaves the decision to the retriever.

IV. A NOVEL REPUTATION SYSTEM FOR LONG-TERM STORAGE

As discussed in the last section, if malicious TSAs issue fake time-stamps, i.e., time-stamps containing the wrong date and time, then retrievers may accept forged documents. Furthermore, the CA trust management system CA-TMS is *only* able to provide trust scores on the ownership of signature keys. Therefore, we propose a reputation-based trust system, LoT, to assess the trustworthiness of the TSAs and time-stamps associated with digital signatures. The proposed system will assign trust scores on the TSAs and time stamps based on the assessment. Typically, reputation-based trust systems are driven by direct experience and indirect experience, obtained via witness referrals [10]. Trust computation in such a system requires three distinct operational steps: i) experience or evidence collection and processing, ii) trust evaluation/assessment, and iii) making a trust-based decision. We next elaborate on these three steps in detail.

A. Experience collection and processing

In the collection phase, direct and indirect experiences provided are collected from the system's participants. An experience – realized as a binary value, either positive or negative – indicates whether a participant believes that a particular time-stamp contains the correct date and time. Participants, in the experience collection and processing phase, are document submitters, storage systems, and TSAs.

Collection phase. To provide their binary experience, participants verify whether the date and time contained in a time-stamp is correct. Initially, the LoT system provides the time-stamp to participants right after the time-stamp is created. Next, these participants verify that the date and time in the time-stamp is reasonably close to the date and time when they received the time-stamp (i.e., the current date and time). How much deviation from the current date and time is allowed is a parameter of LoT and depends on its application. For example, a deviation of half a day may be acceptable for electronic health records, but not for online auctions.

We extend the initialization and renewal procedures presented in Section III-A. The extended procedures use new parameters such as r and δ, where $r > 0$ is the number of TSAs that provide experiences and $\delta > 0$ is the maximum acceptable deviation from the current date and time. In the collection phase, the initialization procedure is as follows:

1) A submitter D sends his or her document d to a storage system.
2) The storage system selects a reputable TSA T from LoT.
3) The storage system requests a time-stamp on d from T.
4) T creates a time-stamp s containing a signature σ and the current date and time τ. T returns the time-stamp s to the storage system.
5) The storage system verifies s. More precisely, it computes an experience $e = \{0, 1\}$ on s such that $e = 1$ if $|\tau_c - \tau| \leq \delta$ otherwise $e = 0$, where τ_c is the date and time when the storage system received the time-stamp s, and τ is the date and time included in s. The storage system submits e, s, D, and T to the reputation system.
6) The reputation system stores e, s, and T together with the participant type *storageSystem*.
7) The reputation system randomly selects r different TSAs other than T that will be allowed to submit their experiences on s. We assume that this number of TSAs can always be found and that they are selected at random to reduce the chance of collusion against or in favor of T. The reputation system notifies the selected TSAs and the document submitter D. Moreover, the reputation system sets a deadline $\delta + \tau_r$ for the selected TSAs and D to submit their experiences, where τ_r is the moment when the reputation system notified D and the selected TSAs. Note that this allows to immediately identify when a time-stamp containing a wrong time has been generated.
8) The selected TSAs and the document submitter D compute their experiences on s as described in Step 5. Next, they submit their experiences to the reputation system.
9) The reputation system stores each submitted experience together with s, T, and the participant type *TSA* or *submitter*.

The same steps are performed during the renewal phase, which is used to generate the subsequent time-stamps. The only difference is that the submitter D does not participate in the renewal phase. This is because he or she may be no longer available after the document has been initially time-stamped. Moreover, LoT can publish the collected experiences, say, on a public board, for accountability reasons. Thus, participants can check that LoT has not changed their experiences.

Processing phase. The reputation system provides trust scores on TSAs and on time-stamps to participants. To compute trust scores, we rely on a well-established trust model, such as CertainTrust [14] or Subjective Logic [15]. In the following, we use CertainTrust. However, Subjective Logic can be readily substituted, as both models are isomorphic.

In CertainTrust model, trust scores are represented by means of the so-called *opinions*. They are represented as tuples $o = (t, c)$, where t represents a trust value and c a certainty value, indicating how confident one is that the trust score is representative. (We use a simplified opinion representation that omits the CertainTrust parameters f and w.)

Trust values are computed as the proportion of the sum of positive experiences, r, divided by the sum of all positive, r, and negative experiences, s, yielding $t = \frac{r}{r+s}$. If $r + s = 0$, $t = 0.5$. The computation of the certainty value is given in CertainTrust as $c = \frac{N\cdot(r+s)}{2\cdot(N-r-s)+N\cdot(r+s)}$. The computation of the certainty value requires an additional parameter N which refers to the *maximal number of expected experiences*. How to set this parameter within LoT will be discussed below.

The trust score o_T on a TSA T and the trust score o_s on a time-stamp s are computed using the experiences the reputation system has collected. While in the latter case, only the experiences collected on s are considered, in the former case the entire history of T with respect to all the time-stamps $s_1, \ldots, s_k$ generated by T is taken into account. The reputation system collects experiences from distinct participants, where one type of participant may be more reliable than another type when providing their experiences. For instance, TSAs may be a more reliable source of experiences than document submitters. Therefore, the reputation system computes three different trust scores o^D, o^S, and o^T, where the labels D, S, and T identify scores derived from experiences given by document submitters, storage systems, and TSAs, respectively.

To compute the trust scores on a time-stamp, N_s can be set as follows. For document submitters and the storage system, N_s should be set to 1 because for every time-stamp only a single document submitter and single storage system can provide an experience. In contrast, we propose to use $N_s = r > 0$ for TSAs because r TSAs are selected randomly by the reputation system to provide an experience on a time-stamp (where r is also a public input parameter). For the trust score on a TSA, N_T can be defined as follows. Assume that the TSA has issued around $k > 0$ time-stamps. Then, N_T is given by multiplying the values of N_s by k.

B. *Trust Evaluation*

Assume a retriever requests a document from the storage system and wants to decide whether this document is a forgery or not. Then, the storage system verifies whether the corresponding time-stamp sequence $s_1, \ldots, s_k$ is valid, i.e., the time-stamps contain valid signatures. Afterwards, it sends the time-stamp sequence to LoT. LoT computes the trust scores on these time-stamps and involved TSAs from the experiences that have been collected so far. Next, LoT signs and returns the resulting trust scores to the storage system. The storage system then returns the requested document and trust scores to the retriever. Finally, the retriever uses the trust scores to decide whether to trust the document.

It may happen that the document has a valid time-stamp sequence, but the decision mechanism suggests that the document should not be trusted. To solve this issue, we propose a trust renewal procedure. Note that the retriever can also perform the above verification of the time-stamp sequences by him- or herself. In this case, he or she obtains the data needed from the storage system. Moreover, the retriever can obtain the experiences LoT published on the public board and run the trust evaluation. Therefore, the retriever neither has to trust the storage system nor our proposed system, LoT.

Next, we detail the trust evaluation of time-stamps and TSAs. After that, we present our decision mechanism and a procedure to renew trust.

Trust evaluation of time-stamp sequences. The trust opinion (score) o_s on a sequence of time-stamps s_i ($i = 1, \ldots, k$) is computed as follows. Assume that weights $w_D, w_S, w_T \in [0, 1]$ represent how much retrievers rely on the collected experiences from submitters, the storage system, and TSAs, respectively. These values can either be provided by retrievers or be public parameters. Initially, the trust scores $o^D_{s_i}$, $o^S_{s_i}$, and $o^T_{s_i}$ on each of the time-stamps s_i are calculated as described before. Then, the overall trust score o_{s_i} is calculated by aggregating the trust scores $o^D_{s_i}$, $o^S_{s_i}$, and $o^T_{s_i}$ on each time-stamp s_i according to the formula $o_{s_i} = o^D_{s_i} \widehat{\oplus}_w o^S_{s_i} \widehat{\oplus}_w o^T_{s_i}$, where $\widehat{\oplus}_w$ refers to the *Weighted Fusion* (W.FUSION) operator as defined in CertainLogic [16], an extension of CertainTrust. Essentially, the weighted fusion operation provides a weighted average over the scores, averaging and combining trust scores into an overall, fused score. This score uses the assigned weights w_D, w_S, and w_T and the certainty values, so that a trust score with a higher weight and/or a higher certainty value has a higher impact on the overall score. Finally, to gauge the trustworthiness of an entire time-stamp sequence, the trust score o_s on the time-stamp sequence is computed from the combined trust opinions $o_{s_1}, \ldots, o_{s_k}$ by calculating $o_s = o_{s_1} \wedge \ldots \wedge o_{s_k}$. Since the overall score should represent how much one can trust that **all** time-stamps contain the correct date and time, the AND operator $\wedge$ as defined in CertainLogic [17] is used. The CertainLogic $\wedge$ operator functions like a probabilistic AND operator over trust scores, considering not only the probabilistic trust value t but also the certainty value c.

Trust evaluation of TSAs. Assume there is a set of l TSAs T_j, where $j = 1, \ldots, l$, $0 < l \leq k$, and each of the TSAs signs at least one time-stamp contained in the time-stamp sequence $s_1, \ldots s_k$. Also, assume weights, $w_D, w_S, w_T \in [0, 1]$, representing how much retrievers rely on the collected experiences from submitters, storage system, and TSAs, respectively. Thus, the computation of o_T is analogous to calculating the trust score on the time-stamp sequence. More precisely, for every TSA T_j, the overall trust score o_{T_j} is calculated using the CertainLogic weighted fusion operator, the individual scores $o^D_{T_j}$, $o^S_{T_j}$, and $o^T_{T_j}$, and the assigned weights w_D, w_S, and w_T. Finally, the trust score o_T on TSAs is computed using the CertainLogic AND operator $\wedge$ and the combined trust scores $o_{T_1}, \ldots, o_{T_l}$, such that $o_T = o_{T_1} \wedge \ldots \wedge o_{T_l}$. The score o_T should tell how much we can trust that **all** involved TSAs generate time-stamps containing the correct date and time.

Decision mechanism. We propose a threshold-based decision mechanism which works as follows. The retriever defines trust thresholds α_s and α_T for the sequence of time-stamps and the TSAs, respectively. These thresholds are in the form of CertainTrust opinions. The values assigned as trust thresholds depend on the time-stamped document. For example, in a hospital using time-stamped electronic health records, thresholds should be as high as possible when the misuse of records are life threatening for patients (e.g., containing the wrong blood type). Other medical records, say, containing blood pressures, might be less harmful and to them a lower threshold can be assigned than to the life threatening ones.

The retriever provides α_s, α_T, o_s, and o_T as input for the decision mechanism. The trust decision is made as follows: if and only if $o_s \geq \alpha_s$ and $o_T \geq \alpha_T$ the mechanism outputs true, i.e., the document is trusted not to be a forgery. Otherwise, false, i.e., the document may be a forgery.

Note that there is a good reason for only the trust opinion o_T on TSAs and the trust threshold α_T for TSAs being not sufficient to make trust decisions. It is because the trust opinion o_s on a time-stamp sequence and the trust threshold α_s for time-stamp sequences can prevent retrievers from accepting, for example, a sequence that contains a wrong time-stamp accidentally issued by a trustworthy TSA.

C. Resetting trust

Even though the time-stamps for a document have valid signatures, the document may not be trusted. We discuss two such situations where this problem may arise. Moreover, we propose a solution to this problem.

Assume there is a document and the corresponding time-stamp sequence in the storage system. The first situation can happen when one or more TSAs, issuing the time-stamp sequence, have bad reputation. The second situation can happen when the time-stamp sequence grows large in size. More precisely, the more time-stamps a sequence contains, the higher the chance that one of these time-stamps have been wrongly issued.

In order to address both situations, we propose the following solution. Assume that a document d has a time-stamp sequence $s_1, \ldots, s_k$ and can no longer be trusted by retrievers. Moreover, assume that there is an expert which is able to check whether the content of d is indeed correct. For example, if d is a document describing a patient's disease, the expert could be a physician that examines the patient to confirm that d is correct. Note that this is a necessary requirement to use the resetting procedure. If there is no expert to check the correctness, then this cannot be done. If there is an expert available he or she first verifies that the content of document d is correct and that it has been legitimately signed, say, by a doctor. If d fails the verification, then the expert alerts the storage system and the procedure ends. Otherwise, the expert re-signs d, generating d'. Then, he or she submits d' to the storage system. The storage system obtains a time-stamp s_{k+1} on d' together with d and $s_1, \ldots, s_k$. Afterwards, the storage system stores d' and s_{k+1} together with d and $s_1, \ldots, s_{k+1}$. Our proposed solution is illustrated in Fig. 4. Next, the storage system requests trust scores on the certificates of the signatures from CA-TMS and collects and stores experiences on s_{k+1} from the reputation system.

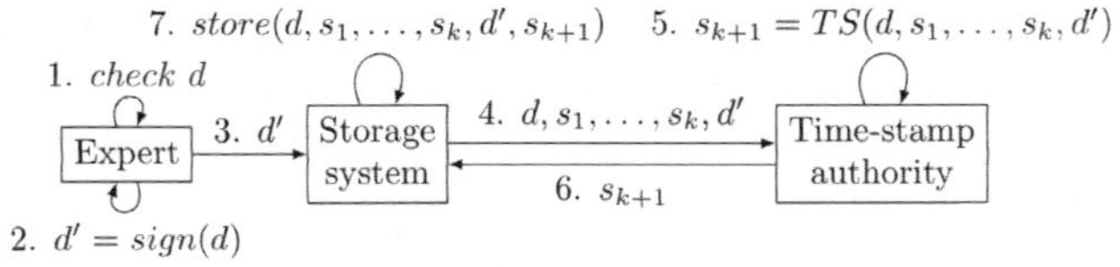

Figure 4. The resetting trust procedure.

Future retrievers use document d' instead of document d. Note that d' is protected by the time-stamps $s_{k+1}, s_{k+2}, \ldots$. The document d and time-stamps $s_1, s_2, \ldots$ can be checked for audit purposes. For example, auditors can check that d and $s_1, s_2, \ldots$ existed before d' and that d and d' are consistent.

V. Evaluation

In this section, we demonstrate the applicability and efficacy of our proposed trust system, LoT. First, we explain an application scenario related to EHRs. Second, we describe the implementation of a demo EHR application. Finally, we simulate the EHR scenario in order to demonstrate the efficacy of our proposed system.

A. Application scenario: Electronic Health Record

Health care institutions (e.g., hospitals) keep their patients' health information in the form of EHRs. An EHR is a container of documents, where each document provides specific information about the patient's health (e.g., the diagnosis of a disease). Additionally, the container includes time-stamp sequences for the documents proving the correctness of the information. The involved parties are storage systems, TSAs, the trust system, and physicians.

Storage systems, TSAs, and the trust system are the same as presented in Section IV. The storage systems can be either hosted by the health care institutions or outsourced to a global service, such as a private health care cloud. The trust system should be hosted by organizations other than the health care institutions and TSAs to prevent collusion. Physicians play the roles of document submitters and retrievers. They are submitters when they update a patient's EHR by adding new documents and are retrievers when they obtain documents from the storage system to learn the health conditions of patients. The EHR software allows to submit and retrieve EHRs and verifies the retrieved documents by checking their time-stamp sequences and trust opinions.

However, issues on performance and trust may occur in this scenario. Performance can be an issue if a retrieved document has a long time-stamp sequence (e.g., it has been stored for decades) and the device running the EHR software has low computing power (e.g., outdated tablet computers). To address this issue, the verification of time-stamp sequences can be pre-computed by the storage systems. Moreover, the computations on trust opinions for each time-stamp and TSA can be done by the reputation-based trust system. Note that in any case the EHR software can perform these verifications by itself, which we recommend for life-critical medical data. Trust issues can happen, for example, when the involved TSAs build bad reputation or time-stamp sequences grow largely (see Section IV-C). Therefore, the EHR software must also show when the retrieved document should not be trusted. Finally, note that physicians may be unable to provide their experiences to the trust system because they might not know how to verify the date and time contained in a time-stamp. Therefore, the EHR software performs such verification automatically when a new document is added to the storage system.

Assumptions. The majority of the involved parties is expected to provide reliable experiences by checking the date and time contained in time-stamps properly. Note that physicians and storage systems are interested in correct time-stamps to avoid being liable for forgeries. In contrast, a TSA wants to build a good reputation but may have no reasons to provide experiences on other TSAs' time-stamps. A possible solution is that the reputation-based trust system only publishes a TSA' reputation if this TSA provides experiences on request.

B. Electronic Health Records Software

We developed a demonstration software to show that physicians can easily use the reputation-based trust system. The demonstrator allows for creating EHRs for new patients, adding documents to existing EHRs, consulting EHRs, and renewing the trust in documents. Due to space limitation, we only describe how physicians consult EHRs and renew trust.

To consult an EHR, physicians use the interface depicted in Fig. 5 as follows. First, they enter the patient's name and birthday. Next, the software retrieves the documents from the patient's EHR found in the storage system. Then, the software obtains the required trust scores from the trust system and uses the decision mechanism to check whether the documents can be trusted. Finally, the software presents the corresponding documents in a table.

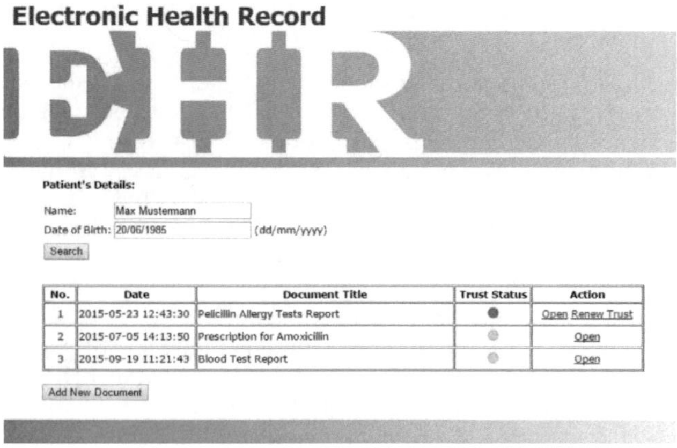

Figure 5. Consulting documents in an EHR.

The table shows for each document the date and time it was initially time-stamped, the document's title, and the trust status. A trust status marked with green means that the time-stamps are correct and that the document has passed the decision mechanism. In this case, physicians can trust the document and open it. In contrast, the red trust status alerts physicians that the document could be a forgery and that its trust should be renewed.

To renew trust in a document, the physician uses the interface illustrated in Fig. 6 as follows. First, the software shows the details and the content of the document. Next, the physician checks that the document contains correct information (e.g., he or she interviews the patient or request new exams). The document can be changed by the physician if necessary. Finally, he or she signs the document and the software submits the document to the storage system.

C. Simulation

To demonstrate the efficacy of the proposed reputation-based trust system in the long term, we simulate the storage of EHRs for 100 years as follows. Initially, submitters (physicians) send $10,000$ documents to a storage system and the initialization procedure is executed for each document. Next, because time-stamps are usually valid for up to five years, the renewal procedure is executed 19 times for each submitted document in order to guarantee its authenticity for 100 years.

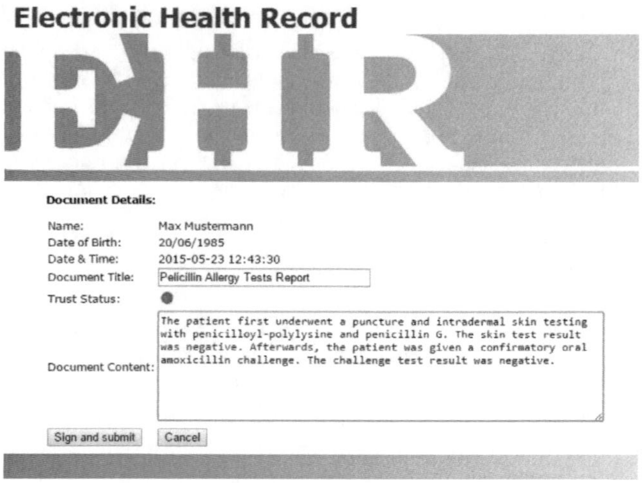

Figure 6. Renewing the trust in a document.

These procedures request time-stamps from a pool of 60 TSAs. From these TSAs, one third issues time-stamps containing correct date and time with a probability of 0.90. The other two thirds issue correct time-stamps with probabilities of 0.85 and 0.80. After a TSA issued a time-stamp, we mimic the collection of experiences from the participants. The submitter, the storage system, and three TSAs check the date and time contained in this time-stamp. The submitter and the storage system do this properly with probabilities p equal to 0.50 and 0.90, respectively. TSAs check it properly with $p = 0.80$. That is, with p they submit *TRUE* to the trust system if the time-stamp contains the correct date and time and *FALSE* otherwise. Furthermore, with probability $1 - p$ they submit *TRUE* if the time-stamp contains wrong date and time and *FALSE* otherwise.

Next, we compute the probability that retrievers obtain a submitted document that has a time-stamp sequence containing at least one time-stamp with wrong date and time. We calculate this probability after executing the initialization procedure, i.e., when the time-stamp sequences of all submitted documents contain only one time-stamp. Furthermore, we compute the same probability every time after running the renewal procedure, i.e., for time-stamp sequences of 2–20 time-stamps.

We compare the calculated probabilities in three scenarios. In Scenario 1, neither our reputation system nor our decision mechanism is available. Therefore, TSAs are selected randomly from the pool and retrievers trust all documents in the storage system. In Scenario 2, only the reputation system is available. TSAs are selected randomly from the set of TSAs having the 10% highest trust opinions. Note that this leads to the *exploration versus exploitation problem* [18] which is also known for other scenarios, such as Amazon or eBay. How to deal with this requires more research and is out of scope for this work. To bootstrap the reputation-based trust system, $10,000$ time-stamps are issued by the TSAs in the pool, the experiences on these time-stamp are collected, and their reputation scores are computed. In addition to the trust system, in Scenario 3 the decision mechanism helps retrievers to decide whether to trust the documents. We use the trust

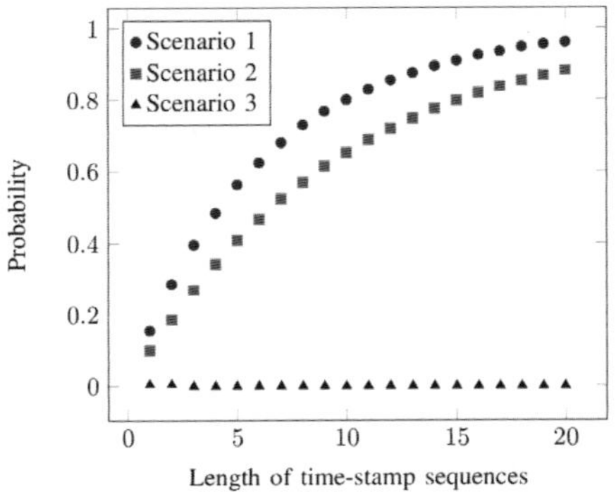

Figure 7. The probabilities that retrievers trust a document that could be a forgery.

opinion $(t = 0.60, c = 0.60)$ as trust threshold for time-stamp sequences and TSAs.

Fig. 7 shows that the probability of retrievers obtaining a forged document grows exponentially for Scenario 1 and 2. However, Scenario 2 is safer for retrievers because the used TSAs are more likely to provide correct time-stamps. By contrast, in Scenario 3 this probability is almost negligible. So it is prevented that a retriever accepts a forged document with high confidence.

However, note that if the trust opinions on time-stamp sequences and TSAs for a document are under the threshold, this does not automatically mean that the document must be a forgery. Therefore, the decision mechanism can produce false negatives, i.e., time-stamp sequences that are indeed correct may not be trusted by retrievers. In this case, if an expert is available the trust can be reset. However, one may want to do this as few as possible and in some scenarios there is even no expert allowing to reset the trust. In this sense, the simulation showed another advantage of using our proposed trust system. More precisely, when selecting preferably trustworthy TSAs, this reduces the chance that a forged time-stamp is generated. Consequently, the trustworthiness of time-stamp sequences decays more slowly.

VI. Conclusion & Future Work

Digital archiving systems store documents in the long term. A serious threat in these systems is that attackers may explore security breaches to tamper with stored documents without being noticed. To address this, a standardized archiving system is available that uses a public key infrastructure, where trusted time-stamp authorities (TSAs) date and sign stored documents periodically. However, in practice TSAs may not be fully trustworthy and could collude with attackers. To cope with this issue, trust models and reputation systems could be used to identify trustworthy TSAs. However, none of the existing systems are designed to run in the long term and to provide trust scores for TSAs.

In this work, we proposed a reputation-based trust system for long-term archiving called *Long-term evaluation of Trust* (LoT). It provides trust scores for TSAs and their time-stamps. These scores are derived from experiences collected from other participants of the system. We demonstrated the applicability of LoT in the use case of electronic health records (EHRs). We described how physicians could use LoT to avoid forged EHRs that, for example, could mislead physicians into prescribing wrong treatments. We presented a demonstration software for physicians and simulated how LoT can reduce the probability of malicious time-stamp sequences generated to forge electronic documents.

This is the first work that shows how to apply reputation systems and trust models to time-stamping-based long-term archiving schemes. Our solution allows to extend the standardized schemes by trust evaluations of archived documents, increasing the chance of detecting maliciously modified or generated documents. This is an important contribution for the practicability of long-term storage, since detecting such misbehavior increases the overall security of archiving systems. Therefore, this improvement allows archiving systems to be used also for the use cases where very sensitive data is processed, such as electronic health records.

Future work. We plan to analyze how to adapt LoT to archiving schemes where multiple TSAs sign a time-stamp together. Moreover, further security analysis on the storage system (e.g., with respect to non-repudiation) is desired. Moreover, we are working on efficient approaches to provide confidentiality together with authenticity for archived documents. Furthermore, it would be interesting to analyze colluding attacks [19][20], e.g., Ballot stuffing, Bad-mouthing, Self-promoting, Slandering, and Sybil attacks, against our proposed reputation-based trust system, LoT. In these types of attacks, attackers can influence the trust scores by sending fake positive or negative experiences to the participants of the system. Therefore, we plan to analyze the attack-resistant trust methods, e.g., similar to [21], in the context of LoT.

Acknowledgments

This work has been co-funded by the DFG as part of projects "Scalable Trust Infrastructures" and "Long-Term Secure Archiving" within the CRC 1119 CROSSING. In addition, it has received funding from the European Union's Horizon 2020 research and innovation program under Grant Agreement No 644962.

References

[1] H. M. Gladney, Preserving digital information. Springer, 2007.

[2] C. Jee, "Nhs promises real-time digital health and care records by 2020," http://www.computerworlduk.com/news/data/nhs-promises-real-time-digital-health-care-records-by-2020-3585822/ [retrieved: June, 2016].

[3] A. J. Blazic, S. Saljic, and T. Gondrom, "Extensible markup language evidence record syntax (xmlers)," RFC 6283, Internet Engineering Task Force, Jul. 2011, https://tools.ietf.org/html/rfc6283 [retrieved: June, 2016].

[4] N. Leavitt, "Internet security under attack: The undermining of digital certificates," IEEE Computer, vol. 44, no. 12, 2011, pp. 17–20.

[5] D. Demirel and J. Lancrenon, "How to securely prolong the computational bindingness of pedersen commitments," IACR Cryptology ePrint Archive, vol. 2015, 2015, p. 584, http://eprint.iacr.org/2015/584 [retrieved: June, 2016].

[6] D. Lekkas and D. Gritzalis, "Long-term verifiability of the electronic healthcare records' authenticity," Journal of Medical Informatics, vol. 76, no. 5-6, 2007, pp. 442–448.

[7] M. Vigil, D. Cabarcas, J. Buchmann, and J. Huang, "Assessing trust in the long-term protection of documents," in ISCC 2013, 2013, pp. 185–191.

[8] M. Vigil, J. Buchmann, D. Cabarcas, C. Weinert, and A. Wiesmaier, "Integrity, authenticity, non-repudiation, and proof of existence for long-term archiving: A survey," Computers & Security, vol. 50, no. 0, 2015, pp. 16–32.

[9] T. Grandison and M. Sloman, "A survey of trust in internet applications," IEEE Communications Surveys and Tutorials, vol. 3, no. 4, 2000, pp. 2–16.

[10] A. Jøsang, R. Ismail, and C. Boyd, "A survey of trust and reputation systems for online service provision," Decision Support Systems, vol. 43(2), 2007, pp. 618–644.

[11] S. M. Habib, S. Hauke, S. Ries, and M. Mühlhäuser, "Trust as a facilitator in cloud computing: a survey," Journal of Cloud Computing: Advances, Systems and Applications, vol. 1, no. 19, 2012, p. 19.

[12] J. Braun, F. Volk, J. Classen, J. Buchmann, and M. Mühlhäuser, "CA trust management for the web PKI," IOS Press: JCS, 2014, Jun. 2014.

[13] R. Canetti, L. Cheung, D. Kaynar, N. Lynch, and O. Pereira, "Modeling computational security in long-lived systems," in CONCUR 2008, 2008, pp. 114–130.

[14] S. Ries, "Extending bayesian trust models regarding context-dependence and user friendly representation," in Proceedings of the ACM SAC. New York, NY, USA: ACM, 2009, pp. 1294–1301.

[15] A. Jøsang, "A logic for uncertain probabilities," INT J UNCERTAIN FUZZ, vol. 9, no. 3, 2001, pp. 279–212.

[16] S. M. Habib, S. Ries, S. Hauke, and M. Mühlhäuser, "Fusion of opinions under uncertainty and conflict – application to trust assessment for cloud marketplaces," in 11th IEEE TrustCom 2012, June 2012, pp. 109 –118.

[17] S. Ries, S. Habib, M. Mühlhäuser, and V. Varadharajan, "Certainlogic: A logic for modeling trust and uncertainty," in TRUST, vol. 6740, 2011, pp. 254–261.

[18] W. T. L. Teacy, G. Chalkiadakis, A. Rogers, and N. R. Jennings, "Sequential decision making with untrustworthy service providers," in Proceedings of the 7th International Joint Conference on Autonomous Agents and Multiagent Systems - Volume 2, ser. AAMAS '08. Richland, SC: International Foundation for Autonomous Agents and Multiagent Systems, 2008, pp. 755–762.

[19] K. Hoffman, D. Zage, and C. Nita-Rotaru, "A survey of attack and defense techniques for reputation systems," ACM Comput. Surv., vol. 42, no. 1, Dec. 2009, pp. 1:1–1:31.

[20] A. Jøsang and J. Golbeck, "Challenges for robust of trust and reputation systems," in Proceedings of the 5th International Workshop on Security and Trust Management (STM 2009), 2009.

[21] S. Ries and E. Aitenbichler, "Limiting sybil attacks on bayesian trust models in open soa environments," in Proceedings of the The First International Symposium on Cyber-Physical Intelligence (CPI-09), 2009.

Security and Safety Requirements for Soft Targets in Czech Republic

Lucia Duricova, Martin Hromada, Jan Mrazek
Faculty of Applied Informatics
Tomas Bata University in Zlin
Zlin, Czech Republic
e-mail: {duricova, hromada, jmrazek}@fai.utb.cz

***Abstract*— This article describes theoretical and management requirements for organizations in the safety and security sector. The aim of this article is to define the primary law framework and to propose evaluation attributes which can help to implement an effective management system in this sector. The article also proposes and describes the solution for system application of security requirements by understanding the soft targets threats. The proposal consists of technical requirements, law requirements and management requirements, as well. The system solution is different for each organization and object; however, the main structure is the same.**

Keywords- Management system; Safety requirements; Soft targets; System solution.

I. INTRODUCTION

Soft targets are objects that do not have special security and safety measures in place. Soft targets are specified objects with a large number of visitors in one place at the same time, and special security measures are not implemented at those locations. One of the main causes of danger is uncontrolled visitors moving in soft targets. People who visit soft targets are a source of risk. Examples of soft targets include: cinemas and theatres, shopping centers, schools, universities and so on [5].

In the Czech Republic, the first security and safety layer is defined by legal measures. In the proposal of the solution, the first security and safety layer is divided into four sections.

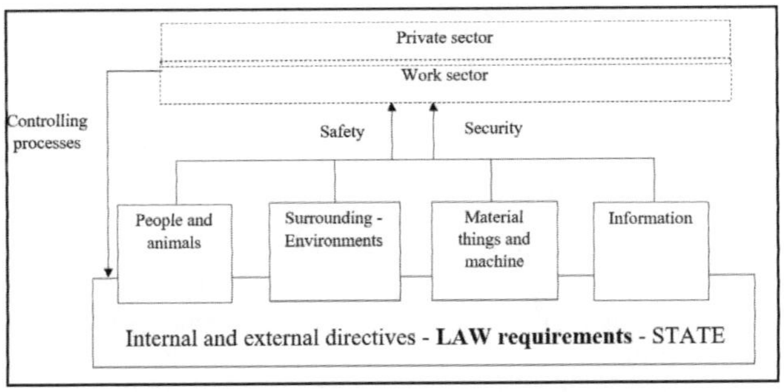

Figure 1. Sectoral breakdown of law requirements.

These four sections are identified in the following paragraphs.

- People and animals – this section is about life and health protection. First is human life, then animal life [4].
- Surrounding and environment – this section is about requirements for safety and security in the surrounding. It is divided in different sections: environment, work places, public places, crowded places and others [1].
- Material things and machines – this section is about using machines and working with things, and about requirements for use and development. Development of things, buildings, machines, as well as product requirements are included in specific requirements [1] [4].
- Information – this section is about classification, use, transfer and about removing information as well [10].

Law requirements and technical information are defined in the first security and safety layer. The technical information is present in the technical standards and European regulations. Currently, our society has a lot of approaches to security and safety solutions with some differences. These differences were identified in risk assessment in the decision making process and terminology. In this research, serious certification standards from special sectors are used, but the work could be exploited for support in other sectors; for example: evaluation of fire risk, more risk analysis, definition of workplaces and machines and others.

After its implementation, software experts could make effective decisions, consequences could be smaller and experts could know the real current status of an object; for example, a building fire. Experts work with software to see the building division, machines and economical risk, calculation of statics and others. As the result, experts could use knowledges from other experts to make a decision. This is the main advantage of this solution.

A. *Typology of Objects*

- Commercial objects – An owner uses legal measures and also technical requirements. Companies identify stakeholder requirements and then they are translated into internal directives. These objects have special operating rules. The commercial objects are divided into two zones: first, the industrial zone and second, the public zone (shops).

- State objects – The state objects are divided into private zone and public zone. Special state objects could be identified with special conditions for use and work with special information and other processes.

The commercial objects can be managed by International Standardization Organization (ISO). ISO standards are international standards that define the organization degree in terms of quality, security, processes and other categories. These degrees are identified by the number of the ISO standard. For example, ISO OHSAS 18001 defines Occupational health and safety in organizations. Every organization that has this certification, has to fulfill the requirements defined in that standard [8].

The reason for ISO certification is business opportunities. Commercial organizations want to achieve better product quality and increase economical profit.

The protective security role of the Security department in any organization is that it is the protector or guardian in charge of company's property, product or merchandise, assets, equipment, reputation, and employees. This responsibility is not limited to the company's assets and employees. It extends to nonemployees as well, regardless of whether they are guests, patrons, customers, or any other visitor on company property [8].

Soft targets are different because of different business aims. A shopping centre does not invest financial resources to implement ISO standards because the customers do not care about ISO standards; however, they care what shopping centres are selling or what the price is. The same is true for theatres, museums and cinemas. These objects do not integrate ISO standards to processes. This research paper proposes an integration to achieve better security and safety in these specific objects.

Legal measures are applied in soft targets. Legal measures consist of Occupational Health and Safety (OHS) requirements and Fire protection (FP) requirements. Secondly, camera systems for monitoring the current situation are present in soft targets. Lastly, technical systems for monitoring closed buildings are present in soft targets. The above conclusions are the results of examination of objects and consultation with the object management.

Our behaviour is the first important aspect in an object. Every visitor must know rules and obligations. This process is in relation with technology and processes that were identified in the object. It is the reason why we must know how the object works. We can identify attributes and processes that are linked with security and safety risks. Every requirement is defined in other sectors (commercial business organization). This research wants to integrate current requirements into one system and its implementation into a software solution. The software solution for soft targets could help experts define reactions to incidents. Our research concentrates on system integration that has been applied into soft targets. The system integration effectively protects soft targets from danger. The software solution contributes to the right decision making and could lead to an improvement of the current situation in soft targets.

The reminder of this paper is organized as follows. The elementary requirements for commercial buildings and legal measures for occupational health and safety are defined in Section 2. In Section 3, the elementary requirements for the fire protection sector are defined. In Section 4, the proposal of management and software solution and the primary principles of fuzzy logic are identified. The elementary principles for the software solution are identified in Section 5.

II. Law Framework

In the Czech Republic, the safety framework is defined in legislative documentation in Occupational Health and Safety and Fire Protection. In businesses and companies, rules are set in place for everyday work. The framework consists of technical requirements that are defined by technical standards.

The input to documentation and rules are management standards in commercial objects. These management standards evaluate companies in the world and grant the quality label. This group (commercial objects) should be divided into the following subgroups:

- Production companies
- Non-production companies = Trading companies

In this paper, the primary lines of defense for specific security and safety options in soft targets are identified. A soft target is an object or place that has borders without special security and safety preventative actions. This is the reason why they are easy targets for our society. Many people have performed uncontrolled actions in an open space or a building. Security or safety incident should occur in this situation, it could be very quick and people could be very threatened.

A. *Occupational Health and Safety*

The legislative framework defines obligations of the employer. The labor code defines employer responsibilities to employees and also defines the system. This part of the paper defines the primary principles which have to be fulfilled.

- If two or more employees are present in some workplace employers must inform each other about risks and measures.
- The responsibility of the employer is to ensure occupational health and safety for every person in the workplace (the employee must be informed about it in writing).
- Risk prevention includes measures that minimize risk to an acceptable level
- Acceptable risk is defined by the law, by calculation or by expert review.
- Expert review is based on experiences and knowledges.

- Every risk must be evaluated, defined, minimized or eliminated.
- Preference is given to collective protection before individual protection.
- Every person that will work at the workplace must be informed about security and safety rules.
- Every employee has to be trained when starting at a workplace, and when changing working process due to new procedure and or introduced technology.
- The employer has to keep a record and evidence of every accident that happened at the workplace in an accident book.
- Employer has to keep evidence documentation for every accident that has been incapacity more as 3 calendar days or in case that injured employee died after accident.
- Minimum for controlling process of OHS is defined once a year [2].

This primary rules could be used to define the system security solution that could be more effective in objects. In working processes, employers have to fulfill more rules, but the only important and useful rules that could be used for every person in the object, are defined in this paper.

- The Czech law defines employees and employers, but in §12 applicable law is understood every person, who must keep this rules (self-employed persons, family of employees, sponsors of building). More law documents apply to construction activities.

In the Czech Republic, special law requirements are defined in legislative documents that have to be kept for working with machines, technical components or other pieces of equipment.

Technical rules for OHS:

- Definition of handling places for working with facilities.
- Definition of technological processes and working procedure according to the producer.
- Definition of installation and removal of protective cover.
- Definition of using operating components without risk's zones on facilities.
- Definition for using actuating devices.
- If a machine or other equipment is not specified by special law, it has to be verified once a year [3].

According to the government regulation no. 361/2007 the collection of Czech Republic laws specifying the temperature for working areas and places is defined. These are divided into three groups:

- Category A - working place with high level of quality.
- Category B - working place with middle level of quality.
- Category C - other places. This definition is known as work classes.

In this paper, two groups are defined and thse are class I. and class IIa. Class I. defines working activities with minimum movement, and it includes administration work activity, control activity, work with computer and so on (Class IIa.) [4].

B. *Occupational Health and Safety Management System*

This standard covers OHS management that provides organizations with the elements of an effective OHS management system that can be integrated with other management requirements and help organizations to achieve OHS and economic objectives. This standard specifies requirement for an OHS management system to enable an organization to develop and implement a policy and objectives which take into account legal requirements and information about OHS risks. This standard is intended to apply to all types and sizes of organizations. The overall aim of this standard is to support and promote good practices, in balance with socio-economic needs [9].

For this research, we have chosen the following terms and definitions from this standard:

- Acceptable risk – risk which has been reduced to a level that can be tolerated by the organization having regard to its legal obligations and its own policy.
- Continual improvement – recurring processes of enhancing the management system (for this policy, it is OHS, although our research could be applied to other groups, too) in order to achieve overall improved performance (in specified group) consistent with the organization policy.
- OHS – Occupational health and safety – conditions and factors that affect or could affect the health and safety of employees or other workers, visitors or any other person in the workplace.
- Corrective action – action to eliminate the cause of a detected nonconformity or other undesirable situation. Corrective action is taken to prevent recurrence, whereas preventive action is taken to prevent occurrence.
- Preventive action – action to eliminate the cause of a potential nonconformity or other undesirable potential situation.
- Nonconformity – non-fulfilment of a requirement [9].

For this research, the process of continual improvement will take place in all areas of activity simultaneously. These rules could be implemented into the system security and safety solution, because this standard is generally accepted in the world and organizations. This standard subscribes to the following approach to reduce the risk:

- Elimination.
- Substitution.
- Engineer controls.
- Signage, warnings and/or administrative controls.
- Personal protective equipment [9].

This framework could be implemented as a management system for solving the risk in the proposed solution. It could be implemented in other kinds of organizations and objects. It is the main reason for implementation. The level of security and safety in a situation in the case of soft targets depends on the correct setting of measures.

III. Fire Protection

In every building, fire protection is defined by the law requirements. In a new object, it is first present in the building documentation. Three groups are identified in the process of construction management:

- Project construction documentation.
- Expression of relevant state administration – the statement of firefighter rescue in which is technical administration fire protection.
- The dealing with construction permits.

If the building is in operation, it means that the building uses legal measures and adheres to fire protection requirements (according to purpose of the object). The purpose of the object is analyzed by fire load which is defined in the fire safety design of the building by a chartered engineer. In the Czech Republic, a fire compartment is defined as bordered unit which should stop spreading of fire to other building units. The zones are bordered by fire barriers; the fire resistance is determined by fire risk, respectively according to the expected duration of the fire. The building structure, which is not divided into fire compartments, is considered as one fire compartment. The building object has to be divided into fire compartments in the case when it exceeds the size of the fire compartment determined by calculation according to CSN 730802 (Fire protection of buildings – non-industrial buildings).

If the object is in operation, the manager has to ensure fire protection by qualified staff. In the Czech Republic, this needs to be done by a professional with qualifications in fire protection. In these processes, a qualified person has to define operation rules that are based on technical administration fire protection, laws requirements and risks in the object. Fire safety equipment, rules of using, and revision interval have to be defined in these processes. Fire management is about proposing effective protection in the object by plans and activities; however, it also involves the training and implementation processes and plans into working process. This is the connection between management of an object and management of an organization.

IV. The Proposal of Safety And Security Management And Software

The current findings were described in the previous section. The main reason is that these findings were confirmed with research and practical use. Fire protection is the main field which we can use to define our new approach. The soft targets were classified in international standards for building. Building requirements in standards are justified. The problems are identified in implication. Experts use the standards as a minimum requirement and therefore they do not integrate them into the system.

The activities that are done in the object have some similar characteristics:

- The emphasis is on preventive actions.
- The four phases could be implemented: Plan, Do, Control, Act. These phrases are common with more sectors.
- Documentation must be implemented to processes and internal politics must involve required measures applied in practice.
- In the object, technical components are used and these components must be analyzed by a qualified person.
- Crisis situation training improves efficient immediate response.

The safety and security management should be effective in objects and organizations. The managers must understand processes that are in the organization and after that, they could see more types of risks. This process where input studying of ties between more as one group of security or safety risks.

As can be seen in Figure 1, there are defending primary groups of security and safety objects. Managers implement protective measures to processes to ensure better security and safety situations in the object. The application of these measures is similar with other measures that are described in international standards and state laws.

People are the main reason security and safety measures are implemented into process or activity. In the analytical part, the ties between people and other attributes are analyzed. Ties are depicted in Figure 2.

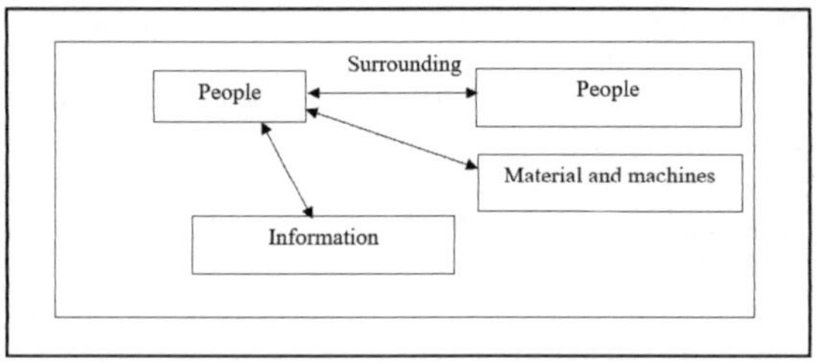

Figure 2. The linkagess beetween four groups of objects.

In these four categories, two procedures that must be identified are proposed. The first procedure is the definition of characteristic and classification. The classification defines attributes which are similar and different. The second procedure is the definition of practice and processes and it has to be followed. The security and safety attributes have to be defined for this security and safety analysis. It means that every process, which could be connected with people and these other four groups of objects, has to be reconsidered according to security and safety attributes. After the definition of the main cause and other causes, the process has to be edited and reintroduced to operation. This solution has analytical part number 1, analytical part number 2 and the last predicting part number 3.

The first part is the study of objective situation and the past actions. The proposed analytical part has the following next steps:

- The analysis of the current state of the object – familiarity with processes in organization.
- The definition of the risks.
- The definition of the main cause and other causes.
- An assessment of the impact of other processes for risk.
- The proposal of permanent corrective action and immediately corrective actions.

The second part will be designed for immediate management in the object. It means that it will be supported with immediately actions, but in real time. This part will be in a continuous process. This part will be similar to the first one; however, inputs will be extended of technical values from technical components. There is a connection with integrated technical measures.

The third predicting part will predict situations and conditions that could happen when operators or managers change attributes, e.g. introducing new machine to object (requirements for using, safety, fire protection, high level of security and others). Each of these solutions shall have a technical and a management part.

V. Software Solution

The disadvantage of this solution is that, for managers and owners to implement this system solution, they must know a lot of specific knowledge and also have experience. This could be solved by one software and systematical solution.

This is the main factor which influences the software solution; therefore, the authors propose fuzzy logic as a tool for realizing software support. Fuzzy logic is based on more options for a solution and supports more experts for solving. It minimizes requirements for managers and operators because managers will be supported by the system. This solution could reduce the incidence of human errors.

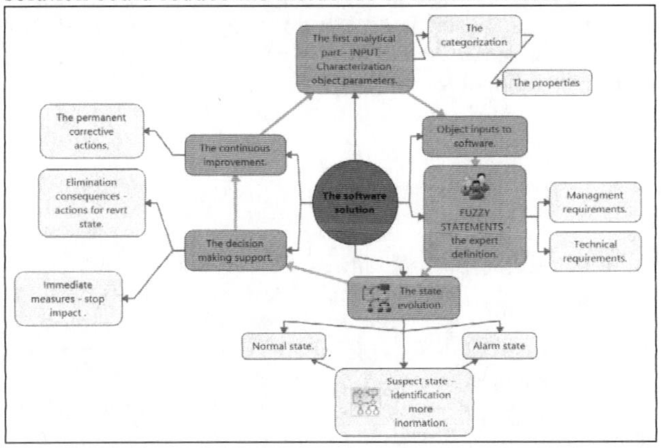

Figure 3. The proposal of software solution.

The proposal integrates management principles and software support into one solution. The proposal of software solution is presented in Figure 3. Fuzzy logic studies a whole range of values in the interval between 0 and 1. The classical logic studies two states. These states can be true (1) or false (0). The expert knowledges and experiences can be coded by fuzzy logic. Fuzzy logic works with fuzzy statements. These fuzzy statements represent degrees of support for the rule.

VI. Conclusion

In this paper, we proposed a software solution for soft targets. The main advantage of our proposal is in the system approach that manages security and safety situations inside an organization. System integration could increase the effectiveness of more security and safety processes, as well as of manager processes. In the presentation of our safety and security solution, we considered different groups of attributes.

The utilization of fuzzy logic is the subject of further research. The proposal takes into account the realization of a software tool that would replace the need for a large number of experts in individual objects by fuzzy logic.

Acknowledgment

This work was supported by Internal Grant Agency of Tomas Bata University in Zlin under the project No. IGA/FAI/2016/012.

References

[1] Act no. 133/1985 Coll. about fire ptorection, Czech Republic.

[2] Act no. 262/2006 Coll. Labour Code, Czech Republic.

[3] Act no. 309/2006 Coll. Act o further terms of safety and health at work, Czech Republic.

[4] Government Regulation no. 361/2007 Coll. establish the conditions of health protection at work, Czech Republic.

[5] L. Duricova Prochazkova and M. Hromada. The Proposal of the Soft Targets Security. Advences in Intelligent Systems and Computing, Automation Control Theory Perspectives in Intelligent Systems. Proceedings of the 5th Computer Science On-line Conference 2016 (CSOC2016), Vol3, Springer, pp.: 337-345. ISSN 2194-5357, ISBN 978-3-319-33387-8, DOI 10.1007/978-3-319-33389-2.

[6] L. Fennely and M. Perry, " The Handbook for School Safety and Security," 1st ed., Elsevier, 2014, ISBN: 978-0-12-800568-2.

[7] L. Prochazkova and M. Hromada, " The Proposal System fot the Safety Assesment of Soft Targets with Focus on School Facilities," Proceeding of 3rd CER Comparative: SCIEMCEE Publishing, Vol. II, pp.: 30-34, ISBN: 978-0-9928772-6-2.

[8] Ch. Sennewald and C. Baillie, "Effective Security Management," 6th ed.,Amsterdam: Elsevier, 2016, ISBN: 978-0-12-802774-5.

[9] ISO 31000:2009, Risk management – Principles and guidelines.

[10] ISO/IEC 27001:2013, Information Technology- Security Techniques- Information Security Management Systems – Requirements.

[11] British Standard BS OHSAS 18001/2007, Occupational Health and Safety Management Systems- Requirements.

[12] ISO 9000:2005, Quality Management Systems- Fundamentals and Vocabulary.

General Model for Personal Data Sensitivity Determination

Marián Magdolen
Department of Security Management
University of Žilina
Žilina, Slovak Republic
email: marian.magdolen@fbi.uniza.sk

Jozef Ristvej
Department of Crisis Management
University of Žilina
Žilina, Slovak Republic
email: jozef.ristvej@fbi.uniza.sk

Tomáš Loveček
Department of Security and Safety Research
University of Žilina
Žilina, Slovak Republic
email: tomas.lovecek@fbi.uniza.sk

Martin Hromada
Department of Security Engineering
Tomas Bata University in Zlín
Zlín, Czech Republic
email: hromada@fai.utb.cz

***Abstract*—This article is a presentation of a general model for personal data sensitivity determination, which is based on early PhD research on personal data protection. Protecting privacy and personal data is in current environment a more and more challenging task not only for government institutions, but for small and large businesses as well. With the information technology advancements more and more personal data are processed automatically each year. That is the reason why effective, adequate and economic security measures have to be adopted to protect privacy of data subjects. But applying security measures blindly without deeper knowledge about sensitivity of such personal data, will not address the expectations for both, processors, for cost and maintenance effectiveness and data subjects, for most secure and trustworthy security measures. To overcome this conflict of expectations, a model for personal data sensitivity was created as a tool to evaluate the sensitivity and assign appropriate security measures.**

Keywords - Personal data protection; security measures, data security; privacy.

I. INTRODUCTION

Right to privacy is one of the fundamental human rights recognized by many international and national conventions, treaties, constitutions and laws. In current security environment and unstoppable information technology development, securing the privacy is one of the grand challenges of today's democracies. General availability of information technology and cloud services, as well as widespread internet usage and increase of web-based transactions, use of social media, targeted advertisement, smart metering and others, create countless opportunities to collect, process, store, analyse and correlate massive quantities of personal data about individuals. To ensure adequate security of this data, processors are forced to ensure their safety by implementing various security measures. Some of the measures are stipulated in the national laws, but others are adopted or just recommended to implement from other sources of information data security documents (e.g., ISO 27 000). We can rarely find an applicable method on how to implement adequate security measures to personal data by taking into account sensitivity and categories of personal data, character of data subject and/or other information relevant for data protection. It is crucial to fully comprehend the interaction between the protection of privacy and the furtherance of security in order to attempt to set appropriate limits [1]. In Section 2 of this article the current process of application of security measures in Slovak Republic with pointing out some of most serious shortcomings of this system is described and later in Section 3 the assessment of the point of view of data subjects for sensitivity of their personal data and in Section 4 and 5 the model for personal data sensitivity determination and its evaluation process is described.

II. APPLICATION OF SECURITY MEASURES IN THE SLOVAK REPUBLIC

Like all European countries, Slovak Republic adopted a law on protection of personal data of individuals as well. Based on the European directive 95/46/EC on the protection of individuals with regards to the processing of personal data and on the free movement of such data (hereinafter referred to as "Directive"), our national legislation tries to issue instructions on how to process and secure personal data by processors to ensure the right balance between privacy and security. Although the European directive 95/46/EC established an obligation for member states to ensure that "appropriate technical and organizational measures should be taken, both at the time of the design of the processing system and at the time of the processing itself, particularly in order to maintain security and thereby to prevent any unauthorized processing;...whereas these measures must ensure an appropriate level of security, taking into account the state of the art and the costs of their implementation in relation to the risk inherent in the processing and the nature of the data to be protected" [2], neither in the directive nor in the Slovak laws or bylaws there is any hint on how to implement these security measures or any explanation of how to determine the appropriateness of security measures to the protected data. In Slovakian act No.: 122/2013 Coll. on personal data protection, our legislators stated that: "the processor is responsible for securing personal data. Therefore, he shall undertake appropriate technical, organizational and personal measures that correspond to the means of data processing, taking into account technical resources employed, confidentiality and importance of processed personal data…" [3]. The extent of appropriate security measures corresponds to specific conditions of processing personal data in filling system, to security risks resulting from the category of processed personal data (e.g., if sensitive data are processed) and to means of processing of such data [4]. However, there is no relevant instruction for processors on the appropriateness of implemented security measures, on the kind of risk assessment method they shall apply and on how to assess confidentiality and importance of processed personal data. Processors can just assume if the taken security measures are appropriate and most of the processors apply the ISO standards on information security to fulfil the requirements. According to our knowledge, there is no other method that would address personal data protection and appropriate security measures assignment along with consideration on data subject sensitivity.

III. Data Subject Point of View

Neither the EC directive nor the Slovak national legislation take into account the perspective of how the data subject feels about the security measures taken by processors. How to include data subjects into the process? The problem regarding personal view on data processing is mainly the possible change in opinions about sensitivity of personal data. People change, circumstances change, the position and situation of individuals change in time. Individual with no interest in special protection of his personal data can, in a few years, become a politician and, as a public officer, his interest to protect his privacy will increase. In that case, from his point of view, the implemented security measures might not be appropriate anymore and it is his prerogative to demand higher level of security. Of course, processors cannot treat each data subject individually when processing large amount of data about undefined number of individuals. But on the other hand, they should take into account sensitivity of personal data not only from their point of view but from point of view of data subjects as well. Assessing such sensitivity level is the very first step for implementation of appropriate security measures which will be not only in accordance with actual legislation but within the expectations of data subjects as well.

IV. Model for Personal Data Sensitivity Determination

Model for personal data sensitivity determination (hereinafter referred to as "model") is a model developed with the aim to include sensitivity of processed data to the data protection, to include data subject specifics and with additional knowledge about processed data to appropriate assign security measures to each specific data filling system. Within the model, various facts are evaluated and as a result, the level of sensitivity of processed data is revealed. With the specified sensitivity level, we can then assign effective, appropriate and adequate security measures to protect personal data in filling system of processor.

If we want to embrace sensitivity as the key factor for security measures implementation, we should use model for sensitivity determination in order to evaluate processed personal data. In order to do so, we should take into consideration a few facts and conditions that are relevant to this process. Legislation requires the processors to establish the conditions for data processing before the processing starts so the processors should evaluate the sensitivity beforehand.

There are three major areas the variables to the model are taken from. The first set is taken from legislation and is obligatory for each processor to include and determine these facts when processing personal data. The second set of variables is based on the type of filling system on conditions and background that are applicable. The third set is based on the knowledge of data subjects and categories of processed data. As the processor shall determine the sensitivity beforehand, it is important to estimate the information carefully and during processing regularly challenge these values to not to underestimate the changes and security measures that have been taken.

First of all first set consist of a few basic legal requirements, that each processor has to fulfil - to determine the nature and purpose of personal data filling system, processors shall define (1) purpose of processing, (2) legitimacy of processing (3) the planned length of time the data are to be stored.

The purpose of processing shall be clearly defined and data collected for specified, explicit and legitimate purpose only. It is forbidden to process data otherwise that is incompatible with those purposes [5]. For data subject, clearly defined purpose of data processing is a first sign of trust when the personal data have been given. The extent of processed personal data (number of personal data collected) is evaluated and the legitimacy of processing is established according the defined purpose.

Personal data may be processed only if the legitimacy of processing is within the Article 6 of Directive. "Personal data may be processed only if: (a) the data subject has unambiguously given his consent; or (b) processing is necessary for the performance of a contract to which the data subject is party or in order to take steps at the request of data subject prior to entering into a contract; or (c) processing is necessary for compliance with a legal obligation to which the controller is subject; or (d) processing is necessary in order to protect the vital interests of data subjects; or (e) processing is necessary for the performance of a task carried out in the public interest or in the exercise of official authority vested in the controller or in a third party to whom the data are disclosed; or (f) processing is necessary for the purposes of the legitimate interests pursued by the controller or by the third party or parties to whom the data are disclosed, except where such interests are overridden by the interests for fundamental rights and freedoms of data subject which require protection…" Slovak act No.: 122/2013 Coll. recognize two types of legitimate purposes for data processing – processing without consent of data subject and processing based on consent of data subject. Processor shall process data without consent of data subject if the purpose of processing, data subjects and the extent of processed data are specified in directly applicable EU law, binding international treaty, law about personal data protection or other particular law [6]. Besides these situations, data shall be processed without consent only in cases mentioned in the Directive, Article 6 and when it is necessary for purposes of journalism or the purposes of literary or artistic expression [7]. Processing data based on consent of data subject is applicable when the consent is freely given, informed and specific and signifies his agreement to personal data relating to him being processed [8].

The planned length of time the data is to be stored is relevant information to assess how long the data are vulnerable. Processors have to ensure that the personal data will be processed no longer than necessary to obtain the purpose of processing [9]. To this first set of information, we have to consider other facts that are subject to the specific settings of personal data filling systems and have relevance to sensitivity determination.

The second set of variables can vary in time but, in the end, the influence on sensitivity is obvious. That includes information about (1) transfer of personal data to other countries; (2) means of processing of personal data; (3) list and nature of third persons or recipients that have access to the data.

Cross-border transfer of personal data "may take place only if the third country in question ensures an adequate level of protection" [10] and "the personal data should be able to flow freely from one Member State to another, but the fundamental rights of individuals should be safeguarded" [11] at all times.

The means of personal data processing are up to processor, whether it is automatic or manual processing. Currently, when everything is online and is processed by information technology, manual processing can evoke more trustworthy and secure way of data processing. On the other hand, many security breaches are still caused not by overcoming the information technological security measures but caused by human error or betrayal.

By processing large amount of data, rarely the processors are able to maintain and administer their filling systems alone. It often depends on purpose but information sharing is often necessary to fulfil the goal of processing and providing access to the data to third persons or other recipients is inevitable. Third party usually means "any natural or legal person, public authority, agency or any other body other than the data subject, the controller, the processor and the person who, under the direct authority of the controller or the processor, are authorized to process the data" [12] and recipient means "natural or legal person, public authority, agency or any other body to whom data are disclosed, whether a third party or not" [13]. Recipients and third parties shall have legitimate reason why to gain access to the data and processors shall very carefully inquire why, when and to what extent to provide the data to such parties.

Third set is based on the knowledge of data subjects and categories of processed data. This is a crucial part as this information is the most relevant to determine whether the processed data are being considered as sensitive from data subject point of view. Processors have to research and gain detailed knowledge about (1) scope of personal data and their category and (2) information about count, nature and character of data subjects.

The directive and Slovak national law about personal data protection stipulate that processors can process only such personal data which scope and content correspond to the planned purpose of processing and are essential to achieve such purpose [14]. Except the proportionality of used data the requirement of using only correct, complete and if necessary up-to-date personal data is applicable and all other data shall be without delay repaired, completed or blocked and subsequently erased [15]. The category of personal data is determined by legislation for regular and special personal data but this division is, in our opinion, not sufficient, very subjective and does not reflect the real opinion of data subjects. Directive forbids to process special data except special circumstances defining special data as data which "reveal racial or ethnic origin, political opinions, religious or philosophical beliefs, trade-union membership, and the data concerning health or sex life" [16]. Slovak national law goes beyond this characteristic and as special category of personal data names - except types of data that are mentioned in Directive as well general identifier of citizens - information about psychical identity and competence, criminal records data, biometric data and image and video files containing any captures of individuals [17]. Extent of such personal data is wide enough to cause problems with processing such data and with assignment of appropriate security measures. For example, photo of individual is so commonly used in many filling systems that assignment of such type of personal data for special category, with strict security rules and permissions to process it, often causes difficulties for processors. Various individuals often have different opinions for special category of data, some of them value more their mobile number than their image/photo or are willing to share the medical data over the credit card number. It is therefore obvious that processors have to evaluate each type of personal data individually and estimate how sensitive such type of data will be for data subjects and accordingly threat (secure) such data.

The last variable relevant for the model is information about count, nature and character of data subjects. Again, processors have to estimate this information beforehand but it is important to update this information regularly in order to assign appropriate level of security to the filling system. Count of data subjects is related to the possible impact of security breach, nature and character of data subjects is relevant to the seriousness of possible security breach.

With all this facts we can estimate the sensitivity of personal data in order to implement such level of security for processor's processing operations that will be adequate, legitimate and appropriate but will also take into account the estimated sensitivity of data subjects.

V. Evaluation of Sensitivity

To evaluate sensitivity of filling system processing personal data, we have to evaluate each factor included into the model. For each factor, one or more questions to be answered are integrated into the model and to each possible pre-set answer there is a certain number of points assigned. After answering all the questions the final value is showing the estimated sensitivity according to the scale. The maximum number of points that are possible to gain is 85. With this high score, it is obvious that processed data are extremely sensitive and in further operation the security measures have to be very exhaustive and other procedures to limit the vulnerability shall be implemented. The minimum number of points that the filling system is able to receive is 18. In such case, most of the data are with low sensitivity and the security measures and vulnerability of the personal data is of low risk. Sensitivity is scaled into five distinctive levels of low, moderate, high, very high and extreme sensitivity.

TABLE I. Sensitivity Evaluation Scale

Evaluation	Points score
Low sensitivity	18 - 25
Moderate sensitivity	26 - 40
High sensitivity	41 - 55
Very high sensitivity	56 - 70
Extreme sensitivity	71 - 85

According to the sensitivity level, we can assign appropriate security measures to each specific data filling system. This is the second part of model where - after thorough risk assessment - effective, appropriate and adequate security measures that are in correspondence with estimated sensitivity of the processed personal data in the filling system could be assigned.

VI. Conclusion

To evaluate sensitivity of filling system processing personal data, we have to address many aspects and steps of processing procedure. Sensitivity level together with later risk assessment allow the processors or data subjects to confirm the expectations for security measures to be taken in any given filling system. Processors are constantly searching for most economical but still sufficient system how to determine and apply security measures for their system and data subjects expect the best security for their personal data. After recent development in massive personal data breaches and mass surveillance affairs, applying adequate security measures will become more and more important to general public in order to ensure their privacy [18]. As the view on personal data sensitivity is changing with various conditions, in the future, there will be more often demand for interactive system that will be able to determine sensitivity level and further help to assign appropriate security measures which will satisfy both processors and data subjects.

Acknowledgment

This work was supported by the research project VI20152019049 "RESILIENCE 2015: Dynamic Resilience Evaluation of Interrelated Critical Infrastructure Subsystems", supported by the Ministry of the Interior of the Czech Republic in the years 2015-2019.

References

[1] S. Stalla-Bourdillon, J. Phillips, M. D. Ryan, "Privacy vs. Security", Springer: London, 2014, ISBN 978-1-4471-6529-3, pp. 5

[2] Directive 95/46/EC on the protection of individuals with regards to the processing of personal data and on the free movement of such data, Paragraph 46

[3] Law No.: 122/2013 Z.z. about protection of personal data, Paragraph 19

[4] Z. Válková, J. Dudáš, J. Palúš, "Zákon o ochrane osobných údajov. Komentár od autorov zákona", Kaštieľ Mojmírovce, 2013, ISBN 978-80-971476-4-8, pp.149

[5] Directive 95/46/EC on the protection of individuals with regards to the processing of personal data and on the free movement of such data, Article 6, Section b)

[6] Law No.: 122/2013 Z.z. about protection of personal data, Paragraph 10

[7] Law No.: 122/2013 Z.z. about protection of personal data, Paragraph 10, Section 3, a)

[8] Directive 95/46/EC on the protection of individuals with regards to the processing of personal data and on the free movement of such data, Article 2, Section h)

[9] Law No.: 122/2013 Z.z. about protection of personal data, Paragraph 6, Section 2, g)

[10] Directive 95/46/EC on the protection of individuals with regards to the processing of personal data and on the free movement of such data, Article 25

[11] Directive 95/46/EC on the protection of individuals with regards to the processing of personal data and on the free movement of such data, Paragraph 3

[12] Directive 95/46/EC on the protection of individuals with regards to the processing of personal data and on the free movement of such data, Article 2, Section f)

[13] Directive 95/46/EC on the protection of individuals with regards to the processing of personal data and on the free movement of such data, Article 2, Section g)

[14] Law No.: 122/2013 Z.z. about protection of personal data, Paragraph 6, Section 2, d)

[15] Law No.: 122/2013 Z.z. about protection of personal data, Paragraph 6, Section 2, f)

[16] Directive 95/46/EC on the protection of individuals with regards to the processing of personal data and on the free movement of such data, Article 8, Section 1

[17] Law No.: 122/2013 Z.z. about protection of personal data, Paragraph 13

[18] S. Stalla-Bourdillon, J. Phillips, M. D. Ryan, "Privacy vs. Security", Springer: London, 2014, ISBN 978-1-4471-6529-3, pp. 93

A Study on User Perceptions of ICT Security

Christine Schuster
Institute for Empirical Social Studies
Vienna, Austria
e-mail: christine.schuster@ifes.at

Martin Latzenhofer, Stefan Schauer
Digital Safety & Security
Austrian Institute of Technology
Vienna, Austria
e-mail: {martin.latzenhofer | stefan.schauer}@ait.ac.at

Johannes Göllner, Christian Meurers, Andreas Peer, Peter Prah
Department of Central Documentation & Information
National Defence Academy of the Austrian Federal Ministry of Defence and Sports
Vienna, Austria
e-mail: {johannes.goellner | christian.meurers | andreas.peer | peter.prah}@bmlvs.gv.at

Gerald Quirchmayr[1], Thomas Benesch[2]
[1]Research Group Multimedia Information Systems
Faculty of Computer Science
[2]Institute for International Development
University of Vienna
Vienna, Austria
e-mail: {gerald.quirchmayr | thomas.benesch}@univie.ac.at

***Abstract*— The human risk factor is a decisive factor in information security but has still not been fully integrated into information security programs and risk management approaches. Based by this lack of integration, we have designed a study on user attitudes to information security issues in Austrian companies. The survey that has been carried out within this study is based on extensive literature research on risk, behavior and trust models. The analysis of the results comprises the identification and confirmation of user perceptions and trustworthiness factors. Building upon the survey results, we propose a set of significant indicators that can help to identify ICT-related misuse and fraudulent behavior as a situation awareness instrument.**

Keywords*— *information security; user perceptions; attitude; human risk factor; work satisfaction; compliance.

I. Introduction

The vital role of trust in an organization's information and communication technology (ICT) systems has been amply discussed in the literature from various perspectives [1][2]. The attitude of employees as an indicator of emerging problems has also been described in recent publications [3][4]. The key issue here is that the human behavior represents a major risk factor and is hard to control from an organization's perspective. Neither can these non-technical vulnerabilities be measured nor is there a real-time early warning system covering this aspect in a sufficiently reliable way. Repetitive awareness measures help to strengthen an organization's culture, but their effectiveness is hard to assess and those measures take a long time and many iterations. So far, there is no satisfying and reliable method that can be applied with reasonable effort to assess the human risk factor in an organization's environment [5][6].

As part of the KIRAS MetaRisk project [7], originally initiated by Johannes Göllner, supported and partially financed by the Austrian National Security Research Program KIRAS, we conducted a survey among employees with and without management functions. Based on the results of this survey, we investigated the situation regarding information security in Austrian companies in 2015. Key topics covered by this survey were how individual staff members applied the safeguards that have been set up, how employees treat security-relevant incidents – especially activities to avoid or circumvent those incidents including activities that cause harm to the organization – and the general relationship between employer and employees. By analyzing the employees' attitudes, tendency of activities and behavior patterns, we have identified possible indicators which can even point to insider fraud in extreme cases.

In the context of information security, the human aspects assume a decisive role as either an early warning of decaying information security awareness or as a careless attitude towards the issue. The continuously growing number of phishing, spear phishing and identity fraud attacks against normal and unexperienced users shows that these types of attacks have recently become even more attractive. With more sophisticated forms of attacks, for example advanced persistent threats (APT) where perimeter controls substantially lose their protective effectiveness [8], the problem becomes more critical. These forms of attacks are trying to obtain an organization's most confidential business information, causing financial damage and in stealing trade secrets. On the other hand, economic pressure is growing in general and both employees and employers are trying to reduce cost, aim for leaner processes and at minimizing efforts, thus making the work environment less comfortable. This is one reason why the potential for misuse, business and cyber-crime is rising [1][6]. A small but significant set of indicators reflects the attitude of the employee towards the information security situation in an individual organization. Consequently, if we look at this set of indicators all together we can identify the principal vulnerabilities of an organization related to the human risk factor. If we link these indicators to particular types of attacks, e.g., social engineering, we can decide whether an organization is more vulnerable than another.

The present paper is structured into five sections. In Section 2, we first present the scientific basis from the relevant literature and our motivation for the study. Section 3 describes the applied methodological approach of the survey performed for the study. In Section 4, we discuss the main results of the study compared to retrospectively documented attack stories from real life. Section 5 proposes aspects for further research and we present concrete indicators that can serve as basis for forming a radar chart and as input for a scorecard. This leads to a general overview of the influence of human risk on information security.

II. Motivation and Background

As amply described in a large number of recent publications including textbooks, information security is an issue of continuously growing importance for organizations of all sizes. Recent trends in Austria [9, p. 8][10][11] and Germany [12][13, p. 7] (the German situation is closely comparable to the Austrian one) have been a shift in attacks towards social engineering and fraud. An analysis of attack types performed in 2014 [14], shows which types of attacks were most successful in affected enterprises (Figure 1). In this context, phishing attacks had the highest success rate, followed by the classic attack types "malware" and "hacking attempts" and by "social engineering". The Austrian internet security report 2015 [10, p. 45] explicitly states that social engineering methods are growing significantly in number and sophistication. This sort of attack can be seen as the currently most dangerous attack type. Therefore, the human factor has turned into the weakest link in the cyber defense chain of an organization.

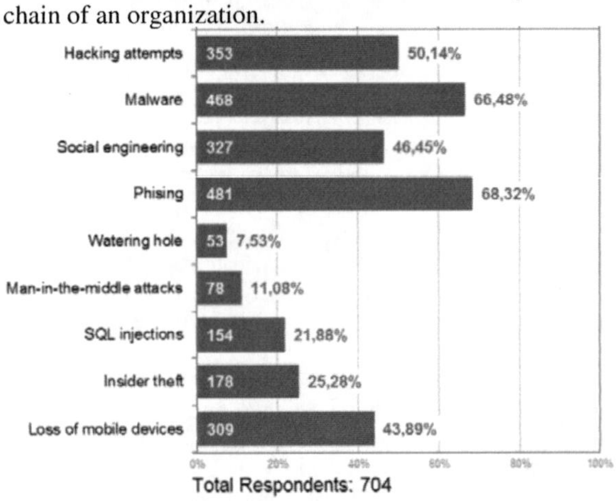

Figure 1. Successful attack types in affected respondent's enterprises in 2014 [14, p. 6]

As these attacks have a significant financial impact on affected companies [14], it is important to know the human vulnerabilities towards social engineering attacks and financial fraud that use information technology as a vehicle to commit crime. In one extreme case, such a financial fraud attack on an Austrian aerospace manufacturer has recently caused an estimated damage of 50 million EUR [15]. To emphasize this financial aspect, Figure 2 points out that almost 50% of US companies suffer financial damage from attacks at least annually, while at the same time employees and managers are more and more ignorant of the impacts of cybercrime.

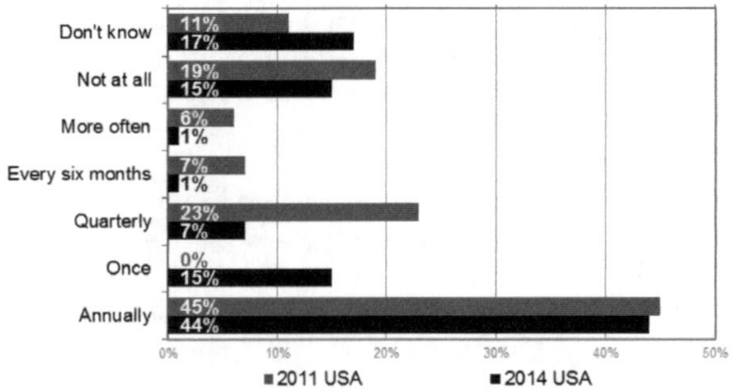

Figure 2. Relative financial impact of cybercrime on organizations [16, p. 28]

Figure 3 clearly shows that insiders – no matter whether they have malicious or non-malicious intents – have made a significant contribution to the damage that enterprises suffered in 2014.

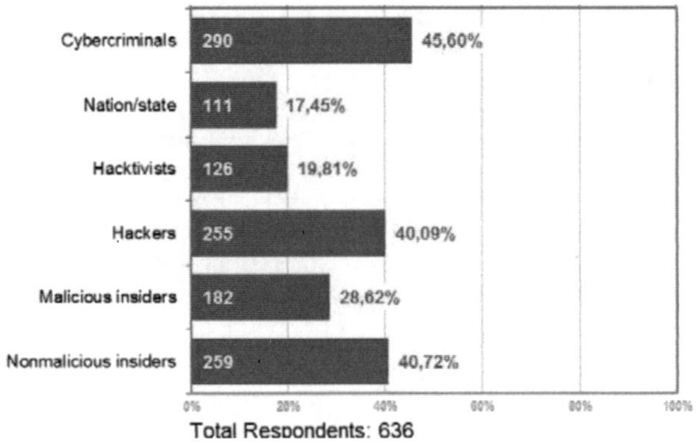

Figure 3. Threat actors [14, p. 5]

The list of threat actors consequently raises the question of how to ensure expected behavior of involved persons in an organization. The term compliance can be defined as the sum of all reasonable measures that address lawful and rule-consistent behavior of a company, its members and employees with regard to legal commands or prohibitions. The business integrity should also be consistent with social guidelines, moral concepts and ethical behavior [17]. In contrast, non-compliance entails all forms of non-observance of guidelines. It can be measured in terms of the seriousness of the infringement and can be categorized into violations that damage the company itself or employees. Three underlying motivational factors for divergent or non-ethical behavior of or within companies have been discussed in the literature: first, non-compliance can be justified by the personal benefit that employees gain by violating regulations. Second, the company as a whole can derive benefits from delinquent behavior. Third, non-compliance can be used to deliberately harm the company or external stakeholders [18, p. 225f]. Various factors might increase the likelihood of non-compliance: difficult working conditions; competitive pressures; unrealistic objectives and focus on simplistic success parameters; too much or too little control within a company's control system; management style; and corporate culture [18, p. 233ff].

In general, working conditions can be divided into three categories; macro, meso and micro level [19]. Raml [20, p. 87ff] allocates economic and social conditions, such as career perspective, economic situation, social status, balancing of family and working life to the macro and meso level. Similarly, work structures and resources (work organization, time models, work atmosphere, career opportunities, bonus payments, information related to work) belong to the macro and meso level [20]. On the other hand, resources and stress are located at the interface between employees and their own work, and are therefore assigned to the micro level [20]. This entails the scope of action, work contents, professional qualification, disturbances and interruptions in daily routine, too many regulations and restrictive surrounding conditions.

It is widely accepted that insiders pose a special form of threat to businesses, institutions and organizations [22][23][24]. Insiders are persons who have a legitimate access to components of the ICT infrastructure. In contrast to external hackers, they have always at least one access point to ICT systems, and thus they do not require time consuming efforts to obtain additional privileges. The predefined trust that insiders must be granted requires more sophisticated security measures. The insider threat is related to the level of their sophistication and depends on the users' breadth and depth of knowledge, as well as their finesse [24].

Insiders can trigger either an accidental or malicious threat, i.e., they can intentionally try to cause harm. Information security measures – e.g., encryption, access control, or least privileges principle – must be implemented regarding to human factors, e.g., with personnel checks or focused risk assessments regarding motivation, opportunity and capability. While these insider threats cannot be eliminated, they can be assessed and managed. Users must understand the reasons for security controls in order to ensure their effectiveness. Hence, they may find ways to circumvent technical restrictions they are faced with [22].

A variety of models addresses the insider issue, either concentrating on certain aspects (e.g., end user sophistication [24]) or more holistic in nature [23][25]. The latter approach incorporates characteristics of the organization, the actor including behavior and attitudes, and the attack itself; overall representing the interdependencies of the different influencing factors [23][25].

Prior national and international studies on insider security threats [25][26][27] have been conducted in the last decade and show the increasing importance of this issue up till now. Despite a good coverage of security policies and measures, the users may obviously work around the controls fulfilling their job objectives in a timely manner. Key issues identified by these studies are data loss prevention, remote information access and the threat against the whole information life cycle. They identified awareness trainings and intensive monitoring measures as effective countermeasures [25][26][27].

Working conditions in Austria are regularly measured by the „Work Climate Index", which was first conducted in 1997 by the Institute for Empirical Social Studies in cooperation with the Upper Austrian Chamber of Labor. It has evolved into a longitudinal study since then and aims at capturing the perception of employees concerning their working conditions, and reveals long-term changes in the structure of employment (e.g., increases in precarious employment), evaluates the subjective situation of Austrian employees, and analyses specific subgroups of employees (e.g., women or older employees). Since 2008, the "Work Climate Index" is complemented with the "Austrian Occupational Health Monitor" focusing on questions of subjective work-related health. Both studies are based on 4.000 interviews conducted annually [28][29][30][31]. Key finding of both studies is the relationship between time related stress and working conditions [28, p. 14]. The stress increasing factors are regulations exceeding the common working time hours Monday to Friday from 7 am to 5 pm (especially working on Saturdays or Sundays or at night) or working over-time regularly. Other factors are contributing to time-stress as well, for example permanent contact to customers, high responsibility, permanent surveillance or a lack of support from colleagues.

As a further step, our study follows a well-founded approach, combining qualitative question technique for discussion rounds and additionally contrasted by the results of a structured and rather restrictive predefined survey with a significant amount of participants. Despite the fact that human behavior can never be modeled accurately through surveys and the results may not be generalized as conclusive evidence for tactical changes in established organizations, the approach reflects a strongly required combination of work satisfaction with information security principles. Due to the extensive survey and the great random sample of respondents, this work might positively influences a proper methodology analyzing the human risk factor in organizations in future, e.g., heuristics, indicators, conditional relationships etc.

Based on attack types documented in recent publications [10][12][14], we have identified a series of major risk factors that contribute to the success of attacks and have consequently derived a targeted list of questions. Some of the most interesting questions that were asked in the study described in this paper are:

- What is the role of ICT security in your company?
- How are security and user guidelines handled?
- What is the current state of awareness among employees?
- Which measures are taken to increase the awareness for ICT security?
- Up to which extent is the private use of company equipment allowed?
- Are there currently any privacy or data loss problems?
- How does the company handle personal data?

- How does the company handle information security?
- Who is responsible for information security in the company?

It is expected that by analyzing the answers to these questions and linking them to attack types, a good assessment of an organization's preparedness for handling attacks can be performed based on organizational vulnerabilities and involving social engineering.

III. STUDY DESIGN AND SETTING

Regarding the design of the study, we followed a well-proven approach that was developed by the Institute for Empirical Social Studies. We decided to use a mixed-method-approach and combine quantitative and qualitative aspects of social research, starting with desk research and following up with two focus groups and questionnaires.

In the desk research, we analyzed current studies on business crime [32][33][34][35], especially concerning (non-)compliance, fraud and personnel risk and summarized key findings. Cases of Business Cybercrime generally have risen over the last years and researchers assume a large estimated number of unreported cases. The offenders are quite often the own employees of an organization, not only caused by intentional acting but carelessness and lack of awareness. We found out that there are some conditions promoting non-compliant behavior: personal characteristics, the own moral awareness, individual situation on a personal level; work conditions, competitive pressure, excessive objective management, lack of internal control, leadership, and organizational culture. Based on these aspects, we derived the security level of the organization and the indicators which determine it. Thus, we were able to develop appropriate interview guidelines as well as questions and answers for the survey. These questions reflect identified key aspects whether an organization is affected by non-compliance more likely or not.

For two focus groups that took place on April 23rd and 29th 2015 we invited both ordinary employees and persons with management functions. The selection process for the participants in the focus groups had two stages and was in line with internal quality standards of the Institute for Empirical Social Studies in order to form optimal focus groups with uniformly distributed attributes, e.g., age, sex, and consuming behavior. In the first group, six ordinary employees (three men, three women) aged between 31 to 62 years took part. The second focus group consisted of eight persons in management position (six men, two women) aged between 42 and 61 years. The group discussions were based on qualitative question techniques and moderated by trained persons following a structured interview guideline, which allowed for an open exchange of opinions. We emphasized on security measures, recent incidents critical for information security, and on the relationship between employer and employee. All members described information and communication activities as main part of their ordinary working routine.

In parallel to the focus groups, we conducted personal interviews with 891 employees of Austrian companies (53% men, 47% women) including persons with management function in the period from January to March 2015. These face-to-face interviews were structured by a prepared survey consisting of 48 questions having either several predefined answer possibilities or offering a five-tier rating. The interviewer leads through the questionnaire, explains, discusses and finally documents the participant's answers. Participants were chosen by a multistage random sampling, where Austrian municipalities were grouped by the total number of inhabitants for each federal state and political district. Then, municipalities from each predetermined group were picked randomly. Within these municipalities, we randomly picked eligible households that again were used as samples for finding further addresses. Target persons were exclusively chosen based on their home addresses. Within each target household, members were assigned by random numbers, and only those were interviewed, whose number matched the one provided by the Kish selection grid [21]. Thus, each stage in the selection process of participants was guided by randomization.

The survey covered central issues of job satisfaction, general health situation, satisfaction with corporate management, security measures within the organization as well as ICT security in general. Twenty-five percent of the respondents were aged below 29 years, 34% between 30 and 44 years, and 41% older than 45 years. Each interview with workers (30%), employees (55%) and members of public administration affiliates (15%) took 25 minutes on average and was performed at the respondent's personal domicile. Most of the respondents had completed compulsory education (9%) or with apprenticeship as craftsmen (42%). 16% of respondents had gone to college and passed their school leaving examination, 16% went to college but did not finish it, and 17% had graduated from university. More than three fourths (76%) of respondents are employed full time, the rest worked less than 36 hours per week (24%). The results are shown separately between persons with a leading function (11%) and those without (89%). 39% of the respondents earn less than 1.500 EUR per month, 39% more than 1.500 EUR per month and 22% refused to indicate their salary.

The study design described above was geared both towards obtaining a better understanding of how information security works in companies and towards determining key indicators of non-compliance by indirectly gathering information of employees of Austrian companies. This benchmark approach aimed at obtaining an accurate and undistorted view of employees older than 16 years within Austria across various organizational sizes and business sectors. The research community could now start follow-up projects with the same or a similar study design, which would enable more detailed analysis of one business sector or company size.

IV. MAJOR RESULTS

The members of the focus groups reported on relevant information security incidents in their organizations, e.g., data loss of emails during archiving, loss of business data due to collapse of servers, stealing of material, sensitive information, and electronic equipment, physical damage by fire, perimeter control vulnerabilities, accounting errors due to account number conversion, and phishing. The members of the focus groups generally point out the need for a balance between scope for development and restrictive measures. Both too much surveillance and the lack of it were considered as problematic. The loyalty of employees suffered when managers enforced strict time recordings, cancelled home office arrangements, and collectively punished employees for the misbehavior of single employees. In contrast, when managers fostered team work, actively took over responsibility and selected the right personnel the sense of responsibility among employees grew.

The personal interviews with employees show that the respondents are most satisfied about the collaboration with their colleagues, the company`s image, the content of their work and the appreciation of their work by colleagues – it is reflected by more than 78% – and 63% of persons with only compulsory education (the latter group reveals comparatively lower values than for the others and is explicitly represented by the second percentage quotation in the following). Respondents indicated medium satisfaction with their line managers, their individual autonomy to take decisions on their working processes, their working time, and the social policies of the company (more than 66% and 45%, respectively). The respondents were least satisfied with training options, workload, employee participation and potential career possibilities (more than 48% and 33%, respectively).

Furthermore, the interviews showed that seven to eight out of ten employees comply with ICT policies, do not cheat the organization, do not take home data or steal anything, do not harm the enterprise intentionally or unintentionally, do not print private documents and do not talk about sensitive information outside of the work. In contrast, up to 7% have committed at least one of those actions. 14% of employees and 19% of managers go to work when they are ill due to their sense of duty, workload and a lack of deputies. In contrast, 9% of the respondents indicated that they had stayed at home at least once in the past although they had not been ill.

Respondents considered ICT services to be a key issue in organizations, regardless of the business sector. Almost half of the respondents indicated that company smartphones are an important topic. The proportion of ICT and smartphone usage is considerably higher in organizations with less than ten employees and only one location. 30% of the employees and 46% of the managers are allowed to use the devices privately. Bring your own device (BYOD) is permitted only for one fifth of employees.

One third of the employees answers company emails outside of working hours. Especially managers often can be reached outside of normal working hours: two thirds of them sometimes and 44% several times a week, whereas only 12% of normal employees work outside of normal working hours. The more the work depends on ICT services, the more the respondents communicate about work after working hours.

Around 15% of employees are allowed to work at home. The proportion raises with the level of education: university graduates telework up to 35% of their working hours. The larger the company and the higher the employee's position in the hierarchy, the more likely is the employee to be allowed to work at home.

More than half of the respondents and three fourths of the interviewed managers consider information security to be an important topic. The survey results indicate that the importance that is attached to information security grows in line with the size of the organization and has special relevance when the company has offices abroad. Almost 75% of the persons working in large-scale companies (more than 100 employees) assess information security's importance to be very high or high, as shown in Table 1. The survey also showed that the sensitivity regarding information security is low among employees of very small organizations and of organizations with a low ICT usage. The first row in Table 1. entitled with "Total" compares the corresponding percentage value without distinction of the organization sizes as reflected by row two to six.

Table 1. Importance of information security divided into company size (n=891)

Company Size (numeric values in %)	very high	high	medium	low	very low	don't know / not specified
Total	28,39	24,55	11,43	5,20	6,90	23,53
Below 10 employees	20,41	17,96	13,87	7,35	13,06	27,35
10 to 19 employees	24,42	26,27	12,44	5,53	5,53	25,81
20 to 49 employees	28,37	27,40	11,54	5,77	6,25	20,67
50 to 99 employees	34,07	30,77	7,69	3,30	3,30	20,87
100 or more employees	47,15	25,20	7,33	0,81	0,81	18,70

Information security was found to have an exceptional standing in companies in the finance and insurance sector (90%), in public administration (77%), and in the health and welfare sector (66%), presumably due to the awareness for processing sensitive data. Nevertheless, one third of the respondents indicated that they have no information security guideline for ICT usage. It is remarkable that especially employees with a lower level of education do not know about any regulations. The information security awareness is comparatively higher in the finance and insurance sector (93%) and in public administration (81%).

A similar picture appears when analyzing the existence of information security awareness measures. Only 28% of respondents reported of (semi-)annual measures, 15% indicated that those measures are rarely performed, one third indicated that no such measures are performed, and one fourth of the respondents did not know whether such measures exist. These results indicate that for almost half of the respondent's organizations no awareness activities are in place. This is emphasized by the results about employee's awareness attitude in Figure 5; almost 60% of the respondents see information security awareness attitudes of their colleagues, but on the other hand 40% do not. The main topics addressed by these awareness measures concern the handling of passwords, behavior during information security incidents and using the internet, awareness concerning the sensitivity of the processed data, risks of mobile ICT devices and data storages, contracts with external personnel, and social engineering strategies.

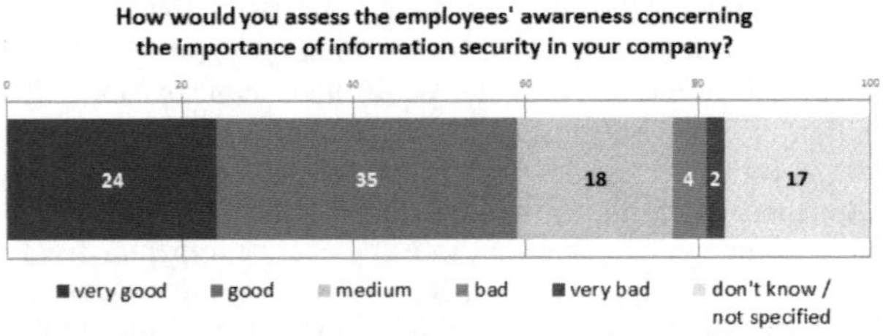

Figure 4. Employees' awareness assessment (values in %; n=891)

Almost half of the respondents answered that internet and ICT services cannot be used for private purposes, whereas the rest of the respondents were not sure about it. Only 17% of the respondents reported that they have an explicit permission to privately use the internet and ICT services provided by their organization. The smaller the organization, the more likely it is that the organization enforces no rules concerning this private use. Companies with offices abroad are more likely to have some rules concerning the private usage of ICT services. Almost three fourths of respondents indicated that there have been no data loss and data protection incidents in their organizations, whereas the rest could not answer the questions. 86% of the respondents trust their employers concerning the processing of their sensitive data, only 8% do not. The proportion of those who do not trust their employers in this regard is higher in public administration: 18% have doubts whether their organization protects data appropriately. 46% of the respondents know which data his or her employer stores, whereas 45% do not know.

The main proportion of the employees uses working time recording systems, either manual recordings (33%) or an electronic badge (41%). In particular, large-scale enterprises use working time recording and access systems, have special visitor regulations, accounting systems for services or telephone cost monitoring. Video surveillance is more common in the finance and insurance sector, whereas Global Positioning System (GPS) locating is more common in transport services. Around 68% of the respondents have no impression that their work place is monitored electronically – this is especially evident for employees from large-scale enterprises. On the other hand, 27% think that they are under surveillance at work.

In companies in Austria, a whistleblower hotline is rather unusual: 72% of respondents indicated that their organizations have no anonymous hotline, whereas 20% of respondents indicated that they do not know whether such a hotline exists. The overall handling of information security differs strongly between managers and employees. The knowledge on information security is substantially lower among employees. The probability, that an organization enforces regulations on information security, increases with the size of the organization or if the organization has offices abroad. Again, the finance and insurance sector, public administration and the health and welfare sector are those business sectors in which information security forms an integral part of organizational culture.

It is remarkable to note that only 15% of the respondents indicated that their organization has defined who is responsible for information security, risk and compliance, whereas 54% reported that their organization has not defined this responsibility and 31% did not know. In different organizations, the responsibility is defined in different ways and may lie with the ICT department, a dedicated person who is responsible for information security, an external company, an audit department or the top management. The likeliness, that appropriate responsibilities are established and enforced, increases with the size of the organization and if the company has offices abroad.

Future research might focus on a comparison of several countries in different cultural areas and within Europe. Another approach we want to follow is to feed an appropriate risk management model with the data presented here. This more systematic research could lead to quantifiable key risk parameters and development of distinct thresholds for the human risk factor of information security. Due to the characteristics of behavior, attitude and perception a heuristic approach could generate input for a scorecard or radar chart with the suggested small set of most interesting questions.

V. CONCLUSIONS

Our findings show that non-compliance is more likely in an environment that is characterized by poor working conditions (inadequate salary, job insecurity, insufficient appreciation of work, lacking support from team members or supervisors, mobbing, and lack of the resources that are necessary to get the work done), competitive pressures, focus on simplistic success parameters, and problems in a company's control system, management style and corporate culture. Favorable working conditions are therefore important in order to enhance the motivation and loyalty of employees. Thus, it is crucial for companies to ensure good working conditions. External regulations and technical solutions, e.g., automated logouts, frequent password changes, access and time badges – are replacing the individual behavioral orientation. Overregulation leads to employees boycotting or bypassing the control system. Excessive control and regulation has a negative impact on the work environment and hampers productivity. Employees often spend working hours with defiant attitudes.

Managers have great influence on the work environment of their employees. Therefore, it is crucial that the managers are selected carefully because they contribute essentially to the company's success and working atmosphere. Good relationships between employees and managers, transparent information and communication structures, transparent work organization and participation in decision-making are necessary to enhance work-life satisfaction and reduce the occurrence of mental disorders. Work life balance in general is considered a necessary requirement for healthy, hard-working, compliant behavior. At the same time, smartphones and laptops enable an integration of work and private life.

The result is that the line between work and leisure is becoming more and more blurred.

Although Austrian companies are in general well-prepared concerning information security, the small and medium-enterprises will have to increase their efforts in order to catch up. Besides the size of the organization, the business sector is decisive for whether information security measures are implemented or not. In sectors where employees are used to handle a lot of sensitive data, such as in the finance and insurance sector, the health sector or the public administration sector, advanced information security measures can be found. Our findings indicate that stronger regulations, monitoring and surveillance measures might not lead to the expected effects in all cases. Consequently, one of the main tasks for human resource management is the selection of loyal employees and the successful integration of employees into the organization.

REFERENCES

[1] M. Plischke, “Company’s Prevention: Risk Management Competing with Technology“ [in German: “Unternehmensprävention: Risikomanagement im Wettlauf mit der Technik”], Inf. Manag. Consult., no. 3, 2009, pp. 57–60.

[2] C. Suchan and J. Frank, Analysis and Design of Powerful IS Architectures: Model-based Methods from Research and Teaching in Practice [in German: Analyse und Gestaltung leistungsfähiger IS-Architekturen: Modellbasierte Methoden aus Forschung und Lehre in der Praxis], Springer-Verlag, 2012.

[3] M. Baram and M. Schoebel, “Safety culture and behavioral change at the workplace” Saf. Sci., vol. 45, no. 6, 2007, pp. 631–636.

[4] C. Buck and T. Eymann, “Human Risk Factor in Mobile Ecosystems“ [in German: “Risikofaktor Mensch in mobilen Ökosystemen”], HMD Prax. Wirtsch., vol. 51, no. 1, 2014, pp. 75–83.

[5] F. W. Guldenmund, “The use of questionnaires in safety culture research–an evaluation” Saf. Sci., vol. 45, no. 6, 2007, pp. 723–743.

[6] B. Fahlbruch and M. Schöbel, “SOL–Safety through organizational learning: A method for event analysis,” Saf. Sci., vol. 49, no. 1, 2011, pp. 27–31.

[7] Federal Ministry for Transport, Innovation and Technology (BMVIT) and Austrian Research Promotion Agency (FFG), “KIRAS Security Research: MetaRisk,” 2016. [Online]. Available: http://www.kiras.at/. [Accessed: 17-Feb-2016].

[8] S. Schiebeck, et.al., “Implementation of a Generic ICT Risk Model using Graph Databases,” presented at the SECURWARE 2015, 9th International Conference on Emerging Security Information, Systems and Technologies, Venice, Italy, 2015, pp. 146–153.

[9] Federal Chancellery of Austria, Ed., “Cybersecurity in Austria” [in German: “Cybersicherheit in Österreich”], Mar-2015.

[10] nic.at and CERT Austria, “Report Internet Security Austria [in German: “Bericht Internet-Sicherheit Österreich 2015”], Feb-2016.

[11] Ministry of Finance, Federal Chancellery of Austria, and A-SIT Center for Secure ICT, “ICT Security Portal – Cybermonitor” [in German: “IKT-Sicherheitsportal – Cybermonitor”], Onlinesicherheit.at, 16-Feb-2016. [Online]. Available: https://www.onlinesicherheit.gv.at. [Accessed: 16-Feb-2016].

[12] Bundesamt für Sicherheit in der Informationstechnik (BSI), “The Situation of IT Security in Germany 2015“ [in German: “Die Lage der IT-Sicherheit in Deutschland 2015”], Nov-2015.

[13] Bundeskriminalamt Wiesbaden, “Cybercrime Federal Overview 2014“ [in German: “Cybercrime Bundeslagebild 2014”], Bundeskriminalamt Wiesbaden, 2014.

[14] Information Systems Audit and Control Association (ISACA), Ed., “State of Cybersecurity: Implications for 2015 - An ISACA and RSA Conference Survey.” 2014.

[15] G. Cluley, “Hackers Steal $55 million From Boeing Supplier,” 21-Jan-2016. [Online]. Available: http://www.tripwire.com/state-of-security/security-data-protection/boeing-supplier-hacked-claims-55-million-worth-of-damage-as-stock-price-falls/. [Accessed: 16-Feb-2016].

[16] Pricewaterhouse Coopers, “Economic crime: A threat to business processes - PWC´s 2014 Global Economic Crime Survey - US Supplement.” 2014.

[17] H. Quentmeier, Practice Manual Compliance: Fundamentals, Objectives, and Practical Advice for Non-lawyers [in German: Praxishandbuch Compliance: Grundlagen, Ziele und Praxistipps für Nicht-Juristen], 1. Edition. Wiesbaden: Gabler, 2012.

[18] W. Schettgen-Sarcher, S. Bachmann, and P. Schettgen, Eds., Compliance Officer: The Augsburg Qualifying Model [in German: Compliance Officer: das Augsburger Qualifizierungsmodell], Wiesbaden: Springer Gabler, 2014.

[19] N. Semmer, “Stress” in Handwörterbuch Arbeitswissenschaft, H. Luczak and W. Volpert, Eds. Stuttgart: Schäffer-Poeschl, 1997, pp. 332–339.

[20] R. Raml, “Positive indicators for health in context of work: an interdisciplinary extension of the term health and its consequences for the differentiation of health situations for employees“ [in German: “Positive Indikatoren der Gesundheit im Kontext Arbeit: eine interdisziplinäre Erweiterung des Gesundheitsbegriffs und dessen Folgen für die Differenzierung gesundheitlicher Lagen bei unselbständig Beschäftigten”], Medical University, 2009.

[21] L. Kish, “A procedure for objective respondent selection within the household,” J. Am. Stat. Assoc., vol. 44, no. 247, 1949, pp. 380–387.

[22] C. Colwill, “Human factors in information security: The insider threat–Who can you trust these days?” Inf. Secur. Tech. Rep., vol. 14, no. 4, 2009, pp. 186–196.

[23] J. R. Nurse, O. Buckley, P. A. Legg, M. Goldsmith, S. Creese, G. R. Wright, and M. Whitty, “Understanding insider threat: A framework for characterising attacks” in Security and Privacy Workshops (SPW), 2014 IEEE, 2014, pp. 214–228.

[24] G. B. Magklaras and S. M. Furnell, “A preliminary model of end user sophistication for insider threat prediction in IT systems”, Comput. Secur., vol. 24, no. 5, 2005, pp. 371–380.

[25] A. M. Munshi, A study of insider threat behaviour: developing a holistic insider threat model, Ph.D. Curtin University, School of Information Systems, 2013

[26] RSA, The Insider Security Threat in I.T. and Financial Services: Survey Shows Employees' Everyday Behavior Puts Sensitive Business Information at Risk, RSA, 2008.

[27] L. Tan, "Asia worried about insider threat. ZDNet Asia.", 2008.

[28] R. Raml, "Working conditions and stress: findings of the Austrian Work Climate Index" [in German: "Arbeitsbedingungen und Stress: Erkenntnisse aus dem österreichischen Arbeitsklima Index"] in "Arbeitsbedingungen und Stress" - Schriftenreihe Österreichischer Arbeitsklima Index 3, 2015, S 12-17

[29] R. Raml, "Scientific fundamentals of the Austrian Occupational Health Monitor" [in German: "Wissenschaftliche Grundlagen des Österreichischen Arbeitsgesundheitsmonitors"] in Schriftenreihe Österreichischer Arbeitsklima Index 2 - Austrian Work Climate Index, 2012, S 12-19

[30] R. Raml, "A theoretical evaluation of the Work Climate Index" [in German: "Eine theoretische Evaluierung des Arbeitsklima Index"] in "Schriftenreihe Österreichischer Arbeitsklima Index 1 - Austrian Working Climate Index", 2009

[31] R. Raml, A. Schiff,: "The localization of the Work Climate Index in a sociologic, psychologic and economic theory spectrum" [in German: "Die Verortung des Arbeitsklima Index im soziologischen, psychologischen und ökonomischen Theorienspektrum"], 2016

[32] Pricewaterhouse Coopers, "Economic crime: A threat to business processes - PWC´s 2014 Global Economic Crime Survey - US Supplement." 2014.

[33] KPMG, "Wirtschaftskriminalität. Deutschland, Österreich, Schweiz im Vergleich. Wirtschaftskriminalität in Großunternehmen und dem Mittelstand." 2013.

[34] A. V. Heerden, F. Weller, and G. Weidinger, „Business Crime. Gemrany, Austria, Switzerland in comparison. Business Crime in large-sized organizations and medium-sized business" [in German: "Wirtschaftskriminalität. Deutschland, Österreich, Schweiz im Vergleich. Wirtschaftskriminalität in Großunternehmen und dem Mittelstand"], KPMG, 2013.

[35] Pricewaterhouse Coopers, "Business Crime 2011. Security Situation in Austrian companies" [in German: "Wirtschaftskriminalität 2011. Sicherheitslage in österreichischen Unternehmen"], PWC, 2011.

Visualization of Privacy Risks in Software Systems

George O. M. Yee

Computer Research Lab
Aptusinnova Inc.
Ottawa, Canada
email: george@aptusinnova.com

Dept. of Systems and Computer Engineering
Carleton University
Ottawa, Canada
email: gmyee@sce.carleton.ca

Abstract—**Software systems can be found in almost every aspect of our lives, as can be seen in social media, online banking and shopping, as well as electronic health monitoring. This widespread involvement of software in our lives has led to the need to protect privacy, as the use of the software often requires us to input our personal information. However, before privacy can be protected, it is necessary to understand the risks to privacy that can be found in the software system. Indeed, such understanding is key to protecting privacy throughout the system's range of application. This paper presents a straightforward method for effectively visualizing and identifying privacy risks in software systems, and illustrates the method with examples.**

Keywords-software; system; privacy; risks; visualization.

I. INTRODUCTION

Numerous software systems targeting consumers have accompanied the rapid growth of the Internet. Software systems are available for banking, shopping, learning, healthcare, and Government Online. However, most of these systems require a consumer's personal information in one form or another, leading to concerns over privacy. For these systems to be successful, privacy must be protected.

Various approaches have been used to protect personal information, including data anonymization [1] and pseudonym technology [2]. Other approaches for privacy protection include treating privacy protection as an access problem and then bringing the tools of access control to bear for privacy control [3]. However, these approaches presume to know where and what protection is needed. They presume that some sort of analysis has been done that answers the question of "where" and "what" with respect to privacy risks. Without such answers, the effectiveness of the protection comes into question. For example, protection against house break-ins is ineffective if the owner only secures the front door without securing other vulnerable spots such as windows. An effective break-in risk analysis would have identified the windows as additional locations having break-in risks (where and what) and would have led to the windows also being secured. The result is a house that is better protected against break-ins. In the same way, privacy risk identification considering "where" and "what" is essential to effective privacy protection - this work proposes a visual method for such identification.

The objectives of this paper are to a) propose an effective method for visualizing privacy risks in software systems to identify where and what risks are present, and b) illustrate the method using examples. The method is limited to the identification of privacy risks. It does not include estimating the likelihood of a risk being realized.

In the literature, there are significant works on security threat analysis but very little work on privacy risk identification using visualization. In fact, the only works that are directly related to privacy risk identification appear to be those on "privacy impact assessment (PIA)", originating from government policy [4]. PIA is meant to evaluate the impact to privacy of new government programs, services, and initiatives. PIA can also be applied to existing government services undergoing transformation or re-design. However, PIA is a long manual process consisting mainly of self-administered questionnaires. It is not focused on software systems nor does it employ visual techniques as proposed in this work.

This paper is organized as follows. Section II defines privacy, privacy preferences, privacy risks, and what they mean for software systems. Section III presents the proposed method for privacy risk visualization, together with examples. Section IV discusses related work. Section V presents conclusions.

II. PRIVACY

As defined by Goldberg et al. in 1997 [5], privacy refers to the ability of individuals to *control* the collection, retention, and distribution of information about themselves. This leads to the following definition of privacy for this work.

DEFINITION 1: *Privacy* refers to the ability of individuals to *control* the collection, purpose, retention, and distribution of information about themselves.

Definition 1 is the same as given by Goldberg et al. except that it also includes "purpose". To see that "purpose" is needed, consider, for example, that one may agree to give out one's email address for the purpose of friends to send email but not for the purpose of spammers to send spam. This definition also suggests that "personal information", "private information" or "private data" is any information that can be linked to a person; otherwise, the information would not be "about" the person. Thus, another term for private information is "personally identifiable information (PII)". These terms are used interchangeably in this paper. In addition, controlling the "collection" of information implies controlling *who* collects *what* information. Controlling the "retention" of information is really about controlling the *retention time* of information, i.e. how long the information can be retained before being destroyed. Controlling the "distribution" of information is controlling to which other parties the information can be *disclosed-to*. These considerations motivate the following definitions.

DEFINITION 2: A user's *privacy preference* expresses the user's desired control over a) *PII* - what the item of personal information is, b) *collector* - who can collect it, c) *purpose* - the purpose for collecting it, d) *retention time* - the amount of time the information is kept, and e) *disclosed-to* - which other parties the information can be disclosed-to.

DEFINITION 3: A *privacy risk* is the potential occurrence of any action or circumstance that will result in a violation of any of the components PII, collector, purpose, retention time, and disclosed-to in a user's privacy preference.

For example, Alice uses an online pharmacy and has the following privacy preference:

PII: name, address, telephone number
Collector: A-Z Drugs
Purpose: identification
Retention Time: 2 years
Disclosed-To: none

This preference states that Alice allows A-Z Drugs to collect her name, address, and telephone number, and that A-Z Drugs must: use the information only to identify her, not keep the information for more than 2 years, and not disclose the information to any other party.

This work considers only privacy risks as defined in Definition 3. The privacy preference components PII, collector, purpose, retention time, and disclosed-to have, in fact, been enacted by privacy legislation as fully describing the privacy rights of individuals in many countries, including Canada, the United States, the European Union, and Australia [6]. Thus, this work is consistent with privacy legislation, and treating only privacy risks defined by Definition 3 does not overly reduce the generality of this work.

III. METHOD FOR PRIVACY RISK VISUALIZATION

The proposed method for privacy risk visualization assumes the following common characteristics of a software system:

a) The software system requires the user's personal information in order to carry out its function. For example, an online bookseller requires the user's address for shipping purposes.
b) The software system may transmit the information (e.g., move it from one group to another within the software system's organization), store the information (e.g., store the information in a data base), and make use of the information to carry out its function (e.g., print out shipping labels with the user's address).

The method is based on the notion that the *location* of personal information gives rise to privacy risks. The importance of location is reflected in physical security, where sensitive paper documents are kept in a locked safe (a location) to protect privacy, rather than being left on a desk (a location). For a software system, storing the user's personal information in an encrypted database with secure access controls is the equivalent of storing it in a safe, with corresponding reduced privacy risks. The method, then, consists of i) determining all the possible locations in the software system where the user's personal information could reside, and ii) evaluating at each of these locations the possible ways in which the user's privacy preferences could be violated. The complete method is as follows:

A. Method for Privacy Risk Visualization

1. Draw the paths of all personal information flows within the software system, based on characteristic b) above, namely, that personal information can be transmitted, stored, and used. Use a solid arrow to represent the transmission of personal information items that are described by privacy preferences. Label the arrow with numbers, where each arrow number corresponds to a description of a personal data item in a legend. Use a square to represent the storage of personal information. Use a circle to denote the use of the information. Use a dashed rectangle to enclose circles or squares into physically distinct units. For example, two circles representing two uses would be enclosed by a dashed square if both uses run on the same computing platform. Physically separate units allow the identification of risks for any data flow between them. Circles or squares not enclosed by a dashed rectangle are understood to be already physically separate units. Label the squares and circles with letters. Each such label corresponds to a description of the type of storage or the type of use as indicated in the legend.
2. Use dashed arrows, numbered in the same way as the solid arrows in Step 1, to add to the drawing all non-personal information flows, if any, that are involved with the transmission, storage and use of the personal information. Non-personal information is information that is not personal or not private, i.e. information that cannot identify any particular individual, e.g., the price of something. The resulting drawing is called a Personal Information Map (PIM). Figure 1 illustrates steps 1 and 2 for the software system of an online seller of merchandise, e.g., Amazon.com, that requires the user's name, address, merchandise selection, and credit card number. These are considered as three personal information items where name and address together are considered as one item. Figure 1 also shows three non-personal information flows (4, 5, 6). The dashed rectangle enclosing A, B, and C indicates that A, B, and C all run on the same physical computing platform.

3. Inspect the PIM resulting from step 2, and for each location (flow arrow, storage square, and use circle) and each personal information item, enumerate the possible ways in which a privacy preference may be violated in terms of violations of any of *PII*, *collector*, *purpose*, *retention time*, and *disclose-to* (see Section II). This may be achieved by asking risk questions for each component, as suggested in Table 1, and drawing conclusions based on security and systems knowledge and experience. The risk questions are "how" questions, based on the idea that a risk arises where there is some way (i.e. how) for a violation to occur. Record the results in a Privacy Risks Table containing two columns: the left column for records of the form "(PII_1, PII_2, .../ locations)" and the right column containing the corresponding privacy risks. The Privacy Risks Table is the goal of the method. Table 2 illustrates this step for the online seller of Figure 1.

It is important to note that the PIM resulting from Step 2 is not a program logic flow diagram and one should not try to interpret it as such. It shows *what* PII is required, *where* PII goes, *where* PII is stored, and *where* PII is used, corresponding to the notion that the location of personal information is key to understanding privacy risks, as mentioned above.

TABLE 1. Risk Questions

Component	Risk Questions
PII	How can the user be asked for other PII, either intentionally or inadvertently?
collector	How can the PII be received by an unintended collector either in addition to or in place of the intended collector?
purpose	How can the PII be used for other purposes?
retention time	How can the PII retention time be violated?
disclose-to	How can the PII be disclosed either intentionally or inadvertently to an unintended recipient?

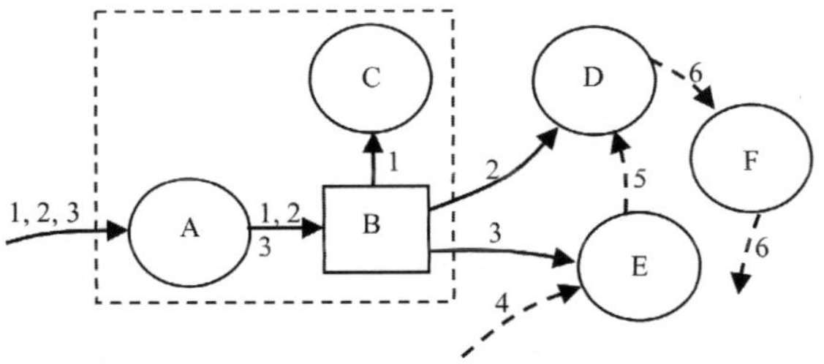

Legend:
A: receive and store data
B: database
C: print shipping label
D: pack item for shipping
E: charge credit card
F: send shipping status to buyer

1: name and address
2: item selected
3: credit card number
4: company account number
5: payment status
6: shipping status

Figure 1. PIM for an online seller of merchandise.

TABLE 2. Partial Privacy Risks Table Corresponding to Fig. 1

(PIIs / locations)	Privacy Risks
(1, 2, 3 / path into A); (2 / path into D); (3 / path into E)	Man-in-the-middle attack violates *collector*, *purpose*, and *disclose-to*; for path into A, user could be asked for personal information that violates *PII*
(1, 2, 3 / A, B); (1 / C); (2 / D); (3 / E)	Trojan horse, hacker, or SQL attack (for B) violates *collector*, *purpose*, and *disclose-to*; for B, information could be kept past *retention time*

Adding non-personal information flows in Step 2 is important to help identify potential unintended leakages of PII. For example, consider a "produce report" use circle that "anonymizes" (any obvious links to the information owner removed) PII and combines the result with non-personal information to produce a report for public distribution. The fact that both PII and non-PII flow into "produce report" could lead to identifying a personal information leakage risk.

It is recommended that this method be applied by a privacy risks identification team, consisting of no more than three or four people, selected for their technical knowledge of the software system and the work procedures and processes of the software system's organization. Good candidates for the team include the software system's design manager, test manager, and other line managers with the required knowledge. The team should be led by a privacy analyst who must also be knowledgeable about security threats and who should have the support of upper management to carry out the privacy risks identification. A definite advantage of the team approach would accrue to step 3, where the enumeration would be more thorough by virtue of more people being involved.

B. A more substantial example

Consider PatientBilling, a patient billing system running in a doctor's office. PatientBilling makes use of two business software systems: an accounting system PatientAccounting and an online payment system PatientPay.

Table 3 shows the user's personal information required by each system. The user provides her private information to PatientBilling which then discloses this information to PatientAccounting and PatientPay.

The proposed method for privacy risks visualization is carried out as follows:

Table 3. Personal Information Required

Software System	Patient Personal Information Required
PatientBilling	name and address, health complaint (patient name, health problem, health problem resolution), method of payment details (name, credit card number, credit card expiry date, health insurance number, health insurance expiry date)
PatientAccounting	name and address, health complaint (as above)
PatientPay	method of payment details (as above)

Steps 1 and 2: Draw the PIM for each software system (see Fig. 2**).** As shown in Figure 2, the following uses of personal information are extra to the core function of each system. First, both PatientAccounting (M) and PatientPay (L) send activity reports back to PatientBilling that contain personal information. These reports contain selections and re-arrangements of personal data (15, 16). Second, PatientBilling produces a publically accessible report for the medical association, giving statistics on the patients seen. To produce this report, PatientBilling (N) selects, re-arranges, and anonymizes personal data (13). Third, PatientAccounting allows its employees to partially work from home (G). Finally, the patient's method of payment details are used without being stored in databases.

Step 3: Enumerate privacy risks at private information locations. Table 4 gives a partial Privacy Risk Table for locations in Figure 2 that have interesting or serious privacy risks. The theft of personal information means that the information is under the control of an unintended party. Clearly, this can violate the corresponding privacy preference or preferences in terms of violating *collector*, *purpose*, *retention time*, and *disclose-to*. The risk of personal information theft arises so often that it is convenient to call it *CPRD-risk*, from the first letters of collector, purpose, retention time, and disclose-to.

To illustrate this step, the risks in the first 3 rows of Table 4 were obtained as follows. For the first row, it was noticed that the personal information flows through transmission paths connecting physically distinct units. The risk questions of Table 1 were then considered, leading to possible man-in-the-middle attacks that give rise to CPRD-risk. In addition, violations of PII are always possible unless strict controls are in place against it. For the second row, it was observed that the associated personal data are input to information use processes (e.g., A, C, D). The risk questions of Table 1 were again considered, leading to possible Trojan horse or hacker attacks that again give rise to CPRD-risk. For the third row, it was noticed that personal data are stored in databases. Once again the risk questions were considered, leading to possible SQL attacks against the databases, giving rise to CPRD-risk. In each of these three cases, knowledge of the system (personal data locations) and knowledge of information security (possible attacks) were needed to identify the risks. The remaining risks in Table 4 were derived in a similar fashion.

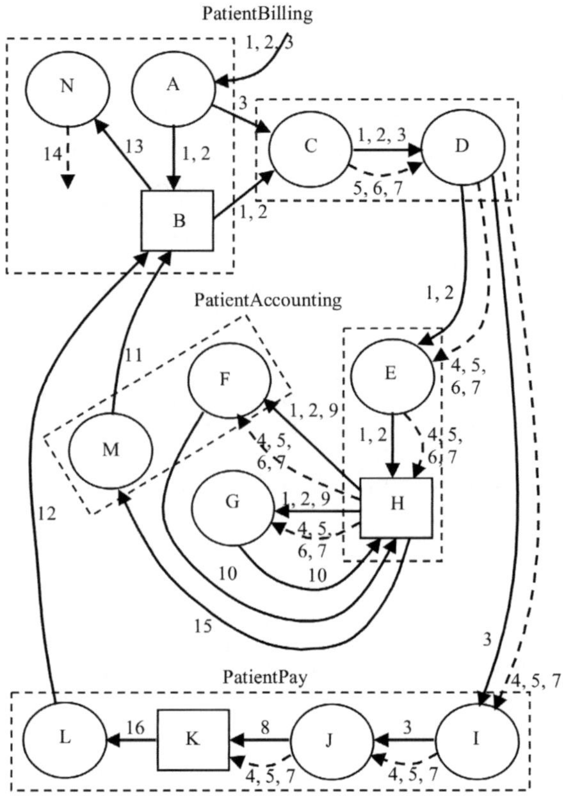

Legend:

A: receive and store data	E: receive and store data
B: database	F: update ledgers at work
C: process billing	G: update ledgers at home
D: disclose data	H: database
1: name and address	I: receive and forward data
2: health complaint	J: charge credit card or insurance; update doctor's account
3: method of payment details	K: database
4: doctor id	L: compose payment report
5: billing id	M: compose accounting report
6: time spent with patient	N: compose report for medical association
7: billing amount	14: anonymized report for medical association
8: doctor account update	15: accounting data
9: current ledger record	16: payment data
10: updated ledger record	
11: accounting report	
12: payment report	
13: patients seen data	

Figure 2. PIM for PatientBilling, PatientAccounting, and PatientPay.

IV. RELATED WORK

The literature on works by other authors, dealing *directly* with privacy risk visualization for software systems, appears to be non-existent. However, the following authors have written on topics that are related to privacy risk analysis. Hong et al. [7] propose the use of privacy risk models to help designers design ubiquitous computing applications that have a reasonable level of privacy protection. Their privacy risk model consists of two parts: a privacy risk analysis part and a privacy risk management part. The risk analysis identifies the privacy risks while the risk management part is a cost-benefit analysis to prioritize the risks and design artifacts to manage the risks. Visualization is not used.

A second class of related work applies privacy risk analysis to specific application areas. Biega et al. [8] propose a new privacy model to help users manage privacy risks in their Internet search histories. They assume a powerful adversary who makes informed probabilistic inferences about sensitive data in search histories and aim

TABLE 4. Partial Privacy Risks Table Corresponding to Fig. 2

(PIIs / locations)	Privacy Risks
(1, 2, 3 / path into A); (1, 2 / path between B and C, path between D and E); (3 / path between A and C, path between D and I); (12 / path between L and B); (11 / path between M and B)	Man-in-the-middle attacks lead to CPRD-risk; corresponding to 1, 2, 3, the patient could be asked for personal information that violates PII (i.e. asked for PII other than 1, 2, 3).
(1, 2, 3 / A, C, D); (13 / N); (1, 2 / E); (1, 2, 9 / F, G); (15 / M); (3 / J); (16 / L)	Trojan horse, or hacker attacks on the personal information use circles lead to CPRD-risk.
(1, 2, 11, 12 / B); (1, 2, 10 / H); (8 / K)	Potential SQL attacks on B, H, and K lead to CPRD-risk.
(13 / N)	A bad anonymization algorithm can expose personal information, leading to CPRD-risk.
(1, 2, 9 / G)	An insecure home environment, e.g., people looking over the shoulder or printed personal information lying on a desk in the clear, can also lead to CPRD-risk.
(1, 2, 9 / G)	If an employee works from home on a laptop and carries the laptop back and forth between home and work, possible theft or loss of the laptop can also lead to CPRD-risk for any of 1, 2, or 9 that might be temporarily stored in the laptop.
(1, 2, 9 / G)	If an employee works from home on a home PC and stores 1, 2, 9 on a flash memory stick, carrying the memory stick back and forth between home and work, possible theft or loss of the memory stick can also lead to CPRD-risk.

for a tool that simulates the adversary, predicts privacy risks, and guides the user. Paintsil [9] presents an extended misuse case model and a tool that can be used to check the presence of known misuse cases and their effect on security and privacy risks in identity management systems. Das and Zhang [10] propose new design principles to lessen privacy risks in health databases due to aggregate disclosure. None of these works employ visualization.

A third class of related work is of course the work on privacy impact analysis (PIA) [4] (Section I).

A fourth class of related work consists of security and privacy threat analysis, e.g., Nematzadeh and Camp [11]. Security and privacy threats are related risks. For example, a Trojan horse attack (security threat) can lead directly to the lost of private data (privacy threat). These works also do not use visualization as described here.

A fifth class of related work concerns earlier work on privacy visualization by this author. Yee [12] presents a notation for representing the software and hardware components of a computer system as well as the data flows between the components. It then checks each component for vulnerabilities that could violate a privacy policy. It differs from this work in terms of the notation (lower level than this work), the method of identifying vulnerabilities, and the use of privacy policies. Yee [13] featured the first use of the PIM but for web services only and involved privacy policies. In this work, we have extended the PIM to software systems in general and removed the need to work with privacy policies.

Finally, there remains a class of related work that also involves visualization of risks but with different goals than in this work. They are works on the visualization of information intended to assist the decision making process under risk or improve the understanding of system security and risks. They differ from this work as follows: a) they concern the visualization of *security* risks rather than privacy risks, b) their goals are to assist in decision making or improve security understanding, whereas the goal of this work is to identify privacy vulnerabilities, and c) their visualizations are lower level in general and resemble more the objects being visualized, whereas this work uses a high level more abstract visualization. Three works representative of this class are Daradkeh [14], Takahashi et al. [15], and Kai et al. [16]. Daradkeh evaluates an information visualization tool for the support of decision making under uncertainty and risk. Takahashi et al. discuss the architecture of a tool for security risk visualization and alerting to increase security awareness. Kai et al. present a security visualization system for cloud computing that displays security levels computed over information gathered at monitoring points. Their visualization system is similar to visualizations provided by a security information and event management system (SIEM) [17].

V. CONCLUSION AND FUTURE WORK

This work has proposed a straightforward method for visualizing privacy risks applicable to software systems, focusing attention on locations involving PII. Although the likelihood of a risk being realized is not covered, identifying the risks is a necessary first step.

Some of the strengths of the method include: a) provides a structured way to identify privacy risks, b) easy-to-use graphical notation, and c) focuses attention on the locations that involve PII.

Some weaknesses of the method are: a) drawing the PIM and filling out the Privacy Risks Table require expertise in how personal information is used as well as expertise in security and privacy, b) the method is manual and is prone to error, and c) the method can never identify all the risks. Weakness a) is unavoidable as even expert systems must get their expertise from people. Also, this "weakness" is common to many analytical methods, e.g., designing good software. Weakness b) can be addressed by building tools for automatically drawing the PIM. Similar tools already exist for rendering a software architecture diagram from the reverse engineering of code, e.g., Nanthaamornphong et al. [18], and it should be feasible to build a similar tool to draw a PIM. Furthermore, automated analysis of the PIM should be feasible by using a rules engine to automate the enumeration of privacy risks, based on machine understanding of the graphical notation in this work. These automations should improve both the accuracy of the PIM and the identification of the privacy risks. Weakness c) may also be unavoidable, as it is due to the nature of security, that no system can be completely secure. However, the above automated tools and rules engine should improve risk coverage.

Future work includes the automations mentioned above, as well as a validation of the effectiveness of the approach. For this validation, it is envisioned that a software system with known privacy risks (reference risks), would be defined to act as the reference system. Different teams of privacy and security experts who do not have prior knowledge of the reference risks would then be invited to apply the approach to the reference system. Their results would be compared to the reference risks to gage the effectiveness of the approach. If the risks found by the teams were fewer than the reference risks, then a follow-up analysis could point to the reasons for the discrepancy and could give insight into ways to improve the approach. On the other hand, if the risks found were more than the reference risks, then it may be concluded that the approach is highly effective.

REFERENCES

[1] V. S. Iyengar, "Transforming Data to Satisfy Privacy Constraints", Proceedings of the 8th ACM SIGKDD International Conference on Knowledge Discovery and Data Mining (KDD'02), Edmonton, Alberta, pp. 279-288, 2002.

[2] R. Song, L. Korba, and G. Yee, "Pseudonym Technology for E-Services", chapter in Privacy Protection for E-Services, edited by G. Yee, Idea Group, Inc., 2006.

[3] C. Adams and K. Barbieri, "Privacy Enforcement in E-Services Environments", chapter in Privacy Protection for E-Services, edited by G. Yee, Idea Group, Inc., 2006.

[4] Treasury Board of Canada Secretariat, "Directive on Privacy Impact Assessment", available as of March 27, 2016 from: http://www.tbs-sct.gc.ca/pol/doc-eng.aspx?id=18308

[5] I. Goldberg, D. Wagner, and E. Brewer, "Privacy-Enhancing Technologies for the Internet", IEEE COMPCON'97, pp. 103-109, 1997.

[6] G. Yee, L. Korba, and R. Song, "Legislative Bases for Personal Privacy Policy Specification", chapter in Privacy Protection for E-Services, edited by G. Yee, Idea Group, Inc., 2006.

[7] J. I. Hong, J. D. Ng, S. Lederer, and J. A. Landay, "Privacy Risk Models for Designing Privacy-Sensitive Ubiquitous Computing Systems", Proceedings, 2004 Conference on Designing Interactive Systems: Processes, Practices, Methods, and Techniques, Cambridge, MA, USA, pp. 91-100, 2004.

[8] J. Biega, I. Mele, and G. Weikum, "Probabilistic Prediction of Privacy Risks in User Search Histories", Proceedings of the 1st International Workshop on Privacy and Security of Big Data, pp. 29-36, Nov. 2014.

[9] E. Paintsil, "A Model for Privacy and Security Risks Analysis", Proceedings of the 5th International Conference on New Technologies, Mobility and Security (NTMS), pp. 1-8, May 2012.

[10] G. Das and N. Zhang, "Privacy Risks in Health Databases From Aggregate Disclosure", Proceedings of the 2nd ACM International Conference on Pervasive Technologies Related to Assistive Environments (PETRA'09), article no. 74, June 2009.

[11] A. Nematzadeh and L. J. Camp, "Threat Analysis of Online Health Information System", Proceedings of the 3rd International Conference on Pervasive Technologies Related to Assistive Environments (PETRA'10), article no. 31, June 2010.

[12] G. Yee, "Visualization for Privacy Compliance", Proceedings of the 3rd International Workshop on Visualization for Computer Security (VizSEC'06), pp. 117-122, Nov. 2006.

[13] G. Yee, "Visual Analysis of Privacy Risks in Web Services", Proceedings of the IEEE International Conference on Web Services (ICWS 2007), pp. 671-678, July 2007.

[14] M. Daradkeh, "Exploring the Use of an Information Visualization Tool for Decision Support under Uncertainty and Risk", Proceedings of the International Conference on Engineering & MIS 2015 (ICEMIS'15), article no. 41, 2015.

[15] T. Takahashi, K. Emura, A. Kanaoka, S. Matsuo, and T. Minowa, "Risk Visualization and Alerting System: Architecture and Proof-of-Concept Implementation", Proceedings of the First International Workshop on Security in Embedded Systems and Smartphones (SESP'13)", pp. 3-10, 2013.

[16] S. Kai, T. Shigemoto, T. Kito, S. Takemoto, and T. Kaji, "Development of Qualification of Security Status Suitable for Cloud Computing System", Proceedings of the 4th International Workshop on Security Measurements and Metrics (MetriSec'12), pp. 17-24, 2012.

[17] Wikipedia, "Security information and event management", available as of June 12, 2016 from: https://en.wikipedia.org/wiki/Security_information_and_event_management

[18] A. Nanthaamornphong, K. Morris, and S. Filippone, "Extracting UML Class Diagrams from Object-Oriented Fortran: ForUML", Proceedings of the 1st International Workshop on Software Engineering for High Performance Computing in Computational Science and Engineering (SE-HPCCSE'13), pp. 9-16, 2013.

Information Security Maturity as an Integral Part of ISMS based Risk Management Tools

Ben Fetler, Carlo Harpes
itrust consulting s.à r.l.
Niederanven, Luxembourg
e-mail: fetler@itrust.lu, harpes@itrust.lu

Abstract—**Measuring the continuous improvement of Information Security Management Systems (ISMS) is often neglected as most organizations do not know how to extract key-indicators that could be used for this purpose. The underlying work presents a six-level maturity model which can be fully integrated in a risk management tool and helps to define key indicators for measuring the improvement of an ISMS. Furthermore, the proposed model establishes on how far the increase of maturity can help to mitigate information security risks and finally, a cost-benefit equation is presented which can be used to quantitatively justify the increase of maturity of an ISMS and to establish an action plan increasing the maturity.**

Keywords-Information Security Management System; Maximal Efficiency Rate; Return On Security Maturity Investment; Information Security Risk Analysis; Security Maturity.

I. INTRODUCTION

The need to set up an Information Security Management System (ISMS) in organizations that treat critical or sensitive information is growing. Constantly new vulnerabilities, exploits and threats express the necessity to set up a managed system that is perfectly adapted to the fast evolving information and communications technology (ICT) environment.

One major difficulty of an ISMS is on how to measure its efficiency, quality or more generically its maturity. By considering the fact that an ISMS is based on continuous improvement, it is important to measure its maturity evolution. The maturity level of an ISMS can be used as a key indicator by Information Security Managers to monitor its efficiency and improvement. For example, young ISMS with low maturity often show similar deficits, such as non-formalized processes or security instructions, untested security procedures or unverified security statements.

A key element of an ISMS that follows the international standard ISO/IEC 27001 [1] is the periodic assessment of risks that includes identification of vulnerabilities, threats as well as estimation of their probability of occurrence and possible impact. During a risk analysis, the organization establishes an overview of currently implemented security controls and sets up an action plan to counteract non-acceptable risks. The aim of the underlying work is to introduce a maturity model that is part of the risk analysis process with the objective to determine the maturity level of security controls, the effect of missing maturity on risks and cost of increasing maturity. Finally, this model allows to define a risk treatment plan combining actions to increase security and actions to increase maturity.

To prove that the security maturity model can be adapted to its context, the model has been tested for a small to medium-sized enterprise (SME).

The rest of this paper is organized as follows. Section II presents related work considered for developing the security maturity model. Section III describes the security maturity model. Section IV introduces the concept of the return on security maturity investment. Section V closes the paper with the conclusion and outlook on further work.

II. RELATED WORK

Several Maturity Models exist for determining the quality of organizational processes. Two common models (Capability Maturity Model Integration (CMMI) [2] and ISO/IEC 15504 – Software Process Improvement and Capability Determination (SPICE) [3]) have been analyzed to collect valuable information that could be reused for the setup of a Maturity model related to Information Security.

The National Institute of Standards and Technology (NIST) developed an IT Security Maturity Model, including several maturity levels and related tasks [4]. These standardized tasks have been reused and partly adapted to fit to the Security Maturity Model described in this paper.

Furthermore, there have already been first tries of including maturity in risk assessment tools [5-6]. Unfortunately, in those tools, maturity is not handled as an evolution indicator but rather as a substitute for indicating the implementation rate of security controls or as a generic and qualitative indicator with no further details on how maturity is measured.

Finally, the quantitative computations that are made to compute the cost-effectiveness of increasing Security Maturity are based on the mathematical models used by the risk assessment methods ISAMM [7] and TRICK Service [8].

III. SECURITY MATURITY MODEL

The elaborated security maturity model is based on a multi-level approach (Section III.A.) with associated Maximal Efficiency Rates (Section III.B.) having a direct influence on the estimated implementation rates of current security controls. This direct influence of maturity levels on the implementation rate of security controls allows establishing a link between security maturity and the assessment of the overall information security status of an organization.

A. Security Maturity Levels (SML)

The elaborated security maturity model contains six levels with associated tasks that have to attain a predefined implementation rate before a higher level can be reached.

The tasks are categorized into five different domains: "Policies" (Pol), "Procedures" (Pro), "Implementation" (Imp), "Test" (Tes) and "Integration" (Int). Every task aims to cover a different aspect of security maturity. The tasks and the different maturity levels are based on the standard NISTIR 7358 [4]. However, the tasks have been reorganized to create an interdependency of the tasks, so that it should not be possible to reach a high SML without fulfilling the tasks of the lower SML's.

In the following, the six SML's and their associated tasks will be presented.

Security Maturity Level 0: Incomplete - No specific tasks available for Security Maturity Level 0, which is reached by default. The associated security controls are quite superficially implemented, typically by a small ISMS team which does not show any systematic approach.

Security Maturity Level 1: Performed - Pol 1: Formal, up-to-date documented policies exist and are readily available to employees; Imp 1: Procedures are communicated to individuals who are required to follow them; Pro 1: Formal, up-to-date, documented procedures are provided to implement the security controls identified by the defined policies; Tes 1: Tests are routinely conducted to evaluate the adequacy and effectiveness of all implementations.

Security Maturity Level 2: Managed - Pol 2: Policies establish a continuing cycle of assessing risk and implementation and uses monitoring for program effectiveness; Imp 2: Information security procedures and controls are implemented in a consistent manner everywhere the procedure applies and are reinforced through training; Pro 2: Procedures clarify where the procedure is to be performed, how the procedure is to be performed, when the procedure is to be performed, who is to perform the procedure, and on what the procedure is to be performed; Tes 2: Tests ensure that all policies, procedures, and controls are acting as intended and that they ensure the appropriate information security level.

Security Maturity Level 3: Established - Pol 3: Policies are written to cover all major facilities in scope; Imp 3: Ad hoc approaches that tend to be applied on an individual or a case-by-case basis are discouraged; Pro 3: Procedures clearly define Information security responsibilities and expected behaviors for (1) asset owners and users, (2) information resources management and data processing personnel, (3) management, and (4) Information security administrators; Tes 3: Effective corrective actions are taken to address identified weaknesses, including those identified as a result of potential or actual information security incidents or through information security alerts issued by national Computer Security Incident Response Teams (CSIRT) or Computer Emergency Response Teams (CERT).

Security Maturity Level 4: Predictable - Pol 4: Policies are approved by key affected parties; Pro 4: Procedures contain appropriate individuals to be contacted for further information, guidance, and compliance; Tes 4: Self-assessments, a type of test that can be performed by company staff, by contractors, or others engaged by company management, are routinely conducted to evaluate the adequacy and effectiveness of all implementations; Tes 5: Independent audits are an important check on company performance, but are not to be viewed as a substitute for evaluations initiated by company management; Tes 6: Information gleaned from records of potential and actual Information security incidents and from security alerts, such as those issued by software vendors are considered as test results. Such information can identify specific vulnerabilities and provide insights into the latest threats and resulting risk.

Security Maturity Level 5: Optimized - Int 1: Policies, procedures, implementations, and tests are continually reviewed and improvements are made; Pol 5: Policies delineate the information security management structure, clearly assign Information security responsibilities, and lay the foundation necessary to reliably measure progress and compliance; Pol 6: Policies identify specific penalties and disciplinary actions to be used if the policy is not followed; Pro 5: Procedures document the implementation of and the rigor in which the control is applied; Tes 7: Evaluation requirements, including requirements regarding the type and frequency of testing, are documented, approved, and effectively implemented; Tes 8: The frequency and rigor with which individual controls are tested depend on the risks that will be posed if the controls are not operating effectively.

B. Security Maturity Parameters

The following section presents the key parameters of the developed security maturity model. All parameters are customizable and can be fine-tuned according to the specificities of the organization in focus.

1) Implementation Scale for Security Maturity Tasks.

This section defines a scale for measuring the implementation rate of the different security maturity tasks. The implementation scale includes five different levels as presented in Table 1 below.

TABLE I. IMPLEMENTATION SCALE OF SECURITY MATURITY TASKS

Level	Explanation	
Not achieved	There exist no proofs that the Security Maturity tasks of the corresponding Security Maturity Level are implemented.	
	Acronym: N	Range: 0%
Rudimentary achieved	There are none or only few proofs available that the Security Maturity tasks of the corresponding Security Maturity Level are rudimentary implemented.	
	Acronym: R	Range:]0%, 20%]
Partially achieved	There are none or only few proofs available that the Security Maturity tasks of the corresponding Security Maturity Level are partly implemented.	
	Acronym: P	Range:]20%, 50%]
Largely achieved	There are proofs available which show that the Security Maturity tasks of the corresponding Security Maturity Level are essentially fulfilled.	
	Acronym: L	Range:]50%, 80%]
Fully achieved	There are proofs available that the Security Maturity tasks of the corresponding Security Maturity Level are fully implemented.	
	Acronym: F	Range:]80%, 100%]

2) *Task Overview per Security Maturity Level*

Each SML has related tasks which have to attain a predefined implementation rate in order to pretend that the SML is reached. The following list exemplary shows the 6 SML's and the related tasks with their required implementation rates:

SML 0: Reached by default – no tasks have to be fulfilled.

SML 1: Pol1, Pro 1, Imp 1, and Tes 1 have to be largely achieved

SML 2: In addition to SML 1, Pol 2, Pro 2, Imp 2, and Tes 2 have to be largely achieved

SML 3: In addition to SML 2, Pol 3, Pro 3, Imp 3, and Tes 3 have to be largely achieved

SML 4: In addition to SML 3, Pol 4, Pro 4, Tes 4, Tes 5, and Tes 6 have to be largely achieved

SML 5: All tasks have to be fully achieved

3) *Maximal Efficiency Rate*

By looking at the previous sections, it is possible to conclude that the higher the reached SML the higher the efficiency of the security treatment in the organization. Hence, a fully implemented security control cannot be fully efficient if the associated SML is not the highest possible.

In order to include these reflections in a risk assessment approach, we introduce the notion of Maximal Efficiency Rates (MaxEffRate) associated with the different SML's (see Table II below).

With the help of collected data during the case study with the SME, the different Maximal Efficiency Rates of Security Maturity Levels can be fine-tuned.

TABLE II. SECURITY MATURITY LEVELS WITH ASSOCIATED MAXIMAL EFFICIENCY RATE

SML	Qualification	MaxEffRate (linear)	MaxEffRate (tailored to our use-case)
0	Incomplete	10%	20%
1	Performed	20%	40%
2	Managed	40%	50%
3	Established	60%	70%
4	Predictable	80%	90%
5	Optimized	100%	100%

The now determined MaxEffRate per SML can be used to calculate the implementation rate of a security control taking into account the SML. For example, this allows to model the fact that a security control can be fully implemented but only have a small efficiency, if the associated SML is low.

The following formula is used to calculate an improved implementation rate of a security control taking security maturity into account, called the Maturity-based Effectiveness Rate (MER):

$$MER = IR * MaxEffRate_{SMLi} \qquad (1)$$

where

- MER= (Maturity-based Effectiveness Rate) be the improved implementation rate of the security control in focus taking Security Maturity into account;
- IR=the current implementation rate of the security control;
- $MaxEffRate_{SMLi}$ be the maximal efficiency rate of the current Security Maturity Level (SML_i).

Example: For the considered SME, we determined that a security control called "Implement an antivirus solution for every system in use" has been applied to 50%. The SML of the antivirus control is 3 because all requirements of SML 3 have been fulfilled (e.g., validated policy in place, requiring the implementation of antivirus solutions) but some tasks of SML 4 are still not satisfied (e.g., no audit was done to verify the well-functioning of the antivirus solution). Thus we have for the antivirus control an implementation rate (IR) of 50%, and a MaxEffRate of 70% which gives a MER of 50%*70%=35% for the antivirus security control.

This example demonstrates that if the maturity of the ISMS in focus has not reached the highest level, the implemented security controls cannot be fully efficient. This conclusion is not astonishing as we can pretend that if for example policies, procedures, implementations, and tests are not continually reviewed and no improvements are made (see Task Int 1 of SML5), the underlying security controls cannot be fully efficient.

Figure 1 illustrates the impact of Security Maturity on the implementation rate of a security control where Security Maturity is taken into account. The figure shows the SME-tailored model.

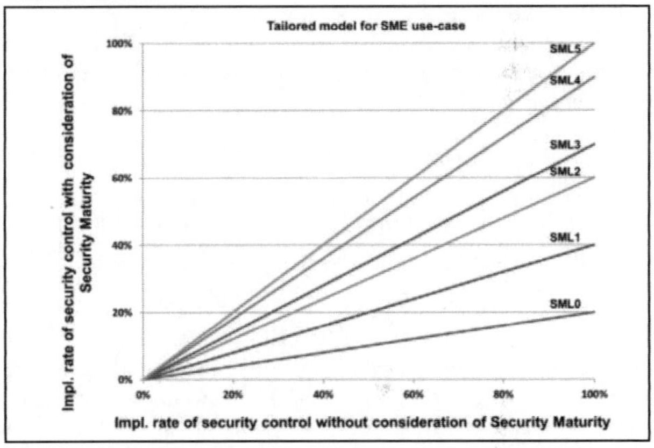

Figure 1. Impact of Security Maturity on implementation rate of security controls (MaxEffRate tailored to SME use-case)

IV. RETURN ON SECURITY MATURITY INVESTMENT (ROSMI)

The introduced maturity model offers the possibility to compute the Return On Security Maturity Investment (ROSMI) which can be used to justify the costs resulting from the resources to invest for implementing the tasks to increase the security maturity (resources are needed to fulfill the different tasks presented in Section III.A.).

The ROSMI is based on the Return on Investment (ROI) and Return On Security Investment (ROSI) concepts [7], [9-10], which consist of investing a certain amount of money with the aim to reduce the risk and such in return save more money than initially invested. This risk reduction is expressed as the difference of the Annual Loss Expectancy (ALE) before, and the ALE after implementing security controls.

The ROSMI, when raising the current SML to the SML above ($ROSMI_{SML_{i \to i+1}}$), is expressed as the difference between the ALE reductions generated by the raise of the current SML ($\Delta ALE_{SML_{i\rightarrow i+1}}$) and the costs incurring by the increase of the SML ($Costs_{SML_{i\rightarrow i+1}}$):

$$ROSMI_{SML_{i\rightarrow i+1}} = \Delta ALE_{SML_{i\rightarrow i+1}} - Costs_{SML_{i\rightarrow i+1}}$$
$$where\ 0 \leq i \leq 4 \quad (2)$$

The ALE Reduction (ΔALE) emerging from the raise of the current SML ($\Delta ALE_{SML_{i\rightarrow i+1}}$) is based on the quantitative risk assessment method, ISAMM [7] and TRICK Service [8].

The first step consists in computing the ALE reduction of every security control based on the increase of the current SML ($\Delta ALE_{M,SML_{i\rightarrow i+1}}$):

$$\Delta ALE_{M,SML_{i\rightarrow i+1}} = ALE_{e_M,SML_i} * RRF_M * e_M * \frac{(maxEffRate_{SML_{i+1}} - maxEffRate_{SMLi})}{1 - RRF_M * maxEffRate_{SML_i} * e_M} \quad where\ 0 \leq i \leq 4 \quad (3)$$

The risk reduction factor of a security control M (RRF_M) is introduced in the TRICK Service methodology [8] and represents a factor which indicates the impact of a security control on the risk exposure of an asset.

The second step consists in summing all ΔALE of the security controls to get the general ALE reduction resulting from the raise of the current SML:

$$\Delta ALE_{SML_{i\rightarrow i+1}} = \sum_M \Delta ALE_{M,SML_{i\rightarrow i+1}} \quad where\ 0 \leq i \leq 4 \quad (4)$$

The resulting ALE reduction gives a clear indication of the influence that the increase of maturity has on risks that a company is facing to and can be used for the ROSMI computation.

V. USE CASE

The underlying maturity model has been applied in the context of a risk analysis for an SME offering trusted third party services. During the risk assessment, the current implementation levels of ISO/IEC 27002 security controls have been estimated and the current SML of each ISO/IEC 27002 chapter has been computed by determination of the implementation rate of the SML related tasks. Based on the now identified SML per ISO/IEC 27002 chapter, it was possible to compare the current implementation rate with the MER. Some chapters showed a high implementation rate but low maturity and revealed the need of incrementing the SML of the different ISO/IEC 27002 chapters to get more efficient security controls having a better mitigation effect on the current risk level of the SME.

The next step consisted in getting an idea about what security maturity tasks to implement first for getting the best effect on the MER of the security controls. For doing so, the workload for implementing the security maturity tasks has been estimated. These information were used as input to compute a prioritized action plan by using the ROSMI formula, showing which tasks to implement first to get the best effect on the effectiveness of the ISO/IEC 27002 security controls.

VI. CONCLUSION AND FURTHER WORK

This work demonstrated that the maturity of an implemented ISMS can be used as a key-indicator with which it is possible to assess the effectiveness of security controls.

Increasing the maturity of an ISMS can by itself be seen as a security control that is used to improve the current security level of an organization.

Furthermore, the presented maturity model enables to illustrate the evolution of information security in an organization and can be used as a basis for taking decisions, related to the continuous improvement of an ISMS.

Finally, the elaborated concept that is already part of the risk assessment tool TRICK Service, now has to be applied for further organizations in order to setup an knowledge base with which it will be possible to adapt the MaxEffRates (see Section III.B.2) to the different types of organizations and proof the feasibility of the tasks related to the different SML's. It is planned to prove the concept for critical infrastructures in the context of further research projects.

ACKNOWLEDGMENT

The research leading to these results has received funding from the European Union Seventh Framework Programme (FP7/2007-2013) under grant agreement n° 318003 (TREsPASS). This publication reflects only the author's views and the Union is not liable for any use that may be made of the information contained herein.

REFERENCES

[1] ISO/IEC 27001:2013 Security techniques — Information security management systems — Requirements

[2] Software Engineering Institute, CMMI® for Development, Version 1.3, "Improving processes for developing better products and services", Carnegie Mellon University, 2010.

[3] ISO/IEC 15504-5:2012 Process assessment – Part 5 : An exemplar software life cycle process assessment model

[4] P. Bowen and R. Kissel, National Institute of Standards and Technology. Program Review for Information Security Management Assistance (PRISMA). NISTIR 7358, Gaithersburg, 2007.

[5] SerNet GmbH. verinice. Retrieved March 28, 2016 from http://www.verinice.org

[6] Microsoft Corporation. Microsoft Security Assessment Tool 4.0. Retrieved March 28, 2016 from http://www.microsoft.com

[7] C. Harpes, A. Adelsbach, S. Zatti, and N. Peccia, "Quantitative Risk Assessment with ISAMM on ESA's Operations Data System," In: The 4th ESA International Work-shop on Tracking, Telemetry and Command Systems for Space Applications, 2007.

[8] European Network and Information Security Agency, Inventory of Risk Management / Risk Assessment Tools - TRICK Service. Retrieved April 8, 2016 from, http://www.enisa.europa.eu

[9] European Network and Information Security Agency, "Introduction to Return on Security Investment - Helping CERTs assessing the cost of (lack of) security,". Retreived April 8, 2016 from: http://www.enisa.europa.eu

[10] W. Sonnenreich, J. Albanese, and B. Stout, "Return On Security Investment (ROSI): A Practical Quantitative Model," Journal of Research and Practice in Information Technology, 2006, vol. 38, pp. 45-56

Modeling Vulnerable Internet of Things on SHODAN and CENSYS : An Ontology for Cyber Security

Marc Arnaert
Univ. Nice Sophia Antipolis, I3S, UMR 7271, 06900 Sophia Antipolis, France
CNRS, I3S, UMR 7271, 06900 Sophia Antipolis, France
e-mail: marc@arnaert.com

Yoann Bertrand
Univ. Nice Sophia Antipolis, I3S, UMR 7271, 06900 Sophia Antipolis, France
CNRS, I3S, UMR 7271, 06900 Sophia Antipolis, France
e-mail: bertrand@i3s.unice.fr

Karima Boudaoud
Univ. Nice Sophia Antipolis, I3S, UMR 7271, 06900 Sophia Antipolis, France
CNRS, I3S, UMR 7271, 06900 Sophia Antipolis, France
e-mail: karima@unice.fr

Abstract—**With the increase of connected devices on the Internet, managing security can become a very difficult task for Information Technology (IT) and security managers. In order to find vulnerabilities for these devices, we can use search engines. Despite the fact that these engines are very powerful, they often propose various and complex syntaxes for queries. Moreover, sorting the results, due to their complexity and quantity, can be challenging and time-consuming for IT & security managers. To overcome these issues, we propose in this paper an ontology that can reduce the complexity and improve the results of search engines to help these managers to detect vulnerable devices.**

Keywords-vulnerability; Shodan; Internet of Things; Censys; ontology; cyber security

I. INTRODUCTION

US research firm Gartner has estimated that 20.8 billions objects will be connected on the Internet by 2020 [1]. This tremendous amount of objects, often referred as Internet of Things (IoT), can be problematic for security.

Indeed, in order to be accessible and operational, these objects need to be connected (for instance, video surveillance, telephony, building management systems, air conditioners, automated doors, etc.). Such quantity of devices can leave a potential open door that can be exploited by intruders.
Moreover, IoT components are heterogeneous and often poorly protected, increasing *de facto* the risk of security breaches (for instance, Fiat-Chrysler has recalled 1.4 Million cars to prevent hacks in July 2015) [2].

To secure connected objects within their companies, security experts or employees in charge of defining security policies can gather information in order to build a vulnerability assessment plan and have a better understanding of the weaknesses of the deployed devices.

In other words, an expert wants to answer the following question: *"Is my device vulnerable and accessible by someone else?"*.

To do so, she/he can use specialized search engines available on the Internet. However, due to the increasing quantity, known vulnerabilities and diversity of connected objects, a basic search can return thousands of results. Such quantity of results can be complex to sort, understand and analyze, especially for non-security experts. Thus, this task can be difficult and time-consuming.

In this article, we propose an ontology that models vulnerabilities of IoT objects. Our ontology is based on existing search engines (Shodan and Censys) and aims at:

- Reducing the number of aggregated results during a search.
- Increasing the relevance of results (i.e., returned vulnerabilities).
- Be usable for non-security experts.

By doing so, we aim at reducing the time-consumption and increase the robustness and feasibility of assisted vulnerability assessments in IoT.

The rest of the paper is organized as follows: Section II presents the related works in the domain of security search engine. Section III describes our contribution, while Section IV discusses future works.

II. RELATED WORKS

A. *Online Databases and tools*

At first, the hackers used specialized security tools software to find potential and vulnerable target, like Kali-Linux [6] the most advanced penetration distribution.

In order to gather information for cybersecurity now, online databases and search engines can be used.

Shodan.io is a search engine designed by programmer John Matherly in 2009. It interrogates devices ports and grabs the resulting banners, then indexes the corresponding public IP address and search into an intern databases for futures lookup. Shodan aggregates a significant amount of information (more than 3.7 billion public IPv4 addresses and also checks hundreds of millions of IPv6 addresses).

Many wonderful works can be found on Shodan. These works encompass vulnerability assessment tool [4], reveals magnitude of IoT [5] and usages in industrial context [3].

Censys.io is a search engine designed by Zakir Durumeric in 2015 [7]. It allows researchers to ask questions about what composes the Internet. Censys collects data through daily Zmap scans of more than 3 Billions IP v4 addresses. Researchers can interact with these data through scripts that can be requested thanks to a SQL engine.

However, using Censys or Shodan can lead to the following issues:

- Results can be too numerous to be efficiently interpreted.
- Results can be irrelevant (i.e., outdated, non-specific, incomplete, etc.).
- Both queries and results can be hard to understand and analyze by non-security experts (i.e., you must know different syntaxes to interact with the two engines, you must sort the results to find the corresponding domain devices, you don't know if these devices are vulnerable and if yes, which vulnerabilities).

B. *Security Ontology*

Existing security ontology covers special domains like networks, architectures, cryptography or resilience domains. Few academic works have been proposed to use security ontology with Shodan ([8][9]) and no ontology has been actually published for Censys. None of them cover the semantic security knowledge to easily find vulnerable devices using Shodan or Censys.

Concerning the IoT domain, several specific ontologies have been proposed (i.e., Iot-ontology [10], SAREF [11] or openiot-ontology [12]). Again, none of them contain the semantic knowledge that could be used with Shodan or Censys to find vulnerable IoT devices into specific domain.

In conclusion, by using existing search engines, we need to know the semantic behind the search engine (in our case, Censys and Shodan) and need to be a security expert to find and understand vulnerabilities on these objects.

Moreover, existing search engines suffer from the following drawbacks:

- There is no correlation with CVE (Common Vulnerabilities Exposure) published by CERTs (Computer Emergency Response Team) [5].
- It is complex to achieve cross-domain and interdatabases operations.
- There is no possibility to reuse the results.
- There is no modeling or automated process.
- Errors or omissions can be done due to human interpretation.
- There is an excessive consumption of time to obtain exploitable results with vulnerable objects.

To overcome previous drawbacks, we propose an ontology that is described in the next section.

III. CONTRIBUTION

As stated previously, we first aim at reducing the quantity of results returned by Censys and Shodan. More specifically, we aim at reducing the complexity of semantic of returned results, increase the relevance of vulnerable objects and ease the use of such tools.

A. *Genericity of the proposal*

Although our contribution focuses on these two search-engines, our model has been implemented to be as generic as possible. Thus, our model can be adapted to the preferred search engine of the IT manager (i.e., Google, Bing, etc.). To facilitate this adaptation, we have used the concept of ontology.

B. *Definition of a cybersecurity ontology*

In order to propose a tool able to model this knowledge semantic, we have created an ontology of research and diagnosis. A graphical representation of such mechanism is depicted in Figure 1. This modeling will allow us to: reuse the field of knowledge, facilitate interoperability and portability, use a reasoning engine to bring new knowledge by inferences, add more accurate descriptions of metadata and facilitate its integration and update in an open and flexible way.

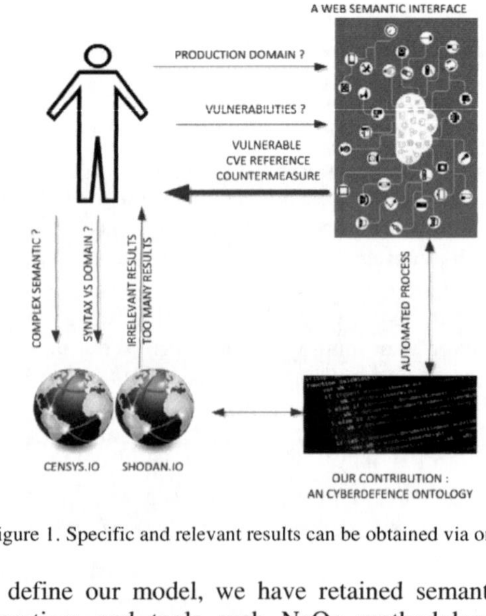

Figure 1. Specific and relevant results can be obtained via ontology.

To define our model, we have retained semantic web best practices and tools such NeOn methodology [13], Linked Data best practices [14].

These works propose methodologies to build well-structured ontologies or datasets from scratch and suggest reusing as much as possible existing works by linking them together.

We have also chosen Stanford's ontology editor 'Protégé 2000' to easily define and improve our ontology. This software is particularly recommended to create a domain ontology [15].

To conclude the main objectives of our work are:

- To create an ontology of research and diagnostic;
- To model a semantic search over Censys or Shodan;
- To include aggregation of existing security vulnerabilities ontologies;
- To validate the syntax of our ontology with W3C (World Wide Web Consortium) tools;
- To evaluate our ontology via standardization tools available on the Internet.

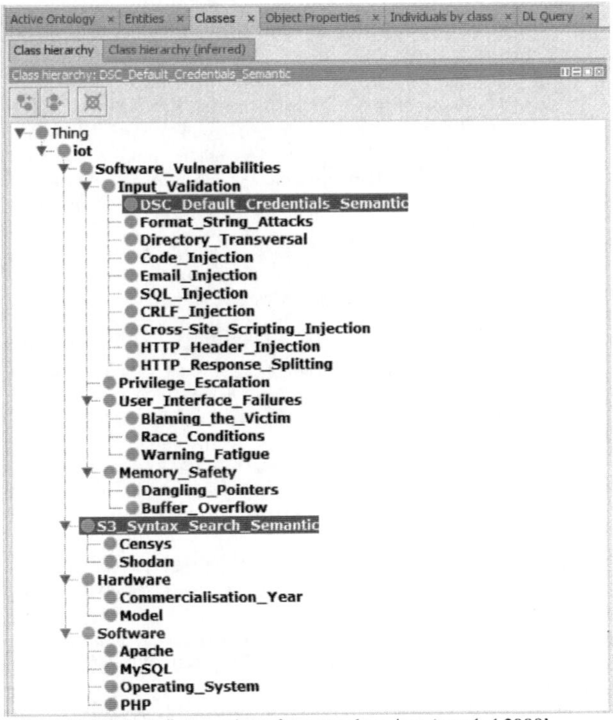

Figure 2. A first version of our ontology into 'protégé 2000'

a) Select semantic for specific domains

To find the semantic related to a specific domain, we have explored publications that define vulnerability semantic [16], projects focusing on Shodan [3], darknet videos [17], deposits of sites (Pastebin), website of published vulnerabilities (db-exploit), and other GoogleDork [18].

The aggregation of these information allowed us to create a primary knowledge base called **S^3 "Syntax Search Semantic"** who can target specific objects in relation to specific research areas. Effectively, using the keywords stored in S^3 in engines such as Censys and Shodan allows users to find the right targeted devices.

b) Select reference vulnerability

In order to test our ontology, we have chosen a reference vulnerability type. For our preliminary tests, we have chosen the *"default credentials"* vulnerability. This vulnerability exploits default logins and passwords. These credentials can easily be found in the manufacturers' documentation that are accessible on the Internet and contain default passwords in clear texts.

Moreover, we have find default credentials lists on the Internet (1000+) and have aggregated them to increase the number of possibilities into our database.
To facilitate our search, we have developed a script that searches documents for specific keywords (i.e., "username", "password", "login", etc.). Thanks to this script, we have generated a database of existing manufacturer's default credentials.

We assume that the person who installed the device has not changed the default password, and we can use it successfully. The advantage of this vulnerability is that it is not iterative and therefore not intrusive and somewhat wordy, in the sense that we do not try repeatedly to penetrate a system. We have created a second database that keeps the *"default credentials"* of associated devices. We will call this second database DCS "Default Credentials Semantic ".

Figure 2, shows a first version of our ontology where S^3 and DCS knowledge can be highlighted to help us to find a field type of vulnerable and assailable IoT device.

c) Validation of S^3 with DCS

We have tested the correlation between S^3 and DCS over Censys. Our ontology will be available on Internet with a specific namespace (URI). It contains S^3 and DCS information. The realization of a first program in Python (both allow on Shodan & Censys), allows us to test our ontology for which the test proves that it is fully functional.

We have obtained at screen a short list of public IP addresses with the open type protocol. Figure 3. shows a textual example of the obtained results. For these preliminary tests, we have validated our proposal by doing a copy/paste of one of the public IP addresses returned into a new browser page. By entering this IP, we have reached the login page of the connected IoT device.

```
CENSYS Request Vulnerable Objects with a research and diagnostic Cyberdefence Ontology
Scientific contribution - Marc ARNAERT -> Tuesday 15th of March 2016 01:07:17 PM

Semantic Search Syntax in Censys.io :
------------------------------------------------------------------
[1] IP: 211.76.13       - Protocol : [u'443/https', u'21/ftp']
[2] IP: 211.21.17        Protocol : [u'80/http', u'995/pop3s', u'25/smtp', u'110/pop3',
[3] IP: 211.21.17        Protocol : [u'80/http', u'443/https', u'21/ftp']
[4] IP: 180.43.28        Protocol : [u'80/http', u'21/ftp']
[5] IP: 202.213.4        Protocol : [u'80/http', u'21/ftp']
[6] IP: 219.103.9        Protocol : [u'80/http', u'21/ftp']
[7] IP: 81.227.90       Protocol : [u'80/http', u'110/pop3', u'21/ftp', u'443/https', u'
[8] IP: 60.249.18        Protocol : [u'80/http']
[9] IP: 106.187.9       - Protocol : [u'80/http', u'22/ssh', u'53/dns']
[10] IP: 210.59.1       - Protocol : [u'80/http']
[11] IP: 210.242.       - Protocol : [u'80/http', u'110/pop3', u'443/https', u'25/smtp',
[12] IP: 59.120.1        - Protocol : [u'80/http', u'110/pop3', u'21/ftp', u'443/https',
[13] IP: 118.99.2       - Protocol : [u'80/http', u'993/imaps', u'995/pop3s', u'25/smtp'
[14] IP: 60.248.1        - Protocol : [u'80/http', u'53/dns']
------------------------------------------------------------------
Number of Vulnerable IOT found : 14
```

Figure 3. Finding Vulnerable Objects in Censys with our application

For these preliminary tests, we have validated our proposal by doing a copy/paste of one of the public IP addresses returned into a new browser page. By entering this IP, we have reached the login page of the connected IoT device.

We have fetched the corresponding login and password in our DCS for this specific device. By entering these credentials, we have obtained a granted access to the full configuration of the IoT device, proving that our solution is quite functional.

In final, we have built a Sparql server [20] and validate basic Sparql queries to obtain the complete list of S^3 and DCS.

IV. FUTURE WORK

In this paper, we have proposed an ontology to obtain more accurate results concerning vulnerable IoT devices, when using search engines such as Censys or Shodan.

For future works, we will create a user-friendly semantic web application that has two goals. The vulnerable domain researching will be unique and user-friendly (i.e., easy to understand and mastered for all types of users). Secondly, the type of vulnerabilities will aim at sorting and obtaining more relevant results.

ACKNOWLEDGMENT

We are extremely grateful to John Matherly for unlimited access to Shodan resources and his precious help and we thank Zakir Durumeric for his wonderful tool Censys.io.

We thank Olivier Corby and Isabelle Mirbel for their help concerning semantic web, Sparql syntaxes and ontologies.

We thank for their inducements, advices and valuable feedbacks Alain Giboin and Frédéric Precioso.

REFERENCES

[1] GARTNER, S. (2015). Gartner Says 6.4 Billion Connected "Things" will be in use in 2016, up 30 Percent from 2015 [interactive].[viewed 2015 m. november 10 d.]. *Access through internet: <http://www. gartner. com/newsroom/id/3165317.*

[2] Miller, C., & Valasek, C. (2015). Remote exploitation of an unaltered passenger vehicle. *Black Hat USA.*

[3] Bodenheim, R., Butts, J., Dunlap, S., & Mullins, B. (2014). Evaluation of the ability of the Shodan search engine to identify Internet-facing industrial control devices. *International Journal of Critical Infrastructure Protection*, *7*(2), 114-123.

[4] Genge, B., & Enăchescu, C. (2015). ShoVAT: Shodan-based vulnerability assessment tool for Internet-facing services. *Security and Communication Networks.*

[5] Radvanovsky, B. (2013). Project shine: 1,000,000 internet-connected scada and ics systems and counting. *Tofino Security, 19.*

[6] Arnaert, M. (2015). Initiating to Ethical Hacking with Kali-Linux. Amazon press.

[7] Durumeric, Z., Wustrow, E., & Halderman, J. A. (2013, August). ZMap: Fast Internet-wide Scanning and Its Security Applications. In *Usenix Security* (Vol. 2013).

[8] Stepanova, T., Pechenkin, A., & Lavrova, D. (2015, September). Ontology-based big data approach to automated penetration testing of large-scale heterogeneous systems. In *Proceedings of the 8th International Conference on Security of Information and Networks* (pp. 142-149). ACM.

[9] Krotofil, M., & Gollmann, D. (2013, July). Industrial control systems security: What is happening?. In *Industrial Informatics (INDIN), 2013 11th IEEE International Conference on* (pp. 670-675). IEEE.

[10] Kotis, K., & Katasonov, A. (2013). Semantic interoperability on the internet of things: The semantic smart gateway framework. *International Journal of Distributed Systems and Technologies (IJDST)*, *4*(3), 47-69.

[11] Daniele, L., den Hartog, F., & Roes, J. (2015). Created in Close Interaction with the Industry: The Smart Appliances REFerence (SAREF) Ontology. In *Formal Ontologies Meet Industry* (pp. 100-112). Springer International Publishing.

[12] Soldatos, J., Kefalakis, N., Hauswirth, M., Serrano, M., Calbimonte, J. P., Riahi, M., ... & Skorin-Kapov, L. (2015). Openiot: Open source internet-of-things in the cloud. In *Interoperability and Open-Source Solutions for the Internet of Things* (pp. 13-25). Springer International Publishing.

[13] Suárez-Figueroa, M. C., Gomez-Perez, A., & Fernandez-Lopez, M. (2012). The NeOn methodology for ontology engineering. In *Ontology engineering in a networked world* (pp. 9-34). Springer Berlin Heidelberg.

[14] Bizer, C., Heath, T., & Berners-Lee, T. (2009). Linked data-the story so far. *Semantic Services, Interoperability and Web Applications: Emerging Concepts*, 205-227.

[15] Noy, N. F., & McGuinness, D. L. (2001). Ontology development 101: A guide to creating your first ontology. *University of Standford.*

[16] Leverett, E. P. (2011). Quantitatively assessing and visualising industrial system attack surfaces. *University of Cambridge, Darwin College.*

[17] Shovgenya, Y., Skopik, F., & Theuerkauf, K. (2015, June). On demand for situational awareness for preventing attacks on the smart grid. In *Cyber Situational Awareness, Data Analytics and Assessment (CyberSA), 2015 International Conference on* (pp. 1-4). IEEE.

[18] Lancor, L., & Workman, R. (2007, March). Using Google hacking to enhance defense strategies. In *ACM SIGCSE Bulletin* (Vol. 39, No. 1, pp. 491-495). ACM.

[19] Cheng, J., Ma, Z. M., & Tong, Q. (2015). RDF Storage and Querying: A Literature Review. *Handbook of Research on Innovative Database Query Processing Techniques*, 460.

[20] Arnaert, M. (2016). Create your own SPARQL web Server for semantic web with DEBIAN & VIRTUOSO. Amazon press.

Energy-aware Security Adaptation in Ubiquitous Mobile Network

Tewfiq El Maliki
Information Technology department hepia, HES-SO
University of Applied Sciences Western Switzerland
Geneva - Switzerland
email:Tewfiq.Elmaliki@hesge.ch

Aïcha Rizzotti-Kaddouri
Haute Ecole Arc Ingénierie he-arc, HES-SO
University of Applied Sciences Western Switzerland
St-Imier – Switzerland
email:Aicha.Rizzotti@he-arc.ch

Abstract — **Data privacy and security are a major concern in any field mainly mobile commerce, Internet of Thing (IoT), and wireless data communication. Classical security is particularly based on encryption to protect data confidentiality, integrity, non repudiation and availability. However, mobile devices are limited in processing, battery life and communication bit rate. Therefore, many security protections are not used in order to save battery life. A new paradigm must be carried out to establish a framework capable to be energy aware when applying a security mechanism. In this paper, we present our Security Adaptation Reference Monitor (SARM). It is based on an autonomic computing security looped system, which fine-tunes security means based on the monitoring of the context including the user environment and energy consumption aspects. Thereafter, we investigate the cost of security and wireless communication related to battery consumption.**

Keywords-framework; autonomic; security adaptation; energy awareness; mobile network

I. INTRODUCTION

As mobile and wireless networks have become increasingly heterogeneous and particularly dynamic, the requirements in terms of security and performance must be addressed in a flexible manner but also in a dynamic way to deal with the evolution of the system in real time according to its context. In addition, the evolution of using smart phones privately and professionally highlights the urgent need of improving security of communication and data.

Currently, mobile phones have become real computers, but unfortunately, with less security. Hence, the existence of multiple flaws such as ease of misuse of resources, total control of communications, especially Short Message, etc.

The increasing number of applications and devices make security more relevant in this field. However, providing security faces challenges because of the severe limitation of CPU utilization related to communications, memory and resources. In fact, security is resources consuming, particularly in wireless Sensor Networks.

We propose a generic Security Adaptation Reference Monitor (SARM) as a compelling solution for this problem. Implementing SARM at each application level is not feasible because the change will interfere in each communication program in each device. The best way to overcome this constraint is to implement SARM in the kernel and consequently having an overall security control. Our work is inspired by the concept of Reference Monitor (RM) that was developed for data access [1].

Thereafter, the basic idea is to integrate SARM, which is an adaptive Security Framework in phones to deal with extremely dynamic security conditions while maximizing performance based on policies, preferences and risks associated with different contexts.

We describe a methodology intended for the use of users or system developers to determine *ab initio* the most suitable adaptive security and access means for different categories of wireless networks. We will also describe some principal resource costs for security and some applications of SARM.

The overall objective of our work is the exploration of SARM to secure transmissions, voice, data of mobiles phone such as Android devices. The principal objective is to use external cryptographic tamper-proof system based on Smart Card (SC) SD, which supports data encryption mechanisms and protected memory.

In Section 2, we survey other related work. Section 3 gives the problem statement, highlighting the motivation of our work then introduces SARM and explains its components and functionalities. Section 4 gives analysis of resource costs for security and explains our experiments. Section 5 addressed simulation implementation to validate SARM. Our simulation results and performance analysis are presented in Section 6 and Section 7 concludes our paper.

II. RELATED WORK

The concept of adaptation security in wireless network is used to mitigate the consequences of a substantial number of runtime threats, when it does not completely eliminate them. Many systems rated at the higher levels of security for data are implemented according to the reference monitor concept. A reference monitor is a concept that has proven to be a useful tool for computer security experts. It is the only effective tool known for describing the abstract requirements of secure system design and implementation.

Reference [2] has proposed an adaptive security application in mobile ad-hoc networks, where network conditions play a role in choosing relevant security mechanisms at runtime.

In Chigan Chunxioo et al.'s paper [3], the authors report that often a highly secure mechanism inevitably consumes a large amount of system resources, which in turn may unintentionally cause a security attack. Consequently, a suitable security service is provisioned in a progressive way to achieve the maximum overall security services against network-performance services throughout the course of Wireless Local Area Network (WLAN) and Sensor networks operation.

Some solutions have already been implemented but they are based on a fixed security scheme and may not be adequate for systems exposed to diverse operating contexts [4] as found in wireless environments and Internet of Things networks.

We can state that current systems either suffer from a number of drawbacks in terms of their overall security capacity and dynamism, or else they are highly specific, addressing a single security issue. Hence with the current setup, total security is far from achievable. We propose a security adaptation Framework for wireless environments, which we call a SARM.

III. MOTIVATION FOR OUR FRAMEWORK

We argue that the spare processing and transmission resources are wasted in mobile environments if security is over-provisioned. Hence, the trade-off between security and performance is essential in the choice of security services. Adaptive security mechanisms are also found in flexible protocol stacks for wireless networks [5], context-aware access control systems [6] and security architectures [7]. This has motivated us for the implementation of a completely reconfigurable architecture [8], which is fundamental to adapt the architecture to the terminal and network variability of the context and particularly in the security field [9]. Seigneur [10] has introduced autonomic security pattern in his security design but only at the authentication level. So, we will use autonomic system to design our framework and take advantage of all the power of it architecture.

A. The system

Three principal components of the autonomic system have been identified in the design of our Framework [11], [12]. These have been extended based on adaptation security architecture.

For the Management unit, we add policies and logs for short- and long-term security or Quality of Service security analysis and monitoring. The block risk, vulnerabilities and performances are based on the risk management module. Risk is in general analyzed as a function of threats and their likelihood, which represents the frequency of hazard [13]. Also, hazard can be broken down into threat and vulnerability components. Each vulnerable element is coupled with an associated safeguard. Finally, risk management is formulated as the maintenance of a set of requirements framed as constraints on the aforementioned factors. If the level of risk falls below a threshold then no action will be taken other than a re-sampling of risk; otherwise, some predefined action will be launched in order to protect assets, and the safeguards related to vulnerabilities will be reviewed. [14]

Policy should be deployed and maintained so as to save time and complexity and make centralized system management more feasible. In addition, risk, performance and vulnerability analysis is a key issue in the Framework because it is responsible for detecting potentially insecure contexts, environments that are potentially wasteful of energy, and/or particularly vulnerable applications. Thus, the analysis could attempt a trade-off between all of these constraints in order to choose an efficient action in the adaptation action to tune the functional unit.

In the end, the functional unit is responsible for selecting adequate security means, like efficient network access. The device will then adapt its security so as to have the most efficient mechanisms. In doing so, the loop will make the communication system more self-managing in terms of security and more accurate in coping with any dynamic changes in context.

This autonomous security Framework is thus well-adapted to react dynamically during runtime, depending on the security parameters and context. In fact, a trade-off between security and performance is also carried out.

We have depicted our generic Framework in Figure 1. It is comprised of two units, which are based on the concept of the reference monitor so as to ensure the security of any network.

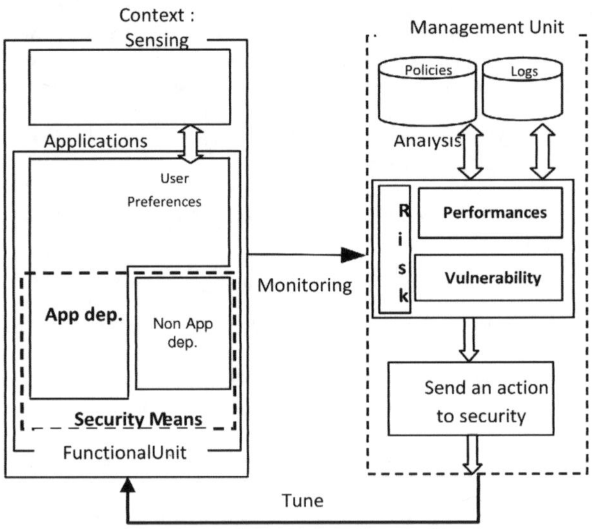

Figure 1. Foundations of our adaptive security Framework

B. Discussion of SARM

The key challenge for SARM is to adapt the Reference Monitor (RM) and autonomic system concepts to wireless communication and beyond, including data access control. The goal of a RM is to enforce security by preventing all processes and users from accessing any data except through the reference itself. The security kernel is managed by security policies.

We have also chosen to apply the autonomic computing security pattern [15] in the design of SARM by dividing it into a functional unit and a monitoring unit. The Framework is adapted to a cross-layer security approach. As a result, the Framework will reduce overheads even at very high levels.

To reduce the system's complexity and to make the system incremental, we propose a feedback loop Framework as introduced in [10] at the authentication level, that is, the system will automatically tune to its best configuration based on its particular monitored context, thus avoiding any static decision making. Hence, the SARM is split into two units looped in a servo control system model in order to fine tune the adequate security measures/means, which we will discuss later. One unit, called the management or monitoring unit, monitors the context by evaluating and analyzing risks, performance, and energy consumption, which are significant for detecting attacks, and tunes the adequate security means using the second module, which is called the functional unit.

C. *Security Means*

As depicted in Figure 2, security means are defined as any algorithm or mechanism that could ensure security but that also has the capacity not to take security action unless it is actually necessary. It also includes the choice of adequate network access, because some network communication technologies are more secure, with higher levels of energy consumption, while others are less secure, with lower levels of energy consumption. Security means can be application-dependent, as in the case of localized trust [16] or distributed trust [17], or application-independent, as with cryptographic protocols. Indeed, localized and distributed forms of trust are good paths to explore because they generate low-computing charges (less energy consumption) and in some cases give better results. Thus they fit the context of Wireless Sensor Network, for example, perfectly.

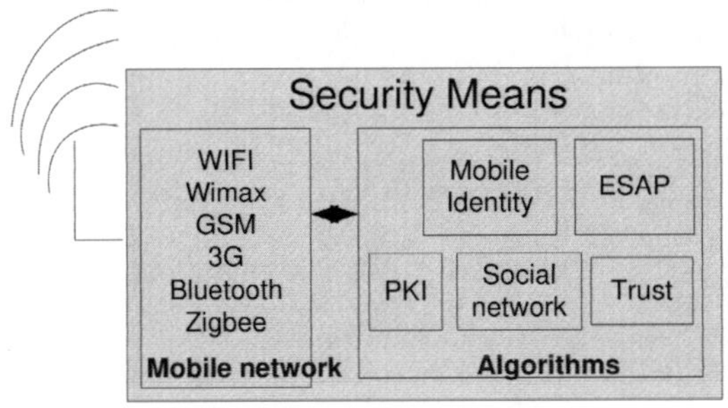

Figure 2. Security Means details

Thus, the analysis could delve into a trade-off between all these constraints to choose an efficient action to tune the functional unit.

IV. Analysis of Resource costs for security

A. *Motivation*

For a long time, security has been treated as a static component in system design, with static security assessment assumed to protect the system throughout its lifetime and assuming that energy is unlimited. However, this assumption does not hold anymore because devices are disconnected from power line and they are in battery mode that has limited live time. Reference [18] declares that Wi-Fi devices consume 30% more energy than normal mode. In [19], we find a complete study of energy consumption in mobile phones and it is proved that a 3G connection consumes from 5 to 10 times more energy than Wi-Fi. In addition, the problem of energy is a key issue in sensor networks and IoT. Therefore, the security cannot be considered without other context aspects especially energy awareness.

B. *Data and telephony*

Data security has become a major concern for all users, particularly for applications in Self-Organization Network field, because they require many security features adapted to their wireless transmission. Different kinds of security mechanisms and strong cryptographic algorithms are available to prevent any violation of data security. Unfortunately, these security capabilities are time and energy consuming. Indeed, certain algorithms and mechanisms are strong enough to protect largely the data but at the same time reduce severely battery lifespan. That is why an adaptable platform for mobile device will save energy and reduce the delay to fit to the limits of a real time range; mainly for telephony application. In this respect, to deploy Voice over IP (VoIP) so that users receive an acceptable level of voice quality, VoIP traffic must be guaranteed certain compensating bandwidth, jitter, and packet loss.

According to G.729 [20], codec requires packet loss far less than **1%** to avoid audible errors. G.114 of International Telecommunication Union [20] specification recommends less than **150 ms** one-way end-to-end delay for high-quality real-time traffic, such as voice; and for Jitter buffers, varying delay, further add to the end-to-end delay, and are usually effective only on delay variations of less than **100 ms**.

Thereby, the delay must be less than 100 ms, which is a significant constraint for mobile device.

C. *Smart Cart*-Secure Digital *(SC-SD) Card*

SC is a card that securely manages and stores information separately from the rest of the device's components. In a SC-SD, man can find security platform delivered through a secure microSD processor. Architecture details are described in Fig. 3. The main objective is to integrate SARM in this smart card to protect voice and data infrastructure, preventing loss or theft of sensible data, vital information and proprietary assets. Another objective aims to increase the awareness of the costs using encryption and access networks.

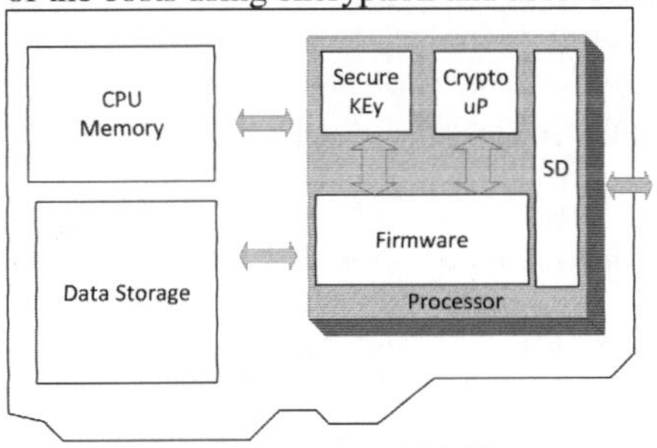

Figure 3. Architecture of SC-SD

D. *Goal of analysis*

The goal of our analysis is to integrate cryptographic algorithms and security mechanisms in SARM in order to implement them in a SC-SD memory card. Thereby, our

SARM means will be chosen perfectly according to context. This will help designers and developers to fit timely the users' preferences and policy in order to have efficiency application and security system. That is why we have carried out experimental measures to compare energy consumption of different algorithms and access networks. Based on the results, we could adapt timely our SARM means to policy and user's preferences. In this respect, we increase the efficiency and validation of the Framework.

Our main goal is to establish a model for the power consumption of phones in many cases to know how to mitigate between security and power consumption in our Framework.

V. ASSUMPTIONS AND EXPERIMENTS

There are three techniques for performance evaluation:

a) Analytical

b) Simulation

c) Measurement

Simulations offer less accuracy than measurements. For this matter, we have previously developed hardware and software to measure energy consumption. That is why we have privileged the measurement instead of analytical or simulation methods. Analytical technique is complicated due to the fact that this method needs more precision and requires more time. We have made several assumptions to limit the scope of the study and also to keep the implementation and complexity reasonable.

TABLE 1. MAIN CHARACTERISTICS OF EXPERIMENTS

Phone	Networks
Galaxy S3; GT9300	WLAN or Cellular network
Android version 4.1.2	803.11g; GSM/UMTS/G4
Battery: 3.8 V; 2100 mAh	Protocols: Data channel (Session Initiation Protocol SIP/RTP); SMS; switched channel, voice PCM G.711 (64 kbit/s)

Further studies are needed to consider an overall evaluation. We use commercially available mobile phones with a SC-SD for the SARM.

A. Metrics and Measurements Methods

Our focus is to determine the impact of cryptographic algorithms and use of different access networks on battery resources. We will explain the methodology of the measurements.

1) Encryption Latency

We will evaluate the latency of some means in SARM, such as identity. The latency is the time to encrypt a block cipher or a file calculated based on a time function.

2) Energy Consumption

To measure the current level, we have developed an electronic card capable to measure a low current level via low precision resistor ($r=50m\Omega$) in series between battery and the mobile phone. The electronic card uses many low noise amplifiers (gain =200) and has an USB interface in order that data will be directly accessed from a PC. The equivalent circuit scheme is shown in Figure 4.

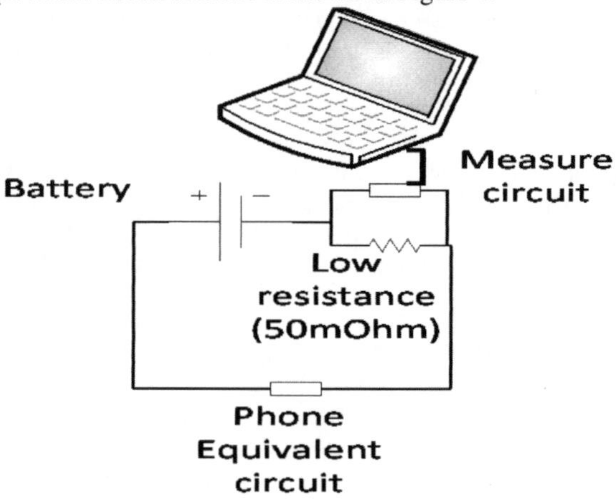

Figure 4- Scheme of experimental energy consumption circuit

The most known problem of battery detection mechanisms was bypassed by using all four battery's connectors; otherwise there will be no power. At the same time, to avoid battery fluctuations we have connected the battery to DC adapter. The time of a single measure is 2500 times by a second. Figure 4 illustrates the details of the experiments. The formulas are only applying Kirchhoff's circuit laws to our circuit. To calculate the power via our method we must: Take the measured voltage via the PC Vpc(t) and divide it by the amplifier gain 200 to have V(t):

$$\mathbf{V(t) = Vpc(t)/200} \quad (1)$$

then apply the equation with V(battery = 3.8)

$$\mathbf{P(t)=U(t).I(t) \approx V.V(t)/r(50m\,\Omega)} \quad (2)$$

Finally, we use (1) and (2) to calculate the power:

$$\mathbf{P(t)= Vpc(t)*0.38} \quad (3)$$

VI. RESULTS AND DISCUSSION

B. Identity management

We have studied all Identity management platforms [21] and we have had a good background in this field as a means in our Framework. We have implemented a test-bed based on WLAN network and mobile phones. The main goal is to know the time consuming difference between a secure and non-secure connection. The results are shown in Figure 5. The requirements of this experience are:

a) E65 telephone

b) WLAN 802.11b, D-link Access Point

c) Tomcat server

d) Security assertion markup language (SAML) [2] Token and Secure Sockets Layer (SSL) connection

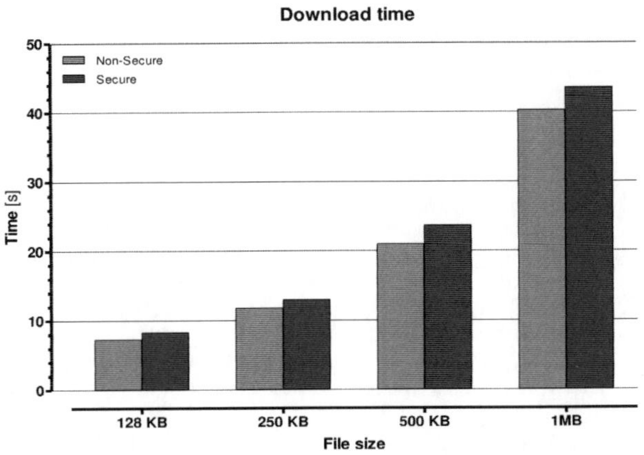

Figure 5. Download time of different files

Figure 5 shows the download time average difference between secure and non-secure for different file sizes. In all cases, the difference between secure and non-secure ranges from 10% to 15%. For each measure, the specific file download is done 30 times. The standard deviation is less than 1.7%.

C. Energy Evaluation

1) Voice Communication energy cost

We have carried out an end to end voice encryption, which is very important to secure in mobile network mainly that any telephony call is not protected at all inside the Global System for Mobile (GSM) network. In Figure 6 we find the network level of our experiment, which contains these elements:

a) Commercially smart card SD for encryption,

b) SIP protocol for signaling,

c) Real Time Protocol RTP for ToIP, and

e) Data channel.

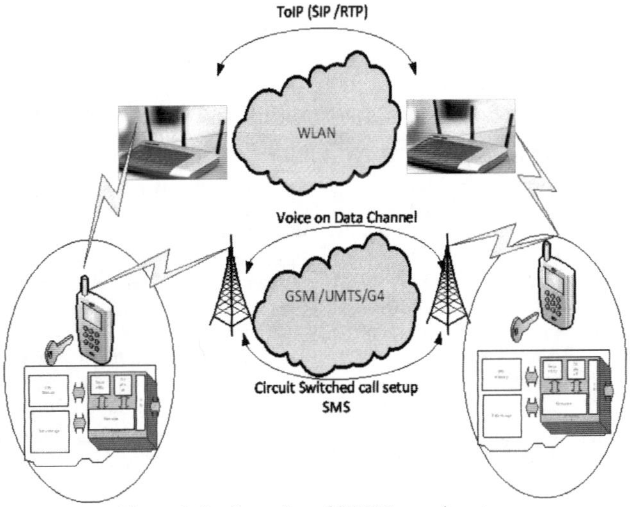

Figure 6: Configuration of SARM experiments

2) Analysis of Results

All energy metrics are based on experiments with Samsung S3 Galaxy. The experiments show power consumption for a voice transmission without and with encryption (Padding and non-Padding). A voice packet is based on 20ms and 64kbit/s, which gives a 160bytes size. Blowfish cipher has the highest encryption energy consuming for 20ms encryption block, which seems to be less efficiently with a small block, because it uses one function to process the entire buffer of plaintext. Figure 7 illustrates that for larger files, Blowfish is more efficient, which is more adequate for voice encryption. Advanced Encryption Standard (AES) is the more energy consuming for long block. However, it is the strongest in terms of cryptographic properties. In all cases, the difference between secure and non-secure ranges from 12% to 20%. Moreover, for each measure, the specific measures are done 30 times. The standard deviation is less than 1%. Therefore, we can state that almost 70% of energy is consumed by transmission and 15% by encryption.

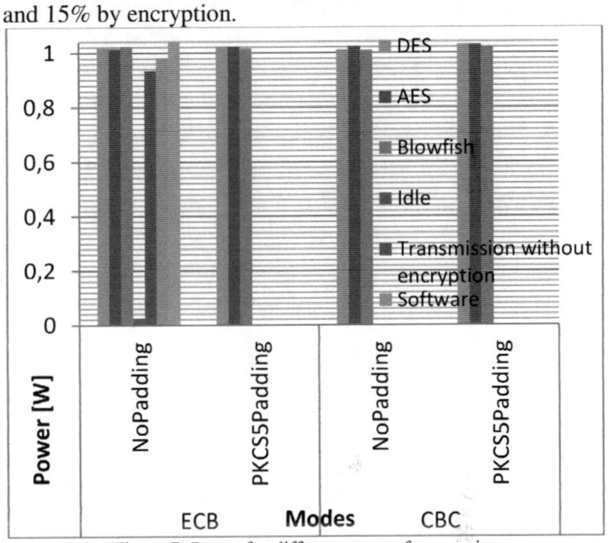

Figure 7. Power for different cases of encryption

3) Access network energy consumption

We must have an overall view about the energy consumption of security utilization in order to tune the best security means and also to choose the best access network depending on the context, user preferences and policies in SARM. That is why we have carried out measurements of energy consumption for Wi-Fi and Bluetooth. The graphs in Fig.8 and Fig.9 show energy consumption (μjoules/Byte). One can see the energy consumption for a file transmission of respectively 100Mbytes over Wi-Fi and 10Mbytes over Bluetooth connections. We have depicted for different distances the average energy consumption, standard deviations (std-dev) and average +2*std-dev -represents 95% of statistical cases-. For short distance -2m line-of-sight-, Wi-Fi energy consumption is higher than Bluetooth. But for higher distances Bluetooth is more energy consuming than Wi-Fi. Please note: The average was carried out over 10 different experiments.

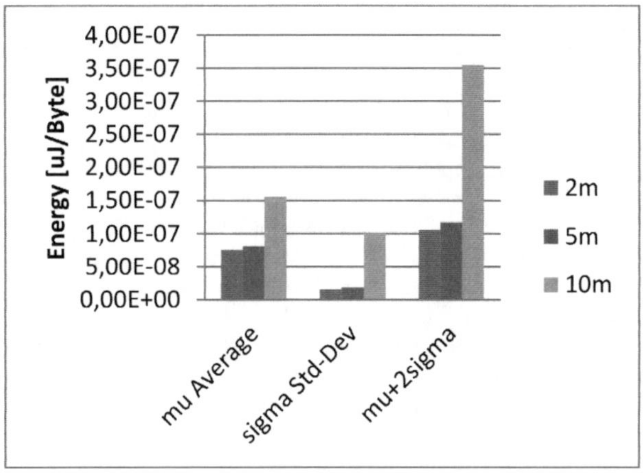

Figure 8. Energy consumption for Wi-Fi 100Mbytes

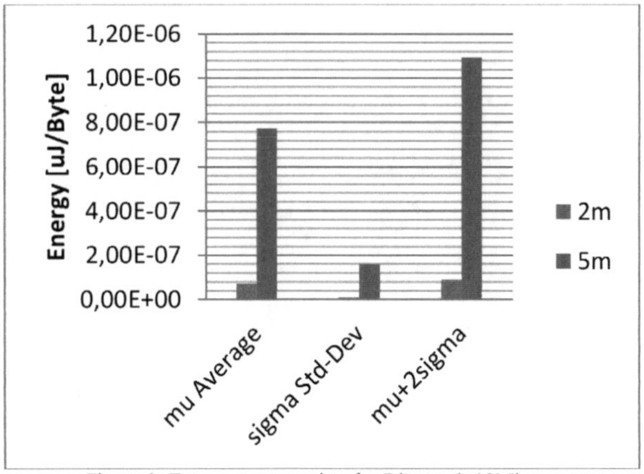

Figure 9. Energy consumption for Bluetooth 10Mbytes

These conclusive and accurate results have been used in one of research projects called iNUIT -Internet of Things and Urban Innovation- [22].

VII. Conclusion and Future Work

The energy consumption is accurately evaluated and is mainly consumed within wireless transmission. These experiments are a foundation for all simulations and evaluations in the future to explore the efficiency of our Framework. Indeed, it gives us a solid background to launch the simulations, of our Framework SARM based on the tuning of the security means related to the accurate energy and access network consumption tradeoffs. Besides, the experiments have given us the opportunity to study a full end-to-end secure telephony connection based also on SARM and SC-SD. Nevertheless, we need further studies of the Framework for real applications, different contexts, and diverse access networks and energy consumption. In short, the proof of concept of SARM was based on implementing it in a tamper resistant security module based on a Secure Digital Card. The results are conclusive and accurate to continue research on efficient energy security adaptation.

References

[1] J. Anderson, "Computer Security Technology Planning," http://seclab.cs.ucdavis.edu/, June, 2016.

[2] C. Chigan, L. Li, and Y. Ye, "Resource-aware Self-adaptive Security Provisioning in Mobile Ad-Hoc Networks," Proc. IEEE Wireless Communications and Networking Conference, 2005, pp.2118–2124.

[3] C. Chigan, Y. Ye and L. Li, "Balancing security against performance in wireless ad-hoc and sensor networks," 60 IEEE Vehicular Technology Conference, USA, 2004, pp.4735-4739.

[4] L. Yuan and G. Qu, "Design Space Exploration for Energy-Efficient Secure Sensor Network," ASAP 2002, pp.88-97.

[5] C. Hager, "Context Aware and Adaptive Security for Wireless Networks," PhD thesis, Virginia Polytechnic Institute and State University, 2004.

[6] M. Lacoste, G. Privat, and F. Ramparany. "Evaluating Confidence in Context for Context-Aware Security," European Conference on Ambient Intelligence (AmI'07), 2007, pp.88-97.

[7] J. Al-Muhtadi, D. Mickunas, and R. Campbell. "A Lightweight Reconfigurable Security Mechanism for 3G/4G Mobile Devices," IEEE Wireless Communications, 9(2):60–65, 2002.

[8] E2R Deliverable D2.2. "Equipment Management Framework for Reconfiguration: Architecture, Interfaces, and Functions," December 2005.

[9] T. Jarboui, M. Lacoste, and P. Wadier, "A Component-Based Policy-Neutral Authorization Architecture," French Conference on Operating Systems (CFSE), 2006.

[10] J.-M. Seigneur, "Trust, Security and Privacy in Global Computing," PhD Thesis, 2005.

[11] T. El Maliki, "Security Adaptation in Highly dynamic wireless", PhD Thesis, Geneva, 2013.

[12] E. D. Sontag, "Mathematical Control Theory: Deterministic Finite Dimensional Systems", Ed. Springer, Jul. 1998.

[13] F. den Braber, T. Dimitrakos, B. A. Gran, K. Stølen, and J. Ø. Aagedal, "Model-based risk management using UML and UP", Issues and Trends of Information Technology Management in Contemporary Organizations, 2002.

[14] A. Gehani, "Performance-sensitive Real-time Risk Management is NP-Hard", Workshop on Foundations of Computer Security affiliated with the 19th IEEE Symposium on Logic in Computer Science (LICS), 2004.

[15] D. M. Chess, C. C. Palmer, and S. R. White, "Security in an autonomic computing environment", IBM Systems Journal, vol. 42, no. 1, pp. 107–118, 2003.

[16] Davis, "A localized trust management scheme for Ad-Hoc networks," in Proceedings of the 3rd International Conference on Networking (ICN '04), March 2004.

[17] X. Titi, T. El Maliki, and J.-M. Seigneur,"Trust-based Hotspot Selection", IADIS International Conference e-Society2010, Portugal. Best Quantitative paper award.

[18] White Paper, "Power Consumption and Energy Efficiency Comparisons of WLAN," Products Atheros Communications, (acceded at: http://www.atheros.com/pt/papers.html), 6/2016.

[19] N. Balasubramanian, A Balasubramanian, and A. Venkataramani, "Energy Consumption in Mobile Phones", IMC'09, 2009.

[20] ITU-T recommendations to find at http://www.itu.int. 6/2016.

[21] T. El Maliki and J.-M. Seigneur: "A Survey of User-centric Identity Management Technologies", Secureware , 2007.

[22] HES-SO, Project iNUIT, to find at http://www.hes-so.ch/data/documents/Brochure-iNuit-web-en-6518. 6/2016.

Security Update and Incident Handling for IoT-devices
A Privacy-Aware Approach

Geir M. Køien

Institute of ICT
University of Agder, Norway
Email: geir.koien@uia.no

***Abstract*—There is a fast-growing number of relatively capable Internet-of-Things (IoT) devices out there. These devices are generally unattended and also relatively vulnerable. The current practice of deploying, and then leaving the devices unattended and unmanaged is not future proof. There is an urgent need for well-defined security update and incident management procedures for these devices. Sensible and secure default settings, as well as built-in privacy must also be included. This is particularly important since the devices are managed by non-professionals. This paper presents an outline of a model to cater to these needs.**

Keywords–Internet-of-Things; Smart home; Incident reporting; Security maintenance; Privacy; Security management.

I. Introduction

A. Background and Motivation

A central assumption in this paper is that IoT devices, whether owned and operated privately or by an organization/company, will be management. The management in question should encompass security functions and sensible privacy setting, and the default settings should be both secure and privacy-respecting. We furthermore assume that the majority of the IoT device owners will be unable to adequately manage and respond to security and privacy requirements.

Web browsers today will quite likely silently install security updates, most operating system will routinely go through security updating procedures as will the smartphone operating system. Some of these require user interaction and consent, while others are fully automated. We postulate that IoT devices will need similar capabilities, and we also believe that these capabilities must be fully autonomous (no user intervention required) since we believe that the largely unattended IoT devices generally cannot rely on user intervention and response.

B. Outline

In this paper, we briefly investigate a class of IoT devices and how these may have full security update management and a minimal security incident and anomaly reporting service. The proposal is still at the modelling stage and the devised model is still work-in-progress. The IoT devices that adhere to our suggested architecture, will feature three information planes:

- User Services Plane (USP)
- User Management Plane (UMP)
- Security Management Plane (SMP)

The services will be realized by a two-tier architecture, separating global and local components, with clear division of authority and assumed trust between them.

The USP and UMP service planes may have cloud-based components, but whatever the case, these planes will have "local" termination with respect to the IoT device. The SMP service will be centralized and "global" in scope.

Privacy is a required property, and our design aim to adhere to the Privacy-by-Design (PbD) [1] tenets. We have therefore taken steps to make the model privacy-aware and privacy respecting, by introducing separation of duties and being particular at what kind of trust is placed in which architectural component/layer.

C. Related Work and Relevant Standards

The field is not yet settled, and the number of papers and proposed standards, of all types, is large and growing. We expect security and privacy to become even more important for IoT in the future

1) Related Work: A few examples.

The survey paper "Security, privacy and trust in Internet of Things: The road ahead" [2] contains a broad overview over the challenges to IoT security. It emphasises that the IoT vision is characterized by heterogeneity, in terms of technologies, usages and application domains. It is also a fast phased and dynamic environment. Traditional security measures still play a large role, but the paper highlights that these are not always complete, sufficient or even appropriate. The authors also point out that scalability and flexibility is essential in this domain.

Another paper which also highlights open issues more than solutions is found in [3]. Also, the authors discusses these and related issues, like vulnerability, threats, intruders and attacks, in [4]. Both papers take a relatively high-level perspective.

In [5], the authors claim that "And as IoT contains three layers: perception layer, transportation layer and application layer, this paper will analyze the security problems of each layer separately and try to find new problems and solutions.". In the end, the authors conclude that IoT devices are more exposed and less capable than other network elements, and that therefore the challenges are both different and more urgent. Trust for IoT devices, both on software and hardware, is discussed in [6].

2) Relevant Standards: There is no shortage of formal standards and industrial standards concerning IoT and security for IoT. The following is an incomplete selected set of standards. There is a bias in the selection towards wireless and cellular communications standards, but this may be well justified as a very large proportion of the IoT devices will have WLAN and/or cellular capabilities built-in.

– 3GPP TS 33.401: 4G Security Architecture

This standard is about the 3GPP 4G security architecture and it encompasses security for the eNodeB (eNB) base (tranceiver) stations (chapter 5.3 in [7]). In a 4G network, to achieve sufficient spatial ($[bit/s]/m^2$) capacity, one needs a densely distributed network of eNB's. There will therefore be a large number of eNB's, and the scenario may be somewhat reminiscent of a managed IoT network. Security for updating and managing the highly distritbuted base stations may be different from many IoT scenarios, but we believe there are many similarities and lessons to be learned here.

– 3GPP TS 33.310: Authentication Framework

This standard [7] specifies, amongst others, roll-out of digital certificates to the 3GPP eNB base stations, using the Certificate Management Protocol (CMP) [8]. This part is highly relevant for IoT devices too, since many of them will indeed be capable of handling asymmetric crypto and digital certificates. Indeed, even the humble SIM card (smart card) is able to do so, and we therefore postulate that this capacity is fully feasible for any IoT device that needs to handle security sensitive data and/or privacy sensitive data. Moore's law also implies that this capacity will only be cheaper over time, and so we fully expect that such capabilities will be commonplace.

– 3GPP TS 33.187: Machine-Type Communications

This standard [9] encompasses security for the so-called Machine-Type Communications (MTC). The standard defines how to allow IoT and machine-to-machine (m2m) devices be connected to a Service Capability Exposure Function (SCEF). Specifically, TS 33.187 requires "integrity protection, replay protection, confidentiality protection and privacy protection for communication between the SCEF and 3GPP Network Entity shall be supported" (Chapter 4.1 in [9]). These aspects are important for all IoT devices and this standard may serve as design input for non-3GPP cases too.

– GSMA CLP.11: IoT Security Guidelines Overview

This document [10] by the GSM Association is a non-binding guidelines document, and is as such not a normative standards document. It may still be quite influential since the GSM Association does have great reach within the community of cellular operators and vendors. The document identifies a set of grand challenges for IoT, and the then proceeds to propose possible solutions. The challenges listed are:

A) Availability
B) Identity
C) Privacy
D) Security

Provisioning of scalable and flexible identifier structures is at the heart of the problem. Similarly, availability and security normally presupposes that the entities (the IoT devices) can be identified. Privacy then adds to this, but presupposing strong security [1] *and* requiring that the long-term identifiers are never exposed in clear (amongst others).

The document pays considerable attention to life-cycle aspects issues. The document also includes a chapter on risk assessment, an aspect which is all too often neglected in standards documents. Would-be IoT system designers are well advised to take this document into consideration. The document seems inspired by the "assumptions must be stated" idea, in a similar vein to the "Prudent Engineering Practice for Cryptographic Protocols" [11] paper. We strongly approve of the need for being explicit about assumptions and conditions.

– NIST: Draft Cyber-Physical Systems (CPS) Framework

The NIST "Framework for Cyber-Physical Systems" document, current in public review draft status, is an ambitious document which is expected to have considerable influence over future products [12].

D. *Paper Layout*

In Section 2, we provide a high-level problem description. This includes the main aspects and high-level requirements. In Section 3, we continue our investigation with a focus on underlying assumptions and premises concerning the devices and the detailed security service needs. In Section 4, we provide an outline of the proposed security management plane model. Here we outline the logical planes, network components and interfaces. In Section 5, we discuss the achievements and in Section 6 we round off with a Summary and Conclusion.

II. High-Level Problem Description

A. *Device Capabilities*

A typical mid-level IoT platform these days would be based on the ARM Cortex family of processors. Here we have the relatively powerful ARM M4 processor (w/floating point and DSP functionality), being both very affordable and surprisingly power efficient [13]. These devices typically sport 32-256KB SRAM memory and up to 1GB flash memory. We assume a device of roughly this capability in our design.

B. *Lightweight, Minimality and Modularity*

The core IoT architecture should be lightweight, including the base protocols. Correctness and efficiency is likely to benefit from this. Basic security and privacy functionality must be included in the core architecture.

Extensibility and additional features will be needed, and this must be designed to be modular. Restraint in adding features is necessary, but is clear that any successful architecture will over time grow more complex and encompass new areas [14]. We advocate a design reminiscent of the microkernel approach to operating systems design [15], in which only a minimal set of functional are at the core, running in supervisor mode, and where other component may be added and where strict rules concerning use of well-defined interfaces and protocols are adhered to. This will, amongst others, facilitate security hardening and it will enable the systems to be deployed on less capable devices.

C. *Connectivity and Exposure*

Commonly the devices will have bluetooth low energy connectivity, WLAN connectivity or even fixed LAN or cellular access. That is, they are reachable over the internet. This also exposes the devices to a whole range of threats, and whenever a device, or a class of devices, gains popularity they are prone to become a target. It is therefore prudent to assume that our IoT devices will, sooner-or-later, become targets.

D. Scalability

Needless to say, any solution that must be able to cope with a large, and fast growing number of devices, must be scalable. That is, the cost model for adding devices/users must be linear and with a low constant factor. The upper limit on the number of devices must be very high as to not prohibit future growth.

E. Explicitness

As a rule, all requirements, including the security and privacy requirements must be explicit. Also, all conditions and premises must be made explicit. Explicitness is also a main lesson from [11] (being essential to Principles 1, 2, 4, 6, 10 and 11 in that paper).

F. Security and Privacy Requirements

Due to the exposure, the devices will need security protection, security supervision and security updating to remove, reduce and mitigate the risks. The devices will need basic capabilities regarding device integrity assurance, and for handling entity authentication, data confidentiality and data integrity.

It is quite likely that the devices will capture, store and transmit privacy sensitive data. We therefore require that a PbD regime should be adhered to [1]. As noted in [16], [17], PbD does not come about all by itself, and considered and careful design, implementation and maintenance is required to create credible privacy solutions.

G. Automation and Autonomy

We cannot expect that the end-users will provide security management for the devices. In fact, the end-user may increasingly be unaware of the presence of the IoT-devices. Effective security management of unattended and highly distributed devices will necessarily have to be automated and autonomous.

H. Challenges

As already mentioned, the GSM Association has recognized four main challenges created by IoT: *availability*, *identity*, *privacy* and *security* [10]. An autonomous security update and incident management system will need to address all these aspects, and provide at least a partial solution to the security aspect. We note that strong security is effectively a prerequisite for availability and privacy.

Trust and trustworthiness are essential elements and even prerequisites for widespread IoT adoption. Trust is a complex matter [6], but suffice to say that credible security management should instill confidence and thereby trust. Trustworthiness is hard to prove, but good security management should provide a measure of assurance.

I. Scope

The proposal made in this paper is an architectural proposal concerning security updating and incident and anomaly reporting. The proposal is, however, not a proposal for a fully fledged architecture, but rather for an architectural component. The proposal may therefore be compatible with other IoT architectures, but may of course also overlap with them or even be at odds with them.

III. Assumptions and Premises

This paper makes a few assumptions about the IoT devices.

A. Internet Connectivity

We assume that the device is connected to the Internet.

B. Hardened OS

The OS is assumed to be hardened. Hardening is also assumed to be carried out when the OS is compiled and built with the program, as is often the case for embedded devices. Unnecessary protocols and services must removed or disabled, and only a minimal set of software be present. A local IPtables firewall may be deployed.

C. Security Capabilities

The devices are assumed to have a trusted platform module (TPM), with basic crypto processing support and secure storage. Preferably, they adhere to standards such as ISO/IEC 11889-1:2015 [18]. A vendor issued device certificate is assumed to be available, or some similar identification that may be used for bootstrapping the CMPv2 protocol [8].

In late 2015, ARM released the ARMv8-M architecture, which is the new baseline Cortex-M architecture [19]. It introduces support for ARM's TrustZone TPM for the Cortex-M processors, and is as such an important step towards credible security for IoT devices. As of yet, there are no commercially available designs, but it is expected that there soon be a plethora of available processors targeted for the security sensitive IoT markets.

D. Power, Processing and Memory Capabilities

The device may have limited capabilities, but we shall assume that the device is not too restricted. That is, we assume it to be roughly at least as powerful as the lower end of the ARM Cortex M3/M4 processor families.

E. Secure Bootloading and Software/Firmware Attestation

A secure bootloader is necessary, and it will likely be using TPM functionality. All software, including firmware and patches, must be signed. All software packages shall have version numbers, and this includes firmware and patches. A TPM may facilitate attestation, but alternatives exists [20].

F. Device Recovery

The device shall feature a secure loader, which facilitates a basic boot strap procedure that can securely rebuild the device software. We expect this to be part of the TPM functionality.

G. Device Identifier

The device must have a unique device identifier. This identifier is assumed to be used in the device certificate, but we shall otherwise be agnostic about the nature of the identifier. The device may also have, or use, higher-layer identifiers, but this is considered outside the scope of this contribution. An example would be a dropbox account identifier.

The device may also have network addresses and cellular identifiers. These *may* uniquely identify the device, but we do not in general consider these to be appropriate for identifying the device (observe the *explicitness* rule).

H. Identifiers and Privacy

A fundamental part of privacy is that there is sensitive data that is linked to a person. If one can break the linkage between the person and the sensitive data, then leakage of the data would not necessarily be (privacy) critical.

We must assume that an intruder will be able to link plaintext device identifiers with the person(s) associated with the device. This capability is after all the core business for enterprises like Google. Consequently, we must assume that the intruder will be able to correlate unprotected data.

It is thus necessary to conceal the permanent device identifier such that no outsider will be able to associate the device identifer with the device or the user/owner. There are several ways to do this, including those described in [21], [22]. The functional split between the global and local services are very much reminiscent of split found in the cellular networks, where the local component necessarily must know the location and where the central component must necessarily know the permanent identity. Here, it has been shown that with proper setup one may achieve both location- and identity privacy [23]. In this paper, we shall ignore the specifics, but we do require that identifier and location privacy is part of the design.

IV. Outline of the Security Management Plane Model

Figure 1 depicts an outline of the Security Management Plane (SMP) model. We have already introduced the logical planes, but shall now take a closer look at how they are arranged. We shall primarily investigate the SMP plane and the associated services.

A. Trust Assumptions and Trust Relationships

We have the following principal entities in our model:

- **USER:** The user and/or owner of the IoT-device.
- **LOCAL:** The local SMP component.
- **GLOBAL** The global (centralized) SMP component.

We assume that the USER is an entity entitled to privacy protection according to the local laws. The GLOBAL entity is assumed to be operated by the IoT device manufacturer or some entity operating on behalf of the device manufacturer. It may also be operated by the software manufacturer. This would be similar to patch update services operated by Microsoft, Google and others.

The LOCAL entity is assumed to be operated by a local entity, perhaps a local branch of the IoT manufacturer or some authority which is legally responsibly, warranties etc., for the IoT devices. It is required that the LOCAL and GLOBAL entities strictly observe the SMP model with regard to information exchange. We have observed that in the post-Snowden era, local authorities have increasingly required critical services to be hosted locally. We therefore have reason to believe that similar requirements may surface for IoT-devices too, or that such services are seen as commercially important to reassure the end-users (building confidence and perceived trustworthiness). We have the following trust assumptions:

- **USER vs. LOCAL**

  The USER trust LOCAL with respect to provided services. This is an asymmetric dependence trust.

- **LOCAL**

  The LOCAL entity must have security trust in the GLOBAL entity. The LOCAL entity shall not trust the GLOBAL entity with respect to USER privacy.
  The LOCAL entity cannot fully trust the USER. The LOCAL entity trust the incident- and anomaly reports, but do not place high significance in individual reports.

- **GLOBAL**

  The GLOBAL entity trust the LOCAL entity with respect to security, but not blindly so. The GLOBAL entity trust the incident- and anomaly reports, mediated by the LOCAL entity, but need not trust any single report and/or report from any single device.

B. The Logical Planes

1) The User Services Plane (USP): USP consists of the data associated with services provided by the IoT-device. We shall not be further concerned with the USP in this paper.

2) The User Management Plane (UMP): UMP consists of the device setup and configuration services provided by the IoT-device. The UMP is specifically about setting up the device end-user functionality. It does not cover basic security or privacy related setup or configuration. The data *may* be privacy sensitive, and the design must reflect this. We shall not be further concerned with the UMP in this paper.

3) The Security Management Plane: The *security management plane* (SMP) is the crux of this paper. It consists of:

- Security setup and configuration
- Security update functionality
- Security incident and anomaly reporting, including local aggregation
- Secure restore functionality
- Identity- and Location Privacy handling

There will be a division of labor:

- Local SMP handling
- Centralized SMP handling

This will facilitate privacy and provide geo-distributed services. Localized processing may easier satisfy national regulatory requirements, while centralized analysis and handling of incidents will provide scalability and efficiency benefits.

C. The Network Components

The division or labor implies a LOCAL component and a centralized GLOBAL component. We observe that the local component will need to have provisions for geographical assurance. Implementation-wise, it will be a matter of policy if there is a need to comply with jurisdictional and regulatory requirements that dictate location of the local SMP handling.

1) The Central/Global SMP Component: The central security update and incident management control function will facilitate both security update production and distribution, and security incident and anomaly analysis.

This function does not need to know the device identifiers, nor does it need to know the associated IoT-device owner or user(s). It may need to know the software version status and any report on incidents and security anomalies associated with

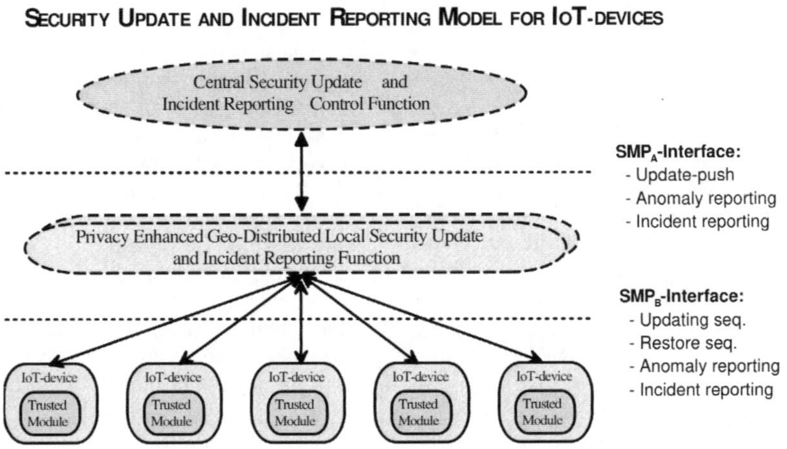

Figure 1. Outline of the Security Management Plane Model.

the devices. For the purpose of the incident analysis, we restrict this function to know the device class and the identity of the local SMP handling component. The true device identifier must never be divulged to the central SMP component.

2) The Local SMP Component: This function handles interactions with the IoT-devices within its geographical coverage area. We expect this area to coincide with regulatory or jurisdictional borders.

The IoT-devices will communicate with the local SMP component. The local component will therefore know both the IP-address and the device identifier. The IP-address may be concealed if one uses Tor services [24], but the device identifier must be known to the local SMP component.

The local SMP component will communicate with the central SMP component, and it will receive protected security patches and software packages from the central SMP component. The local SMP component will aggregate and anonymize incident- and security anomaly reports from the IoT-devices before forwarding them to the central SMP component. The local SMP component may use temporary synthetic alias identifiers for a device, if there is a need for device references. This identifier must never be allowed to become an emergent identifier, and it must be fully de-correlated from the true device identifier. The de-correlation must be complete with respect to the full context given by the message exchange.

D. The SMP-Interfaces

1) The SMP_A-interface: This is a fully authenticated and security protected interface between the local SMP component and the central SMP component, as depicted in Figure 1.

2) The SMP_B-interface: This is a fully authenticated and security protected interface between the IoT-device and the local SMP component, as depicted in Figure 1.

3) Realization: The abstract SMP protocols should be agnostic about the underlying security transport protocol. Suffice to say, that strong security and credible privacy must be assured. The ENISA recommendations for cryptographic protocols, algorithms and key lengths provides good advice in this respect [25], [26]. ENISA is an EU agency, and the recommendation therefore carry some significance.

E. The SMP Services

1) Security Update – Local provisioning: One can have both push and pull mechanisms for security updates, but for IoT devices we do not generally recommend push solutions since it probably require more resources from the device. Push solutions may of course be appropriate for zero-day vulnerabilities, but scheduled pull solutions would likely suffice for patches that are less urgent and less critical. The scheduled pull frequency should reflect the security policy for the particular device class and according to usage, availability, etc.

In either case, signed security updates will be received by the IoT device. All updates must be numbered, and the device will log the date/time and update number before implementing it. The local SMP shall not maintain logs about device status unless required to do so by the IoT device.

2) Security Update – Central provisioning: Whenever a security update patch is produced, the central SMP component will distribute the security update to the local SMP components. We recommend update frequencies to reflect the common vulnerability scoring system (CVSS) [27], although the CVSS system has been criticized for not properly reflect IoT devices [28]. The normal "serious vulnerability" score of 7 may therefore not properly reflect IoT concerns.

3) Incident- and Anomaly Reporting: Security incidents and anomalies are detected and reported by the TPM. This information is used by the SMP components to uncover large scale attacks and emerging attack trends. The ENISA publication [29] provides valuable guidance as to EU regulatory input on incident reporting.

4) Local Incident and Anomaly Reporting: This service will include software status, including patch levels etc. The device identifier is part of the security context, but should not be part of the incident/event report itself. A synthetic referential identifier may be provided by the local SMP.

It may, subject to authorization, be beneficial to store the incident history of the devices at the local SMP. This may allow the local SMP to detect if certain devices are specifically targeted. If so, one may speculate that the IoT device is an advanced persistent threat (APT) target. This in turn may trigger increased supervision and alarms.

5) Central Incident and Anomaly Reporting: The local SMP component will forward incident reports to the central SMP component. The local SMP component shall take steps to replace identifiers, if any, such that the central component never learns the true device identifier behind a reported incident. The local component *may* aggregate certain events and may delay reports to provide further de-correlations.

6) Device Attestation: The IoT device may request attestation services from the local SMP component. This service will need to be based on TPM functionality and permitting the local SMP component to survey the state of the IoT device. It may be part of a forensics service or a device recovery service.

7) Device Recovery: The IoT device may subscribe to recovery services at the local SMP component. As a minimum the local SMP should provide services to restore the device to a pristine condition, with all recent security update patches being implemented.

8) Device Backup: The local SMP component may provide a secure backup procedure, covering all or selected data data elements. The device backup data should be encrypted and protected by the TPM, using unique device specific keys. Only the TPM should be able to restore the backup data.

9) Device Decommissioning: Life cycle considerations implies that one will need an explicit way of clearing all information on the target device. This will in effect clear all data and restore initial factory settings. This procedure must be resilient enough to withstand efforts from ordinary forensic tools to restore the information. The procedure may be triggered by a request via the local SMP component. The TPM should be responsible for carrying out the task.

V. Discussion

This paper describes an outline of an architectural component. Quite a few of the characteristics described below cannot be fully judged on the basis of the outline.

A. Lightweight, Minimality and Modularity

Our architectural component outline is both lightweight and relatively minimal. It is also modular, in the sense that it will build upon basic identifier structures and cryptographic capabilities, and delivers higher-level services.

B. Explicitness

This is related to requirements and conditions, including preconditions and postcondition. Essentially we have a "Mean what you say and say what you mean" situation. Use of formal methods may help verifying that captured requirements are adhered to, but these tools cannot in general help out with the "capturing" part. Explicitness must be enforced in any further development of the architectural component and in any implementation.

C. Scalability and Exposure

The division into a local-global split will facilitate scalability, as well as improving error resilience and thereby improving availability. Exposure is a necessary evil, but conscious design and appropriate use of cryptographic protocols can significantly reduce the unwanted effects of exposure.

D. Security and Privacy

The concrete security mechanisms is not specified in our proposal. Hence, more work is needed here for a concrete realization. However, there is no grand challenge here, only work that must be done precisely and consistently. Identity privacy and unlinkablity is mainly addressed through the local-global functional split. Data privacy is primarily by means of encryption. The requirements for the split is important, and schemes and measures that enforce the split must be encouraged. It would seem prudent to have this as a contractual requirement, and local regulatory requirements may also be an instrument in enforcing the functional split. Still, in the end, there must also be an economical incentive to manage and run both the local and the global infrastructure.

How credible is the privacy?

Clearly, it depends on the split between the local and global component being fully respected. There exists other solutions that would avoid this. These would be *privacy-preserving* and tend to be based on secure-multiparty computation and/or homomorphic cryptography. However, as argued in [30], strong irrevocable encryption may in the end provide less security and privacy. Governments are claimed to act a long the lines of "If we cannot break the crypto for a specific criminal on demand, we will preemptively break it for everybody." [30]. So, privacy must be balanced and possibly revoked, and this is achieved in our proposal.

E. Challenges: Availability, Identity, Privacy and Security

"Identity" is the only aspect that has not been addressed by our proposal. That is, we have identified this as a building block that our proposal depends upon.

F. Scope and Completeness

The scope is limited to a high-level model. Within the scope the proposal is reasonably complete, but there are many parts to be resolved, and the details have not yet been fully worked out.

G. Further Work

The model presented is an architectural component of a security architecture. Further work is needed to fit this component into a complete architecture. In particular, the concrete implementation of the security requirements should be aligned to the use in other areas. This is particularly relevant for identifiers and for basic services such as entity authentication, and integrity and confidentiality services.

Key agreement and key distribution must also be addressed and aligned to the overall security architecture. Preferably, one also wants to have a well-defined, effective and efficient security protocol to be the backbone of the services. As of today, one is often advised to use the Transport Layer Security (TLS) protocol [31] or the IPsec security protocols [32]. However, these are poor choices for IoT, and TLS are also broken [33], [34], and should probably be phased out. That is, a dedicated, effective and efficient privacy-aware security protocol will probably have to be designed for this purpose. This will be a difficult task, but following advise from [11], [25] and applying state of the art tools, it is also clearly doable. Privacy, if it is to be credible, must be strongly aligned and be consistent over the full architecture to avoid leakage of sensitive data.

Smart metering or remote home monitoring would be examples of IoT systems that could benefit from the capabilities of the model. As such they would make good candidates for a pilot implementation to feature the model architecture.

VI. Summary and Conclusions

In this paper, we have identified the need for autonomous security update and incident/anomaly reporting for IoT-devices. In particular, we have addressed relatively capable IoT devices that ordinarily will be unattended devices, very much in line with a significant segment of the smart home devices.

This paper has provided a rough outline of a model in which IoT security update and incident handling is separated from normal user functionality, including user functionality setup and configuration. We believe that this is necessary since security management is becoming too complex to handle for end-users, and that the consequence of not managing security will be too severe. The current deploy-and-forget regime does not play out well for security functionality.

We have also provided a model in which there is a clear distinction between the centralized function and the local function. The main benefits of this arrangement is that one can more easily adhere to local regulatory requirements and one can provide identity- and location privacy solutions. This facilitates unlinkability, which is essential for credible privacy. It also enables scalability, which is ever so important for the IoT domain.

This paper represents an initial investigation of a new model for security update and incident handling for IoT devices. The model is by no means complete as it stands, but we believe that it has great promise for both better and more flexible security update and incident handling, in addition to catering to local regulatory requirements and being able to provide much needed privacy by design features.

References

[1] A. Cavoukian, "Privacy by design; the 7 foundational principles," [retrieved: 06-2016] www.ipc.on.ca/images/Resources/7foundationalprinciples.pdf, 01 2011.

[2] S. Sicari, A. Rizzardi, L. A. Grieco, and A. Coen-Porisini, "Security, privacy and trust in internet of things: The road ahead," Computer Networks, vol. 76, 2015, pp. 146–164.

[3] M. Abomhara and G. M. Køien, "Security and privacy in the internet of things: Current status and open issues," in Privacy and Security in Mobile Systems (PRISMS), 2014 International Conference on. IEEE, 2014, pp. 1–8.

[4] ——, "Cyber security and the internet of things: Vulnerabilities, threats, intruders and attacks," Journal of Cyber Security, vol. 4, 2015, pp. 65–88.

[5] Q. Jing, A. V. Vasilakos, J. Wan, J. Lu, and D. Qiu, "Security of the internet of things: Perspectives and challenges," Wireless Networks, vol. 20, no. 8, 2014, pp. 2481–2501.

[6] G. M. Køien, "Reflections on trust in devices: an informal survey of human trust in an internet-of-things context," Wireless Personal Communications, vol. 61, no. 3, 2011, pp. 495–510.

[7] 3GPP TSG SA3, "3GPP System Architecture Evolution (SAE); Security architecture (Release 13)," 3GPP, TS 33.401, 03 2016.

[8] T. Kause and M. Peylo, "Internet X.509 Public Key Infrastructure – HTTP Transfer for the Certificate Management Protocol (CMP)," IETF, RFC 6712, 09 2012.

[9] 3GPP TSG SA3, "Security aspects of Machine-Type Communications (MTC) and other mobile data applications communications enhancements (Release 13)," 3GPP, TS 33.187, 01 2016.

[10] GSM Association, "IoT Security Guidelines Overview Document; CLP.11, Ver.1," [retrieved: 06-2016] www.gsma.com/connectedliving/wp-content/uploads/2016/02/CLP.11-v1.1.pdf, 02 2016.

[11] M. Abadi and R. Needham, "Prudent engineering practice for cryptographic protocols," IEEE transactions on Software Engineering, vol. 22, no. 1, 1996, pp. 6–15.

[12] Cyber Physical Systems Public Working Group, "DRAFT: Framework for Cyber-Physical Systems," NIST, USA, Public Review Draft v0.8 Framework, 09 2015.

[13] ARM Ltd., "Cortex-M4 Processor," [retrieved: 06-2016] www.arm.com/products/processors/cortex-m/cortex-m4-processor.php, 2016.

[14] G. M. Køien, "Reflections on evolving large-scale security architectures," International Journal on Advances in Security Volume 8, Number 1 & 2, 2015, 2015, pp. 60–78.

[15] A. S. Tanenbaum, "Lessons learned from 30 years of minix," Communications of the ACM, vol. 59, no. 3, 2016, pp. 70–78.

[16] S. Spiekermann, "The challenges of privacy by design," Communications of the ACM, vol. 55, no. 7, 2012, pp. 38–40.

[17] D. Le Métayer, "Privacy by design: a formal framework for the analysis of architectural choices," in Proceedings of the third ACM conference on Data and application security and privacy. ACM, 2013, pp. 95–104.

[18] ISO/IEC, "ISO/IEC 11889-1:2015," ISO, Geneva, Switzerland, Standard 11889-1:2015, 08 2015.

[19] ARM Connected Community., "Whitepaper - ARMv8-M Architecture Technical Overview," [retrieved: 06-2016] https://community.arm.com/docs/DOC-10896, 2015.

[20] F. Armknecht, A.-R. Sadeghi, S. Schulz, and C. Wachsmann, "A security framework for the analysis and design of software attestation," in Proceedings of the 2013 ACM SIGSAC Conference on Computer Communications Security, ser. CCS '13. New York, NY, USA: ACM, 2013, pp. 1–12.

[21] G. M. Køien and V. A. Oleshchuk, Aspects of Personal Privacy in Communications-Problems, Technology and Solutions. River Publishers, 2013.

[22] G. M. Køien, "A privacy enhanced device access protocol for an iot context," Security and Communication Networks, vol. 9, no. 5, 03 2016, pp. 440–450.

[23] ——, "Privacy enhanced cellular access security," in Proceedings of the 4th ACM Workshop on Wireless Security, ser. WiSe '05. New York, NY, USA: ACM, 2005, pp. 57–66.

[24] "The Tor Project," [retrieved: 06-2016] www.torproject.org, 2016.

[25] N. P. Smart, V. Rijmen, M. Stam, B. Warinschi, and G. Watson, "Study on cryptographic protocols," ENISA, Report TP-06-14-085-EN-N, 11 2014.

[26] N. P. Smart et al., "Algorithms, key size and parameters report 2014," ENISA, Report TP-05-14-084-EN-N, 11 2014.

[27] First, "Common vulnerability scoring system, v3," [retrieved: 06-2016] https://www.first.org/cvss, 06 2015.

[28] D. J. Klinedinst, "CVSS and the Internet of Things," SEI Insights, [retrieved: 06-2016] insights.sei.cmu.edu/cert/, 09 2015.

[29] M. Dekker and C. Karsberg, "Technical guidance on the incident reporting in article 13a (ver.2.1)," ENISA, Report, 10 2014.

[30] P.-H. Kamp, "More encryption means less privacy," Commuications of the ACM, vol. 59, no. 4, 04 2016, pp. 40–42.

[31] T. Dierks and E. Rescorla, "The Transport Layer Security (TLS) Protocol; Version 1.2," IETF, RFC 5246, 08 2008.

[32] S. Kent and K. Seo, "Security Architecture for the Internet Protocol," IETF, RFC 4301, 12 2005.

[33] H. Krawczyk, K. G. Paterson, and H. Wee, "On the security of the tls protocol: A systematic analysis," in Advances in Cryptology–CRYPTO 2013. Springer, 2013, pp. 429–448.

[34] C. Hlauschek, M. Gruber, F. Fankhauser, and C. Schanes, "Prying open pandora's box: Kci attacks against tls," in 9th USENIX Workshop on Offensive Technologies (WOOT 15), 2015, pp. 1–15.

Attacker-Parametrised Attack Graphs

Alastair Janse van Rensburg*, Jason R.C. Nurse and Michael Goldsmith

Department of Computer Science, University of Oxford, Oxford, UK
Email: alastair.jansevanrensburg@cs.ox.ac.uk*

***Abstract*—Computer network attackers chain system exploits together to achieve their goals, which range from stealing data to corrupting systems. Attack graphs represent these paths through the network, and provide the basis for calculating many security metrics. In this paper, we seek to extend graph-based analysis from the consideration of single graphs to the consideration of multiple. By performing analysis on many graphs at once, we consider the range of threats faced and avoid the downsides of several current techniques, which focus purely on known and expected attackers. In particular, we propose a novel method of generating a set of attack graphs, parametrised by attacker profiles. Our technique would enable security analysts to consider the security of their network from the perspective of many attackers simultaneously. This contrasts with existing techniques, which typically analyse attacker-independent graphs or graphs constructed around predefined attacker profiles. We analyse the resulting set of graphs first through deterministic methods and then using a probability measure.**

***Keywords*–Attack Graphs; Attacker Profiling; Intrusion Detection.**

I. INTRODUCTION

Attack graphs are a useful tool for network security analysts, facilitating quantitative study of computer network security. The graph acts as a map of the vulnerabilities in the network, revealing how attackers can combine exploits to achieve their goals. Attack graphs are the basis for calculating many security metrics which provide the analyst with practical information [5].

There are many approaches to attack graphs, and one of the most relevant to our work is presented by Dantu *et al.*, who examine attack paths using three attacker profiles [1]. Their approach examines the risk posed to assets from attackers matching each profile, which represent the network's most significant adversaries. Zhang *et al.* use modelling artefacts to capture relationships between exploits, in a manner similar to our method's *capabilities* [9].

Another area of relevance to our work is metrics on graphs. Wang *et al.* emphasise the importance of careful composition of individual metrics, and demonstrate that poor interpretation of metrics can decrease security [8]. Homer *et al.* present a probabilistic method to quantify risk on attack graphs [3]. They observe that assuming attack paths have independent probabilities will most likely not lead to the correct conclusion. They also claim precise that estimates are not required to take action; it is sufficient to be able to class vulnerabilities as "high risk" or "low risk" if, for example, this facilitates patching of "high risk" vulnerabilities first.

The contribution of this paper is towards expanding profiling techniques: generating complete sets of profiles instead of choosing them individually; defining a probability measure to enable a risk-centric analysis; and making these large sets practical by aggregating metrics across them. This paper represents a work-in-progress, and challenges with the current method and potential future work are discussed at the end.

The remainder of this paper is structured as follows: in Section II, we provide context for our approach. Section III introduces our technique. In Section IV, we discuss applications, in particular looking at ways our method can be applied deterministically and probabilistically to provide actionable information to analysts. Finally, in Section V, we reflect on our method, providing a summary of the benefits and challenges.

II. CONTEXT

The precise definition of attack graph varies between authors. With this in mind, our technique aims to avoid being prescriptive – it can be adapted to any typical definition (e.g. [4][7]). For clarity, we choose a definition of attack graph that will be used throughout the paper. Specifically, an *attack graph*, $G = (V, E)$, is a graph consisting of a vertex set V and a (directed) edge multiset E. It may be a multigraph (with multiple edges between the same vertex pair). A simple example graph is presented in Figure 1.

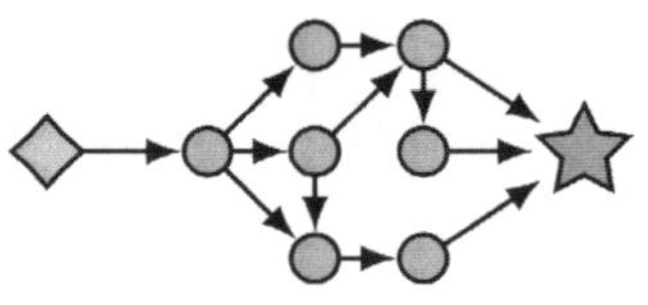

Figure 1. An example attack graph; the initial state is a diamond, the attacker's goal is a red star.

Vertices correspond to states of the network and attacker, and edges correspond to actions that the attacker can take. The attacker seeks to move the network between states, starting from the *initial state* and potentially reaching the *goal*. The presence of an edge indicates a possible action that an attacker could take, but not necessarily an action that they will take. We do not have a strict definition of state – but these typically reflect both the condition of the network and the attacker's access to it. A state might be, for example, that the attacker has root access to a given server, or it might be that a piece of software has been crashed by the attacker.

A. Attacker Profiling

Attacker profiling brings knowledge of the attackers into the modelling process. Network intruders have varying abilities and resources – nation states are likely to have vastly different capabilities to disgruntled ex-employees, who might have subtly different capabilities to those who deface websites. As a result, each attacker has a different set of exploits available to them. Essentially, for each attacker we can derive an individual attack graph, containing only the actions they can perform.

It is impractical, however, to predict precisely the attributes of attackers who will attack the network. Instead, attackers are usually categorised into more general profiles. (This is not necessarily a loss of accuracy; if an exploit requires £500 to perform it is not important whether an attacker has £1,000 available to them or £1,000,000. It is sufficient to know that they have *more than £500*, and so our attacker profile need only contain this fact.)

Existing work uses a variety of methods to decide how these attack profiles are created – typically focused around contributions from experts. The aim is to focus analysis: creating profiles to disregard unlikely exploits and give more attention to exploits that attackers are capable of. To facilitate this, a small number of profiles are designed: Grunske and Joyce illustrate their method with two pre-determined profiles [2]; Dantu *et al.* create three profiles based on a survey [1]. These techniques capture the risk posed by these profiles, but with a loss of generality – it may be true that attackers primarily fall into expected categories, but it is not certain that every attacker will. Additionally, if the wrong profiles are chosen then the analysis will be inaccurate as a result.

Our technique seeks to benefit from attacker profiling without neglecting unexpected attackers. To achieve this, we generate a profile for each possible combination of attributes. We restrict ourselves (for the sake of practicality) to binary facts about the attackers. This, we feel, is justified because the impact on the resulting attack graphs is also binary – either an exploit is possible or it is not; either an edge is present or it is not. Using this large and complete family of profiles we aim to have considered the network's security from the perspective of any possible attacker.

III. Attacker Parametrisation

To perform our technique, we require a well-structured set of attacker profiles, and a map from these attacker profiles to attack graphs. With these, we will be able to move from conclusions about individual graphs (corresponding to individual attackers) to conclusions about the set of graphs (corresponding to all attackers). A well-structured set of attackers allows us to translate observations about the resulting graphs to observations about the underlying structure.

To achieve our method, we first define an **attacker profile** as a set of *capabilities*. Each capability is a property which the profile either has or does not have. Such a capability might be "physical access", representing attackers who can gain physical access to the relevant hardware, or "access to X hacking toolkit", representing attackers who can use a specific piece of software. From a set of n capabilities, we generate a total of 2^n attacker profiles, corresponding to each different combination of capabilities. By defining the profiles in this way, we have a set of profiles which is as complete as possible – every combination of capabilities is represented, regardless of how likely or expected they are. Some of these profiles will be those we expect, possessing some (but not all) the capabilities. Others will represent much less plausible attackers; one profile has every capability, one has no capabilities at all.

To utilise the profiles, we use a **base attack graph**. This is the attack graph generated through standard methods, without of consideration of the attackers. We then augment this graph by assigning each edge a condition on profiles. These conditions represent the ability to perform the corresponding attack. A condition could be "does the profile have capability X?", but they do not need to be simple – a complex condition could require multiple capabilities: "does the profile have X, or Y and Z?". For example, pressing a hardware reset button on a piece of equipment would require physical access, so the corresponding edge might have the condition "does the profile have the *physical access* capability?".

We then prune the base attack graph with respect to a profile in order to create an **attacker-profile graph**. This graph corresponds to only the attacks of which the profile is capable. To perform the pruning, we simply remove all edges whose conditions are not satisfied by the profile. We can create such a graph for each possible profile (i.e., each possible combination of capabilities). Consequently, we have converted a base attack graph and a collection of capabilities into a complete set of attacker-profile graphs. Each graph in this set represents how our network appears from the perspective of an attacker with a particular set of capabilities. This is illustrated in Figure 2.

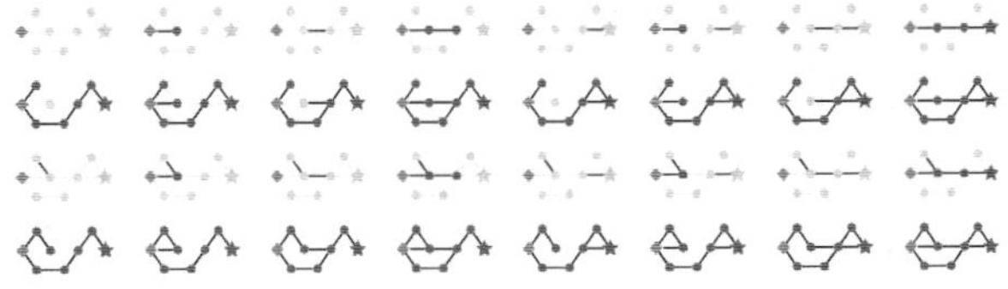

Figure 2. The attacker-profile graphs drawn out for each profile, corresponding to the example in Figure 3.

Formally, we will let C denote the set of all capabilities. An attacker profile is then a subset of C, containing the capabilities of the profile. An attacker-profile graph for the profile $A \subseteq C$ will be denoted G_A. This is the graph that contains only edges whose condition is satisfied by the profile A. We will also use μ to denote a metric on attack graphs, so that $\mu(G) \in \mathbb{R}$, for an attack graph G. For example, μ could be the number of paths from the initial state to a given goal vertex.

IV. Application of the Approach

Using every possible attacker-profile graph ensures the analysis is general. However, considering a large number of profiles requires special techniques, as it is impractical to individually examine each graph. Analysis of a single attacker-profile graph may be beneficial, and standard techniques can be applied to these. However, the key benefits of our method will be gained when analysts are able to consider every graph simultaneously, minimising the additional work while still treating every attack profile separately for as much of the process as possible. To this end, we first explore key properties of the set that may be useful to analysts. We then investigate the effect of defining a probability measure on the set of capabilities, which will enable a risk-centric examination.

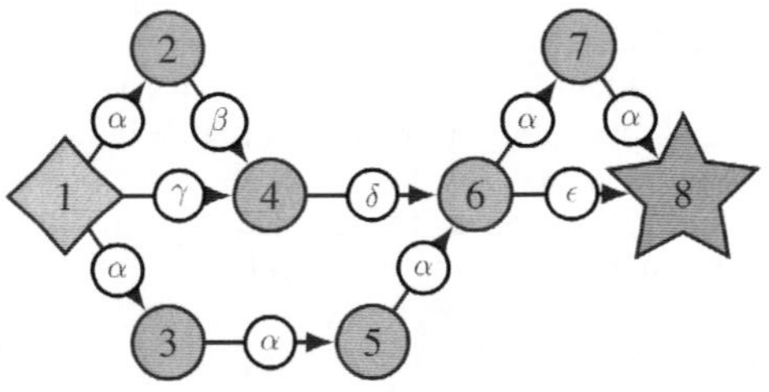

Figure 3. An attack graph, each edge labelled with a single capability that is sufficient and necessary to perform that edge. Vertex v_i is labelled i.

To illustrate the following techniques and to demonstrate them, we will refer to the example attack graph in Figure 3, in which each edge has been labelled with the capability from the set $\{\alpha, \beta, \gamma, \delta, \epsilon\}$ that (alone) enables it (i.e., each edge has the condition "does the profile have capability X?", where X is the label in the corresponding white circle on the graph).

A. Deterministic Analysis

Security analysts may be interested in how well their network is defended against different combinations of capabilities. Which sets of capabilities (there may be multiple) are sufficient to reach the goal? Which capabilities are necessary? By determining these, analysts can examine which capabilities they need to concern themselves with the most. If it is discovered that physical access is necessary to reach the goal, then they may be well-advised to increase their protection of physical systems. Conversely, if physical access is not necessary nor in any of the sufficient sets then it may be that their efforts are better focused elsewhere.

In the example, $\{\alpha\}$ is a sufficient set: an attacker with this capability would be able to reach the goal. From a network-defence standpoint this may be a concern is a sufficient set – attackers need only one capability to reach the goal. This would be of particular concern if α is a simple capability (e.g., access to a common piece of hacking software), but may be of less concern if α is an unusual capability or one that can perhaps be controlled (e.g., physical access to a server room).

This can be generalised to looking at vertices other than the goal node. For a vertex $v \in V(G)$ we can define $n(v)$ to be the set of necessary capabilities that an attacker must have in order to reach the vertex v. If an attacker had been detected (through, for example, an Intrusion Detection System) as having reached a set of states $\{v_1, v_2, \cdots v_k\}$ then it can be inferred that they have, at least, the capability set $\bigcup_{i \in [k]} n(v_i)$. Subsequent decisions on how to react to the attack, or where else the attacker might have reached, can be informed by this. Any state for which this capability set is sufficient to access is a target which the attacker has shown they have the ability to reach.

Relating this again to our example above, we can see that $n(v_2) = \{\alpha\}$ (v_2 is labelled simply as "2" in Figure 3). This, together with the fact that $\{\alpha\}$ is a sufficient set for the goal, implies that an attacker who is detected at v_2 has the capability to reach the goal. Even if the system is only capable of detecting attackers reaching v_2 and not the other states, then a detection at v_2 is a suggestion that the attacker may have also reached the goal, as they have demonstrated the capability to do so. This could act as an early warning when reacting to live events – especially if an attacker demonstrates unusual capabilities early in their intrusion.

B. Probabilistic Analysis

Many existing attack graph techniques use probability to capture the uncertainty in predicting the attributes of attackers. We define a probability measure, $\mathbb{P}$, on the set of attack profiles, weighting the profiles according to the likelihood that an attacker matches them. For a profile $A \subseteq C$, $\mathbb{P}[\{A\}]$ is the probability that an attacker has the capabilities in profile A (and no other capabilities). $\mathbb{P}[\{B \cup \{\alpha\} : B \in \mathcal{P}(C)\}]$ is the probability that an attacker has, at minimum, the capability α.

For the example, we will assume that each capability has a probability of $\frac{1}{2}$, and that each capability is independent of the others. From this, we can derive the probability of each profile – in this example, we see that each profile has the same probability, $2^{-5} = \frac{1}{32}$.

By assigning probabilities to profiles we capture some dependencies between exploits. Compare the two paths to the goal $v_1 \to v_4 \to v_6 \to v_8$ and $v_1 \to v_3 \to v_5 \to v_6 \to v_7 \to v_8$. The first path consists of 3 actions (or edges) and the second path consists of 5. If independent probabilities were assigned directly to edges, this would imply that the probability that an attacker can successfully perform the first path is $\frac{1}{8}$ and the second path is $\frac{1}{32}$ – leading to the conclusion that the first path is the more likely. However, by assigning probabilities to profiles we see that in fact all the actions in the second path are similar; an attacker who can perform one of the attacks can perform the rest. As a result, they all require the same capability and so the probability that an attacker can perform the entire path is the probability that an attacker has that capability: $\frac{1}{2}$. By factoring in this additional information we reach a contradictory (but more accurate) conclusion: the second path is, in fact, more likely despite being longer.

Using the probability measure we are able to generalise any metric on a single attack graph to being a metric on the whole set of attack graphs. Let μ be a metric that maps a graph to a number, representing some property of the graph. Then we can extend μ to the set of graphs by taking its expectation. If the probabilities and capabilities are accurate, this gives a much more representative value than applying the metric to the base attack graph directly. Indeed, the base attack graph assumes the worst-case scenario: it assumes every attacker has every capability. By splitting the attackers into profiles and applying the metric to each profile, we capture interactions between different profiles and exploits. By weighting them with the probability measure and aggregating them, we create a risk-centric summary of the metric.

One metric we can apply to our example is the *number of paths*, that is, we let μ_1 be the number of paths that exist from the initial state v_1 to the goal state v_8. For the base graph, $\mu_1(G) = 6$. In contrast, $\mathbb{E}[\mu_1(G_.)] \approx 1.19$, a considerably lower value. This is because the vast majority of attackers do not have every capability. By treating each profile separately and then combining the results of the metric, we get a much more reasonable answer – the expected number of paths an attacker has to the goal is about 1.19. This is a much more meaningful (and potentially reassuring) statement than the conclusion that any attacker can choose from 6 paths to the goal, which the base attack graph might suggest.

We can also define metrics that are not particularly useful on individual graphs but aggregate to give useful results. For instance, we define μ_2 to be 1 if there is any path to the goal and 0 otherwise. Unsurprisingly $\mu_2(G) = 1$, telling us that, for the profile with every capability, there is at least one path to the goal. On the other hand, $\mathbb{E}[\mu_2(G_.)] \approx 0.56$, which indicates that about 44% of attackers have no path to the goal. Such a value might be useful when evaluating the security of two possible network configurations.

Modelling each profile with a separate graph enables us to look at properties which depend on the whole graph. It may be the case that the system administrators are able to fix some small set of exploits, but not all of them (it could be too cost prohibitive, or impact usability too much). Attack graphs provide an excellent basis for making this decision; the graph shows the consequences of each exploit and demonstrates the impact of removing it. However, using a base attack graph for this decision is equivalent to making your decision solely around attackers with every capability. Through our method, we can make this decision to target as many attackers (weighted by probability) as possible. As a result, the exploits removed will lead to the greatest reduction in risk.

In the example, removing the edge from $v_4 \rightarrow v_6$ appears to have the most benefit to the base attack graph. It removes the shortest path, and can only be circumvented by the comparatively long route $v_1 \rightarrow v_3 \rightarrow v_5 \rightarrow v_6$. The *number of paths* metric supports this: removing $v_4 \rightarrow v_6$ has the greatest effect, lowering the metric from 6 to 2 – the next-best removal only lowers the metric to 3. If we use the *expected* number of paths instead, we see that removing edge $v_4 \rightarrow v_6$ does lower the metric to 0.75, an improvement on the original 1.19. But this is not the optimal edge removal: removing $v_5 \rightarrow v_6$ lowers the expectation even further to 0.44. This is because attackers only use edge $v_4 \rightarrow v_6$ when they also have other capabilities (a successful attack via this edge requires γ or both α and β to reach the edge, and then α or ϵ to reach the goal). So its removal has significant impact for the few attackers with many capabilities, but little or no impact for the majority. Conversely, removing $v_5 \rightarrow v_6$ prevents the most likely attack path, and has the greatest impact for typical attackers.

V. CONCLUSION AND FUTURE WORK

In this paper, we proposed an extension of existing attacker-profiling techniques on attack graphs. Our method improves on existing methods by constructing profiles from a set of capabilities, resulting in a complete collection of profiles for analysis, providing a more rounded consideration of attackers.

A. Contribution and Summary of Benefits

Our method has two main improvements over existing techniques. Firstly, we model each profile with its own attack graph, giving us a conclusion based only on attacks from that profile. These conclusions are then aggregated to give an overall picture of the network. In this way, we avoid conflating attacker profiles and over- or underestimating attackers.

Secondly, we define profiles as collections of capabilities and generate a complete set of profile. This ensures analysis is not only about expected attackers. We use flexible definitions of *capabilities* to allow analysts to model attackers in as much (or as little) detail as required. Considering attackers in terms of their capabilities leads to useful statements about these capabilities. Necessary or sufficient capability sets provide information to analysts which can aid them both when designing and evaluating networks, and when reacting to live incidents.

We avoid complex probability assignments by shifting probabilities from edges to capabilities. In particular, we do not require many large conditional probability tables, as in Bayesian Attack Graphs [6]. The number of capabilities is also much smaller than the number of edges, meaning fewer probability assignments must be made. A typical attack graph could have hundreds or thousands of edges [4], but could be modelled with far fewer capabilities. By assigning probabilities to a smaller set we make it feasible for analysts to spend more time on each value and consider each dependency. Capability probabilities may also be reusable between different networks and potentially even between similar organisations. This would result in significant reductions to the work required.

As demonstrated above, applying metrics to the base attack graph assumes the worst-case scenario. While this evaluation is useful, an expectation-based method gives more realistic results, factoring in knowledge about the attacker to provide a risk-based summary of the network. Our method allows the extension of any metric on individual graphs, enabling use of the substantial existing work on attack graph metrics.

B. Challenges for Future Work

Future work in this area will seek to address several key challenges: Firstly, it is not yet clear how best to build capability sets. These are crucial for successful application, so a framework for finding them would be greatly beneficial. It is expected that this process could be supported by automated techniques, or by shareable and reusable templates.

Secondly, it is not straightforward to assign probabilities. In any probability-based attack graph, considerable effort must be applied to assign probabilities. This is particularly true when dependencies between values are considered. We believe our method alleviates this difficulty by reducing the number of required assignments (other methods require thousands of edges to have assigned probabilities, while our method only requires them for capabilities). However, this is still a challenge which could be improved with further work.

Thirdly, as our method is still at an early point, we have not undertaken testing to validate results. We do not believe our method will have significant computational overhead, but it may require additional effort from experts compared to some existing methods.

REFERENCES

[1] R. Dantu, P. Kolan, and J. Cangussu, "Network risk management using attacker profiling," *Security and Communication Networks*, vol. 2, no. 1, pp. 83–96, Jan. 2009. [Online]. Available: http://doi.wiley.com/10.1002/sec.58

[2] L. Grunske and D. Joyce, "Quantitative risk-based security prediction for component-based systems with explicitly modeled attack profiles," *Journal of Systems and Software*, vol. 81, no. 8, pp. 1327–1345, Aug. 2008. [Online]. Available: http://linkinghub.elsevier.com/retrieve/pii/S0164121207003056

[3] J. Homer, X. Ou, and D. Schmidt, "A sound and practical approach to quantifying security risk in enterprise networks," *Kansas State University Technical Report*, pp. 1–15, 2009.

[4] S. Noel and S. Jajodia, "Managing attack graph complexity through visual hierarchical aggregation," in *Proceedings of the 2004 ACM workshop on Visualization and data mining for computer security*. ACM, 2004, pp. 109–118. [Online]. Available: http://dl.acm.org/citation.cfm?id=1029225

[5] ——, "Metrics suite for network attack graph analytics," in *Proceedings of the 9th Annual Cyber and Information Security Research Conference*. ACM, 2014, pp. 5–8. [Online]. Available: http://dl.acm.org/citation.cfm?id=2602117

[6] N. Poolsappasit, R. Dewri, and I. Ray, "Dynamic Security Risk Management Using Bayesian Attack Graphs," *IEEE Transactions on Dependable and Secure Computing*, vol. 9, no. 1, pp. 61–74, Jan. 2012.

[7] L. Wang, A. Liu, and S. Jajodia, "Using attack graphs for correlating, hypothesizing, and predicting intrusion alerts," *Computer Communications*, vol. 29, no. 15, pp. 2917–2933, Sep. 2006. [Online]. Available: http://linkinghub.elsevier.com/retrieve/pii/S014036640600137X

[8] L. Wang, A. Singhal, and S. Jajodia, "Toward measuring network security using attack graphs," in *Proceedings of the 2007 ACM workshop on Quality of protection*. ACM, 2007, pp. 49–54. [Online]. Available: http://dl.acm.org/citation.cfm?id=1314273

[9] S. Zhang, X. Ou, A. Singhal, and J. Homer, "An empirical study of a vulnerability metric aggregation method," DTIC Document, Tech. Rep., 2011.

Study on Dual Data Structure in Enterprise Information Security Architecture

Mikio Suzuki
President of eVan TEC, Ltd.
Tokyo, Japan
e-mail: mikioszk@evan-tec.com

Fumihiro Kubota
eVan TEC, Ltd.
Tokyo, Japan
e-mail: fkubota@evan-tec.com

***Abstract*— Security Operation Center is known as a centralized team within the organization working against critical cyber threat by mainly analyzing logs. This paper points out the duality of information on Security Operation Center and proposes several issues according to its new security scheme and also raised awareness to protect confidential business information and employees' rights of privacy.**

Keywords*—*Security Operation Center; logs; Dual Data Structure; Information Security Policy.

I. Introduction

An increase in sophisticated cyber attacks seems to be all over the world. The essential cause of this fact is that the Internet is open and free. Although this aspect brings great advantages in our highly informed society, it causes the threat of cyber attacks. Security Operation Center (SOC) specializes in investigating cyber attacks by analyzing logs [1]. Security Information Event Management (SIEM) is a related technology for analyzing logs automatically [2]. In other words, analyzing the logs is essential to make counter strategies against cyber attacks. However, the results of analyzing of logs include not only cyber attack data, but also confidential business intelligence and private information. This paper points out the recognition of dual data structure in data flow of SOC and the necessity of developing an information security policy on SOC.

II. Data Structure

A. Dual data structure on the information security

To study the data flow in an enterprise computer system, we consider the Enterprise Architecture (EA), which is a methodology or a guideline for entities in an enterprise to normalize information and optimize business strategies [3]. Then, we study the data flow among the entities which compose the EA. As depicted in Fig. 1, data flow between entities is an objective of our study. Business process causes data flows between entities. At the same time, the result of observing or monitoring the data by SOC includes business data flow as well as intelligence data or private data. In this study, we refer to this fact as "dual data structure".

Let us take an example to understand the duality of data mentioned above. One might easily recognize that most of the log data might be business relating data. However, very small combinations of log data, very difficult to find, might possibly be related to cyber attacks, although each log does not indicate the illegal action. This means the log data has another aspect of information relating to business intelligence as well as cyber attack information.

Data confidentiality should be classified into three ranks (High, Middle, and Low) in designing of an information security policy [4]. It seems that the low rank data takes a low risk; however, it might be reclassified into a high risk data after being analyzed by SOC. This implies low rank data cannot be assumed as low risk data without analyzing.

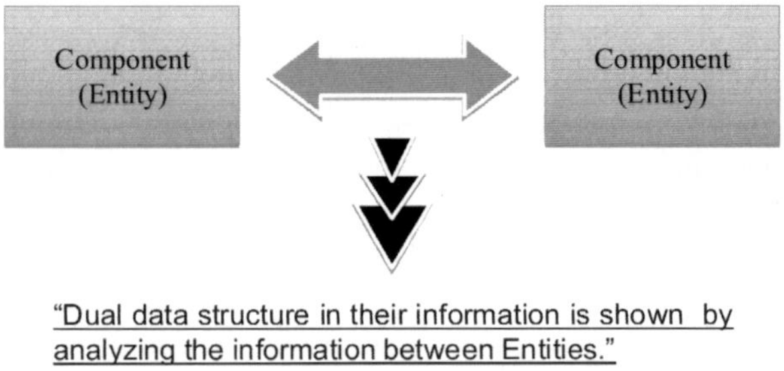

Figure 1. Dual Data Structurer generated by two entities

B. Several effects on the information security caused by Dual Data Structure

Dual Data Structure changes several aspects in information security architecture as follows.

1) Dual Data Structure in SOC changes Reference Monitor Model (RM)

In designing SOC and the related RM concept [5], technical qualification needs to be reconsidered as an essential security model. In Fig. 2, the log database is produced by each monitoring log data and, after analyzing the log database, new confidential information will emerge. It indicates that security requirements have to focus on the issue of dual data structure when building SOC scheme as well.

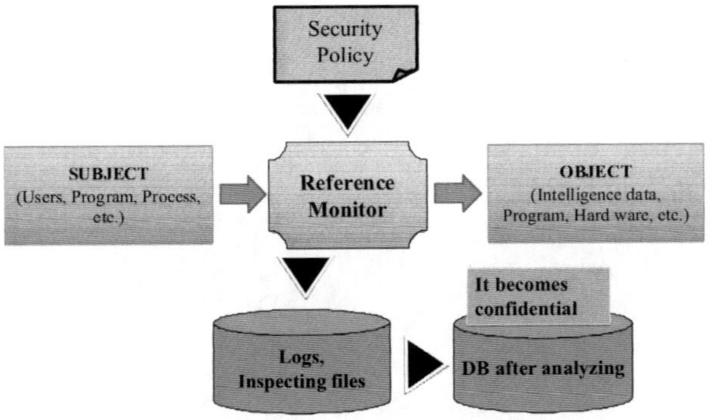

Figure 2. Information Reference Model [4].

2) Dual Data Structure in SOC relating privacy

The basic structure of log data contains the user information, such as, ID information, or name, time, subject, object and behavior as depicted in Fig. 3. This issue should be under the privacy impact assessment [5] and Tokenization or Anonymous is also under the consideration to be introduced into the log data structure.

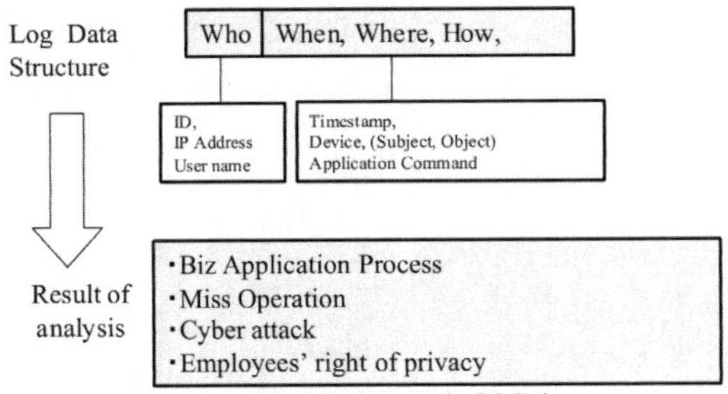

Figure 3. Dual Data Strucuture in SOC data.

C. Understanding Dual Data Structure

To understand the essential meaning of Dual Data Structure, we suppose the concept of "Unknown unknowns" [6]. Critical targets of SOC are "Unknowns". They are almost impossible to identify. In other words, under the condition of "unknown unknowns", SOC is working on daily missions to analyze unknowns of cyber attacks.

Professionals of Information Security in SOC should transfer the status "Unknown unknowns" to the status "Unknown known". This means that they present the actual attack evidence from the results of SIEM by their experience or the outside information, and transfer findings to managerial persons of the enterprise. In case of both outside or inside SOC analyzing log data which belongs to an enterprise, a professional has the responsibility to analyze the results.

D. The issue of security policy relating to SOC

We have studied several aspects of data relating to SOC in terms of RM, privacy rights. Further discussions about information security policy related to duality are as follows.

1) Data handling policy of DB based on log data

Those data should be kept in highly confidential status and integrity of the data should be kept safe.

2) Review of Privacy impact assessment

Privacy impact analysis should be studied in design stage of SOC as well as operational stage.

3) Outsourcing of SOC work

Review the risk of outsourcing of SOC taking into account the duality of SOC data. We would like to suggest that outsourcing of SOC work had better be avoided.

III. CONCLUSION

This paper points out a duality in EA data. From the comprehensive thoughts, it is concluded that recognition of dual data structure and necessity of developing information security policy regarding SOC must be argued.

This idea contribution raised the importance to consider the dual aspect in information security. The followings are expected for further study.

1) Information security policy of SOC

To the best knowledge of the authors, there is no security policy relating to SOC which is taking duality into account.

2) Advanced analyzing logs in duality

Maching learning is the new trend in analyzing logs. Duality in the result of analyzing logs must be governed by the above information security policy.

REFERENCES

[1] Barbara A Nadel, "Building security: handbook for architectural planning and design", McGraw-Hill, 2004, p.220.

[2] David R. Miller, Shon Harris, Alan Harper, Stephen VanDyke, and Chris Blask "Security information and event management implementation" McGraw-Hill Education; 2010

[3] Col Perks, and Tony Beberidge, "Guide to enterprise IT architecture" Springer-Verlag New Yourk, Inc., 2003.

[4] US Department of defense, "Trusted computer system evauation criteria (TCSEC)", DoD 5200.28-STD, December 26, 1985.

[5] CISSP® Common body of knowledge review, "Security architecture & design domain" Version 5.10, P.65.

[6] David Wright and Paul de Hert, "Privacy Impact Assessment (Law, Governance and Technology Series)", Springer; 2012 edition (July 22, 2012).

[7] Charles Saatchi, "Unknown unknowns", Booth-Clibborn; First Edition, 2015.

International Academy, Research,
and Industry Association (IARIA)
412 Derby Way
Wilmington, DE 19810

ISBN 978-1-5108-2693-9

CURRAN ASSOCIATES INC.
proceedings.com

13th Ranshofen Light Metal Days 2024

IOP Conference Series: Materials Science and Engineering
Volume 1315

Saalfelden, Austria
26-27 September 2024

IOP
Institute of Physics